Teacher as Inquiring Learner Activity

Like the think-aloud activity in Chapter 1, the purpose of this activity is to help you begin to explore a student's strategies. (Again, at this point, describe the student's strategies in your own words. Don't peek ahead!)

Find a middle school or high school student who is willing to help you learn. Ask the student to pick out an easy text and a hard text. Have the student read the easy text aloud first for about fifteen minutes and then switch to read the hard text for another fifteen minutes. If the student is clearly frustrated by the hard text, try to find a less difficult text to read or stop after eight to ten minutes.

As the student reads aloud, ask him or her to stop and tell you what he or she is thinking. If the student doesn't think aloud periodically, stop the student and ask what he or she is thinking about or what connections he or she is making to the text. Take notes on a copy of the text or perhaps tape-record this session. After the session with the student, go over your notes or the tape.

- From ideas and comments the student stated, what reading strategies can you infer that the student used?

For example, if the student said he or she thought the book would be about how paleontologists searched for dinosaurs, you could infer that the student used prediction as a strategy.

Inquiry Activities About Your Learning

1. Choose a diversity characteristic and learn about it. Visit a community organization that serves that particular population. Interview the staff about the lives of the people in the community. What contributions are the people making to their community? What issues do they face? Try to find a member of the community who is willing to be interviewed about the story of her or his life.

2. Research the contributions of diverse people to your content area. What have people from a minority culture, women, and people with disabilities accomplished? Look for biographies or news reports about their accomplishments. Identify organizations related to your content area for contacts that could inform you about the contributions of their members.

Inquiry Activities About Your Students' Learning

1. Observe two classes—a low-track class and a high-track class—in your content area. If possible, observe the same teacher for both classes. Compare the content being taught and the instructional methods used. Compare the students' and the teachers' behavior. How do they affect each other? What does the teacher do differently in the two groups, and why? What are your conclusions about the teaching and learning in the two tracks?

2. Interview a teacher about his or her students. First, ask the teacher to describe the students in his or her different classes. Second, ask the teacher to describe a few students whom she or he finds interesting. Third, ask a series of questions about those students. What content knowledge do they bring to class? What strategies do they use to learn and study? What attitudes toward learning do they bring to class? What standardized tests does the teacher need to give? How do the students score on the tests? What decisions are made based on the scores? Does the teacher think the scores and tests are used fairly? How does the teacher learn about his or her students?

The text's *Inquiry into Learning and Teaching* theme promotes study of how content-area teachers and students learn, and how teaching strategies work.

Inquiry Activities encourage analysis of literacy strategies and teaching practices.

Literacy and Learning

Literacy and Learning:
Strategies for Middle and Secondary School Teachers

Karen Kuelthau Allan
Lesley College

Margery Staman Miller
Lesley College

Houghton Mifflin Company BOSTON NEW YORK

Sponsoring Editor: Loretta Wolozin
Associate Editor: Lisa Mafrici
Project Editor: Kellie Cardone
Production/Design Coordinator: Jennifer Meyer Dare
Senior Manufacturing Coordinator: Marie Barnes

Cover Designer: Nina Wishnok/Dynamo Design

Printed in the U.S.A.

Library of Congress Catalog Card Number: 99-72022

ISBN: 0-395-74646-9

123456789-DC-03 02 01 00 99

Contents

Preface   xii

PART ONE   **The Contexts of Teaching and Learning**   **3**

1   **Teacher as Learner**   **4**

Becoming a Content-Area Teacher   7

Knowledge of the Content Area 8   Knowledge About Learners 10
Knowledge of Content Pedagogy 10   Knowledge About Curriculum
Materials 11   Realistic Learning About Teaching 12

How Learning and Literacy Fit with Content-Area Teaching   14

The Role of Literacy in Learning Content 15   Strategies to Support
Learning in Content Areas 16   Teaching Literacy Strategies for
Learning Content 19

Education for the Twenty-First Century   22

Middle Schools and High Schools for the Twenty-First Century 22
Teaching for the Twenty-First Century 23

2   **Students as Learners**   **27**

Who Are the Students in Classrooms?   28

Diversity of Race and Ethnicity 30   Diversity of Language 32
Diversity of Socioeconomic Class 34   Diversity of Gender 35
Diversity of Special Needs 36   Teaching Diverse Students 37

What Do Students Bring to Classrooms?   39

Content Knowledge in Schemata 39   Strategies for Learning 41
Attitudes, Beliefs, and Values for Learning 42

How Standardized Tests Can Be Used Fairly for Your
Students as Learners   43

3   Choices and Decisions for Content Learning   **50**

Choices and Decisions About Materials   53

Rationale for a Variety of Texts in the Content Areas 53
Types of Texts 54   Selecting Appropriate Texts for Students 59

Choices and Decisions About Pedagogy   65

Communication Roles in Classrooms 66   Grouping for Learning 68
Teaching Tools for Literacy 73   Assessment Tools for Literacy 75

Lesson Plans: Combining Content, Strategies, Materials,
and Pedagogy   79
A Generic Lesson Plan Format as Applied to Modeling and
Explaining Content and Strategy in Tandem   80

Sample Lesson Plan   80

Goals and Objectives 80   Pedagogy or Teaching Procedures 81
Assessment and Evaluation 83

Information and Resources   85

PART TWO   Teaching Tools for Strategic Learning   **89**

4   Generating Ideas: Building on Background Knowledge   **90**

Strategies and Tools for Activating Prior Experiences and
Prior Knowledge   91

Modeling and Explaining Strategies for Activating Prior Knowledge 93
Activating Prior Knowledge in Every Content Area 97   Three Scenarios
of Students' Prior Knowledge 99   Teaching/Assessing Tools for Prior
Knowledge 100   Direct Teaching Tools for Prior Knowledge 105
Focus on Writing: Journals 106

Strategies and Tools for Previewing and Predicting   108

Modeling and Explaining Strategies for Previewing and Predicting 109
Teaching/Assessing Tools for Previewing and Predicting 113   Focus
on Writing: Freewriting 116

Strategies and Tools for Exploring New Vocabulary   117

Concepts and Vocabulary 118   Guidelines for Preteaching Selected
Vocabulary for Important Concepts 119   Modeling and Explaining

Strategies for Exploring New Vocabulary 120   Assessment Tools for Exploring New Vocabulary 123   Teaching/Assessing Tools for Exploring New Vocabulary 125   Direct Teaching Tool: Morphemic Analysis 129   Focus on Writing: Using New Vocabulary 133

Purpose Setting and Monitoring: Two Underlying and Ongoing Strategies   134

Modeling and Explaining Strategies for Purpose Setting and Monitoring 134   How Purpose Setting and Monitoring Are Presented in This Book 135

A Checklist for Monitoring Strategies for Generating Ideas   136

5   Interacting with Ideas: Comprehending and Constructing Knowledge   139

The Overall Strategy: Finding and Interpreting Information— Making Connections   142

Constructing Meanings: Text-Based and Schema-Based Connections 142   Using Three Supporting Strategies to Help Construct Meaning 145   Modeling and Explaining Strategies for Finding and Interpreting Information 146

The Importance of Questioning   152

Types of Questions and Answers 153   How Questioning Can Facilitate (or Hinder) Students' Understanding 156   Observing the Role of Questioning in This Chapter 159

Strategies and Tools That Emphasize Text-Based Connections   159

Modeling and Explaining Strategies That Emphasize Text-Based Connections: A Review of the E-car Script 161   Teaching/Assessing Tools That Emphasize Text-Based Connections 162   Assessment Tools That Emphasize Text-Based Connections 170   Focus on Writing: Writing to Learn in Journals, Learning Logs, and Lab or Field Notebooks 173

Strategies and Tools That Emphasize Schema-Based Connections   174

Modeling and Explaining Strategies That Emphasize Schema-Based Connections 176   Teaching/Assessing Tools That Emphasize Schema-Based Connections 179   Assessment Tool for Strategies That Emphasize Schema-Based Connections 183   Focus on Writing: Journals and First Drafts 184

Three Supporting Strategies and Tools   187

Capitalizing on Text Organization 188   Constructing Auxiliary Aids 194   Independent Learning of New Vocabulary 198   Focus on Writing: Supporting Strategies and First Drafts 206

Purpose Setting and Monitoring During the Interacting with Ideas Phase (Underlying and Ongoing Strategies)   207
A Checklist for Monitoring Strategies for Interacting with Ideas 208

6 **Refining Ideas: Studying and Clarifying Knowledge**   **213**

Strategies and Tools for Organizing Ideas and Enhancing Prior Knowledge   217

Modeling and Explaining Strategies for Organizing Ideas and Enhancing Prior Knowledge 217   Teaching/Assessing Tools for Organizing Ideas and Enhancing Prior Knowledge 227   Assessment Tools 235   Focus on Writing: Summaries for Readers 237

Strategies and Tools for Evaluating Ideas and Reconstructing Prior Knowledge   240

Modeling and Explaining Strategies for Evaluating Ideas and Reconstructing Prior Knowledge 241   Teaching/Assessing Tools for Evaluating Ideas and Reconstructing Prior Knowledge 248   Assessment Tools 253   Focus on Writing: Revising First Drafts Through Conferences 253

Communicating Learning to Different Audiences   255

Communicating Learning Through Speaking Opportunities 256   Communicating Learning Through Dramatic Opportunities 257   Communicating Learning Through Art and Music Opportunities 258   Communicating Learning Through Writing Opportunities 258

Purpose Setting and Monitoring During the Refining Ideas Phase (Underlying and Ongoing Strategies)   260
A Checklist for Monitoring Strategies for Refining Ideas   260

7 **Linking the Phases: Learning Through Research Projects**   **264**

Using Research Projects for Learning   267

Different Purposes for Research Projects 267   The Role of the End Product in a Research Project 270

Sample Lesson Plan One: A Research Project to Assemble Known Facts and Interpretations   274

Researching and Planning the Project 274   Generating Phase: Introducing the Project 275   Interacting Phase: Understanding the Subject 278   Refining Phase: Organizing Understandings 283   Communicating Learning: End Products for the Project 285

Sample Lesson Plan Two: A Research Project to Investigate an Issue or a Problem   286

Researching and Planning the Project 287   Generating Phase: Introducing the Project 288   Interacting Phase: Initial Understanding of the Issue 290   Refining Phase: Organizing Initial Understandings 294   Recycling to Generating Phase Strategies 295   Recycling to Interacting Phase Strategies 298   Recycling to Refining Phase Strategies 299   Communicating Learning: End Products for the Project 300

Information and Resources   302

PART THREE

Enhancing Learning Through the Disciplines   307

8   Designing Curriculum for Learning: Teaching for Major Understandings   308

Defining Curriculum   309

The Teacher's Role in Designing Curriculum 313

The Standards Movement and Curriculum   314

The Current Movement 314   Standards for Selected Specific Disciplines 318   Concerns and Questions About the Standards 330

Models for Curriculum Development   331

Three Curriculum Models 331   The Unit Plan 335

Applying Standards to the Teaching Profession: A Look Ahead to Chapter 12   341

9   Single Discipline-Based Learning and Literacy   345

Common Concerns Among the Disciplines   348

Content and Understandings 350   Strategies 351   Planning for Coherence 352   Acting on Teachers' Concerns: Making Changes 354

Discipline-Specific Concerns and Related Literacy Strategies   354

Science 357   Mathematics 358   English/Language Arts 360 Social Studies 362

Sample Unit Plans: Sample Single Discipline Unit for the Middle School   364

Major Understandings 364   Resources 366   Individual Lessons 367 Student Evaluation 370   Making Connections Among the Disciplines 371

Sample Single Discipline Unit for the High School   373

Major Understandings 375   Resources 375   Individual Lessons 376
Student Evaluation 378   Making Connections Among the
Disciplines 379

**10   Coordinated Curriculum: Enhancing Learning
Among Disciplines   383**

An Overview of Coordinated Curriculum   386

Benefits of Coordinated Curriculum 387   Planning and Scheduling
for Coordinated Curriculum 389

Sample Unit Plans: **Sample Coordinated Discipline Unit for
the High School   392**

How the Teachers Came Together 393   The Teachers' Goals,
Planning, and Scheduling 394   High School English Literature
Course: Women's Literature 395   High School Biology/Health
Course: AIDS Education 398   How the Teachers Carried Out the
Coordination of Their Disciplines 404

**Sample Coordinated Discipline Unit for the
Middle School   405**

How the Teachers Came Together 407   The Teachers' Goals, Planning,
and Scheduling 407   Middle School English/Language Arts Course:
Historical Fiction and Letter Writing 408   Middle School Mathematics
Course: Geometry 412   How the Teachers Carried Out the
Coordination of Their Disciplines   414

11   Integrated Curriculum   421

What Do We Mean by Integrated Curriculum?   422

Interdisciplinary, Integrated, and Thematic Study: Similarities
and Differences 424   Rationale for an Integrated Approach to
Curriculum 430

**One Model for the Design and Development of Integrated
Curriculum   431**

The Miller-Allan Model for Developing Curriculum 431
Preplanning: Finding Worthwhile Themes 432   Planning for
Integrated Curriculum 436   Implementing the Integrated Unit 442
Assessing Students' Understandings and the Outcomes of the Unit
as a Whole 446

Working with Other Teachers: The Importance of Teams to Integrated Curriculum   451

Guidelines for Interdisciplinary Teams 452 Allowing Sufficient Time 453 Assessment Questions 455 A School Vision 455

Two Sample Integrated Thematic Units   456

Sample Unit Plans   457

Sample Middle School Unit: "Our Environment: Home, School, Town, Planet Earth"   457

Preplanning 457 Planning 457 Implementing 459 Assessing Student Understanding and Outcomes of the Unit as a Whole 461

Sample High School Unit: "Immigration and Cultural Diversity: Are We Still a Nation of Immigrants?"   462

Preplanning 462 Planning 463 Implementing 465

12 Continuing to Grow as a Reflective Professional   473

Thinking About Your Own Teaching and Learning   476

Professional Standards for Teachers 476 Content Knowledge 477 Knowledge of Your Students/Learners 478 Content Pedagogy 479 Selecting Materials and Resources to Fit Content and Learners 480

Taking an Inquiring Stance: Learning from Your Own Teaching and from Your Learners   480

Applied Educational Research 481 Becoming a Teacher Researcher: Inquiring into Your Own Classroom 485 A Middle School Student Teacher Engages in Classroom Inquiry 491

Joining Additional Communities of Learners   493

Information and Resources   496

References   499

Index   512

Preface

In this century, information sources have changed from the 1900s newsboy hawking "EXTRA!! EXTRA!!" on the local corner to the 2000s global, grass-roots Internet where every Web site shouts "EXTRA!!" *Information explosion* has become a commonplace twentieth-century phrase, but information will exponentially expand in the twenty-first century. That information will include not only data-based research and thoughtful dialogue but also sound bites, info-tainment, and hearsay. In the twenty-first century, everyone will need literacy strategies to construct meaning from the information maze they will encounter in both school content-area subjects and in their daily lives.

We wrote *Literacy and Learning* to show content-area teachers that literacy strategies and teaching tools would support their students' construction of meaning in their specific subject area. Although this book especially supports novice teachers, experienced teachers and reading specialists have found our focus on students' literacy strategies useful in their professional development in this information age.

Approach

▶ ▶ ▶ ▷ **When Do Literacy Strategies and Teaching Tools Support Content Learning?**

The second part, and core of this book, *Teaching Tools for Strategic Learning*, contextualizes the use of strategies and tools. Our organization—***before*** learning to generate ideas, ***during*** learning to interact with ideas, and ***after*** learning to refine ideas—demonstrates how the infusion of literacy strategies and teaching tools enhance content learning.

We explain literacy strategies and teaching tools for *Generating Ideas: Building on Background Knowledge* (Chapter 4), *Interacting with Ideas: Comprehension and Constructing Knowledge* (Chapter 5), and *Refining Ideas: Studying and Clarifying Knowledge* (Chapter 6), by using the phases of before, during, and after. Chapter 7 *Linking the Phases: Learning Through Research Projects* links these phases together and shows how literacy strategies and teaching tools are embedded in research projects. Part Three, *Enhancing Learning Through the Disciplines,* further applies the phases of generating, interacting, and refining ideas in content-area units. In addition, we supply many activities in a range of disciplines—science, social studies, math, English, and more—to anchor student learning.

▶ ▶ ▶ ▶ Metacognitive Awareness of Strategies and Learning

Although preservice teachers are accustomed to reading and writing throughout their own schooling, many have not thought consciously about *how* they read and write to learn in their content areas. Our goal is to build teachers' metacognitive awareness of their own literacy strategies so that they can nourish their students' strategic learning.

To build preservice teachers' metacognitive awareness of not only their own reading strategies but their students' strategies, in Part Two, we *model and explain* reading strategies using different types of texts from a variety of content areas. Within the context of learning from texts, we model and explain strategies that emphasize generating ideas (such as, previewing and predicting), interacting with ideas (such as, finding and interpreting information), and refining ideas (such as, organizing ideas). Discussions about strategies that percolate in college courses and field experiences lead to meaningful use in content-area classrooms—that is our aim.

▶ ▶ ▶ ▶ Teaching and Assessing Tools with Content-Area Standards and Instruction

This book is about strategies and tools. In every chapter in Part Two we emphasize *when* teachers use specific teaching tools to support students' learning. We include teaching tools for before reading (e.g., brainstorming, vocabulary), during reading (e.g., DRA, comprehension guides), and after reading (e.g., summaries). We also integrate writing (e.g., journals, first drafts) into the same chronology to complement the reading teaching tools. Furthermore, we interweave assessment with instruction by describing how teaching tools can be used concurrently to instruct and to assess learning and by presenting assessment only tools, such as retelling.

We continue to interweave teaching and assessing tools into the content-area units of Part Three, *Enhancing Learning Through the Disciplines*. Recognizing that content-area teachers need to respond to the *standards* devised by professional groups and state departments of education, we first discuss the curriculum standards for the major disciplines. Then, combining the literacy strategies and teaching tools with curriculum standards, we show preservice teachers how to build curriculum units that correspond to three configurations in secondary schools: 1. preservice teachers commonly find themselves in subject departments and need *single subject units;* 2. preservice teachers in different content areas, interested in teaching the same topic, may plan a *coordinated unit* on the topic for teaching in their own content-area field placement; or, 3. they may find themselves in a school, most likely a middle school, in which the teachers periodically create integrated units that combine several subject areas. Thus, they need to know how to participate in planning an *integrated unit* with the other teachers.

▶ ▶ ▶ ▷ Inquiry into Learning and Teaching

Throughout *Literacy and Learning*, we want content-area teachers to inquire into 1. how they learn, 2. how the teaching they observe and conduct works, and 3. how their students learn. Through reflecting on teaching and learning, content-area teachers will continually learn to improve their teaching practice and their students' strategic learning.

We open the book in Part One, *The Contexts of Teaching and Learning,* by addressing the facets of teaching that will last throughout an individual's teaching career: knowledge in a content area, diversity of student population, choices of pedagogical tools and curriculum materials. Thus, we ask these new teachers to think about how they will design their own classrooms to provide greater learning opportunities for their students.

Throughout the book both within and at the end of chapters, we offer readers *inquiry activities* that encourage them to interview teachers, test teaching tools, examine students' strategies, and reflect on their own learning and literacy. With these inquiry activities, we ask these new teachers to develop a habit of reflection on teaching and learning.

Building upon the inquiry activities interwoven throughout the book, we close Chapter 12 *Continuing to Grow as a Reflective Professional,* by showing preservice teachers how those inquiry activities are like classroom inquiry projects. We also show how teachers could conduct inquiry in their field experiences and in their own classrooms. We aim for these twenty-first-century teachers not to just meet the professional standards but also to inquire into their teaching and their students' learning so that a community of learners exists in their classrooms.

Content and Organization

We begin *Literacy and Learning* with Part One, *The Contexts of Teaching and Learning,* to present the facets of teaching and to challenge preservice teachers to be responsive in teaching their students of the twenty-first century.

- Chapter 1, *Teacher as Learner,* defines content-area teaching, defines literacy strategies and teaching tools and how they fit with content-area teaching, and sets goals for teaching in the twenty-first century.

- Chapter 2, *Students as Learners,* describes student diversity and offers teaching suggestions; discusses students' schemata knowledge, strategies, and attitudes; and outlines how standardized tests affect students.

- Chapter 3, *Choices and Decisions for Content Learning,* describes the variety of texts and selection criteria, discusses communication roles and groupings for learning, defines the types of teaching tools and assessment tools in Parts Two and Three, and offers a sample lesson plan for teaching strategies and content in tandem.

We have organized Part Two, *Teaching Tools for Strategic Learning,* to emphasize when learners use strategies to learn and when teachers use teaching/assessing tools to support students' learning of content.

- Chapter 4, *Generating Ideas: Building on Background Knowledge,* focuses on **before reading and writing**, models strategies of activating prior knowledge, previewing and predicting, and exploring new vocabulary; and explains tools like brainstorming, graphic organizers, anticipation guides, concept of definition, morphemic analysis, and freewriting.

- Chapter 5, *Interacting with Ideas: Comprehending and Constructing Knowledge,* focuses on **during reading and writing**. This chapter explains text-based connections and schema-based connections and types of questions; models strategies of finding and interpreting information, capitalizing on text organization, constructing supporting aids, and learning new vocabulary independently; and explains teaching tools, such as, DRA, study guides, peer-led discussions, text pattern guides, note-taking system, graphic organizers, vocabulary self-selection, semantic feature charts, context clues, and first drafts.

- Chapter 6, *Refining Ideas: Studying and Clarifying Knowledge,* focuses on **after reading and writing**, models strategies for organizing ideas and evaluating ideas, explains teaching tools—like categorization charts, summary writing, post reading study guides, and PORPE—and describes communicating learning to different audiences through speaking, drama, art, music, and writing opportunities.

- Chapter 7, *Linking the Phases: Learning Through Research Projects,* melds the previous three chapters and foretells the units in Part Three. Chapter 7 discusses the purpose of research projects and types of end products, describes a middle school research project for Women's History month, and a high school research project that investigates the issue of child labor.

Part Three, *Enhancing Learning Through the Disciplines,* embeds literacy strategies and teaching tools within curriculum development of content-area units. It also defines the range of curricula units that teachers may choose to embark upon at different times in the year or in their career.

- Chapter 8, *Designing Curriculum for Learning: Teaching for Major Understandings,* compares the curriculum standards in the major disciplines, defines three curriculum models—single discipline, coordinated, and integrated— and outlines a general unit plan useful across the disciplines.

- Chapter 9, *Single Discipline-Based Learning and Literacy,* recognizes the importance of major understandings in each of the content areas and the department organization in secondary schools. It presents a middle school social studies unit on conflict between nations and a high school geology unit on fossils.

- Chapter 10, *Coordinated Curriculum: Enhancing Learning Among Disciplines,* describes how two teachers plan a unit together from their respective discipline's perspective but teach students separately in their own content-area classrooms. This chapter presents a high school unit on women scientists that links biology/health and literature and a middle school unit on quilts in historical fiction that links geometry and English/language arts.

- Chapter 11, *Integrated Curriculum,* describes the study of issues, problems, or themes without discipline demarcations, delineates planning with other teachers through a model for designing and implementing an integrated unit, and presents a middle school integrated unit on the environment and a high school one on immigration.

- Chapter 12, *Continuing to Grow as a Reflective Professional,* describes professional standards for teachers and the areas of continuous learning— content, students, pedagogy, and materials—and emphasizes reflection on teaching through classroom inquiry.

Special Learning Features

To emphasize our dual themes of learning about one's own literacy strategies and learning about teaching literacy and content in tandem, we have integrated special learning features into the text.

- *Modeling and Explaining Scripts* exhibit how literacy strategies are used in the act of reading different types of content-area texts. These scripts build readers' metacognitive awareness of their own literacy strategies and show how to model and explain strategies with students. Throughout the chapters in Part Two, these scripts emphasize specific strategies appropriate for the three phases—before, during, and after reading.

- *Teaching and Assessing Tools* are integrated to emphasize how instruction is based on student learning. In presenting teaching/assessing tools, we describe how to use the teaching tool, such as a comprehension guide, to support students' learning and also how it can be used to assess students' learning. In addition, we present direct teaching tools, like teaching about word parts, and assessment tools, like retelling. Matched to the three phases of reading, these tools are the focus of the chapters in Part Two and are incorporated into the curriculum units in Part Three.

- *Focus on Writing sections* are integrated to emphasize the reading–writing connection. Emphasizing writing to learn, we discuss journals, first drafts, revisions of first drafts, and end products in the chapters in Part Two and we incorporate writing into the units in Part Three.

- *Checklists for Monitoring Strategies* serve as a tool for the readers' metacognitive awareness of their literacy strategies and as a teaching tool for students to gauge their use of literacy strategies. Since we view monitoring as ongoing throughout the three phases, we include checklists at the end of those chapters in Part Two.

- *Content-Area Curriculum Units* exemplify the three curricula models found in middle schools and high schools—single discipline units (Chapter 9), coordinated units (Chapter 10), and integrated units (Chapter 11). Presenting both a middle school and a high school example for each model, we demonstrate how to meet content-area curriculum standards, incorporate literacy strategies and tools to support content learning, and assess the outcomes of student learning.

- *Three types of Inquiry Activities* occur within every chapter: *Teacher as Inquiring Learner Activities, Inquiry Activities About Your Learning,* and *Inquiry Activities About Your Students' Learning.* We designed these inquiry activities to reinforce our themes of investigating one's own and students' literacy strategies and of investigating teaching practice by reflecting on one's own teaching and on experienced teachers' practices. Tied to the content of each chapter, readers could use these activities as the basis for class discussions and as field-based assignments.

In addition, we have included the following learning pedagogy and resources to assist readers' comprehension of the chapters:

- *Chapter Graphic Organizers* are designed to give readers an overview of the chapter's content and to encourage readers to use previewing strategies.

- *Purpose-Setting Questions* are designed to help readers predict the contents of the chapter, activate their own prior knowledge about the content of the chapter, and guide their comprehension of the chapter.

- *Selected Information and Resource bibliographies* at the conclusion of Parts One, Two, and Three are designed to encourage readers to continue their learning about specific topics. Chosen specifically for content-area teachers, we included books, journals, and Internet sites that represent different content areas.

- *Examples of Specific Teaching Tools* from different content areas make concrete the explanations of reading and writing teaching tools in Part Two.

Acknowledgments

Writing, like teaching, is a collaborative process. We have many people to thank. First, we thank our students with whom we tried our germinating ideas and our approach to content-area reading. Our students, in becoming teachers, brought literacy strategies and tools into their teaching and their classrooms. Many students understood that metacognition and strategy instruction could be transferred from literacy into math, science, and social studies. We also thank experienced teachers who lent us their expertise, who refined our strategy instruction with their students, who supplied us with curriculum ideas and classroom examples, and who collaborated with other teachers to continually improve their practice.

Second, we thank our colleagues at Lesley College. Our faculty colleagues participated in conversations about teaching, learning, and literacy and encouraged us throughout the project. Our Ludke Library colleagues assisted us in our varied searches. The Russell Professional Development Grants and Lesley College Sabbaticals provided us time to research and write at crucial points in the project. Dean William Dandridge kept his watchful eye on our progress and encouraged us.

Third, we thank the following reviewers:

Pam Cole, Kennesaw State University

Mary Ann Dzama, George Mason University

Bruce Foster, Rowan University of New Jersey

Barbara Guzzetti, Arizona State University

Dennis Jacobsen, California State Polytech University, Pomona

James Martin-Rehrman, Westfield State College

Margaret McIntosh, University of Nevada, Reno

Linda Molner, University of Colorado

Candace Poindexter, Loyola Marymount University

Mary Ann Wham, University of Wisconsin

They thoughtfully and thoroughly challenged our thinking and so strengthened the book. We thank them for the time they willingly gave, their thorough comments, and their knowledge of literacy, teachers, and college students.

Fourth, we thank the people at Houghton Mifflin Company. Most importantly we thank Loretta Wolozin, Senior Sponsoring Editor, who supported the original idea of a new vision of content-area reading and advocated for the realization of that vision from the proposal to the actual book. We also could not have brought this book to fruition without Merryl Maleska Wilbur, Development Editor, who insightfully comprehended our major themes and who helped us solve numerous puzzles encountered in communicating our themes. Lisa Mafrici, Associate Editor, who steered us carefully throughout the publishing process, kept us buoyed up through every deadline with her very cheerful, positive manner. Kellie Cardone, Project Editor, skillfully shepherded us and the book through the details and deadlines of production.

Finally, we thank our extended families and close friends who have experienced this project with us. Margery expresses deep gratitude to her parents who have always encouraged her to pursue new challenges and to her husband, Lee, who has offered his understanding throughout this project. Karen dedicates this book to the memory of her late husband, Andrew A. Allan, who celebrated the initial endeavors and drafts of this book and who devoted his life to students' and teachers' learning.

Karen Kuelthau Allan
Margery Staman Miller

Literacy and Learning

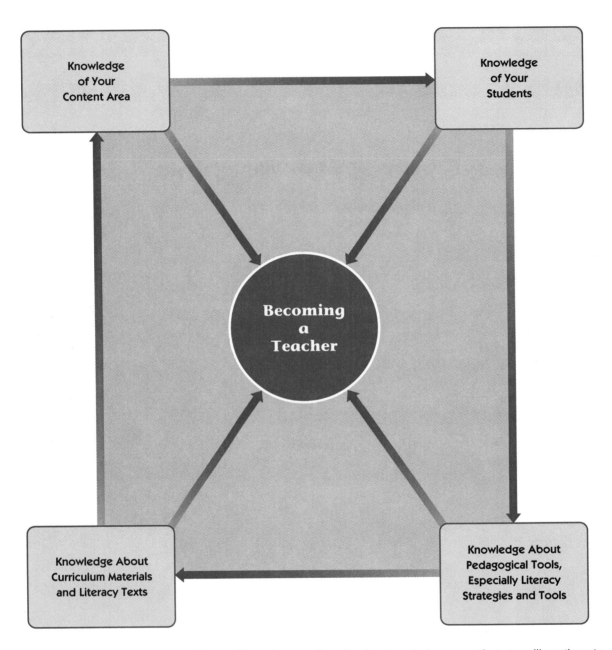

In Part One, The Contexts of Teaching and Learning, we describe four knowledge areas that you will continue to learn about throughout your teaching career. In Chapter 1, Teacher as Learner, we give an overview of the four areas and define how literacy supports content-area teaching. In Chapter 2, Students as Learners, we focus on diversity in today's classrooms. In Chapter 3, we describe literacy texts, communication roles and groupings, and literacy teaching tools.

The Contexts of Teaching and Learning

Chapter 1:

Teacher as Learner

Chapter 2:

Students as Learners

Chapter 3:

Choices and Decisions for Content Learning

Information and Resources

1

Teacher as Learner

Congratulations! You have decided to become a teacher! Although you were born in the twentieth century, you will spend your teaching career in the twenty-first century. What changes will you experience and witness in the next century? Like you, Louise Kuehlthau (the grandmother of one of the authors) had a teaching career that crossed two centuries; born in the nineteenth century, she taught in the twentieth. Think about the changes she experienced. Born when horses drew carriages, she drove a car across the country. Born when kerosene lamps lit houses, she watched Neil Armstrong walk on the moon on her new color television set. Born during the Impressionist art period, she witnessed the pop art of Andy Warhol. Beginning her teaching career in a one-room schoolhouse, she concluded it by chairing the school committee of a burgeoning town with a large high school. She never would have predicted the magnitude of those changes when she began teaching. Where will science, current events, art, music, and literature take you and your students in the twenty-first century?

One prediction that you can make is that knowledge will continue to expand exponentially. Grandmother Kuehlthau probably could have made a reasonable attempt to cover a content area; now we hold no such expectations. The curriculum has become increasingly packed as more and more topics have been added; teaching has become more swiftly paced and learning more superficial. The result is that teachers can no longer pretend to cover a content area. Instead, teaching must focus on strategies that will allow people to continue to learn beyond the time when they are students. Thus, the heart of this book is literacy strategies for lifelong learning in all content areas.

We titled this first chapter "Teacher as Learner" because we view teaching as a lifelong learning process. First, we discuss becoming a content-area teacher by increasing your knowledge of your content area, your knowledge about students, your knowledge about pedagogy or teaching tools, and your knowledge about curriculum materials. Although you want to learn as much as you can in these four areas now, even experienced teachers continue to learn in these four areas. Therefore, we conclude this section with a discussion of how you can realistically learn about teaching while you are teaching.

Second, we define how this text, *Literacy and Learning*, fits with content-area teaching. We define the role of literacy in learning, that is, how speaking, listening, reading, and writing are used to learn and communicate content ideas. Since effective learners and communicators use strategies, we describe the concept of strategy and students' use of literacy strategies. Then, we introduce you to how we teach and assess literacy strategies within the context of your content area—the heart of the whole book.

Finally, we conclude by discussing education in the twenty-first century. In each century, and sometimes each decade, educators develop new beliefs and goals for schools. As the United States has changed from an agricultural society, to an industrial society, to a knowledge-based society, schools need to change too. We discuss changes you may participate in and encourage you to think about your goals as you become a teacher in the twenty-first century.

Purpose-Setting Questions

1. Why did you choose to become a content-area teacher? What topics in your content area do you feel knowledgeable about, and what areas do you need to learn more about?

2. Think about what you have learned about students, pedagogy or teaching practices, and curriculum materials in your college program. In what areas would you like to learn more?

3. How do you use literacy (that is, speaking, listening, reading, and writing) to learn in your content area? What have you read that has intrigued you? How do you use writing to help you understand your thinking in your content area?

4. Think about the best teacher you have had in your schooling experiences. What happened in that classroom that made this person an outstanding teacher? How would you describe the teacher you aim to become in the twenty-first century?

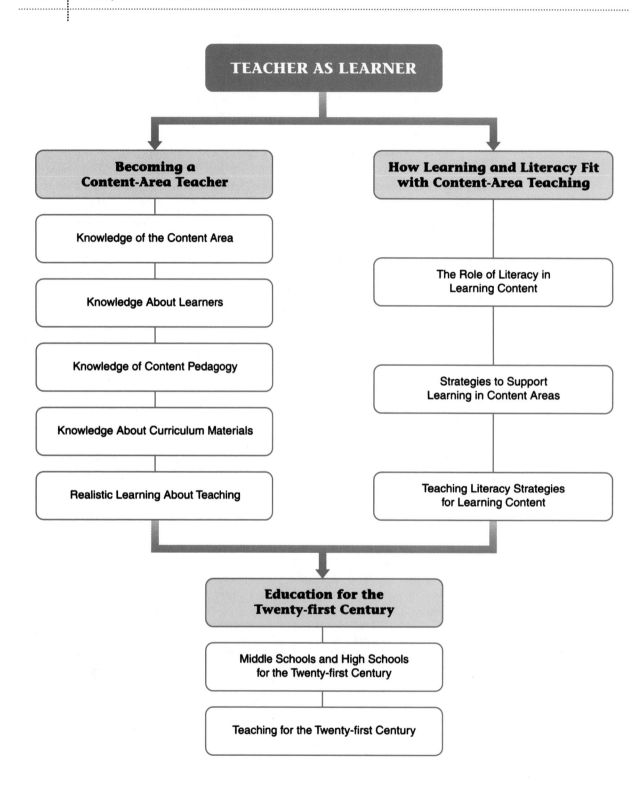

Becoming a Content-Area Teacher

Y ou have decided to become a teacher because you enjoy your content area; maybe you are even passionate about it. You like investigating and predicting weather, enjoy reading and discussing Jamaica Kincaid's books, find mathematics in everyday situations, or carry a sketchbook with you everywhere. But more than being engrossed in your content area, you want to communicate that content to young people. You hope to interest students in applying your content area to their everyday lives and to interest at least a few of them in pursuing the subject in a career.

Your combined interest in your content area and your students sets you apart from other people majoring in your field. In many jobs and professions, workers are continually updating their knowledge; anthropologists continue to study their cultures, economists the theories of the marketplace, poets poetry. Unlike these and other workers, middle school and high school teachers not only continue to learn in their subject area, they also study teaching-learning events in their own classrooms. Recognizing the need for knowledge in subject matter and in teaching the subject matter, the Carnegie Commission states:

> Teachers must think for themselves if they are able to help others think for themselves, be able to act independently and collaborate with others, and render critical judgment. They must be people whose knowledge is wide-ranging and whose understanding runs deep. . . . They must be able to learn all the time. . . . Teachers will not come to school knowing all that they have to know, but knowing how to figure out what they need to know, where to get it, and how to help others make meaning out of it. (Carnegie Commission, 1986, p. 25)

Since both the knowledge in your content area and the students in your classes continually change, teaching is a continuous and career-long learning experience. We agree with Shulman (1986, 1987) and Cochran, De Ruiter, and King (1993) that teaching requires learning in four areas:

- Knowledge of the content area: Content, strategies, and attitudes of the subject area and connections to other subject areas
- Knowledge of learners: Cognitive and affective development of students as well as their cultural environments
- Knowledge of content pedagogy: Teaching tools at the confluence between content and students
- Knowledge of curriculum materials: Textbooks, curriculum guides, computer programs, and primary sources, among others

Educators in different content areas have also described teaching as learning in the four areas (for example, mathematics—Ball, 1991; English—Grossman, 1991; science—Hollon, Roth, & Anderson, 1991; and history—Wineburg & Wilson, 1991). You have begun learning in the four areas in your college preparation, but even as you gain experience, you will continue to learn in each of these same areas.

▶ ▶ ▶ ▶ Knowledge of the Content Area

In preparing to be a middle school or high school teacher, you have been majoring in a field and probably specializing in a specific area. When you teach, you may have studied some of the topics in the curriculum but not others. For example, suppose you are a political science major or an American Revolution specialist. As a social studies teacher, you will need to broaden your knowledge of American history. Or perhaps you decide to teach a new topic, like asteroids, because you're interested in it, your students are interested in it, or the topic is in the news or movies now. You will need to update your knowledge about asteroids. Becoming a continuous learner in your content area may require you to learn new topics, build on your current knowledge, and learn about new ideas and theories in your field.

Rather than communicating a list of isolated facts as a content-area teacher, you want to communicate the major ideas in your content area as well as the strategies to learn in your area (McDiarmid, Ball, & Anderson, 1989). What are the major themes in history, styles and media in art, or theories in earth science? How are the major ideas in your content area related to each other? In addition, think about what "doing" or learning your content area means—what a mathematician does or what a historian does. Does mathematics consist of algorithms and theorems to be solved or a means for describing different patterns in the world? Is history the interpretation of people's actions, the chronological representation of factual events, or a framework for understanding current policy and social issues? Is literary analysis one absolute interpretation of a book or one individual's response to the book among other possible responses?

We do not mean to imply that there is necessarily one way to view your content area. In some content areas, experts disagree about "doing" their domain; in others experts generally agree. Furthermore, views change as new theories are considered. We recommend that you begin to think about your personal view of your content area and how you want your students to view it. Although you will have curriculum mandates to meet, we think that how you view your content area will influence the ideas and concepts you teach, how you teach those ideas, and the learning you reward.

Teacher as Inquiring Learner Activity

Find a partner whose field is the same as yours, and together discuss and take notes about the views each of you holds about your content area.

• What are the major topics, ideas, and theories in your content area? How do they relate to one another and extend into the everyday world? How do experts tackle questions or problems in your field? What strategies do they use to investigate or learn? How do new ideas or theories become accepted in your field? How do experts "do" your content area?

After you have listed your ideas, describe your view of your content area to partners in a different field.

• How is your description of your content area different from and similar to their descriptions of theirs? Do you have any revisions to your own description?

Think about how you want to introduce your students to "doing" your content area. You might want to keep these notes and revise them as you become a continuous learning professional.

Knowing his subject matter, his student, and curriculum materials, the teacher created a problem-solving activity for these students.

© Michael Zide

▶ ▶ ▶ ▷ **Knowledge About Learners**

In your teacher preparation program, you probably have taken a course on adolescent psychology and read research and theories of cognitive and emotional development. Maybe you have had the opportunity to take a multicultural course and recognize that students bring diverse cultural heritages to schools. Although you have learned general information about development and diversity, you will be continually learning specifically who your students are and what previous learning they bring to classrooms (see Chapter 2, Students as Learners).

Your students may look similar, but in fact they have diverse characteristics, such as race or ethnicity, language, income levels, gender, and special needs, and in unique combinations. In addition to their previous learning in and out of school, they bring unique knowledge, strategies, and attitudes to your classroom. You will want to discover what information (or even misconceptions) your students have before you teach a topic. You will also want to discover what typical strategies they use for tasks, such as solving algebra problems or writing a persuasive letter to the editor. If you teach in the same school for a number of years, you will become adept at predicting your current students' diverse characteristics and background knowledge. Even so, you will continue to learn about your students because students are different and unique, and they are always changing.

Our major focus in this book is on strategies: literacy strategies that help students learn content (we discuss them in Part II). Most middle school and high school students use some strategies, but they may not be aware of how they use them. Less successful students do not use effective strategies and usually are unaware that strategies even exist (Garner, 1987; Garner & Alexander, 1989). You will want to learn what strategies your students use and what strategies can help them learn better.

You may or may not be aware of the strategies that help you learn in your content area. Actually, learning about a new topic to teach will give you a chance to become more aware of your own learning strategies. What strategies do you use when you read an article in your content area or write a term paper? You will need to become aware of your own literacy strategies because strategy teaching means making your own strategies visible to your students.

Thus, the part of the continuous learning we focus on in this book is investigating literacy strategies for learning content—your own strategies and your students' strategies.

▶ ▶ ▶ ▷ **Knowledge of Content Pedagogy**

Content pedagogy is the area that makes you a teacher. Positioned at the confluence between knowledge of content and knowledge of students, teachers make decisions about teaching-learning events: the teaching tools, student activities, and curricular materials to use. In making these decisions, you are communicating your passion about your field and your description of "doing" your field.

For example, both an English major and an English teaching major study Shakespeare, but only an English teacher decides how to communicate to students the universal themes of Shakespeare. Unlike a Shakespeare professor who begins with Act I, scene 1 of *Romeo and Juliet*, an English teacher might bring to class news articles about Serb and Croat lovers in Sarajevo to discuss before reading the play. Similarly, although both history majors and history teaching majors study the Civil War from primary source materials, a history teacher selects sources that project clearly either a Northern or a Southern point of view. After studying the sources, the students would role-play both Union and Confederate people to interpret the effect of the war on our nation and to learn what "doing" history is.

In bridging content and students, teachers make instructional decisions about teaching tools and student activities that support and enhance students' learning. In our examples above, the teachers chose discussion and role play. You have probably learned about teaching methods in your own content area. In Part II, we focus on teaching tools for literacy strategies that support learning your content area.

When teachers think about bridging content and students, they also make decisions about the communication roles students and teachers play in the social environment of the classroom (see Chapter 3). Teachers decide when to lecture and when to have the students work in small groups. They think about when student-to-student exchanges of ideas will enable students to clarify, evaluate, and revise their thoughts and positions about the content under study. In our examples above, what decisions about communication roles do you think the teachers made?

Beginning teachers usually focus on their own teaching actions—what they are doing in the classroom. We encourage you to focus as quickly as possible on students' actions—what particular students are doing—because knowledge about your students' learning will inform you about your teaching. Studying specific teaching-learning events and particular students will become an absorbing learning experience that will last all of your career.

▶ ▶ ▶ ▶ Knowledge About Curriculum Materials

Learning about curriculum materials, one aspect of content pedagogy, is a continuous pursuit of teachers. Whether suitable materials are available is often the deciding factor about whether to teach a particular topic. Even in their "leisure" time, teachers serendipitously search for a more current article, a more accessible primary source, or a new author that will better support teaching-learning in their classrooms.

In your subject-area methods courses, you probably examined specific materials. Although beginning teachers usually rely on textbooks, we encourage you to incorporate other sources, such as library books, primary sources, and on-line texts (see Chapter 3). As you expand your knowledge of the variety of materials available, you will need to evaluate their contents and usefulness carefully (see Chapter 3).

▶ ▶ ▶ ▶ **Realistic Learning About Teaching**

You may be wondering how you can possibly juggle all of the day-to-day work of teaching and keep learning about all four knowledge areas: content, learners, content pedagogy, and materials. Actually, your path for continuous learning will follow from your day-to-day juggling of teaching work. You will meet a puzzling student who intrigues you, use a teaching tool that works one period but not the next, or become dissatisfied with how students learn with a curriculum material. From those wonderings about students, reflections on your teaching, and trying out different curriculum materials, you will choose paths for your professional growth—collaborating with other teachers, reading professional journals, and attending conferences, for example. Teachers direct their continuous learning to topics that affect their daily lives by reflecting on their own teaching, students, and classrooms (see Chapter 12).

As you begin teaching, we expect you to work on becoming a reflective practitioner about your teaching, your students, and your classroom. You can observe your students, analyze how they are learning and how you are teaching, and reflect on how your practice can improve.

To start you on becoming an observant and reflective teacher, we offer three types of inquiry activities throughout the book: Teacher as Inquiring Learner Activities, Inquiry Activities About Your Learning, and Inquiry Activities About Your Students' Learning. These activities will give you opportunities to examine content-area teaching, specific teaching-learning events, your learning and literacy strategies, and your students' learning and literacy strategies. As you engage in those activities, we recommend keeping a field notebook in which you record what you do and observe, the data you collect, as well as your thoughts, analysis, and reflections about what you're learning. For example, look ahead to the Teacher as Inquiring Learner Activity on page 16. If you choose to do that activity, your field notebook might look like Figure 1.1.

We offer you the inquiry activities so that you begin your career-long search to understand your teaching, your students' learning, and events in your classroom better. Teaching is an uncertain craft (McDonald, 1992) at which teachers first apprentice and then spend their careers practicing.

Figure 1.1

Sample Field
Notebook for
Inquiry Activities

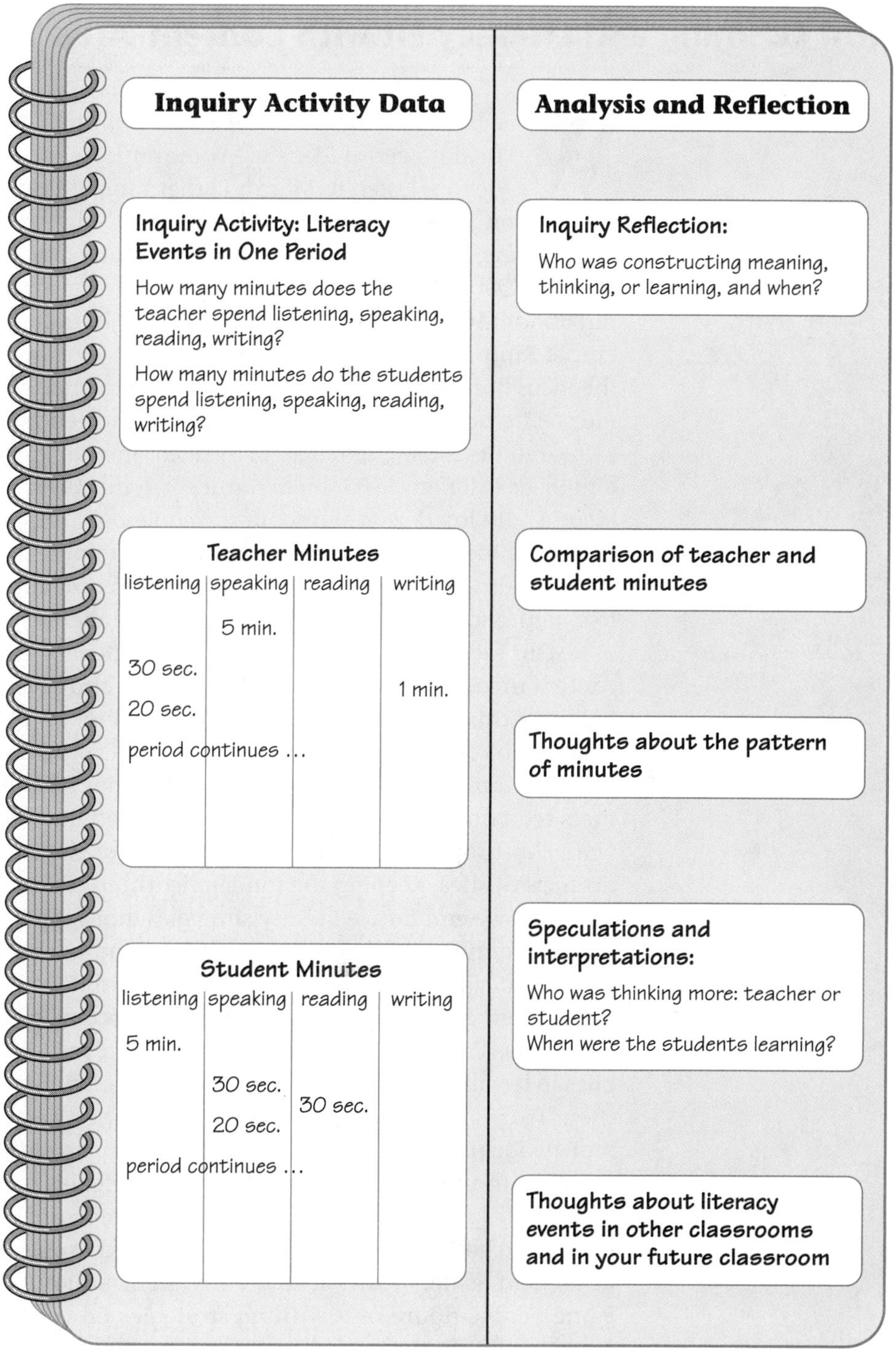

Inquiry Activity Data

Inquiry Activity: Literacy Events in One Period

How many minutes does the teacher spend listening, speaking, reading, writing?

How many minutes do the students spend listening, speaking, reading, writing?

Teacher Minutes

listening	speaking	reading	writing
	5 min.		
30 sec.			
20 sec.			1 min.
period continues …			

Student Minutes

listening	speaking	reading	writing
5 min.			
	30 sec.		
	20 sec.	30 sec.	
period continues …			

Analysis and Reflection

Inquiry Reflection:

Who was constructing meaning, thinking, or learning, and when?

Comparison of teacher and student minutes

Thoughts about the pattern of minutes

Speculations and interpretations:

Who was thinking more: teacher or student?
When were the students learning?

Thoughts about literacy events in other classrooms and in your future classroom

How Learning and Literacy Fit with Content-Area Teaching

We have joined the concepts of learning and literacy because in every field powerful ideas are communicated to others through a literacy action. Listen to Martin Luther King's "I Have a Dream" speech, and you can only be persuaded by the power of his ideas. Read Rachel Carson's *Silent Spring*, and you can only decide to take action against DDT or Agent Orange. Debate welfare policies with friends, and you hone your own thinking about the controversies in public policy. In taking literacy actions, Martin Luther King, Jr., Rachel Carson, and you and your friends think about not only the ideas but the purposes for communicating and the audiences to receive the ideas. Literacy actions are social actions in which the speaker or writer of the ideas and the listener or reader of the ideas interact through the message or content ideas (Moffett, 1983/1968; Barnes & Todd, 1995). Without literacy actions, ideas would lay dormant and inert. People pursue literacy actions to construct their own ideas and to communicate ideas to others in society. You and your students also will engage in literacy actions to construct ideas for yourselves and to communicate ideas to each other and to audiences beyond the classroom.

Our focus in this book is on literacy strategies that support learning in the content areas and complement the learning strategies you use in your specific field. We think that reading, writing, speaking, and listening (or literacy) are avenues to *communicate* content; they are not content in themselves. For example, mechanics read directions and warranties for parts. Computer programmers read and write computer languages and the documentation about software. Anthropologists read about cultures as well as write field notes about artifacts at sites. Keeping the tandem learning of strategies and content in the forefront, we emphasize literacy strategies that support the content areas.

We emphasize three aspects of learning in this book: (1) your learning with literacy in your content area, (2) your students' learning with literacy in this content area, and (3) your learning to become a content-area teacher. The old adage, "You can lead a horse to water but you can't make him drink," applies to learning too. We can present information to people, but we can't make them learn. That is why we subscribe to the theory that people construct knowledge, actively build and rebuild their knowledge, when they learn. In constructing their knowledge, they use strategies to remember, incorporate, and apply knowledge to situations, problems, and issues. In every field, experts have both a large knowledge base and a range of strategies that they use in tandem as they learn or create new information (Alexander & Judy, 1988). Some people figure out learning strategies on their own; others do not and could benefit from instruction. Therefore, our emphasis in this book is on the tandem teaching of both content knowledge and strategies.

▶ ▶ ▶ ▶ **The Role of Literacy in Learning Content**

Literacy, or listening, speaking, reading, and writing, is the means for communicating ideas to yourself or someone else. Literacy has no content (that is, unless you study language for its own sake, as a linguist or a lexicographer does). Therefore, the content must come from the subject area. In math, students record how they solved the problem in a process journal—that's using literacy. In social studies, students interview a community member, such as a Vietnam veteran or protester—that's using literacy. In both examples, the content plays the dominant role by providing the message; but without the supporting role of literacy, students could not examine or communicate the content.

In the ongoing life of the classroom, speaking and listening occur almost automatically. In traditional classrooms, the teacher controls who speaks when, as well as the pace and the topic of the interchanges; students are expected to listen, absorb information, and produce the answers teachers expect. Do you think those students are constructing knowledge or memorizing information? To engage students in constructing knowledge, we prefer student-to-student exchanges that analyze the information and evaluate the strategies they use. In addition, we encourage activities (when they are germane to the curriculum) that use speaking and listening in situations that occur normally in adult society, like interviewing community members, experts, or other students either in person or on-line. Whether with students in the class or with people beyond the school, speaking and listening play important roles in generating, interacting, and refining ideas in your content area.

Since curriculum materials are used in teaching-learning events in classrooms, reading plays a prevalent role. In traditional classrooms, the textbook dominates the curriculum. Students read each chapter and answer the review questions. Although we recognize that as a beginning teacher you will rely on textbooks, we encourage you to supplement them with other materials (see Chapter 3). For example, in English, you can relate journals and newspaper articles to the literature students read. Social studies teachers can provide opportunities to read a variety of texts: primary documents, newspaper articles, historical fiction, biography, on-line references. Science teachers can incorporate a variety of texts—for example, students' journals, on-line data, magazines, and informational books—as resources to support hands-on learning. Foreign language teachers can have students read on-line text from other students. Throughout Part II, we address reading strategies for obtaining, analyzing, and evaluating the ideas from a variety of texts so that students thoughtfully construct their learning in your content area.

Writing occupies an interesting role in our schools. Traditionally, students write term papers and essays, and teachers correct and grade them. Content-area teachers rarely have used writing except for testing purposes.

Instead, we encourage all content-area teachers to focus on writing as an avenue for exploring tentative ideas during learning and less as a product to be examined. Since English teachers emphasize the writing process—drafting, revising, and editing—all content-area teachers can emphasize the types of writing used to learn and communicate in their content area. Throughout Part II in Focus on Writing sections, we present teaching tools that use writing to generate ideas, record and think through ideas, compare one's ideas with a text's, and communicate one's more refined ideas to an audience or to pose questions that can guide further study.

In this book, we emphasize literacy strategies that support the learning of your content. As a learner and a teacher, you should select the strategies, from among the ones we discuss in Part II, that suit your students and the learning tasks in your content area.

Teacher as Inquiring Learner Activity

Observe a classroom in your content area, and record your observations of the types of literacy events that occur and their participants. Within one period, track the number of minutes the teacher spends listening, speaking, reading, and writing. Also track the number of minutes the students spend listening, speaking, reading, and writing. Think about the learning goals and objectives you think the teacher had for the period.

• How would you assess who was constructing meaning and when was it occurring?

▶ ▶ ▶ ▷ **Strategies to Support Learning in Content Areas**

In this book, we ask you to think about what strategies you use to learn in your content area, and especially what literacy strategies you use. We think that if you are aware of your own learning and literacy strategies, you will be better able to teach strategies to your students. You also will be better able to decide when a particular strategy would be appropriate and how it is used in a specific situation. In essence, you will be able to make your invisible strategies visible to your students in the context of learning content knowledge.

Strategic learners are conscious of what they know, how they learn, what tasks require, and how they are progressing. Educators call this consciousness—metacognitive awareness, or thinking about thinking (Flavell, Miller, & Miller, 1993; Garner, 1987). We picture metacognitive awareness as working like the control panels in a computer that oversee how programs function. Think back to a time when you were confused about what was required for an assignment. In metacognitive terms, you monitored your thinking: you recognized what you did not know and determined what strategies were necessary to do the assignment. In contrast, think about a time when you were completely absorbed in a novel or were solving a problem smoothly. In metacognitive terms, you monitored your progress or recognized that you were progressing well and need not change strategies.

Not all students are metacognitively aware, although the older the students are, the more likely it is that they are aware (Garner & Alexander, 1989). Teachers often assume that students are aware of what they know and don't know—their content knowledge. In fact, poor students often do not recognize that they do not understand a text, and not all students recognize when they are confused or need to study more. Furthermore, we think that many students are unaware of their strategy knowledge—in other words, how they learn. For some students, learning has come so easily that they have not considered how they learn. For others, learning has been so difficult that they attribute any learning success to luck rather than to their own efforts. Certainly some students are aware of how they learn, but we think that most students do not think strategically about how to accomplish a learning task or use a small repertoire of strategies for every task without regard to the different requirements of each specific task.

Let's define what we mean by *strategy*: a conscious plan of action for achieving an activity or goal (Dole, Duffy, Roehler, & Pearson, 1991; Duffy & Roehler, 1989; Paris, Lipson, & Wixson, 1983/1994; Pressley, Goodchild, Zajchowski, & Evans, 1989). People choose a strategy to use based on their assessment of what the task requires and their purposes for completing the task. Rather than just plunging ahead, strategic learners stop and think about how to proceed. Sometimes they invent a new strategy, at least for them, or adapt a strategy they already know to fit the task better. Thus, the key words for describing strategies are *conscious, selective, useful for the situation,* and *adaptive.*

We think that metacognitively aware learners are conscious of their strategies when they encounter a new or a difficult task. But when they face a familiar or easy task, we think they routinely apply strategies that have been successful for them in the past (Pressley et al., 1989) and consider adapting those strategies only when problems arise. For example, chess players have familiar strategies that they successfully use, especially when facing an easy opponent. They make their moves routinely until, by luck, the easy mark makes a challenging response. Then they must reconsider more consciously and deliberately their strategies to achieve checkmate.

In the research on strategies, two recurring questions arise: (1) What is the difference between strategies and skills? and (2) Are strategies general and applicable across all disciplines or specific and applicable to only a particular discipline? Neither of these questions is easily or definitively answered. Let's outline our position on each question.

First, *what is the difference between strategies and skills?* You have probably heard the term *skills* applied regularly—for example, to arithmetic skills, reading skills, soccer skills, basic skills. Educators and researchers used the term *skills* before they used the term *strategies,* and in some cases people have just substituted the term *strategy* for *skills* (such as *reading strategies* for *reading skills*). We, however, define a *skill* as a discrete action in isolation (Dole et al., 1991; Duffy & Roehler, 1989; Paris et al., 1983/1994). For example, knowing addition facts is an arithmetic skill. But you need a problem-solving strategy to know when using addition would be appropriate to solve a problem. Or you may learn the skill of heading the soccer ball, but in the context of a game, you need to know when to head the ball instead of kicking it—a strategy. Or when you encounter an unknown word in a book, you may decide to skip it, or decipher the letter sounds (phonics), or figure it out from the surrounding context, or look it up in the dictionary. If you can easily decipher the sounds of unknown words in isolation, you will choose the strategy of using letter sounds (phonics) to identify the word when you need to. If you are unsuccessful, you may change to another strategy. Thus, for us, the key words that describe "skill" are *discrete, isolated action* and for "strategy" *planned, useful action in context.*

Second, *are strategies general and applicable across all disciplines, or specific and applicable to only a particular discipline?* This discussion has been swinging back and forth for decades (Perkins & Salomon, 1989). As an example, physics experts use specific strategies, and yet when they come upon an unfamiliar problem, they may use a general strategy, like thinking of an analogy. Recognizing what information is relevant to the problem—content knowledge—makes both general and specific strategies effective. Therefore, Perkins and Salomon argue for a consensus position of general strategies applied in specific contexts. We agree.

We think that literacy strategies are general strategies for using in specific contexts. As a content-area teacher, you will want to teach literacy strategies in tandem with your content-area texts. Therefore, you will use strategies in a specific, contextual setting and concentrate on the strategies that are useful to your students' doing learning and literacy tasks in your content area.

When you work with a teacher in another content area, you both may discover that a general strategy is useful in both content areas, although you each apply the strategy in a discipline-specific manner. For example, a general literacy strategy is to preview or get an overview of the text (see Chapter 4). Mathematicians preview or quickly read the entire problem through before deciding how to solve it. Poets preview or read aloud a poem in its entirety before they read to interpret it. When the mathematician and the poet preview their respective texts, both are striving to get a general sense of their texts. However, they notice different aspects or features about their texts, based on their knowledge of their respective fields. Since the particular features significantly contribute to their understanding, the strategy of previewing is specifically applied, in a very contextual manner, to their respective texts. Thus, content knowledge and strategy knowledge are intertwined, one reinforcing the other.

By the way, both teachers will need to apply the strategy because students will rarely independently transfer the previewing strategy from a math class to an English class. Both teachers need to remind the students of the other teacher's application of the strategy.

In this book, we emphasize general literacy strategies that can be specifically applied across different content areas. The literacy strategies function to support learning in specific contexts—your content area—and so we have included examples from different content areas. We expect you to construct your knowledge of strategies—both literacy strategies and strategies more specific to your content area—and to select or adapt useful ones.

▶ ▶ ▶ ▶ Teaching Literacy Strategies for Learning Content

We are interested in your becoming an effective content-area teacher. Thus, we focus on content pedagogy, the instructional tools that use literacy to support learning content. We use the term *tool* to refer to the instructional activities that constitute the teaching-learning events in classrooms.

As a content-area teacher, you concentrate on the content you want your students to learn. Concurrently, you need to think about the literacy and learning strategies your students need to use to learn that content. Once you have decided what content and what strategies will be in your lesson, you need to choose the tools you will use to teach. As you can see in Figure 1.2, the tool should fit your purposes and your students because each tool has different purposes. In Chapter 3, we fully define each tool, and in Part II we present specific tools in each category. Now, because the major focus of this book is literacy strategies in the context of learning, we want to explain the teaching tool of modeling and explaining, which we highlight with specific examples or scripts in Part II.

Athletes, carpenters' apprentices, and chefs' assistants have been instructed through modeling and explaining for a long time, but the academic areas have only recently begun to incorporate the coaching or apprenticeship type of instruction (Collins, Brown, & Newman, 1989). When you choose the teaching tool of modeling and explaining, you aim to make your invisible literacy strategies visible to your students by using a book or an article they will read—a specific, contextual setting (Duffy et al., 1987). Becoming metacognitively aware of your use of learning and literacy strategies will help you model and explain, discuss, and even trade strategies with your students.

Figure 1.2

Choices of
Pedagogical Tools

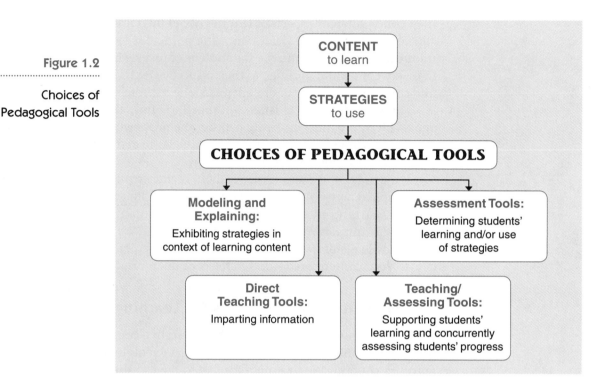

To teach students how to use strategies, you would read modeling or demonstrating strategies, and interrupt your reading to explain your thinking and your strategies. You explicitly discuss with your students:

- What the strategy is and does
- When and why to use the strategy
- How to use the strategy

If you modeled strategies without explaining, you would exhibit their use with a specific text. But the students would have to infer from your model what strategies were used, how they were used, and why they were used. Because the strategies are embedded in your reading (modeling), they may not recognize that you are using strategies. Therefore, you should both model and explain specific strategies you use with particular texts. (We provide example scripts in Part II.)

After modeling and explaining a strategy, you need to coach students as they try out using the strategy in a similar contextual situation. As they practice the strategy (often with partners at first), you and their peers can offer suggestions or pointers. Finally, students independently recognize when and where to incorporate the strategy (Pearson & Gallagher, 1983).

When teachers (or even students) model and explain their literacy strategies, they are demystifying their processes by making their strategies visible. Let's consider an example of modeling and explaining from physical education: learning the lob shot in tennis. The tennis coach begins by explaining what a lob is; this is *declarative knowledge.* She then sets up game scenarios and explains the purpose of the lob and when to use it—*conditional knowledge.* Next, she describes how to execute a lob—*procedural knowledge*—by elaborating on how to stand, hold the racket, and hit the ball. As she does so, she demonstrates (or models) the lob by actually executing a few lobs. (Note that hitting a lob in isolation is a skill. When the player knows not only how to lob but selects when and where to use the lob in a particular situation, then the lob can be called a strategy.)

If the tennis coach just modeled the lob in a game, the players would have to figure out the hidden or implicit techniques that the coach used. They would have to infer how to execute the lob and when to use the lob in a game. Some players would figure out the techniques. Others would not.

When content-area teachers use modeling and explaining, they need to select which literacy strategies fit the text. What strategies will be most useful for the texts that students read? What strategies will expand the students' repertoire of literacy strategies? What literacy strategies are most important for the goals and objectives in the unit of study?

Teacher as Inquiring Learner Activity

The purpose of this activity is to help you become metacognitively aware of your literacy strategies so that you can model and explain them to your students. (At this point, we do not expect you to name specific literacy strategies. In Part II, we present literacy strategies, but don't peek ahead. This is an exploration activity—not a test!)

To complete a think-aloud activity, select an easy text and a hard text in your content area. First read the easy text aloud for fifteen minutes. As you read, stop and voice your thoughts into a tape recorder, or jot your thoughts in the margins of the text.

* What are you thinking about as you interact with the text? For example, what did you think when you read the title?

Repeat the think-aloud activity with the hard text. Then analyze your reading and thinking with the easy text and the hard text.

* What strategies did you use with each text? Were your strategies different with the hard text than the easier text? Why?

Education for the Twenty-First Century

We have emphasized the continuous learning experiences involved in becoming a content-area teacher and the intersection of learning and literacy strategies because your students will live in a changing world. What must schools, teachers, and curricula become to prepare those students for the twenty-first century? What beliefs and assumptions do you hold from your own experiences in middle school and high school? What are your beliefs about those schools in the future? What goals do you hold for your future teaching?

▶ ▶ ▶ ▶ Middle Schools and High Schools for the Twenty-First Century

What do you want middle schools and high schools to be like in the twenty-first century? Do you envision the traditional middle school and high school that has fixed forty-one-minute periods on a rotating schedule and students in rows facing the teacher, who remains at the chalkboard throughout the class period? Or do you envision reforms that will help every student, raise the quality of learning, and silence the criticism of education by the public, by foundations in their reports on reforms, and by educational researchers in their studies of schools?

In *Turning Points: Preparing American Youth for the 21st Century* (Carnegie Council on Adolescent Development, 1990), which presents recommendations for transforming the middle school, and in *Breaking Ranks: Changing an American Institution* (National Association of Secondary School Principals, 1996), with recommendations for the high school, we found similar reforms that relate to learning and literacy:

- Smaller student bodies or schools within a school and a team of teachers working with no more than ninety students so that a caring community of learners can develop

- Flexible scheduling, so that classes could extend over fifty minutes as warranted, and flexible grouping, without restricting the range of courses, rather than tracking

- Where practical, integration of content areas or connections within and across content areas—math and science as well as biology, chemistry, and physics—and, again where practical, applications to real life

- Where appropriate, the integration of technology

- Instruction that develops reasoning, problem solving, and strategies to learn

These reforms are being implemented now in some middle schools and high schools. Some middle school teachers are working together and coordinating or integrating their curriculum units. In some high schools, smaller schools within a school exist. In many high schools, two teachers work together in a common course, such as English and social studies teachers teaching an American studies course.

What kind of school will you teach in for your preservice work and for your first employment?

As you move into teaching, we encourage you to find a similarly minded colleague or two and work to introduce changes in your schools.

▶ ▶ ▶ ▶ Teaching for the Twenty-First Century

Given that you won't change the school on your first job, you *can* decide how you will teach in your classroom. Do you remember which junior high or middle school and high school teachers inspired you, bored you, or challenged you? What did you do in those classes: take notes from lectures or discuss in small groups? Did the teacher incorporate teaching tools, like study guides, to support your learning? Did you discuss strategies for learning the content? Did you relate the course content to issues or events outside school or to other courses?

Think about a worst-case and best-case scenario from your secondary schooling. We remember a worst scenario: an American history teacher who wrote an outline of facts on the board and elaborated that outline as his lecture, while students silently copied the outline in notebooks. He would interrupt his lecture periodically with questions, to which students responded with one word or one phrase. If a student answered incorrectly, he called on another student until he got the answer he was looking for. At night students read the chapter and answered the chapter review questions. In that class, students learned that "doing" history was memorizing isolated facts.

In contrast, we remember a best-case scenario: a high school social studies teacher who challenged students to relate the curriculum to current events. During the civil rights unrest of the late 1950s, the class discussed the Preamble to the United States Constitution, "We, the people . . ." in terms of Alabama's stand against integrating public schools. Students argued whether Alabama could invoke the Preamble and secede from the United States. In that class, students learned that "doing" social studies was analyzing current and historical problems using factual knowledge and critical thinking.

Those worst- and best-case scenarios can still be found today. Walk into any school, and you will find teachers who lecture while students passively take notes. According to researchers (Goodlad, 1984; Alvermann, O'Brien, & Dillon, 1990) teacher talk still dominates elementary and secondary classrooms. Rarely does a discussion involving connected dialogue interrupt the teacher, and even more rarely does a discussion among only students occur. Yet you can also find teachers who challenge students to work with the material by incorporating discussion, projects, current events or issues, and related disciplines.

Among the recommendations on instructional strategies in *Breaking Ranks* are ones that strive to change high school classrooms dominated by teachers who are dispensing information. Teachers need to use a variety of student-centered teaching tools and judiciously use the teacher-centered lecture. Teachers are encouraged to become coaches and facilitators, assisting students to build their knowledge actively instead of passively receiving facts. Teachers should provide students with experiences in making judgments about facts, drawing inferences from facts, solving problems with facts, and using logical reasoning with facts, for example. And finally, teachers should integrate assessment with instruction so that the instructional activities inform both the students and the teacher about the status of learning and also inform future instruction.

What kind of teacher do you aim to be? We expect that you will aim to involve your students with the content in your subject area so that they will construct ideas and maybe become interested in pursuing the subject in a career. Beyond those aims, we advocate the teaching of strategies in tandem with the content. A secondary teacher's statement, " I have to cover biology; it is the last time they may have the subject," will not hold in the twenty-first century. Every student will encounter biology after that course in the form of personal or societal issues—for example, questions about diseases, nutrition, lifestyle, or the effects of pollution. Educators need to teach students strategies to acquire knowledge in the content areas so that they can continue to learn when faced with new information and issues in the future.

We are asking you not only to interest students in subject matter but to equip them with strategies they can use with future content. Our aim is to help you acquire literacy strategies and teaching tools that will help you teach and help your students learn in your content area.

Summary of the Chapter

One goal for this chapter was for you to begin thinking about teaching in the twenty-first century. We also wanted to introduce you to what you will learn about in this book and your course.

We discussed that to become a content-area teacher now and in the future, you want to learn continually in four areas:

- Knowledge of your content area
- Knowledge of learners
- Knowledge of content pedagogy
- Knowledge of curriculum materials

We encouraged you to begin reflecting on teaching through the inquiry activities in every chapter.

Next, we discussed how literacy fits with content-area learning:

- The role of literacy in learning content: speaking, listening, reading, and writing as avenues for learning and communicating ideas to oneself and others
- Strategies as conscious plans of action for achieving a task
- Teaching literacy strategies for learning content

Finally, we asked you to speculate about middle schools, high schools, and teaching in the twenty-first century. Rather than automatically teaching as you were taught, we urge you to consider the reforms advocated. As you begin your career in teaching, we hope you will become a broker of change to make your students' education better.

Inquiry Activities About Your Learning

1. Interview an experienced teacher in your content area. How does the teacher want his or her students to view the content area? What are his or her major goals for the students that underlie his or her teaching? What does the teacher consider the major themes or ideas in the content area? How do those major ideas relate to one another and to the everyday world? Can the teacher sketch a diagram or model of the essence of the content area, the relationships among the major ideas, or what it means to "do" the content area?

2. Write your literacy autobiography. How did you learn to read and write? Both in school and out of school, what texts have you enjoyed reading or shared with your peers as you've grown up? What types of writing do you do in school and out of school? In school, were you taught strategies for reading, writing, and studying? Describe what you remember about learning literacy strategies.

Inquiry Activities About Your Students' Learning

1. Ask a student to sketch a picture of life in middle school or high school. (Reassure the student that drawing ability is not expected.) In the student's view, what are the important places in the school? What are the significant activities in school?

How would the student draw a typical classroom in the school? How would the student draw a typical student learning in a typical classroom? How would the student draw a typical teacher teaching in the school?

Now ask the student to draw his or her ideal school, ideal classroom, ideal activities, and ideal teacher. Did the student make any changes? Ask the student to describe the similarities or differences in the two drawings.

2. Interview a student about his or her literacy activities in and out of school. What does the student read and write in school? What speaking and listening activities does the student engage in during school? Outside school, what reading and writing, speaking, and listening does the student engage in? Does the student use literacy to accomplish everyday activities, like ordering a hamburger or using a computer program? Does the student use literacy as a hobby, such as reading a book for pleasure or keeping a diary? How would the student assess the importance of literacy to his or her everyday life and to his or her learning in school?

2

Students as Learners

As a Native American friend of mine says, you will be the children's teacher when you learn to accept their gifts. (Featherstone, 1995, p. 18)

Your students' gifts are their identities, their cultures, their knowledge, their strategies, and their attitudes for learning that they bring to your classroom and develop within it. As their teacher, you can gain the understanding to be able to respond to the unique gifts and needs of your students, even when you have 100 or 125 students. When you are able to "see students individually," you will have become a responsive and reflective teacher. This will not happen on the first day or in the first month. Teaching is not a recipe or "one size fits all" (Reyes, 1992). Teaching is learning about and with students.

In this chapter, we present three major aspects of Students as Learners (see the chapter opening graphic). First, we focus on who the students are in classrooms today and in the future because understanding the diversity characteristics of your students will help you teach your content. We will discuss five categories of diversity—race/ethnicity, language, income levels or socioeconomic status (SES), gender, and special needs—because you are likely to teach students who represent those diversity characteristics. We conclude with suggestions for teaching all students, but especially diverse students. As we will repeat throughout the chapter, we want you to remember that not everyone with the same diversity characteristic is alike. Students are individuals with unique combinations of characteristics.

Second, we define what students bring to classrooms from their previous learning. Educators no longer view students as blank slates on which to write new knowledge; now educators recognize that students enter their classrooms with previous knowledge, strategies, and attitudes. As a content-area teacher, you need to think about what students bring so that you can build on the content they have already learned, the strategies they use to learn, and the attitudes they hold about learning.

And finally, we discuss standardized tests because they have consequences for your students' lives and for the schools in which you work. You need to understand what they are, how they are used and misused, and how you can use them fairly.

Purpose-Setting Questions

1. What is your cultural background? How do you define yourself in terms of race, ethnicity, language, socioeconomic status, gender, and special needs? How has your background influenced your views, interests, values, choice of college, and decision to be a teacher?

2. Whom have you met in college who is different from you? How has that person's school experiences been different from and similar to yours? Do you hold different or similar views about the opportunities that schools offer students? Can you explain how those differences or similarities originated?

3. Can you remember what background knowledge you brought to your high school or college classes in your content area? For example, can you remember what elementary geometry knowledge helped you understand geometry in secondary school or college? Do you remember teachers' building on your previous learning?

4. What standardized tests have you taken, such as the SATs? How do you perform on standardized tests? Why do you find them easy or difficult to take? How were your scores on standardized tests used to make decisions about your schooling?

Who Are the Students in Classrooms?

The population in the United States is becoming more diverse racially and ethnically. If you look at the public school enrollment data for 1986 and 1994 (see Table 2.1), you will see that the white student population has decreased while the other racial/ethnic student populations have increased. Because these trends are expected to continue, more classrooms will have students from diverse backgrounds.

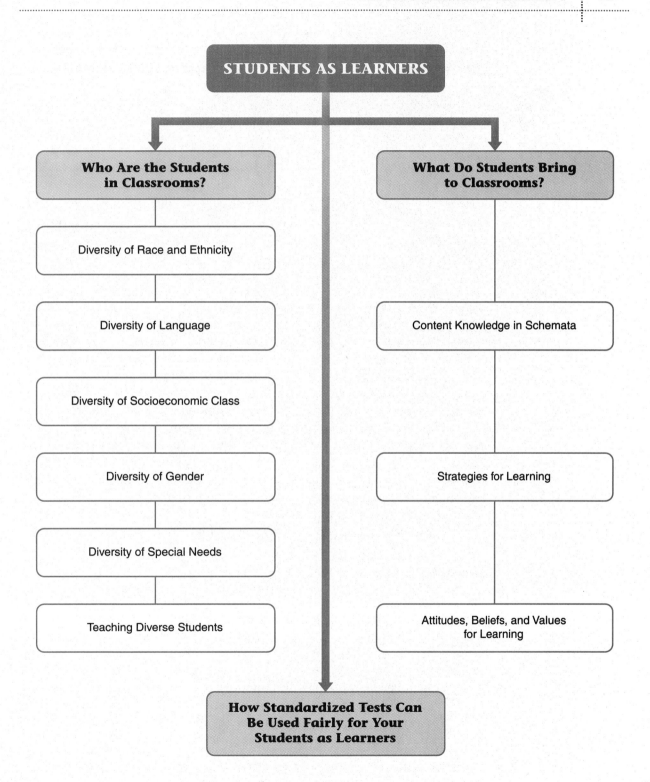

STUDENTS AS LEARNERS

Who Are the Students
in Classrooms?

What Do Students Bring
to Classrooms?

Diversity of Race and Ethnicity

Diversity of Language

Content Knowledge in Schemata

Diversity of Socioeconomic Class

Diversity of Gender

Strategies for Learning

Diversity of Special Needs

Teaching Diverse Students

Attitudes, Beliefs, and Values
for Learning

How Standardized Tests Can
Be Used Fairly for Your
Students as Learners

Table 2.1   Enrollment in Public Elementary and Secondary Schools, by Race or Ethnicity

	White	Black	Hispanic	Asian or Pacific Islander	American Indian/ Alaskan Native
% in 1986	70.4	16.1	9.9	2.8	.9
% in 1994	65.6	16.7	13.0	3.6	1.1

Source: National Center for Education Statistics (1996).

Students are diverse in characteristics other than race and ethnicity. Students speak different languages, come from families with different income levels or socioeconomic status (SES), have gender differences, and may have special learning needs. Each of these diversity characteristics brings challenges and gifts to teaching and learning in content-area classrooms.

Although some people use the term *multicultural*, we prefer the word *diversity* to refer to the broad range of differences among students in classrooms. We begin by presenting an overview of diversity in regard to only five categories—race and ethnicity, language, SES, gender, and special needs—although we recognize that people have these characteristics in combination as well as other characteristics we do not address. You also know that people are individuals, and so although we discuss groups, we do not mean to stereotype an individual. We follow the overview with a general discussion of teaching diverse students. In Part Two on specific teaching tools, we will refer back to this diversity discussion.

▶ ▶ ▶ ▶   **Diversity of Race and Ethnicity**

Everyone belongs to several cultural groups (Gollnick & Chinn, 1994). Our various cultures define the ways we perceive and behave in the world, as well as our beliefs and values. People define themselves in terms of the microcultures, different cultural groups with which they identify, such as race and ethnicity, gender, class, religion, language, occupation, age, learning ability or achievement, personal hobbies and interests, or personality traits. People with different cultural group identities can experience the same situation differently. For example, males and females (gender culture) often experience events in the workplace differently (the business culture).

If you are a white American of European descent, you may not think much about your race or ethnic culture's characteristics because it has been the dominant majority culture in the United States. If you are an African American, Asian American, Hispanic American, or Native American, you probably do realize that you participate in two cultures: your minority culture as well as aspects of the majority culture.

A simple example of a majority perspective is the Mercator map projection of the world. You have probably seen Mercator's map with the Americas and Europe near the center and Asia split between the right and left sides. Because a map projects the mapmaker's concept of the world, Mercator must have believed that North America and Europe were more important than Asia. Have you ever seen a map with Australia at the top instead of the bottom? We have, and it surely communicates Australia's "minority cultural" perspective!

Teacher as Inquiring Learner Activity

List the specific cultural groups that define you—for example, "white, male, student teacher, athlete." Think about the characteristics we will discuss— race/ethnicity, language, SES, gender, and special needs—as well as others that may define you, such as career choice, religion, age, interests, or hobbies. Draw a circle or pie chart. Allocate sections of the pie chart to each cultural identity.

- Which of these cultures are most important to defining you?

Our country has struggled with the ideal of equality and the reality of a diverse, immigrant population since its beginnings. Remember that the U.S. Constitution stated that only propertied, white males could vote. Although education is meant to provide equal opportunity, minority culture students, who are often also poor, dominate the lowest track in high schools, are numerous in special education classes, are scarce in advanced placement courses, and have high dropout rates (Oakes, 1992).

Why do some minority culture populations succeed in school while others fail? Ogbu (1993) argues for a theory that contrasts the identities of voluntary and involuntary immigrants. Voluntary minority people (for example, some Europeans and Central Americans) have come to the United States to be more successful than they could be in their homeland. Keeping their original identity, they add a second identity of the majority culture which helps them succeed in school. In contrast, involuntary minority people (for example, Native Americans and African Americans) create their identity in opposition to the white American identity. When they view school success as part of the white identity but not part of their own minority identity, they may decide not to excel in school.

Ogbu's theory may be reflected in urban secondary schools, since many urban high school students view dropping out as political action against the school and see no benefits in continuing their education (Fine, 1991). Nevertheless, we caution against automatically applying the theory to groups, and especially to individuals. Voluntary minority students can struggle in school, and involuntary minority students can thrive there (Nieto, 1996). School success or failure is probably a combination of "personal, cultural, political and societal processes in which all of these factors affect one another in sometimes competing and contradictory ways" (Nieto, 1996, p. 246).

To ignore race and ethnicity is to deny a person's heritage or identity. As the student population becomes increasingly diverse, all educators need to strive to understand their own culture and their students' cultures and how this identity can affect teaching and learning. For example, providing science education for culturally diverse students is complicated and requires sensitivity on the part of teachers (Lee & Fradd, 1998). McDiarmid recalls his scientific discussion with Yup'ik Eskimo students in which they analyzed how the refrigeration system worked and why it was broken. At the end of the discussion when McDiarmid asked why the cooler broke, "one of the students who had been most involved in the conversation replied, 'Ghosts'" (1991, p. 257). Recognizing the clash between the scientific, majority culture and a spiritual, minority culture did not solve McDiarmid's teaching dilemma, but at least he understood the cultural clash he faced.

▶ ▶ ▶ ▷ Diversity of Language

Whether we are a nation of one language, English, or a nation with diverse languages is a hot political debate. Usually because majority culture people have immigrant ancestors who learned English on their own, they think recent immigrants need only to be surrounded by English speakers to learn English. However, both in the past and now, language-minority students are more likely to drop out of school; in fact, Hispanic youth are more than twice as likely to drop out (Crawford in Tinajoro & Hurly, 1997; National Education Association, 1997).

You may have met different terms describing various second-language programs and students. In *transitional bilingual programs* with bilingual teachers, the students read, write, and learn content in their first language as they begin to learn English; then they use both languages to learn and finally use primarily English. In *English as a Second Language* (ESL) classes, the teacher speaks only English, and the students learn content and literacy in English. Finally, the term *limited English proficiency* describes the amount of English language that students speak, not their ability to learn English. When many students speak the same first language, schools often establish transitional bilingual programs. When only a few students speak one language or when many students speak different languages, schools usually establish ESL classes. In Part Two, we will use the term *ESL* to refer to students' learning English in either bilingual or ESL programs.

In evaluating various bilingual and ESL programs, researchers have not determined which program teaches students more English, more quickly (Moran & Hakuta, 1995). Therefore, some researchers are investigating classroom-based questions about teaching and learning (Moll, 1992; Minami & Ovando, 1995). For example, researchers have found that Spanish/English bilingual students who are successful English readers use strategies in both languages and use their Spanish knowledge to support their English (Langer, Bartolome, Vasquez, & Lucas, 1990; Jiménez, García, & Pearson, 1996). We think this recent research supports our focus on strategies in Part Two.

As you think about language diversity, consider several factors that are involved in learning a second language (García, 1999). To start, students' first language is a part of their cultural identity. Second, students learn conversational language for specific situations (say, ordering a hamburger) more easily than the abstract language of content areas (studying ions). Third, students usually understand more of what they hear and read in English than they can express in speaking and writing. And last, if students have studied the content and learned to read and write in their first language, then learning in the second language can be easier.

Diversity of Dialect.   Most languages have different dialects or versions of the language that have small differences in pronunciation, vocabulary, and grammar. In language terms, different dialect speakers can express ideas equally well and understand each other. However, in many languages, one dialect has acquired more social prestige than the others. Standard American English is the dialect the majority culture has accepted for public oral and written communication. Therefore, schools and textbooks use standard American English. Among the dialects in the United States, Black English dialect (most recently called Ebonics) and Appalachian English have not been attributed social prestige, even though their linguistic differences with standard English are small (Warren & McCloskey, 1997). In most schools, those dialect speakers are expected to learn standard English.

Dialect, like language, communicates home culture and is a part of our individual identity. Some people choose to be bidialectical, just as they are bicultural, using the dialect that fits the social situation. For example, one dialect is used for peer conversations and another in more formal situations, such as in job interviews. Like cultural diversity, educators need to be sensitive to their perspectives of language and dialect differences and assist students in adding, not eliminating, the languages or dialects that are appropriate for various social situations (Crawford, 1993).

▶ ▶ ▶ ▶   **Diversity of Socioeconomic Class**

Americans, and especially educators, want to believe our society is a meritocracy: If students study and work hard, they can succeed in society. In fact, educational success can often be predicted by SES, and low SES students are more likely to drop out (Committee for Economic Development, 1987).

Although society as a whole has a range of SES levels, many residential communities are not very diverse economically. Wealthy suburbs have public schools with more resources; poor cities have schools with fewer resources (Committee for Economic Development, 1987). These resource differences have

An ongoing goal of every teacher is to learn about the individuality of each student in his or her diverse student population.

© Mary Kay Denny/PHOTO EDIT

resulted in differing educational opportunities (described as *Savage Inequalities* by Kozol, 1991) and lawsuits about educational financing in several states.

Within a school population, the low SES students dominate the low groups in elementary schools, the low tracks in secondary schools, and the special education or compensatory programs throughout the grades. Although the tracks or programs were established to meet student needs, these instructional differences result in different educational experiences. In the high tracks, the teacher's instruction focuses on conceptual understandings, includes a variety of academic tasks and less lecturing (although still plenty), and communicates respect and self-worth to the students. In the low tracks, the teacher's instruction focuses on basic skills, isolated facts, and fewer topics; includes more repetition and lecturing; and communicates disrespect and low expectations to the students (Knapp & Woolverton, 1995). Educators at all levels need to examine their good intentions for meeting student needs and determine if their instruction expands, rather than limits, students' opportunities.

▶ ▶ ▶ ▷ **Diversity of Gender**

Many educators began to examine their classrooms and their teaching for gender patterns when *The AAUW Report: How Schools Shortchange Girls* (American Association of University Women, 1992) and *Failing at Fairness: How America's Schools Cheat Girls* (Sadker & Sadker, 1994) were published. Most educators believe they are fair until they look closely; ourselves included. When we examined our college classrooms, we found the male students talked and asked questions proportionately more, thereby dominating the class conversation. Although schools have made progress toward equity (American Institutes of Research, 1998), teachers at every level need to examine the gender patterns in their classrooms and how the patterns influence communication roles and grouping decisions (see Chapter 3).

Although gender achievement differences are narrowing in beginning math, science, and computer science courses, enrollment differences still occur in the advanced courses. Girls are more likely to take advanced placement biology but less likely to take physics or calculus. Without the advanced courses, women do not have an adequate background for math, science, or computer careers (American Institutes of Research, 1998). And often even high-achieving young women do not elect to pursue math or science majors or careers unless they have a parent's or teacher's encouragement (American Association of University Women, 1992).

In contrast, reading/language arts or verbal achievement has been touted as the area where women achieve more than men. More girls than boys take courses in English, foreign languages (French and Spanish), and the Fine Arts and they take more courses in those areas (American Institute of Research, 1998).

In every content area, educators need to ask if the students of nonstereotype gender feel welcome and have the same opportunities to learn.

▶ ▶ ▶ ▶ Diversity of Special Needs

As defined by Public Law 101:476 in 1990, the Individuals with Disabilities Education Act (IDEA), special needs or disabilities categories include learning disabilities, mentally retarded, hearing impairments, speech or language impairments, visual impairments, serious emotional disturbance, orthopedic impairments, autism, traumatic brain injury, and other health impairments. Although not listed in IDEA, the U.S. Department of Education allows students with attention deficit disorder (ADD) and attention deficit–hyperactivity disorder (ADHD), which often occur in conjunction with learning disabilities or emotionally disturbed categories, to receive special education services.

Because you will most likely meet students with learning disabilities, who account for 51.2 percent of the total disability population (U.S. Department of Education, 1997), and because this book is on literacy, we focus on students with these disabilities. Although there are various definitions of what constitutes a learning disability, most states use the IDEA definition that contains four major identifying characteristics (Lerner, 1993). First, the student has a disorder in one or more basic psychological processes, such as memory, auditory perception, or visual perception. Second, the student has learning difficulties in speaking, listening, reading, writing, and/or mathematics. Third, the learning problem is not caused by other disabilities, such as visual impairments or mental retardation. And fourth, the student is severely underachieving compared to his or her projected potential.

In accordance with the law, students with special needs receive appropriate education in the least restrictive or separate environment and are mainstreamed, or learn in regular classrooms, whenever possible. Since 1986, the Office of Special Education and Rehabilitative Services has encouraged the regular education initiative or serving students with special needs primarily within the regular classroom (Will, 1986). Therefore, in your content-area classrooms, you will teach students who have literacy and learning difficulties. They may need additional instruction from a special education teacher either in your classroom or in the resource room. Granting that more collaboration between regular and special education is needed, Lerner (1993) recommends that both regular and special education teachers have adequate time and support to prepare and collaborate; moreover, students with difficulties need to exhibit acceptable classroom behaviors, and they will continue to need supportive services from the special education teacher.

Middle and high school students with learning disabilities most likely bring many experiences with academic failure, poor self-concepts, and inept social skills in addition to the usual characteristics of adolescent development (Lerner, 1993). Furthermore, they may be at a disadvantage for content-area learning. In the elementary grades, they often were at the resource room during science or social studies periods. In their reading instruction, they often read stories, not content material, and they learned isolated reading skills, like sequencing, instead of strategies to understand content-area ideas (Bos & Anders, 1990).

You will want to collaborate with the special education teacher in providing for learning for students with learning disabilities. You might ask the special education teacher to investigate strategy instruction programs (Harris & Pressley, 1991; Gaskins & Gaskins, 1991) that will coordinate well with the strategies we will teach you in Part Two.

▶ ▶ ▷ ▷ ## Teaching Diverse Students

Agreeing with Sleeter (1997), we do not set out a list of special methods for teaching diverse students. Instead, teaching all students, and especially diverse students, is accomplished by listening to and understanding students, building a dialogue with students, and sharing decision-making power with students. By incorporating the following general suggestions into your content-area teaching, you will communicate to your students that you have high expectations for them and that you will provide the opportunities to learn the content they will need:

- **Build your cultural awareness.** Recognize your own combination of cultural heritages, such as race and ethnicity, gender, and SES, as well as others we have not discussed. Acknowledge your cultural perspectives and become aware how your perspectives influence your attitudes, values, and behavior.

- **Learn about the other cultures in your school.** You may begin with cultural festivals and music, but delve beyond those common cultural characteristics into more subtle characteristics, like conceptions of adolescence or gender roles and patterns of conversation.

- **Find role models.** Search for racial/ethnic, gender, and special needs role models who have contributed to the knowledge in your content area.

Enlisting the help of a librarian and community members, you can find role models your students can read about or interview in class.

- **Encourage student participation.** Observe the ways that students participate in class, and discuss with them any patterns you've noticed. Ask the students for suggestions on improving communication opportunities for all students in both whole class and small group discussions.

- **Know students as individuals.** You can quietly and personally encourage diverse students—not only those you think can excel in your subject area but also those you might be able to interest in your subject area. Become an advocate for your students.

Special Issues for Teaching Students with Diversity of Language and Dialect.
Like culture, language is a part of personal identity. Respect the language or dialect students bring, and add standard English to their repertoire. We recommend the following practices (adapted from Sullivan cited in E. García, 1999, and Crawford, 1993):

- **Wait for answers.** When you ask a question or present a task, wait a long time for a response. Give second-language speakers more time to formulate in English what they know.

- **Respond to the speaker's meaning.** Continue the dialogue by expanding on the content of the response instead of correcting the grammar.

- **Don't force a reticent student to speak.** In second-language acquisition, like first-language acquisition, learners understand more than they can express. Think of ways other than speaking that students can show they understand, such as drawing.

- **Create opportunities to use language.** Instead of listening to the teacher talk or lecture, students can work in pairs or in cooperative learning groups. (See Chapter 3.)

- **Demonstrate or use pictures and objects** to communicate concepts if possible.

- **Correct grammar in written text instead** of oral language. Because students' written texts are concretely displayed on paper, the students' written language can be more easily edited into standard English than their oral language. Provide students with opportunities to write to students in other classsrooms and schools and to people in the community (see Chapter 6), so that they will have a purpose for editing into standard English.

The gifts students have are many and diverse. As you accept their gifts, you will provide learning opportunities for them to enhance those gifts. Now let's discuss what learning experiences students bring to classrooms.

What Do Students Bring to Classrooms?

lthough your students may appear similar to each other, each brings a unique constellation of learning experiences to class. Before you meet them, they have accumulated these characteristics:

- **Content knowledge** from past school experiences and from their everyday experiences
- **Strategies** for learning that may be conscious or intuitive
- **Attitudes, values, beliefs** about their own learning ability, your content area, and school in general

Cognitive psychologists theorize that people organize knowledge into what they call *schema* or *schemata* (plural of *schema*). A schema is an organized network of ideas, concepts, data, and experiences. You could picture the schemata in your brain as different web sites linked together on the Internet. People have different schemata for different areas of knowledge (mathematics) and different experiences (viewing the president on television) and make connections among schemata (using mathematics to interpret presidential polling data).

▶ ▶ ▶ ▷ **Content Knowledge in Schemata**

Content knowledge schemata are what you know about the world (Anderson, 1994). What schema do you activate when you read the following passage? Who and where is Rocky?

> Rocky slowly got up from the mat, planning his escape. He hesitated a moment and thought. Things were not going well. What bothered him most was being held, especially since the charge against him had been weak. He considered his present situation. The lock that held him was strong but he thought he could break it. He knew, however, that his timing would have to be perfect. Rocky was aware that it was because of his early roughness that he had been penalized so severely—much too severely from his point of view. The situation was becoming frustrating; the pressure had been grinding on him for too long. He was being ridden unmercifully. Rocky was getting angry now. He felt he was ready to make his move. He knew that his success or failure would depend on what he did in the next few seconds. (Anderson, Reynolds, Schallert, & Goetz, 1977, p. 372)

Some students think Rocky is a convict planning an escape; others think he is a wrestler in a tough match; still others have different interpretations.

Who you thought Rocky was depended on the content knowledge in your schema.

Throughout their lives, people build schemata from direct experiences with natural phenomena, from their social and cultural experiences within their communities, and from their learning experiences in school. When you have a new experience, for example, seeing a movie (perhaps *Armageddon*), you search for an appropriate, matching schema in your brain (action movies). That schema allows you to recognize which details are important (asteroid and special effects) and to fill in details that may have been omitted. Later when you want to tell someone about the movie, you will refer to the schema to help you recall the special effects. You may even talk about special effects from other movies that are part of your schema but were not actually part of that new movie (Anderson, 1994)!

Schemata can lead people astray when their schemata do not match the new information. Students may ignore a scientific explanation that seems to contradict their previous knowledge (Alvermann, Smith, & Readance, 1985). For example, even though current college students have listened to their past elementary, middle, and high school teachers explain the cause of the earth's seasons, a number still incorrectly think the cause of the seasons is the earth's distance from the sun. They continue to forget the teacher's scientific explanation—the earth's tilt—in favor of their own misconceptions (Schneps, 1988; Atwood & Atwood, 1996).

Cultural schemata can both help and hinder understanding of different texts. For example, Indian people comprehended a passage about a wedding in their home country better than a passage about an American wedding. In recalling the American wedding, they mistakenly included some Indian wedding customs that were not in the passage (Steffenson, Joag-Dev, & Anderson, 1979).

Learning is constructing knowledge by adding new schemata, recognizing gaps in and enhancing existing schemata, recognizing mismatches and reconstructing schemata, and making new connections among schemata. Naturally as a content-area teacher, you will want to know what content knowledge students bring to your classroom so that you can build from their existing schemata.

Furthermore, you will want to help students organize their content knowledge in their schemata. In deciding what content to teach, you will want to focus on significant ideas and understandings that relate to each other instead of fragmented, isolated facts. For example, if you state that arteries are elastic and veins are not, students will try to memorize those isolated facts. Suppose instead that you elaborated on the significance of elasticity: since arteries lead from the heart, they need to accommodate the pressure from a pumping heart; veins, going to the heart, do not. Then students could integrate the concept of elasticity with the operations of the circulation system. The result would be a more elaborate and organized schema (Bransford, 1994).

We will return to the topic of schemata and building on and refining prior knowledge throughout Part Two. However, in your campaign to build schemata and dispel any misconceptions that students may have acquired, remember McDiarmid's dilemma with the Yup'ik Eskimo students. In our opinion, different worldviews, in that case a scientific worldview and a cultural-religious worldview, are but contrasting schemata of the world, not misconceptions. Only students can resolve that dilemma of contrasting worldviews, and they may decide to live in two worlds.

▶ ▶ ▶ ▷ ## Strategies for Learning

We think that all students bring ways of learning or strategies to classrooms from their learning experiences at home and in the community. In some cultures, children learn using a "watch–then do" strategy, while others are encouraged to learn by trial and error (Nelson-Barber & Estrin, 1995). Students also bring strategies from past learning experiences in classrooms, such as the strategy of cueing into the teacher's questions to locate important information.

You recall from Chapter 1 that we define a strategy as a conscious plan of action for achieving an activity or goal. We predict that you use learning strategies that are effective in your content area. We want you to become aware of what strategies you use and when you use them so that you can teach them to your students.

In this book (especially in Part Two), we focus on literacy strategies that support students in learning and communicating content knowledge. We do not divorce strategies from content; instead, we select literacy strategies that will support learning content. We think some students have discovered literacy strategies on their own, perhaps from wide reading of texts. However, we think most students—your average students and maybe even your above-average students—use only a few strategies repeatedly for most tasks. Moreover, we think most students are not very metacognitively aware of how they learn and what literacy strategies they use or don't use. Thus, when we write about nonstrategic learners, we picture most of your students. These students need to be taught a variety of effective literacy strategies so that they will match their strategies to specific tasks. And all students need teachers' asking metacognitive questions such as, "How are you going to find that out?" or "What strategies will help you understand that article?"

We are concerned about the diverse students—especially students with learning disabilities, students from a minority culture, and students with low

SES—who have not previously performed well in school. Both Delpit (1988), from the African-American perspective, and Reyes (1992), from the Mexican-American perspective, argue for the explicit and direct teaching of literacy strategies and standard English within classrooms that are respectful and welcoming to the culture and language/dialect of the students. Students with learning disabilities, who struggle to learn from print, also need explicit and direct teaching of literacy strategies (Gaskins & Gaskins, 1991). If teachers and schools are to provide equal educational opportunity to learn, then teachers need to build on the strategies students bring by teaching strategies that support learning content.

Teacher as Inquiring Learner Activity

Like the think-aloud activity in Chapter 1, the purpose of this activity is to help you begin to explore a student's strategies. (Again, at this point, describe the student's strategies in your own words. Don't peek ahead!)

Find a middle school or high school student who is willing to help you learn. Ask the student to pick out an easy text and a hard text. Have the student read the easy text aloud first for about fifteen minutes and then switch to read the hard text for another fifteen minutes. If the student is clearly frustrated by the hard text, try to find a less difficult text to read or stop after eight to ten minutes.

As the student reads aloud, ask him or her to stop and tell you what he or she is thinking. If the student doesn't think aloud periodically, stop the student and ask what he or she is thinking about or what connections he or she is making to the text. Take notes on a copy of the text or perhaps tape-record this session. After the session with the student, go over your notes or the tape.

• From ideas and comments the student stated, what reading strategies can you infer that the student used?

For example, if the student said he or she thought the book would be about how paleontologists searched for dinosaurs, you could infer that the student used prediction as a strategy.

▶ ▶ ▶ ▶ Attitudes, Beliefs, and Values for Learning

Throughout elementary school, students evaluated themselves during different tasks, compared themselves to their peers, and received feedback from teachers and parents (Ames & Ames, 1991). By the time you meet students, they have formed their self-concepts about their ability to learn in your content area, about the value of investing effort in learning, and about their expectations or goals for learning (Wigfield, 1997).

Students commonly define their ability to learn by whether they are smart. When students meet with success in school tasks, they come to believe that they can learn. This belief, called *self-efficacy*, influences the tasks that students choose, the amount of effort they will exert, their persistence when difficulties arise, and their achievement. Belief in the ability to perform well is important, but it is not sufficient. Students also need to have the strategies and knowledge required for the task (Schunk & Zimmerman, 1997).

Students perceive the value of a task in terms of its usefulness, interest, and importance (Wigfield, 1997). The value they place on a task is related to their goals or the outcomes they expect. Some students study for the grade (an extrinsic reward), while others study just to learn or for curiosity (intrinsic rewards). When students' goals are grades, they concentrate on their performance, place value on their ability, compete with and compare themselves to other students, and become anxious about mistakes. In contrast, when students' goals are knowledge, they concentrate on the learning process, value effort and challenge, and consider mistakes part of the process (Ames & Ames, 1991). Of course, adolescents are often influenced by how their peers value school tasks and their desire for peer acceptance.

As a content-area teacher, you probably will vary the rewards you offer. At times you may offer extrinsic rewards and reinforce performance goals, such as the number of experiments completed or an excellent example of work (Ames & Ames, 1991). At other times, when you focus on strategies and students' self-evaluations, you will emphasize intrinsic rewards and competency or learning goals (Schunk & Zimmerman, 1997). With your students, you will discuss the criteria for a successful outcome before they begin and teach them to examine their work in terms of the criteria. You will ask students how they are pursuing the task and whether their strategies are effective or producing progress. Finally, you will ask your students to reflect on how they learned the last time, what is different or similar this time, and what they would do next time.

Our goal (and we hope yours) is that all students will build schemata that contain the important concepts, acquire useful strategies for learning concepts, and have the attitudes that will sustain their learning in school and beyond.

How Standardized Tests Can Be Used Fairly for Your Students as Learners

For decades, students have taken standardized tests, and school officials have made decisions about students based on their scores. For example, Scholastic Assessment Test (SAT) scores have been a part of the requirements for admission into colleges; achievement test scores have been a part of tracking decisions in high schools. In the past, test scores were one factor used in conjunction with other factors, like grades. Now the stakes seem higher because a single test score can have enormous consequences for students and schools. Based on their scores, students may not be promoted or may not graduate. Schools may be rewarded for high scores, or censored and taken over by state education agencies for low scores. Because more minority culture students score low and more majority culture students score high, the stakes are even higher for students with diverse backgrounds (Darling-Hammond, 1991). Since decisions are made about all students based on standardized test scores, we need to explain standardized tests to you and present both misuses and uses of standardized test scores.

Standardized tests are formal tests published by commercial companies. Usually in multiple-choice format, the tests are designed to be equivalent or standard across all schools. They are intended to compare the achievement of one group of students to another and schools in a district or state to one another (Mitchell, 1992). To establish the comparisons, the test developers give the test to a typical group or sample of students who demographically represent all students in the country. The high to low range of scores from that typical sample establishes what is the normal range, and the test is called *norm referenced*. Future test takers' scores are compared to that normal range of scores to determine where they stand as high, average, or low in achievement.

In addition to the SATs, you can probably remember taking achievement tests like the Comprehensive Test of Basic Skills (CTBS) or the National Assessment of Educational Progress (NAEP) tests. The legislatures in thirty-eight states now have state-mandated assessment tests, usually administered in the fourth, eighth, and tenth grades (Jerald, Curran, & Olson, 1998). Most likely you are required by your state to take standardized teacher certification tests in literacy and your subject area. At every level of American schools, a typical student takes standardized tests (see Table 2.2).

Standardized tests have typical characteristics (see Table 2.3) that make them easy to use and to misuse. Because they are considered standard, objective, and norm referenced, funding sources, like state legislatures and federal agencies, use test scores for accountability in an effort to determine whether money has been well invested (Olson, 1998). When students' scores have not improved, the funding source may intervene to change how the school is educating their students. In the drive to reform education, standardized test scores are often the sole criterion used to determine a successful school or program when other factors, like problem solving, might be more useful.

When schools are judged by students' standardized test scores, then every school wants to be "above average." Mathematically, of course, the whole student population can't be above average. If tenth graders' scores av-

Table 2.2   A Typical Student's Standardized Testing Experiences

Grade	Test
Elementary school	
Third grade	Comprehensive Test of Basic Skills (Reading, Language, and Math)
Fourth grade	State-mandated competency tests National Assessment of Educational Progress Tests
Fifth grade	Comprehensive Test of Basic Skills (all content areas)
Middle school	
Seventh grade	Comprehensive Test of Basic Skills (all content areas)
Eighth grade	State-mandated compentency tests National Assessment of Educational Progress Tests
High school	
Tenth grade	State-mandated competency tests
Eleventh grade	Preliminary Scholastic Assessment Test
Twelfth grade	Scholastic Assessment Tests Advanced Placement Tests
Postsecondary	
	Professional certification exams
	Graduate Record Exams

eraged 70 last year and 80 this year, then the average score moved higher. But when the test is recalculated for its normal range of scores, then 80 will be the average, not above average. When you read about the goal for schools to be "above average," remember that standardized tests are designed to produce a range of high to low scores.

In trying to reach the goal to be "above average," teachers may change the way they teach or teach to the test (Darling-Hammond, Ancess, & Falk, 1995). For example, they may take instructional time for students to practice the test's format. Some teachers change the content of their curriculum from in-depth study to a memorization of facts (Darling-Hammond et al., 1995). Particularly teachers of low SES students use standardized tests to develop

Table 2.3   Characteristics of Standardized Tests

Characteristic	Comment
Norm referenced	Compares a student's score to scores of a typical group of students in the same grade to determine whether the score is high, average, or low
	Assesses recognition, not production, of facts
Short answer (usually multiple-choice)	Assesses knowledge of isolated facts and basic skills rather than problem-solving and analytical thinking
Sample of student achievement at a single point in time	Cannot assess progress over a semester or the school year
Independent of the curriculum in the school	May contain content that students have not studied
Viewed as objective and not influenced by the judgments of teachers	Reflects the judgment of the test maker in deciding what facts and skills to test
Yields a numerical score that can be used to make decisions about student placement, retention, and graduation	Can reward or censor schools and teachers based on students' scores

Sources: Darling-Hammond (1991); Wolf & Reardon (1996).

curricula and determine their instruction (Center for Study of Testing, Evaluation and Educational Policy in García & Pearson, 1994).

When funding sources and the schools themselves use only the standardized test score to evaluate curricula and teaching, they have defined quality education as basic skills. Certainly students need to learn facts, but they also need to learn how to frame problems, solve problems, and think critically. Although some standardized tests, like the NAEP, have added analytical essays, most standardized tests do not measure inquiry skills and higher-level thinking.

And finally, majority culture students and minority culture students perform differently on standardized tests. Historically, every immigrant group has performed poorly on standardized tests (Figueroa & García, 1994). Several reasons can account for the poor performance of diverse students (García & Pearson, 1994). First, diverse students do not bring the same prior knowledge to the tests that majority culture students bring and so do not recognize or understand some of the content. Second, the tests are timed, and bilingual students, who use both languages to understand the content, are often unable to complete the tests. Third, standardized tests, even math tests, are reading tests. Diverse students may not understand the vocabulary in the test directions or in the test items (García, 1991).

When you are faced with the uses and misuses of standardized tests scores, how can you use them fairly? First, you can acknowledge what the tests evaluate and don't evaluate. Although we don't recommend ignoring their content, especially when the tests are tied to state-mandated curriculum standards, we think facts should not be isolated but be used in problem solving (see Chapter 5). We encourage you to include in-depth study and critical thinking in the curricula you offer to all your students.

Second, you can use the score as a relative gauge of where students were that day. But the score doesn't determine where students will be tomorrow. Furthermore, the score doesn't measure the students' attitude or determination to learn. You can motivate and teach your students.

Third, although standardized tests are used to assess students' final achievement, you can use other assessment tools to evaluate both their ongoing learning and their final understandings. Those teaching/assessing tools in your classroom can supplement the single test score, describe different qualities of students' learning, and exhibit both the process and the products of students' learning. We define both ongoing and final assessment tools useful to your instruction in Chapter 3 and present specific assessment tools in Parts Two and Three.

Summary of the Chapter

As a content-area teacher, you are at the confluence between your content area and your students. To teach your content effectively, you will need to learn about your students. Every school population has diverse students, even those populations that superficially appear to be homogeneous. You will want to delve beneath the surface to discover the diversity in your school population and also to discover each student's individuality.

In this chapter, we have first described who student populations are in terms of only five diversity characteristics:

- Race/ethnicity
- Language

- Socioeconomic status
- Gender
- Special needs

In our discussion, we presented the major ideas or theories, new terms, and educational issues related to each diversity characteristic. In addition, we offered general suggestions to help you meet diverse student needs in your content classroom. In Part Two, we will present specific literacy strategies as well as teaching and assessment tools that will help all students learn your content. Remember that as the U.S population becomes more diverse, groups are not homogeneous and individuals are unique.

Second, we discussed students' diversity in terms of the content knowledge, strategies, and attitudes they bring to classrooms:

- Students' background knowledge in their schemata may be different depending on their everyday and school experiences.
- Students bring strategies for learning, although they may not be aware of the strategies they use.
- Most students need to be taught literacy strategies that will help them learn content more effectively.
- Students bring attitudes about themselves as learners and about learning in your content area.

As a content area teacher, you will want to assess what your students bring to your content classroom and then provide instruction to further their learning. The literacy strategies and tools in Part Two and the Units in Part Three will help you.

Third, we discussed standardized tests because you and your students are affected by them:

- You need to understand what they test and how they are used and misused.
- You can make decisions about classroom assessment tools that inform you (and your students) about how they are learning as well as what they are learning.

If you are like most teachers, you decided to become a teacher because you liked students. Even though you are teaching content, you are really teaching students. We know you will enjoy learning about your students and learning with your students. We have, and we still do.

Inquiry Activities About Your Learning

1. Choose a diversity characteristic and learn about it. Visit a community organization that serves that particular population. Interview the staff about the lives of the

people in the community. What contributions are the people making to their community? What issues do they face? Try to find a member of the community who is willing to be interviewed about the story of her or his life.

2. Research the contributions of diverse people to your content area. What have people from a minority culture, women, and people with disabilities accomplished? Look for biographies or news reports about their accomplishments. Identify organizations related to your content area for contacts that could inform you about the contributions of their members.

Inquiry Activities About Your Students' Learning

1. Observe two classes—a low-track class and a high-track class—in your content area. If possible, observe the same teacher for both classes. Compare the content being taught and the instructional methods used. Compare the students' and the teachers' behavior. How do they affect each other? What does the teacher do differently in the two groups, and why? What are your conclusions about the teaching and learning in the two tracks?

2. Interview a teacher about his or her students. First, ask the teacher to describe the students in his or her different classes. Second, ask the teacher to describe a few students whom she or he finds interesting. Third, ask a series of questions about those students. What content knowledge do they bring to class? What strategies do they use to learn and study? What attitudes toward learning do they bring to class? What standardized tests does the teacher need to give? How do the students score on the tests? What decisions are made based on the scores? Does the teacher think the scores and tests are used fairly? How does the teacher learn about his or her students?

3

Choices and Decisions for Content Learning

As you will soon find out, if you haven't already, teaching is not a simple task. Experienced teachers can make teaching appear easy because they have a repertoire of teaching tools and a reservoir of knowledge. First, they have learned about their students, especially if they have been teaching in the same school and same grades for several years. Not only do they know what to expect from tenth-grade students and what will challenge them, they are attuned to their students' background, as we discussed in Chapter 2. Second, experienced teachers know the content required by state and local mandates. They have decided which areas to teach in depth and which to "cover." Third, experienced teachers have acquired materials, such as textbooks, magazines, and artifacts, that support the content they are teaching. Fourth, experienced teachers have refined their pedagogy and may even have preferred teaching tools, like small group discussions or whole class brainstorming, that work well for them and for their students. To you, experienced teachers may seem to have solved many of the day-to-day teaching questions in your discipline. Because most experienced teachers have a repertoire of preferred teaching tools and reservoirs of knowledge, their choices and decisions often seem invisible.

Often spurred by questions from student teachers, their own professional reading, and new issues and trends in the field, teachers, who are continuous learners, regularly reexamine their practices and investigate new teaching practices, content, and materials. They make some choices and decisions before a lesson, some during the planning phase, and some after the action of teaching, when they may revise their plans for instruction. And sometimes they make split-second decisions in the middle of teaching on the basis of their repertoires and reservoirs. You will gain your own repertoire and reservoir just as they did, with experience. In this chapter, we concentrate on the choices and decisions you will make as you plan your instruction.

In the chapter opening graphic we have shown the decision-making areas that a teacher is involved with when designing a lesson for a particular class or group of students. We have placed students in the center of the triangle because what you know about your students influences every decision you make.

We have placed strategies supporting content at the top of the triangle. You know from Chapter 1 that we advocate teaching content and strategies for learning that content in tandem. You have probably learned about content and strategies in the discipline-based courses in your program. In Part Two, we will discuss literacy strategies, as well as teaching and assessment tools, that support your students' learning the content in your particular discipline.

At the base of the triangle we placed materials and pedagogy. Both of these areas support teaching your students content and learning strategies. First, we discuss the variety of literacy materials you can choose from to engage students with content and a rationale for using each material. We also discuss characteristics to consider when you evaluate and choose specific literacy materials. Having suitable materials for your students often affects your decisions about what content you teach and how you teach it.

Second, we discuss the variety of pedagogical decisions teachers make. In the confluence between students and content, teachers decide how best to teach and communicate with their students about content. Finally, we present grouping choices that range from whole class, to small group or cooperative learning, to individual learning.

In this chapter, we present a rationale and overview of materials, teaching tools, and assessment tools. In Part II, we examine many of these materials and explain specific teaching and assessing tools you can use. You will make decisions about materials as well as the teaching and assessing tools to use based on the demands of your subject matter and the needs of your specific students.

Purpose-Setting Questions

1. What different types of texts do you usually read in your content area? Are there some different types of texts you could incorporate into your content-area learning and teaching?

2. What makes a text readable, considerate or user-friendly, and fair or representative of diverse populations? How do you use this information to match texts to students?

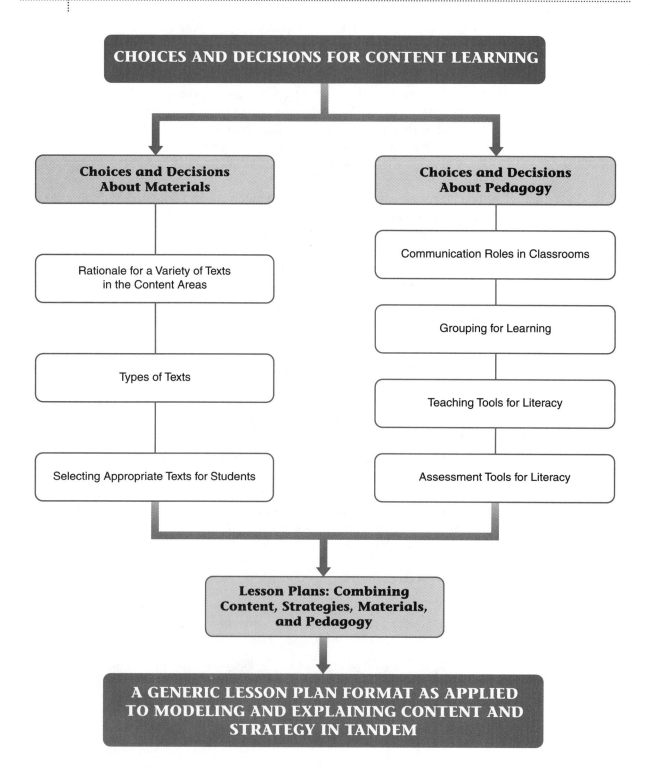

3. Who governs communication patterns in classrooms: teachers or students? And what role can grouping patterns play in determining the learning and the communication in a classroom?

4. How can a teaching tool become an assessment tool?

5. What are the roles and importance of lesson plans for experienced teachers? What are the roles for you as a beginning teacher?

Choices and Decisions About Materials

When we use the terms *materials* or *resources* (in the unit plans in Part Three), we mean the objects you need to carry out your lesson. Materials could be beakers, spatulas, acrylic paints, tennis rackets, video cameras, as well as the more typical textbooks, pencils, and paper. Remembering to gather all necessary materials together and to have enough for every student makes a period go smoothly.

In this book, we use the term *text* to mean any material that is composed of words. A text could be a textbook, fiction or nonfiction books (often called trade books), a magazine, a newspaper, a primary source (a diary or document), student writing, or on-line text. We use this general term because we don't want to limit your thinking to only printed matter, only textbooks, or only fiction. We want you to think broadly about the types of texts your students could read and could write.

▶ ▶ ▶ ▶ ## Rationale for a Variety of Texts in the Content Areas

In encouraging you to think broadly about types of texts, we want you to begin that lifetime process of collecting a variety of materials suitable to your content and your students. We recognize that not every type of text is suitable for a specific content area, unit of study, or particular student in your class. We also recognize that you know of specific texts in your field, such as manuals or computer documentation, that we have not mentioned. We encourage you to begin your search for a variety of materials or resources that will complement your content area.

Your students will benefit from the incorporation of multiple resources in their classes in a number of ways:

• They will gain more in-depth knowledge because they have read more widely.

- They will remember concepts and important vocabulary because they have met them repeatedly in different contexts.
- They will have the opportunity to explore and practice a variety of literacy strategies as they learn from different types of texts.
- They will learn they can express their own ideas and knowledge through a variety of texts.
- They will recognize that authors write for different audiences and that they may too.

If students read only health textbooks, when will they learn how to evaluate the conflicting health advice that is often reported in news articles? Increasing the variety of texts will allow you and your students to explore different literacy strategies that support learning your content. In the next section, we briefly describe the variety of texts you might consider.

▶ ▶ ▶ ▶ Types of Texts

Walk into most classrooms, and you will find textbooks (Goodlad, 1984). Often required by local or state boards or chosen to support districtwide curricula, textbooks are still the most prevalent curriculum material in every grade (Palmer & Stewart, 1997). In addition to textbooks, however, there are a number of other texts you might explore to enhance your content-area teaching.

Textbooks.   In discipline-based courses and methods courses that you have taken, your professors may have expressed their views about the suitability of textbooks as a major source of content. Some may have criticized them and encouraged you to develop your own materials and to teach with a more hands-on science approach (Ball & Reiman-Nemser, 1988). We strive to seek a balance. We acknowledge the reality of getting to know the content in your courses and therefore think beginning teachers appreciate the organization and coverage that textbooks contain. As a preservice mathematics or science teacher, you probably have not studied every topic in your discipline in depth and will value the breadth of content that textbook writers provide. We also do not think you will be in a position as a beginning teacher to change state and district requirements for the courses you will teach. You may in fact be required to incorporate textbooks into your teaching. Therefore, we encourage you to view the textbook as a resource for you and your students that you can supplement and adapt as you get to know your content and your students.

Remember that textbooks are designed to survey content and present a synthesis of agreed-on information. In this survey format, important understandings related to a topic may be glossed over or omitted entirely. Once you recognize where textbooks have not treated an important understanding well, you can engage your students in a thoughtful study of that topic. Additionally, since it usually contains synthesized, agreed-on information, the textbook often presents a rather static view of your field. You will want to motivate students to be more active learners themselves by exploring the controversies, conflicting theories, and the tenuous facts about the content they are studying.

Informational Books.   We can probably find informational books, or nonfiction books, on every content area. A major advantage of most nonfiction books written for children as well as adults is that they can treat a narrow subject in depth. For example, James Cross Giblin in *The Riddle of the Rosetta Stone: Key to Ancient Egypt* (1990) researched and wrote a book on the Rosetta Stone, a narrow topic usually treated in a page or less in a textbook. By writing about a narrow topic in depth, authors discuss, rather than mention, concepts. Students read the important vocabulary for those concepts in different contexts. To understand concepts, students need the sustained exposure to those concepts and vocabulary that can be provided in a nonfiction book (Alvermann, 1994).

Another advantage is that nonfiction books about important topics are written on different reading levels. You may be able to find books on related topics that meet the reading needs of different students in your class. For example, just by thumbing through *I Am an American: A True Story of Japanese Internment* (1994) by Jerry Stanley and *Voices from the Camps: Internment of Japanese Americans during World War II* (1994) by L. D. Brimner, informational books written about the Japanese internment in the United States during World War II, you can surmise that one is easier to read than the other and that they would enable students of differing abilities in a history course to study the same topic and contribute to whole class or small group work. Table 3.1 lists additional resources that can assist you in finding informational texts, as well as fiction, poetry, and picture books that will enhance your content-area teaching and help you meet the interests and reading needs of your students too.

Fiction Books.   Science fiction, fantasy, historical fiction, and realistic fiction can capture the mood of an event, not just the facts (Speigel, 1987). Reading an entire work or a selection from fiction aloud may lead your students to recognize the human side of your content. Furthermore, fiction writing often is more descriptive than nonfiction, so readers gain a more vivid picture of an event, which may entice them to read more and learn the actual facts. Imagine your students' reactions if you started an astronomy unit by reading aloud from H. G. Wells's *War of the Worlds* or Ray Bradbury's *Martian Chronicles* each period. If you are studying ratios in math, you could sample sections of *Gulliver's Travels* and determine the ratios between Gulliver's world and that of the Lilliputians.

Table 3.1 Resources for Choosing Selected Texts to Complement Content-Area Learning

Sources	Informational Books	Fiction and Poetry	Picture Books
Books			
Beyond Words: Picture Books for Older Readers and Writers, by S. Benedict and R. Carlisle (1992)	x	x	x
Connecting Informational Children's Books with Content Area Learning, by E. B. Freeman and D. G. Person (1998)	x		
Eyeopeners, II, by B. Kobrin (1995)	x		
High Interest–Easy Reading, by P. Phelan (Ed.) (1996)	x	x	
Making Facts Come Alive, by R. A. Branford and J. V. Kristo (1998)	x		
Magazines for Kids and Teens, by D. R. Stoll (Ed.) (1997)	x	x	
Rip-Roaring Reads for Reluctant Readers, by G. W. Sherman and B. D. Ammon (1993)		x	
The Story of Ourselves: Teaching History Through Children's Literature, by M. O. Tunnell and R. Ammon (1993)	x	x	
Teens' Favorite Books, by International Reading Association (1992)	x	x	
Articles			
"Developing Social Studies Concepts Through Picture Books," *Reading Teacher* (1994)	x	x	x
"Nonfiction Tradebooks in Content Area Instruction: Realities and Potential," *Journal of Adolescent and Adult Literacy* (1997)	x		
"The Place of Picture Books in Middle Level Classrooms," *Journal of Adolescent and Adult Literacy* (1998)	x	x	x
"Pirates, Baseball and Explorers," *NERA Journal* (1996)		x	x

Poetry and Picture Books. Using poetry and picture books in middle school and high school classrooms can add another dimension to an area of study. For example, students could read from Paul Fleishman's *Joyful Noise: Poems for Two Voices* (1988) when they are studying insects in general science or biology or selected poems from Nora Panzer's *Celebrate America in Poetry and Art* (1994) when studying historical events or different regions of the country in their history or geography classes.

Although picture books were originally written and designed for very young readers, today some are appropriate for older readers, even adults. Picture books, nonfiction and fiction, provide rich details and data by combining words and strong visual images of people and places, such as those found in *A River Ran Wild: An Environmental History* (1993) by Lynne Cherry, *Castles* (1977) and *Pyramids* (1975) by David Macaulay, *Lincoln: A Photobiography* (1993) by Russell Freedman, and *Nettie's Trip South* (1987) by Ann Warren Turner. Picture books can also make difficult or sensitive concepts more palatable, such as the images of war conveyed in *The Wall* (1990) by Eve Bunting or *Rose Blanche* (1985) by Roberto Innocenti and Christophe Gallaz. Picture books can also pique students' interest in a new topic or provide background knowledge for a new unit of study.

Magazines. We recommend incorporating magazines into your content area for several reasons. First, for some students, reading a short selection, like a magazine article in a familiar format, is more appealing than facing an entire book. Second, magazines usually contain current information that supports or serves to bring textbook information up to date. Third, magazine articles focus on topics using photographs, graphics, and interviews, which help students gain additional information related to the central topic. As with

When students read a variety of texts, they learn more content, increase their vocabulary, and practice a range of literacy strategies.

© David Young-Wolff/PHOTO EDIT

nonfiction books, students have the opportunity to meet the important vocabulary and concepts related to the topic in a user-friendly context.

You can probably find a suitable magazine for every content area given the number of adult and adolescent magazines published today. In addition to the general adult magazines like *Time* and *National Geographic*, you can find magazines written for students, such as *Ahora,* written about a range of age-appropriate topics for teens in Spanish class; magazines that publish student fictional or informational pieces such as *Merlyn's Pen*; or a science-oriented magazine like *Wildlife Conservation*, whose major purpose is to inspire young people to become active conservationists. A useful resource for you as a teacher seeking resources for your students is Stoll's recent *Magazines for Kids and Teens* (1997), which annotates a variety of magazines and organizes them by subject area and age appropriateness.

Newspapers.   Like magazines, newspapers contain current information, and they employ a variety of visuals as well as different formats to convey their message. We recommend national or large city newspapers because they contain articles relating to every content area likely to be in any middle school or high school curriculum. These newspapers have articles or entire sections devoted to current science, technology and health-related discoveries and events, reviews of books and arts events, and, of course, sports articles, opinion columns, and cartoons. We also recommend that you and your students read local or regional newspapers because they focus on local issues and events. These newspapers in particular allow you to extend your curriculum beyond the classroom walls into the everyday world and community in which your students live.

On-line Texts.   The World Wide Web or Internet is another source of text that in the future may capture the interest of more readers than printed text. Newspapers and magazines, or 'zines, are on line, and home pages have been created by cities and towns, state and federal agencies, and organizations or societies related to every content area to provide information to interested individuals across cyberspace.

If you have searched on the Internet, you have already discovered that quality varies greatly among web sites. Second, you know that you can get lost among all the links to other sites and that you can mistakenly or inadvertently travel to sites requiring parental consent. Therefore, we recommend that you locate a few productive sites before students begin their own searches for additional sites related to a topic being studied.

You also need to teach students to evaluate sites. A useful home page maintained by middle and high school students, "KIDS: Kids Identifying and

Discovering Sites" (**http://www.scout.cs.wisc.edu/scout/KIDS/index.hmtl**), issues bimonthly evaluation reports about sites and includes site evaluation criteria as well.

Primary Sources.   These texts are often the most difficult of the listed types of texts to find and to read. Historical primary sources, like journals, may be written in script that is hard to decipher and language that is hard to understand. Other journals that support the various content areas, such as artists' sketchbooks, athletes' record books, and scientists' journals, can be difficult to locate.

Public documents, census records, town maps, death certificates, legislative laws, the *Congressional Record,* research reports to governmental agencies, and, most important, letters are primary sources that support the content areas. These primary sources often make history, science, or mathematics come alive through their descriptions and their documentation of real people's everyday endeavors. Song lyrics, posters, ads, and maps can be classified as primary sources and literacy texts too. Finally, photographs and portraits, documentary films, and even drawings on buildings and on ceramics are sources of firsthand data that can supplement the usual texts and print media.

Student Texts.   We include student texts because students are worthwhile audiences for each other, whether the communication is on-line or in print. We encourage students to share and help each other, with everything ranging from a first draft to a finished article. In our experience, even the most recalcitrant students write more and better when they are communicating with other students.

Students' notes, journals, records of observations, and interviews are examples of writing to learn or writing while learning. Sharing these tentative writings can help students recognize what and how they are learning. Sharing ideas from tentative writings during learning allows students to receive support and challenge from other students as well as from you. Students will also create published writing and end products in various forms that they may share with appropriate audiences both in school and beyond the classroom setting. Students often choose these end-of-unit products to demonstrate their understandings as well as their best work for inclusion in their portfolios.

▶ ▶ ▶ ▶ Selecting Appropriate Texts for Students

The surest way to match a text to students is to ask the students to read the text and tell you what they understood. Sometimes school districts ask teachers to pilot a new textbook before they purchase it for all teachers. Then teachers can evaluate the match of the textbook to their particular students and their curricular goals. Unfortunately, when many teachers and textbook selection committees make decisions, teachers and students do not have the opportunity to try the books out. Instead, selection committees estimate the level of difficulty and the appropriateness of the textbooks.

When researchers first began to consider the importance of knowing the level of the texts their students were using, they measured textbooks for *readability*. More recently, researchers have examined textbooks for *considerateness* and *fairness*. We emphasize the importance of combining all three factors in order to obtain a good measure of a book's overall appropriateness for your students.

Readability.   If you have used the grammar check on your computer, you may have seen a statistic that indicates the grade level of your text (you probably paid no attention to it). That statistic is a *readability score*. Textbooks from the beginning readers to high school physics textbooks have a readability score.

Readability formulas are designed to estimate what reading level a student would need to read a given text successfully. The most commonly used language variables are sentence length, number of syllables, and number of words.

The assumptions underlying readability formulas are not infallible. First, multisyllabic words, like *atmosphere* and *constitution*, are repeated often in a text, and explanations as well as supporting graphic aids may be provided. Second, because ideas are connected and explicated in longer sentences, sometimes readers find longer sentences easier to understand than short, choppy ones (Pearson & Johnson, 1978). Third, because language and dialect differences can change the number of syllables that individuals assign to a word, a particular text may be assigned different levels of difficulty by different individuals. Therefore, we examine the text's language and use the readability score in combination with considerateness and fairness.

The Fry Readability Formula is widely used to assess content-area materials, and you can easily calculate it using the graphic provided in Fig. 3.1. Remember that the score you find from most readability formulas represents a range of about plus or minus one grade for elementary texts and plus or minus two grades for high school texts—not the precise grade of the particular text throughout. Readability formulas are meant to be predictive devices to help you match materials and students; they are not meant to be exact (Conard, 1984).

As a consumer of materials for your students, you need to understand how to figure readability so that you can make informed decisions when a sales representative tells you the textbook is on a ninth-grade reading level. Remember that readability formulas are used on a number of representative

Figure 3.1 Fry Readability Formula and Graph

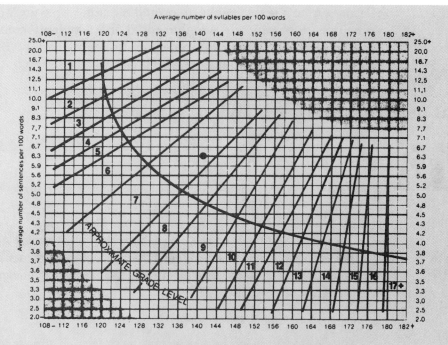

Average number of syllables per 100 words

Expanded Directions for Working Readability Graph

1. Randomly select three (3) sample passages and count out exactly 100 words each, beginning with the beginning of a sentence. Do count proper nouns, initializations, and numerals.
2. Count the number of sentences in the hundred words, estimating length of the fraction of the last sentence to the nearest one-tenth.
3. Count the total number of syllables in the 100-word passage. If you don't have a hand counter available, an easy way is to simply put a mark above every syllable over one in each word, then when you get to the end of the passage, count the number of marks and add 100. Small calculators can also be used as counters by pushing numeral 1, then push the + sign for each word or syllable when counting.
4. Enter graph with *average* sentence length and *average* number of syllables; plot dot where the two lines intersect. Area where dot is plotted will give you the approximate grade level.
5. If a great deal of variability is found in syllable count or sentence count, putting more samples into the average is desirable.
6. A word is defined as a group of symbols with a space on either side; thus, *Joe, IRA, 1945,* and & are each one word.
7. A syllable is defined as a phonetic syllable. Generally, there are as many syllables as vowel sounds. For example, *stopped* is one syllable and *wanted* is two syllables. When counting syllables for numerals and initializations, count one syllable for each symbol. For example, *1945* is four syllables, *IRA* is three syllables, and & is one syllable.

Note: This "extended graph" does not outmode or render the earlier (1968) version inoperative or inaccurate; it is an extension. (REPRODUCTION PERMITTED—NO COPYRIGHT)

Source: From "Fry's Readability Graph: Clarifications, Validity, and Extension to Level 17," *Journal of Reading,* 21 (December 1977), 249.

selections from a text to derive an overall estimate of the text's difficulty. They do not measure every variable that could affect students' comprehension of the text, such as the particular content or the chapter format (IRA, NCTE position statement on readability, 1984).

Teacher as Inquiring Learner Activity

Using the Fry Readability Formula and Graph, calculate the readability range for a textbook in your content area.

● Does the score include the grade the textbook is intended for?

Look at the multisyllabic words in the samples of text you chose.

● Would the words be familiar or unfamiliar to your students? Are the words so important that you would teach them in a prereading activity, or would you expect students to read them independently and figure out their meaning from the context?

Look at the length of the sentences.

● Are the ideas in long sentences clear or confusing? Are ideas in the short sentences clear or choppy? Are the ideas in the sentences connected to each other?

We think a readability range is one measure of a level of a text, but only one measure. Considerateness and fairness are the two other criteria to use to assess the text and to match them with your students' learning needs. Fig. 3.2, a sample checklist you might use in evaluating texts, shows that the interconnection among these variables determines a text's overall appropriateness for use with your students.

Considerateness.   When you are deciding how considerate a text is, examine *format variables* and *content variables* to determine how well topics are explained (Armbruster, 1984). Remember that your students will bring various background knowledge to the text and often they have little familiarity with content-area topics and specialized graphics and visuals.

Let's begin with the *format variables* of considerate textbooks and informational books (see Figure 3.2). First, the whole book should have aids for the reader. The table of contents should inform readers what content is covered and in what order. A glossary, index, and bibliography or references should aid readers in finding or extending specific ideas.

Figure 3.2

Selecting Literacy
Materials: A Checklist

Selecting Literacy Materials: A Checklist

Readability Range _____

Would you teach the multisyllabic words?
Would you expect students to read them independently?
Do the long sentences have too many ideas, or do they clearly connect ideas?
Do the short sentences seem choppy or clear?

Considerate Format

Does the Table of Contents show an orderly sequence?
Does the book contain reader aids, like an index, bibliography, and glossary?
Do the introduction and subheads clearly represent the chapter's organization?
Are the illustrative materials clear and connected to the text?

Considerate Context

How many ideas are presented? Is that number reasonable?
Are the ideas explained clearly and connected explicitly?
Do the examples and analogies match the students' background knowledge?
Is an overarching principle evident?

Fairness

Do the illustrations have a fair representation of race or ethnicity, gender, and class?
Do the illustrations have people in nonstereotypical roles?
Do the examples and problems in the text represent a fair and nonstereotypical representation of race or ethnicity, gender, and class?
Does the text use nonsexist language?

Second, within each chapter, an introduction should alert the reader to what information will be covered and how the information is organized. Purpose-setting questions might be included to guide the reader to significant information on the topic. Subdivisions or subheads should also indicate the organization of the chapter and alert readers to significant content. Illustrative material, such as pictures, tables, and graphs, should be explained in the text and in the caption as well. Finally, a chapter summary should remind readers of the major points.

Now let's discuss the *content variables* of considerate texts (see Figure 3.2). First, the purpose of content writing is to explain facts, events, people, actions, and ideas clearly so that students understand their significance. An entire textbook may present unifying themes or theories within the content area.

Any such framework should be explicitly stated so that students understand how information presented throughout the text will be connected. Individual chapters may be *constructed* around an overarching principle or understanding. For example, a chemistry text could be built around major principles or theories of chemistry (Singer, 1992). In a history text the theme of gaining an American identity could unify a description of events leading to the American Revolution (Beck, McKeown, & Gromoll, 1989).

Second, the manner in which specific facts, events, and concepts are connected to each other and to the overarching understanding should be explicitly explained. For example, a high school history text that describes the French, English, Russian, and American revolutions should explicitly point out their similarities and differences. A science text explaining the functions of arteries and veins should highlight and clarify their differences in function in the human body (Singer, 1992). In physics textbooks (and we think math textbooks as well) the words in the text should be explicitly connected to the formulas presented (Alexander & Kulikowich, 1994).

Third, new concepts or ideas need to be spread out and elaborated rather than presented in rapid fire succession. The number of details or concepts should be carefully considered based on the topic and the assumed background knowledge of the students for whom the book was written.

Finally, any examples and analogies used in the text need to fit with the students' background knowledge if they are to assist in clarifying a point. If the examples or analogies are too abstract or unfamiliar, students will not understand the concept they are supposed to explain (Alexander & Kulikowich, 1994).

Although textbooks are usually examined for considerateness, we advise you also to examine for considerateness other texts that you plan to use with your students. We think informational books, newspaper articles, and magazine articles can be more considerate than traditional content-area texts to your students because their content is often more focused and often is supported by helpful visual aids. Adapted primary sources, rather than actual primary sources, are more considerate because the language and spellings are modernized. With the explosion of the availability of text on the Internet, considerate format and content such as the criteria—design features, ease of use, content, and credibility—developed by the students at KIDS should be used to assess the texts found on the Internet. And, finally, students should learn how to create considerate text of their own by organizing their content, including a reasonable amount of detail, evidence, or facts, and making explicit connections for their readers. You might want to develop a list of user-friendly criteria with your students for the texts they write.

Fairness. As our school population becomes more diverse (see Chapter 2), we certainly want texts that treat race or ethnicity, gender, disability, and class fairly. But what is *fairness*? How important is it for students to see themselves or others like them in the texts they use? Is there a specific list of books or set of facts every student in the United States should know (Bloom, 1987; Hirsh, 1988)? Should required book lists and sets of facts be expanded to include the contributions of groups that heretofore have been underrepresented, and should they be more representative of the demographics of the country as a whole as we enter the twenty-first century than they are now (Sleeter & Grant, 1991)? Educators on both sides have weighed in on this debate. Students need texts that serve as mirrors of themselves and texts that serve as windows to others. Therefore, we define fairness in text as being able to see oneself in some texts and being able to learn about others in other texts.

Compared to textbooks decades ago, textbooks appear to be fairer today. Sleeter and Grant (1991) found that for the most part, the textbooks they analyzed used nonsexist, nonstereotypic language. Furthermore, the distribution of pictures by race and gender closely reflected their percentage in the general population, although white males still dominated. Nevertheless, the texts they analyzed still did not reflect the distribution of class and disability found in the overall population. The middle class dominated, and persons with disability were almost completely ignored.

Just like textbooks, other texts such as trade books, magazines, and online sites, should be evaluated for nonsexist language and fair representation of people (see Figure 3.2). You and your students could evaluate the different texts they read for fairness.

In summary, we encourage you to examine texts using all three factors—readability, considerateness, and fairness—when you are deciding on texts for your students. Remember that all students benefit from a variety of texts—different types of text as well as both challenging and easy texts. As a teacher and lifelong learner, you should read widely in your content area and constantly be on the lookout for suitable materials for your students. Many of the sources listed in Table 3.1 can assist you in this pursuit.

Choices and Decisions About Pedagogy

You know what content you want to teach and you have found materials to use. Now you are ready to think about how you will teach. Your choices and decisions about pedagogy will define you as a teacher, and they will reveal your expectations and views of your students. Clearly pedagogical decisions are important.

We suggest that you think about four interlocking teaching decisions when you plan for a class period or lesson:

- Communication roles for the teacher and for the students
- Grouping patterns for learning
- Teaching tools for literacy
- Assessment tools for literacy

Within a single period, you and the class may experience several communication roles, groupings, and teaching and assessment tools. In order to cover the content and give your students opportunities to apply strategies and understandings, few lessons use a single mode of instruction for the entire period. In fact, we recommend that you plan on using a variety of roles, groupings, and tools in one period whenever possible.

▶ ▶ ▶ ▶ **Communication Roles in Classrooms**

By *communication roles in the classroom,* we mean who decides who can talk and actively participate. As the teacher, you can decide whether communication will be (1) teacher directed, (2) teacher-student interchanges, or (3) student-to-student interchanges. Each has its purpose as well as advantages and disadvantages.

Teacher-Directed Communication.   In this communication pattern, the teacher decides who talks and when; often the teacher does most, if not all, of the talking. No doubt you have experienced the formal lecture in your own education. A second form of teacher-directed communication you have probably experienced is recitation, or in-class response to teacher-directed questions. In recitation, the teacher asks questions of students, a single student responds, and the teacher evaluates the response. If the student gives an incorrect response, the teacher will often continue asking the same question until a student gives the "correct" response. As every student knows, recitation is often focused on the students' remembering facts and details related to a topic, and it sometimes deteriorates into a situation where students are merely trying to guess what answer the teacher is looking for rather than to demonstrate the understandings they have gained about a topic of study.

We object to lectures or recitation for an entire period because most students are passive during these times. Therefore, if you choose to use either of these direct approaches, we recommend that you intersperse your lectures with questioning and that during the questioning or recitation, when you call on a student for a response, you then ask another student to confirm or refute the answer. This sort of alternate response keeps the students on their toes and encourages them to be active listeners and learners during teacher-led communication.

Short teacher-directed communication can be useful. We like the term *mini-lesson* because it implies that the activity takes place for part of a period. Students may need clarification of specific content, so you explain the content in a mini-lesson of ten to fifteen minutes. You may decide to demonstrate an experimental procedure in science, a safety procedure for the bandsaw in vocational education, or how to interview someone or revise writing in a mini-lesson in language arts. In a teacher-directed mini-lesson, the teacher dominates the communication to explain or demonstrate specific concepts or strategies. Science, vocational education, home economics, arts, and physical education teachers have been conducting such short demonstrations or mini-lessons for many years. They give direct instruction, and then students do similar activities in order to practice and apply their new knowledge and strategy.

To free yourself and your students from teacher-directed lessons, you need to believe that students learn from each other and not just from you. If you want to build a community of learners in your classroom, you need to see yourself and your students as important participants and contributors to the construction of meaning. We suggest that you try a variety of options when planning communication within your own classroom to maximize your students' acquisition of the strategies and skills, as well as ownership of the content knowledge being covered.

Teacher-Student Interchanges.   In these interchanges, the teacher and students share the communication decisions about who talks, when, and for how long. Instead of the one-word response often expected in the recitation pattern, the students are encouraged to explain and give reasons or evidence for their thoughts and understandings. The teacher assumes different roles depending on the situation.

Suppose you want to be sure your students understand the geographical concept of region. You might lead a discussion by asking students to give characteristics of regions they are familiar with. Using their examples, you then probe for students to summarize the features that can be used to define a region. In that situation, you are the *guide*; you direct the discussion, but the students are talking most of the time, to either you or other students.

In another teacher-student interchange, you could be a *coach* or *facilitator*. Suppose the students are designing models of aerodynamic flight in their science or physics class. You would ask questions or make statements that would lead the students to consider their design carefully, such as, "Will that wing span provide the lift needed?" When coaching, a teacher speaks very little and focuses on listening to the students' discussions with their peers or may wait for the students to initiate an interchange when they need assistance to answer a question or solve a problem.

Student-to-Student Interchanges.   We think teachers should provide for more opportunities for student-to-student interchanges in which the students govern who talks, when, and for how long in the classroom. In these instances the teacher is either an observer or a participant-observer. In the role of *observer,* the teacher does not interject comments into the students' interchanges. Instead the teacher operates like an anthropologist collecting data about a cultural event. When the teacher adopts the role of *participant-observer,* the teacher takes on no more decision-making power than any student participant. For example, in a discussion of an issue, such as, "Does a dress code violate student rights?" you can express your views as a participant-observer. However, you would choose an opportune time so that you do not extinguish student-to-student interchanges, especially because students rarely forget who's the teacher!

▶ ▶ ▶ ▶ **Grouping for Learning**

Although educational reforms call for less tracking, we acknowledge that tracking will continue in some form in many junior high, middle schools, and high schools. And although you will probably not change school policy and how students are assigned to classes and courses, you can usually determine the grouping patterns within your own classroom. You need to decide whether whole class, small groups, pairs, or individual configurations will best serve your teaching-learning purposes and, most important, the learning needs of your students.

We think the purpose for instruction should determine the grouping pattern chosen for any specific lesson. At certain times, either high- or low-achieving students need direct instruction, so perhaps you will carry out a mini-lesson on specific content or a strategy in a homogeneous small group. At another time, high- and low-achieving students have information about a topic to contribute to each other in heterogeneous small groups. Especially in science or math classes, you may find that same-sex small groups may allow girls more opportunity to learn actively (Guzzetti & Williams, 1996; Jones & Wheatley, 1990). The grouping patterns you choose should vary during a lesson, a unit, or a course. You should always be flexible with your grouping decisions so that they best meet instructional and student needs, and be ready to revise your plan.

Whole Class.   When everyone needs to learn or to share similar information, teachers keep the whole class together. Teachers conduct whole class mini-lessons and whole class teacher-led discussions when a new topic or strategy is being introduced, such as at the beginning of a new unit or theme study or when a new text is introduced. Teachers also hold class meetings when students need to plan research projects or divide up learning tasks in the classroom. Another use of whole class grouping is when the students participate in a culminating activity, such as a debate or discussion, which gives them a chance to use their understandings or new knowledge. Also, as a culminating activity for a unit, the whole class might share their finished products—art works, research projects, or written texts—with each other.

Small Groups.   Teachers usually choose to divide the class into small groups to meet different instructional purposes and to meet different student needs. Teachers make these decisions because of the advantages for students' learning that are inherent in small group structure:

- Students learn by interacting with each other cooperatively.

- Students construct meaning more actively by interacting with the materials and each other.

- Students with different information and strengths (heterogeneous groups) can contribute to each other.

- More students find it easier and more comfortable to talk and listen in a smaller group than in a whole class setting.

- Student participation in homogeneous groupings enables them to accomplish content-area goals and objectives more effectively and efficiently.

Teacher-Led Small Groups.   We think that the purpose for a small group governs the teacher's particular communication role with that group. We have already mentioned teacher-directed mini-lessons to a small group when students need specific instruction. When students are learning together in a group, a teacher can be a coach, helping the students accomplish their task. For the same reason, teacher-led discussions could help a small group accomplish their task. For example, a teacher could act as a coach with a small group by teaching the students a process, such as how to comment on a peer's writing or how to compare different problem-solving approaches in mathematics, so that the students can be more effective in their own learning and more helpful to each other.

Student-Led Small Groups.   Although we use the generic term *small groups,* you will encounter special terms that refer to particular types of small groups where students take on a variety of roles in support of learning with one another. Cooperative learning groups (Johnson, Johnson, & Holubec, 1990; Slavin, 1988) and peer-led discussion groups are two student-led groupings that we find particularly useful. Perhaps you have participated in one or more of these small group settings while taking your college or university courses.

Peer-led discussion groups: Reader response. In small group discussions of their texts, students share reactions to the text, clarify understandings and information gained from the text, and extend their thoughts and opinions to other texts and real-life situations. Sometimes mistakenly construed as a "jam session" in which students expound on their feelings, the goals of peer-led discussion (based on Rosenblatt, 1983) are the examination of audience reactions and an analysis of how the writer induced those reactions. Students could discuss the evidence for and the validity of the author's conclusions in nonfiction text. For fiction text, the students may discuss the believability of a character's change justifying their responses with citations from the text. We will more fully discuss peer-led groups in Chapters 5 and 6.

Peer-led discussion groups: Writing response. In writing conferences or small groups, students comment on each other's writing to help the writers revise their first drafts. Elbow (1973) suggests that peers first comment on what is working or what they like about the draft, since everyone needs positive reinforcement. Next, peers ask one another questions about points that confuse them, places in the written piece where more detail or information is needed, or places in which the sequence seems confusing. Peers respond as a real audience to help each other communicate more clearly what they intended. We discuss such writing conferences in Chapter 6.

Cooperative learning small groups. Johnson et al. (1990) emphasize that students of differing achievements, interests, and knowledge can contribute to the learning of everyone in a group. They stress that students must be taught to work cooperatively, such as learning to clarify the purpose or goal of the small group, how to create a group response or product, and how to evaluate their own process as well their products. In the cooperative learning model that Johnson et al. proposed, generic roles—leader, reader, recorder, checker, and encourager—are assigned to group members. While we prefer to have students create and assign roles as necessary for the particular learning task, we like cooperative learning groups for discussion purposes, research projects, science investigations, and math problem solving.

Another version of cooperative learning for small groups, known as the *jigsaw approach* (Aronson, 1978), is a two-step procedure for students to use when sharing knowledge about different topics in a unit of study. First, students in a group focus on and learn about a specific subtopic related to a common area of study; these groups are referred to as *expert groups* for this reason.

For example, expert groups in an American history class could learn about different events in the civil rights movement; expert groups in a science class could learn about different astronomical bodies. After the expert groups have completed their learning, the class regroups into what are known as *teaching groups*. Each teaching group includes a member from each of the expert groups, who teaches the other members about the subtopic his or her expert group had focused on. For example, the student who was the asteroid expert would teach about asteroids and then learn about comets, black holes, supernovas, and neutron stars from the other experts. Chapter 7 contains specific instances of jigsaw groups' working together to do research on a multifaceted topic.

Pairs and Partners.   Sometimes even a small group is too large for the purpose; in this case, it may be advantageous to have students work with only one other person. When students share ideas with a partner, they can trigger each other's ideas. In other instances, a student might benefit from having a *tutorial partner*—a peer who can help with the content or the processes in a particular discipline or within a particular unit of study. Such peer-aged tutoring has been particularly successful at the middle school level because both students, the tutor and the tutee, demonstrate increased self-confidence and higher motivation (Wagner, in Alexander & George, 1993). We prefer students working in pairs rather than alone to edit the mechanics of their peer's writing to produce a final product. Additionally, pairs of students can help each other understand difficult text, work on a science project, and research a topic, especially when they have the same or complementary interests.

Although we have emphasized the value of small groups, pairs, and partners, students do learn individually, and you want to know your students as individuals. We strongly suggest that you mix independent or individual work into your grouping designs. Furthermore, some students have unique interests that no other student shares. Those individuals benefit from pursuing their interests in depth. Content-area teachers also have the opportunity to foster those individuals whose unique interests relate to their own interests.

Practical Considerations for Grouping Decisions.   The major purpose for any grouping decision is to allow the teacher to meet the instructional purposes dictated by the content being studied and the objectives given the needs and strengths of the students in their class. If you teach several sections of the same course, you may have to change the grouping arrangements you chose for a lesson, a series of lessons, or for the entire unit because the students are different and require different teaching and learning arrangements in order for them to meet the instructional goals.

First, the size of the group can make or break the success of small group work. We envision a variety of groups: two individuals working as partners or pairs, cooperative groups of four students, and small reading and writing discussion groups made up of five or six students. The size of a group should be determined by the complexity of the learning task at hand, the materials that are being used, and the outcomes that you desire, as well as the needs and strengths of the students. Groups are not meant to be static or permanent. They may vary in size and composition during the course of a series of lessons, a unit, or a semester in order to meet instructional goals and student learning needs that often become apparent as the lesson or unit is in process.

Second, you may wish to assign students to groups that are balanced by gender, race, achievement, and other factors that make them representative of the class as a whole (see Chapter 2). At the beginning of the year, you might want to allow students to choose their own partners or groups because you don't yet know the students and their learning needs. After you have had time to observe the students as they participate in their self-selected groups, you may choose to reassign them to groups. At this time you may want to act as a guide for the small groups or even for partners, modeling for students how to participate more effectively as a speaker and as a listener. Although we prefer not to assign roles, in our role as teacher-guide, we have done so when students needed to learn how to contribute to a group or when they needed help in identifying what roles might be useful to carry out a task or move a particular project forward. It is important that students know that the grouping patterns during the year will vary. You may want to return to self-selection of partners or groups later in the unit, the semester, or the year as the students get to know each other better and the course content and the classroom expectations more fully.

Third, we think one of the most useful ways to teach students about working cooperatively is to create a list with students of the behaviors that contribute to learning—for example, simple items like listening to each other, reading directions, and ensuring that everyone participates. You know from groups or pairs you've participated in that even simple behaviors can be difficult at times. Therefore, either during or at the end of an activity, each group or pair should evaluate how well they have cooperated. In all small group work, it is important that each student learns how to assess his or her own contributions as well as what the group or partnership has accomplished. Coming together as a class to share the positive instances as well as the instances that need improvement, the class can pick one or two behaviors to stress in their next session with their small group or with their partner. Finally, these same criteria can be incorporated into self-assessment checklists for students to use in evaluating their own performance.

Finally, you know from your own group work that it is not difficult to stray off task. Few students, yet alone adults, work solidly on a single topic for forty minutes! Every group or partnership does stray, and sometimes the tangents taken are very beneficial. However, when students govern the cooperative groups or the pairs they are in, the crucial criterion for the teacher to determine is whether the students are returning to the task and whether they are using the grouping interactions in a purposeful manner related to the topic and content being studied. Such observation and reflection allow the teacher to determine the benefit of the grouping patterns chosen in terms of the meeting of both the instructional goals and the learning needs of their students.

Teacher as Inquiring Learner Activity

One of the decisions you will make over and over again during your teaching career is how best to group your own students to maximize their learning experiences. Later in this chapter, you will see how this consideration is incorporated in a sample lesson plan. For the next week keep track of the different ways students are grouped in your university classes and labs or in your field placement settings.

Create a checklist using the categories for grouping that have just been described, for example, whole class, small groups, pairs and partners. Leave room also for comments and reactions about how you think these decisions about grouping helped you or got in the way of your learning or that of your students. Share your findings with other students in your discipline, for example science, art or math, or with other students at your level, for example middle school or high school.

▶ ▶ ▶ ▷ **Teaching Tools for Literacy**

Because your students will have a range of literacy needs, you will need a repertoire of teaching tools to support their reading and writing in your content area. In Part Two, we present many specific teaching tools from which you can select. Here we define the three categories of teaching tools you will meet in Part Two.

Modeling and Explaining.   Because we emphasize the process of learning content, we consider the modeling and explaining teaching tool to be a primary teaching tool. The objective of this tool is to make literacy strategies visible and explicit so that students are aware of strategies they should or do use.

In modeling and explaining strategies, you both show your process of literacy learning and hold a running commentary on your process. Using the text your students read, you express out loud how you are learning (your strategies) and what you are learning (the content). As we stated in Chapter 1, you explicitly name each particular strategy and what it does (*declarative knowledge*), tell why and when to use the strategy (*conditional knowledge*), and show how you use the strategies (*procedural knowledge*). If you use your strategies without explicit explanations, your students may not recognize the strategies or learn why, when, and even how to use them.

You will want to model and explain the use of strategies with the different texts your students read throughout the year. To build your students' metacognitive awareness of strategies at the beginning of the year, you will model and explain your own strategies in a teacher-directed mini-lesson. Throughout Part Two, we include scripts in order to model and explain to you specific literacy strategies useful with different content-area texts.

As your students become more metacognitively aware, you may choose to hold a teacher-guided discussion in which you and the students identify the strategies to use, tell what the rationale is for their use, and decide when to use them. Perhaps at this stage a student could demonstrate how to use the strategy with the material and content at hand. You may even initiate student-to-student interchanges in which students model and explain their strategies in small groups and pairs for one another. Whenever your students face a difficult text, you may decide to model and explain your strategies in order to teach them useful strategies for that text. Remember also that your students will need guided practice or coaching in using strategies before they can use them independently (Pearson & Gallagher, 1983).

Direct Teaching Tools.   Like a teacher-directed lesson, a teacher uses a direct teaching tool selectively to impart information to students. For instance, you may directly teach word parts—root words, prefixes, and suffixes—so that your students can decipher unknown multisyllabic words when they meet them in the content-area texts. Because the students receive information only when a direct teaching tool is used, you will want to follow up with an activity in which students use the information or content in a meaningful situation. In the word parts example, you would have your students collect and define additional words with similar word parts when they read their own texts.

Teaching/Assessing Tools.   We like teaching/assessing tools because they serve two functions in instruction. First, they are teaching tools that support students' learning of content and use of strategies. Second, while the students use the tools to understand text or content, the teacher can assess the students' learning, turning a teaching tool into an assessing tool. From that assessment, the teacher can make decisions about what and how to teach next.

For example, to support your students in finding and interpreting important information in a new text or selection, you may decide to use the teaching/assessing tool of teacher-guided discussion or a directed reading activity (explained in Chapter 5). As the students read the text, you periodically ask questions about the text and discuss with the students how purpose-setting questions support their learning. As a teaching tool, your questions help the students identify the important details and interpretations. The discussion among students helps them to comprehend the content. As the students discuss, you notice who comprehends the text, what ideas are understood, and where there is confusion, thus turning the teaching tool into an assessment tool.

In addition to informing you and your students about the direction of instruction, teaching/assessing tools are effective because the students operate on the content. Instead of just passively receiving the content through lecture or other direct instruction, the students are being engaged in a process in which they construct their own version of the content. For example, in the teacher-guided discussion, the students explain their understanding of the content and how they interpret the information. Because the students are transacting with their ideas, they can also assess what strategies and content they know and what they need to learn. Specific teaching/assessing tools are included in every chapter in Part Two because they inform teachers and students how learning and instruction are progressing.

▶ ▶ ▶ ▶ **Assessment Tools for Literacy**

If you think of assessments like standardized tests, weekly quizzes, and end-of-unit tests, then our use of assessment with pedagogy may seem unusual to you. However, we prefer different assessment tools: ones that inform students and teachers about ongoing learning and that exhibit the content students have learned. When students and teachers use assessment tools in this manner, then assessment is interactive with instruction.

Assessment tools chosen to measure both literacy and content-area learning, during individual lessons or a series of lessons (Part Two) or at the culmination of a unit (Part Three), should be decided on based on four guidelines.

The assessment tools and end products that are chosen should exhibit that the
    goals and objectives of a lesson or unit were accomplished

Students should be required to demonstrate their use of knowledge, not just their acquisition of facts

The degree of choice or how an assessment tool is chosen, and who—the teacher, the student, or the teacher and student in collaboration— decides how students' understandings will be demonstrated should vary according to student needs and teacher objectives

Finally, students should have the opportunity to share their new understandings and knowledge with appropriate audiences

The tools we have chosen to emphasize throughout this text are all *performance assessment measures*—they exhibit student learning. In the lessons described in Part Two and the units designed for different curriculum approaches in Part Three, students are required to demonstrate their knowledge by showing ongoing learning (a journal entry, graphic, model) or creating a product (video, diorama, essay, poem). We prefer such performance assessments because they inform students about their own learning and inform teachers about what and how to instruct students. In Part Two of this book, we present primarily teaching/assessment tools that you and your students can use to inform each other about literacy and content-area learning and conclude with a focus on end products in Chapter 7. In Part Three, we incorporate both teaching/assessment tools and end products or culminating activities into different content area units.

Formative Assessment Tools for Ongoing Learning.   Assessment that occurs while a task or project is still progressing is called *formative* (McMillan, 1997). Formative assessment, detailed more fully in Chapter 8, allows the teacher to modify goals, directions, and assignments before a task or project or unit of study is completed. In both Parts Two and Three, we present four types of formative assessment tools: teaching/assessing tools, assessment-only tools, monitoring and self-monitoring questions, and working or collection portfolios.

Teaching/Assessing Tools.   We have already discussed how you can use these tools to teach your students as you keep an eye on assessment. We repeat these tools here to stress that assessment angle: good teaching concentrates on students' responses. You have a wonderful opportunity to observe students' active learning when they are working or with a teaching/assessing tool. Most beginning teachers concentrate on their own teaching, their role during the lesson, and what they are doing in the lesson. However, we want you to learn to attend to what your students do—their ongoing learning— which you can determine as you observe your students working alone or in small groups, as well as in whole class settings. Using teaching/assessing tools such as the ones described in detail in Part Two will allow you to be informed about your students' learning of both strategies and content throughout a given lesson or unit.

Assessment-Only Tools.   As the name denotes, assessment-only tools indicate how or what a student is learning or has learned; they do not teach. Although you probably think of end-of-unit tests, assessment-only tools can be used during learning too. For example, in Chapter 4, we present an assessment tool in which the students rate how well they understand the important vocabulary you have selected from a particular unit or chapter. If a student doesn't know a specific word, this type of rating sheet or assessment tool doesn't teach the word. But you can examine the rating sheets to assess what words you need to teach for the student's future study.

Monitoring and Self-Monitoring.   During every task, strategic learners are metacognitively aware, and they are able to monitor their own progress toward learning. These students stay with successful strategies, abandon unsuccessful ones, and change strategies as they work on different parts of the task. In the modeling and explaining scripts in Part Two, you will find statements that monitor what strategies are useful. Also, at the end of each chapter, you will find a monitoring checklist that lists questions to ask to help students monitor their ongoing use of strategies. We suggest that you select monitoring questions to use with your students during modeling and explaining lessons, as well as with your coaching or guided practice sessions and even when your students are independently applying their strategies and understandings.

Collection Portfolios and Ongoing Performance Evaluation.   Also called *documentation* or *working portfolios*, these portfolios contain the artifacts students produce as they learn in any content area—for example, a word map (see Chapter 4), a study guide with their responses (see Chapter 5), or a summary (see Chapter 6) that students have completed in whole class, small group, partner, and individual work during their study. Students and teachers can review their working portfolios to assess progress in learning, such as their understanding of the issues surrounding the Vietnam War, their competency in expository writing in both language arts and across the content areas, and their application of mathematical calculations during their science investigations. Periodically as the year progresses, students will need to weed their working portfolios to discard insignificant artifacts and save clear examples of significant learning. We discuss the collection portfolio more fully in conjunction with the integrated curriculum approach in Part Three.

Summative Assessment Tools for Evaluating Learning.   When assessment occurs primarily as a concluding or culminating activity for a series of lessons or a unit, it is called *summative assessment* (McMillan, 1997). Summative assessment is usually based on students' ability to synthesize knowledge and demonstrate their understanding in some concrete product that can be shared with others—teachers, peers, parents, and administrators. In Parts Two and Three, we present three forms of summative assessment tools: end products such as research papers and projects, as well as performances, classroom- and teacher-made tests, and showcase portfolios.

End Products and Performances That Actively Demonstrate Learning.   Students can demonstrate what they have learned to audiences other than the teacher. Students can apply what they have learned in projects that inform other students in class, in other classes, and in other schools. Their projects could inform the local citizens, a historical group, or an ecology society. Students may present to the local planning board their research on the ecological status of a wetland and their positions on a new highway proposed to run through it. Students may write reviews for school or local newspapers, applying their understandings of responding to literature and writing in review format.

In Chapters 6, on refining ideas, and 7, on learning through research projects, and throughout the chapters in Part Three, we present a variety of products and projects that are used as assessment tools. For example, debates, newspaper articles, and an ad campaign are end products suggested in Chapters 9, 10, and 11. The term paper (both the traditional and several alternative forms), summaries and abstracts, reviews, and annotations are the focus in Chapter 7. Finally, dramatic as well as art and musical opportunities to communicate learning are presented in Chapter 6. Each of the products enables the learners to communicate their unique understanding of content to different audiences, one of whom is always the teacher. Although the unit has ended, the teacher can use the information to inform future units and to design new learning opportunities for individual students or groups within the class.

Classroom and Teacher-Made Tests.   Lessons, units, and semesters do end, and students need to demonstrate what they have learned. Think about the tests you have taken and the learning you demonstrated on them. On multiple-choice tests, you demonstrated how well you could memorize facts and figure out the choices given. On essay tests, you had the opportunity to synthesize ideas, critique works, or substantiate theories or positions you held. When tests are given, we prefer the essay because students construct their own meaning by writing their understandings. We do acknowledge the difficulty in grading a large number of essays.

We always prefer assessments that match with learning goals and actively engage students. However, paper-and-pencil assessment of a task may be useful in certain instances. Essay tests in particular, which prompt students to think critically and creatively as they synthesize information from their study of multiple sources, can be very useful and appropriate in all of the content areas (see Chapter 6 and all of the chapters in Part Three). Short-answer tests that demonstrate students' knowledge of facts and details related to a particular time period or event in history, science formulas, chemistry notations, and math theorems may assess a student's repertoire in a given content area.

Showcase Portfolios. Showcase or "best-work" portfolios are summative assessment tools because their purpose is to display the culmination or synthesis of a student's work in a course, a semester, or an academic year. Often the showcase portfolios are referred to as display portfolios because other individuals—teachers, parents, administrators—will see and respond to them. In addition to the products themselves in the showcase portfolio, students are expected to provide written commentary to explain why they have chosen the particular pieces of work in their portfolio and to include some comments about their own growth and development as a reader and writer, a mathematician, a scientist, or an artist as displayed in the products they have chosen for display. In this way, the summative portfolios demonstrate not only a student's competency in a content area or several content areas, but also their ownership of their own work and their reflective and evaluative competencies.

Lesson Plans: Combining Content, Strategies, Materials, and Pedagogy

Student teachers and interns often ask us, "If experienced teachers don't write lesson plans, why do we?" Our answer is that experienced teachers do create lessons, based on their repertoire of teaching tools and their reservoir of knowledge about their content and their students. In addition, they think about the purpose or objective of every lesson, the materials they need to have prepared, the groupings that will occur, and the teaching/assessing tools they will use. Often these experienced teachers write notes for themselves as they think through these components of a lesson. The only difference from you is that these experienced teachers are not required to write the plans for an outside audience, such as their supervisor or cooperating teacher or even their peers. Although their plans may seem invisible, they most assuredly are there.

In this section, we outline a generic lesson plan format and accompany it with a sample lesson plan. We do not expect you to understand many of the teaching tools and assessing tools in the lesson plan; we will explain those tools in Part Two. For now, we give you the lesson plan format so that you will have the structure in which to place the teaching and assessing tools described in detail in Part Two.

A Generic Lesson Plan Format as Applied to Modeling and Explaining Content and Strategy in Tandem

Lesson plans are not written in narrative paragraphs; they are organized lists or directions that you can refer to quickly. Everyone develops his or her own style of lesson plan; however, you may be required to use a preferred department or district format when you are a teacher in a particular middle school or high school. Most lesson plans have four basic parts: (1) goals and objectives, (2) materials, (3) pedagogy or teaching procedures, and (4) assessment or evaluation. When you write lesson plans, you preplan the content and strategies you expect to accomplish. Although we estimate one period for each lesson, we know that some plans will take more than one period to complete because of either the nature of the activities or the students' performance and responses during the lesson.

In the sample lesson plan that follows, we emphasize using a strategy to support the learning of content. The lesson proceeds from a teacher-directed mini-lesson where the teacher models and explains for the students to the students working with each other.

Sample Lesson Plan

Goals and Objectives

We think this is the most important section of a lesson plan: Why are you and the students learning the content and the strategy? If you don't have an important reason, then you are wasting both the students' and your time. We think lessons begin with a teacher goal or goals and student learning objectives:

- A *goal* is your overall purpose for the lesson: what you want to accomplish and in a broad sense what you expect your students to learn.

You may state the goal in general terms, like understand or *know.* As you will see in Chapter 8, lesson goals are derived from even larger unit goals.

- *Objectives* are more detailed statements of what students are to learn about content and strategies. For objectives, you use more specific verbs, like *predict* or *diagram.* Objectives are derived from lesson goals and can help you focus your instruction. You will see how goals and their accompanying objectives operate in the lesson plan that follows. You can also look ahead to Figures 8.1 and 8.2 to see how goals and objectives fit and work within the broader unit framework.

For example, in a science/health lesson for high school students, the teacher's lesson plan includes the following goals and objectives:

Goal (major understandings; overall purpose of lesson)**:** To change students' eating habits by building their understanding of the new nutritional guidelines

Objectives (specific student learning and/or performances expected to be gained from the lesson)**:**

Content: Students will compare the old nutritional guidelines to the new ones.

Strategy: Students will interpret the designs of the two graphs for how they portray information about nutritional value.

Materials

The materials or resource section is a list of what you and the students need that period. The sole purpose is to ensure that you gather all the necessary materials for the lesson. For example, in the sample lesson the teacher would need the following items:

Magazine articles such as "Watch What You Eat!" *Time,* May 11, 1992, and "A Pyramid Topples at the USDA," *Consumer Reports,* October 1991

Transparency of circle or pie graph and pyramid graph of nutritional diets

Pedagogy or Teaching Procedures

This section is a step-by-step outline of the activities that will happen during the period, assuming that you and the class don't get off on a tangent or don't decide to change the activity on the spot. Both of these do happen.

The first step is so important we call it *previewing*. Previewing occurs when you bridge the students' prior knowledge (Chapter 2) with what they will learn in this lesson. If you are beginning a new topic, you may want to spend a whole period bridging between their background knowledge and the new topic (Chapter 4):

Teaching Procedures

Preview: Whole class

Students will write a list of what they ate yesterday and estimate the nutritional value of each food. As a class, discuss why their diets are or are not nutritional.

In the subsequent steps, you list the teaching tools and student groupings for learning that are most appropriate for the topic and the students. The second step in the lesson might be a mini-lesson on a specific topic. The third step might be to guide pairs of students to work with a text or to participate in small group discussions about the text. Following the advice given to us when we began teaching, we always plan more than time allows. Nothing is worse than to have students complete in ten minutes what you thought would take forty-five minutes! Besides, you can always use tomorrow what they didn't do today.

Mini-lesson on reading graphs: Whole class

Teacher displays transparency of circle or pie graph. Elicits from students what facts are portrayed on the graph. Asks what nutritional message is portrayed on the graph and what about the graph's design gives that message.

Teacher displays pyramid graph transparency. Asks how the message has changed. Asks students to think about why the government didn't just change the proportion on the circle graph.

Teacher discusses how the manner in which graphs illustrate information affects the way we interpret facts.

Guided practice: Pairs

Students read both articles and the text on the pyramid graph.

Students are guided by purpose-setting questions such as: What points about a healthful diet does the government think is portrayed well by the graph? What evidence supports the government's healthful diet? Is the pyramid persuasive?

Peer-led Discussions: Small groups engage in considering the following:

1. The pros and cons of the pyramid graph.
2. Why they think the meat and dairy products industry originally opposed changing from the circle pie chart to the pyramid.
3. How their diets yesterday fit with the pyramid. Put items on a pyramid.

Reporting out of small group discussions: Whole class

Assessment and Evaluation

We divide this category into student assessment and lesson evaluation. First, student assessment should answer the question, "How will my students demonstrate they have accomplished the student objectives?" In order to do this, you can look at student responses on the teaching/assessing and assessing-only tools developed for the lesson. You can add information you have gained from your own observations, anecdotal records, and field notes.

Second, you want to evaluate the lesson as a whole. What helped the students understand? How long did the students need? Did the sequence fit the students' learning needs? You also want to evaluate the student assessment data carefully. Based on your assessment of the students' learning, you determine what the next teaching-learning experiences should be and what should be included in future lessons.

Assessment and Evaluation

Tools and criteria to evaluate students:

1. Students' list of items in yesterday's diet and placement of items on a pyramid.
2. Individual student comments about the message of the graphs during mini-lesson.
3. Individual student comments during discussions and reporting out of main points of their discussions—identify pros and cons; speculate on industry objections; evaluate diets.

Lesson evaluation—questions to ask yourself as a teacher:

1. Did the students practice the strategy of interpreting graphs during the reading of the articles?

2. Were the articles appropriately matched to the students' interest and reading ability?

3. Did the mix of groupings and activities support the students' learning of content and strategies?

Finally, remember that teaching is learning. Try to focus on your students and the information they are giving you about their learning rather than what you are doing. By focusing on students' learning in process as well as the outcomes or products, you will increase your reservoir of knowledge and be better able to select from your repertoire of teaching tools for the next lesson you plan and carry out.

Summary of the Chapter

In this chapter about choices and decisions, we are advocating for variety and against the traditional educational routine: read the textbook at home, lecture next day, and test soon thereafter. Using a variety of texts will give your students the opportunity to:

- Meet the content in different contexts
- Meet different points of view
- Recognize that the field still entertains questions to be asked and answered.

Using a variety of communication roles and groupings will support different purposes for learning:

- Teacher-directed, whole class, or small group mini-lesson learning purposes
- Teacher guided or coached, small groups, pairs, or independent learning purposes
- Student centered, small groups, pairs, or independent learning purposes

As you begin your teaching career, we recommend preplanning your choices and decisions using the lesson plan format. As you build a repertoire of teaching tools and a reservoir of knowledge, you will adopt an abbreviated form. To assist you, in Part Two we concentrate on teaching and assessment tools that support literacy strategies. As you read Part Two, think about your content area, and select the literacy strategies and tools that support learning in that area. Once again, you will need to make choices and decisions.

Inquiry Activities About Your Learning

1. Choose a topic in your content area that you enjoy but haven't had the chance to study in depth. How many different types of texts can you find on that topic? What different information does each text provide? How fair and considerate are the different texts? Would some match well to your students?

2. In one of your college classes or even in a social situation, observe who governs the talk. Does the teacher or the individual respond differently to men than women? Do the men in class act differently than the women do? Interview a talkative man and a talkative woman. How do they view the communication in the classroom? In a social situation, who governs the topic of conversation? Does anyone interrupt?

Inquiry Activities About Your Students' Learning

1. Observe a science or math class and a social studies or English/language arts class. Tally whom the teacher calls on, who receives reprimands, who speaks out. Tally which gender talks more to the whole class or in small group work, or goes unnoticed by the teacher. Did you find gender differences? Did you find gender differences in science or math compared to social studies or English, or did the genders talk the same regardless of the class? Do you think the teacher's gender made a difference?

2. Select a text in your content area. Determine its readability, considerateness, and fairness using the questions for selecting literacy materials in Table 3.1. Then interview two students about the text: a successful student and a student who is struggling a little. Have each one read the text aloud. Ask each one questions about whether the text was hard or easy to read, about their understanding of the content, and about their opinions of the fairness of the text. Do their views correspond to yours? Why or why not?

Information and Resources

Professional Books

Alvermann, D. E., Hinchman, K. A., Moore, D. W., Phelps, S. F., & Waff, D. R. (Eds.). (1998). *Reconceptualizing the literacies in adolescents' lives.* Mahwah, NJ: Erlbaum.

Presents issues and ideas for thinking about literacy in every classroom and discusses the know-how and perspectives that diverse adolescents and their teachers bring.

García, E. (1999). *Student cultural diversity: Understanding and meeting the challenge* (2nd ed.). Boston: Houghton Mifflin.

Defines cultural and language diversity and discusses teaching diverse students. Of particular interest are two secondary projects.

Grant, C. A., & Sleeter, C. E. (1998). *Turning on learning: Five approaches for multicultural teaching plans for race, class, gender, and disability* (2nd ed.). Columbus, OH: Merrill.

For each approach, such as studying single groups or taking social action, gives a rationale and specific lesson plans (K–12).

Shulman, J., Lotan, R. A., & Whitcomb, J. A. (Eds.). (1998). *Groupwork in diverse classrooms: A casebook for educators.* New York: Teachers College.

Looks at the open-ended dilemmas faced when teachers use group work instead of traditional teaching. Invites readers to submit their reactions to the authors' web site, **http://www.WestEd.org.**

Professional Journals

Anderson-Inman, L., & Horney, M. (1997). Electronic books for secondary students. *Journal of Adolescent and Adult Literacy, 40*(6), 486–490.

Discusses the advantages and disadvantages, the embedded resources, and evaluation criteria for electronic books.

Benjamin, B., & Irwin-DeVitis, L. (1998). Censoring girls' choices: Continued gender bias in English language arts classrooms. *English Journal, 87*(2), 64–71.

Reports middle school girls' comments about gender issues, such as being smart, and male characters in books, and concludes with teaching suggestions.

Lester, J. H., & Cheek, E. H. Jr. (1998). The "real" experts address textbook issues. *Journal of Adolescent and Adult Literacy, 41*(4), 282–291.

Surveyed forty-four high school students for their opinions of and suggestions for their content-area textbooks.

Lord, T. (1998). Cooperative learning that really works in biology teaching: Using constructivist-based activities to challenge student teams. *American Biology Teacher, 60*(8), 580–588.

Discusses the rationale for, problems of, and solutions to group work. Suggestions given on types of questions and activities, like concept maps, charts, and diagrams.

White, J. (1998). Helping students deal with cultural differences. *Social Studies, 89*(3), 107–111.

Discusses culture as defined by anthropologists and describes a student inquiry project about how different people view personal space.

Internet

http://www.memory.loc.gov/ammem/ammemhome.html (American Memories).

A national digital library of its photos, prints, documents, maps, motion pictures, and sound recordings that the Library of Congress is creating. The Educator's Page has specific classroom ideas and search help for using the collection.

http://curry.edschool.Virginia,EDU/go/specialed/ (special education).

A comprehensive web site that organizes and updates information into five major areas related to special education. Particularly useful for K–12 and postsecondary educators.

http://curry.edschool.Virginia.EDU:80/go/multicultural/ (Multicultural Pavilion).

A comprehensive, interactive educational Internet project useful for both K–12 and college educators, with links to other web sites. See the Teacher's Corner archive and database of multicultural activities, songs, historical documents, and literature.

http://www.inform.umd.edu/Diversity/ (Diversity Database).

A reference for research and policy information on diversity covering age, class, gender, ethnicity, and race.

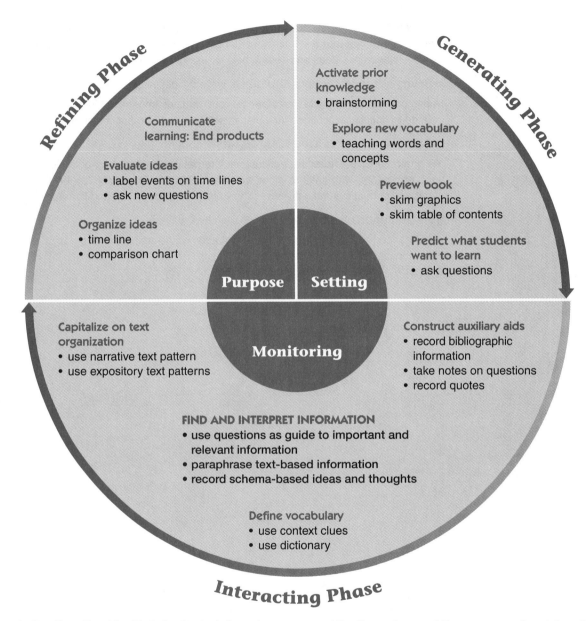

Refining Phase

Generating Phase

Activate prior knowledge
• brainstorming

Communicate learning: End products

Explore new vocabulary
• teaching words and concepts

Evaluate ideas
• label events on time lines
• ask new questions

Preview book
• skim graphics
• skim table of contents

Organize ideas
• time line
• comparison chart

Predict what students want to learn
• ask questions

Purpose | **Setting**

Monitoring

Capitalize on text organization
• use narrative text pattern
• use expository text patterns

Construct auxiliary aids
• record bibliographic information
• take notes on questions
• record quotes

FIND AND INTERPRET INFORMATION
• use questions as guide to important and relevant information
• paraphrase text-based information
• record schema-based ideas and thoughts

Define vocabulary
• use context clues
• use dictionary

Interacting Phase

In Part Two, *Teaching Tools for Strategic Learning,* we present the three phases of literacy: generating, interacting, and refining. Chapter 4, *Generating Ideas: Building on Background Knowledge* (the generating phase), focuses on the strategies and tools used before reading a text. Chapter 5, *Interacting with Ideas: Comprehending and Constructing Knowledge* (the interacting phase), discusses strategies and tools used during reading. Chapter 6, *Refining Ideas: Studying and Clarifying Knowledge* (the refining phase), presents strategies and tools used after reading. Chapter 7, *Linking the phases: Learning Through Research Research Projects,* demonstrates how strategic learners cycle through all three phases.

Teaching Tools for Strategic Learning

Chapter 4:

Generating Ideas: Building on Background Knowledge

Chapter 5:

Interacting with Ideas: Comprehending and Constructing Knowledge

Chapter 6:

Refining Ideas: Studying and Clarifying Knowledge

Chapter 7:

Linking the Phases: Learning Through Research Projects

Information and Resources

4

Generating Ideas: Building on Background Knowledge

What do you do to prepare yourself for taking a new course? When you register for the course, do you read over the course description to learn what will be covered? Do you think about how this course will build on your previous courses and fit into your college program or your career plans? After groaning about the cost of the books, do you skim the Table of Contents or leaf through the textbook to get a more detailed overview of the course? On the first day of class, do you skim the syllabus to find out what topics are covered and what the assignments are? If you do any of these things to prepare yourself, you are using strategies to generate ideas or building on your background knowledge.

We define *generating ideas* as encompassing three major strategies that serve as springboards from which to launch new learning. First, before they embark on reading or writing a text, strategic learners *activate prior experiences and prior knowledge*. They search their schemata for one that will match, or come close to, the text they're about to begin. Second, strategic readers *preview and predict or survey the text* and think about what they are likely to learn. Third, as strategic readers activate their background knowledge and preview the text, they may notice unfamiliar words. They may decide to *explore new vocabulary* before they read, or wait until they come to the new words during their reading of the text. Although we have separated these three major strategies in order to analyze and discuss what a strategic learner can choose to do, you will find that they overlap and intertwine. Strategic learners flexibly skip from one strategy to another, or use all three in combination.

Underlying the literacy strategies are two ongoing strategies, *purpose setting* and *monitoring*, which begin in this generating phase and continue throughout a task. At the beginning of a task, strategic learners set their purpose, which guides their selection of effective strategies. They also begin to monitor their progress (or are metacognitively aware, a term we introduced in Chapter 1) to determine whether they have selected effective strategies.

In this chapter and subsequent chapters in Part Two, we introduce you to the specific teaching tools that we defined in Chapter 3, as you can see from the Chapter Graphic. First, to make the strategies visible to you, we model and explain each of the three major literacy strategies—activating prior experiences and prior knowledge, previewing and predicting, and exploring new vocabulary—with three different content-area texts. Second, we describe a variety of specific teaching and assessing tools that support your content-area students as they learn literacy strategies. We also focus on writing that complements the literacy strategies. And finally in this chapter, and in every other chapter in Part Two, we discuss the underlying ongoing strategies of purpose setting and monitoring and provide a checklist that you may use with your students.

Purpose-Setting Questions

1. How do you generate ideas when you begin to read a new book or text-book, write a poem or nonfiction article, observe a science phenomenon, research a historical event or person, solve a mechanical or mathematical problem, create an art object or a special meal?

2. Think about a text you have read in your content area. What prior experiences and prior knowledge did you bring to reading that text? Did you consciously think about your background before you read the text?

3. When you approach a new text, do you preview or skim the text, predict the content of the text, or skim the vocabulary? If you do, how does that help you? If you do not use these strategies, think about why you find no such need.

4. For your assignments, how do you devise your own purpose, within your professors' guidelines, and how do you monitor whether your work is proceeding well?

Strategies and Tools for Activating Prior Experiences and Prior Knowledge

You probably activate your prior experiences and knowledge every day of your life when you face new experiences. For example, when you order from a restaurant menu, do you choose the steak, which you know,

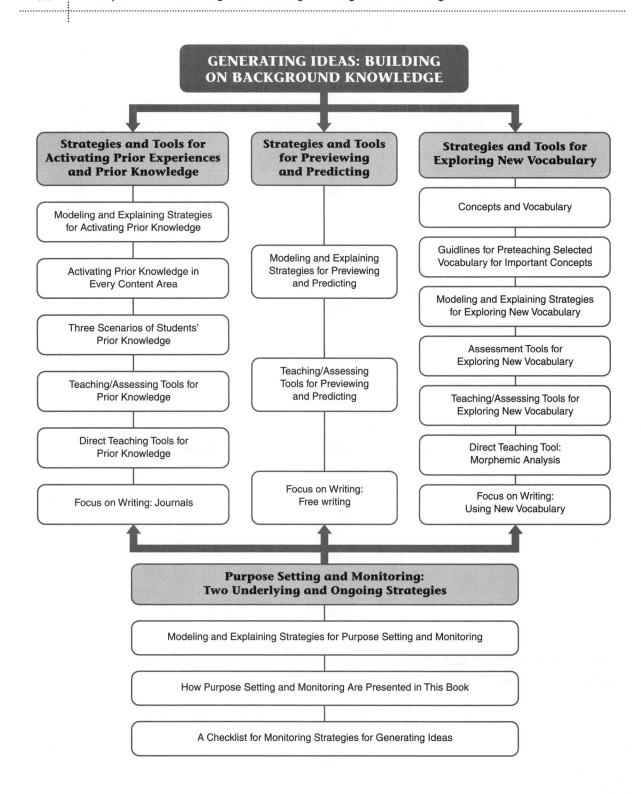

GENERATING IDEAS: BUILDING ON BACKGROUND KNOWLEDGE

Strategies and Tools for Activating Prior Experiences and Prior Knowledge

- Modeling and Explaining Strategies for Activating Prior Knowledge
- Activating Prior Knowledge in Every Content Area
- Three Scenarios of Students' Prior Knowledge
- Teaching/Assessing Tools for Prior Knowledge
- Direct Teaching Tools for Prior Knowledge
- Focus on Writing: Journals

Strategies and Tools for Previewing and Predicting

- Modeling and Explaining Strategies for Previewing and Predicting
- Teaching/Assessing Tools for Previewing and Predicting
- Focus on Writing: Free writing

Strategies and Tools for Exploring New Vocabulary

- Concepts and Vocabulary
- Guidlines for Preteaching Selected Vocabulary for Important Concepts
- Modeling and Explaining Strategies for Exploring New Vocabulary
- Assessment Tools for Exploring New Vocabulary
- Teaching/Assessing Tools for Exploring New Vocabulary
- Direct Teaching Tool: Morphemic Analysis
- Focus on Writing: Using New Vocabulary

Purpose Setting and Monitoring: Two Underlying and Ongoing Strategies

- Modeling and Explaining Strategies for Purpose Setting and Monitoring
- How Purpose Setting and Monitoring Are Presented in This Book
- A Checklist for Monitoring Strategies for Generating Ideas

or the ostrich, which is unfamiliar? In school, you also activate your past knowledge, as you do when you think about last semester's foreign language course to make this semester's course easier. When strategic learners begin a new course for which they have little prior knowledge, they search their memory for any ideas that might be related to the course. When they activate their prior knowledge and experiences, they search their schemata for a match. When they find a schema that matches, then they have *hooks* on which to attach new learning.

We discuss strategies for activating prior experiences and prior knowledge first because as a content-area teacher, you want to figure out what schemata your diverse students bring to your content area. Figure 4.1 shows the variety of pedagogical tools that you can select to use in your classroom. Because in this book we focus on literacy strategies that support content learning, first we present the teaching tool, modeling and explaining, to demonstrate how a strategic reader activates prior experiences and prior knowledge.

▶ ▶ ▶ ▶ Modeling and Explaining Strategies for Activating Prior Knowledge

Throughout this chapter, and all the other chapters in Part Two, you will find modeling and explaining scripts that illustrate literacy strategies in action. Before we present the first one to you, we need to clarify three points.

First, you recall from Chapters 1 and 3 that modeling and explaining is a teaching tool that seeks to make literacy strategies visible. Using material that the students might read in different content areas, we select specific literacy strategies and explicitly identify the strategies and tell why, when, and how to use them (Paris, Lipson, & Wixson, 1994). Remember that nonstrategic learners, who may not be metacognitively aware, need clear, direct statements. Because we are communicating to you in print, we present primarily teacher-directed mini-lessons in our modeling and explaining scripts because they are the clearest to demonstrate in a textbook. However, we also recommend teacher-guided mini-lessons in which you and your students discuss the strategies to use, as well as why, when, and how to use them. Students could also model and explain strategies to each other. Depending on how strategic your students are and how difficult the text and the content are, you will decide whether to model and explain through teacher-directed, teacher-guided, or student-to-student mini-lessons.

Second, you will notice that we use the "I" pronoun in the modeling and explaining scripts because on the printed page only one person's use of strategies can be visible. For example, although we both would activate prior

Figure 4.1

Strategies for
Activating Prior
Experiences and
Prior Knowledge

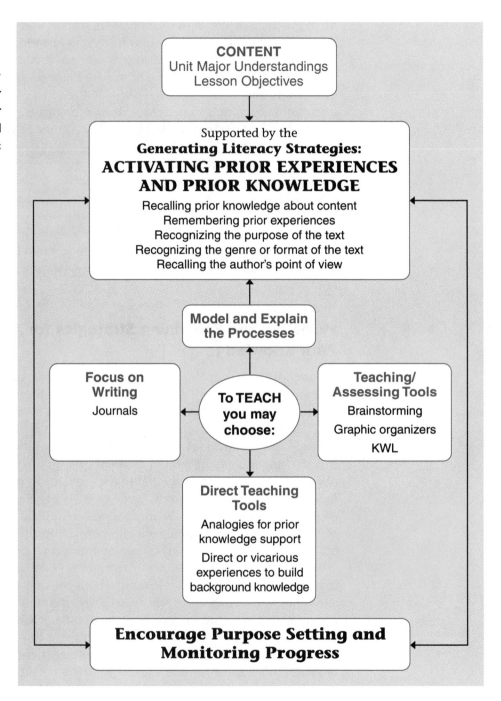

In a brainstorming activity, the earth science teacher records the students' prior knowledge about the types of rocks in the earth's crust.

© Michael Zide

experiences and knowledge, the specific knowledge would vary depending on which of us modeled because each of us has different schemata.

Third, in order to model and explain to you, the reading process needs to be slowed down. The newspaper editorial in the first script is not difficult to read, so we use our strategies automatically. For example, we know that an editorial tries to persuade, so we would not explicitly explain that to ourselves. But to model and explain to you, or any other student, we need to be explicit so that our automatic strategies are visible. When you model and explain strategies for your students, you will need to slow down your literacy process too, so that your students can see your strategies.

For this modeling and explaining script, pretend that your class is studying the Constitution and the Bill of Rights. Your major understanding or goal is for students to recognize that these are living documents that continue to affect our lives today. For this lesson, your *content objective* is for the students to take a position on firearm legislation in the light of the Second Amendment, the right to keep and bear arms. You also have a *strategy objective*: for the students to recognize how to activate prior knowledge before reading.

As you read this script, notice that I am activating my prior knowledge about the topic, the source or author, and the purpose of the text:

Modeling and Explaining Prior Knowledge Strategies

Modeling and Explaining How I Use
My Prior Knowledge

Because the *Boston Globe* is my hometown news-paper, I read it regularly. I often agree with its opinions, although not always. **My first strategy is that I recognize the source or author**. Since I have read editorials before, I know an editor's purpose is to persuade readers to support the opinion or take an action in the community. When I read, I will look for the editor's opinion and reasons and then decide whether I agree. **My second strategy is that I recognize the purpose of an editorial: to persuade.**

I expect the title to inform me about the topic of this editorial, but this title does not.

Since I don't have enough information to **tap into my background knowledge**, I will read the first paragraph to find the topic.

Newspaper Editorial

The Boston Globe

Self-deception, not self-defense

The exchange between US Reps. Patrick Kennedy and Gerald Solomon last week in Congress showed the powerful emotions unleashed by the Republicans' attempt to repeal the law banning assault weapons. The ban, approved in 1994, is a modest attempt to rein in lethal violence, and it deserves more than a few months to show its worth.

Kennedy, nephew of two murdered political leaders, was expressing a sentiment common to many relatives of victims when he said: "Families like mine, all across the country, know all too well about the damage these weapons can do."

"The law banning assault weapons" tells me that the topic is gun control, and so I **activate my prior knowledge about the topic**.

I recall that I supported the passage of the bill to ban assault weapons, the Brady bill. The Brady bill was named after Jim Brady, who was shot, along with President Reagan, and severely injured. Because I have that background

"The exchange between US Reps. Patrick Kennedy and Gerald Solomon last week in Congress showed the powerful emotions unleashed by the Republicans' attempt to repeal the law banning assault weapons. The ban, approved in 1994, is a modest attempt to rein in lethal violence, and it deserves more than a few months to show its worth."

knowledge, I support the law that bans assault weapons.

From my prior experiences, I remember the assassinations of President Kennedy and Senator Robert Kennedy and exactly where I was at both times. Furthermore, I have read newspaper accounts of drive-by shootings in cities and the grief of families. Thus, I have more knowledge to support my position.

Being against the repeal of the law, I agree with the editor's position. I decide to look for the editor's reasons against the repeal and see if they are similar to mine. Thus, I have **set my own purpose** for continuing to read.

Patrick Kennedy, nephew of two murdered political leaders, was expressing a sentiment common to many relatives of victims when he said: "Families like mine, all across the country, know all too well about the damage these weapons can do."

"Self-Deception, Not Self-Defense," *Boston Globe*, March 30, 1996, p. 10. Reprinted courtesy of *The Boston Globe*.

To summarize, in this generating ideas phase at the beginning of reading the editorial, I explicitly modeled and explained my strategies for activating my prior knowledge and for the underlying strategy of setting a purpose. When I read the editorial:

1. I **activated my prior knowledge about the source**, the *Boston Globe* (I often read and agree with my hometown newspaper).

2. I **activated prior knowledge about the purpose of an editorial** (to persuade readers), and so I knew to search for the editor's opinion.

3. I tried to use the title **to tap into my background knowledge** about the topic. (The title did not inform me of the topic.)

4. Finding the topic, I **recalled prior knowledge and experiences** (knowledge about the Brady Bill and memories of the Kennedy assassinations).

5. I **set a purpose** for continuing to read the editorial (to compare the editor's reasons not to repeal to my own reasons).

In every content area, you can model and explain activating prior knowledge about the content, the source, and the intent or purpose.

▶ ▶ ▶ ▶ **Activating Prior Knowledge in Every Content Area**

Let's take a look at how readers use this strategy in some of the content areas. For instance, in math, strategic students employ their prior knowledge about sources and contents when they complete problems in math textbooks. They know the problems will relate to only the topics in the chapter and will conform to the problem types discussed in the chapter. They know the purpose is to practice solving those types of problems. However, nonstrategic students may not recognize the uniformity of textbook problems because they don't look back in the chapter for help (Garner, 1987).

In English and language arts, strategic readers know that particular authors write in a certain style, and so they seek out books by their favorite authors. English teachers encourage students to read critically for an author's style. For example, if you are an avid reader of novels by Stephen King or viewer of his movies, you have prior knowledge of him as an author and the content of his books. You know he intends to arouse frightening emotions in his readers or viewers, and although the specific content changes, you expect horror and suspense from him. If you read his serial novel, *The Green Mile*, did it match your prior knowledge? Because it was in serial format, were you annoyed that you couldn't peek ahead to the end, or did that increase your suspense?

When strategic learners study a primary document in social studies, they search their prior knowledge for information about the source or author and the purpose or intent of the author, in addition to their content knowledge. Consider this excerpt from Patrick Henry's speech:

> Gentleman may cry, peace, peace—but there is not peace. The war is actually begun! The next gale that sweeps from the north will bring to our ears the clash of resounding arms! Our brethren are already in the field! Why stand we here idle? What is it that gentlemen wish? What would they have? Is life so dear, or peace so sweet, as to be purchased at the price of chains and slavery? Forbid it, Almighty God! I know not what course others may take; but as for me, . . . give me liberty, or give me death!

Readers would search their prior knowledge to place this speech in its historical context. They might remember that he spoke to the Virginia Convention on March 23, 1775, one month before the British and colonials clashed at Lexington and Concord. Knowing that the author, patriot Patrick Henry, was an eloquent orator, readers would remember that his intent was to persuade reluctant Virginians to align themselves with the Massachusetts patriots and establish a Virginia militia to defend themselves against the British.

In addition to modeling and explaining strategies, you will want to know what prior knowledge your students bring to your content area. Below you will find three common scenarios of students' prior knowledge.

▶ ▶ ▶ ▷ **Three Scenarios of Students' Prior Knowledge**

You want to know what knowledge your students are bringing to your content areas so that you can plan instruction to match what the students need. When teachers assess students' prior knowledge, frequently they are confronted with three different scenarios (Graves and Slater, 1987, 1996).

Little Prior Knowledge.   This scenario is particularly common the first time students study a content area in school. For this scenario, you will search for any related knowledge that might serve as a bridge between what the students are to learn and what is familiar to them. Or you may provide direct experiences that will build the students' background knowledge for the unit of study. For example, in conjunction with their study of the biological structure of trees, inner-city sixth-grade students throughout the spring tapped maple trees in an abandoned lot and then boiled the sap to make maple syrup. As the leaves began to bud, the students could taste the difference in the sweetness of the syrup due to the chlorophyll.

You will want to know if your students have little prior knowledge so that you can build and organize their new schemata by teaching not only the facts but also the relationship among the ideas.

Elaborate Prior Knowledge.   In this second scenario, the students have a substantial amount of prior knowledge about the subject, accumulated from a variety of sources. For example, from many previous experiences, students have heard, viewed, and read stories in which a main character has a problem that eventually gets resolved. Although they may not be aware of the narrative organization, they bring an elaborate knowledge of stories to a teacher's instruction of story organization. These students need opportunities to extend their story schema to more complex plot organizations, like foreshadowing, and to more in-depth understanding of stories, like a study of theme. Whenever students bring elaborate prior knowledge to any content area, they need opportunities to investigate the topics in depth through problem-solving situations and investigations in the community and through contact with outside experts on the topic.

Superficial Prior Knowledge, Misconceptions in Prior Knowledge, and Mismatches Resulting from Prior Knowledge.   You recall the discussion in Chapter 2 of how a mismatch between the student's schema and the content-area information can lead students astray. Let's look at three examples because a mismatch occurs commonly in the content areas.

In the superficial knowledge version of this scenario, the students have only meager knowledge about the topic, although they have heard of it. For example, eleventh-grade students studied the westward movement back in the fifth and eighth grades, but not in enough depth so that they can compare the stories of the families on the Oregon Trail, the religious refugees on the Mormon Trail, the gold-seeking men on the California Trail, and the different Native American nations along the trails. If this is the case, your instruction could provide that in-depth knowledge.

In a similar situation, the students have misconceptions in the knowledge they do have. Remember the example of misconceptions about the earth's seasons in Chapter 2. If you are a science teacher, you will encounter students who have naive or everyday explanations for the scientific concepts. Social studies and English and language arts teachers will encounter students with misconceptions about different cultures and people. Whenever students have misconceptions in their prior knowledge, your instruction would aim to refute their misconceptions.

In the mismatch version of this scenario, cultural or language examples are most common. From Chapter 2, you recall that the Indian readers' schemata of weddings interfered with their reading about an American wedding. When students read literature by Shakespeare or Zora Neale Hurston, they may experience a mismatch between their own language and culture and the author's. ESL students, naturally using expectations from their first language and culture, may experience a mismatch with the second language and culture. Since the students may be unprepared for or confused by the mismatch, your instruction would aim to clarify the cultural and language differences.

In each of these scenarios, you will want to determine your students' prior knowledge so that you can work from their background knowledge during subsequent instruction. The teaching/assessing tools in the next section will help you determine their prior knowledge.

▶ ▶ ▶ ▷ Teaching/Assessing Tools for Prior Knowledge

Assessing a student's or a class's prior knowledge is not a simple task. Sometimes, teachers discover students' misconceptions and mismatches during instruction rather than before. Nevertheless, teachers still try to assess prior knowledge in order to plan instruction better.

Since we present tools for the first time in Part Two, remember how we defined teaching/assessing tools in Chapter 3. You recall that you can assess and teach simultaneously, depending on your purpose or point of view in a particular situation. For example, using brainstorming, you teach your students to activate their prior knowledge so that they can use their schemata to learn the information in the text. At the same time, you use brainstorming to evaluate what background knowledge your students bring to a new unit—using the tool for assessment.

Remember too that your goal is to foster independent, strategic learners. You want to encourage learners to use these tools to activate their own prior knowledge, first under your guidance and then independently. Thus, as you use these teaching/assessing tools, you can also model and explain to your students why and how to use them independently.

Brainstorming. *Brainstorming,* or compiling a list of all the words associated with or related to a topic, is a common activity for exploring what students already know. You will want to notice what type of words the students are listing: everyday words or specialized words. For example, a teacher asked students to list all the words they associated with Native Americans, the topic of the new unit, because he wanted to know what factual information and what misconceptions the students had. The teacher found that the students' prior knowledge came from westward expansion texts and movies and that they had little cultural knowledge about the different nations.

English and language arts teachers often use brainstorming when students use dreary words in their writings. Students can be encouraged to rehabilitate tired words, such as *said* and *went,* by brainstorming lists of more descriptive, precise, and livelier alternatives. (A mini-lesson on the thesaurus could be combined with this brainstorming.)

Graphic Organizers. You will find that educators use many terms for schemata representations. Science educators refer to *models* or *concept models*; for example, they will ask students to draw a model of what the inside of the earth looks like. English and language arts educators often refer to *semantic maps*; they place the topic in a center circle, with categories radiating out (Fig. 4.2 is an example). Math and science educators often refer to a *hierarchical representation*; they subdivide categories in a tree branching form. We will use the term *graphic organizer* to refer to all categorization systems, whatever the particular shape—whether radiating suns, hierarchical trees, or a unique design. We have included graphic organizers as a teaching/assessing tool in many chapters (and in different sections in this chapter) because we have found them to be useful representations of students' schemata at various points in the learning process. You may also have noticed that we use

Figure 4.2

Seventh Graders'
Graphic Organizer of
Their Prior Knowledge

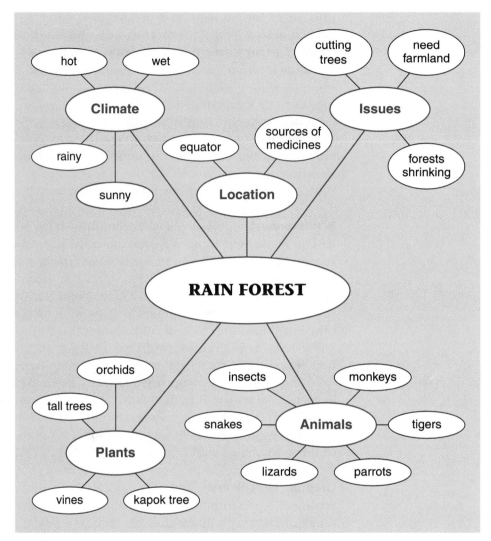

graphic organizers at the beginning of every chapter, as well as inside the Part Two chapters, to help you organize your schema for the upcoming information in the chapter.

In many content areas, if the students categorize the words in a brainstorming session, you could consider the categorization as a representation of their schema. In assessing graphic organizers, you are interested in discovering what categories of information the students have and what information is in each category without any hints from you. When a seventh-grade teacher used a graphic organizer in a lesson on the rain forest (see Figure 4.2), she noticed the students had no categories for different layers of the rain forest and had only superficial knowledge of the plants and animals.

When we teach, we ask students to categorize their ideas in any design that shows how the categories might be related. As the students develop their graphic organizers, they talk about the categories and the items in specific categories. That discussion of their prior knowledge is often a more important learning experience than creating the actual graphic organizer. As the students learn, they often revise these graphic organizers, both during the study and at the end.

KWL (Know—Want to Know—Learned). KWL was designed to elicit students' prior knowledge and to arouse their curiosity about a text through exploring three separate topics: What We Know, What We Want to Find Out, and What We Learned and Still Need to Know (Ogle, 1986). First, the class brainstorms

Figure 4.3

KWL Chart About
Children's Jobs

What We Know	What We Want to Find Out About Past Jobs	What We Learned and Still Need to Learn
paper route	1. Where did children work?	
baby-sitting	2. How many hours?	
raking leaves	3. How old were they?	
mowing lawn	4. How did they go to school?	
walking dogs		
getting good grades	5. How hard were their jobs?	
washing dishes	6. How much did they get paid?	
cleaning my room		
farm chores	7. Did they have to work?	
delivering things	8. What kinds of work did they do?	
house chores		
sewing		

Categories

1. Jobs we do
2. Jobs in the past
3. Conditions of work
4. Schooling

What We Know about a topic—children's jobs in Figure 4.3—as you record their ideas. After students have generated their prior knowledge, they organize their ideas into categories of information and add categories they predict will be subtopics in texts they'll read. Using their categories and any confusing or conflicting ideas that have emerged, you help the class formulate questions for What We Want to Find Out. From the whole class discussion, the students individually could record their prior knowledge, questions, and categories on their own KWL sheets. After reading a text or different texts, they record What We Learned and Still Need to Learn or notes and new questions on their sheets. Finally, you and the class would discuss the information gained, any questions not answered, and new questions that arose. Thus, KWL begins with students' activating their prior knowledge and continues to support their learning during the interacting phase (examined in Chapter 5) and the refining phase (in Chapter 6).

Two expansions have been suggested for the original KWL. In KWL Plus (Carr & Ogle, 1987), the students organize What They Have Learned in a graphic organizer and then write a summary about the topic. We encourage students to summarize both the information learned and the new questions they now have. When students write summaries, they have the opportunity to integrate their prior knowledge and newly learned information into their schemata, which helps them remember the information (see Chapter 6).

KWL has also been adapted to serve as a research tool. (Remember this tool when you read Chapter 7.) When students list how they will find information (Ogle, 1996), you can assess their prior knowledge about reference sources. Depending on the reference sources listed, you might introduce students to different reference sources in mini-lessons.

Teacher as Inquiring Learner Activity

Assess the prior knowledge a middle school or high school student has about a topic in your content area. Ask the student to complete one of the teaching/assessing tools, like a brainstorming list or a graphic organizer. Let him or her work independently for a while. When you think the student has no more ideas, then ask him or her to tell you about what is written. New ideas may occur to the student during the telling. When you think the student really has no more ideas, you could ask a few questions about the topic to probe for any remaining knowledge. You may also want to ask the student where or how he or she gained this knowledge—in school or from the Internet, for example. When you have finished, analyze the student's knowledge.

- What did the student know well, and what not at all? Did the student have any misconceptions? In what aspects of the topic would you instruct the student?

▶ ▶ ▶ ▷ **Direct Teaching Tools for Prior Knowledge**

You recall from Chapter 3 that we define *direct teaching tools* as when the teacher imparts specific information to students. When you use these tools, you dominate the communication more than you do with the interactive teaching/assessing tools.

Analogies for Prior Knowledge Support.   Teachers use familiar topics and experiences from their students' prior knowledge and cultural backgrounds to create analogies. The purpose of an analogy is to use a familiar topic as a bridge to the unfamiliar, new topic. Obviously analogies must make sense to your students (Brown, 1992). Does the following example make sense to you?

> If you know how to skateboard, then you will find snowboarding simple to master. In both skateboarding and snowboarding, you place your feet and balance your weight similarly on a board. In both, jumps and stunts use the contour of the terrain as the basis for the stunt. However, in skateboarding, your feet are not attached to the board, while in snowboarding your feet are fixed to the board with a binding system. As a result, you will be able to do different types of stunts in snowboarding than skateboarding and won't land without your board.

You may understand the target topic, snowboarding, if you are familiar with skateboarding. If you are not familiar with skateboarding, the analogy will not be helpful to you. Notice in the example that we pointed out the similarities as well as the differences. No analogy is a perfect match, so students need to distinguish how the target topic is different from the familiar one. The familiar topic is only a bridge, not a replica.

Science teachers use analogies to explain phenomena that students cannot observe. They also use models as analogies for phenomena. For example, when thinking about carbon atoms, scientists pictured Buckminster Fuller's geodesic dome and named the model "Bucky Ball." That model served as an analogy while they tried to find evidence for the structure of carbon atoms.

Direct or Vicarious Experiences to Build Background Knowledge.   When ideas are abstract for students, they may need more direct experiences with a concept to understand it. Art teachers, music teachers, physical education teachers, vocational education teachers, and computer teachers consistently incorporate hands-on or direct experiences into their curricula. Science teachers provide demonstrations, lab experiments, and field studies; social studies teachers incorporate primary sources, oral history research, and survey research. English and language arts teachers incorporate real purposes and audiences into their writing assignments. In each of these content domains, the direct experiences help students experience learning in the content area as an adult in that field would.

When direct experiences are not feasible, simulations, role playing, videos, and guest speakers are useful. With computer technology, students can observe simulations of various conditions in science experiments or access primary documents on CD-ROMs or at web sites. We encourage you to supplement the textbook with direct and vicarious experiences.

▶ ▶ ▶ ▶ ## Focus on Writing: Journals

Journals (also called *learning logs*) are places for students to record the evolution of their thinking and express their personal reactions to both the content and the process of their learning. Thus, journals are a hybrid between diaries, which contain only subjective, personal reactions to events, and class notebooks, which contain only objective, subject matter notes (Fulwiler, 1987). Journal entries may include drawings, diagrams, models, math problems, lists, phrases, sentences, or even paragraphs. The form of this writing is unconstrained and free-wheeling because the purpose is to understand one's thinking.

As part of your instructional plans, you may assign *prompts,* or questions, to direct students' entries. An ESL teacher asks his students to write their ideas in their native language on the left page and then in English on the facing page, providing a tool for the students to use their native language to support their growing English vocabulary. Teachers often ask students to record their brainstorming, graphic organizers, or KWLs in journals because the students can reread and revise them later as they learn.

At Grandma's House, FOXHILL

big rooms

long driveway

fish ponds in front of house

sardines

Christmas

walking through the woods

going to tea

play jump rope in the front hall

the playroom upstairs

butterfly room

annual pictures

Grannie breaking her hip

eating cheese meatloaf and getting sick

Figure 4.5   Significant Positives and Negatives Time Line

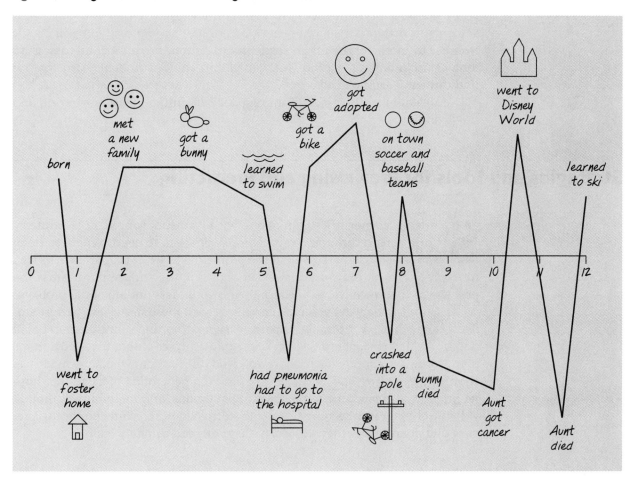

Journals can also be a source for writing ideas when students compose their own entries. Students often brainstorm topics for writing and their knowledge about each topic in journals. After brainstorming many childhood memories at her grandmother's house called Foxhill (see the list in Figure 4.4), the student chose one memory to write about: the taking of annual photographs of all the cousins in the family.

Sometimes composing a graphic organizer helps students find a specific focus within a broad topic when they are generating ideas for a composition. A specific graphic organizer could be a positive and negative time line (Reif, 1992). For example, Tom used the time line graph shown in Fig. 4.5 to record the high of being adopted and the low of his aunt's death.

We use journals not only for generating ideas but also in interacting with ideas (Chapter 5) and refining ideas (Chapter 6), and so we will return to journals periodically in this book.

These tools for activating prior knowledge and prior experiences will tell you what your students bring to your content area. When you teach your students to activate their prior knowledge and experiences, you will decide whether to model and explain strategies in action, use a teaching/assessing tool, or use a direct teaching tool, depending on your students' strategy use and content learning needs.

Now let's turn to a second strategy for generating ideas: previewing and predicting.

Strategies and Tools for Previewing and Predicting

Strategic learners try to figure out what is ahead. For example, strategic learners read through a mathematics problem to get a general sense of what information is given in the problem and what is unknown, as well as to predict or estimate an answer. In addition, they might paraphrase the problem in their own words to check their own understanding of the problem.

Figure 4.6 the ways you may choose to teach those strategies. Because students rarely preview textbook chapters (except perhaps to count the number of pages), we first present a modeling and explaining script that takes advantage of the format or chapter aids. Before you read, think about whether you use the chapter aids that we have included to assist your generation of ideas: the chapter graphic overviews, the purpose-setting questions, and the subheads that divide the chapter into sections. Strategic learners quickly skim chapters to preview and predict what they will learn; they will read carefully later.

Figure 4.6
....

Strategies and Tools
for Previewing and
Predicting

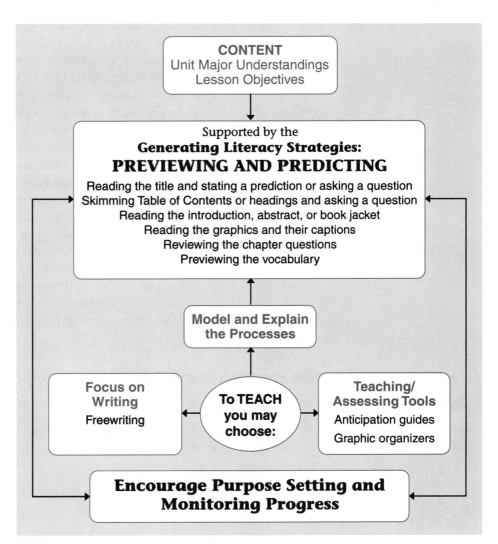

▶ ▶ ▶ ▶ **Modeling and Explaining Strategies for Previewing and Predicting**

Before we presented the first script in this chapter, we stated that most of our modeling and explaining scripts would be teacher directed because we are communicating to you in print. However, since we recommend that you use teacher-guided modeling and explaining mini-lessons, we present a teacher-guided one in this second script. When you want to involve students in an interactive discussion of strategies some of them might be using, then you would choose a teacher-guided modeling and explaining mini-lesson. Because the students are directly involved here in a back-and-forth exchange, this think-aloud script reads a bit differently from the previous script and most of the other modeling and explaining scripts in this book. In this script, my students and I (the "we" in the script) worked on the strategies together. I have also excerpted the chapter because you don't need every example of a strategy to understand its use. When you model and explain with your students, you would include as many instances of the strategies as your students need and may be every instance.

Pretend for this script that the unit's major understanding is how different cultures influence each other: Egypt and Nubia in ancient times as well as the United States and other countries today. The students will begin by reading the textbook and then read additional resources. For this chapter, the *content objective* is a comparison of the cultures of Egypt and Nubia, and the *strategy objective* is for students to recognize how to preview and predict using chapter aids. For this modeling and explaining script, assume the students have little or only superficial prior knowledge about ancient Egypt and none about Nubia. As you read the script, notice the chapter aids I incorporate into my previewing:

Modeling and Explaining Previewing and Predicting Strategies

Modeling and Explaining with Students

Social Studies Textbook

Textbook chapters have several aids that help readers understand their content. When we read or **preview** those aids first, we prepare ourselves to read the whole chapter more easily. So let's discuss how we can use the **strategy of previewing** with each chapter aid.

The first aid to **preview** is the chapter title to learn the major topics of the chapter and then to use the strategy of **activating our background knowledge**. Who knows what and where the Nile is? What else do we know about the Nile River? What kingdoms are located on the Nile? Okay, Egypt is obviously one; do we know any others? No? Okay; so we have a question to answer when we read.

That's another strategy: **asking questions** to predict what we might learn.

The second aid to **preview** is the Thinking Focus box. The authors are **setting a purpose** for our reading. When we have a purpose, we stay focused on our task.

What do the authors think is the most important information to learn from this chapter? Yes, our purpose is to compare Egypt and Nubia, the second kingdom.

The third aid to **preview** is a list of key vocabulary. Let's see if we can define the words. . . .

Let's read page 84, where *dynasty* is defined. Who can state the definition in his or her own words?

Where have you heard *dynasty* used? Why did basketball fans refer to the Chicago Bulls as a dynasty?

LESSON 1

Kingdoms on the Nile

THINKING FOCUS

Describe differences in the way kingdoms developed in ancient Egypt and ancient Nubia

Key terms
- delta
- cataract
- dynasty
- pharaoh

If you stood on the green banks of Egypt's Nile River and began walking west, the green under your feet would vanish within a few miles…

Prehistoric rock paintings show that the Sahara once supported human and animal life. Colorful paintings have been found throughout the desert.

Thinking Focus: Describe differences in the way kingdoms developed in ancient Egypt and ancient Nubia.

Key terms: *delta, cataract, dynasty, pharaoh*

UNDERSTANDING DYNASTY

What Is a Dynasty?

A dynasty is not the same as a king. A dynasty is a series of rulers who descended from the same person. Egypt's First Dynasty had eight rulers. The Thirteenth Dynasty had about 70 rulers.

The fourth aid to **preview** is the headings and subheadings that divide the chapter into sub-topics. We should skim them to figure out **how the chapter is organized** and to see if we have any **prior knowledge**. Remember the purpose? What do you predict the topics of two sections will be?

Let's find the headings on pages 84 and 85.

What **predictions** can we make about what will be covered?

"Who are the kings of Egypt?"

Look at the time line on page 85.

Previewing a graphic can help us predict or ask questions about what we want to learn. Does anyone have a question about the time line?

"Why did Egypt rule Nubia and then Nubia rule Egypt?"

Egypt, Land of the Pharaohs

Trapping and storing the floodwaters of the Nile was a mighty job. Leaders emerged to organize such big projects. Between 4000 and 3000 B.C., some of these leaders grew very powerful.

No one knows exactly how kingdoms developed along the Nile. Some experts now believe that a group of people in Lower Nubia had the first government with kings of great power. These scholars also say that Egypt's first kings may have descended from Nubians. Such ideas are being hotly debated today.

The Beginning of History

A clearer picture of the history of kings emerges after about 3000 B.C. That is when the first written records appear. Historians are now debating whether the first writing is Egyptian, as is generally thought, or whether it is actually Nubian.

Kings and Kingdoms

Thirty dynasties ruled Egypt for nearly 3,000 years. Historians divide Egypt's ancient past into three periods, called kingdoms. On the timeline below, trace Egypt's Old, Middle, and New kingdoms.

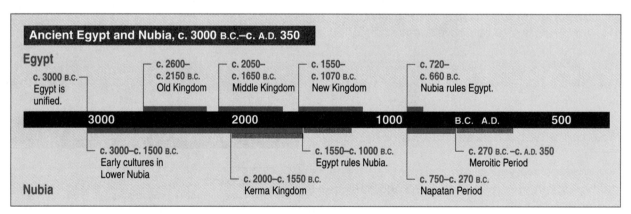

Ancient Egypt and Nubia, c. 3000 B.C.–c. A.D. 350

Egypt

c. 3000 B.C. — Egypt is unified.

c. 2600–c. 2150 B.C. Old Kingdom

c. 2050–c. 1650 B.C. Middle Kingdom

c. 1550–c. 1070 B.C. New Kingdom

c. 720–c. 660 B.C. Nubia rules Egypt.

3000   2000   1000   B.C. A.D.   500

c. 3000–c. 1500 B.C. Early cultures in Lower Nubia

c. 2000–c. 1550 B.C. Kerma Kingdom

c. 1550–c. 1000 B.C. Egypt rules Nubia.

c. 750–c. 270 B.C. Napatan Period

c. 270 B.C.–c. A.D. 350 Meroitic Period

Nubia

In this modeling and explaining script, I **previewed** the chapter aids, eliciting student contributions as I guided them through the following strategies:

1. After introducing them to the usefulness of chapter aids, the class and I **previewed** the chapter **title** to **activate prior knowledge**: Egypt. We also **asked questions to predict** what we might learn (the second kingdom).

2. We **previewed** the **Thinking Focus box** to clarify the **purpose for reading** the chapter (comparing the kingdoms of Egypt and Nubia).

3. We **previewed** the **key vocabulary words** to define them (*dynasty*, for example).

4. We **previewed** the **major headings to predict** the chapter organization (a section on Egypt and another on Nubia).

5. From the **subheadings**, we made **predictions** or **asked questions** about what we might learn (the kings of Egypt).

6. And finally, we **previewed the graphics** (the time line) and **predicted or asked questions** about what we wanted to learn (Why did Egypt rule Nubia and then Nubia rule Egypt?).

Thus, by skimming the chapter aids, we gained an overview of the information and set a purpose. In addition, we activated what prior knowledge we had, made predictions, and asked questions.

When you use the previewing strategy, you apply the general strategy to specific clues in particular texts. In experiments, recipes, and directions, readers usually preview the materials or ingredients required and the steps involved before they carefully read and follow the directions to complete the task. In mathematics, strategic learners estimate (or predict) what the solution might be. In science, strategic learners hypothesize (or predict) what their observations will be or what will occur in their experiment. When reading a novel, strategic learners predict what will happen in the plot or what the characters might be like. After reading several works by the same author, strategic readers make predictions about subsequent works by this same author, even though they may be fooled because the author may have chosen to write differently.

Now let's discuss teaching/assessing tools that you may select to support your students' predictions about texts.

▶ ▶ ▶ ▶ **Teaching/Assessing Tools for Previewing and Predicting**

Because students tend to plunge right into their reading without previewing or predicting, you may decide to introduce a teaching/assessing tool: anticipation guides or graphic organizers. When you introduce the tool, you will explain to the students that previewing and predicting will alert them to the content of the text.

Anticipation Guides for Making Predictions.   Sometimes students need hints to access their prior knowledge. To get thoughts and opinions flowing, students could complete an *anticipation guide* in pairs or independently.

The following steps for creating an effective anticipation guide (Duffelmeyer, 1994) are based on Herber's (1978) ideas about using prediction to arouse students' interest:

1. Determine the most important ideas to be learned.

2. Write five to seven statements about the important ideas that:

    a. activate the students' prior knowledge.

    b. invite students' opinions.

    c. challenge students' beliefs and misconceptions.

3. Reproduce the statements on a worksheet and add "agree" or "disagree" columns, which students will check. (see Figure 4.7). Individually or in small groups, students indicate whether they agree or disagree with the statements. In addition, they must defend their responses to their peers.

Figure 4.7

Anticipation Guide for a Study of Gandhi

Agree	Disagree	Statements
_____	_____	1. Gandhi came from a prosperous and influential family.
_____	_____	2. While in law school, Gandhi dressed and behaved like a British gentleman.
_____	_____	3. In South Africa, Gandhi did not suffer the discrimination that blacks did.
_____	_____	4. In South Africa, Gandhi found his voice and acted against prejudice.
_____	_____	5. After witnessing the brutal treatment of Zulus, Gandhi agreed that violence should be met with violence.
_____	_____	6. Gandhi was never taken seriously by the British government.
_____	_____	7. Hindus and Muslims learned to coexist in India.

You can assess your students' predictions right away by observing how they respond and defend their responses in pairs, small groups, or whole class discussions. You might infer how their prior knowledge and diverse backgrounds might have influenced their predictions.

Instead of statements about content, you might create a variation. For a math problem or a science investigation, an anticipation guide could present a problem and possible approaches for solving it. Students could check what they think is the most reasonable course of action and defend it. In another variation, an anticipation guide could focus on an issue, such as smoking, by presenting opposing opinions or perspectives of different people. After predicting the opinions of smokers, nonsmokers, cigarette makers, doctors, restaurant owners, and attorneys general, students could gather information on the issue and debate the differing perspectives.

Anticipation guides can go beyond generating ideas to refining ideas (the topic of Chapter 6). By changing the guide to include a "before reading" column to be checked first and then an "after reading" column to be checked later, students can record whether they changed their predictions. A further extension would have students write why they did or did not change their predictions and what information supported their stance (Duffelmeyer, Baum, & Merkley, 1987). You and your students can evaluate how their ideas changed, turning a teaching tool into an assessing tool.

Teacher as Inquiring Learner Activity

Construct an anticipation guide. Find an informational book, a magazine article, or a newspaper article about a topic, issue, or problem related to your content area. Think about what prior knowledge, opinions, beliefs, and misconceptions students might have. Using your best estimate of their prior knowledge and opinions, write five to eight statements that invite students to think about the topic and even to take a position. Add "before" and "after" columns for students to check. You could construct an anticipation guide for a problem and possible solutions or an issue and various perspectives if you wish.

If you have the opportunity, use your anticipation guide with a small group of students. Have them discuss and complete the "before" column in pairs. After reading the text, the pairs complete the "after" column and discuss their answers. When everyone has finished, the whole group would compare their answers and discuss their reasons.

Think about what the group predicted and what they learned.

- How would you change the guide the next time?

Graphic Organizers for Previewing and Predicting.   Do you use the graphic organizer at the beginning of each chapter in this book to preview the whole chapter before you begin to read? Each graphic organizer shows you the chapter's organization—how the parts relate to each other and comprise the whole—instead of letting you guess the organization as you read. When you want students to learn a specific organization or structure, you present that organization in a graphic organizer.

For example, if you are studying digestion, you would present a diagram of the digestive system. The students could label the parts they knew and add what they knew about each part's function. Don't forget that you would assess what they wrote so that you could build on their prior knowledge during instruction.

As another example, let's say you are studying the biological taxonomy. Scientists have expanded the number of kingdoms and debate the classification of particular species, but they have never changed the taxonomy itself. You would present the taxonomy as a graphic organizer (see Figure 4.8) and have students add their prior knowledge to it.

▶ ▶ ▶ ▶ Focus on Writing: Freewriting

We have chosen to categorize freewriting as a tool for predictions, but we use it for other purposes as well. As originally designed (Elbow, 1973), students were asked to write on any topic for about fifteen minutes without interruption to increase their writing fluency. Teachers have since adapted freewriting for other purposes, such as to set a purpose for the class, cue prior knowledge, and make predictions about upcoming content.

For example, before beginning a new novel, Robin McKinley's *The Hero and the Crown*, an English/language arts teacher asked the students to complete a freewriting on the question, "What makes a hero?" After writing, the students shared their characteristics that define a hero and their examples of heroes. Based on the characteristics of known heroes, the students predicted what the characteristics of Aerin, the heroine, would be.

Using freewriting in a political science class, a special needs high school teacher asked her students to respond to the following questions before they began a study of the Middle East and the U.S. role there:

1. Do you think we should work to convert other countries to democracies?
2. Can you think of any situation in which you would interfere in a fight or argument between two people you didn't know?

Their responses indicated their prior knowledge and predicted the issues that would be discussed during later study.

Figure 4.8

Graphic Organizer for
Biological Taxonomy

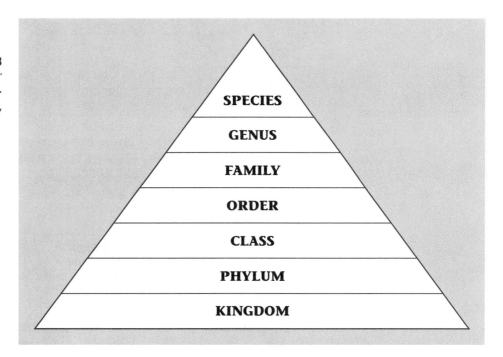

After observing scientific phenomena, students could complete a free-writing about their observations and predictions regarding subsequent observations or investigations. For example, after working with parallel electrical circuits, students could diagram and write their predictions for serial circuits.

In summary, the strategy of previewing and predicting is often used in concert with activating prior knowledge because strategic learners preview in order to learn what schemata to search for. Furthermore, strategic learners often preview the vocabulary in a text to determine whether the text contains known or new words and to determine the difficulty of the text for them to read. Let's now examine the strategies for exploring new vocabulary.

Strategies and Tools for Exploring New Vocabulary

I f you have no clue as to what a word means, you can ask someone who is nearby, look it up in a dictionary or glossary, or deduce the meaning from the sentences surrounding it. In this section, we look at the strategy of asking someone or preteaching vocabulary so that students will understand the content more easily when they read the text (see Fig. 4.9). Because strategic

Figure 4.9

Strategies and Tools
for Exploring New
Vocabulary

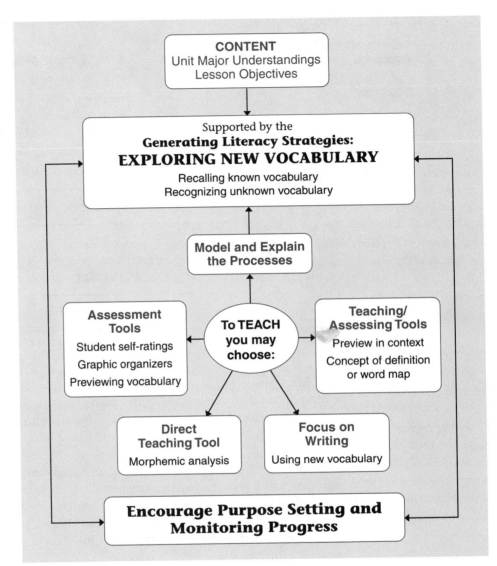

readers use the dictionary and the surrounding sentences or context while they are reading, we will return to the topic of vocabulary in Chapter 5.

However, before we begin to discuss preteaching vocabulary, we need to define concepts and the words that label them.

▶ ▶ ▶ ▶ **Concepts and Vocabulary**

We define *concepts* as categories of real and vicarious experiences in schemata. One experience does not form a concept; it's just an instance or an example. For example, to form a concept for "dog," people need repeated experiences (with spaniels and boxers and other breeds) to deduce the common or essential attributes (domesticated, mammal) from the variable and idiosyncratic attributes (large, short haired) that pertain to only particular instances. Concepts can be concrete and simple, like *pencil,* or abstract and complex, like *freedom.*

Concepts, and the words used to represent them, have features or characteristics that people in a particular culture or community have agreed on. When enough people use a word to express the same concept, the meaning becomes standardized, and lexicographers will add the word to dictionaries. These defining features or essential attributes constitute dictionary definitions and textbook explanations of concepts. For example, in the first exhibition of thirty-nine renegade artists in France in 1874, Claude Monet included a painting entitled *Impression: Sunrise.* Using the term *impressionists,* a critic derogatorily reviewed the works by these painters who strove to catch their immediate impressions of light and color interactions as they painted outside. Now, *impressionists* refers not only to that group of painters but to that style of painting.

In math, "infinity" and "pi" are agreed-on concepts, and their symbols (∞ and π, respectively) function just like words. Mathematical notations function like sentences and paragraphs containing mathematical concepts or mathematical descriptions of scientific phenomena. Mathematicians compose the community of people who define and redefine the concepts and words in their domain. Thus, one part of content-area teaching is inducting students into that community by building and enriching their schemata with concepts and vocabulary important to your content area.

▶ ▶ ▶ ▶ Guidelines for Preteaching Selected Vocabulary for Important Concepts

Most likely somewhere in your schooling, you had a teacher who passed out a list of twenty words for you to define, use in sentences, and be tested on. Instruction in definitions and one or two exposures to the words, however, will never solidify vocabulary meaning or integrate words (concepts) into anyone's schemata (Stahl & Fairbanks, 1986).

The first guideline for vocabulary building is to ask, "What concepts are crucial to students' learning?" Then teach the most important words (concepts) and words that relate to one another so that students build or extend their schemata (Nagy & Herman, 1987). Since you and your students will frequently use those most important words when talking and writing about the topic, the definitions will become well known or established. All students, and especially students with learning difficulties (Bos & Anders, 1990), benefit from schemata-building vocabulary instruction.

Figure 4.10

The Balancing Act
of Selecting
Vocabulary to Teach

Content
Key concepts,
specialized meanings

Students
Prior knowledge,
learn words independently

Teacher
Selects the vocabulary
to teach before reading

Second, determine what related words extend and elaborate concepts or schemata. You need to decide whether to teach some related words or whether students can learn them independently. You may decide not to teach the related words because students could understand them within the context of a discussion or the text.

Third, because it is impossible for you to teach every word, ask yourself what words are less important to the text. Some students will learn these words through their reading (Nagy & Herman, 1987). We return to using context to learn words during reading in Chapter 5.

Thus, in selecting vocabulary to teach, you are balancing the concepts important to the unit of study and your students' prior knowledge (Herber, 1978), as depicted in Fig. 4.10.

Now let's look at a modeling and explaining lesson in which the teacher explores new vocabulary with the students.

▶ ▶ ▶ ▶ Modeling and Explaining Strategies for Exploring New Vocabulary

You recall in the modeling and explaining script for Kingdoms on the Nile that the key term *dynasty* was defined using background knowledge and the context of the chapter before reading. The purpose of exploring new vocabulary is to have definitions in place so that students' comprehension flows more smoothly during reading. Let's look at another modeling and explaining script; in this one, we use an analogy to explain the new math vocabulary. (Remember the direct teaching tool of analogies in activating prior knowledge strategies?)

Suppose you are starting a math unit on the use of variables in algebra. The first chapter in the textbook unit discusses the order of operations, beginning with a vocabulary section. To assist your students with the vocabulary, you have decided to model and explain with them, defining the important vocabulary introduced in the first section:

Modeling and Explaining Strategies for Exploring New Vocabulary

Introduction to a Modeling and Explaining Mini-lesson on New Vocabulary: Using an Analogy to Activate Prior Knowledge

Teacher: Everyone has several names; for example what name do your friends call you?

Student: Beth.

Teacher: What name did your family call you when you were little?

Student: Bethie.

Teacher: That was a nickname or a sign of endearment, used by your family. What did your mother call you when she was mad or serious?

Student: Elizabeth Laura Holmes.

Teacher: Beth, Bethie, and Elizabeth Laura Holmes are three names that refer to you. When a particular name was used in a specific situation, you knew exactly what feeling was implied by that name! Particular names are used in specific situations. With that example in mind, let's discuss the new vocabulary on page 176 of our new chapter, "Order of Operations."

My Modeling and Explaining

This section of the chapter introduces the new vocabulary.

Thinking about my introduction to the lesson, how would you define *numerical expression*?

Yes, it is a name for a number.

A number could have different names or have different expressions. **[paraphrasing definitions into own words]**

Mathematics Textbook

Numerical Expressions

A **numerical expression** is a combination of symbols for numbers and operations that stands for a number. The **value** of a numerical expression is found by performing the operations. Performing the operations is called **evaluating the expression.** For example, the seven expressions here all have the same value, 2.

2	$5 - 3$	$20/10$	$5 \times 2 - 8$
2^1	$347.8 - 345.8$	$10^0 + 10^0$	

My Modeling and Explaining

Again thinking back to our name analogy, what is *value* similar to?

Yes, the person all the different names refer to. **[connecting definition to analogy]**

Evaluating the expression is like figuring out the situation: why did your mother use that name? Just like your names, each expression is used in a specific situation.

Let's discuss a few examples and the different "names" or expressions that stand for "2."

1. The first name, 2, represents the whole number.

2. 5 – 3 is a subtraction expression (or situation) for "2."

3. 20/10 is a division or ratio expression. A situation might be that you have 20 cookies and 10 friends and so 2 cookies per friend.

4. Let's go to 347.8 – 345.8, a decimal expression that could describe a 2-degree difference in temperature.

5. $5 \times 2 - 8$ is an algebraic expression. To ensure that all of the expressions mean the same for everyone across the world, mathematicians have agreed on rules for the order of operations. So, to get 2 in this expression, what operation would we do first?

[define examples of the concept]

Mathematics Textbook

The **value** of a numerical expression is found by performing the operations.

Performing the operations is called **evaluating the expression**.

For example, the expressions here all have the same value, 2.

2
5 – 3
20/10
347.8 – 345.8
$5 \times 2 - 8$

Source: A. Usiskin et al., *Transition Mathematics* (2nd ed.) (Glenview, IL: Scott Foresman, 1995), p. 176.

Let's review the strategies and tools used in the modeling and explaining script for exploring new vocabulary:

1. I **activated prior knowledge** by using an **analogy** (a student's nickname).

2. The class and I **paraphrased the definitions** by stating them in our own words ("A numerical expression is a name for a number").

3. I **connected the definitions to the analogy** (different numerical expressions to different names).

4. I **defined the different examples** of the numerical expressions (concept) for the number 2 (5 – 3 is a subtraction expression for 2).

During that modeling and explaining, I defined words with the students. Before you teach words, you might want to assess what words they need to learn.

▶ ▶ ▶ ▶   Assessment Tools for Exploring New Vocabulary

You recall we discussed assessing the words students used to determine the prior knowledge in their schemata. Before you teach vocabulary words, you want to assess whether the students know the specific words for important concepts or if they use everyday words for the concepts. For example, do they use the everyday words *crackling noise* instead of the specialized word *static*?

Since some everyday words also have a specialized meaning in a particular content area, you want to assess whether students know that specialized meaning. Students may know the everyday meaning or the primary meaning of *line*, for example, but may not know the specialized meanings for *line* in math, geography, or music. Students may not understand words or phrases, like *Cold War* and *common market*, that have specialized meanings but use everyday words in a figurative rather than a literal sense.

Depending on the grade you teach, you might not expect students to know the specialized words in your content area. On the other hand, you know students should have learned the words *longitude, latitude, equilateral triangle,* and *parallelogram* before high school.

Student Self-Ratings.   Most students can rate their own knowledge of words accurately (Beck, McKeown, McCaslin, & Burkes, 1979). Thus, one way to begin assessing specific vocabulary knowledge is to ask the class as a whole or the students individually to estimate whether they know well the important conceptual words for a unit or text (they can give a definition), are somewhat familiar with the words (they are acquainted with them and may recognize them in context), or have no idea of what the words mean. For an upcoming science unit, a teacher made the rating chart in Figure 4.11.

After the students rate their knowledge of the important conceptual words, you and your students know which words to concentrate on learning. Some students may just need to refine their definitions, while others may need instruction in the concepts represented by the words. All students will need many opportunities to read and write those important words so that their meanings become established.

Figure 4.11

Student Self-rating
Chart

Word	Well Known: Please Define	Familiar: Take a Guess	Unknown
Ecology			
Photosynthesis			
Population			
Community			
Biome			
Biosphere			
Ecosystem			
Biotic			
Abiotic			
Respiration			

Graphic Organizers with Teacher-Selected Vocabulary.   Once you have decided on the most important words for the concepts and schema in the unit of study, you could ask the students to construct their own graphic organizers using the vocabulary you've selected. Your purpose is to assess the representations of their schemata when you have given them clues—the important conceptual vocabulary.

We recommend using the following steps:

1.   Write each important word on an index card and make a packet of vocabulary words for each small group of students.

2.   Give each group a packet, and instruct the students to create their own graphic organizer that illustrates the relationships among the words. The group members may add new words on cards or delete a word card.

3.   As a group, the students arrange the cards and come to a consensus about the design of their graphic organizer, a task that usually involves them in much discussion. The students' discussion of their concepts and vocabulary allows them to explore their prior knowledge (Stahl & Vancil, 1986).

4.   After drawing their graphic organizer on chart paper or an overhead, the students must explain the relationships that their design sets out to the whole class.

5. As each group explains its graphic organizer, the students in the full class compare the different graphic organizers and explanations composed by the other groups. The different designs indicate the different interpretations that students have made. At this point, you are not looking for a correct design; you are assessing their prior knowledge of the words.

Previewing Vocabulary to Match Selections Appropriately with Particular Students. You also want to know whether a specific text contains too many unknown words for the students or for particular students (such as students with learning disabilities or ESL students) to understand the text. If your students regularly stumble over the words, they will not be able to concentrate on understanding the ideas. If the text is inappropriate, you need to plan alternatives, like finding an easier selection, reading with a partner, or taping the selection for the student. None of these alternatives is easy to accomplish.

In a small group session with struggling students, you would preview a text together and ask them to rate their knowledge of the vocabulary by asking, "Are there words or concepts on this page that you don't know?" "Are the unknown words defined within the text so that you can learn them on your own?" "Are there too many unknown words [typically five to eight per page] for you to understand this selection?" As the teacher, you make the judgment as to whether the unknown words are important or minor concepts. If they represent minor concepts, the students would likely be able to read the selection well enough so that you do not need to come up with alternative measures.

▶ ▶ ▶ ▶ ## Teaching/Assessing Tools for Exploring New Vocabulary

We stated earlier in this chapter that you will decide whether to teach important new vocabulary before reading or whether students could independently learn vocabulary during their reading. Most likely both will occur because you and your students will encounter six different vocabulary learning situations; they are set out in Table 4.1.

When students are learning new concepts, new words, or new meanings, teachers decide to preteach the most important conceptual words. You may decide to use a teaching/assessing tool—either *preview in context* or *concept of definition.*

Preview in Context. In the Kingdoms of the Nile script when *dynasty* was defined, the script modeled the preview-in-context tool for teaching new vocabulary (Readence, Bean, & Baldwin, 1989). Drawing on the students'

Table 4.1   Tasks, Students, and Tools for Vocabulary Learning in Content-Area Classrooms

Task and Example	Typical Students	Teaching Tool
Learning new words for new concepts. Examples: *vassal, lithosphere, algorithm, tesselation.*	All students encounter these words in every content area every year.	Use the teaching/assessing tool of concept of definition (this chapter). Teach deciphering word parts: root words and affixes (this chapter). Use graphic organizers to show how new words are related (this chapter).
Learning new words for known concepts. Examples: *dissident, condensation, digit, estimate.*	All students expand their vocabularies with these words every year. For ESL students, the new words are English words for concepts they know in their native language.	Use the teaching/assessing tool of preview in context (this chapter). Read text in which words are defined in context (Chapter 5). Teach how to find specific meanings or synonyms in the dictionary or glossary (Chapter 5). Teach deciphering word parts: root words and affixes (this chapter). Label known concepts on graphic organizers with new words (this chapter).
Learning new meanings for known words. Examples: *front* in science, *tribute* in social studies, *hack* in rugby, *volume* in math.	All students learn the specialized meanings used in specific content areas for everyday or familiar words.	Give the new definition, and compare the two meanings. Read in context and compare new to familiar meaning. (See preview in context, this chapter). Teach how to find specific content-area definitions in the dictionary or glossary (Chapter 5).
Clarifying and enriching the meanings of known words. Examples: the difference between *hilarity* and *joviality*; that *virtuoso* refers to musicians and not athletes.	All students expand their vocabularies by learning more precise words and the particular nuances in the meanings of words.	Read widely to meet words in different contexts (Chapter 3). Use the teaching/assessing tool of a graphic organizer of central concept and related categories (this chapter).

Using the new words in speaking and writing.	All students need encouragement and support in using new words in different situations.	Incorporate journals in which students explain what they are learning (Chapters 4 and 5). Have multiple opportunities for student-to-student discussions (Chapter 5). Provide opportunities to write for different purposes and different audiences (Chapter 6).
Learning to read known words.	Less able readers may not easily read known content words or even the everyday words in their speaking or listening vocabularies.	Read words in a variety of considerate, appropriate texts (Chapter 3). Teach deciphering word parts: root words and affixes (this chapter). Provide opportunities for students to write and read in each other's journals (Chapters 4 and 5).

Source: Adapted from Graves & Slater (1996, pp. 264–265).

prior knowledge and the immediate context in the reading selection, the teacher and the students compose probable meanings for new vocabulary. Readence et al. outline the following steps, which are repeated for each new word:

1. *Preparation.* The teacher selects important vocabulary from the reading text.

2. *Establishing context.* Pointing out the first word in the text, the teacher and students read aloud or silently the surrounding sentences or context.

3. *Specifying word meaning.* The teacher questions the students to help them compose a probable definition for the word based on their interpretation of the text and their prior knowledge.

4. *Expanding word meanings.* After the students have arrived at a definition for the word in that context, they can extend their understanding by discussing synonyms, antonyms, or other contexts in which the word could occur.

During the previewing, you assess the students' prior knowledge, use of context, and resulting definitions. If your students have difficulty composing a definition, one student could consult the dictionary, and then you and your students could discuss how to select the appropriate definition for the specific context. Once you have modeled and explained previewing in context with your students, you remind them to use the tool in paired reading and independent reading.

Concept of Definition or Word Map. Replicating a concept learning model (Frayer, Frederick, & Klausmeier, 1969), the *concept of definition* (also called a *word map*) can be used to teach concepts as well as to teach what constitutes a complete definition (Schwartz, 1988). Essentially the teacher (and the students if they have prior knowledge) build a specific type of graphic organizer for the concept (see Figure 4.12) while previewing the chapter:

1. The teacher identifies the target concept and places it in the center of the graphic organizer. (*igneous*)

2. The teacher writes the general class to which the concept belongs—the superordinate category. (*rocks*)

3. The teacher (and possibly the students) explains the target concept by identifying its essential attributes or properties. (*made from magna*)

4. The teacher (and possibly the students) cites examples of the target concept. (*granite*)

Figure 4.12

Concept of Definition for Igneous Rocks

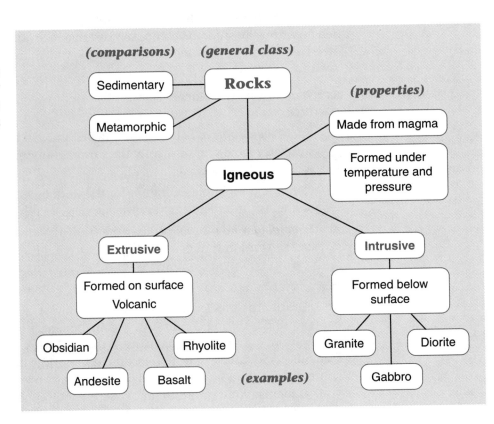

5. The teacher (and possibly the students) compares the target concept to related yet different concepts in the same superordinate category. (*sedimentary*)

In the initial teaching of concepts and words, as in our earth science example on rocks, you would model and explain how to complete the graphic organizer. As the unit progresses, students may encounter additional properties as well as more examples and comparative examples, which they can add to the graphic organizer. They should have opportunities to present and explain their additions. In our example, when they read, students could complete a word map for sedimentary rocks, and you would assess the properties and examples. Naturally, if particular students, like students with learning disabilities, need support, you would build the word map or graphic organizer interactively with them.

After students understand the format of the concept of definition, Schwartz (1988) recommends that students use the word map structure to evaluate definitions presented in textbooks. Does a definition identify the superordinate class and describe the essential attributes of the concept? Does the definition give examples and related concepts? If definitions are incomplete, students can decide where to search for the needed information.

Teacher as Inquiring Learner Activity

Make a concept-of-definition or word map for a concept from your content area or from everyday life that interests you—for example, *explorer, texture, villain, amphibian, patriot, kangaroo court, jump shot, novel, polygon,* or *integer.*

- What is the superordinate class for the concept? What are the essential attributes or properties? What are examples of the concept? What concepts are related to your target concept?

You may also find it helpful to think of contrasting examples or nonexamples of the concept, such as *hero* for *villain* or *loyalist* for *patriot.*

▶ ▶ ▶ ▶ **Direct Teaching Tool: Morphemic Analysis**

If you had to memorize the meanings of Greek and Latin roots, prefixes, and suffixes in high school, you've had experience with *morphemic analysis* or *structural analysis*. Morphemic analysis means breaking words into their meaningful parts. A *morpheme* is the smallest unit of meaning; it could be a whole word, like *atom,* or the parts of a word. *Hydrocarbon* has two morphemes—*hydro* and *carbon*—and *atoms* has two also—*atom* and *-s.* In content areas, morphemic analysis can allow readers to understand the meanings of new words. For example, very few students in our classes know the word *gynecocracy,* yet many figure it out from *gyne-* and *-ocracy.*

A special case of morphemic analysis is the recognition of *cognates,* or words from two languages that are familiar in form and meaning. Cognate examples from English and Spanish are *species/especies* and *naturally/naturalmente.* Although you can see the similarities between the cognates, and successful bilingual readers do also, intermediate bilingual students and older low-literacy bilingual students do not easily recognize cognates (Jiménez, García, & Pearson, 1996; García & Nagy, 1993).

Your direct teaching of morphemic (and cognate) analysis will help students when they read independently because they can recognize familiar parts of words and deduce the meaning, as you did for *gynecocracy.* Using the criteria of frequency and usefulness to choose words, you would model and explain how to analyze a word. Beginning with clear examples, you would model and explain how to detach the prefix from the root word, how to detach the suffix if necessary, how to recall the meanings for the different word parts, and how to infer the new meaning for the whole word. For cognates, you would highlight the similarities and differences between the two languages.

Root Words.   In the content areas, you want to model and explain common root words or morphemes that occur in your content area—for example, *chromo-, anthro-, helio-, cardio-,* and *magni-.* Your goal is for students to be able to generate new meanings based on the familiar morpheme. For example, once the students know the math word *centimeter,* you can teach them to determine the meanings of several related words (see Figure 4.13).

Prefixes.   You want to teach that common prefixes have more than one meaning and more than one spelling (*in-, im-, ir-, il-*). Sometimes when a prefix is removed, the root word is unknown (*-trigue* in *intrigue*) or the meaning of the root word is unrelated to the whole word (*-vented* in *invented*) (White, Sowell, & Yangihara, 1989).

Suffixes.   You may need to teach some students that there are two types of suffixes. *Inflectional suffixes*, the first type, occur most often and are different forms of the same word indicating verb tense (convers**ed**) or number (pencil**s**). ESL students may need mini-lessons in recognizing inflectional endings

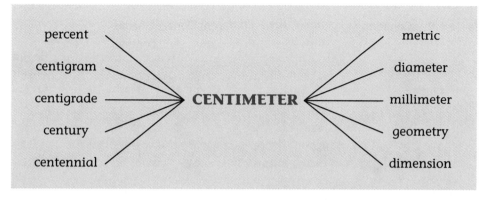

Figure 4.13

Words Related
to <u>Centimeter</u>

in text and in writing them in their own texts. *Derivational suffixes*, the second type, change the part of speech (*converse* to *conversation*) and may change the pronunciation and spelling (*sane* and *sanity*), and the meaning relationship may not be predictable (*vital* and *vitality*) (White, Sowell, & Yanagihara, 1989).

After mini-lessons in how to use morphemic and cognate analysis, students would apply the strategy independently during their reading. You could make a class chart of the important or frequent morphemes, and add words to the list as you and your students encounter them throughout the year (see Table 4.2) Most important, as you and your students explore morphemes, remember that the importance of morphemic analysis is *not* knowing a list of affixes and root words but *applying* known prefixes, suffixes, and roots to learn new words.

Teacher as Inquiring Learner Activity

Think about how many words you know that use the prefix -*trans* or the suffix -*ology*. You could compose quite a list. Think about your content area. You might want to survey the glossary of a textbook in your content area.

• What are the common prefixes, suffixes, and roots?

Begin a list or maybe a graphic like the one for *centimeter* (see Figure 4.13). If you are keeping a journal, you could devote a few pages to your collection. Clearly you will continue to build your collection throughout your teaching career.

Table 4.2   Common Morphemes Across Different Content Areas

Morpheme	English	Social Studies	Science	Math	Health and Physical Education	Other
anti-(against)	antagonist anticlimax antihero antithesis antonym	antifederalist antipoverty anti-Semitic antitrust	antibody antidote antitoxin	antiderivative antilogarithm	antiseptic antibiotic antiperspirant antacid	antifreeze
auto-(self)	autobio-graphy autograph	autocracy autonomy	automation autopsy			automatic automobile
circum-(around)	circumflex circum-locution	circa circum-navigate circumpolar	circulation circuit circumlunar	circumference circumcenter		circus circumspect circuitous circumstance
graph (to write)	biography monograph paragraph orthography	demography topography graffiti	photograph graphite seismograph telegraph geography	graph	choreograph	phonograph
mono (one)	monolingual monologue	monarchy monopoly monolith	monochro-matic monogenesis monomolecular	monomial	monocular mononu-cleosis	monotone monogram monorail monastery
scrib, script (to write)	ascribe description manuscript scribble	conscription proscribe	prescription	circumscribe		postscript subscribe transcribe scripture

sym, syn (together)	synonym	syndicate	symbiosis	symbol	symptom	symphony
	synopsis	synthesis	synapses	symmetric	syndrome	synagogue
	syntax		synthetic	asymmetric		sympathy
	symbolic					synchronize

Source: Selected from L. E. Burmeister, *Reading Strategies for Middle and Secondary School Teachers* (2nd ed.) (Reading, MA: Addison-Wesley, 1978), pp. 366, 367, 369, 374, 378, 384, 385.

▶ ▶ ▶ ▶ **Focus on Writing:**
Using New Vocabulary

In previous Focus on Writing sections, we included journals, brainstorming, graphic organizers, KWL and its variations, and freewriting. For any of those tools, you could note the vocabulary that students use. In addition, students could keep a vocabulary section in their journals. They could rate their knowledge of vocabulary, record their probable definitions (preview in context), or collect common morphemes they discover.

For example, at the beginning of a math unit, students were asked to define *decimal* and compare it to *fraction*. The fifth- and sixth-grade students exhibited a range of definitions for the term:

> c. I think decimals are little dots that can mean so much. I really don't no [sic] what decimals are. I think they are like fractions because they both make shapes. I think decimals and fractions are not alike because a decimal is small and a fraction can be any size.
>
> d. A decimal is a fraction. We use decimals to show part of a number. Decimals are like fractions except the lines separate the numbers and the dots separate the decimals. (Gordon & Macinnis, 1993, p. 39)

In summary, we have focused on assessing students' knowledge of important vocabulary and preteaching only those important words they don't know or would have difficulty learning on their own. Remember that you are building background knowledge or schemata through the vocabulary teaching/assessing tools you use. When the words are related to the important concepts you are teaching, you and the students will be expressing them often in both speech and writing, and the students will remember them.

Purpose Setting and Monitoring: Two Underlying and Ongoing Strategies

D o you use the purpose-setting questions at the beginning of each chapter in this book to guide your learning? During a learning task like reading this book, do you monitor how your learning is progressing? If you engage in purpose setting and monitor your progress during literacy tasks, you are metacognitively aware.

Throughout all three phases of learning and literacy tasks—generating ideas, interacting ideas, and refining ideas—strategic learners keep their purpose in mind and monitor their use of specific strategies until they decide they have accomplished their purpose and the task. Thus, we view purpose setting and monitoring as underlying and ongoing strategies in all phases.

In this section, we will discuss modeling and explaining these two underlying and ongoing strategies, discuss their importance, and outline how we will present them in the rest of the chapters in Part Two.

▶ ▶ ▶ ▶ ## Modeling and Explaining Strategies for Purpose Setting and Monitoring

Because purpose setting and monitoring are underlying and ongoing strategies, whenever we model and explain literacy strategies, we include them. For example, editorial purpose setting and monitoring were embedded in the first script in this chapter.

Purpose Setting.   In the editorial script, the reader began with a general purpose related to the persuasive purpose of an editorial:

- "to look for the editor's opinion and reasons and to decide whether I agree."

    As the reader proceeded, a more specific purpose was stated:

- "to look for the editor's reasons against the repeal [of the gun law] and see if they are similar to mine."

    When strategic readers are presented with unfamiliar topics, they often refine their purposes as they learn more. For example when researching new topics, students often begin with general purposes and then refine to more specific purposes when they narrow their research topics.

    Purpose setting is important to model first because strategic learners determine what schemata to activate, what knowledge to seek, and what information to remember based on their purposes. When learners have a purpose, they construct meaning and build their schemata purposefully rather than aimlessly memorize facts. Second, strategic learners use purpose setting to determine which strategies to use. For example, since reading for entertainment and reading to analyze an argument are two different purposes, strategic readers select different literacy strategies. And finally, strategic learners know when their tasks are completed because they know they have accomplished their purposes.

Monitoring Progress.   You recognize that monitoring is really being metacognitively aware of both content and strategies. First, you want your students to be aware of the content they know and what they don't know. Then they can construct meaning and build their schemata. When students can identify their misunderstandings or errors, then you will have clear direction for your instruction.

Second, strategic learners are aware of their strategies and monitor how well their strategies match the specific task. If their progress is smooth, then strategic learners may let their strategies work automatically. However, when their progress is stymied, strategic learners try to figure out why their strategies are not working and often do change strategies. Remember this from the editorial script:

I expect the title to inform me about the topic of this editorial, but this title does not. Since I don't have enough information to tap into my background knowledge, I will read the first paragraph to find the topic.

In most of the modeling and explaining scripts, our monitoring statements indicate successful learning of content and highlight successful use of different strategies. However, since students benefit from seeing what strategic learners do when they are confused or not comprehending, don't hesitate to model how to remediate confusion.

▶ ▶ ▶ ▶ How Purpose Setting and Monitoring Are Presented in This Book

In Chapters 4 through 6, you will find purpose-setting and monitoring statements in each of the modeling and explaining scripts. You will also find a monitoring checklist at the end of each chapter. Each checklist contains generic statements related to purpose setting and monitoring progress appropriate for that literacy phase: generating, interacting, or refining. We present a checklist for you to use with your students because we have found a monitoring checklist useful in building metacognitive awareness, especially among less strategic learners.

A Checklist for Monitoring Strategies for Generating Ideas

Purpose Setting

✓ Have you set a purpose for reading or writing?

Activating Prior Knowledge

✓ Do you have any background knowledge you can activate?

✓ Do you recognize the purpose, genre, or format of the text?

✓ Have you read this author before and so know the author's likely point of view?

Previewing and Predicting

✓ Have you previewed the text to help you activate your background knowledge?

✓ Did you find the title, subheads, graphics, or other chapter aids helpful in predicting what the text would contain?

✓ Did you skim the table of contents and ask questions to guide your reading?

Exploring New Vocabulary

✓ Did you preview the vocabulary to see if the text was comfortable or too difficult for you to read?

✓ Do you need to define some words before you read?

Summary of the Chapter

In this chapter, we have concentrated on the first phase of a literacy task: generating ideas or building background knowledge. We have emphasized four categories of strategies:

- Activating prior experiences and prior knowledge
- Previewing and predicting
- Exploring new vocabulary
- Purpose setting and monitoring

Strategic learners select specific strategies and use them in concert to build their background knowledge when they are beginning a literacy task. To teach these strategies, we have described specific pedagogical tools:

- Modeling and explaining the processes with texts the students read in your content area to make the strategies visible to students
- Teaching/assessing tools to support students' learning of strategies and content, such as brainstorming, graphic organizers, KWL, anticipation guides, and concept of definition
- Direct teaching tools to impart information to students, such as direct experiences and morphemic analysis
- Assessment tools to inform your instruction, such as student self-rating of new vocabulary
- Focus on writing by incorporating tools, such as freewriting and journals

You will choose what strategies to model and what teaching tools to use based on the content objectives you have, the texts you use, and your particular students' needs.

As we end the generating phase in this chapter and begin the interacting phase in Chapter 5, remember that we have artificially separated the phases so that we could explain strategies to you. Strategic learners move naturally between phases and even recycle through phases guided by their purposes and their monitoring of their progress as they tackle learning tasks, read nonfiction books, write research reports, or evaluate web pages.

Inquiry Activities About Your Learning

1. Research a new area, issue, or topic in your content area. To choose, think about what you might need to teach that you have not studied in depth in your college program. Or what interests you personally that you haven't researched yet but might like to teach in the future? Keep a journal to track the generating strategies you use. How do you activate your prior knowledge, preview and predict, and explore vocabulary? What specific strategies do you select in each category (remember that you need not use every one). Write your reflections about how you used the strategies, and assess their effectiveness. Review the teaching/assessing tools sections, and try using a few tools yourself. Write your reflections about the tools too. Having personal experience with strategies and tools will help you make your process visible when you model and explain with your students.

2. Choose a trade book (fiction or nonfiction) or a magazine article appropriate for your content area. Identify the most important information in a nonfiction text or the most important element (imagery, character) in a fiction text (that becomes your content objective). Select the ten most important content words for the vocabulary words you might preteach. If you selected a chapter book, you might decide to

choose words from a few chapters. Do not select ten words for each chapter; remember the guidelines!

Design a graphic organizer that depicts the relationships among the important content vocabulary.

Inquiry Activities About Your Students' Learning

1. Interview a middle school or high school student about the generating strategies he or she uses when beginning to read or write in your content area. You might want to provide a specific scenario—perhaps a topic the student will be studying in your content area or a particular reading or writing task. Begin with open-ended questions, such as, "What do you do to prepare to read or write?" Then ask about whether the student activates prior knowledge, previews or predicts, explores vocabulary, sets a purpose, or monitors his or her progress. For example, you could ask, "Did you think about what you knew before beginning?" Depending on the answer, you could ask more specific questions, for example, "Did you read the book jacket to see if you knew anything about the content or knew the author?"

Summarize what generating strategies the student uses. Based on what you have learned, what strategies would you model and explain to the student?

2. Think about a topic in your content area and find a text—a web site, a newspaper article, a book. Choose a teaching/assessing tool described in this chapter, for example, graphic organizers, KWL, preview in context, analogies, or freewriting. Create a lesson plan with a content objective, and incorporate one of the teaching/assessing tools.

If you have the opportunity, use your lesson plan with students. Afterward assess what the students learned and your plan. Reflect on the changes you would make next time. Remember that teachers often revise their lesson plans, both during teaching and afterward, for the next time they teach the material—either next period or next year.

5

Interacting with Ideas: Comprehending and Constructing Knowledge

"The facts, ma'am. Just the facts," stated the detective dryly. "Now what was the man wearing?" If you watch late-night reruns of old television shows, you may have heard the detective on *Dragnet* admonish witnesses to tell only the facts. But telling just the facts is harder than it seems. People *interpret* facts, which results in differing accounts of everything from car accidents to history. People find and interpret facts while observing scientific phenomena, viewing an art object, or solving a mathematics problem. They relate one fact to another, attach significance to particular facts, and incorporate facts into arguments, solutions, or beliefs. In other words, they *con-* *+ knowledge*; they don't just list facts. In some classrooms, teachers require stu- *list* facts, and so students have an unrelated set of facts. But in real life, *st* list facts; they seek to understand or comprehend information, and *nsion* of information, they construct knowledge.

have generated ideas, either independently by predicting from *cipating* in a class brainstorming session to activate prior knowl- *enter* the heart of the learning process: interacting with ideas, com- *d* constructing knowledge. We chose the word *interacting* to empha- *ncepts*, ideas, and information flow between the text and the learner's *he* background knowledge in the learner's schema influences how the learner comprehends the text, and the information in the text influences how the learner constructs, adds to, and redesigns his or her schema. This transactional view of the process (Rosenblatt, 1994; see Chapter 1) holds that meaning doesn't reside in just one place—on the page, for instance. Instead, meaning is constructed by the reader after thinking about schema-based ideas and interpreting text-based ideas.

You know from our discussion of schema in Chapter 2 and our discussion of activating prior knowledge strategies and tools in Chapter 4 that strategic learners make connections between their schemata and the text information before they read the text. Now, in this chapter, we are concentrating on comprehending text and thus constructing knowledge about the subject while reading text.

Can you remember when you learned a subject or a sport for the first time? Perhaps in your first encounter with physics, Spanish, or jazz, you felt adrift in a sea of information. Inundated with information, you may have had difficulty figuring out what information was important, what was supporting or related information, and what was nonessential information. The first time middle and secondary students study a content area, they often decide they must remember everything because they do not know which information is the most important. As a content-area teacher, you will want to use teaching/assessing tools that help your students find and interpret information by making text-based and schema-based connections.

Although finding and interpreting information is the overall strategy in interacting with ideas, strategic readers incorporate three supporting strategies to help them construct meaning. First, they *search for how the text is organized* in order to find the information the author considers important more easily. Second, knowing that remembering complex information can be cumbersome, if not difficult, strategic readers *construct auxiliary aids*, like notes, to help them construct meaning. Finally, strategic readers are *alert for new vocabulary or concepts*. They know that learning new conceptual words will assist them in constructing their knowledge. For each of these supporting strategies, you will want to use teaching/assessing tools, particularly with students who have difficulty finding and interpreting information independently.

Don't forget the underlying and ongoing strategies of purpose setting and monitoring progress, for how will your students know what the important ideas to look for are if they haven't set a purpose? How will they know if they have comprehended ideas if they don't monitor the interaction between the text and their schema? Strategic readers monitor whether the text makes sense to them or whether they need to change their strategies, their purpose, or the text.

Purpose-Setting Questions

1. When you read a text in your content area, do you concentrate on the author's ideas (text-based meaning)?

2. When you read a text in your content area, do you converse with the author's ideas by agreeing or disagreeing based on your schema knowledge?

INTERACTING WITH IDEAS: COMPREHENDING AND CONSTRUCTING KNOWLEDGE

The Overall Strategy: Finding and Interpreting Information—Making Connections

Constructing Meanings: Text-Based and Schema-Based Connections
Using Three Supporting Strategies to Help Construct Meaning
Modeling and Explaining Strategies for Finding and Interpreting Information
The Importance of Questioning
Types of Questions and Answers
How Questioning Can Facilitate (or Hinder) Students' Understanding
Observing the Role of Questioning in This Chapter

Strategies and Tools That Emphasize Text-Based Connections

Modeling and Explaining Strategies That Emphasize Text-Based Connections

Teaching/Assessing Tools That Emphasize Text-Based Connections

Assessment Tools That Emphasize Text-Based Connections

Focus on Writing: Writing to Learn in Journals, Learning Logs, and Lab or Field Notebooks

Strategies and Tools That Emphasize Schema-Based Connections

Modeling and Explaining Strategies That Emphasize Schema-Based Connections

Teaching/Assessing Tools That Emphasize Schema-Based Connections

Assessment Tool for Strategies That Emphasize Schema-Based Connections

Focus on Writing: Journals and First Drafts

Three Supporting Strategies and Tools

Capitalizing on Text Organization

Constructing Auxiliary Aids

Independent Learning of New Vocabulary

Focus on Writing: Supporting Strategies and First Drafts

Purpose Setting & Monitoring Progress During the Interacting with Ideas Phase (Underlying and Ongoing Strategies)

A Checklist for Monitoring Strategies for Interacting with Ideas

3. In your past schooling, did teachers assign texts to be read independently, or did they incorporate teaching tools, like discussions or study guides, to help you find and interpret the content?

4. Do you use a text's organization to help you locate important information to understand?

5. What system do you use to take notes in classes or from texts?

6. What do you do when you meet a new word while reading: skip it, figure it out from context, or look it up?

The Overall Strategy: Finding and Interpreting Information—Making Connections

I n the central phase of the learning and literacy task, interacting with ideas, strategic readers negotiate their understanding of the text and of their schemata. Guided by their purposes and monitoring their progress, strategic readers concentrate on the overall strategy of finding and interpreting information, thereby making meaningful connections in both the text and their schemata (see Fig. 5.1). In the interplay between the text and their schemata connections, strategic readers comprehend and construct their knowledge.

▶ ▶ ▶ ▷ Constructing Meanings: Text-Based and Schema-Based Connections

Every student needs both text-based connections and schema-based connections to construct meaning. To learn, text-based information must be sorted—to distinguish what's important and what's not, what's understood and what's not, what's conflicting or what's not—and integrated from different places—the graphic and text, the beginning and end of text. However, text-based information is important only if it can be used to solve problems or issues, understand another human being, clarify a perspective, substantiate a theory, or provide a reason for action. To accomplish any of those purposes, schema-based connections need to be engaged. Inferences, elaborations, alternatives, themes, or issues need to be considered; comparisons to other sources of information need to be weighed; and applications to real situations need to be pursued.

What is interesting is when and how strategic readers make connections between the text and their schemata. Analyzing the think-alouds of only

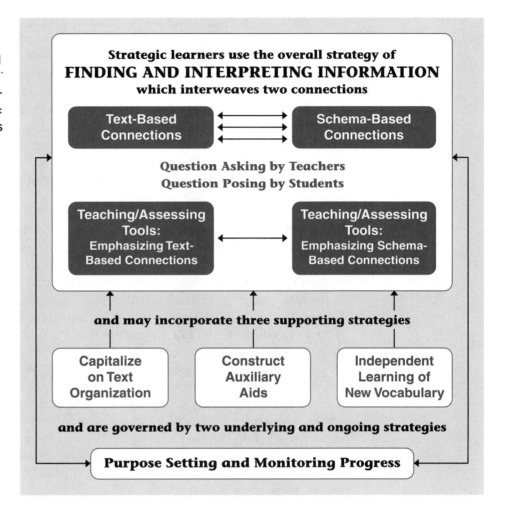

Figure 5.1

Finding and Inter-
preting Information:
Making Connections

eight capable high school readers, Hartman (1995) found three continuously
made both connections, four made text-based first with some schema-based
connections, and one concentrated on schema-based connections. Even
though we hesitate to generalize from Hartman's small study, we think strategic readers do choose how and when to make both text-based and schema-
based connections.

**Continuously Making Both Text-Based and Schema-Based Connections
Scenario.** Having activated their background knowledge during the generating phase, strategic readers concentrate on negotiating both text-based and
schema-based connections for meaning during the entire text. As they read,

they sift through the ideas in the text and weigh the relevance of information as they make text-based connections. They are doing more than absorbing the text information; they are making connections to their schemata. Referring to their prior knowledge, they consider different interpretations from other sources and their own experiences and begin to alter their schemata.

We think strategic readers continuously make text-based and schemata-based connections when they have sufficient background knowledge about the content and when the difficulty level of the text is comfortably matched to their reading strategies. Although we'd like to think this scenario represents capable reading, we recognize that the two other scenarios are equally legitimate.

Concentrating on Text-Based Connections with Some Schema-Based Connections Scenario.   Strategic readers decide to concentrate on the text because their purpose is to gain information or to understand the author's meaning. They make connections among the text information using their schemata primarily to verify whether they understand what the author has stated. During the interacting phase, strategic readers decide to hold other schemata connections, like connections to other sources or to their life, in abeyance until after they have finished reading.

We think one instance when strategic readers decide to concentrate more on the text-based connections is when they discover they have meager prior knowledge. Clearly they know they need to add information to their schemata. Another instance is when they read nonfiction text, such as, a scientific report, a set of directions, or an editorial about a community issue. Although they could continuously make text-based and schemata-based connections, they decide to concentrate primarily on text-based connections to make sure they understand the author.

Concentrating on Schemata-Based Connections Scenario.   In this scenario, strategic readers focus on interpreting and reacting to the author's meaning using their background knowledge of other sources and their experiences. They are involved primarily in using their schemata as a guide to particular information or in rethinking their schemata-based information while grazing over text-based information.

We think this scenario can have positive and negative instances. When strategic readers have substantial prior knowledge, they use their schemata-based connections to react to new, contradictory, or even incorrect information. When the text contains information, issues, or themes that resonate with the reader, strategic readers may concentrate more on their schema-based connections. Both editorials and novels are texts that strategic readers may react strongly to and so focus on their schema-based connections. On the negative side, when readers ignore contrary reasons or uninteresting information, we could not call that concentration on schema-based connections strategic.

Thus, in these three scenarios, strategic learners make both text-based connections and schema-based connections as they find and interpret information. Although the balance may differ in three scenarios, connections between text and schema are made in a symbiotic process of finding and interpreting information.

When you teach your students, you want to use teaching/assessing tools that engage both text-based and schema-based connections and help students decide how to balance those connections. Since many of those tools use questions, either asked by teachers in teacher-led discussions or posed by students in peer-led discussions, we discuss the importance of questioning first. Then we present tools that emphasize text-based connections and use teacher-led discussions and follow with tools that emphasize schema-based connections and use peer-led discussions.

Every student needs both types of discussion: teacher led and peer led. At times, with difficult text (a primary source, for example), students may benefit from a teacher-led discussion to make connections. At other times, students need to take responsibility for their thinking about text. If given the opportunity, they will challenge each other by offering their constructions of meaning. In both types of discussion, teachers and students concentrate on finding and interpreting information by making text-based and schema-based connections. Discussions are not the only tools students need to make connections about meaning. They need instruction in the three supporting strategies as well.

▶ ▶ ▶ ▶ Using Three Supporting Strategies to Help Construct Meaning

As strategic readers find and interpret information through text-based and schema-based connections, we think they use three supporting strategies to assist them.

1. *Strategic learners capitalize on the organization of the text* to help them locate the important information in the text and to recall that information (Richgels, McGee, Lomax, & Sheard, 1987). Using their schemata-based knowledge of text organization gained from previous reading, they search for clues to how the author's important ideas can be connected, related, and interpreted. Sometimes readers meet a unique organization. For example, a scientist may

first state the conclusion and implications, or a novelist may state the final outcome in the first sentence, as Toni Morrison does in *Paradise*. Then strategic readers concentrate on text-based connections to figure out the text's organization and its meaning.

2. Strategic learners construct auxiliary aids by taking notes; drawing a diagram, model, or graphic organizer; and picturing the ideas in their minds. With concrete auxiliary aids, like notes or diagrams, strategic readers can review the aids and add schema-based connections to assist their comprehension.

3. Strategic learners independently learn new vocabulary or concepts because if they skip important words, they will miss text-based connections. Thus, they look for highlighted words or repeated words, use the context around a word to figure out its meaning, figure out word parts, and consult a dictionary or glossary. They incorporate those new words into their schemata so that they can communicate their ideas more precisely and clearly. You know from Chapter 4 that you may decide to preteach important concepts and vocabulary. However, some words are best taught within their context, such as figurative language or connotations.

If your students don't efficiently capitalize on text organizations, construct auxiliary aids, or learn new vocabulary independently, you will want to model and explain the advantages of those strategies and assist them with teaching/assessing tools.

In summary, in this chapter, we focus on the overall strategy of finding and interpreting information through making both text-based and schema-based connections. To help make those connections, we present three supporting strategies: capitalizing on text organizations, constructing auxiliary aids, and independently learning new vocabulary.

Before we move on to the teaching/assessing tools for each of these strategies, we present a modeling and explaining script in order to make specific strategies visible to you.

▶ ▶ ▶ ▶ **Modeling and Explaining Strategies for Finding and Interpreting Information**

Suppose that you are teaching a unit on pollution that focuses on the question, "Will pollution in the United States be at an acceptable level in the year 2005?" You plan to have your students do research to find information on various pollution problems and related solutions. In preparation for their independent research, you plan to teach the students how to conduct research on the Internet. To get them started, you have gathered a list of useful sites, and you plan to model and explain how to find and interpret important information using an article from one web site, *The Why Files* (**http://whyfiles. news.wisc.edu**), that posts science articles for secondary students.

To begin, you review generating strategies. Pretend that you and your class have brainstormed a list of pollution problems and related solutions. One problem on the list is car pollution, and one solution might be electric cars, especially for urban areas where people drive in short trips. Therefore, the purpose of reading the article, "Can Electric Cars Help Me Breathe Easier?" is to evaluate whether electric cars would be an effective solution to car pollution. As you read the script, notice when schema-based and text-based connections occur.

Modeling and Explaining Strategies for Finding and Interpreting Information

Strategies I Chose to Use

I have **schema-based connections** that I will keep active as I read this article. I know that gasoline cars pollute the air. I have seen smog over many urban areas and even in rural mountain areas. My opinion is that electric cars will be an effective solution to pollution.

In addition, from my **schema**, I know this article is written to inform readers, and my purpose is to learn information. So I plan to search for **text-based connections** that may change my existing schema.

This **text-based information** I recognize. From my **prior knowledge**, I know California passed a law about zero-emission cars and that the goal of 2 percent in 1998 wasn't met.

I wonder if the goal of 10 percent in 2003 still might be kept and what states are working toward that goal. Thus, I have **new questions because I recognize what I don't know**.

Article from a Web Site

Can Electric Cars Help Me Breathe Easier?

The push for electric cars grew out of persistent air pollution in the Los Angeles basin, which led California's erstwhile plan to require that 2% of new vehicles sold in 1998 be "zero-emissions vehicles." (That proportion is still supposed to rise to 10% by year 2003.) In addition, several Northeast states signed on to the California standards, enlarging the market push for e-cars.

Strategies I Chose to Use

This **information is irrelevant**. I know e-cars are available, but my purpose is not to research sales information. I'm going to skip this paragraph.

This is the article's main question—and mine too. With this main question (or main idea) in mind, I'm going to seek supporting details to answer yes or no.

Thus, from my **schema-based connections**, I think the **text organization will compare the pros and cons of e-cars**. I will **capitalize on the comparison organization** to find and interpret information.

Here is the quick answer: It depends! That **text-based information** about coal and oil generators is a con for e-cars. From my **schema-based information**, I suppose hydropowered generators for e-car electricity would reduce pollution—a pro for e-cars.

However, I had not connected the electric car to electricity-generating plants. That's **important information**.

Now I have another **new question**, to answer before I determine e-car effectiveness: How is local electricity generated?

Now I'm trying to find **specific details** about the pros and cons of e-cars. I read that e-cars change the chemicals in pollution. I ask is that good (pro) or bad (con)? To help me understand Wang's results, I'm going to **construct an auxiliary aid** or take notes on a chart [see Fig. 5.2].

Article from a Web Site

(If you want to order an electric car, you don't have to wait that long.)

However, nobody is in a position to coerce consumers to buy these cars, so the car-makers face the prospect of subsidizing the new vehicles—which they are less than eager to do.

But can electric vehicles deliver on their promise to reduce emissions? Are they even "zero-emission" vehicles to begin with? In other words,
Can e-cars doom the fume?

That depends on where the electricity originates. If it is from a coal- or oil-fired generator, the answer is "Not." In this case, the electric vehicle shifts the pollution from the tailpipe to the generating plant.

They also alter the chemical composition of the pollution. Michael Quanlu Wang of Argonne National Laboratory used a computer simulation to compare the use of electric and gasoline cars in four large U.S. cities.

Figure 5.2

Comparison Chart
for Notes

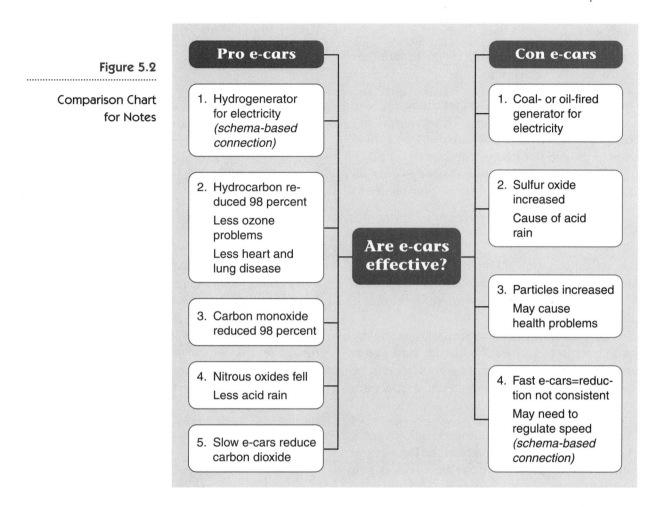

Now, although I can write the names of the chemicals on my chart, I need to make sure I understand them. So I will use my **vocabulary learning strategies** to check the meanings.

When I click on *defined,* the computer switches me to the **glossary.** I learn that *hydrocarbon* is defined as 1 hydrogen element combined with 1 carbon element and is found in fossil fuels. I know carbon monoxide is a poisonous gas.

Nitrous oxide is not defined in the glossary. So I examine the **root words**: *nitrous* could be *nitrogen,* and *oxide* must be *oxygen* since it was in

The results showed the electric vehicles would reduce hydrocarbon (*defined*) and carbon monoxide (*defined*) by 98%: see *Magnitude and Value of Electric Vehicle Emissions.* (Hydrocarbons create ground-level ozone, which causes cardiac and respiratory disease.) Emissions of nitrous oxides, another cause of ozone and acid rain, also fell.

Strategies I Chose to Use

Article from a Web Site

the word *monoxide*. I need to go to another source for a fuller definition.

I notice the **signal word** *But*, indicating opposite results: what e-cars increase. This confirms my **comparison text organization**. I add these notes to the con side of my chart [see Figure 5.2].

Again I meet **new vocabulary**—*particulates*. From the **context**, I define *particulates* as "fine soot particles."

But Wang found that emissions of sulfur oxide (a key cause of acid rain), and particulates would actually increase. (The health effects of these ultra-fine soot particles are now under increasing suspicion.)

Here is information about carbon dioxide. Although I don't find a signal word, the phrases *at slow speeds* and *at higher speeds* surely signal a comparison.

I add these conflicting results to my comparison chart [see Figure 5.2]. I could **add from my schema** that e-car speed would have to be regulated since we already have a speeding problem on highways.

I recall my purpose: to evaluate the effectiveness of e-cars as a solution to pollution. As I survey my comparison chart, I weigh the **text-based pro and con details** for e-cars as an effective solution. I conclude that e-cars may not be effective for where I live—**restructuring my schema**.

So I need to investigate **new questions**:

1. What are the pollution controls on gas cars?
2. What is the source of electricity that would charge e-car batteries?

The story for carbon dioxide, the greenhouse gas that's taking heat for causing global warming, was more complex. At slow speeds, electric vehicles greatly reduced carbon dioxide; the effect was less dependable at higher speeds. As you read them, remember that all calculations of pollution trade-offs will depend on the age and pollution controls of the gasoline autos and the electric-generating plants in question.

Clean? That depends on **where** you live . . . (Sound Familiar?)

Source: Excerpted from "Can Electric Cars Help Me Breathe Easier," *The Why Files* (**http://whyfiles.news.wisc.edu/055electcar/ whywewant.html**). © 1999, University of Wisconsin Board of Regents. Used by permission.

Let's review and summarize my example of modeling and explaining. Don't forget that before the modeling and explaining script, generating strategies were reviewed: the purpose for reading the article and prior knowledge of pollution problems and solutions. As you read the strategies used to find and interpret the important information, think about the interplay between text-based and schema-based connections:

1. I began with **schema-based connections** (what I knew about pollution and my opinion of e-cars).

2. **From my schema**, I knew the purpose of the article and so knew to search for text-based connections.

3. During reading, I **recognized text-based information that was also in my prior knowledge or schema** (California had passed a law about zero emissions).

4. Using **text-based information**, I also **recognized what I didn't know and asked new questions** (whether states are working to meet the 2003 goal and the connection between generating plants and e-cars).

5. I skipped **irrelevant text information** (purchasing an e-car).

6. I found and interpreted **text-based information** and **specific details** (the pros and cons about e-cars).

To help me make text-based connections, I used the three supporting strategies:

7. I **capitalized on text organization** because I predicted a comparison organization from my **schema-based knowledge**—determined the article would give pro and con details about e-cars. I also recognized that the word **but signaled comparison**—an opposite result.

8. I **constructed an auxiliary aid** (made a comparison chart for my notes about e-cars).

9. I used **independent strategies for learning new vocabulary** (the web site glossary, the context, and word parts).

10. Finally, I **reviewed my purpose** (evaluate e-cars), **drew a conclusion from text-based information that changed my schema-based information** (e-cars may not be effective), **and asked new questions**.

In using these strategies, I was interacting with the ideas. Because the purpose was "to evaluate whether electric cars are an effective solution," I judged the importance of the facts and how they would fit the purpose. If the purpose had been "to determine what emissions electric cars reduce," I probably would have just memorized those facts in the article. Thus, to interact with ideas, learners need a challenging purpose or thoughtful question to address. Let's examine the types of questions teachers ask and the types of answers students give, keeping in mind a goal of critical thinking during interacting with ideas.

The Importance of Questioning

Questions have been a part of a teacher's repertoire since Socrates used them as a teaching tool to help students think. Many teachers use questions as an assessment tool: they initiate with a question, a student responds, and the teacher evaluates (this is known as the *I-R-E pattern*). (You recall our discussion of communication roles in Chapter 3.) In I-R-E, or recitation, classrooms, questions are assessment tools used to determine whether the students have retained the information from the text (Alvermann, O'Brien, & Dillon, 1990). Students clearly recognize that the teacher knows the right answer and will keep asking the question until a student gives that answer.

In contrast to the I-R-E classroom, people in their everyday life ask questions because they don't have the answer. They seek unknown information, want to compare their understanding to another person's, or want another person's opinion or interpretation. Real questions instigate conversations, discussions, or even arguments. In everyday life, people ask questions to find and interpret unknown information.

Look back at the e-car script and find where and why questions were posed. In finding and interpreting information, real questions were asked for these reasons:

- Guide comprehension or set a purpose—"Are e-cars an effective solution?"

- Flag unknown information—"I wonder if the goal of 10 percent in 2003 is kept?"

- Highlight an important connection and unknown information—"How is local electricity generated?"

- Highlight an alternative solution to investigate—"What are the pollution controls on gas cars?"

When you model and explain interacting with ideas, you will want to ask real questions so that students understand that posing questions helps negotiate between schema-based meaning and text-based meaning. Furthermore, because nonstrategic students tend to assume they understand the text, you will want to pose real questions that will assist them in making text-based and schema-based connections.

In this introduction to questioning, we have used the term *real questions* to contrast with the test situation or the I-R-E pattern of classroom talk. Let's now look at questions more closely and define different types of questions.

Our purpose is for you to recognize that different types of questions help students to negotiate text-based and schema-based information. After we have discussed types of questions, we will discuss using questions in teaching.

▶ ▶ ▶ ▶ **Types of Questions and Answers**

We acknowledge that students need to retain factual information in order to interpret. However, we think teachers can ask critical thinking questions that will require students to exhibit their factual knowledge while they interpret the information. The e-car question, "Are electric cars an effective solution to air pollution problems?" requires both factual information and critical thinking. Thus, we think you should be aware of different types of questions and answers so that you can adjust your questioning pattern when you use questions to teach and to assess. You will also want to teach your students about different questions so that they pose questions that activate their thinking while they are reading.

In content-area materials, you may find types of questions labeled with different terms. We think you should know those terms and the critical thinking that they imply. In addition, we will outline how we think the levels correspond to text-based and schema-based connections.

Question-Answer Relationship (QAR) Framework. We like the QAR framework because it corresponds to the different scenarios of reading in which strategic readers negotiate text-based information and schema-based information. Raphael (1986) suggests that teachers and students discuss where answers to different questions are located using the QAR classification scheme:

- *Right There*—Students can underline in the text the words in the question and for the answer. Both are explicitly in the text or text based. Using the e-car text, the question, "What emissions do electric cars reduce?" and its answer, "hydrocarbons," are in the text.

- *Think and Search*—Students must find the answer by integrating information from different places in the text so the answer is text based. We have found that readers encounter two situations in content-area texts. First, in some texts, the *author has explicitly linked the information across the text* so that the reader's task is to recognize those text-based connections, like Right There. For the e-car text, the question, "Will electric cars help reduce acid rain?" can be answered by locating information in two separate places in the text where the author explicitly refers to acid rain. In the second case, the author has not explicitly linked the information and so the *reader must infer the connections or use his or her schema-based information*, as in Author and Me (the next point). In the e-car text, to answer the main question "Can e-cars doom the fume?" the reader must assess detailed information from several paragraphs and then judge whether e-cars would be an effective solution. Thus, we can align Think and Search with either Right There or with Author and Me, depending on whether the author or the reader makes the connection across the text-based information.

- *Author and Me*—Students must have read the text to understand the question but use their schemata knowledge to answer it. For the e-car text, the question, "Should drivers in your community purchase an e-car?" would require the students to think about the text information but answer from their schemata knowledge about their community's electrical sources.

- *On My Own*—Students can answer the question using their schemata without having read the text. For the e-car text, the question, "How is electricity produced in your community?" cannot be answered from this text but might be answered from the students' schemata.

We have found that QAR is a useful framework for making the process of negotiating text-based meaning and schema-based meaning visible to students when we model and explain. We also use the QAR framework to teach students to recognize where their answers to our questions come from and to pose a variety of questions that use both the text and their schemata.

Three Levels of Comprehension.   We include Herber's comprehension levels (1978) because he applies the levels to a useful teaching tool: the levels of comprehension study guide for content materials. However, before we introduce his guide in the teaching tools section, we need to explain his three levels so that you can compare his levels to other classifications of questions.

Consolidating past reading research on levels of comprehension, Herber applied three levels to content-area reading. As you read the definitions for Herber's three-level classification, think about how the terms correspond to the QAR framework:

- *Literal.* The reader determines the essential information presented in the text. This is also referred to as "reading the lines" (text-based connections).

- *Interpretive.* Because of background knowledge, the reader recognizes the author's implied meanings by integrating information from sections of the text—also known as "reading between the lines." Although the author hasn't stated the relationship, the reader can infer the meaning (text-based connections and schema-based connections).

- *Applied.* The reader synthesizes new text information with background knowledge to extend existing schema knowledge and generalizes that knowledge to new situations or abstract principles—"reading beyond the lines." The reader thinks about the significance of text-based and schema-based connections to contemplate broader concepts, such as justice, or to understand community or global issues and problems (schema-based connections).

You might want to look back at the examples of questions about the e-car text that we gave with the QAR framework. Where would you place those questions in Herber's classification?

A More Elaborate Taxonomy of Questions. Commonly referred to as *Bloom's Taxonomy* (Bloom, Englehart, Furst, Hill & Krathwohl, 1956), this classification system for educational objectives has been applied to formulating questions. We have added the translation level (Sanders, 1966) because we often ask students to restate text-based ideas in their own words. Think about diversity students, especially ESL students, who can recite an author's words but may not really understand their meaning. You will want not only ESL students but many other students to express their text-based information in their own words so that both you and the students can assess their comprehension. When we work with teachers, we incorporate key words for questions:

1. *Literal*—Recall the author's exact words or statements. Key words: *what, when, who, where, how, list, name, label, define, recall.*

2. *Translation*—Change ideas into a parallel form. Key words: *paraphrase, illustrate, tell in your own words, rephrase, draw, make a chart, diagram, or model.*

3. *Interpretation*—Link facts, ideas, or experiences to show a relationship. Key words: *distinguish, predict, estimate, rearrange, infer, explain, describe.*

4. *Application*—Transfer ideas, rules, or principles to solve a new situation. Key words: *apply, test, solve, demonstrate, build, plan, choose, construct.*

5. *Analysis*—Explain how to break down the concept into component parts. Key words: *analyze, categorize, classify, contrast, compare, discriminate, debate.*

6. *Synthesis*—Explain how to combine separate elements into a new idea, new product, or new relationships. Key words: *synthesize, conclude, create, put together, suggest, formulate, hypothesize, generate solutions, review.*

7. *Evaluation*—Devise criteria or standards and determine or measure if criteria are met. Key words: *evaluate, judge, decide, defend, select, consider, critique, determine appropriateness.*

We include this more elaborate taxonomy of questions because you will find content-area materials that use these levels as objectives or identify questions according to these levels. You may also find the categories useful when you formulate questions or tasks for your students.

In summary, we think that although people use different terms, they are referring to similar concepts, which we have outlined in Table 5.1. We have used dotted lines to indicate that categorizations are not exact in practice. Remember that the importance of questions is not to categorize them but to use them to assist students in making connections as they find and interpret information. We encourage you to try out different taxonomies to determine which one you find most useful. We will discuss using questions in classrooms in the next section.

▶ ▶ ▶ ▶ **How Questioning Can Facilitate (or Hinder) Students' Understanding**

When teachers ask questions, they are pointing to what they consider to be important information. When teachers ask literal questions, they are communicating to students what facts are important. When teachers ask questions requiring connections among text or schema information, they communicate what relationships, connections, and applications among facts and concepts

Table 5.1   A Comparison of Terms for Types of Questions

Our Terms	QAR Terms	Three-Level Terms	Seven-Level Terms
Text-based connections	Right There	Literal	Literal
Integrate across text-based connections	(author's text connections) Think and Search (reader's inferred connections)		Translation
Text and schema connections	Author and Me	Interpretive	Interpretation
Schema-based connections	On My Own	Applied	Application Analysis Synthesis Evaluation

are important. Unfortunately, teachers ask primarily literal, text-based questions (Alexander, Jetton, Kulikowich, & Woehler, 1994). We presented you with different classifications of types of questions because we want you to ask more than literal, text-based questions. We expect you to engage your students in negotiating meaning, and so you will ask questions that require connections. Before we insert questioning types into different teaching/assessing tools, we need to offer you some general ideas about using questions in your classroom.

A Caution About Taxonomies. Any taxonomy of question types can be misleading, even dangerous. First, sometimes teachers think they should always ask one question from each category. Second, teachers ask unrelated questions without considering that the questions should point to important and related information (Alexander et al., 1994). Since you will be teaching important related concepts, ideas, and generalizations—not isolated, unconnected facts—you will want to ask related questions that build those concepts, ideas, and generalizations. In planning your questions, begin with a higher-level question; then ask only the lower-level questions that help answer that higher-level question. We will return to this technique when we insert questioning into teaching tools in the next section.

Think Time or Wait Time. Have you noticed how quickly most teachers fire off questions? Rowe (1974) found that teachers waited less the one second after asking a question and after a student responded to the question. We tease teachers by comparing them to radio disc jockeys—afraid of dead air when no sound is going over the air waves.

In classrooms, silence can mean that students are thinking! If you have asked a higher-level question, students need to integrate text-based information or reconstruct their schema-based information in the light of the new text-based information. An ESL student may need to negotiate meaning in two languages or translate meaning back and forth between the two languages. Thinking situations require time. To help you wait in silence, count to 5 or 10 slowly—that is a long time—or wait even longer. And after a student has responded, wait again. That student may elaborate on the answer, or another student may respond to the first student, creating a conversation or discussion.

Avoiding the I-R-E Pattern. Usually the I-R-E pattern occurs when teachers ask literal questions or allow only one correct answer. You want to use your questions to initiate, facilitate, and sustain your students' discussion of their ideas or their construction of meaning. If you ask higher-level questions, then students can make a variety of connections among text-based and schema-based information. Their connections may trigger connections from other students, allowing students to respond to each other instead of directing their comments to you. We will discuss first teacher-led discussions and then peer-led discussions in this chapter.

Questions Can Occur in All Phases.   Teachers find that when they ask literal questions before reading, students read only for those details, paying scant attention to the rest of the chapter. Now that you know about levels of questions, you might want to think about what questions to ask before reading.

Here, in the interacting phase, teachers' questions serve to alert students to important text-based and schema-based connections. These questions can also probe for students' misconceptions so that confusions can be clarified as they occur. Of course, students' questions can also lead to discussions of connections and confusions. Because this is the middle of the task, the students' connections may be viewed as tentative, temporary, or in construction until they have completed more of the text and had time to reflect on the text as a whole.

And finally, since the connections during this middle phase of interacting with ideas are tentative, temporary, or in construction, teachers ask questions after reading in refining ideas (the subject of Chapter 6). Teacher questions that come after reading help students consolidate their understanding, reflect on their understanding, and consider the text as a whole. Students may have questions after they have finished reading because they need more information or because they are still restructuring their schema. If questions persist, as can occur in real-life learning, the students can recycle through the generating, interacting and refining phases again.

Teacher as Inquiring Learner Activity

Observe a teacher while he or she is questioning students. Using one of the taxonomies, keep track of the types of questions the teacher asks.

- How many text-based or literal questions are asked? What questions above the literal level are asked?

  Try to determine whether the answers are text based, schema based, or integrate text and schema.

- How long does the teacher wait after asking a question? Which students answer questions: boys or girls, diversity students, learning disabled students, "smart" students? Can you determine if the teacher is using questions to assess the students (an I-R-E pattern) or to teach the students how to find and interpret information?

▶ ▶ ▶ ▶ **Observing the Role of Questioning in This Chapter**

Have you noticed how we use questions in this book? You might want to skim this chapter to locate where we ask questions. We use questions for different purposes, but all of the purposes aim to encourage you to make connections.

First, we include purpose-setting questions at the beginning of each chapter. Those questions are to encourage you to activate your prior knowledge and preview and predict what we consider to be important information for you to find and interpret.

Second, we sprinkle questions throughout a chapter. Usually those rhetorical questions are meant to help you make schema-based connections to the text-based information. As you read, we hope you are making text-based and schema-based connections about your reading process, your past school experiences, and your future teaching of students.

Third, in Teacher as Inquiring Learner Activities, we ask questions to help you apply the information to a new situation. The questions may ask you to observe specific facts or interpret particular actions. Our aim is for you to integrate connections between text-based information and real-life information outside of this book.

And finally, we hope you pose your own questions as you read this book. We hope you ask questions about what strategies you use to learn in your content area, about strategies your students might use to learn, and about teaching tools that you might use with your content area.

Now, after thinking about text and schema connections in finding and interpreting information and different types of questions, let's turn to strategies and tools that incorporate those connections and questions.

Strategies and Tools That Emphasize Text-Based Connections

We used the word *emphasize* in the subhead just above because, in addition to text-based connections, schema-based connections will occur. In your content-area teaching, you will meet students who would benefit from finding and interpreting text-based information (see Fig. 5.3).

When your students bring little prior knowledge to your content area or to specific topics within your content area, you will assist them in learning by using teaching/assessing tools that point to the important information and to interpretations among text-based information. You want them to add information to their schemata in a well-organized manner that will serve them well the next time they study the topic.

Figure 5.3

Finding and Interpreting Information: Strategies That Emphasize Text-Based Connections

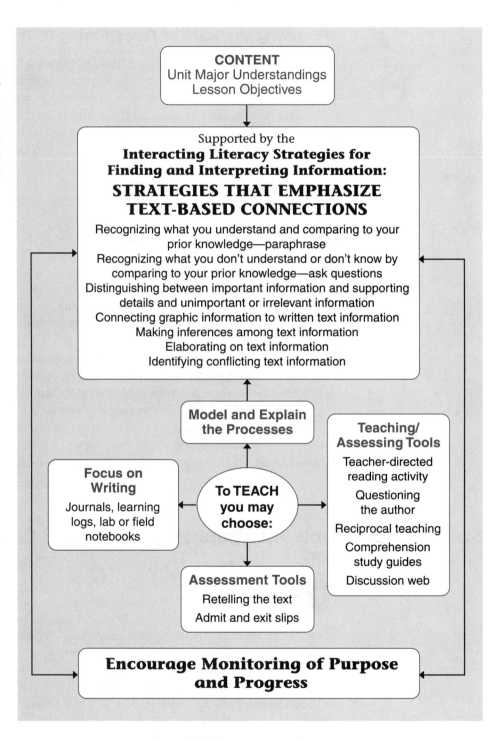

Although your students recognize that they are to learn information from nonfiction texts, especially textbooks, they may not make connections among the text-based information. They may proceed through the task without really thinking and then wonder why they can't recall information or why they missed the significance of the United States' not joining the League of Nations, for example. Many students would benefit from teaching/assessing tools that encouraged them to respond to the text as they read.

▶ ▶ ▶ ▶ ## Modeling and Explaining Strategies That Emphasize Text-Based Connections: A Review of the E-car Script

We positioned the e-car script early in the chapter so that you would gain an overview of the reading process we have labeled as "interacting with ideas." To model and explain the whole process, we included both text-based and schema-based connections, as well as the three supporting strategies. Now let's reexamine that script, concentrating on the text-based connections made.

- *Recognized the article was nonfiction and written to inform.* The clue: The title, "Can electric cars help me breathe easier?" Since strategic readers determine whether the text will match their purpose, they look for text-based cues about the source or author and type or genre of the text. Since the university-based web site was created to inform high school teachers and students about science topics, the source should be reputable. Factual information was presented in the first paragraph, confirming that the article would be informative.

- *Recognized text information that also was in prior knowledge.* The clue: "laws on car emissions." Strategic readers recognize familiar text-based information that is in their schemata. Sometimes readers paraphrase the text-based ideas in their own words to reinforce their understanding.

- *Decided information was irrelevant or not connected to important information.* The clue: "purchasing an e-car." Strategic readers sift through information, and when the author includes interesting or "seductive" details (Garner, Gillingham, & White, 1989), determine the relevance of that information. In this case, buying an e-car may be a future consideration, but it does not directly pertain to the effectiveness question. Strategic readers skip irrelevant information.

- *Identified a new important connection from the text.* The clue: "the relationship between electricity generating plants and e-cars." When using the overall strategy of finding and interpreting important information, strategic readers flag new text-based connections. In this case, the article points out that the origin of electricity is a factor in the effectiveness of e-cars—not just the e-car alone. Strategic readers know to investigate new connections.

- *Categorized specific details.* The clue: "pro facts and con facts regarding e-cars." Strategic readers search for text-based information on which to base their interpretations. Furthermore, strategic readers don't just memorize facts in the order that they read them. Instead, from different sections of the text, they organize the factual details so that they can draw inferences and analyze or synthesize the information—that is, make text-based connections. In this case, the benefits and liabilities of e-cars were categorized so that a comparison could be made and a conclusion about their effectiveness drawn.

- *Reviewed and analyzed the conflicting information.* The clue: "pros and cons of e-cars." Having categorized the text-based information, strategic readers begin to operate on that text-based information. In this case, reviewing the comparison chart led to the identification of conflicting information or no clear-cut conclusion about the effectiveness of e-cars. Strategic readers decide if further research is needed to draw a reasonable conclusion.

Although we have highlighted text-based connections, remember that schema-based connections were present, if to a lesser degree, in the script. Prior knowledge about pollution, car emission laws, and type of text supported the reader's focus on text-based connections. As the reading proceeded, the reader checked into schema-based information to recognize new information and add a problem to the comparison chart. And finally, all of the learned information was added to the schema and actually restructured the old schema, since e-cars may not be as beneficial as they were previously thought to be.

▶ ▶ ▶ ▶ **Teaching/Assessing Tools That Emphasize Text-Based Connections**

Before interacting with ideas, remember that you and your students would have generated ideas by activating prior knowledge, previewing and predicting, and preteaching unknown vocabulary. From generating teaching tools, you might have discovered that your students had meager prior knowledge and that the vocabulary and concepts in the text were difficult for them. When you make those discoveries, you will decide to emphasize text-based connections.

To guide their students in text-based connections for finding and interpreting information (see Figure 5.3), teachers choose to model and explain the strategies so that the connections are visible to students. Teachers also choose to use teaching/assessing tools, when students need more guidance. With some teaching/assessing tools—directed reading activity and questioning the author—the teacher asks questions to guide the students' comprehension as they read. With the teaching/assessing tool of reciprocal teaching, the teacher begins to guide, and then the students take over the guidance. With the tools of comprehension study guides and discussion webs, the teacher structures the students' independent reading and peer discussion. Since the teacher needs to plan the objectives and questions before class, we begin with a section about planning for all of the tools.

Planning for Text-Based Teaching/Assessing Tools. Since these five tools—directed reading activity, questioning the author, reciprocal teaching, comprehension study guides, and discussion webs—are teacher directed or guided, you need to plan your instruction before class. Here is the process you can follow:

1. *Decide the main content objective or understanding for the entire text.* What major idea or theme do you want students to learn or focus on?

2. *Compose one or two higher-level questions* using one of the taxonomies to help you frame the question. Higher-level questions would be at least at the interpretive level and integrate text-based and schema-based connections and set the purpose for reading the entire text. (See Table 5.1.)

3. *Formulate the supporting questions* to help students answer your higher-level question(s). Supporting questions could be literal questions or interpretive text-based connections. Remember that all questions should relate to one another so that your students will build their schemata. (See Table 5.1.)

4. *Decide what vocabulary is important* for your main content objective and the questions you'll be asking. Then you need to decide whether to teach some words before the students read. (Refer back to Chapter 4.)

5. *Decide how to link students' prior knowledge to the information in the text.* (Refer back to Chapter 4.)

6. *Decide whether the students will read the text in its entirety or in sections.* If you divide it into sections, mark the appropriate places to stop and discuss the text.

As we describe using each of the five tools with students and give examples, remember the planning that needs to be done first. We also assume that you and your students will have completed generating activities before using any of these tools.

Directed-Reading Activity (DRA).   Most likely you have experienced the DRA in elementary school when you met with the teacher in reading groups. If you read teachers' manuals for your content area textbooks, you will no doubt realize that their lesson plans are just like the DRA. The manual directs you how to introduce the textbook chapter (prereading), what to emphasize and ask in sections of the chapter (during reading), and, finally, what to review and extend through questions or activities (after reading).

If the text is difficult to read—perhaps it is a primary source document, a scientific report, or even a textbook—then you may decide to guide your students' reading through a whole class DRA. If you have ESL students, students with learning disabilities, or perhaps students who ignore their homework, you may decide to provide direct support in a small group DRA. While you work with this small group, other students may support each other with a comprehension guide (an up-coming guide), for example, or be able to work independently.

Because you guide the students, you also assess how they are learning. If the students are unclear, you would need to stop and explain or provide further information. You also may need to rephrase your questions or ask new questions to help students comprehend the information. Use your content objective to keep yourself focused on what the students are to learn as you assess their progress. When teaching students to find and interpret important information with the DRA, you would use the following steps.

1. *Begin with generating tools, which may be done in any order:*
    a. Introduce the text by activating the students' prior knowledge that relates to the text.
    b. Preteach important, unknown vocabulary words.
    c. Set the purpose for reading the text by stating your higher-level question(s) that will guide the students' comprehension of the entire text.

2. *Use the teaching tool of asking questions.*
    a. Ask a supporting question to guide the students as they read a section of text silently.
    b. Repeat the supporting question and ask additional supporting questions as needed based on your assessment of the students' answers. Use your questions to give students feedback on their understanding. Ask them to clarify their answers, explain their reasons, explain the source of their answer (QAR), and/or read aloud, supporting sections of text. Ask the students to respond to each other's answers, even though in this teacher-centered DRA, students will probably direct their comments to you.

c. Repeat a and b until the text is completed.

d. Return to the higher-level question(s) and discuss the whole text.

3. *Assign refining activities*—for example, summarize the text, write a poem, or draw a map.

Teacher as Inquiring Learner Activity

Select any text appropriate for your content area: a magazine, newspaper, or on-line article; a chapter from a book or textbook; a primary source. As you read the text, think about what is most important for students to learn from the text. Compose your content objective(s).

- What is a higher-level question you could ask? What related supporting questions will help students answer the higher-level question?

    If possible, do a directed reading activity with a small group of students and a text they need to read.

- Do your questions help students find and interpret the important information? Would you change any questions for the next time?

Questioning the Author.   Designed to help students make text-based connections, we think questioning the author (QtA) (Beck, McKeown, Hamilton, & Kucan, 1997) is a useful tool because students typically do not challenge authors, especially textbook authors (Wineburg, 1991). Usually when they read textbooks, students assume that all information is thoroughly explained. However, you know that not all textbooks explain concepts completely, and they make assumptions about students' prior knowledge that might be right or wrong.

Like the DRA, you decide what the important information is and where to segment the text. In deciding the sections, you would note places where you think students should express their understanding of the text, might need more information than the text offers, could be confused by the author's information, or might miss text-based connections across different sections of the text.

At those points in the text, you ask general queries, instead of content questions, to probe students' understanding of the text. Beck et al. (1997, pp. 34, 45) suggest two types of generic queries: initiating queries and follow-up queries. Here are some *initiating queries*:

- What is the author trying to say here?
- What is the author's message?
- What is the author talking about?

For *follow-up queries,* they propose one set for nonfiction text and a different set for fiction text:

Queries for Nonfiction Text

- What does the author mean here?
- Did the author explain this clearly?
- Does this make sense with what the author told us before?
- Does the author tell us why?
- Why do you think the author tells us this now?

Queries for Fiction Text

- How do things look for this character now?
- How has the author let you know that something has changed?
- How has the author settled this for us?
- Given what the author has already told us about this character, what do you think he's up to?

As with the DRA, you need to be ready to respond to students' specific answers with a query tailored to their thinking. You can also ask them to clarify their answers, explain their reasons, or find support in the text. This can be challenging but exciting because you need to assess their thinking in the midst of teaching.

When you decide to use the directed reading activity or questioning the author tools, you have decided that your students need direct teacher support in order to comprehend the text. In the next tool, the teacher models and explains the support and then turns the responsibility over to the students to provide support for each other.

Reciprocal Teaching.   The teaching/assessing tool of reciprocal teaching (Palinscar & Brown, 1984) uses questioning and adds predicting, clarifying, and summarizing. Palinscar and Brown recommend that first the teacher model and explain the comprehension strategies in the following order:

1. Using the title, graphics, subheads, you predict the content of the text selection and explain what clues give you information. (Recall previewing and predicting in Chapter 4.)

2. You and the students read a section of text.

3. You ask the students questions about the section of text. You can explain to the students that the questions point to important text-based and schema-based connections and teach them QAR.

4. You pick a vocabulary word or a section of text to exhibit confusion or misunderstanding. You ask the students to clarify the point for you or search the section of text for information to clarify the point. You would also ask the students if they need clarification about any information. Needless to say, if the point is not sufficiently clarified, then you and the students have a question for the next section of text.

5. You summarize the section of text by stating what you learned or what text-based information was important to remember. You would also explain why the information is important and what text clues you used to summarize. (We discuss more on summaries in Chapter 6.)

6. Having completed one cycle with a section of text, your students now assume the role of the teacher.

We would begin the second cycle by asking the students as a group to contribute their predictions, questions, points needing clarification, and summaries. This collaborative reciprocal teaching could easily continue for a number of lessons with different content-area texts.

As the students gain ease with the four comprehension strategies, different students can assume the role of teacher and lead the group through a section of text. You would participate and offer support or feedback as needed, gradually fading out until the students have complete responsibility for conducting the session with each other. You and the students can also gradually lengthen the sections of text covered in each cycle as students become more adept with the process.

Although we have described reciprocal teaching in a small group situation, we know teachers who have used reciprocal teaching successfully in whole class, partner, and tutorial situations too. Furthermore, teachers have used it successfully with a wide variety of students in many grades: students who are poor comprehenders, students with learning disabilities, and ESL students. A well-researched tool (Rosenshine & Meister, 1994), reciprocal teaching encapsulates the comprehension process and directly teaches those strategies. You know we like tools that make the mystery of reading visible!

So far, we have suggested teaching/assessing tools in which you guide students' reading in class. However, you know that most content-area teachers assign reading to be completed as homework. You also know that some students don't complete that homework, and other students need more support to complete the reading successfully. Completed either in or out of class, study guides provide students with written support during their reading. Study guides can take many different forms. We present two comprehension study guides next, and later in the chapter we present text organization study guides.

Comprehension Study Guides.   In essence, a comprehension study guide is a directed reading activity on paper. We will present two types of comprehension study guides: levels of comprehension guide and learning from text guide.

Levels of Comprehension Guide.   You recall that in the Types of Questions and Answers section, we set out the three levels of comprehension—literal, interpretive, and applied—because Herber (1978) uses those three levels to create his Levels of Comprehension study guides. Although questions can be used for each level, Herber's unique contribution is his recommendation to use statements instead of questions. He maintains that students who have trouble answering questions need to be shown what answers are and how answers for each level differ (see Fig. 5.4).

Before reading the text, the students read the statements on the study guide. Then the students read the text to find supporting information for the statement. After reading the text, the students check the statements they can support with text- and schema-based information. In addition, Herber recommends that the students discuss whether and how they support or don't support the statements. We think this discussion is important because students must defend their answers. Inferential statements can initiate interesting dis-

Figure 5.4

Excerpts from a Levels of Comprehension Guide

Literal Level
_____ 1. Many of the 800,000 children working in agriculture are doing so legally.
_____ 2. Workers are protected from pesticides.

Interpretive Level
_____ 1. One of the reasons Americans can buy inexpensive vegetables is that farmers can hire children to work for them very cheaply.
_____ 2. The large farm owners are more concerned with the welfare of children than with economic competition.

Applied
_____ 1. Sometimes it's okay to break the law if it's the only way you can help your family.
_____ 2. We are all responsible for what happened to Rosa Rubio's son.

cussions as students defend what they think the author implied. As the students defend their answers, you would observe and assess the ideas they support and the reasons they present. You want to know if they can locate appropriate text-based ideas and connect their schema-based ideas to the text.

We have found that creating a three-level guide with statements is an interesting task for teachers because teachers usually ask questions rather than find answers. You create the study guide in the same way you plan for a DRA. Herber recommends these guidelines:

1. Begin with the inferential level, writing statements that connect text-based information and connect the text with the students' schemata.

2. Think about the essential literal information needed for those inferences, and write statements containing that text-based information.

3. Think about how the information could be applied or generalized to broad concepts, abstract principles, or other situations in the community or world.

Although the statement guide is to show students the correct answers, most teachers slip in a statement that cannot be supported by the text. They want to keep the students thinking rather than automatically checking every statement.

Learning-from-Text Guide.   Like Herber's study guide, the learning-from-text guide proceeds from the literal level, to the interpretive level, to the applied or evaluative level (Singer & Donlan, 1980). The difference is that this guide uses questions instead of statements (see Figure 5.5).

Discussion Web.   Look back to the e-car script at the pro and con comparison chart; we used the graphic of *discussion web* (Alvermann, 1991). If the students had read the text independently, they would answer the central question, "Are e-cars an effective solution to pollution?" listing text-based information on opposing sides of the web. After gathering opposing information from the text, students would come to a consensus about their position or a conclusion about e-car effectiveness.

To foster more student participation, Alvermann recommends that the teacher gradually increase the discussion group size (also called Think, Pair, Share by Gambrell & Almasi, 1994). First, pairs of students read the text, individually or together, and record their ideas on a web. Then two pairs meet as a small group to compare their webs. After debating their reasons, the students reach a consensus on the issue. Each small group then presents its conclusion, solution, or point of view to the whole class. If a group can't reach a consensus, the dissenters may present their point of view in a minority report.

Figure 5.5

Learning-from-Text
Guide

Following the Stock Market

In the stock table in the business section of the newspaper, locate one of your stocks, and answer the following questions with your partner. When you finish, find your partner's stock and again answer the questions.

Literal Level
1. What is the name of the stock you're checking?
2. What stock market is the stock traded through?
3. What was the highest price paid for the stock during the past year?
4. What was the closing price of the stock yesterday?

Inferential Level
1. Will you buy or sell the stock? Why or why not?
2. Should you have bought more stock last year?
3. How does your stock compare to a stock in a similar company—for example, Apple and Intel?

Generalization or Evaluative Level
1. Do you think this is a bull or bear market? Support your opinion.

Once again, you would assess the students' defense of text-based connections and schema-based connections to the text. You can encourage different solutions from different groups. Primarily you want to know if the groups reached reasonable solutions that they can support.

Alvermann suggests adaptations of the discussion web for different content areas by changing the labels on either side of the central question. For math word problems, the problem's question would be in the center and the side labels would be "Relevant Information" and "Irrelevant Information." In science, the labels could be opposing hypotheses—"Hypothesis 1" versus "Hypothesis 2." For social studies and English, the names of people or characters, respectively, with different points of view would be the two labels.

▶ ▶ ▶ ▶ **Assessment Tools That Emphasize Text-Based Connections**

We predict that you have regularly experienced questions as an assessment tool during your schooling. We know that many teachers give a "Friday quiz" or an end-of-unit test. But in this chapter, we are looking at questions as part of the teaching/learning experience. We advocate that you use questions to help students find and interpret information by giving them feedback. Questions that produce discussion about the information help students comprehend text-based connections and help them make schema-based connections.

Retelling.   We use retelling when we want students to recall what they have read without any clues from our questions. Because a *retelling* is usually an individual assessment, we use it when we are puzzled about how well a student comprehends a text independently. Our purpose is to learn what the student thinks is important to remember—that is, the student's text-based connections.

In our experience, students often give very short answers when asked to retell. They state the topic of a nonfiction text without any details or elaboration. For a fiction text, they identify the main character and mention an event. Unlike a summary, a retelling of nonfiction should contain not only the topic but the main ideas and the details that explain that important information. A retelling of a fictional text should include main characters and the details of the setting, plot, and problem the plot turns on.

Students may give short answers because they have not been asked to retell before. To cue the student that you want an elaborate retelling, you may want to phrase your request like:

- "Tell me everything you remember about . . . "
- "Start from the beginning and tell me everything that has happened so far."

You may also ask the student to tell you more about a concept or a character he or she mentioned. Until the student clearly can recall no more, you can continue to ask:

- "What else do you remember about the topic?"
- "What did the character do next?"

Then you can ask the student questions about important information he or she neglected to mention. The student may be able to recall more information after you have prompted with your questions.

Since students usually retell only literal information, you may want to ask questions beyond that literal level—questions about text-based connections and questions about schema-based connections. You will want to know if the students can offer an opinion about the action or a character or relate actions or characters to their own lives. With nonfiction text, you will want to know if students can connect information across text or relate the information to their observations or experiences.

Admit and Exit Slips.   Teachers often want a quick reading on their students' understanding of the concepts, readings, and assignments. *Admit* and *exit slips* are quick comments written on index cards at the beginning or end of class, respectively. Anonymously students tell the teacher their confusions, their reactions, their frustrations, and even their celebrations.

For example, math teacher Don Schmidt uses admit slips as an avenue for students to communicate anonymously with him and as a tool to build a sense of community among the students (see Figs 5.6-5.8). At the beginning of class, every student writes a quick note anonymously, but it can't contain nasty language or hurtful comments about another person. After shuffling the notes, Schmidt reads a random selection aloud to the class (Schmidt, 1985). From these three figures, you can see that Schmidt thus learns about his students' feelings about math, their understandings of concepts, and their

Figure 5.6

Admit Slip Example

> *Page 227 was hard.*
> *Mr. Schmidt,*
> *Can you explain 227 to me today?*
> *Thanks.*

Source: From *Roots in Sawdust: Writing across the Disciplines* by A. R. Gere. Copyright © 1985 by the National Teachers of English. Reprinted with permission.

Figure 5.7

Admit Slip Example

> *Hi class,*
> *Friday's algebra homework was too difficult for the average dumb student.*
> *Dumb student*

Source: Ibid.

Figure 5.8

Admit Slip Example

> The math test I thought was a good idea. It helped me to see what I had to review before going into algebra next year. I don't think I did too well on the second and third pages, but now I know what to expect in algebra. Now I can review all of it before going to high school. (p.107)

Source: Ibid.

reactions to tests, activities, and assignments. The students learn that others are either struggling or celebrating too. The opportunity to write allows students to reflect on events and reconsider their opinions.

Exit slips are the reverse of admit slips. Students write a quick note at the end of class. You may want immediate feedback before you plan the next day's lesson. What did they understand, have problems with, need help on, or complete easily? You could read the exit slips aloud at the beginning of the next class and use them to lead into the day's agenda.

▶ ▶ ▶ ▶ ### Focus on Writing: Writing to Learn in Journals, Learning Logs, and Lab or Field Notebooks

Teachers sometimes ask students to record their information, explain their understanding, and examine their learning processes in journals. You want students to express in their own words how they understand the text and how they understood class discussions and activities.

In science classes, students can record their procedures and their observations in a lab or field notebook. As the science teacher, you would review these notebooks for the students' understanding of the concepts and their learning processes. Have they entered predictions or hypotheses? Are they appropriately reconsidering their previous ideas? Notice the questions or hypotheses the high school student records in this entry:

> In lab, we are making models of molecules with different bonds, and have just made a butane molecule that has free bond rotation. Even though they have the capability of doing so, why would they? Also what makes them move? Kinetic energy? I wonder what the world would be like if there was not free-bound rotation—really cold? (Lozauskas & Barell, p. 44)

In math, students can record how they solved a particular set of problems. As the math teacher, you would assess how effective their strategies were in solving the problem. Did they find the important information and ignore irrelevant information? You and the students would assess not just whether the answers were correct but how they arrived at their answers. Students could compare the strategies they used to arrive at their answers. They may discover that they could solve the problems in more than one way. In the following entry, a high school student records her problem-solving process:

> To find the x-intercepts for a problem like this,
> $(x + 2)(x + 3) = x^2 + 5x + 6$.

> You would set it up equal to 0 and you would get −2 and −3. You need to find the x-intercepts so you can graph it. If you get a trinomial that you cannot

set equal to zero, you will have to use the quadratic formula. Finding the y-intercepts, you look at the equation and take the number without the x. Such as above, 6 would be the y-intercept. (Pugalee, 1997, p. 309)

English teachers want students to explain their understanding of characters, events, the author's choice of words, and the author's use of literary devices. Students could also speculate on what they expect to happen or how they expect characters to act or change.

Although we have emphasized text-based connections in this section of the chapter, we hope you recognize that schema-based connections should be made too. You want your students to negotiate between text and schema whenever they read and at any point during their reading. So although we have emphasized text-based connections, we welcome schema-based connections whenever they foster a more complete understanding of content information. At times, we emphasize schema-based connections, the next topic.

Strategies and Tools That Emphasize Schema-Based Connections

You recall that we discussed schema-based connections in Chapter 4 when we looked at activating prior knowledge. As we return to a discussion of schema, we assume that students' schemata have been activated using generating strategies.

Earlier in this chapter in the e-car script, you found that schema-based connections were made even though text-based connections were more prevalent:

- From the schema, **prior knowledge was activated** about e-cars and about the purpose and type of text—an information article.
- **Schema-based information was matched to text-based information**—California law about car emissions.
- **Schema-based information about how texts can be organized** was used to recognize that the e-car text had a comparison organization.
- At the end, **schema-based information was reconstructed** by the new text-based information.

Just as schemata were not ignored when text-based connections dominated, text-based connections cannot be ignored when schema-based connections are made.

Figure 5.9

Finding and Interpreting Information: Strategies and Tools That Emphasize Schema-Based Connections

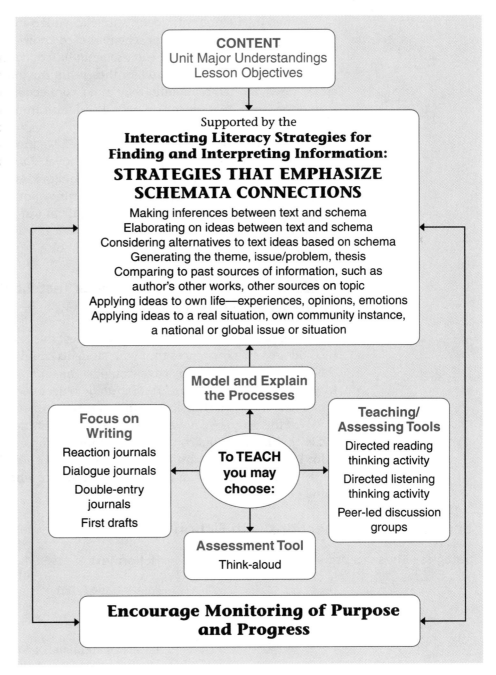

When interacting with ideas, strategic readers make inferences and elaborate on ideas, connecting their schema-based knowledge to the text-based information (see Fig. 5.9). From their schema-based ideas, they think about implied ideas like the theme, issue, or thesis that the author does not explicitly state. Based on their schemata, they make connections to other sources of information, their own life, or an actual situation in their community, the nation, or the world.

To demonstrate some of these strategies, we present a modeling and explaining script with an excerpt from a first novel, *Parrot in the Oven mi vida,* by Victor Martinez, who won the 1996 National Book Award for young adult literature. A Mexican American himself, Martinez portrayed a year in Manuel Hernandez's life through scenarios with his out-of-work father, his trailer-cleaning mother, his older sister and brother, his toddling sister, as well as friends and gang members in and out of school.

▶ ▶ ▶ ▶ **Modeling and Explaining Strategies That Emphasize Schema-Based Connections**

If you are an English teacher, you might select this book because Martinez depicts adolescent experiences that your students could compare and contrast to their own. Your content objective would be the understanding that fiction portrays the human condition. Your strategy objective would be for students to make schema-based connections to their own lives.

For this script, we have skipped generating strategies because we want to focus on schema-based connections within finding and interpreting information. You know that in an actual situation, we would have generated ideas with students first. As you read this script, notice where the reader begins to think about the theme:

Schema-Based Connections with Fiction Text

Strategies I Chose to Use	Fiction Text
	Parrot in the Oven mi vida by Victor Martinez
	To Mom's surprise, Dad actually found a job doing office work for the Awoni Building Company. To everyone's surprise, Nardo got a job delivering medicine for Giddens's Pharmacy. I helped him with his route on Saturdays. (p. 159)
Remembering when I was a teenager, I worked Saturdays and summers as did my friends. **(connecting to my life)**	

I **visualize** a small-town drugstore with a mousy Mr. Giddens in the back filling prescriptions.

I have an ominous feeling reading this text—"against the nagging in my head" and "sizing me up." I sense a conflict between Manuel and Mr. Giddens that's based on cultural differences. **(making inferences between text and schema)**

Here is confirmation of my feeling: trouble is coming. Why does Mr. Giddens want to introduce Manuel to his daughter?

Not knowing Manuel's last name is a signal of class and cultural differences. I think an underlying prejudice is operating here. **(inferring alternatives to text ideas based on schema)**

Why is Mr. Giddens inviting Manuel? This is a cultural clash. Dorothy doesn't want to bridge their differences. Manuel can only get hurt. Can't he see the danger? **(thinking about the theme or issue)**

. . . [A]gainst the nagging in my head, I stepped inside [the drugstore]. . . .

From the corner of my eye, I saw Mr. Giddens sizing me up. (p. 161) . . .

[Then] I saw Dorothy, Mr. Giddens's daughter, although I didn't know her name or who she was at the time. (p. 163)

. . .

When she saw me, she smiled, like she recognized me, then turned back around to Mr. Giddens who looked at me like suddenly an idea had popped into his head.

"Oh, Manuel! Could you come over here a minute," he said, sending his arm around in a little corral. "I want to introduce you to my daughter."

He kept circling his hand for me to come over, but I couldn't get my shoes to budge. Something was screwed on wrong. Mr. Giddens inviting me over to introduce me to his daughter wasn't natural. . . .

"Dorothy, this is one of my delivery boys, Manuel, uh, Hernandez—or is it Herrera?" . . .

"Hi, Dorothy!" I said, anxious to meet her, yet stiffening a little against Mr. Giddens's push.

"Hi," she said smiling.

She wanted to talk more with her father, but he didn't want to. (pp. 164–165)

"Would you like to come to Dorothy's party? Lots of food and punch?"

He said this enthusiastically, wiping his face with a handkerchief, but while he did, Dorothy was tightening her shoulders and her smile collapsed a little. "Dad!!" she said, stressing her voice. (p. 166) . . .

"Well," I said. I didn't know what to say, really; didn't know what was going on. Whatever was going on, though, I knew words wouldn't help.

Strategies I Chose to Use

I remember the feelings of being outside the popular group. At times, I wanted to be inside, like Manuel, while at other times, I was content to have fun with my own friends. **(connecting ideas to own life)**

From my vantage point, I want Manuel to resist, but I know I probably would not have when I was a teenager. The desire to be accepted is too strong for teenagers to resist.

He vaguely recognizes the prejudice of the Giddenses now. Later when he's hurt, he has directly experienced prejudice. **(applying ideas to a real situation and issue)**

Fiction Text

"But he won't *know* anybody," Dorothy pleaded.

"That's what you'll be there for, honey," Mr. Giddens said with assurance, "to introduce him around, make him feel welcome. I'm positive he'll have a good time."

"Okay . . . okay. I give up!" Dorothy said, gritting her teeth and dropping her arms, exasperated. She handed me an invitation card. "Here, you're invited," she said halfheartedly. (p. 167)

. . .

Before walking out of the door, Dorothy turned and smiled. It was a smile that would tumble around inside my brain for days. I wanted to believe that it meant that somehow she'd changed her mind about me, and that I'd be welcome at her party, but deep down I knew it didn't. In any case I didn't care, and only later, when I realized that I *should* have cared, did it really hurt. (pp. 168–169)

Source: Text copyright © 1996 by Victor Martinez. Used by permission of HarperCollins Publishers.

In summary, when I read *Parrot in the Oven* I made schema-based connections and linked them to text-based connections in order to find and interpret the information:

- I **applied ideas to own life** (recalled my high school experiences).
- I **elaborated on ideas** from the text (remembered teen jobs).
- I **made inferences** between my text and schema (ominous feeling about an impending clash of cultures).
- I **generated a theme or issue** for the chapter (encountering cultural clash).
- I **applied ideas to real situations** (realistically knew Manuel couldn't resist, although I wished he would).

Earlier in this chapter, we emphasized teaching/assessing tools in which the teacher directs the focus of the discussion through questions. Now we focus on connections that students initiate. When you teach, you will decide when to be directive, because your students need to understand particular concepts and when to be open-ended, because you want to follow your students' selection of concepts and their reactions or their thinking about those ideas.

▶ ▶ ▶ ▶ **Teaching/Assessing Tools That Emphasize Schema-Based Connections**

Although these tools are student centered, emphasizing their schema-based connections, you would be wise to prepare backup questions or prompts in case a group is floundering. The first tool is a hybrid because the teacher guides the students' responses. The second tool, peer-led discussions, is obviously student centered. The students pose the questions, govern the course of the discussion, and challenge each other's understanding of the text. You may be a participant or provide support if necessary, but the students have the major responsibility for learning. For these discussions, you may decide to have the students read the same text or read a variety of texts on a theme.

Directed Reading (or Listening) Thinking Activity. This activity is similar to the teaching/assessing tools in the text-based connections section, but remember that the DRA and QtA, as well as the others, were focused on the teacher's objective. We have classified the DR-TA/DL-TA as student centered because the students make and verify their own predictions about sections of the text (Stauffer, 1969). Because sometimes students understand texts better when those texts are read aloud to them, we have included the DL-TA as an alternative. As the students read (DR-TA) or listen (DL-TA) to text, the teacher guides the process but follows the students' understanding of the text.

In the DR-TA with either fiction or nonfiction text, you would use the following steps:

1. You *elicit your students' predictions* based on their schemata and the clues from the title, graphics, subheads, or even the opening paragraph. You may want to encourage divergent predictions. You may ask:
   - "What do you think the story will be about?"
   - "What do you think you will learn from this text?"
   - "Why do you make that prediction?"

2. You ask the *students to read silently to an appropriate stopping place* using their predictions as the purpose for their reading.

3. After reading that section, you *ask the students whether their predictions still make sense* and discuss what in the text leads them to support, reject, or modify their predictions. You can also ask whether they found unexpected information or events. If students express confusion, you would refer them to the text or another student for clarification. Their confusions might become purposes or predictions to guide their reading of the next section of text.

4. You *ask the students to keep, modify, or devise new predictions* for the next section of text.

   • "What will happen next? What will the character do in this situation?"

   • "What will be the significant information we will learn about next? What information do you need to support your hypothesis or generalization? What information do you need clarified?"

5. You and the students *recycle through the steps* to the end of the text.

6. At the end, the students can *discuss their reactions* to the text and extend their learning to other situations—schema-based connections.

For nonstrategic learners, the DR-TA/DL-TA tool is an intermediate step combining teacher support and independent student thinking about text. As students become experienced in making, verifying, and modifying their predictions, they could lead the discussion in small groups or pairs.

While you are guiding students through the text, you are certainly assessing what schema-based and text-based connections the students make. You want to notice what clues students use to make the predictions; what support they cite for keeping, rejecting, or modifying their predictions; and how reasonable, sensible, and thoughtful their thinking is.

Now let's turn to peer-led discussions in which the teacher may be an equal participant, or maybe not a member at all.

Peer-Led Discussions.   In the teaching/assessing tools for text-based connections, we presented the DRA, QtA, reciprocal teaching, and discussion webs; in all of these, the teacher governs the discussions. Although we labeled those events as discussions, they are definitely school discussions designed to accomplish the teacher's objective. Outside of school, real discussions are governed by the participants who often have differing views about the topic.

We use the general term *peer-led discussions* because we want to refer to every content area. English and language arts teachers may encounter other similar terms, such as *book clubs* (McMahon & Raphael, 1997), *literature circles* (Short & Pierce, 1990), and *grand conversations* (Eeds & Wells, 1989). Most other content areas use the term *small group discussion*, although *idea circles* has been coined for discussions of science texts (Guthrie & McCann, 1996).

In discussions, equal participants address a common issue—for example, math proofs, scientific evidence, or poetry reactions—in which the exchange of different views will augment the participants' understanding, appreciation, or actions (Dillon, 1994). We classify discussions as peer led when the following characteristics are present (Dillon, 1994):

As equal participants in the group, the teacher and the students discuss their understandings, reactions, and questions regarding the book being studied in their content-area class.

© Joel Gordon

- Students talk directly to each other.
- Students ask questions of each other.
- Students' statements are longer than two or three words.
- Teachers ask questions for which they honestly don't know the answer (real questions!).
- Teachers are mostly silent and do not direct the speaking turns.
- Teachers occasionally reflect or rephrase a student's thought, connect two students' statements, or state their own genuine thoughts or interests.

As you see, we don't eliminate the teacher as a participant; however, the teacher is only a facilitator or coach. In essence, by offering statements and evidence to support their statements, students discover what they think and are challenged by what other students think.

Initiating Discussions. We think that genuine discussion can occur when a teacher initiates the discussion by asking a higher-level question, stating a problem or issue, or simply asking for student reactions. Although teachers may initiate peer-led discussions with a prompt, experienced discussants may find their own reactions or issues more engaging and ignore the prompt (Alvermann et al., 1996). When that happens, teachers must remember that the objective is for students to react thoughtfully, not necessarily to address the prompt.

Genuine discussion can occur as well when students initiate the issues. Peer-led discussions can lead to more complex and longer student responses, more questions, and more alternative interpretations than the teacher-led discussions primarily because teachers dominate their teacher-led discussions with text-explicit questions (Almasi, 1995). Your students can lead discussions if you help them prepare for the discussions.

Teachers require students to come prepared to the group discussion (students don't always comply!). Sometimes students respond first in their journals as they read (see the Focus on Writing section below for more information). Students may complete freewriting or a drawing in class before the discussion. Teacher Eric Paulsen has students mark important passages with small sticky notes on which students write a key word to remind them of the idea they want to discuss (Daniels, 1994).

When students are just beginning to work in peer-led discussions, teachers may assign roles to the students and rotate the roles among the students for each discussion session. Daniels (1994) assigns roles to the group members, for example, Discussion Director (asks questions), Vocabulary Enricher (defines words), Connector (links book to the world and other books), and Summarizer. During peer-led discussions, each student presents his or her contribution for the group to discuss. After students have experienced the different roles and practiced them in several peer-led discussions, they know how to respond during their own reading and how to participate in groups. Then the roles are no longer formally assigned. Instead, students assume a role whenever they have that information to contribute.

Guidelines for Holding Peer-Led Discussions.   Forming the group is the first task. We prefer small groups of about five students—large enough to produce different views and small enough so that each student has a reasonable chance to speak. Depending on the class or the particular unit, we sometimes assign students to groups and at other times allow students to form friendship groups. Experienced discussants prefer to work with peers who contribute to the discussion, whether they are friends or not (Alvermann et al., 1996).

1.   You know that the first guideline is for all students to talk without fear of put-down or ridicule. Only then will diverse views be expressed.

2.   Students need to listen to understand the meaning, not just the words, of every student's contribution. You know that some students, like ESL students, are particularly reluctant to speak out even in small group dis-

cussions. When ESL students and students with learning disabilities gain experience with small groups, they will participate and maybe even lead them (Goatley, Brock, & Raphael, 1995).

3. Students need to be clear about the task before the group in order to be productive. Whether the task is to explore diverse reactions or to focus on the teacher's prompt, the students learn to monitor their on-task production. Students learn that they have complementary responsibilities—to talk and to listen, as well as to focus on the topic and explore different perspectives. In an exploratory mode (Short, 1992), students wander off topics, meander around various topics, and appear not to complete topics they begin to explore. Nevertheless, engaged students return to important connections, keep each other centered on important questions or positions, and reintroduce burning issues. When students know that the expectation is a mutual exploration of ideas and the topic is interesting or debatable, they will keep each other reasonably on task (Alvermann et al., 1996).

4. The last task in peer-led discussions is a debriefing session in which each group evaluates how the discussion proceeded compared to a list of criteria for the whole class. When a particular criterion is hard to achieve, such as valuing everyone's point of view, then we make that an objective to focus on during the next discussion. Sometimes we have used the *fishbowl technique*. A small group sits in the center and holds their discussion. In a circle around the center group, the rest of the students sit and take notes on how the discussion is proceeding. After the discussion, the class debriefs, citing the criteria met and the criteria needing improvement. At no time should an individual be singled out by name; instead students describe behaviors that did or did not contribute to the discussion.

▶ ▶ ▶ ▶ Assessment Tool for Strategies That Emphasize Schema-Based Connections

The purpose of the think-aloud tool is to determine the reader's strategies and the schema-based and text-based connections he or she makes. Thus, we could have placed the think-aloud with text-based connections just as easily.

For inquiry activities, we suggested in Chapter 1 that you complete a think-aloud and in Chapter 2 that a student complete a think-aloud. You might want to have another student complete a think-aloud now that you have been reading about strategies.

When teachers are puzzled about a student's learning process, they may ask that student to think aloud as he or she works on a task. Then the teacher can figure out the strategies and the information that the puzzling student is using during the task. A teacher we know asks her whole class to think aloud quietly with text. The students write their thoughts, questions, and reactions on sticky notes, which they stick on the pages. Later she carefully examines the comments written by the one or two students who were puzzling her and only quickly surveys the comments from other students.

When you use a think-aloud to assess whether students find and interpret important information, you are noticing examples of both text-based and schema-based connections outlined in Table 5.2. After the think-aloud, you would discuss the student's specific comments with the student. You want the student to be aware of the strategies that he or she used well. You might also ask questions about strategies that could be used.

▶ ▶ ▶ ▷ Focus on Writing: Journals and First Drafts

Journals and first drafts of a writing are often exploratory. The writer is investigating ideas, discovering meaning, and making connections between the text he or she is writing, the text he or she has read, and his or her own schema-based ideas.

Reaction Journals, Dialogue Journals, and Double-Entry Journals. Teachers often use journals when they want students to make connections as they interact with ideas. They model and explain with students how to respond in journals by writing in a journal themselves. Since the management of many

Table 5.2   Connections to Assess During a Think-Aloud

Text-Based Connections	Schema-Based Connections
Comments on the important information	Comments by inferring or elaborating on ideas
Translates information into their own words	Speculates on the theme or thesis of the text
Comments on what they don't understand	Suggests alternative actions or solutions from own experiences or knowledge
Comments how later text relates to previous text	Comments on ideas from past sources read
Comments how the graphics clarify or augment the words	Comments on real situations from own life or own community

journals from different classes becomes a juggling act, you will want to devise a reasonable schedule for assessing their journals. Some teachers respond during class, ask students to label certain entries to which they respond, or respond to five journals per class each night. We know that finding time to respond can be irksome; however, students will use their journals more thoughtfully if you carve out time to respond.

We have already suggested that students prepare for discussions by writing in journals. Students can respond in three versions of journals:

- *Reaction journal* (the generic version). The student records questions, ideas, thoughts, drawings, comments, predictions, or any other connections to the text.

- *Dialogue journal*—a reaction journal that has a respondent. Usually the teacher responds, but peer respondents work too. The student and the respondent hold a written conversation about the text. In conversing with the students, teachers build on the students' connections, offer connections to their own lives, probe for more information, and question the students' thoughts.

- *Double-entry journal*, in which the page is divided in half vertically. In Chapter 1, we suggested that you keep an inquiry field notebook in double-entry form. As a reaction journal, the student uses one side of the page to write a summary of the text or notes about the text. On the opposite half, the student records his or her reactions triggered by that text.

When Whitin (1996) used reaction journals in her seventh-grade class, the students responded to literature with both writing and drawing. Using the *sketch-to-stretch* technique (Harste, Short, & Burke, 1988), the students drew their interpretations of themes, characters, conflicts, and feelings using symbols, colors, shapes, lines, and textures. Whenever they drew, the students explained how their drawings represented their ideas to Whitin, the class, or their collaborative group. Heidi, one of the students, chose to sketch a pie chart to represent the feelings of Perry in *Fallen Angels* by Walter Dean Myers. She explained the chart also in her journal (see Fig. 5.10).

Let's look at the two scripts you already read in this chapter and the reactions we might look for if students were writing in journals. First, for the excerpt about Manuel, you might assess the types of connections that students included in their journals:

- Did they apply the events and emotions to their own lives?
- Did they make inferences about the characters and their actions? For example, did they discuss why Mr. Giddens is insisting that Manny be invited?
- Did they elaborate on or discuss the prejudicial behavior of the characters or of people in their own lives?

Figure 5.10

Pie Chart and Journal
Response for <u>Fallen
Angels</u>

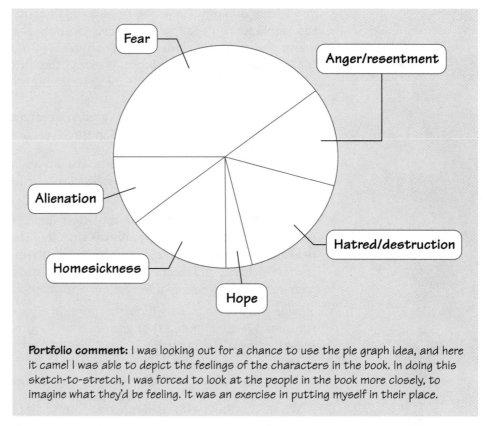

Portfolio comment: I was looking out for a chance to use the pie graph idea, and here it came! I was able to depict the feelings of the characters in the book. In doing this sketch-to-stretch, I was forced to look at the people in the book more closely, to imagine what they'd be feeling. It was an exercise in putting myself in their place.

Source: From *Research in the Teaching of English*, 30,(1), p. 124. Copyright © 1996 by the National Council of Teachers of English.

- Did they suggest any alternatives for Manny to consider? What would they do in his situation?
- Did they identify any elements in Martinez's prose?
- Did they make any connections among the chapters in the book to form any thematic statements about the book or generalizations about life?

Second, for nonfiction text, such as the e-car text, you would assess students' journals for the concepts that they understood. You might look for the following connections:

- Did they understand the overarching concept: e-cars' effectiveness depends on the local source of electricity?
- Did they make connections among the concepts and compare the pros and cons?

- Did they elaborate on the concepts or just reiterate the information literally?
- Did they make connections to their chemistry knowledge?
- Did they include graphic information or make connections to graphic information?
- Did they compare current concepts and information to past sources of information, such as class activities or other readings on pollution solutions?
- Did they apply the concepts to events, observations, or real situations in the natural world or in their society? Did anyone comment about pollution in their own community or in places like Los Angeles or Aspen?

From reading students' journals, you would assess what connections the students make independently. Then you would emphasize text-based and schema-based connections they don't make in a mini-lesson and encourage those connections in your responses in their journals.

First Drafts. Writing a first draft means interacting with ideas—figuring out what ideas are important and how to interpret that information. Some writers explore their major ideas and even details when they generate ideas. Writers who know their purpose, their audience, and their genre or format can generate most of the ideas they will include in their drafts. Nevertheless, turning notes into sentences is not always a simple task, and a first draft can go easily or bumpily. We recommend using graphic organizers or outlines to flesh out ideas to include (refer back to Chapter 4).

Some writers need to compose a *discovery draft* to find ideas—that is, a very tentative draft written after generating sketchy ideas and by means of which the writers seek to discover new ideas and meanings. Sometimes a discovery draft is a freewriting. A discovery draft is useful because the writer can actually see the ideas in sentences and revise them.

All first drafts, especially discovery drafts, are just that: drafts meant to be revised. (We discuss revision in Chapter 6.) Now let's turn to the three supporting strategies that students may need to find and interpret important information.

Three Supporting Strategies and Tools

When people interact with ideas, their goal is to find and interpret information by negotiating text-based and schema-based information. Not all texts are easy to read and not all information is simple to remember, so strategic learners rely on three supporting strategies to assist them in finding and interpreting information: they capitalize on text organization, construct auxiliary aids, and independently learn new vocabulary (see Fig. 5.11).

▶ ▶ ▶ ▷ Capitalizing on Text Organization

Sometimes readers have difficulty finding where important text-based information is located or separating important information from less important or irrelevant information. In this situation, strategic readers use their schema-based knowledge to capitalize on text organization to assist them in finding and interpreting important information and in recalling that information later (Myer, Brandt, & Bluth, 1980; Taylor, 1980). Before we begin our discussion of tools, let's examine two basic categories of text organization: narrative text organization and expository text organization.

Two Basic Categories of Text Organization.   We usually divide text organization into narrative (fiction) organization or structure and expository (non-fiction) organizations or structures. However, authors are not so cleanly categorized. For example, journalists sometimes use the narrative organization to communicate factual information. We will present only generic text organizations for narrative and expository texts, but we encourage you and your students to explore specific organizations that authors use in your content area.

Narrative Text Organization.   From the Iliad to current movies, people have encountered original variations of the generic *story structure* or *story grammar* (Stein & Glenn, 1979; Mandler & Johnson, 1977)—for example:

- Setting—time, place, main characters

- Problem and goal

- Plot or sequence of events
  Event 1—attempt and outcome
  Event 2—attempt and outcome
  Event 3—attempt and outcome

- Resolution of problem and attainment of goal

Not every author follows these elements; for example, some books have an unresolved ending. However, you can probably name books and movies that exhibit those elements.

Figure 5.11   Three Supporting Strategies and Teaching Tools

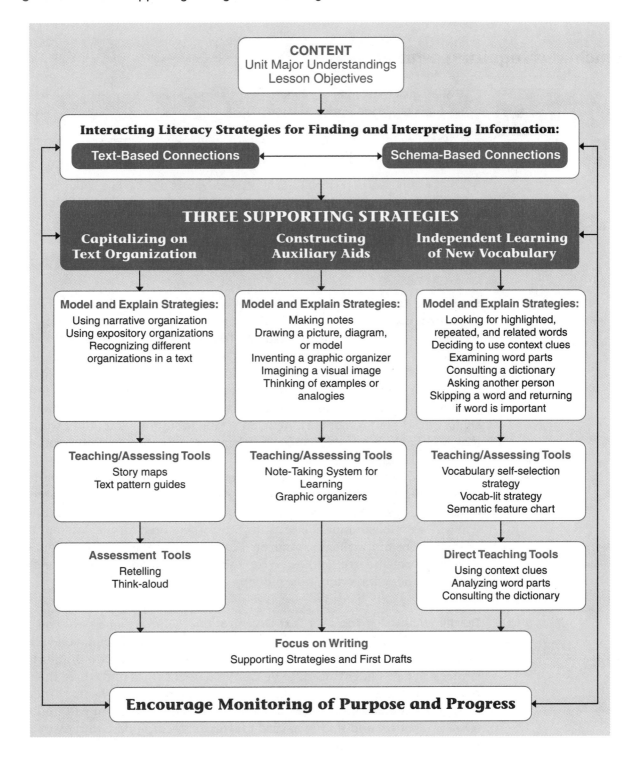

Teacher as Inquiring Learner Activity

Explore different types of fiction or short stories to see how the types compare to the generic story grammar.

- What elements do different authors include? What elements do different authors change?

   Alternatively, you may want to compare fables and folktales from different cultures. For example, the librarian could help you find the cultural variations of the Cinderella story.

- Do tales from different cultures exhibit similar elements?

Expository Text Organization.   Nonfiction writers use a wide variety of text organizations. Think about how differently front-page news reports and directions for a game are organized. Writers may use a single organization throughout the text, although often writers combine different text organizations. For example, authors writing history often combine chronological and cause-and-effect organizations when they explain the events leading to the American Revolution. Sometimes authors indicate the text's organization by signal words—but sometimes they don't. (See Table 5.3.) You might want to look back to the e-car script and note when the comparison organization was signaled and when it was not.

   Whether the writer used a single organization and signal words or multiple organizations without signal words will determine how difficult the comprehension task will be for your students (Hare, Rabinowitz, & Schieble, 1989). You will want to examine the texts in your content area for the different text organizations that writers in your field commonly use. In addition, you will want to model and explain how to capitalize on text organization for finding and for recalling important information. (See the e-car script.)

Teaching/Assessing Tools for Text Organization.   From the questions you ask during a DRA or QtA or from a student's retelling or think-aloud, you will be able to assess whether a student uses text organization as a supporting strategy. When students seem to be confused about what and where the important information is, we recommend introducing a guide to the text's organization. Although we have used the term *text organization*, you will find the terms *text pattern* and *story map* used to refer to specific guides that assist students with text organization.

Table 5.3   Expository Text Organizations and Common Signal Words

Text Organization	Signal Words
Sequence, chronology, biography, life cycle, procedures	*a specific date, now, then, before, after, when, first, second, finally*
Cause and effect, causal chain of events	*because, consequently, as a result, thus, therefore, since, if . . . then*
Problem-solution, hypothesis-results	*because, consequently, as a result, thus, therefore, since, if . . . then*
Persuasion, argument	*therefore, thus, if . . . then, because, since*
Comparison and contrast, similarities and differences	*but, although, yet, however, while, either . . . or, neither . . . nor, on the other hand, more than, less than*
Main idea and supporting details, topic and attributes or examples	*for instance, for example, one . . . another*
Collection or topic and list of items in no particular order	*next, then, and, one . . . another*

Story Maps for Narrative Texts.   From their past fiction reading, many of your students will have the common elements of a story in their schemata. However, you will want to use a *story map* to support their reading in the following situations:

- Your students cannot recognize story elements in familiar books.
- Time switches like flashbacks or foreshadowing complicate the text's plot.
- Significant events, like a character's mental states, are difficult to follow.

Even high school students have difficulty following the mental states of Henry Fleming in *The Red Badge of Courage*.

A story map can take different forms. Some teachers outline the story elements, as we did earlier in the chapter. After each element, the students record the specific details as they read. When students read quest, survival, or adventure stories, a circle graphic organizer may capture the character's journey from "home," through trials, and back to "home." "Home" may be a physical place, or it could represent a mental state, with the events serving as episodes in the character's development or growth.

Text Pattern Guides for a Single Organization Pattern.   We think expository text organization is more difficult than narrative text organization because students have less experience with nonfiction texts. Even if students haven't themselves read many stories, they have heard stories when people talk about events in their lives. But people don't talk in expository organizations, giving the main topic and then supporting details. Therefore, we prefer to teach expository text organizations directly by modeling and explaining, discussing text organizations with students, and creating text pattern guides for students to use while they read (Armbruster, Anderson, & Ostertag, 1987; Taylor & Beach, 1984).

When you create a *text pattern guide* for students, your goal is to show students how text organization can lead to the important information and how to connect information across sections of the text or interpret information. You will want to begin with a text that has a single, clear organization. Here are the guidelines:

1. Examine the text to determine how the author organized the information: sequence, cause and effect, problem solution, comparison and contrast, main idea and supporting details, persuasion or argument, listing or collection.

2. Determine whether the author used signal words explicitly to highlight the text organization.

3. Create a graphic organizer that depicts the text organization. You may decide to complete part of the graphic organizer to assist the students or have the students fill in all of the graphic organizer. The graphic organizer in Fig. 5.12 is designed to guide students in describing the roles and hierarchy of ancient Egyptian society.

4. Have the students read the text and fill in the text pattern guide.

When they have completed the guide, you would have the students discuss the information in small groups or with the whole class.

Text Pattern Guides for Discerning Mixed Organization Patterns.   Many texts, in particular textbooks, are not pure; that is, different sections of the text may use two or more organizations. Your students may become confused by mixed organizations and need help in locating the important information. In such cases, you could create a text pattern guide to direct students to the information you want them to concentrate on.

For example, in "Traveling the Long Road to Freedom, One Step at a Time," the author, Donovan Webster, relates historian Anthony Cohen's experiences in retracing the routes runaway slaves took on the Underground

Figure 5.12

Graphic Organizer for
Text Pattern Guide

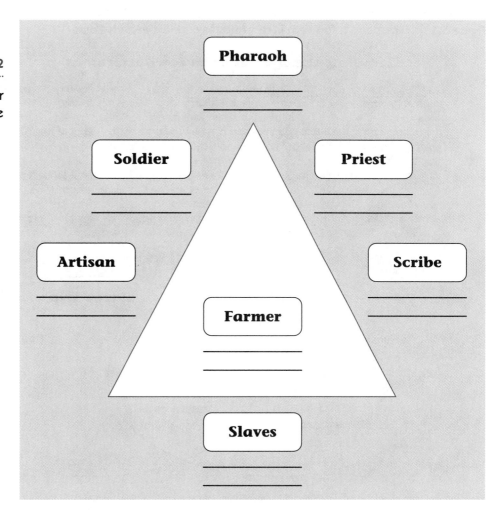

Railroad. From the title, we expected that the essay would be a chronology of Cohen's journey (*sequence pattern*). However, in addition, Webster contrasts Cohen's trip to the runaways' trips (*comparison pattern*) and periodically explains a specific topic (*main idea* and *supporting details pattern*)—resulting in three text organizations. (See Fig. 5.13 for an excerpt from the article in which the comparison pattern is in boldface and the sequence pattern is underlined.)

Suppose your students will read this text in their study of the Civil War. You would choose one organization to emphasize and give them a text pattern guide to assist them in locating the factual information you want to emphasize. We would use a comparison pattern guide to emphasize the similarities

Figure 5.13 Excerpt from Text with Mixed Patterns and Text Pattern Guide

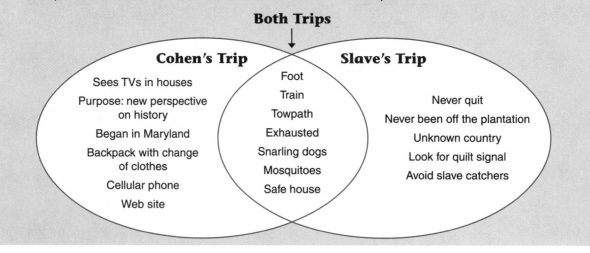

Traveling the Long Road to Freedom, One Step at a Time

Through a dark midnight drizzle, Anthony Cohen is on the run. **Like a slave escaped** from a plantation in the antebellum South—**only 150 years later**—Cohen is testing his fate on the Underground Railroad. He has **now** spent 700 miles and six weeks engaged in hook-or-crook transport, moving fast and light, **retracing a route once used by runaway slaves** as they sought refuge in Canada.

As it was for his predecessors, Cohen's trip has been difficult. "I'll go by foot, boat, train, horse, buggy, **any historically accurate way** I can hitch a ride," he's fond of telling listeners. . . .

Right now, though, Cohen is traveling by every escaped slave's most standard means: his feet. In tonight's case, he's hoofing a rainy towpath along the Erie Canal in western New York State. He's exhausted and behind schedule. He's a little discouraged, too, though he's trying not to show it. Earlier tonight, he'd been buoyed by the prospect of making the nearly 40-mile trip to his next stop by boat, but departure time came and went—and he never heard from the captain.

Both Trips

Cohen's Trip
- Sees TVs in houses
- Purpose: new perspective on history
- Began in Maryland
- Backpack with change of clothes
- Cellular phone
- Web site

(Both Trips — overlapping section)
- Foot
- Train
- Towpath
- Exhausted
- Snarling dogs
- Mosquitoes
- Safe house

Slave's Trip
- Never quit
- Never been off the plantation
- Unknown country
- Look for quilt signal
- Avoid slave catchers

Source: D. Webster, "Traveling the Long Road to Freedom, One Step at a Time," *Smithsonian* 27 (1996): 48–49.

(and differences) of Cohen's trip to the runaway slaves' trips on the Underground Railroad (see Figure 5.13).

Thus, although the author of this text combined three text organizations, in our instruction we would guide students to the comparative information because it would be most useful to their study of the Civil War.

▶ ▶ ▶ ▶ **Constructing Auxiliary Aids**

We have already modeled and explained constructing an auxiliary aid in this chapter with the electric cars script. Do you remember the different emissions—hydrocarbon, carbon monoxide, sulfur oxide, and particulates—and which ones e-cars reduced or increased? Knowing those details would be hard to recall; we took notes but didn't just jot them down in linear fashion on a page. Instead, we organized the notes into a comparative chart (or graphic organizer) of the pros and cons of e-cars so that we could draw conclusions more easily. Taking notes is a common strategy, but people also draw pictures, make diagrams, construct models, visualize images, or think of examples and analogies to assist their memories and study ideas. We recommend teaching note taking, graphic organizers, models, and diagrams rather than highlighting the text with a special marker because students who have little prior knowledge tend to highlight nearly everything and wind up with a text that is nearly solid yellow!

Teaching/Assessing Tools for Constructing Auxiliary Aids.   How did you learn your system for taking notes? Most of our college students invented their own system, although a few were taught outlining or the note-taking system for learning. Many novice students have a disorganized array of notes. Because note taking is an individual process, we recommend modeling and explaining note taking interactively with students, comparing students' notes to yours and to each other's, and incorporating note-taking practice situations not only with texts but with videos, guest speakers, and observations.

Note-Taking System for Learning.   Like the double-entry journal, the *Note-Taking System for Learning* (Palmatier, 1973) helps students organize lecture notes and textbook notes into a format useful for studying. This system is particularly helpful when students need to integrate two sources of information, like lecture and readings, but it can be easily used with one source too.

Using a notebook page with a wide 2-inch left margin, the Notetaking System for Learning involves four steps (see Fig. 5.14):

1. Students record notes from their first source on the right-hand side of the notebook, using subordination, numbers, and other format clues. They leave space for additional notes from a second source if another is used. They leave the back of the paper blank and number the pages.

2. Students organize the information by labeling the major topics in the left-hand margin.

3. In the spaces left in the notes from the first source, students add information from their second source. If they need more space, they write on the back of the page.

Figure 5.14

Note-Taking System
for Learning

1. **Record notes** from first source—lecture, video, textbook, reference book, informational book. For each major topic, leave space if another source is used.

2. **Label units** to organize information

3. **Add information** from a second source.

4. **Study** Turn labels into questions and recite the notes that are covered up.

4. Students study the information by covering their notes, leaving only the labels on the left visible. Turning the labels into questions, students recite the answers they recorded in their notes on the right side.

Assessing the quality of students' notes requires evaluating each individual student's notes. Therefore, we recommend that students work in pairs, comparing their notes or comparing their notes to your model. You will want to discuss the criteria of useful notes—the format, the organization, and the content. You and your students could develop your own criteria or use the rating scale in Table 5.4 We would discuss with the students why some characteristics are rated higher than others. Students may have differing opinions about the advantages and disadvantages of some rankings. For example, we consider using a pen better than a pencil but a few of our college students do not.

Graphic Organizers, Diagrams, Models, or Pictures.   You have no doubt figured out by now that we like graphic organizers. Often in content areas, drawing a diagram, model, or picture and labeling it is more useful than notes in only words. If you have introduced a graphic organizer in generating ideas, then your students could take notes on that graphic organizer as they interacted with the ideas in the text. If you have created a graphic organizer as a text pattern guide, your students will use it for their note taking. When students have many experiences with both graphic organizers and text organization, they can create their own graphic organizer for their notes.

Table 5.4   Notes Evaluation Criteria

	4 Points	3 Points	0 Points
Format			
Use of Ink	I use pen consistently.	I use pen and pencil.	I use pencil.
Handwriting	Others can read my notes.	Only I can read my notes.	I can't read my notes.
Notebook	I use a looseleaf binder.	I use a spiral notebook.	I don't use a notebook.
Use of Page	I leave enough space for editing.	I leave some space for editing.	My notes cover the page.
Organization			
Headings	I use new headings for each main idea.	I use headings inconsistently.	I don't use headings for changes in main ideas.
Subtopics	I group subtopics under headings.	I don't indent subtopics under headings.	My subtopics are not grouped.
Recall column	I use cue words and symbols to make practice questions.	I use cue words in a recall column.	I do not use a recall column.
Abbreviation	I abbreviate whenever possible.	I use some abbreviation.	I don't abbreviate.
Summaries	I summarize lectures in writing.	I write a list of summary lecture topics.	I don't summarize.
Meaning			
Main points	I identify main points with symbols and underlining.	I list main points.	I don't list main points.
Supporting details	I show the relationships between main ideas and details.	My notes list details.	I don't list details.
Examples	I list examples under main points.	I list some examples.	I don't record examples.
Restatement	I use my own words.	I use some of my own words.	I use none of my own words.

Source: Table from Stahl, Norman A., King, James R., and Henk, William A. (1991, May). "Enhancing students notetaking through training and evaluation," from *Journal of Reading, 34* (8), 614–622. Reprinted by permission.

Another use of graphic organizers for notes is to teach the formal outline. That formal outline, with its Roman numerals, capital letters, and numerals, is clear only when the student understands how the text (and content) is organized into subcategories. Many middle school students cannot visualize subcategories in a formal outline but can in a graphic organizer. Therefore, we recommend you first use a graphic organizer to illustrate the subcategories. Then, directly on the graphic organizer, you write Roman numerals on the major categories and capital letters on the first layer of subcategories. And finally, you convert the graphic organizer into the formal outline format.

When you are assessing students' notes on graphic organizers, you again are assessing how adequately they have recorded information—enough information, that is, but not too much. We have found that an advantage of graphic organizers is that students record primarily essential information instead of reams of details. If you have given your students a graphic organizer, then you are evaluating whether they recorded the major categories and the essential supporting details. If they have created their own graphic organizer, you will assess how they have shown the relationship of major ideas and details.

▶ ▶ ▶ ▶ Independent Learning of New Vocabulary

Even when you have taught the important words for the content area, you will return to vocabulary when students interact with ideas, for several reasons. First, you want to teach students how to learn words independently rather than skipping unknown words. You want to model and explain how readers use the context to guess the meaning, try to decipher the meaning from the word parts—root, prefix, suffix—and consult the dictionary or glossary when they need a specific definition for that context. Second, after teaching deciphering word parts, using the context, and consulting a dictionary (see below), you want to assess whether students apply those strategies independently.

Third, for some words, like figurative language or connotative meaning, readers need the context to understand the author's implied meaning. When texts have figurative language or implied connotations, you need to teach context clues, or determining meaning from the surrounding words and sentences, while the students read the text.

Therefore, you will want to model and explain learning new vocabulary by using the context, deciphering word parts, and consulting the dictionary or glossary while reading a text. You may need to teach information directly about those strategies; in addition, you will want to emphasize using that information strategically during reading.

Modeling and Explaining Strategies for Independent Vocabulary Learning. For this mini-lesson, let's say that you and your students are studying the issue of reintroducing species into environments where they existed in the past. After researching factual information supporting the different perspectives, you plan to hold a debate about the issue of reintroduction. Because students are reading a variety of texts, you decide to model and explain vocabulary learning strategies. One group of students is researching the reintroduction of wolves in Yellowstone that is in litigation. You have selected a passage from one of their texts, *The Return of the Wolf to Yellowstone*, to use:

Modeling and Explaining Strategies for Independently Learning New Vocabulary

My Independent Vocabulary Learning Strategies

Translocation is a new word for me. I would use two strategies to figure out its meaning. First, I would **analyze its word parts**. I know the prefix *trans* means "across" from words like *transport*. I also know the word *location* means "place."

Second **using the surrounding context**, obviously Canada is one place and Yellowstone is another place.

So, I decide the meaning of *translocation* is the movement of wolves from the Canadian site to the Yellowstone site.

Viability may be a new word for students. I know that it has a **suffix**, *-ability*, but that leaves the **root**, *vi-*. I'm not sure I know that root word.

I need to **consult the dictionary**. In my dictionary, I don't find the word *viability* as an entry. It is listed under the entry for viable. I learn *viable* means "capable of living," and the root word means "life."

Excerpt from:
The Return of the Wolf to Yellowstone

These fourteen wolves are meant to be only the beginning of a minimum of three to five years of **translocation** of Canadian wolves to Yellowstone—fifteen or so more every year until the recovery goal is met.

Let's assume that at least some of these first fourteen do settle down and breed here. If they are the only wolves we ever import, and no others arrive by natural means, then the genetic diversity of the future Yellowstone wolf population will be so low that its chances of long-term **viability** could be slim to none, for one of the principal effects of inbreeding is a declining reproductive rate. There are many

My Independent Vocabulary
Learning Strategies

Returning to the context, "long-term via-bility could be slim to none" means the chances of the Yellowstone wolf population's having the ability to live would be small because of the lack of gene diversity.

Harrying is a new word for me; the only Harry I know is a name. From previous context, I know the park people want the wolves to leave the pens in which they have been living in Yellow-stone and live freely in the environment. But the wolves aren't leaving the pens. So my guess is that *harrying* means "pushing," but I need to look it up.
My dictionary lists more than one def-inition, and I must select the one that fits this context:

1. "to make a destructive raid."
That doesn't fit; the park people don't want to destroy the wolves.

2. "to force (a person) to move along."
That fits; the park people want the wolves to move out into the park but they think forcing them to move would be wrong.

Excerpt from:
The Return of the Wolf to Yellowstone

other effects of small population size, none of them good.

In short, the wrong move now—**harrying** the wolves out of the pens, for example, and thereby setting off an exodus or damaging the packs' social structure— could mean that some of the wolves will kill livestock, the politicians will make the most of it, the reintroduction will be over, and there will be a very good chance that wolves may never be reestablished in Yellowstone.

Thomas McNamee, *The Return of the Wolf to Yellowstone* (New York: Henry Holt, 1997), pp.115–116.

In summary, to learn the new vocabulary in the passage independently, I used three word learning strategies:

- I used **morphemic analysis** or **word parts** to decipher the meaning of roots, prefixes and suffixes (*translocation*).

- I **consulted the dictionary** and had to **select which definition fit the context** (*harrying* means "to force to move").

- For the new words, I also used the **context** of the passage to check that the meaning made sense.

Now let's turn to teaching/assessing tools and direct teaching tools for learn-ing new vocabulary.

Teaching/Assessing Tools for Students' Independent Vocabulary Learning.
To emphasize the importance of learning new vocabulary, teachers often have students record new words in a section of their journal or notebook. The three tools we present could easily be used in conjunction with journals.

Vocabulary Self-Selection Strategy.   When you want students to locate the important words and yet have a common class list of words to study, you could use the *vocabulary self-selection* (Haggard, 1982, 1986). In the beginning, you would model and explain the strategy with your students:

1. You select a target word—the most important conceptual word.
2. You and the students, in pairs, read the text to identify related words important for learning the content, stopping when a student pair finds an important word.
3. When a student pair locates a word related to the target word, they nominate it for the class list. The teacher writes the word on the board. The class defines the words from their prior knowledge and the context.
4. The class proceeds through the text, nominating and defining words until the reading is complete.
5. Student pairs consult glossaries or dictionaries to refine the class's definitions.
6. The class and the teacher narrow the list to a reasonable number of words. We suggest around ten words.
7. The students record the final list in vocabulary journals and use the words in future study.

During the interactive modeling and explaining mini-lesson, you would notice who is able to locate important vocabulary related to the target concept you selected. You could also ask students why they selected their words and how they know they were important. In this way, students would be teaching each other about locating words. Remember that you can nominate words too, especially when you think the students have skipped an important word.

Vocab-Lit Strategy.   Chase and Dufflemeyer's (1990) *vocab-lit strategy*, designed as an adaptation of the vocabulary self-selection strategy for English classes, emphasizes vocabulary that can help students understand literary elements like characterization. To introduce the strategy, Chase selects a vocabulary word and explains how to complete the entry in a journal or on a study sheet as the students complete their own entry (Fig. 5.15). In subsequent classes, a student nominates a word and, with Chase's help, conducts a class discussion around completing the entry. Thus, the class builds a list of vocabulary words as they read the novel.

Figure 5.15

Vocab-Lit Entry for
<u>Chocolate War</u>

Word	My Knowledge	Context
ingratiating	_____ unknown	On the surface, he was one of those
	_____ acquainted	pale, ingratiating kind of men who
	_____ established	tiptoes through life.

Definition
To work oneself into someone else's good graces

Group Strategy
_____ experience

_X_ context

_X_ dictionary

What We Learned
Brother Leon uses people. He puts on an appearance to get his own way.

Source: Figure from Chase, Ann C. and Duffelmeyer, Frederick A (1990, November). "VOCAB-LIT: Integrating vocabulary study and literature study" from *Journal of Reading 34*, (3), 188–193. Reprinted by permission.

We particularly like the vocab-lit strategy for several reasons. First, it combines estimating the students' knowledge of the word, recording the strategies they use to define the word, and recording how learning the word furthered their understanding of the text. Second, we could adapt the entry format to nonfiction texts by asking students to record how the word furthered their understanding of the topic. And finally, we could narrow the students' selections to words related to a target concept, as in the vocabulary self-selection strategy, such as an author's imagery for fiction or the central concept for nonfiction.

Semantic Feature Charts.   When teachers focus on a specific category of concepts, like clouds or character traits, they want students to learn the names (examples) that identify different items and the descriptive words (attributes or features) that distinguish among the examples. Related to the word map (see Chapter 4), the *semantic feature chart* is a grid on which examples (cirrus, cumulus clouds) are listed vertically and features or attributes (wispy, rising towers) are listed horizontally. If an example has a particular attribute, students record a plus (+) in the square; if not, a minus (–). (Cirrus clouds would have a plus in the "wispy" and a minus in the "rising towers" columns.) By surveying the patterns of pluses and minuses, students can compare the variation in attributes and draw conclusions about similar examples (Johnson & Pearson, 1984).

In introducing the semantic feature chart, we recommend that you model and explain how to compose and complete this chart. Thereafter, students could use it as a study guide for a text. Depending on the text and your students, you may decide to list all of the attributes and require students to find the examples in the text and then mark the chart. Or you may decide that your students need more support: both the examples and the attributes

Figure 5.16   Semanitc Feature Chart for Connotations

Feature

Synonym	positive	negative	loud	meaningful	mindless	redundant	articulate
verbose	–	+	–	–	–	+	–
talkative	–	–	–	–	–	–	–
voluble	+	–	–	+	–	–	+
garrulous	–	+	+	–	+	–	–
loquacious	+	–	–	+	–	–	–

Source: From R. S. Baldwin, J. C. Ford, and J. E. Readance, (1981) "Teaching word connotations: An alternative strategy," *Reading World*, 21 (2), p. 107. Used by permission of the College Reading Association.

on the grid. Then the students would mark the grid while they read the text. After your students have completed the semantic feature chart, the class should discuss and assess how they defined the concept and allocated the attributes. This discussion can be more important than marking the charts because students verbalize their understandings.

A semantic feature chart (see Fig. 5.16) could also be used to depict the shades of meaning among words or connotative meanings (Baldwin, Ford, & Readence, 1981). *Denotation* is the general meaning of words, while *connotation* is the subtle meaning. For example, you know the difference between *scent* and *odor* and when to say and not to say each word. However, ESL students may need to be taught the subtle, culturally tied, connotative meaning of words.

In this chapter, we are recommending that students using semantic feature charts while they interact with text. However, we also recommend using semantic feature charts after students have read the text. At that time, students can review and refine their ideas.

Direct Teaching Tools to Foster Students' Independent Vocabulary Learning. As you model and explain strategies for learning unknown words while reading, you want to include information about context clues, word parts, and consulting the dictionary or glossary.

Using Context Clues.   We think that using context clues is the preferred strategy for most experienced readers. For many new words or new definitions for familiar words, readers infer the meanings because they understand the topic and the surrounding text. From the context, readers learn the connotations of words and the figurative meaning of words and phrases. Even when using other tools to learn the meaning of words, you will want your students to refer to the context in order to check that the meaning makes sense.

We think modeling and explaining the use of context clues is the most realistic way to encourage students to adopt the strategy (Buikema & Graves, 1993). When an author has clearly defined a word in context, we would point that out to students and discuss how the author is defining the word. Was a definition given? Was the concept described? Through a discussion with the students, we would identify the specific context clue and how it informed us of the unknown word's meaning.

In Table 5.5, we have listed five types of context clues that we think are the most useful for your students to be taught to use (adapted from Vacca & Vacca, 1999). Teaching the list in isolation will not encourage your students to use context clues. However, like you, they can use the list to recognize and point out context clues when they meet them in text. Your students could create their own lists and examples.

Table 5.5   Context Clues

Clue	Clue Defined	Example
Definition	The author tells the definition within the same sentence as the unknown word.	The longest side of a right triangle **is called** the *hypotenuse.*
Description	The author gives additional information of category, examples, or attributes.	Martha Graham was an influential *choreographer,* **inventing movement that united dance steps and emotions**.
Synonym	The author links the unknown word with a known synonym or restates the concept.	The *Emancipation* Proclamation did not give **freedom** to all the slaves on January 1, 1863.
Contrast	The author gives an antonym or opposite phrase.	Unlike the **extensor** muscle, the *flexor* does not extend the arm.
Cause-effect	The author implies the meaning by denoting a cause-effect relationship.	*Physical weathering* **produces soil by** breaking down rock and mineral matter into smaller pieces.

Source: From Richard T. Vacca and JoAnne L. Vacca, *Content Area Reading*, 6th edition. Copyright © 1999 by Addison Wesley Educational Publishers Inc. Reprinted by permission.

A note of caution is in order: using context clues alone will only acquaint students with the unknown word. Students will need to meet the word many times and may need to consult the dictionary for a precise definition if unknown words are to become established as a part of their vocabulary.

Analyzing of Word Parts (Morphemic Analysis).   In Chapter 4, we discussed teaching word parts when you have selected vocabulary that contain useful word parts for students to know. Now you will model and explain using word parts to decipher unknown words. As your students meet new words, they can create a class list of common roots, prefixes, and suffixes useful in your content area.

Consulting the Dictionary or Glossary.   In our opinion, most students view consulting the dictionary as drudgery because they have been required to look up twenty words for a Friday test. Therefore, we view the dictionary as a reference tool to consult—not use—for specific information.

We assume that your students know basic word finding skills, such as using guide words. We think the most important strategy for your students is *selecting the meaning that fits the context*. If the text has a glossary, then the author has already selected the appropriate definition for that subject. When consulting a dictionary, students need to learn to consider all of the definitions and to read the complete entry carefully. Students can focus on a familiar fragment of a definition (Scott & Nagy, 1997). For example, a student wrote the sentence, "My family erodes a lot," from the dictionary definition of "eats out" or "eats away" (Miller & Gildea, 1987). Integrating a specific definition with the particular context may be more difficult than many teachers have realized.

Four characteristics of dictionary entries will assist students and are worth modeling and explaining:

1. The definitions are listed in a particular order depending on the specific dictionary—frequency of use, primary meaning first, or historical order.

2. The part of speech may determine the meaning.

3. Subject labels indicate the meaning for specific content areas.

4. Derivations can be a clue to meaning.

As we have stated when you teach the important words you've selected, students need to use new words in many settings—reading, speaking, writing, and listening—if they are to incorporate them into their permanent vocabularies (Stahl & Fairbanks, 1986).

Teacher as Inquiring Learner Activity

Survey a text in your content area.

- What are the important vocabulary words you would preteach? What words would you think students would need to learn independently?

   Select about ten words that you think students are unlikely to know.

- Does the text provide clues to the meaning of the unknown words?

   Determine whether the unknown words have known word parts that the students could use to decipher the meanings. Consult the dictionary to find out how the dictionary defines the words.

- What order does the dictionary list meanings for its entries? Could a student find and understand the dictionary definition that fits the context?

   Decide whether your students could learn words independently or whether you should teach additional words as they read the text.

▶ ▶ ▶ ▶ **Focus on Writing: Supporting Strategies and First Drafts**

Each of the supporting strategies—capitalizing on text organization, constructing auxiliary aids, and independently learning new vocabulary—can assist students in interacting with ideas not only during reading but also when writing a first draft.

When students learn how stories, recipes, or arguments can be organized from their reading, they can use those text patterns to plan, compose, and revise their written texts (Allan & Miller, 1995; Englert, Raphael, Anderson, Anthony, & Stevens, 1991). We recommend adapting generic graphic organizers to fit the particular format or genre that the students are writing. For example, we previously suggested the circle graph as a story map for fiction or quest stories. Students could also use the circle graph to represent a life cycle for biography and an autobiography or a seasonal cycle to chronicle a specific species or habitat.

The graphic organizers used to plan text patterns can also serve as auxiliary aids. Students would make notes on the graphic organizers as they generated ideas for their writing or took notes from different sources. Thus, before they begin to write, they would have a concrete picture of the information they have and how they will organize it in their first draft. They may also refer back to the graphic organizer to evaluate whether they have included enough information and followed that organization in their draft.

Since first drafts are written to communicate the students' ideas, students should include not only the important vocabulary you have selected but the new vocabulary they have learned independently. Students can review their graphic organizers to assess their use of new vocabulary. When they write, they will want to check that the new words are used in the appropriate context.

We discuss revising first drafts and communicating learning to different audiences in Chapter 6.

Purpose Setting and Monitoring During the Interacting with Ideas Phase (Underlying and Ongoing Strategies)

You know that we consider purpose setting and monitoring to be ongoing, underlying strategies throughout all three phases of learning and literacy. You know that strategic readers set their purposes for reading in the generating phase. Now, in the interacting phase, they monitor those purposes, checking to see if they can accomplish their purposes. If not, then strategic readers decide whether to find a different text or to change their purposes. In addition, their generating strategies of activating prior knowledge, previewing and predicting, and exploring new vocabulary provide the initial ideas that they will continue to monitor during their interacting with ideas.

Throughout the interacting with ideas phase, strategic readers monitor their progress in constructing meaning. As they negotiate text-based and schema-based meaning, they determine how well they understand the connections among the ideas. Strategic readers concentrate on finding and interpreting text information to add to their schemata and on searching their schemata for information that helps them understand the text. When comprehension is proceeding smoothly, strategic readers focus on understanding the information. When they discover puzzling information, in either the text or their schemata, then strategic readers focus on their strategies and decide how best to change strategies.

Strategic learners also monitor their progress in finding and interpreting information by determining when and how to use three supporting strategies. When they capitalize on text organization to locate and recall important information, they monitor what the organization is and where the signal words or clues about the organization are. Depending on how complex the ideas are, strategic readers recognize when they need to construct auxiliary aids in order to understand and recall the information. Furthermore, when readers spot unknown words within text and decide what strategy to use to define them, they monitor the importance of the new vocabulary for interacting with ideas.

People usually think reading means to proceed from page 1 straight through the text in order. However, when their purposes are served better, strategic readers move around in text. During interacting with text, strategic readers regulate their pace through the text by rereading, reading on, reading aloud, skimming, skipping parts, jumping back to parts, reading ahead and around, or pausing to think. For example, strategic readers often read the conclusion section of a research report first, especially when no abstract is available. Some mystery readers read the ending first, although many others wouldn't want to spoil the plot by reading the ending first. When readers adjust how they are interacting with text, they are monitoring their progress.

Thus, once again, monitoring progress is pervasive when strategic learners tackle texts.

A Checklist for Monitoring Strategies for Interacting with Ideas

Monitoring Purpose

✓ Can you accomplish your original purpose with this text?

✓ Should you change texts or modify your purpose?

Monitoring Text-Based Connections for Finding and Interpreting Information

✓ Can you paraphrase the information in the text in your own words?

✓ Are you asking questions about information you don't understand?

✓ Can you distinguish the important information and supporting information from the unimportant or irrelevant information?

✓ Does the graphic information help you understand the text?

✓ Can you elaborate or make inferences on the ideas in the text?

✓ Do you find conflicting information in the text?

Monitoring Schema-Based Connections for Finding and Interpreting Information

✓ Can you elaborate or make inferences between text ideas and your schema ideas?

✓ Do you know of alternative ideas that the text doesn't consider?

✓ Can you state the theme, thesis, or issue or problem that the text centers on?

✓ Can you describe how other sources of information or authors are similar to or different from this source?

✓ Can you describe how the text could apply to your own life, your community, or the world?

Monitoring Capitalizing on Text Organization

✓ Can you recognize the overall organization of the text?

✓ Can you follow the different organizational patterns that the author includes?

Monitoring Constructing Auxiliary Aids

✓ Do you need to take notes to study or recall the information?

✓ Do you need to draw a diagram, model, or graphic organizer?

✓ Can you think of examples or visualize an image to interpret the information?

Monitoring Independently Learning New Vocabulary

✓ What words in the text are unknown to you?

✓ How do you determine if the unknown words are important?

✓ What strategy can you use to learn the words: skip unimportant words, context clues, word parts, dictionary or glossary?

Summary of the Chapter

In this chapter, we have focused on the middle of a literacy task, when strategic readers are constructing their knowledge by making connections between text-based and schema-based information. First, we emphasized the interplay between text-based and schema-based connections with the overall strategy:

• Finding and interpreting information.

We also discussed types of questions and answers so that you could guide your students in finding and interpreting important information.

Second, we explained three supporting strategies that help strategic readers find and interpet information:

- Capitalizing on text organization
- Constructing auxiliary aids
- Independently learning new vocabulary

You know that readers choose particular strategies to match the specific text they are reading because they continually:

- Monitor their purpose and their progress.

To teach these strategies, we described teaching/assessing tools:

- Modeling and explaining the overall strategy and supporting strategies to make the entire process visible, like with the e-car script.
- Modeling and explaining specific strategies to concentrate on making particular strategies visible—like the Manuel script or the wolf script.
- Teaching and assessing tools to assist students in finding and interpreting information, for example, the DRA, reciprocal teaching, comprehension guides, and peer-led discussions.
- Assessment tools like admit slips to gauge the class's understanding or retellings and think-alouds to figure out a puzzling student's strategies.
- Teaching and assessing tools to help students use the supporting strategies, like text pattern guides, a note-taking system, or context clue signal words.
- Focusing on writing with journals and first drafts.

You recognize that you must select when to model and explain, when to use a teaching/assessing tool, and when to focus on writing. Over the course of the year, you will use some teaching tools over and over again, and others you will use as your students need them with specific texts. You want students to be comfortable with classroom procedures, yet engaged by the variety of strategies and tools you infuse in your content instruction.

As we move from interacting ideas to refining ideas, the subject of Chapter 6, many of the strategies begun in this middle phase will continue. In the interacting phase, many of the text-based and schema-based connections in finding and interpreting information are tentative. Strategic readers begin to make those connections to construct their understanding, but they hold those connections in abeyance. When strategic readers finish the text, they refine those ideas. When they are dissatisfied with the information they have found and interpreted, they may recycle back to the generating stage with new questions for a new text. Thus, you remember that these phases are artificial and that strategic readers move among them naturally, governed by their purposes and their progress.

Inquiry Activities About Your Learning

1. Plan a modeling and explaining mini-lesson with a text from your content area. Find a text that is interesting to you or that your students might read. Read the text, thinking about different strategies you are using either automatically or consciously to understand the text. (Do a think-aloud.) What strategies would be particularly useful for students to use with the text? Does the text lend itself to particular strategies, like vocabulary strategies in the wolf script? Or does the text lend itself to a variety of strategies, like text-based, schema-based and supporting strategies in the e-car script? Choose which strategies to model and explain, and make notes on the text. Think about how you will explain the usefulness of the strategies and how it is helping you understand the content. With another college student in your class, model and explain your texts to each other, and offer each other advice on how to explain strategies to students.

2. Choose a fiction or nonfiction book about a subject in your content area, and write a reaction journal as you read it. Maybe two of you want to read the same book or complementary books and exchange dialogue journals. What do you think about while you read certain sections? What do you question? What reactions, opinions, and feelings does the book arouse? How does the book relate to your own life or your community? What do you notice about the content or the author's writing? Would you use the book with students? How do you think students would react to the book? What would you discuss with students when they read the book?

Inquiry Activities About Your Students' Learning

1. Create a comprehension study guide or a text pattern guide for a text in your content area. You could choose a textbook, but especially for the text pattern guide, we recommend choosing a magazine or newspaper article or a chapter from an informational book, if you want nonfiction text. If you choose a fiction book, you may decide to make a guide for one chapter, several chapters, or the entire book. Decide your content objective for the text or what is important to learn from the text. For the comprehension guide, devise the higher-level questions or statements first and then the supporting questions or statements. For the text pattern guide, create a graphic organizer that depicts how the text is organized. Have a small group of students read the text and complete your study guide. Evaluate your guide to determine whether to change it for another group.

2. Plan and hold a small group discussion about a text in your content area. Discuss with the teacher what text to have the students read, when they should read it, and whether to conduct a teacher-led discussion or to participate in a peer-led

discussion. If you choose the teacher-led discussion, you need to plan your questions that will initiate and facilitate discussion—higher-level question(s) and supporting questions. You also need to decide what teaching tool to use, for instance, the DRA or a discussion web. If you choose a peer-led discussion, you also need to plan a prompt to initiate the discussion and comments or questions to facilitate discussion. You want to be prepared in case your students don't lead the discussion or finish the discussion too quickly.

6

Refining Ideas: Studying and Clarifying Knowledge

If you have ever been in a heated discussion with friends who refused to change their opinions in spite of the evidence you presented, then you know how difficult refining ideas can be. The same process of weighing evidence that occurs in a discussion among friends also takes place in courts of law and at science conferences. In our courts, people on the jury hold their beliefs, opinions, and theories in abeyance while they consider which side has the preponderance of evidence. At scientific conferences, scientists want verification from more than one research study before they are convinced to alter their theory or to adopt a new theory. When new information jars or contradicts everyday experiences, then people have even more difficulty changing their prior knowledge. For example, although researchers have proved that the *Heliobacter pylori* bacteria cause ulcers, some people still attribute their ulcers to stress and eating spicy foods. At other times, people hold on to their theory or belief in spite of everyday experiences to the contrary. In World War II, the U.S. government interred Japanese Americans based on the theory they would be more loyal to Japan than to the United States despite evidence of their business and community contributions. People hold on to their prior knowledge, theories, and beliefs tenaciously; nevertheless, people do learn and change, enhancing and reconstructing their prior knowledge and beliefs in the process.

Walk through any school, and you will find many students who slam books shut after reading a chapter and students who copy over a first draft without any revisions. Just having read a text once doesn't necessarily mean that you will remember the ideas, even if you have interacted with the ideas. Just having put ideas on paper doesn't necessarily mean that you have expressed your ideas clearly enough for a reader to understand. Nonstrategic learners consider their tasks finished when they make the first, and sometimes only, pass. Strategic learners, on the other hand, know they don't just absorb ideas but must study the information if they want to learn it. If you want your students to refine their schemata, you will want to plan opportunities for them to study and clarify their knowledge.

Remember that generating, interacting, and refining ideas are not separate phases; rather, they form an accumulative process, perhaps even a cyclical one. When strategic learners generate ideas, they build the springboard from which to interact with new information. When strategic learners interact with ideas, they begin to reconsider their prior knowledge in the light of new information and begin to make decisions about revisions to their knowledge. In this phase also, strategic learners make tentative hypotheses, interpretations, or conclusions. At the refining phase, strategic learners have the advantage of viewing the text as a whole. They can take the time to review, reflect on, or revisit without being immersed in the text. They may decide that they missed some information and so reread to interact with text. Or they may ask a new question and search for a new source, returning once again to the generating phase after refining ideas. Thus, strategic learners build on the knowledge gained in the previous two phases to refine their knowledge now.

We think strategic learners refine their ideas in two ways: *enhancing prior knowledge* and *reconstructing prior knowledge* (see the chapter opening graphic). We use the word *enhancing* because it connotes adding new information to what one already knows or expanding an existing schema—a common experience. Examples of enhancing are adding clearer details to a first draft, repeating a science experiment to confirm evidence, and confirming what you know about Abigail Adam's character after reading her letters. We view *reconstructing* as altering one's schema through a major revision—a rare event. When nutritionists replaced the circle with the pyramid diagram for daily nutritional requirements, they sought to reconstruct people's schemata of the major food groups. In science, examples of reconstructing ideas are Einstein's theory of relativity and the controversial theory that dinosaurs and birds are related. A social studies example is the revision of the country's concept of what *equal education* means as a result of the U.S. Supreme Court 1954 decision in *Brown v. Board of Education*. Both enhancing and reconstructing are constructive learning processes in the content areas.

We have organized refining strategies into two major categories in this chapter (see the chapter graphic). The first refining strategy is organizing ideas and enhancing prior knowledge. Having finished reading or writing a text, strategic learners stand back and think about or categorize ideas, elaborate on ideas, summarize, and draw conclusions. They also confirm their understanding of the text by comparing it to other works they know and their own life and incorporating that new understanding in their schemata. The second refining strategy is evaluating ideas and restructuring prior knowledge. Strategic learners critically think about what they

REFINING IDEAS: STUDYING AND CLARIFYING KNOWLEDGE

Strategies and Tools for Organizing Ideas and Enchancing Prior Knowledge

Modeling and Explaining Strategies for Organizing Ideas and Enhancing Prior Knowledge

Teaching/Assessing Tools for Organizing Ideas and Enhancing Prior Knowledge

Assessment Tools

Focus on Writing: Summaries for Readers

Strategies and Tools for Evaluating Ideas and Restructuring Prior Knowledge

Modeling and Explaining Strategies for Evaluating Ideas and Restructuring Prior Knowledge

Teaching/Assessing Tools for Evaluating Ideas and Reconstructing Prior Knowledge

Assessment Tools

Focus on Writing: Revising First Drafts Through Conferences

Communicating Learning to Different Audiences

Communicating Learning Through Speaking Opportunities
Communicating Learning Through Dramatic Opportunities
Communicating Learning Through Art and Music Opportunities
Communicating Learning Through Writing Opportunities

Purpose Setting and Monitoring During the Refining Ideas Phase (Underlying and Ongoing Strategies)

Checklist for Monitoring Strategies for Refining Ideas

already know and decide to reconsider or refute their old ideas. They may decide they need more information, ask new questions, apply evaluation criteria, or review points of view. And finally, they apply the information to new situations in their own life, their community, or the general society.

You will notice from the chapter graphic that we include the now-familiar modeling and explaining teaching tool, teaching/assessing tools, assessment tools, and the Focus on Writing section. Within the teaching/assessing tools, you will find familiar tools discussed in previous chapters. Since refining is at the end of a continuous process, you might choose to proceed with a tool you began using in a previous phase. We have also included familiar tools, like graphic organizers, that now serve a refining purpose. And finally, you will find new tools for teaching, assessing, and writing.

Since the refining phase occurs at the end of a lesson, a series of lessons, or a unit, we close the chapter with a section on communicating learning to different audiences. In the refining phase, teachers want students to synthesize their learning in an end product. These end products, which we call speaking, dramatic, art and music, and writing opportunities, often reveal to the students as well how much they have learned.

And finally, since we emphasize metacognitive awareness, we close the chapter with the underlying and ongoing strategy of purpose setting and monitoring during the refining phase.

Purpose-Setting Questions

1. Thinking about your past learning experiences, can you remember a time when you have enhanced your prior knowledge (a common experience) and when you have restructured your prior knowledge (a rare experience)?

2. How do you organize ideas that you need to study? Would a tool, like a graphic organizer or postreading guide, help?

3. When you finish reading a lengthy text, do you summarize the ideas in writing? How do you think summarizing texts would help you study the information?

4. When you finish writing a first draft, what do you do to evaluate whether you expressed your ideas clearly? Have you ever asked a peer to read your draft and offer revision suggestions?

5. In your secondary schooling, how did teachers ask you to communicate your learning: through tests or through communication activities and projects? What did you learn by completing different end products?

Strategies and Tools for Organizing Ideas and Enhancing Prior Knowledge

When strategic learners organize their ideas and enhance their prior knowledge (see Fig. 6.1), they are really studying information to understand it better and to remember it. Using strategies like categorizing ideas, summarizing, drawing conclusions, or rereading and reciting, strategic learners strive to increase their knowledge or augment their schemata. Your strategic ESL students might translate and transfer ideas between their two languages to refine their ideas (Jiménez, García, & Pearson, 1996).

When you skim Figure 6.1 for organizing and enhancing ideas, you will notice we emphasize strategies and tools that usually occur at the end of a task. For example, strategic learners usually summarize at the end of a text, even though they may summarize periodically when reading a long text. Similarly, they determine their conclusions at the end, even when they have drawn tentative conclusions earlier. In addition, you will notice familiar strategies and tools that we have discussed in Chapters 4 and 5. We have restated previous tools, like KWL and text pattern guides, to remind you that you may revisit them during the refining phase.

Before we discuss teaching/assessing tools, we will use the teaching tool of modeling and explaining to make organizing and enhancing strategies visible for you. In this refining phase, you will find that we present two scripts together—first a script for categorizing information and second a script for summarizing information.

▶ ▶ ▶ ▶ **Modeling and Explaining Strategies for Organizing Ideas and Enhancing Prior Knowledge**

Pretend that you and your class will study a unit on ecology centered on this major issue: "How can societies balance human, plant, and animal needs to ensure sustainable habitats for all species?" The class will study different habitats around the world, including the rain forests, but you think students should also study the conditions of habitats and species in the United States, especially local habitats. As a part of the unit, you've decided students will investigate local habitats and species to determine their present condition and whether recovery projects exist or are needed. In preparation for that investigation, your students will read an article to learn about recovery and reintroduction projects so that they will be able to ask informed questions during their local investigations.

Figure 6.1

Organizing Ideas and
Enhancing Prior
Knowledge:
Strategies and Tools

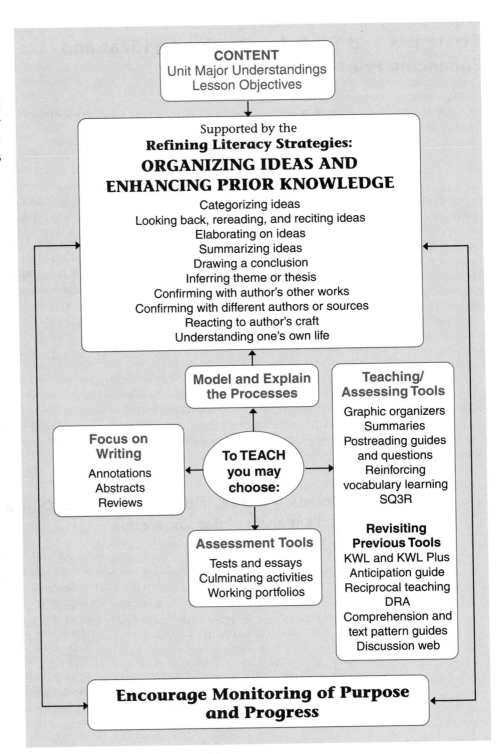

CONTENT
Unit Major Understandings
Lesson Objectives

Supported by the
Refining Literacy Strategies:
ORGANIZING IDEAS AND
ENHANCING PRIOR KNOWLEDGE

Categorizing ideas
Looking back, rereading, and reciting ideas
Elaborating on ideas
Summarizing ideas
Drawing a conclusion
Inferring theme or thesis
Confirming with author's other works
Confirming with different authors or sources
Reacting to author's craft
Understanding one's own life

**Model and Explain
the Processes**

**Teaching/
Assessing Tools**

Graphic organizers
Summaries
Postreading guides
and questions
Reinforcing
vocabulary learning
SQ3R

**Focus on
Writing**

Annotations
Abstracts
Reviews

**To TEACH
you may
choose:**

**Revisiting
Previous Tools**
KWL and KWL Plus
Anticipation guide
Reciprocal teaching
DRA
Comprehension and
text pattern guides
Discussion web

Assessment Tools

Tests and essays
Culminating activities
Working portfolios

**Encourage Monitoring of Purpose
and Progress**

Figure 6.2

Plan Book for Day 1

Day 1

Introduce "Returning the Natives" article by teacher-led, whole class discussion.

Generating Strategies

1. Review unit's purpose: Local habitats sustainable?
2. Review prior knowledge
   Endangered Species Act
   Examples of bald eagle and condor
3. Preview and predict
   Source—The Audubon Society's position
   Illustrations—4 animals
   Topic—reintroduction problems and solutions

Interacting Strategies

1. Find and interpret information on each reintroduction project—problems, solutions
2. Use text organization: categorization
3. Use supporting aid: check important information in the margin

Since the students will be reading a variety of sources, you have decided to model and explain the strategies for organizing ideas and enhancing prior knowledge. Depending on how independent your students are, you will decide whether also to model and explain particular generating and interacting strategies in order to prepare them for refining strategies.

Let's assume that your students can successfully read the text you have chosen, and so you plan to discuss generating and interacting strategies with them briefly and have them read the text independently on the first day (see Fig. 6.2). On day 2, you plan to model and explain refining strategies. So that you understand the categorization chart we use (see Table 6.1) and the summary in the modeling and explaining scripts, we have excerpted one section of the article, on the Delmarva fox squirrel project, for you to read. We have highlighted information recorded on Table 6.1:

Excerpt from "Returning the Natives"

On a cool, windy morning last April on the Delmarva Peninsula, I pulled on a pair of hip boots and followed retired U.S. Fish and Wildlife Service biologist Guy Willey into a partially flooded pine woods. Willey, now a consultant to the service, had set 25 traps at dawn, baiting them with corn, and now he was checking them. These Maryland woods held one of the **few remaining natural populations of the endangered Delmarva fox squirrel**, one of the 10 subspecies of the Eastern fox squirrel. Unlike the more common gray squirrels, with which they share their range, fox squirrels do **not adapt well to forest fragmentation** and are unlikely to venture far from the woods. One will not find a fox squirrel eating peanuts in a city park. They remain wild; thus their current crisis.

Heavy spring rains had left water in every depression, some ankle deep, some above the calf. We sloshed along, from one empty trap to the next. Willey, a congenial, talkative man and a native of the area, has had a lifetime of experience with the Delmarva fox squirrel. "**Delmarvas prefer mature hardwoods**, where the understory is more open," he told me. "We've found some in pines like these, but we **don't really know whether or not a pine woods can sustain a population**."

. . .

At the turn of the century the Delmarva fox squirrel could be found throughout the Delmarva Peninsula. . . . By **the 1960's more than three-quarters of the hardwoods** that once covered much of the peninsula had been **cut**, and only a few populations of Delmarva fox squirrels remained, 80 percent of them in Maryland's Dorchester County, where Willey and I had spent the morning.

. . . In 1978, in a sweeping effort to reestablish the fox squirrel throughout its historical range, the U.S. Fish and Wildlife Service approved a plan to trap Delmarvas in their few remaining populations and translocate them. Between **1978 and 1991 nearly 300 squirrels were translocated to 17 sites throughout the Delmarva Peninsula**. Finding suitable habitat was the principal challenge. **All but 3 of the 17 sites were on private land**. "Trying to **convince landowners to allow** the government to place an endangered species on their property, well. . . ." [Biologist] Therres shook his head, leaving the sentence unfinished.

. . .

. . . When Therres found a landowner who would cooperate, they **settled the matter with a handshake**: "People don't like to sign a piece of paper with the government, and the squirrels don't care." Therres admits this was hardly ideal. In one case **a site was logged** five years after a group of squirrels had been released on it.

The translocation effort was halted in 1991, but not because of sites threatened with logging. In fact, the project appeared to be successful. The problem was that no one knew with certainty what constituted a "successful" population of Delmarva fox squirrels because so many questions about natural populations remained unanswered. **How many squirrels are needed for a healthy population, and how many acres do they require?** The facts are limited— squirrels don't attract many researchers. Thus, each spring for the past four years, Guy Willey has trapped and tagged Delmarva fox squirrels from five undisturbed natural populations, accumulating data.

Source: Reprinted with permission from the November/December 1996 issue of *Audubon Magazine*. To subscribe to Audubon call (800) 274-4201.

On day 2, you would model and explain categorizing ideas with the chart (see Modeling and Explaining Script for Categorizing Ideas) in order to prepare the students for writing a class summary of the article. The class would be divided into four expert groups of six to eight students each to record information about one animal to study. Then, in jigsaw manner, pairs from each expert group would regroup into new teaching groups to teach each other about their animals. Thus, all students end up with information about all four animals on their categorization chart (see Table 6.1) and are prepared for the subsequent summary writing. Here is the teacher's first script:

Modeling and Explaining Script for Categorizing Ideas

We will study this material in two ways. First, we will complete a categorization chart that will describe the important information about each project. Second, we will compose a class summary of the article.

As you can see from my chart on the overhead and the charts you have, I have labeled the categories of information you are to record. [See Table 6.1.] Why did I label the rows with the names of the four endangered animals? Yes, obviously, the **text was organized** primarily around the four animals: the fox squirrel, the butterfly, the falcon, and the prairie chicken.

What are the labels for the four columns, and why did I choose those labels? For each column, I have labeled **categories of important information that describe** the research on each project: the original problem, the method of reintroduction, the reintroduction problems, and new questions. How will those labels help us? Yes, we will be able to **compare** the research across the four different projects and learn what to ask about our local habitats and species.

In your expert groups on one animal, you and a partner will **record** information about your animal's project on your categorization chart. You may **look back at** the checks marking important information that you made as you read. You may need to **reread** the text for missing information. Your expert group will compare charts and come to an agreement about the information about your animal. Then we will form jigsaw groups so that each pair can teach the other pairs about their animal project. You will end up with a completed chart for all four animal projects.

Table 6.1   Categorization Chart for Reintroduction Projects

	Descriptions of Research			
Species	Original Problem of Species and Habitats	Method of Reintroduction	Reintroduction Problems Encountered	New Questions and Research
Delmarva fox squirrel, Delmarva Peninsula, Maryland	1) Not adapt to fragmented forest 2) '60's, ¾ of hardwood forest cut 3) Only few populations left	1) Translocation 2) Between '78 & '91, 300 squirrels trapped, relocated to 17 sites	14 sites were on private land Needed permission from owners to put squirrels on property; owners reluctant to sign; did agree with a handshake 1 site logged 5 years after relocation	Trap and tag squirrels: 1) How many squirrels constitute a healthy population? 2) How many acres do they require in their range? 3) Do they prefer hardwood or pine forests?
Schaus swallowtail butterfly, Biscayne National Park, Florida	1) loss of hardwood hammocks to residential development 2) '84, endangered, range 4 sites 3) '92, 1 site 4) 8/92, Hurricane Andrew hit site, killing butterfly pupae	1) For 8 years requests to breed butterflies from collected eggs denied 2) 6/92 request granted; eggs collected	1) '93, lost 50% of pupae because kept in air-conditioned room 2) At what stage should butterflies be put out? a) '95, put out pupae & warblers, ate 60–99% b) '96 put out adult butterflies	After release of tagged adults, recapture What is a butterfly's range?

Table 6.1 (continued)

	Descriptions of Research			
Species	Original Problem of Species and Habitats	Method of Reintroduction	Reintroduction Problems Encountered	New Questions and Research
Northern Aplomado falcon, South Texas and Louisiana coast	1) Coastal grasslands become farmland or urban development 2) Last nest found in '52	1) Captive propagation and release program 2) Offspring taken from Mexican birds and bred 3) '95, 39 falcons released	1) '96 virus in birds' food killed some falcons 2) Must learn to fly at release site: a) Put in box on tower and fed b) Slowly open door of box; falcons panic; biologist sprays water to calm them c) Falcons practice flying for increasing distances	Habitat changed to ranches and farms Can falcon adapt to new habitat?
Attwater's prairie chicken, South Texas and Louisiana coast	1) Loss of coastal grasslands 2) '80's, drought 3) '92, 456 chickens 4) Currently 70 chickens	1) Captive propagation and release program 2) '92, 49 eggs from wild, 7 chicks survived	Houston Zoo biologist asks, How to breed wild chickens? 1) Devised breeding cage to ensure genetic diversity 2) Raising chicks in different conditions and taking notes	1) How to teach chicken to drink dew from plants? 2) What do you feed chickens? Crickets 3) What do you feed crickets?

While the students are working, you would circulate to observe their progress and help pairs as needed. If you thought the students were struggling, you and the students would complete the charts together in an interactive manner: your chart on the overhead with the students at their desks. After the students completed their categorization charts (perhaps on day 3), you would model and explain summarizing ideas into a written summary. Here is the script:

Interactive Modeling and Explaining Summarizing Ideas

My Prompts to Students for Summarizing

The **purpose for writing a summary** is to help you organize and study information from the text. If you are reading several texts, then a summary of each will help you compare and integrate information from the different texts. Let's compose a summary of this article together using the categorization charts to help us organ-ize and compare information to include in the summary.

Often in writing summaries, we begin with a statement that **synthesizes or integrates** all of the information—a **thesis or theme**. I can either write the thesis now or after I have summarized sections of the article. What does the author want us to remember about reintroducing all four species? Does anyone have a thesis statement?

The information I **include** and **exclude** in the summary will vary depending on my **purpose.**

1. If my purpose is to describe each project, then my strategy would be to follow the organization of the text or use the rows on the chart. I would include information about each project separately.

2. However, the class's **purpose** is to learn questions to ask about local habitats. So, I want to **include** information that describes the research across projects. So I will **summarize the categories that describe research**—the columns on the chart.

Examples of Sentences in Class Summary

Repopulating an endangered species in its historical habitat is not a simple or easy task. Just ask the biologists who have encountered problems in their repopulation programs for the Delmarva fox squirrel, Schaus swallowtail butterfly, northern Aplomado falcon, Attwater's prairie chicken.

Look down the first column and compare the original problem of each species. Who can **draw a conclusion** about the common cause for the four animals to be endangered? What is a second cause? Can someone compose a sentence or two about the causes?

Turning to the second column on the chart, how have biologists tried to reintroduce the animals? Who has a **summary sentence**?

Reread the third column. Did each project encounter the same problem? No, each project had unique problems; so I can't generalize from one project to another or **draw a conclusion**. I will have to list the major difficulty each project had, but I can say every project had difficulties to solve. For each project, how can I summarize the problem or challenge the biologists encountered?

Why would I want to list each problem? Yes, I might want to ask local biologists about the problems and see if our local problems are similar or unique.

The fourth column is like the third column. Each project has unique questions and new research to conduct. So again I can't **draw a conclusion** except to say every project continues to research.

Again, studying these new questions may help the class ask questions of our local biologists. What questions are biologists involved in these four projects still asking?

The loss of habitat is the primary cause for the four animals becoming endangered. Weather events have also contributed to endangering the butterfly (a hurricane) and the chicken (drought).

Biologists use two types of programs to repopulate species:

1. translocation for the squirrel and

2. captive propagation and release programs for the butterfly, falcon, and chicken.

In each program, the biologists encountered problems:

1. getting permission to release squirrels on private land,

2. learning at what stage to release the butterflies,

3. learning that the falcons needed practice flying before fully released, and

4. learning how to breed chickens.

In each program, biologists continue to ask research questions:

1. How many acres and what type of forest does a healthy population of squirrels need? How many is a healthy population?

2. What is a butterfly's range?

3. Can falcons adapt to a non-native habitat?

4. Can bred chickens be trained to live in their "historic" habitat?

If I hadn't composed a **thesis** statement at the beginning of the summary, I would go back to that now. Since I did that already, let's think about how to conclude the summary.

Near the end of the article, a biologist at the Houston Zoo asks whether a habitat is really wild habitat when people have put telephone poles in it? The biologist also asks what is the goal of the projects? **Reread** her questions and use them to compose a final conclusion for the summary.

Let's reread the summary and see if it's clear and complete or if it needs some changes.

When we reintroduce endangered species to their "historic" habitat, we should consider whether the habitat is wild or have we already changed their native habitat. What is our goal?

1. to keep a habitat or species wild or unchanged, or

2. to be able to sustain the life of the habitat or species even when the habitat has changed?

For students to study and clarify their knowledge in the refining phase, we think students need to revisit the information through strategies, like categorizing information on a chart and writing a summary. Therefore, we presented two examples of modeling and explaining strategies to organize and enhance prior knowledge. Let's now review and summarize both of those examples:

To Categorize Ideas in Preparation for Summarizing

- Set a **purpose** for using a categorization chart (to compare projects)
- Used **text organization** to identify categories (rows in Table 6.1 represented the four endangered animal projects)
- Used **important information that described** the research (column categories in Table 6.1 described attributes of the research projects)
- **Recorded** information for each animal project in the corresponding category (used jigsaw groups or expert groups and then teaching groups to complete categorization chart)
- **Looked back** at checks made on the text that marked important information to record that information
- **Reread** as necessary to record missing information.

To Summarize Ideas

- Set a **purpose** to decide what information to include and exclude in summary

- Found or **interpreted thesis** of article
- **Reread** columns in the categorization chart to try to compare information
- **Drew conclusion** about the common cause of becoming endangered
- **Summarized** two reintroduction methods
- **Could not generalize or draw a conclusion** about reintroduction problems or new questions and so listed the unique information for each project
- **Reread and drew conclusion** for summary—new questions

Now let's turn to teaching/assessing tools that support students in organizing ideas and enhancing their prior knowledge.

▶ ▶ ▶ ▶ Teaching/Assessing Tools for Organizing Ideas and Enhancing Prior Knowledge

Whether your students begin with little knowledge or substantial knowledge about your content area, most frequently you will have students enhancing, rather than reconstructing, their prior knowledge. As they learn new concepts and new vocabulary and make new connections among text-based and schema-based information, they increase their knowledge about the topic. Now, in the refining phase, you will use teaching/assessing tools so that students can study and remember the information or enhance their schemata.

Because the refining phase occurs after the generating and interacting phases, you can continue with the teaching/assessing tools that the students have already used (refer back to Figure 6.1). They could revise a graphic organizer or an anticipation guide that they worked on in the generating phase. They could finish their KWL Plus, directed reading activity, or reciprocal teaching by reviewing what they learned. And finally, students could discuss the comprehension guides, the text pattern guides, or the discussion webs that they completed during the interacting phase. Students can organize, clarify, and study information with these same teaching/assessing tools.

At other times, you may want to introduce different teaching/assessing tools by having students create a new graphic organizer, summarize the text, or complete a postreading guide. You will also want to reinforce the new vocabulary and make sure the students use their new vocabulary to express their understanding. And finally, you may teach them SQ3R (survey, question, read, recite, review) to study the information. In the next sections, we discuss those different teaching/assessing tools.

Preparation for Summarizing: Categorization Chart. Writing a summary is not an easy task because you need to be both concise and complete at the same time. We think that when students complete a graphic organizer first, they distill the information down to the most important facts and interpretations needed in a summary. For texts of any length, students need a preparation step to help them determine what to include in and what to exclude from the summary.

Although graphic organizers can take many forms, we chose to use a categorization chart when we modeled and explained with the endangered species article because it matched the text's organization. You already know that you would select the graphic organizer that best depicts how important information is organized. We will discuss graphic organizers again in a later section.

The graphic organizer serves as a tool on which students can reduce and organize the extensive information given in a text. By reviewing the text in order to complete the graphic organizer, students clarify what is important information to include in a summary and concurrently study the information as well. You recognize that nonstrategic students, especially students with learning disabilities, will need a tool to revisit and study information.

Summary Writing. Writing a summary helps students study information because they review their notes on graphic organizers and compose an even more concise version of the author's important ideas. Again the students need to determine what information to include in and exclude from their summaries and how to organize those ideas clearly and succinctly. The graphic organizer should contain all of the most important information; an ideal summary, however, could combine and synthesize information, but that is difficult even for high school and college students to do (Brown & Day, 1983).

Your students' purpose for learning the information will determine what they include in their summary and how they organize the material. In the Modeling and Explaining Script for Categorizing Ideas on endangered species, we could have summarized each project separately following the text's organization if the purpose had been to catalogue repopulation projects. However, since the purpose was to determine questions to ask about local habitats and species, we summarized information across projects.

The audience who will read the summary also determines what information students include (Hidi & Anderson, 1986; Hill, 1991). If the students are writing for themselves to help them remember the information that they intend to use later, their summaries could contain the important ideas they need to study. A concise summary in this situation would not be as important as a complete one. In contrast, if they are writing a summary to inform a reader, as in a review, then the students need to be concise and yet also give the reader a complete picture of the text. We discuss writing summaries for readers in the Focus on Writing section later in the chapter.

When you discuss the main idea or moral of a story with your students and when you ask them what a text is all about, you are beginning to teach summarization. When you and your students find and interpret important supporting information, once again you are beginning to teach summarization. Building on those strategies, you want to teach students to write a summary as a tool for studying independently.

When you teach writing a summary, you would begin by modeling and explaining with a, short, well-organized text that your students can comprehend easily. For both the graphic organizer and the summary, you would emphasize four guidelines (adapted from Hidi & Anderson, 1986):

- Include only the most important ideas.
- Exclude unimportant and redundant information.
- Use the organization of the text to help organize the summary.
- Combine, integrate, generalize, or synthesize information.

You could write a whole class summary, as in the modeling and explaining script, or have individuals or pairs of students write summaries.

When individuals or pairs write summaries, then you and the class would compare several students' summaries, anonymously, and discuss the similarities and differences. Following are the topics to address in this review:

- What information (including concepts and vocabulary) did most students include? Did they include that information because it was a main idea? Did they think details were needed to support that main idea?

- What information did only some students include? Why did they think those details were important to include?

- What information did students exclude? Was more information needed?

- How did students combine information?

- Did students write a thesis or theme statement that synthesized the text?

Your nonstrategic readers will have more difficulty than strategic readers in both finding the important ideas and writing those ideas in their summaries (Winograd, 1984). A comparison of students' summaries for different texts over time can help the students learn the variety of ways that their peers compose summaries. They can experiment with different combinations of information and recognize that completeness and conciseness can be achieved in different ways.

Expanding Students' Summary Writing.   After your students have written summaries for clearly organized texts, you will want to model and explain writing summaries for texts that contain less familiar content and less clear or mixed organization patterns. With less clear texts, your students will have more difficulty deciding what information to include and exclude. So in addition to modeling, you will want your students to compare and evaluate their summaries to learn from each other.

You will also want to model and explain how to synthesize, generalize, and integrate information in summaries. You would model how to combine the information, reorder information, or invent a new version of the information. When you summarize text, you may find generalizing, and synthesizing the information more difficult than condensing the author's information and organization, and your students will too. After all, integrating, generalizing, and synthesizing information is higher-level thinking.

When you teach students to summarize, do not expect them to write complete and concise summaries easily. You probably find writing summaries challenging yourself. We suggest that you spend the whole year writing summaries for different types of texts. One teacher we know saves the students' summaries in their working portfolios and has the students compare their June summaries to their September ones. Students easily recognize their progress.

Teacher as Inquiring Learner Activity

We encourage you to write summaries as a studying tool. Write a summary of a chapter or a text in your content area.

- What strategies do you use? Does a graphic organizer help you distill information before you write the summary? Why do you include or exclude particular information? Do you follow the organization in the text, or do you use a different organization? Do you integrate information from different sections of the text? Do you synthesize ideas in your statements?

  When we assign our students a written review of the research on a topic of their choosing, we ask them to complete a categorization chart first. On the chart, the columns are labeled with the components of the research—question or hypothesis, method, results, conclusions—and the rows are the different studies. Using their categorization charts, our students write a summary or a review of the research. Instead of writing a summary of one text, you might choose to summarize several texts or write a review of the research.

Graphic Organizers.   When you use graphic organizers in generating ideas, in interacting with ideas, and now in refining ideas, you and your students would revise them to incorporate new information. Reviewing a graphic organizer from the generating phase, students would eliminate the misconceptions or incorrect information from their prior knowledge and add newly learned information. They could elaborate on the earlier information to create a more complete representation of their current knowledge. Similarly, if, during the interacting phase, students used a graphic organizer as a text pattern guide or for note taking, they would review their graphic organizers and the text to see that they recorded all the necessary important information and what they need to add or revise.

For some texts, you may decide to use graphic organizers only in the refining stage because you want to help students study the information (Peresich, Meadows, & Sinatra, 1990). Because students are engaged in organ-izing the information into another form, they are more likely to remember it or enhance their schemata. You could ask the students to create their own graphic organizer that would represent how they've added ideas to their schemata. Or you could provide the students with a blank graphic organizer, like a semantic map, a flowchart, a cause-and effect chain for events, a story map, or a Venn diagram, which represents how the information is organized in your content area. For example, after studying the digestive system, a biology teacher presents a diagram of the digestive system on which students must describe the sequence of consuming an ice cream cone. First, students write what they recalled and then they review the text to add any missing information.

Whether your students are revising earlier graphic organizers or reating new ones, you want to assess how they organize and represent information:

- Have they included the important information and added new information?
- Have they used the new vocabulary for the important concepts?
- Have they shown relationships among concepts by how they have placed them on the graphic organizer?
- Can they explain how their graphic organizer represents the concepts they've been learning?

From the vocabulary the students use for the newly learned information and their explanations of the relationships on their graphic organizers, you will be able to decide how clearly and completely they understand the concepts. You may decide that the graphic organizer is an end product representing the students' learning, or you may use it as a tool to prepare for other end products, as we did in summary writing.

Postreading Guides and Questions.   You may choose to use study guides and questions as you do graphic organizers: to interact with ideas or to refine ideas after reading. By using guides and questions now, you provide your students support in organizing the information and their thoughts. If your students are reading several texts, then postreading guides and questions will help them integrate information across the different texts. For example, Peters (1996) recommends postreading guides for a Civil War unit that focuses on two questions: (1) "Should individuals use violence to prevent the enforcement of laws they reject? and (2) Was the Civil War inevitable?" (p. 185). To assist students in organizing what they have read about several events, Peters suggests a cause-and-effect reading guide (see Fig. 6.3)

Since the materials students would have read did not explicitly state all of the reasons or results, students would need to interpret the information they already have. After completing the guide, the class would discuss their different responses and assess the plausibility of their reasons for the results of each event. Clearly, what Peters advocates is for students to learn how to interpret events as historians do.

Another example of a postreading guide is from a unit on the homeless. Each group of students read a text about a different homeless population. The questions on the postreading guide in Figure 6.4 helped the students organize the factual information and their interpretations about homeless people. After completing the guides, the class pooled their information and conclusions about homeless people.

SQ3R.   You have already learned the concepts that this somewhat strange-looking acronym represents: **s**urvey, **q**uestion, **r**ead, **r**ecite, **r**eview (Robinson, 1961) from previous chapters. We present it here because most of the strategy is about organizing and enhancing prior knowledge. The first step is to *survey* the text (covered in Chapter 4), and the second is to ask *questions* (covered in both Chapters 4 and 5). Step 3 is to *read* or interact with text (covered in Chapter 5). Both steps 4 and 5, to *recite* the information read and to *review* the information, are strategies for refining ideas.

Although we consistently use the SQ3R strategy because we have more reading to do than we have time, we have met few secondary or college students willing to invest the time in using this strategy. That said, we still advise teaching secondary students SQ3R as an investment in the future when they have more reading than they have time. If you incorporate the teaching/assessing tools we've suggested that are similar to the steps of SQ3R, then students may recognize the value of SQ3R (or, in our terminology, of generating, integrating, and refining strategies).

Figure 6.3

Cause-and-Effect
Postreading Guide for
a Civil War Unit

> **Causal Reasoning:**
>
> **Event:** Publication of *Uncle Tom's Cabin*
> **Reason:** _____
> **Result:** _____
>
> **Event:** Free Soil Dispute
> **Reason:** _____
> **Result:** _____
>
> **Event:** John Brown's Raid
> **Reason:** _____
> **Result:** _____
>
> **Event:** The South views slavery differently from the North.
> **Reason:** _____
> **Result:** _____
>
> **Event:** Plantation owners had most of the political power in the South.
> **Reason:** _____
> **Result:** _____
>
> **Event:** Most Southerners did not own slaves.
> **Reason:** _____
> **Result:** _____

Source: From D. Lapp, J. Flood and N. Farnan, *Content Area Reading and Learning: Instructional Strategies* Second Edition, pp. 200–202. Copyright © 1996 by Allyn & Bacon. Reprinted by permission.

Reinforcing Vocabulary and Concepts. We have already discussed preteaching vocabulary and previewing vocabulary in Chapter 4 and independently learning vocabulary through context and the dictionary in Chapter 5. If students are going to remember the new vocabulary for new concepts, they will need to study and use the words in a variety of ways.

Figure 6.4

Postreading Guide for
a Text on Homeless
People

1. What homeless group is the focus of this report?

   _____

   _____

2. What percentage of the general population does this group make up?

   _____

   _____

3. What percentage of the homeless population does this group make up?

   _____

   _____

4. Where did members of this group live before they became homeless?

   _____

   _____

5. What are their family backgrounds?

   _____

   _____

6. List three reasons that members of this group became homeless.

   _____

   _____

   _____

7. List three facts that you think are important to share with other students.

   _____

   _____

   _____

8. List three things that members of this group have in common with
   you or someone you know.

   _____

   _____

   _____

9. If you could pick only one word to describe members of this group,
   what would it be?

   _____

One natural way to reinforce vocabulary and concepts is for you and your students to use the words in speaking and writing. ESL students benefit from using the new vocabulary in context, and students with learning disabilities benefit from the repetition in different contexts. When students are recording in their journal entries, composing first drafts, and discussing their interactions with text, you can encourage (or require) them to use the new vocabulary. You might ask them to compose freewriting using the vocabulary words, use new vocabulary in exit slips, include new vocabulary in the predictions and summaries of reciprocal teaching, or count every time a new vocabulary word entered the peer-led discussions. Semantic feature charts could be used now to reinforce vocabulary so that students could revisit and discuss how the features of the concepts or examples compared. Students with learning disabilities learned more vocabulary with semantic feature charts than with definition activities (Bos, Anders, Filip, & Jaffee, 1989). Students could revise an earlier graphic organizer to include the new vocabulary and concepts. And when writing summaries of texts, students should use the new vocabulary.

Some students may need additional practice to learn the words. Familiar activities, like crossword puzzles or matching exercises, help students study words because students must link the words with definitions. We introduce a less familiar tool, the word continuum, because it can reinforce the connotations of words.

Word Continuum. A *word continuum* is like a number line in mathematics (see Fig. 6.5). Students order the words from negative to neutral to positive meanings or from less to more of a characteristic. Thus, a word continuum visually depicts the shades of connotations or the nuances in the meanings of similar words for a concept. At the end of a unit on nutrition, students completed a word continuum from junk food to healthy food. In English, a word continuum of adjectives could depict the nuances of descriptive words.

▶ ▶ ▷ ▷ **Assessment Tools**

You know that we have been discussing assessment tools (and teaching/assessing tools) in every phase because we view assessment as informing both a teacher's instruction and a student's learning. However, since this refining phase occurs at the end of a lesson, the end of a series of lessons, and the end of unit, both teachers and students expect an assessment of what was learned. We have already mentioned revisiting teaching/assessing tools, like KWL or

Figure 6.5   Word Continua

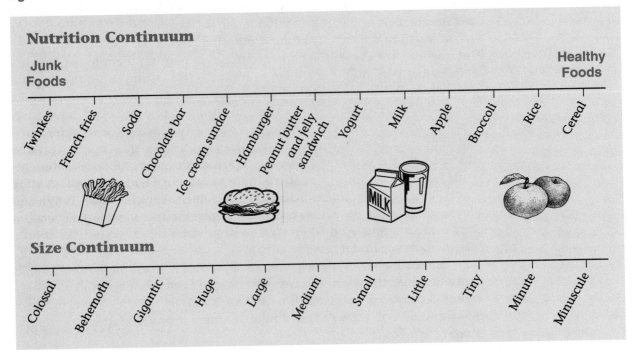

graphic organizers, so that students can assess for themselves how they have enhanced their prior knowledge. Students working together can compare summaries and postreading guides to help each other assess what they have learned. In addition, teachers and students use tests and essays, communication activities, and portfolios to evaluate learning.

Tests and Essays.   Tests are common in middle and secondary classrooms. Certainly students need practice in taking tests, but we remind you that some students do not perform well on tests or perform well on only certain types of tests, such as multiple-choice tests. You know how you perform on tests and you may know friends who say they test well or poorly. So we encourage you to create different testing formats—true-false, multiple choice, and essay— and to evaluate students through class work, communication activities, and portfolios as well.

When you create tests, we recommend that you return to the Types of Questions and Answers section in Chapter 5. You will want to consider carefully whether to ask literal questions or higher-level questions. Think about your major understanding or objective and what type of question would allow students to exhibit their understanding of content. Questions that ask students to explain, interpret, compare, analyze, or describe will allow students to organize their ideas and show how they have increased their prior knowledge.

Communication Activities.   At the end of this chapter, we have included a section describing a sampling of communication activities. Communication activities are speaking, drama, art and music, and writing projects in which students express their learning or enhanced knowledge. Now, we want to encourage you to use those activities or projects as assessment tools. To complete those activities, like a debate, a collage, a rap, or a front-page news article, the students will need to organize their ideas and exhibit whether they have increased their knowledge. To be fair to your students, you need to be clear in your directions about what you require in each activity. In addition, you and your students can determine the criteria both of you would use to evaluate the projects. However, also allow for creativity and individuality because the advantage of these activities over tests is that students will create unique products. In Part Three, we present units that include communication activities in the refining phase of the units.

Collection Portfolios.   When you want students to evaluate their own progress, we recommend portfolios. A *collection portfolio* contains work that students have completed during all three phases of study: generating, interacting, and refining. A student's portfolio could contain a brainstorming list, a study guide, journal entries, notes from conferences or discussions, and communication activities. At various points in the semester, you will want students to review the portfolio contents and weed out less significant items. Students should keep items that demonstrate how they have progressed and refined their knowledge over time. From the collection portfolio, students would select items for their *showcase portfolio*—exhibitions of learning progress. They also would write essays evaluating the items and telling how the items demonstrate their learning progress. In Part Three, we return to collection and showcase portfolios when we present units for different content areas.

▶ ▶ ▷ ▷   ## Focus on Writing: Summaries for Readers

Previously, we discussed composing summaries for oneself—to organize and study information—that are not constrained by length. Summaries written for readers—the annotation, the abstract, and the review—are constrained in length. The students must represent the author's ideas very concisely and yet also completely enough to inform the audience.

Annotations.   *Annotations* of the sources in a bibliography succinctly relay to readers the content of the sources. When you search computer databases or card catalogues, you probably use the annotation of a source to decide if it contains the information you need. A persuasive form of an annotation is the blurb on a book jacket. Publishers write blurbs to inform potential readers and entice them to buy the book. Students could write annotations to inform other students about whether to select a book to read. The second student could evaluate whether the annotation represented the book clearly and in an interesting manner.

Abstracts.   Often around one hundred words in length, *abstracts* are written to inform readers about the contents of research articles. Following the format of the research report, the researcher summarizes the hypothesis, research design, results, and conclusion of the study. If your students are reading research reports, you may want them to evaluate how the author summarized the research in the abstract and compare it to the detailed information in the article. When your students write reports of their research, they could compose an abstract for their final draft.

Reviews.   *Reviews* contain a short summary or synopsis of a work, an analysis of its strengths and weaknesses, and opinions of it or advice to the reader about purchasing or attending the work (an art show or play, for example). You and your students could examine the reviews written by both students and critics that are published in newspapers, magazines, and on-line sites and decide how persuasive they are (see Figs. 6.6, 6.7, & 6.8).

Students could write reviews of books, videos, movies, CDs, software, or events. In assessing either published reviews or other students' reviews, students would consider the following questions:

- In the synopsis or summary, does the reviewer provide a clear overview of the entire work?
- Does the reviewer discuss the strengths and weaknesses of the work?
- Does the reviewer offer convincing opinions about the work or advise you about attending or purchasing the work?

If the reviewer is experienced or knowledgeable in the field, then the review often compares the work to other similar works in the field. For example, a critic may compare the current movie to past movies in the same genre. Students who are well versed in a field could include comparisons in their reviews.

Figure 6.6

Student Web Site Review: Hill Aerospace Museum

This site, "Home of the *SR-71 'Blackbird' Spy Plane*," is for people interested in fighter aircraft and air shows. When you visit you will find pictures of planes, missiles, and bombs. We recommend this site to fanatics of air force equipment. Included here are pictures of the *SR-71C Blackbird* and the *Dragonfly*.

We were very excited to find this site because we have been to this museum. If you can, visit the museum, which is located at a large Air Force field outside of Salt Lake City, Utah. There you will see the real *F-15 Eagle, F-16 Falcon, SR-71C Blackbird*, and the *T-38 Talon*.

If you can't visit the Hill Aerospace Museum, a great museum to visit virtually is the National Air and Space Museum. Exhibits at this museum follow our nation's history of flight. At this site you can visit all the exhibits that are currently on display at the museum. The newest exhibit, "Star Wars, The Magic of the Myth," is now on-line. You don't even have to wait in line to see it!

URLs: Hill Aerospace Museum: **http://www.hill.af.mil/museum/**
National Air and Space Museum: **http://www.nasm.si.edu/**

From Copyright Internet Scout Project, 1994–1999. **http://scout.cs.wisc.edu/.** Used with permission. This issue of KIDS, dated November 12, 1997, was written and produced by the third, fourth, and fifth grade students of Nederland Elementary School in the Boulder Valley School District, located in Nederland, Colorado. The KIDS Report is published with the support of the Internet Scout Project and the National Science Foundation.

Figure 6.7

Student Web Site Review: NASA's Home Page

The NASA Homepage has everything you want to know about NASA and space. It posts information on the latest flight and provides updates on the latest projects, like the Mars landing project and the Hubble Telescope. There are all sorts of in-flight and ground images, including ones of astronauts, vehicles, and buildings. If you have a question, you can get your answer from an expert from NASA. You can even ask astronauts questions!

We recommend this site because it's fun and educational for children. The information is reliable and kept VERY current. Exploring NASA can keep you entertained for hours. The only down side of this site is that some of the images load really slowly.

URL: **http://www.nasa.gov/**

From Copyright Internet Scout Project, 1994–1999. **http://scout.cs.wisc.edu/.** Used with permission. This issue of KIDS, dated November 12, 1997, was written and produced by the third, fourth, and fifth grade students of Nederland Elementary School in the Boulder Valley School District, located in Nederland, Colorado. The KIDS Report is published with the support of the Internet Scout Project and the National Science Foundation.

Never Cry Wolf, by Farley Mowat
Report by: A High School Student
Rating: Two Thumbs Up
Category: Adventure

Never Cry Wolf is a true story about a man named Farley Mowat who is sent up north to study some arctic wolves, because he works for the wildlife association. The wolves weren't as dangerous as he had feared they would be, and he ended up really understanding the wolves' behavior.

The main character in the book is Farley Mowat who is a mammalogist with the Wildlife Association. The wolf family that Farley is studying are not like the other wolves because this family of wolves are nice and act like he's not even there. He tries a lot of different experiments to try and trick the wolves. For instance, when the wolves left one day, he urinated in a circle around his tent to mark off his territory to see what the wolves' reaction would be.

The author's writing style really gets you into the story and he uses some descriptive words. He gives you an idea of what the Arctic is like, since most of us have never been there. I think that I would recommend this novel to the type of reader who likes true stories, or stories about wolves and wildlife.

Source: BookNook, **http://i-site.on.ca/booknook.html**

Strategies and Tools for Evaluating Ideas and Reconstructing Prior Knowledge

By separating strategies for evaluating ideas and reconstructing prior knowledge from strategies for organizing ideas and enhancing prior knowledge, we are emphasizing that strategic learners may completely revise their schemata. They critically think about the new information and reconsider their prior knowledge in the light of that information. When your students begin with misconceptions about content, you want them to reconstruct their schemata, not just to add new information to erroneous information. You will recall from Chapter 2 that students probably retain prior knowledge that stems from their cultural beliefs, even though you think the evidence refutes those beliefs. In this situation, you and your students need to recognize the cultural differences.

Reconsidering and refuting prior knowledge are the primary strategies (see Fig. 6.9), but strategic learners also figure out what information is missing or what they need to know and ask new questions about the topic. In comparing the new information and their prior knowledge, strategic learners evaluate the different ideas they encounter by using criteria they have devised or learned. They review their own and the author's purposes, point of view, or bias in evaluating the new information. They may also apply their reconstructed ideas to new situations or examples and to events in their own lives, their community, or global society.

As you survey Figure 6.9, you will find familiar teaching/assessing tools and several new ones. You may want your students to revisit their brainstorming lists from the generating phase to revise their prior knowledge. You may continue using tools begun in the interacting phase, like peer-led discussions or DR-TA, in order to have students evaluate their ideas now that they have finished reading. In the refining phase, they can reflect on the entire text and may reconstruct their view of the text or apply the ideas to other texts and other situations in their lives or in the community.

As before, we will present the tool of modeling and explaining strategies first because we want to emphasize how to make strategies visible to your students. We include an excerpt from the text, a categorization chart, and questions for the class to discuss.

▶ ▶ ▶ ▶ Modeling and Explaining Strategies for Evaluating Ideas and Reconstructing Prior Knowledge

We chose the article "Rewriting Southwestern Prehistory" because the author presents evidence to support a new theory that could revise how archaeologists view Pueblo civilization. When teaching students, we like to use texts that show how people reconstruct knowledge and that show what people hold as factual evidence does change.

Suppose you plan to study ancient civilizations around the world. You could decide to organize the study around the major understanding or question, "What is a civilized society?" In the generating phase, your students will brainstorm their ideas about what constitutes a civilized society today. During the interacting phase, the students will read a variety of sources about ancient

Figure 6.9

Evaluating Ideas and
Reconstructing Prior
Knowledge: Strategies
and Tools

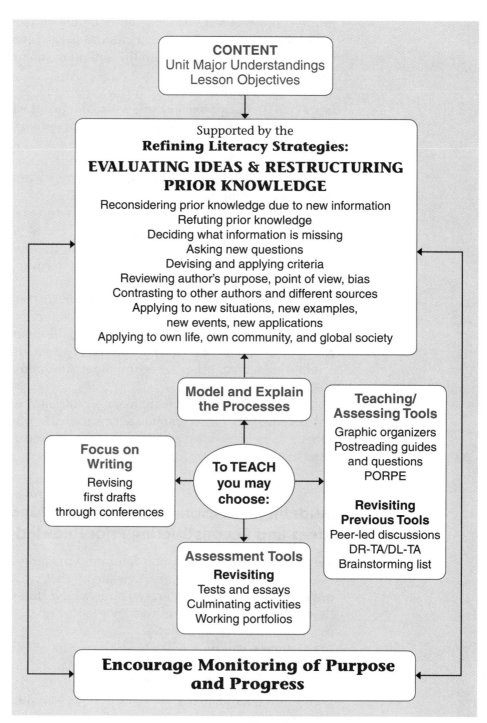

peoples who lived on every continent. In the refining phase, they will devise criteria to reconstruct their definition of a civilized society. You have decided you will model and explain how to revise or reconstruct ideas about civilization using the article "Rewriting Southwestern Prehistory."

To introduce the article and set a specific purpose for reading, you would call the students' attention to the first paragraph, where the author informs readers of the old and new theories about Pueblo ruins. You would have the students identify the three Pueblo centers mentioned—Chaco Canyon, Aztec Ruins, and Casas Grandes—in the paragraph and on a map. You would point out that the text is probably organized around the three centers. As they read, the students' task is to mark where the author states the old and new theories and cites the evidence for the theories. Later they will use the evidence to define what a civilized society is. Here is an annotated excerpt of the article for you to read:

Modeling and Explaining Script for Evaluating Ideas and Reconstructing Prior Knowledge

My Notes

Excerpts from "**Rewriting Southwestern Prehistory**"

New studies suggest an overarching political system dominated much of the Southwest from a.d. 850 to 1500.

Old theory

The ancient Southwest has long been viewed as a patchwork of boom-and-bust cultures. Pueblos were thought to have come and gone independently of one another and archaeologists rarely looked beyond the areas immediately surrounding their excavations.

New theory

But a new study of the Southwestern landscape has revealed that **three of the largest and most important ancient centers were linked by a 450-mile meridian line**—Chaco Canyon, in New Mexico; Aztec Ruins, 55 miles due north near the Colorado state line; and Casas Grandes, 390 miles due south in Chihuahua, Mexico.

My Notes	
	Excerpts from "**Rewriting Southwestern Prehistory**"
Archaeological evidence	Chaco and Aztec were also **connected along the meridian by a road,** known today as **the Great North Road**. . . . Tree-ring dates indicate that Chaco was occupied mainly from A.D. 850 to 1125 (after which its population was greatly diminished), Aztec from 1110 to 1275, and Casas Grandes from 1250 to 1500. Since these sites did not flourish simultaneously, **the road and meridian may have served to commemorate cultural and historical continuity.**
New theory	
First center	The first and largest of the three centers, **Chaco Canyon** is notable for ten huge buildings called Great Houses in and around an 11-mile stretch of canyon. . . .
Archaeological evidence	These **Great Houses** were oval, rectangular, or D-shaped sandstone structures several hundred feet across and up to five stories tall, with hundreds of rooms ranged around two or more sides of an open plaza. The canyon also had a number of **Great Kivas**, circular, roofed ceremonial buildings about 55 feet in diameter. These larger structures dominated hundreds of smaller buildings, . . .
Geographical evidence	plazas, and roadways, all arrayed around a **north-south axis** joining two Great Houses. . . .
New theory	But Chaco's influence did not stop at the canyon's edge, because it was also the **hub of a Chacoan Regional System**, defined in the late 1980's by a small group of National Park Service, Bureau of Land Management, and university archaeologists. This regional system included about **150 communities** with thousands of individual settlements stretching across more than 35,000 square miles in the Four Corners area (where New Mexico, Colorado, Utah and Arizona come together). Each of these sites had **a Great House** . . .
Archaeological evidence	and most of them had **a Great Kiva**. . . . . . .

New question about missing evidence

. . . Efforts are under way to survey the corridor between Chaco and Casas Grandes, by aerial and satellite photography, **to see if a "Great South Road" linked the two sites** as the Great North Road linked Chaco and Aztec. . . . The area covered by the Chaco-Aztec-Casas Grandes meridian and adjacent sites is more than 100,000 square miles—two and one-half times the size of the Chacoan Regional System and 1,000 times that of the typical survey area around a Southwestern archaeological site. **The existence of a political system encompassing so great an area will require the review and revision of almost every aspect of Southwestern prehistory.** The abandonment of the Four Corners ca. 1280, for example, remains largely unexplained, though **archaeologists have proposed droughts and new religions as possible causes.** Aztec Ruins came to an **end,** the Four Corners was **abandoned,** and Casas Grandes **began** at **almost exactly the same time.** Clearly something momentous happened, but no one yet knows what. Collaboration with Pueblo scholars will do much to clarify this new history of the ancient Southwest.

Other theories or hypotheses

Unanswered question

Excerpted from Lekson, S. H., "Rewriting Southwestern History," *Archaeology Magazine 50,* (1) pp. 52–55. Reprinted by permission.

After the students have read the article, you would introduce a blank categorization chart by defining the labels on the columns and rows. (For a completed chart, see Table 6.2.) The purpose of the chart is to help students organize the evidence so that they can evaluate whether the new theory about Pueblo civilization has sufficient support (the question in Table 6.2). In pairs or independently, the students may complete the chart, or you may want to model and explain how to complete the chart by discussing the evidence from the first civilization, Chaco Canyon. While the students work, you would circulate to observe their progress and offer assistance as needed.

When the students have finished their charts, you could fill in a blank chart on the overhead, if the students need that reinforcement. If the students

Table 6.2   Categorization Chart of Evidence for the New Theory

	Does the evidence support the new theory that an overarching political system linked three large regional centers?			
	Archaeological Evidence	Geographical Evidence	Astronomical Evidence	Oral History Evidence
Chaco Canyon, 850–1125	1) Great Houses 2) Great Kivas 3) 150 communities with Great Houses and Kivas 4) Great North Road 5) Macaw skeletons	1) Located on meridian 2) Buildings on north-south axis 3) Great North Road on meridian	Southwestern sky: All 3 centers have a daily rotation of sky on north-south axis around the meridian.	Today's Acoma and Zuni live near the meridian. They have similar oral histories.
Aztec, 1110–1275	1) Black and white ceramics 2) Great Houses	1) Located on meridian 2) No geographical advantage to location		Some people went south from a great center to find macaws.
Casas Grandes, 1250–1500	1) Pueblo-style buildings 2) Macaw pens 3) Macaw skeletons	1) Located on meridian 2) Is there a Great South Road?		They returned with macaws.

completed their charts well, then you would begin a discussion. In this script, a teacher-led discussion, the strategies to evaluate and reconsider ideas are triggered by the teacher's prepared questions. Additional supporting questions may need to be asked, depending on the students' answers.

Here is the script of the teacher's prepared questions:

Modeling and Explaining Script for Teacher-led Discussion

- Is the evidence sufficient to support the new theory? What additional evidence is needed? What new questions should archaeologists ask? (**evaluate evidence**)

- What is the difference in the viewpoints between the archaeologists who believe the old theory about the Pueblo civilization and those who support the new theory? (**reconsider point of view**)

- What is the author's point of view of Pueblo society? What does his use of the word, "prehistory" connote about his point of view? (**reconsider point of view**)

- How do you evaluate or define the Pueblo society? Is it civil and by what criteria? How does your criteria compare to the archaeologists' and the author's? (**evaluate and reconstruct**)

Let's review and summarize not just the example of modeling and explaining to evaluate and reconstruct ideas but the strategies that would come before it:

Generating Phase Strategies
- **Set a purpose** specifically for the article (to note the old and new theories and to find evidence for the new theory)

Interacting Phase Strategies
- **Capitalized on text organization** (three Pueblo centers)
- **Found and interpreted important information** (old and new theories and evidence)
- **Constructed auxiliary aids** (marked important information on copies of the article)

Refining Phase Strategies
- **Reread** and **organized** evidence on a **categorization chart**
- **Evaluated** the evidence for the new theory, **missing evidence**, and **new questions**
- **Reconsidered point of view** of archaeologists supporting old theory and those supporting new theory
- **Reviewed point of view** of author of article and use of word *prehistory*
- **Reevaluated** and **reconstructed** own definition of civilization

Now let's turn to teaching/assessing tools for evaluating ideas and reconstructing prior knowledge. We think that many students will benefit from the support of teaching/assessing tools because discarding or revising prior knowledge is not easy.

▶ ▶ ▶ ▶ ## Teaching/Assessing Tools for Evaluating Ideas and Reconstructing Prior Knowledge

In reconstructing and evaluating ideas, we want students to reconsider the positions presented in texts as well as their own perspectives, which is a difficult task (Chambliss, 1994). When students read only textbooks, they may be unaware of the controversies surrounding events or that differing perspectives abound in every field. For example, in social studies, students may have read the facts about the Lend-Lease Act but little about the reasons for and political controversies behind the act. In art, they may learn about Andy Warhol, but do they compare the critics' reactions to his Campbell soup can picture to earlier critics' reactions to cubism or to impressionism? As students evaluate the controversies in the events, theories, works, or positions of people in every content area, they can formulate their own positions and test out their ideas with their peers.

We think many students need support in organizing the important ideas to evaluate and then to reflect and reconsider those ideas. In addition, they need opportunities to experiment with their positions by discussing them with other peers. In explaining and defending their positions, students reconstruct their knowledge. Therefore, we will present the familiar tools of graphic organizers and postreading guides and questions and one new tool, PORPE, that helps students write essay exams. You may decide to revisit previous tools, like peer-led discussions or brainstorming lists as well.

Preparation for Evaluating Evidence: Categorization Chart. You undoubtedly noticed that we again used a categorization chart for the modeling and explaining script, but this time we used it to evaluate ideas for reconsideration. We think most students don't automatically challenge factual information but rather accept facts as unassailable. They accumulate factual information without sorting it into categories that can be reexamined. By providing students with a graphic organizer or a study guide, you can support their organizing of information so that they can focus on evaluating and reconsidering that information. Therefore, the teaching/assessing tools we examine here are not new; we are just using them for a different outcome.

Figure 6.10   Understanding Conflicting Perspectives: Civil War Unit

Event	North	South	Consequence
Dred Scott case	Position Reason for position Values, beliefs, underlying position	Position Reason for position Values, beliefs, underlying position	Immediate impact Long-term impact
Firing on Fort Sumter	Position Reason for position Values, beliefs, underlying position	Position Reason for position Values, beliefs, underlying position	Immediate impact Long-term impact
Uncle Tom's Cabin	Position Reason for position Values, beliefs, underlying position	Position Reason for position Values, beliefs, underlying position	Immediate impact Long-term impact
Kansas-Nebraska Act	Position Reason for position Values, beliefs, underlying position	Position Reason for position Values, beliefs, underlying position	Immediate impact Long-term impact

What were the different regional perspectives underlying the four conflicting events?

What democratic values were in conflict?

Was violence a response to the resolution of these events?

Focus Question: Can the use of violence be justified?

Source: From D. Lapp, J. Flood, and N. Farnan, *Content Area Reading and Learning: Instructional Strategies*, Second Edition pp. 200–202. Copyright © 1996 by Allyn & Bacon. Reprinted by permission.

Postreading Guides and Questions.   Although we used a categorization chart, we could have used a *postreading guide* to help students evaluate and reconstruct their own and the text's ideas.

For the same Civil War unit mentioned earlier, Peters (1996) guides students to organize information about four events—the *Dred Scott* case, the firing on Fort Sumter, publication of *Uncle Tom's Cabin,* and the Kansas-Nebraska Act—so that they can analyze the conflicting perspectives of the North and the South (see Fig. 6.10.) By identifying the reasons for and values and beliefs underlying the positions that the North and the South held, students would organize the important information and begin to interpret and reconsider the individual events. Then the students would answer three questions about all four events: "What were the different regional perspectives underlying the four conflicting events?" "What democratic values were in conflict?" and "Was violence a response to the resolution of these events?" The students would then interpret the two perspectives of the Civil War and reconstruct their own positions to answer the focus question of the unit: "Can the use of violence be justified?"

As the students complete the postreading guide, you and the students would assess how clearly they stated their positions and whether the positions, reasons, and underlying values correspond with each other. Students could also complete the guide together and compare each other's interpretations. To

Figure 6.11

Point-of-View Guide

America After 1941

America's Huge War Needs (pp. 617–618)

1. As a worker in a U.S. defense plant, tell what effect the War Production Board has had on you, your co-workers, and the soldiers overseas.

Americans Go Back to Work (p. 618)

2. As one of the leaders in a national labor union, what is your reaction to the need for war supplies?
3. As a farmer, tell how your life has changed from the Depression days to the present days of wartime.

Opportunities for Blacks (pp. 618–619)

As a black person from the South:
4. Tell why you and others moved to the Northeast and Midwest sections of the United States.
5. Describe the effect of Hitler's racist doctrine on your situation at home.
6. Tell why Executive Order 8802 was important to you.

Source: Excerpt from Wood, Karen D., Lapp, Diane and Flood, James (1992). *Guiding Readers Through Text: A Review of Study Guides* (Newark, DE: International Reading Association). Reprinted by permission.

reinforce refining ideas after students have completed the postreading guide, we would hold a debate in which students would represent the two perspectives. At the close of the debate, the class would discuss their own positions on the use of violence in contemporary society and their own lives.

Another example of a postreading guide is a *point-of-view guide* in which students take on the role of a person or character (Wood, 1988). Using their schema-based connections, they elaborate on, interpret, and speculate on text-based information. By creating the perspective of a particular role, they reconstruct and reconsider the ideas they have read about in their textbooks. For example, in Figure 6.11, students take the point of view of different workers in the United States during World War II (Wood, Lapp, & Flood, 1992).

English teachers can create a guide in which students take the role of a specific character in a novel and speculate about the character's actions and perspectives toward a new situation—one that is not in the book. Alternatively, the students could choose a minor character in the book and relate that character's point of view toward the main characters and the events. You could read your students *The True Story of the Three Little Pigs,* a picture book by Peter Scieszka, written from the wolf's point of view, as a fun, mood-setting example.

If you can accept a little anthropomorphism in science, you could create a guide on which students would take the perspective of an animal in an environment, a chemical in a solution, or an asteroid in space. Students would describe their surroundings and the events that might occur, as well as their reactions to those events and surroundings.

Both you and your students would assess the reasonableness of the point of view or new perspective. Did the students incorporate the important information that would support the particular perspective taken?

Teacher as Inquiring Learner Activity

Find a text in your content area that your students could read, and create a postreading study guide for it. You could think of an issue or problem in your content area and find one or two texts that address the issue. You could rephrase a topic like the Civil War into a contemporary issue, as Peters did. Or you could examine the theme or issue in a novel.

Consider different perspectives on the issue, problem, or theme, and create a study guide on which students would organize the information. You could create a pro/con chart, a semantic web for several positions, or a decision tree for different options, for example.

• What questions could you ask so that students would evaluate, apply, or reconsider those perspectives and their own?

If you have the opportunity, try your postreading guide with your students, and discuss what they learned.

• How would you revise the guide and your questions?

PORPE.   Designed to assist students in studying for essay exams (Simpson, 1986), *PORPE* consists of five steps: **p**redict, **o**rganize, **r**ehearse, **p**ractice, and **e**valuate. You would need to model and explain each step with your students and allow for much collaborative or partner work for students to gain competence in writing essays:

1. *Predict* potential essay questions. Students can find predicting potential essay questions difficult. If you have asked both text-based and schema-based questions and discussed different types of questions during the interacting phase, students may have less difficulty devising likely essay questions. As you model and explain potential essay questions with them, you would also explain the key words used in essay questions, such as *explain, compare and contrast, discuss,* and *critique.*

2. *Organize* information to answer the predicted questions. Just as we used the two categorization charts, you would present a graphic organizer for students to use. If students have had experience in organizing information, they could create their own graphic organizers to depict the important information and supporting details or examples they will need in their essays.

3. *Rehearsal* of the organized information. The students would study the information by reciting from memory the major ideas on their graphic organizers. Gradually over several days, they would recite more and more details. We recommend that students work in partners, quizzing each other on the information.

4. *Practice* writing the essay. Having rehearsed the information, the students are ready to write their answers to the questions from memory. You would model and explain the sections of an essay: the opening statement that rephrases the question or takes a specific stand; the paragraphs, each containing a major point and supporting details; and the concluding or summarizing paragraph. Or you and the students could compose the opening statement together and perhaps the first paragraph. Then the students could compose the rest of the essay in pairs or independently. On subsequent essays, students could work in pairs or independently to practice writing the entire essay.

5. *Evaluate* the practice essay. Students would compare their written essays with their graphic organizers to see if they included the important information. They also would evaluate whether they answered the question, whether their major points were clearly supported, whether they used transitions between paragraphs, and whether their position was clear in the opening and concluding paragraphs. You would want to model and explain how to evaluate an essay using examples of class work (anonymously, of course) or even a poorly written one you created specifically for this purpose. Subsequently, students could evaluate and give revision suggestions to each other.

▶ ▶ ▶ ▶ Assessment Tools

We have already discussed the assessment tools of tests and essays, communication activities, and collection portfolios in the earlier assessment section of this chapter. Obviously, those same tools can be used to assess whether students can evaluate ideas and whether they have restructured their prior knowledge. However, if students are to demonstrate how they have evaluated and restructured knowledge, then they need to be asked higher-level questions for tests and essays, need to have opportunities for challenging communication activities, and need to assess their collection portfolios thoroughly.

▶ ▶ ▶ ▶ Focus on Writing: Revising First Drafts Through Conferences

We could have discussed revising first drafts in the previous Focus on Writing section as easily as here. However, we want students to do more than consider how they have organized and elaborated on their ideas; we want them as well to evaluate those ideas critically and even to restructure their first drafts. To emphasize that revision of first drafts, a very difficult act for most writers, we have placed it here.

Most writers, especially students, consider their first draft to be clear and complete. Some writers have learned to set aside a first draft for a few days so that they can reread the draft more critically or more like a reader would. Most writers need another reader to ask questions about specific information or to state where they experienced confusion while reading. From that reader's questions and comments, writers learn where to revise their drafts.

In schools, particularly in English classes, teachers confer with students about their drafts, and students confer with each other. These conferences could occur during prewriting (generating) and during composing of the first draft

These students are helping each other refine their ideas in their written drafts.

© Susie Fitzhugh

(interacting) as easily as now, during revising (refining), because the purpose is not merely to have students rewrite. Instead, the conferences are to assist the students in expressing their intended meaning clearly and completely.

We encourage you to model and explain revising conferences so that your students can conduct peer conferences. In revising conferences, you would concentrate on the ideas and information, saving editing comments (for example, spelling and punctuation) for after the ideas presented in the writing are clear. Conferring with students both individually and in small groups, you would ask questions and point out confusions that you have. You would also model and explain several strategies and suggestions for them to use when they revise their drafts.

Whether students are writing nonfiction, fiction, or poetry, we recommend that you selectively model and explain revision categories focused on exploring the following questions (Allan & Miller, 1995; Atwell, 1998):

- What is the purpose and meaning or subject of the draft: to tell a story, to give directions, to explain a subject or topic, to persuade, to create poetry?

- Who is the audience: peers, a specific person, people in the community?

- How is the text organized: sequence, problem solution, or some other way?
- Is the amount of information or detail enough, accurate, and specific but not too much, too general, or too redundant?
- Is the information focused and not tangential to the purpose?
- Is the beginning engaging and the ending fitting?
- Are the words and sentences clear, specific, precise, and flowing?
- Does the writing have voice—personality, uniqueness, character—instead of being dry, listless, and dull?

You would not explore all of these revision categories in one conference because that could overwhelm the student; rather, you would choose the ones that are most important to the student's draft. Whether each student has chosen his or her own type of text (poem, fiction narrative, biography, personal memory) or you have assigned the same type of text (reporting information, eyewitness accounts, letters to the editor), you will confer on only the most important category. Over the course of a year, you would model and explain different categories for revision. As students gain experience, they may come to a conference with their peers knowing they need help on a specific category of problems.

Communicating Learning to Different Audiences

Throughout these three chapters in Part Two, we have concentrated on constructing knowledge by first generating ideas, then interacting with ideas, and finally refining ideas. Now, at the end of refining, you will want students to take stock of the learning that has occurred over several lessons or at the end of a unit in a culminating activity.

While the test is a prevalent tool on which students demonstrate their learning, we recommend offering students a variety of communication options over the course of the year. Sometimes you may assign one communication activity; at other times, you may allow students to choose from several activities or let students devise their own communication vehicle. Clearly all of these choices depend on the major understandings and objectives that you have set out for students, as well as their competencies and needs.

Key to the students' motivation and investment in any communication activity is the audience. Proving learning to the teacher on a test or piece of writing has the reward of a grade, which is motivating for the college-bound students. However, in our experience, when students communicate to specific audiences, they invest more in the activity and so refine their learning even more. Aside from the teacher, peers in the classroom are the most convenient audience for students' communications. You could arrange for students in other classes, different grades, or even different schools to be the audience. Student audiences are particularly appropriate when the students apply their learning to their own lives in and out of school. When the students' learning can be applied to their community or society in general, then not only are student audiences appropriate, but you could arrange interesting specific audiences, such as the mayor or the members of a local historical society. Students could also communicate with the general public in the community through the local newspaper, poster campaigns, or presentations at town meetings, for example.

When you offer a variety of communication options to students, you and your students will uncover the different strengths of particular students. The public speaker, the computer graphics person, or the investigative reporter in your class could have the opportunity to demonstrate knowledge because the option matches his or her strengths. Therefore, to pique your interest, we will present a sampling of opportunities through which students could communicate their learning to different audiences: speaking, drama, the arts, and writing.

▶ ▶ ▶ ▶ **Communicating Learning Through Speaking Opportunities**

Speaking activities can range from a simple reading of a text to peers to the more complicated presentation of research evidence at a public meeting.

When students have read a variety of texts, they could simply read aloud significant passages and tell why those passages were significant to their learning. A small group of students could perform a choral reading of a poem or a section of text. Students could give book talks about the texts they read to persuade other students to read that text. Through each of these activities, students can exhibit their interpretations of the text.

When students have held peer-led discussions about a text or a variety of texts, they may have explored different reactions and opinions. The small group could turn that discussion into a panel presentation of their differing reactions and opinions. Students could present their particular reaction and the evidence to support that reaction. After the panel presentation, their peers could ask them questions.

When the students have researched a topic or investigated a local issue, they could present their results and conclusions in a panel presentation, similar to panel presentations that are regular parts of professional conferences. To classmates, other students, or specific interested citizens, students could report the results of their surveys about an issue, their interviews of people's oral histories, or their directions for an experiment, recipe, or hobby activity.

Finally, we suggest that students who have researched a topic hold a debate on an issue. Presenting a position, marshaling evidence to support the argument, and rebutting opponents' arguments with evidence is a challenging activity. Opportunities to practice formulating arguments orally can help prepare students for presenting arguments in writing.

▶ ▶ ▶ ▶ Communicating Learning Through Dramatic Opportunities

We think that most content-area teachers are more comfortable with informal drama activities than formal play productions. Our informal drama suggestions could be performed within class or before other audiences even when the trappings of productions are minimal. Procedures, systems, and observations in many content areas could be informally dramatized. For example, a biology teacher asks her students to dramatize the circulation system. The students figure out how to represent the organs and the movement of blood, oxygen, and nutrients, and then they present their improvisations to the whole class.

Role play or simulations and pantomimes are informal drama too. Students could do a pantomime or role-play of a specific person or event in any content area, such as a particular scientist's making a discovery or an ordinary person in history. In an English class, students participated in a lottery for grades to simulate the situation in Shirley Jackson's famous short story, "The Lottery" (McQueen, 1996). Marrying characters from different novels or famous people from different eras or different fields into an improvised role play of an event or controversy can offer students challenging opportunities.

Another informal drama is *readers' theater*, in which students read a story by taking the parts of the characters in the story. Short stories that have a substantial amount of dialogue for characters work well for readers' theater. Assuming the roles of the characters and a narrator, the students read the story as they would read the script of a play. Students learn how to portray their characters through their voice only.

And finally, in this video age, students could video their speaking or dramatic endeavors to present in class or on local cable television.

▶ ▶ ▶ ▶ **Communicating Learning Through Art and Music Opportunities**

Art media offer students the opportunity to express feelings and sensations they may find difficult to communicate with words. If some students are reluctant to draw, sketch, or paint representations of their learning, reactions, or feelings, they could create collages, abstract representations, or computer graphics. Students can be encouraged to sketch their ideas by viewing the working sketches or models of scientists as well of artists.

Music offers similar opportunities to students. Some students may choose to compose a musical selection for their instrument or compose a selection on the computer. Raps are now the most common song form that students use to communicate their learnings. Have your students compose a rap for a chemical reaction or a historical event, for example.

Students who are not artistically or musically venturesome could select a painting reproduction or a musical recording that represented their learning, reactions, or feelings. In addition to sharing the music or art, the students could tell how it represents their topics and why they selected it.

Finally, students can persuade other students and the general public to become aware of specific issues and take action through poster campaigns and musical jingles or songs. In those artistic activities, students would learn to present their position and their evidence in an entertaining and attention-getting manner.

▶ ▶ ▶ ▶ **Communicating Learning Through Writing Opportunities**

Because our field is literacy, we could make a long list of writing suggestions. Instead we will offer a few suggestions in four categories: poetry, narrative, expository, and persuasive. Any of these opportunities could be published in print or on-line.

First, poetry can express learning as well as images and feelings. You might want to revisit the poetry books suggested in Chapter 3. Three poetry forms adaptable to many content areas are bio-poems, found poems, and diamantes. First, in *bio-poems*, each line describes the topic. The name of the topic is printed vertically, one letter per line. Using the letter on the line for the first word, each line tells information about the topic. A second poetic form is *found poems*: free verse composed from vocabulary words or words randomly selected from texts. Choosing from a large variety of words, students would create a line or a stanza of poetry. A third form, *diamantes* are five or seven lines in a diamond shape. In the five-line diamante, the first line is one word naming a thing and the fifth is another word for it. The second line contains two descriptive words; the third line three action words; and the fourth two descriptive words relating to the fifth line. Tiedt (1970) invented the seven-line diamante. It begins describing one subject and ends with its opposite as follows: one noun for the first subject, two adjectives, three participles, four nouns (two for first subject and two for the opposite subject), three participles, two adjectives, one noun for the opposite subject.

Second, although narrative forms are most common in English and language arts classes, other content areas can also incorporate the narrative sequence, even for nonfiction writing. Students might write a personal narrative about an experience in their life in an English class. Or they could write a narrative about how they learned as well as what they learned about a topic in any content area. For example, they could write their experiences and learnings when they did field observations or when they interviewed a person. A narrative suggestion for students to demonstrate their knowledge of history is to write fictional journals for ordinary people of that time. Students could depict the everyday life of a soldier in World War II or a laundress in the Gold Rush, for example. Finally, in every content area, students could write character sketches or biographies about important people who have contributed to the field.

Third, the most common expository form in schools is the traditional report or term paper (which we will present in Chapter 7). For now, we want you to think of alternative forms of informing audiences about subjects or topics. A student's personal letter to a friend or relative can exhibit what the student has learned. Students could explain information to each other through front-page news articles, eyewitness reports, or even a textbook chapter (Sosenke, 1994). In every content area, newsletters, magazine articles, and pamphlets are published to report information to specific audiences. Students could either write their own or send contributions to be considered by the published ones.

Finally, in persuasive forms, whether a letter, editorial, or review, students evaluate ideas and seek to refine their audience's knowledge and opinion on the subject. We find that writing persuasive letters prepares students for writing essays since both seek to convince the reader. In letters to specific people, such as parents, school personnel, or governmental officials, students must state the problem and their position, offer major points to support, and conclude with their solution or recommendation. When students want to reach the general public or peers, letters to the editor of the local paper and editorials in the school newspaper, respectively, are useful forms. And don't forget reviews, which we discussed earlier.

Since we have offered you only a few suggestions for speaking, drama, art, music, and writing opportunities, we encourage you to explore other communication activities so that your students can demonstrate their learning of your content area in a variety of ways.

Purpose Setting and Monitoring During the Refining Ideas Phase (Underlying and Ongoing Strategies)

At the refining phase, strategic learners monitor whether they have accomplished their purposes. They may decide that they accomplished their purpose satisfactorily and their strategies were successful. They may decide that they have discovered a new purpose (question) worth exploring and begin thinking about strategies for their new purpose. They may decide that their purpose has not been accomplished satisfactorily, and they need to recycle to generating or interacting strategies.

In deciding about whether they have accomplished their purposes, strategic learners monitor or assess what they know now compared to their earlier knowledge. They decide how to organize the information clearly so that they can study it. They monitor themselves as they review the information, checking to see if they can recall most of the information. Strategic learners also think critically about the information by evaluating the ideas. They reconsider their own prior knowledge, the author's ideas and bias, and the ideas in other sources. Throughout the phases but especially in the refining phase, strategic learners monitor whether they have enhanced or restructured their prior knowledge.

Thus, strategic learners are really engaged in self-evaluation and goal setting for future learning.

A Checklist for Monitoring Strategies for Refining Ideas

Monitoring Purpose

✓ Have you accomplished your original purpose?

✓ Have you accomplished the purpose you changed to during the interacting phase?

✓ Have you discovered a new purpose to pursue?

✓ Do you need to recycle to generating or interacting phases?

Monitoring Organizing Ideas and Enhancing Prior Knowledge

✓ Can you organize the important ideas into categories that build your schema?

✓ Can you elaborate on the important ideas?

✓ Can you summarize the important information for your purposes?

✓ Can you draw a conclusion, infer a theme, or determine the thesis?

✓ Can you confirm the information with other works or sources?

✓ Do you need to review important vocabulary?

✓ Do you need to reread, look back, review, or recite the information to study?

Monitoring Evaluating Ideas and Restructuring Prior Knowledge

✓ Have you changed, reconsidered, or refuted your prior knowledge based on the new information?

✓ Do you know what information is missing or have new questions to ask?

✓ Have you applied criteria to evaluate the information?

✓ Do you recognize the author's point of view, bias, intent, or purpose?

✓ Can you contrast these ideas to ideas in other works or sources?

✓ Can you apply the ideas to your life, your community, or society in general?

✓ Can you imagine new situations, events, examples, or application for these ideas?

✓ What communication activity do you choose to express your learning, and who is your audience?

Summary of the Chapter

This chapter represents the last of the three phases, the refining phase. We have emphasized two major strategies that strategic learners use:

- Organizing ideas and enhancing prior knowledge
- Evaluating ideas and restructuring prior knowledge

We think your students will more frequently increase their prior knowledge than restructure it. However, when they bring misconceptions to your content area, you will strive to reconstruct their prior knowledge. In either case, strategic learners monitor their purpose and their progress to see if their strategies fit their tasks.

To help students use refining phase strategies, we presented both new and familiar teaching tools:

- Modeling and explaining to make visible both major strategies
- New teaching/assessing tools, like the summary, SQ3R, and PORPE
- Familiar tools now serving the refining phase, like graphic organizers and postreading guides
- Continuing tools begun in an earlier phase, like KWL Plus
- Assessment tools: tests, communication activities, and collection portfolios
- Focus on writing: summaries for readers and revising first drafts
- Communication opportunities for students to express their learning

Once again, we remind you that you must select the strategies to model and explain, as well as the teaching/assessing tools to use. You will make those decisions based on your content objectives, your students' needs, and the curricular materials you use.

You have now come to the end of the generating, interacting, and refining phases. You know that we separated these three phases in order to model and explain the strategies and to explain teaching/assessing tools. In reality, you and your students would seamlessly move from one phase to the next and even recycle through phases. Therefore, in Chapter 7, we will demonstrate that continuous flow through the three phases when we describe two research projects.

Inquiry Activities About Your Learning

1. Write a review of a curriculum material in your content area: for example, a text, computer software, web sites, teacher's guides, or textbooks. Summarize the material concisely yet completely, so that your peers understand its contents. Identify the strengths and weaknesses in the material. If possible, compare it to other curriculum materials you know. Finally, offer suggestions on how and with whom to use (or not use) the curriculum material. You might want to compile your classmates' reviews into a curriculum resource booklet.

2. Find a text in your content area that might cause you to reconsider your prior knowledge. The text could be a research paper that presents an opposing or new theory, a magazine article, a position paper or an editorial about a controversial issue, or a novel set in an unfamiliar culture. What is your view or position before you read the text—your prior knowledge? After you have read, think about the author's position. What information supports that perspective? Do you agree or disagree with that perspective, and why? What in the text might cause you to reconsider your position?

Inquiry Activities About Your Students' Learning

1. With a small group of students, write a summary for a text they need to study. Choose a text that is well organized and contains information they will understand easily. Devise a graphic organizer that will help them organize the information. You can decide whether they should complete the graphic organizer as they read or afterward. After they have organized the ideas, you might want to discuss the information before writing the summary. Depending on the students, you may decide to write a summary together, in pairs, or independently. Guide the students through sections of the summary: writing the opening overview sentence, summarizing sections of the text, and composing a concluding sentence. Have the students share their summaries and discuss the similarities and differences. Can you tell if they condensed information or synthesized information?

2. With a classmate in your content area, brainstorm a list of communication activities that could be end products for a topic or a unit in your content area. Think of a variety of speaking, drama, art, music, and writing activities. Think about different audiences who would be interested in receiving the students' products. Pick four communication options. Write directions for each option. Devise criteria you and the students could use to evaluate the products. You might want to try doing the communication activities yourself so that you know if your directions are clear and your criteria appropriate.

7

Linking the Phases: Learning Through Research Projects

You know that we have artificially separated the generating, interacting, and refining phases in the previous three chapters. We separated the three phases so that we could analyze specific strategies for you. On the basis of that analysis, we expect you to select strategies to model and explain that fit the literacy tasks you will assign your students. In addition, we anticipate that you will choose from among the teaching/assessing tools in order to support your students' learning.

In this chapter, we link the three phases together because strategic learners use literacy strategies in concert. You recall that in Chapter 5, we always included a brief generating phase before we modeled strategies for the interacting phase. In Chapter 6, we outlined the generating and interacting phases before we modeled strategies for the refining phase. We do not want you to forget that strategic learners use strategies in all three phases with every literacy task: when reading science experiments or newspaper articles and when writing geometric proofs or poems. In this chapter (see graphic), we will analyze two research projects as we model how the generating, interacting, and refining phases work in concert.

Before we present the two research project scenarios, we explain the different purposes of research projects in content areas and the role of end products in research projects. You know your students need to learn more knowledge in your content area and how to learn content independently or to research information. We will explain how research projects can address those goals in the purposes for research projects. Then, after reviewing the discussion presented in Chapter 6 on end products, we examine the role of end products in research projects and present three new types of end products. When you plan research projects for your students, you will carefully consider both the purpose of and the end product options for the project.

Most of this chapter consists of two types of research projects. First, considering middle school students who are relatively less experienced researchers, we outline a research project focused on assembling known facts and interpretations. We define assembling known facts and interpretations as researching information that others have discovered. In our fictionalized scenario, middle school students locate known information from sources in the school's library in conjunction with Women's History Month.

Second, we focus on secondary students, who are more experienced researchers. We describe a research project focused on investigating an issue or problem with unknown solutions. Therefore, the students have the chance to conduct a real investigation by gathering and analyzing new data. In this fictionalized scenario, students research the issue of child labor, first with library sources and then with community sources: people in businesses, government agencies, labor unions, hospital emergency rooms, and schools.

For this chapter, imagine that the students are in the middle of the year when they are incorporating strategies in research projects. Moving seamlessly from phase to phase, teacher and the students select specific strategies as needed. During each phase, the teacher monitors the strategies that the students use, models and explains strategies that the students need to learn, and selects teaching/ assessing tools to support the students' learning. In both project scenarios, we discuss modeling and explaining selective strategies, as well as specific teaching/ assessing tools that you have read about in previous chapters.

Purpose-Setting Questions

1. What kinds of research projects have you done: assembling known facts and interpretations or investigating an issue or a problem with unknown solutions, or both kinds?

2. What strategies have you used in the generating phase of a research project? How do you begin to research a topic or question?

3. During the interacting phase, what strategies do you use to find and interpret information? What supporting strategies do you use to help you comprehend your research? Where did you learn strategies to conduct research?

4. In the refining phase, what strategies help you organize and evaluate your research? When do you discover a theme or express a thesis?

5. What types of end products have you completed? What did you learn from the different end products?

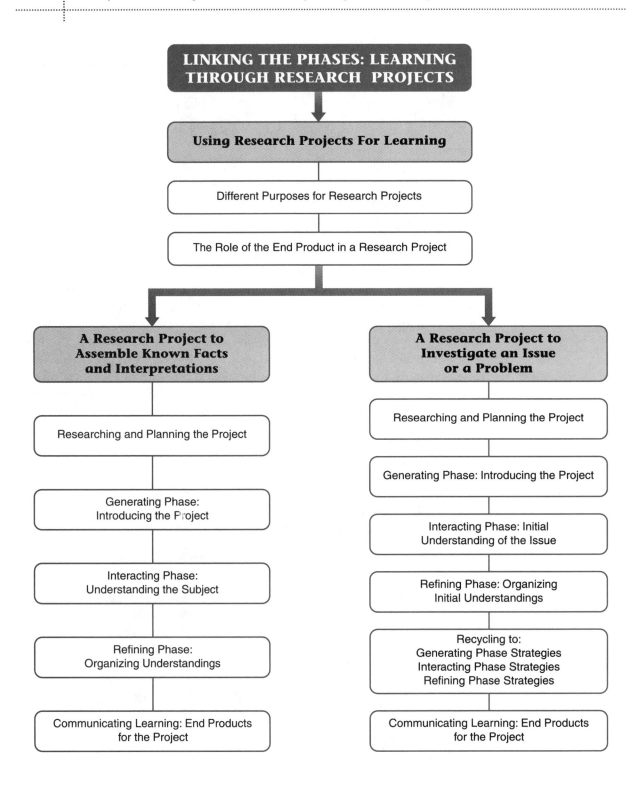

Using Research Projects for Learning

You know from your own school experiences that many teachers initiate research projects in conjunction with their mandated curriculum, such as westward expansion or weather. At other times, teachers use research projects to supplement the curriculum with topics, such as Black History Month or the problem of homelessness. In both cases, the teachers have two goals for the research project. First, they want their students to gain in-depth learning about a particular topic and communicate that knowledge to others. Second, they want their students to gain expertise in conducting research not only from library sources but, when appropriate, from original data sources as well.

You also know from your own school experiences that research projects usually have end products. In many cases, the traditional report or term paper is assigned. However, as we suggested in Chapter 6, learning may be communicated through many different end products and to various audiences.

Thus, before we present the two scenarios of research projects, let's discuss the purposes for the research projects and the role of end products.

▶ ▶ ▶ ▶ Different Purposes for Research Projects

As a content-area teacher, you have the dual goals of extending your students' knowledge of content and increasing their ability to conduct research. Research projects can serve both goals.

Extending Knowledge and Information. Your first purpose of research projects is to build your students' knowledge about specific topics in your content area. You may ask students to choose specific topics related to a curriculum area they have studied; for example a student may choose to research Louis Howe, political advisor to Franklin Roosevelt, during a study of U.S. history in the 1920s and 1930s. Sometimes you may broaden the choice spectrum so that students may research any topic that interests them within your content area. Offering choice, even within a limit like a historical era, will increase your students' motivation to enhance their knowledge about your content area.

Whatever topic choices you offer, you and your students need to be clear about your aims and expectations for the content to be learned. You may expect students to enhance their prior knowledge by assembling known facts and interpretations. As we stated in Chapter 6, enhancing prior knowledge is a worthy goal in the content areas, especially when students have little in-depth knowledge before they begin the study. Furthermore, assembling a coherent review of known information is a useful goal in some of life's research projects. Suppose you want to buy a car; you would research consumer information to assemble known facts and interpretations that inform your decision. However, you would be unlikely to make a new or original discovery that would revolutionize other consumers' purchases. In the first scenario that follows, we present a research project that asks students to assemble facts and interpretations from known information in library sources.

You may aim for students to restructure their prior knowledge by investigating an issue or question that has no known solution. In researching an unknown solution, students can produce unique insights, make original discoveries, or establish their own positions by collecting their own data from observations, experiments, interviews, or surveys. For example, students may provide evidence for local options about a national problem, like homelessness. Or their local experimental evidence could provide support for influencing U.S. policy on global warming. In the second scenario in this chapter, we present a research project to investigate an issue or problem in which students collect new data in order to formulate their own positions on the unresolved issue.

Learning to Conduct Research.   Your second purpose is to teach students strategies and tools for conducting research so that they can learn content independently. At every level, teachers need to model and explain strategies, to incorporate other teaching tools in support of their students' learning, and to assess or monitor their students' use of strategies and tools. In the middle school grades, teachers need to devote considerable class time to modeling and explaining strategies and to teaching/assessing tools. In the high school grades, teachers can use class time to assess and monitor the strategies that their more experienced students use and to incorporate modeling and other teaching tools based on specific students' needs. Thus, we are clearly stating that teachers need to use class time to instruct students in the process of research, rather than simply assigning the research project for homework. Of course, students will do additional work after school as well on their research project.

Researching Known Data.   When researching known data, students learn what others have discovered by reading library sources, the starting place for most research. When conducting research with library sources, students have a real purpose for exploring a wide variety of sources: informational books, magazine articles, and specialized works, like atlases, among others. As your students locate their sources, you emphasize applying literacy strategies for those specific texts in each of the three phases: generating, interacting, and refining.

When your students are less experienced researchers, you might concentrate on one or two types of texts to model and explain specific strategies. As your students gain research experience, you expand their research strategies because they can delve more deeply into their topics. Then students apply strategies across multiple sources, such as, on-line documents, informational books, and magazine articles, in order to gather sufficient information on the topic. Synthesizing known information from multiple sources is more complicated because the students must decide what information is similar, different, complementary, and contradictory.

In the first scenario that we present in this chapter, a research project to assemble known facts and interpretations, the teacher and his sixth-grade students conduct research with one or two library sources.

Researching New Data.   Real investigations in your field necessitate asking questions or tackling problems for which new data are needed. By doing real investigations, you introduce your students to the research strategies and research sources used in your field. Often these real investigations require students to seek sources beyond the school. The students may conduct experiments or observations locally, interview or survey people in the community, or locate primary documents from local historical societies and on-line sites. Since the sources may be unfamiliar to the students, you may need to model and explain strategies for finding and interpreting data from these sources.

Like any real investigation, the students use the research strategies through the three phases. In the generating phase, they ask their questions or define their problems and identify their data sources. During the interacting phase, they determine what data are relevant and analyze and interpret their data. In the refining phase, they synthesize and draw their own conclusions about their data. In each of the three phases, no one else has examined precisely their same data. For instance, other researchers have investigated monarch butterflies, but only your students research them in their own town. Your students' data are new and their results and conclusions unknown until they make them. Thus, even when their investigations corroborate other researchers' work, the students analyze new data and so conduct a real investigation.

To give your students the opportunity to experience real investigations, we encourage you to locate questions, problems, or issues in your curriculum for which students can research new data. In the second scenario in this chapter, a research project that delves into an issue, the teacher presents the issue of child labor in conjunction with a curriculum unit on the Industrial Revolution. Cooperative groups research new data on different aspects of the issue.

▶ ▶ ▶ ▶ The Role of the End Product in a Research Project

Remember that one goal is to teach students to conduct research independently. Therefore, the entire research project—every step along the way, not just the end product—is worthy of assessment by both you and your students. You might ask students to keep working portfolios, which are useful vehicles for collecting the ongoing learning during a research project.

Although we have emphasized the process of learning by concentrating on strategies, we think most people have a reason, a goal, or a product in mind when they embark on a project. For example, both the athlete and ordinary jogger have goals for their training: to be physically fit, to perform well, or to live a healthier life. Few run just to run without regard to a distance, time, or performance goal. Therefore, the product or goal can provide the motivation for the process, especially when you embark on an extensive project like a research project.

The end product also serves to give students a sense of accomplishment. Because they communicate what they have learned, the students have verification that their strategies resulted in increased knowledge. If students have the opportunity to communicate their learning in different end products, they exhibit different strengths and accomplishments. So, let's discuss alternative end products as well as the end product of term paper.

Alternatives to the Traditional Term Paper.   At the end of Chapter 6, we discussed communicating learning through different opportunities in speaking, drama, art and music, and writing and to appropriate audiences. As you plan research projects for and with your students, you can explore the variety of opportunities through which students can communicate their learning to others. When students engage in an extensive research project, they will be prepared to inform their peers, community citizens, or local officials in various ways: through panel presentations, front-page news reports, eyewitness reports, interview articles, biographies, or pamphlets, for example. They can use their research to persuade peers, citizens, officials, or national leaders through letters, poster campaigns, songs or jingles, debates, or other vehicles. Demonstrating their learning through the arts, they could entertain, inform, and perhaps persuade through end products like informal drama, videos of reenactments, paintings, computer graphics or music, poems, and fictional journals or memoirs.

When your students choose their own research topics based on their individual interests, the element of choice should extend to end products as well. For each of the alternative end products we briefly describe next—I-search papers, multigenre papers, and murals representing literature—the element of choice in the creation of the end product is crucial. For each product, the students conduct research, record their learning in journals, and design end products suited to their understanding of their topic. Those end products also have the unique voice or expression of the students because they chose the topic and chose to create the specific expression of their learning.

I-search papers (Macrorie, 1988) begin with topics or issues of central importance to the students. Recording their search in a journal, they consult different sources—for example, they may interview experts, read library sources, or observe people engaged in the topic. They also chronicle the changes in their thinking as they gain more and more information. In writing the I-search paper, the students narrate the stories of their searches and their ideas. We think the I-search paper resembles KWL because the students narrate what they knew in the beginning, tell about the search, and conclude with what they learned and did not learn, and what they gained from the experience.

Modeled after Michael Ondaatje's book *The Collected Works of Billy the Kid,* Romano's (1995) *multigenre paper* is a collection of different genres of writing. Romano thinks that "each genre offers me ways of seeing and understanding that others do not" (p.109). As the students research their topic and record their learning in journals, they try out different genres—news articles, poems, dialogues, interviews, narratives, informational essays, songs—to express their information. In the final multigenre paper, they compose or revise several genre pieces to communicate different aspects of their topics.

A mural representing literature is a more unusual end product. In the "Art of Literature" project, Rief (1992) and her students worked in tandem with the art teacher. In cooperative groups, the students chose one work of literature to represent in a mural. They brainstormed and drafted visual ideas (generating phase); studied artists, their paintings, and art elements such as colors, lines, and abstract versus representational symbols (interacting phase); and finally analyzed and revised their artistic expressions of the literature (refining phase). Although the students wrote about their creative process for their teachers, they wanted their murals to evoke reactions from their peers without statements of their intents, as most artists prefer. Rief summarizes their learning:

> These students created startling new ways, ways beyond words, to look at three books—to look at the human experience in these books through their own personal experiences and personal knowledge. And they made meaning so effectively that viewers bring their own meaning to, and take their own meaning from, the experience. (1992, p. 161)

These three alternative research projects and end products take time. In fact, Rief's took two trimesters. In addition, students find them more challenging than the term paper (Romano, 1995), primarily because they create an original end product and assume real ownership over the product.

Making the Most of the Traditional Term Paper.   In many classrooms, from elementary school through graduate school, students assemble known facts and interpretations in written reports or term papers. If only because of the prevalence of written products, students need to learn to write term papers in the standard format, consisting of title page, introduction, subtopics or categories of information, synthesis or conclusion, and bibliography.

You might assign the other traditional reports in your field that are based on the term paper, especially when your students research new data. Research reports in the sciences and social sciences published in professional journals are variations on the term paper. Journalistic articles published in specialized magazines for specific audiences, like *Smithsonian, Scientific American,* and *Canoe,* report and synthesize information, albeit more informally in some sources.

When students enter the refining phase, they need to begin thinking about composing their term papers. The strategies to organize and evaluate ideas discussed in Chapter 6 are useful when writing term papers. You can support students by having them complete a graphic organizer of their information. The advantage of a graphic organizer is that it encapsulates or distills the reams of information in the students' notes. By viewing the whole report on one page, students can decide which subtopics (or questions) have more information, which need more information, which should be eliminated, and which should be highlighted. Based on the evaluation of the subtopics, students can decide how to sequence the subtopics before they begin to write.

The next challenge is turning their notes into sentences and paragraphs. You can review the Focus on Writing sections in previous chapters for tools, like freewriting (Chapters 4 and 6) and discovery drafts (Chapter 5), that support students' composing. When students write in the almost stream-of-consciousness style of freewriting and discovery drafts, they may jump-start their composing and find the important ideas, themes, or theses for their papers. In addition, your students may offer suggestions, like writing several titles or writing the most important part first, that help each other begin to compose.

And finally, you will want your students to share sections of their first drafts in peer conferences in order to help each other revise and edit their papers. A term paper is a published document and so needs to contain complete and well-organized information expressed in standard grammar, spelling, and punctuation.

Assessing End Products.   Naturally the criteria you and your students use to assess end products will depend on the types of end products they produce. And whether your students complete alternative end products or term papers, you should discuss with them the criteria both of you will use to assess the products.

For every end product, students should communicate the overall topic or issue, the most important information, and a synthesis or conclusion. We think a creative art project, a poem, and a term paper can communicate those three aspects, although each will communicate the same aspects very differently.

When your students complete alternative end products in speaking, drama, art, music, and writing, they should assess their products considering the following focused questions:

- Can the audience recognize the central idea, thesis, theme, and position in the product?

- How or where does the audience learn about the important aspects, characteristics, and information?

- What aspects of the product contribute to the audiences' being more informed or persuaded to the creator's position?

- How does the product accomplish the creator's goal and demonstrate the creator's new learnings?

When your students write term papers, they should assess their first and final drafts using the following focused questions:

- Is the overall topic (theme or thesis) clear to the reader?

- Can the reader tell when each subtopic is introduced?

- Does the order of the subtopics make sense to the reader?

- Does the reader have enough information about each subtopic? Where does the reader need more information? Where is there extraneous information?

- Are the introduction and conclusion satisfying to the reader?

Teacher as Inquiring Learner Activity

Reflect on your research experiences in a freewriting.

- Were you taught strategies or guided through your first research report? Did you always write the traditional report, or did you sometimes present your information in a skit or a poem? Did your motivation change when you could choose your topic rather than being assigned a topic? How do you research topics now in college? Have you found a way to change an assigned topic into a personally meaningful topic? Do you think your professors are asking you to assemble known facts and interpretations? When have your professors asked you to research new data? How can you learn from your experiences to provide research opportunities for your students?

In the rest of the chapter, we present two specific examples of research projects: first a middle school research project to assemble known facts and interpretations and second a high school project to investigate an issue with unknown solutions.

Sample Unit Plans

A Research Project to Assemble Known Facts and Interpretations

In this fictionalized sixth-grade classroom scenario, the social studies/English teacher introduces a research project on outstanding women during Women's History Month. His content major understanding for the unit is for students to answer this question: "Why are the women outstanding in their fields?" He also wants to emphasize strategies for reading biographies and for doing library research.

Choosing the particular woman they want to learn about, the students research known information from sources in their school library. The teacher emphasizes not just literal information but interpreting that factual information. To help students interpret the information about the women they are studying, the teacher asks students to compare their subjects in an alternative end product.

Researching and Planning the Project

Once the teacher decides on the curriculum topic for the unit, he has three tasks: increasing his own knowledge of the topic, checking on available sources for students, and outlining the activities in the unit. Particularly for this topic, he collects information from newspapers and magazines throughout the year, continually learning about the topic. In addition to increasing his general knowledge, he chooses to research outstanding women photographers because of his interest in photography. He plans to use his own research as a model for his students.

Although the students will find their own sources of information, the teacher wants to be assured that the school library has enough different biographies on women to meet the wide range of reading levels in his classroom. The school librarian suggests displaying the biographies since she is going to feature Women's History Month too. In addition, she will contact the local library for books to supplement the school's collection. She also suggests biographical encyclopedias and *Faces* magazine as additional sources.

Satisfied that the students will have enough sources available to them, the teacher sketches a plan for the unit. Although these sixth graders have written research reports before, his experience tells him that they need guidance and instruction during the research process. During each of the three phases, he decides to model and explain the specific strategies he uses to research two women photographers, Dorothea Lange and Margaret Bourke-White, as the students concurrently research the women they have chosen to study.

Since he wants the students to interpret the women's lives—not simply report events in their lives—the teacher plans a collaborative end product. Students who are researching women in related fields will form cooperative groups. In their groups, the students will compare the lives of their subjects and find significant similarities and differences. The groups will then decide how to communicate their learnings about the women—perhaps a role play, a collage, or an interview.

Having a general plan and being assured of sufficient sources, the teacher begins to plan specific lessons for the generating, interacting, and refining phases of the research project. You might want to look ahead to Figure 7.2, which lists selected strategies for three phases for an outline of the research strategies.

Generating Phase: Introducing the Project

During the generating phase, the teacher plans first to introduce the research project to the students using teaching/assessing tools. After the students have chosen which women to research, he plans to model and explain his strategies as he begins to research the lives of photographers Dorothea Lange and Margaret Bourke-White.

Teaching/Assessing Tools. To open the unit, "Why are the women outstanding in their fields?" the teacher holds a **brainstorming discussion** with the whole class **to assess the students' prior knowledge**. On chart paper he draws a **semantic map** with the topic, outstanding women in different fields, in the middle and different fields radiating outward (see a sample map in Figure 7.1). He asks his students to contribute the names and accomplishments of the important women they know. He expects that some fields, like math or computers, will be empty, and many interesting women he knows, like Rear Admiral Grace Hopper (U.S. Navy, Retired) who invented the computer language COBOL and the term *bugs*, will not be mentioned.

Figure 7.1   The Teacher's Brainstorming Map of Outstanding Women

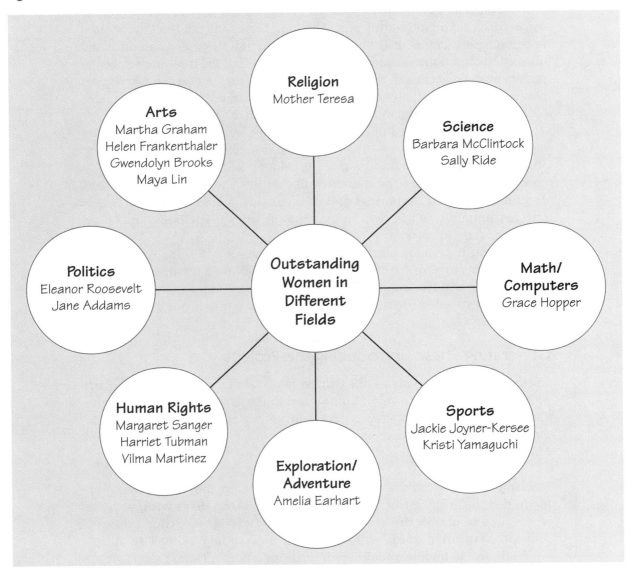

Teacher as Inquiring Learner Activity

With your peers, you might see how many outstanding women you could contribute to the sample semantic map in Figure 7.1.

- What names can you add? What other fields can you add? Do you know of outstanding women in your own field?

  Most people don't know many outstanding women unless they have researched the topic. You might want to take this opportunity to research famous women in your field. Start by skimming the biographical encyclopedias in the library. Make a list of the women in your field and their accomplishments. Perhaps you can find a full biography written about one woman to read. Save your list, because you might find it useful in the future.

After the students have contributed the names of the outstanding women they know to the class's semantic map, the teacher takes the students (and the semantic map) to the library. The librarian gives a **book talk to preview** the biographies: for some just mentioning the woman's contribution; for others giving a brief biography. As the librarian mentions each biography, the teacher adds the name to the semantic map. After the book talk, the students begin thinking about which women they want to research and browse among the books.

In a few days, after the students have had time to mull over their choices, the teacher asks them to write three choices on a piece of paper (**choosing a topic**). After matching the students and their choices as best he can, he begins to model and explain his research process.

Modeling and Explaining Strategies. The previous weekend, the teacher planned the strategies he wanted to model and explain. Now, while he models and explains, he refers to those written plans to make sure he covers every strategy.

First, he relates to his students his **prior knowledge** about photographers and famous pictures. He knows Alfred Steiglitz's and Ansel Adams's photographs, remembers the name Margaret Bourke-White but not her photographs, and recalls seeing Dust Bowl photographs, especially one of a worried mother with her children, but not the photographer.

Second, he models and explains **previewing a book**. He **skims** through the book on Dorothea Lange, looking at the **pictures**, and finds the Dust Bowl photograph he recalled; he learns the title, *Migrant Mother*. He also **skims** the **Table of Contents** and finds a chapter about the photograph.

Third, after skimming the book and thinking aloud about the overall question for the research project ("Why are the women outstanding in their fields?"), he models and explains how to **predict** what he'll learn. In addition, he models turning those predictions into **questions that he will research**:

- How did Lange decide to become a photographer?
- What obstacles did Lange encounter as she practiced in the field?
- How did Lange happen to photograph the mother for the famous photograph, *Migrant Mother*?

When he finishes modeling and explaining, he initiates a similar process for his students using selected teaching/assessing tools.

Returning to Using Teaching/Assessing Tools.   The teacher outlines the activities the students will engage in to **activate their own prior knowledge** and **to preview and predict** what they will research:

- Tell your partner what you already know about the woman you will research.
- Skim through your book on the woman you will research, looking at the pictures and captions. Look at the book jacket too.
- Skim your Table of Contents to make predictions about what topics will be covered in the book.
- Write your questions to research, and share them with your partner.

During this time, the teacher circulates to help the sixth graders, especially when they compose their questions. Once they have shared their questions with their partner, the students begin their research. They are now in the interacting phase.

Interacting Phase: Understanding the Subject

The teacher knows that some students will charge ahead in their research, while others will lag behind. He decides to make a **checklist as an assessing tool** to monitor where the students are in their research and what strategies they are using. On graph paper, he writes the strategies in the three phases (see Figure 7.2) across the top and the students' names down the page. When he confers with individual students, they will check the strategies they discuss so that the checklist serves as an ongoing **monitoring tool** for both of them. He will also note what strategies to model and explain and what teaching/assessing tools the student might need.

"Migrant Mother" by Dorothea Lange.

Copyright The Dorothea Lange Collection, The Oakland Museum of California, City of Oakland, Gift of Paul S. Taylor

Modeling and Explaining Strategies. The teacher decides to model and explain **finding and interpreting information, capitalizing on text organization,** and **constructing auxiliary aids—note taking**—using his research on Lange. He plans to spread out the modeling and explaining lessons over the many periods that the students are researching.

First, he models how to record the sources of information on a **bibliography page** as he writes his source on the overhead:

Meltzer, Milton. *Dorothea Lange: Life Through the Camera.* New York: Viking, 1985.

Figure 7.2   Selected Strategies for the Three Phases

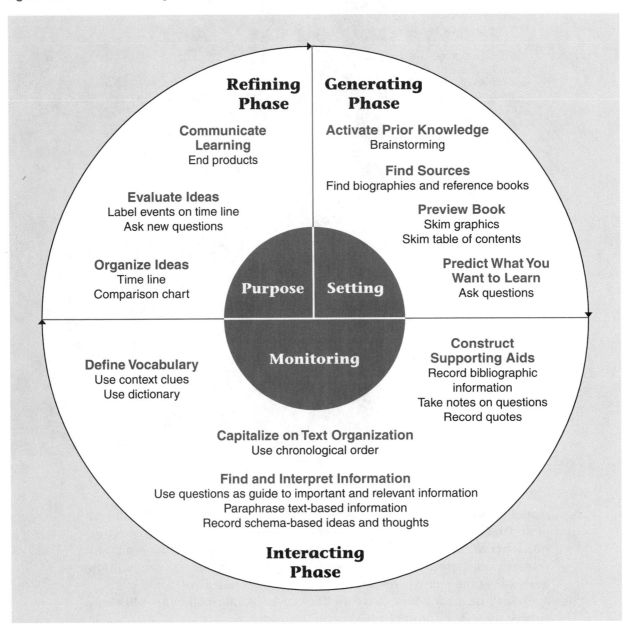

He also explains why the students need to give credit to the authors they read.

Second, he models and explains how to begin **finding and interpreting important information** by writing each of his **questions** on a separate transparency. Beginning with his first question, How did Lange decide to become a photographer? he asks the students where in the book he is likely to find that information. Referring back to the Table of Contents, he and the students discuss **capitalizing on the text organization—in biographies, usually chronological order**.

Third, the teacher models and explains **making text-based connections** and **schema-based connections** and **taking notes** about those important connections. Reading the students the first chapter in the Lange biography aloud, the teacher stops periodically to have the students suggest notes to write under the first question on the transparency. The teacher discusses the following points when writing his notes (see Figure 7.3):

- If the **text-based information was important and relevant** to answering the question

- What words to write (how to **paraphrase text-based information**)

- How to record **schema-based connections** or your own ideas and questions in brackets to distinguish them from text-based information

Fourth, he models and explains how to **record quotations** using his third question: How did Lange happen to photograph *Migrant Mother*? He

Figure 7.3

Taking Notes

> **1) How did Lange decide to become a photographer?**
>
> As a child:
> > looked in people's windows and watched them
> > studied photographs in the library
> > cut out photos from newspapers and magazines; put on bedroom wall
> > never owned a camera or took a picture
>
> After graduation:
> > announced to mother wanted to be a photographer
> > mother made her go to teacher-training school but she quit
>
> Took jobs in photographers' studios and camera shops to learn
> Took a course with Clarence White, School of Photog.
>
> [Amazing that she did not have a camera and never took pictures—how did she know she wanted to be a photographer? What fascinated her?]

explains *when* to use quotations—for an especially unique or memorable statement—and *how often*—sparingly. (See Figure 7.4.)

Teaching/Assessing Tools.   Using his assessment tool, the strategy checklist, the teacher determines which students to support with additional teaching/assessing tools. He recognizes that the students' research questions operate like **comprehension study guides** for finding and interpreting both text-based and schema-based connections. As he circulates through the classroom reading students' notes, he initiates a modified **reciprocal teaching** or **DR/TA** with specific students. He asks them to summarize what they've learned so far, to point out any confusing information, and to predict what they're likely to learn next. In addition, he discusses specific students' **note-taking process** and suggests a note-taking system to some students.

During one period, the teacher asks the class to use the **vocabulary self-selection strategy** and record new words to learn. After collecting words

Figure 7.4

Quotations in Notes

---

3) How did she come to photograph *Migrant Mother*?

1. Job for govt. agency to photo migrant life in Calif.
   Drove past sign "PEA PICKERS CAMP"
   20 mi. later turned back and drove into camp
   "'I was following instinct, not reason,' she recalled later. 'I drove into that wet and soggy camp and parked my car like a homing pigeon.'
   'I saw and approached the hungry and desperate mother, as if drawn by a magnet. I do not remember how I explained my presence or my camera to her, but I do remember she asked me no questions.'
   Dorothea made five exposures, working closer and closer to her subject. 'I did not ask her name or her history. She told me her age, that she was thirty-two. She said they had been living on frozen vegetables from the surrounding fields, and birds that the children had killed. She had just sold the tires from her car to buy food. There she sat in that lean-to tent with her children huddled around her, and seemed to know that my pictures might help her, and so she helped me. There was a sort of equality about it.'" (pp. 35, 37)
2. Pea picker story and photo reported in San Francisco paper.
   Fed. govt. sent food to feed migrants

from students, he reviews with the students how to **use context clues, word parts, and the dictionary** to define unknown words independently.

The teacher knows the students need many class periods and homework time to complete their research. Yet to prevent the project from dragging on too long, he encourages, supports, and pushes the students toward the refining phase.

Refining Phase: Organizing Understandings

Nearing the end of the research project, the teacher wants students to organize and to evaluate their ideas in order to enhance their prior knowledge and maybe even restructure it. Once again, he will model and explain his strategies and provide teaching/assessing tools to support the students' use of strategies.

Modeling and Explaining Strategies.   The teacher plans to model and explain how he has enhanced and restructured his prior knowledge through his research on Lange.

During one period, he **organizes** his information about Lange on a **time line,** which serves as a **summary** of her life. (See Figure 7.5.) He **evaluates** the events in her life as either obstacles (below the line in Figure 7.5) or as opportunities (above the line in the figure). Then he discusses how he expected a woman photographer to confront more obstacles than Lange actually did and must **restructure** his prior knowledge because Lange's life was filled with opportunities.

During a second period, he and the students **study** his time line and discuss two interesting **themes**. One theme is that Lange's career had two parts: a studio portrait career that was funded by paying customers and then portraits of ordinary people in the field career that government grants funded. Another interesting theme is how her career changed after she photographed *Migrant Mother*. Formulating **new questions**, he asks whether *Migrant Mother* was a career-making photograph for her and whether other photographers have career-making photographs.

Teaching/Assessing Tools.   To assist his students in organizing and summarizing, he asks the students to record major events in the lives of their outstanding women on **time lines**. He suggests either dividing their time lines into different periods, like childhood years and early career years, or recording specific years. When the students have completed their time lines, he introduces the comparison activity.

Figure 7.5   Partial Time Line of Lange's Professional Life

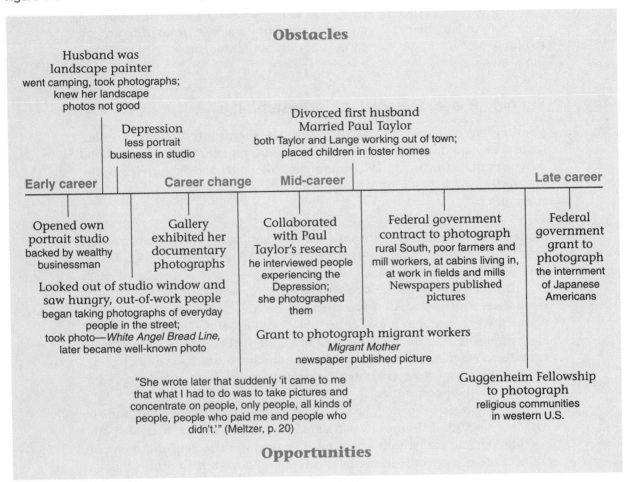

A Comparison Activity.   The teacher's objective is for the students to compare the women's lives by searching for the commonalties and the differences in their experiences. To model comparing two women's lives, he shows his time lines of Lange's and Bourke-White's lives. Studying the two time lines for similar events, he and the students create a comparison chart (see Table 7.1.)

Then, the students meet in their cooperative groups (those of students researching women in related fields) and spread out their time lines. Looking across the several time lines, the students search for similarities and differences in the lives of their outstanding women and record their interpretations on a comparison chart.

Communicating Learning: End Products for the Project

Throughout the research project, the teacher shares his checklist with his students so that everyone can assess and monitor the use of strategies and their progress in the project. In his conversations with students and from their notes, time lines, and comparison charts, he knows they have been increasing their knowledge about outstanding women. Although the students have assembled enough known information to write a traditional term paper, he offers the students the opportunity to interpret creatively what they have learned about the women.

The class brainstorms end product ideas, such as these:

- A skit of a real or fictional event at which the women in the same field meet
- A collage to show how the women changed their field
- Character sketches that highlight a comparison of the character traits of women in a particular field

Table 7.1   Comparison Chart of Lange and Bourke-White

	Lange	Bourke-White
Early interest	Drawn to photos Never used a camera	No early interest Earned money with camera
Learned photography	From working in studios Took course by Clarence White	From taking pictures for pay Took course by Clarence White
Subjects	People	Industry
Funding	Government grants	Primarily commercially employed, some grant work
Famous photos	Documentary photos of poor and ordinary people	Photo essays of industry and world events
Locations	Primarily United States	All over the United States and rest of world
Sacrifices	Family life when children young	Divorces

The teacher decides to create a collage of Lange's and Bourke-White's photographs that represent the most interesting similarities and differences between the two women. The cooperative groups meet to brainstorm how they will communicate the lives of the women they studied.

When the cooperative groups have decided on their end product, the teacher convenes the whole class to discuss evaluation criteria. The teacher and the students devise the following criteria:

- Can the audience identify the women and what field they represent?
- Can the audience tell what contributions each woman makes to the field?
- Can the audience identify some similarities and differences among the women?
- Does the creation entice the audience to think more thoughtfully or more appreciatively about the group of outstanding women?

When the cooperative groups complete their end products, the class shares them with each other. The teacher videotapes their performances and projects, which are then displayed in the school library.

Sample Lesson Plan Two

A Research Project to Investigate an Issue or a Problem

When students investigate an issue or problem for which the solution is unknown, they not only assemble facts that other people have researched, but they collect their own facts or new data as well. From the data they collect and analyze, they discover new information, formulate their own positions or conclusions to share with appropriate audiences, and take appropriate actions on the issue or problem. Combining known data with their new data, the students investigating an issue or problem conduct real research as it is done in every field.

Teacher as Inquiring Learner Activity

Some of you may know of research projects that involve students in collecting new data. Ornithology research at Cornell University and Mississippi River research at the University of Southern Illinois are two examples. In both of these research projects, students collect field data from their local area and transmit the data to the researchers at the university. The university researchers benefit because they receive data from sites they could not feasibly observe. The students benefit because they participate in answering scientific questions for which the answers are unknown.

- Are professors at your college conducting research that middle school or high school students might participate in?

- Do your professors know about any cooperative research opportunities at another university?

- Can you find web sites on the Internet that offer cooperative research opportunities for your future students?

In this fictionalized high school scenario, the social studies/political science teacher introduces an investigation into child labor that connects with the Industrial Revolution in the curriculum and with the current controversy over child workers in the manufacture of clothing and sports equipment. The teacher's major goal is for students to express their own informed position on child labor today through answering this question: "Should businesses employ minors or child labor in the United States and abroad?" Using a checklist, the teacher plans to help her students monitor their strategies and progress and to tailor her modeling and explaining and other teaching/assessing tools to the specific needs of students.

To build their background knowledge, the students first assemble known information from library sources on the issue. In the second half of the unit, the students collect new data by surveying local businesses, local and state agencies, and other people who have information on child labor. Finally, based on their research of known data and their new data, the students formulate their own positions on child labor in our global society. They decide how to communicate their positions—as a class, small groups, or individuals—and to whom.

Researching and Planning the Project

Although the teacher has taught the Industrial Revolution for several years, she is intrigued with the child labor issue because she has read newspaper articles about Nike and other manufacturers that employ children in their overseas factories. Since she regularly connects historical and current issues in her classes, she decides to research the issue and revise her unit.

In the library, she first finds the original law on child labor, Title 29, Fair Labor Standards Act of 1938, in the reference section:

Title 29, Fair Labor Standards Act of 1938, in T. A. Jacobs (ed.), *Legal Directory of Children's Rights*, Vol. 1: *Federal Statutes* (Frederick, MD: University Publications of America, 1985).

Using Search Bank on the library computer, she skims numerous newspaper and magazine articles written on different reading levels—for example:

N. Gibbs, "Cause Celeb: Two High-Profile Endorsers Are Props in a Worldwide Debate over Sweatshops and the Use of Child Labor," *Time,* June 17, 1996, pp. 28–30.

S. Greenhouse, "Accord to Combat Sweatshop Labor Faces Obstacles," *New York Times*, April 13, 1997, pp. 1, 20.

Through the Internet, she visits the Department of Labor web site and finds information about working teens and the No Sweat label—for example:

Department of Labor, *Protecting Working TEENS,* **http://dol.gov/dol/ opa/public/summer/facts.htm**.

Finally, she checks out two library books to skim:

Russell Freedman, *Kids at Work: Lewis Hine and the Crusade Against Child Labor*. New York: Houghton Mifflin, 1994.

Milton Meltzer, *Cheap Raw Material: How Our Youngest Workers Are Exploited and Abused*. New York: Viking, 1994.

Concluding that her students can find plenty of resources, she begins to plan the investigation that follows.

Generating Phase: Introducing the Project

In the generating phase, the teacher uses several teaching/assessing tools to captivate the students' interest. In addition, she uses tools to emphasize the strategies of **activating prior knowledge and experiences** and **previewing and predicting** content to learn.

Teaching/Assessing Tools.   In introducing the new unit, the teacher seeks to assess what knowledge the students have about the general topic of child labor, what personal work experiences they've had to support their own or their family's expenses, and whether they have read about child labor issues in the news media. She plans to have the class survey their experiences, brainstorm their prior knowledge, ask initial questions to research, and determine useful library sources.

Surveying the Class.   Since the teacher knows that many high school students work to support either their families or their recreational interests, she surveys the class's work experiences by tallying their answers to the following questions:

- Who holds a summer job? Who holds a year-round job?

- What type of job do you hold?

- What tasks do you do on the job?

- What days do you work? What hours do you work?

- If we surveyed students in other classes, would we obtain the same results?

- Is our class typical or representative of this school's population?

For homework, she asks the students to read the labels on their clothes and to list the countries where their clothes were made. The next day, the students compile their data in a frequency table and determine not only the variety of countries in which their clothes are made but which countries make most of their clothes.

Brainstorming.   After introducing the two surveys, the teacher states the **purpose** of their investigation: "Should businesses employ minors or child labor in the United States and abroad?" Using the first part of KWL, she asks the students to write, **"What I know about child labor,"** and to jot down any questions they might think of as they write. When the students have finished freewriting, they share what they know, such as information about work permits or news about sweatshops.

Asking Initial Questions to Research.   After sharing the class's collective knowledge, the teacher turns to **what we want to know (KWL)** or **initial questions** to guide the investigation. As a whole class, the teacher and students brainstorm questions, such as those listed below:

- What are the federal and state regulations on child labor?

- When and how were these regulations passed?

- Do U.S. businesses follow the regulations?

- Do other countries have regulations on working conditions that protect children?

- In the past, what industries or businesses employed children?
- In the past, why did children work? Are the reasons different today?

When the class has compiled a list of questions, the students group them into four categories:

- Federal and state laws and regulations
- Working conditions of U.S. teens and business's policies on the working conditions of minors
- Working conditions of minors overseas and business's policies on the working conditions of minors
- History of child labor

The students choose which category they want to research and form research groups.

Determining Library Sources.   Assessing the students' background knowledge, the teacher finds the students have personal knowledge from their work experiences but little general knowledge. She states that each group will begin its investigation with library sources to build background knowledge. Based on the information the groups uncover in their library research, they will gather new data by interviewing people in agencies and businesses about child labor.

Each research group lists possible library sources—the computerized card catalogue, the general reference database in Search Bank, the newspaper database in Search Bank, the Internet home pages of government agencies, and reference books—and decides which members will search what source.

Interacting Phase: Initial Understanding of the Issue

Keeping in mind that their ultimate purpose is to take a position on whether businesses should employ minors, each research group gathers background information about its topic. The teacher monitors and assesses the strategies students use to decide if she needs to teach specific students particular strategies (see Figure 7.6).

Asking Specific Questions for Each Subtopic.   Building on the class's brainstorming of initial questions, each research group brainstorms specific questions to guide research into its category. For example, the federal and state law and regulation group asks the following **specific questions to research**:

- What is the federal law on child labor? Where can we get a copy of it?
- Are any types of employment exempted from regulation?
- Does the law define what days and hours children can work? Do these allowable working hours change during school vacations?

Figure 7.6   Initial Strategies for the Three Phases

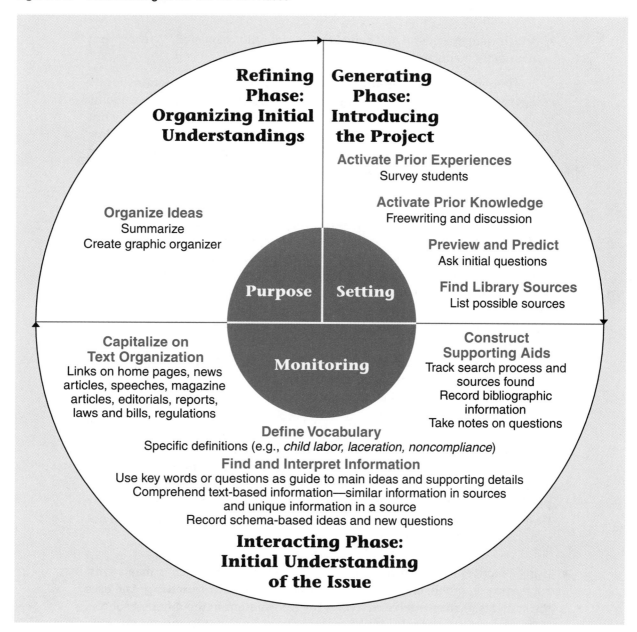

Refining Phase: Organizing Initial Understandings

Organize Ideas
Summarize
Create graphic organizer

Generating Phase: Introducing the Project

Activate Prior Experiences
Survey students

Activate Prior Knowledge
Freewriting and discussion

Preview and Predict
Ask initial questions

Find Library Sources
List possible sources

Purpose   Setting

Monitoring

Capitalize on Text Organization
Links on home pages, news articles, speeches, magazine articles, editorials, reports, laws and bills, regulations

Construct Supporting Aids
Track search process and sources found
Record bibliographic information
Take notes on questions

Define Vocabulary
Specific definitions (e.g., *child labor, laceration, noncompliance*)
Find and Interpret Information
Use key words or questions as guide to main ideas and supporting details
Comprehend text-based information—similar information in sources and unique information in a source
Record schema-based ideas and new questions

Interacting Phase: Initial Understanding of the Issue

- What are our state's law or regulations? Where can we get a copy?

- Do our state regulations differ from the federal ones? Which takes precedence?

- When were the federal and state laws or regulations enacted? Why or what caused their enactment?

After each research group has listed possible research questions for its category, the whole class composes a graphic organizer so that the students can see where similar questions occur. For example, the question about what caused the enactment of child labor laws could be researched by the law group and the history group. Rather than duplicating their efforts, these groups can coordinate or pool their efforts.

Focusing on the Strategies for Making Connections.   Since these are high school students, the teacher knows they have researched topics before. However, she also knows that the issue of child labor will introduce the students to new sources and to sources that may be hard for individual students to understand. In addition to circulating at the beginning of each period, she plans to meet with one research group each period to determine its progress in understanding its subtopic. She plans to check on the group's overall strategy—finding and interpreting important information—as well as its use of the three supporting strategies—constructing auxiliary aids, capitalizing on text organization, and defining vocabulary independently. For each of the strategies, she has **specific monitoring questions** to ask the students and **teaching/ assessing tools** to assist them if needed.

Monitoring the Strategies for Making Connections.   The teacher and the students know that making **text-based and schema-based connections** is their primary undertaking. The students know to use the **key words** in their specific questions for the **main ideas** and how to take notes on the **supporting details**. In addition, they know how to record **new questions or new information** that reveals an aspect of their topic that they had not considered.

Using Teaching/Assessing Tools as Needed.   When the teacher meets with each research group, she follows the steps in **reciprocal teaching**. She asks the students to **summarize or retell** the information in the different sources they are reading, to **seek clarification** about any confusions, and to **predict** what they will learn next. If particular students are having difficulty understanding their specific text—for example, the original law on child labor—she is ready to conduct a **directed reading activity** with them.

Throughout the project, the teacher uses the following specific monitoring questions to guide the group's discussion of its progress:

- Have the students found **productive sources** to answer their specific questions?

- Can each student productively **comprehend the text-based information** in a source?

- Are the students finding **similar information** in different sources to conclude they have enough information on the question?

- Are they finding **unique information** in a particular source?

- Have they discovered **new questions** to research in other sources?

- What are their own **schema-based ideas** on the subtopic?

While she emphasizes the overall strategy of finding and interpreting both text-based and schema-based connections, she also occasionally monitors the students' use of the three supporting strategies.

Focusing on the Supporting Strategies.   Because the students are reading a variety of different sources, the teacher early on checks to see if they can **capitalize on text organization**. She expects that only some students will need support with **constructing auxiliary aids** strategies. Because child labor is a new topic for the students, she plans to have the students **define the new vocabulary** they encounter.

Capitalizing on Text Organization.   The teacher knows that most students are familiar with the **text organizations** of magazine and newspaper articles, speeches, and editorials, but she expects students may need assistance with reading laws and bills. Most students know how web sites can be organized and how to link to various other sites. However, the teacher reminds them to keep track of where they have visited!

As the students read their different sources, she shares the following specific monitoring questions to help them determine if they are taking full advantage of text organization:

- What is the purpose of the text or the intent of the author?

- Is the author expressing opinions, reporting information, or both?

- Where are the most important ideas located in the text?

- Can the students find subsections of the text?

- Can the students locate the details for important ideas?

She plans either to conduct a **directed reading activity focusing on text organization** or make a **text pattern guide** for students who are grappling with difficult materials.

Constructing Auxiliary Aids.   Especially at the beginning of the research project, the teacher and the students monitor the students' note taking:

- Have they taken **bibliographic** information first, even if they are not sure they will use the source?

- Are they **keeping track of their search process**—the key words they used to find the sources and a list of possible sources?

- Do they have a **system for note taking** that indicates the specific source, paraphrases the text-based information, identifies quotations, and identifies their own schema-based ideas?

- Do their notes match the specific question? Do their notes contain irrelevant information?

Although the teacher has a survey of **criteria for evaluating notes**, she gains enough information by reading a few notes and through her discussion of the students' understanding of the information they are finding. If a student is having difficulty, she will suggest talking into a tape recorder or taking notes on a graphic organizer she helps the student design.

Independent Vocabulary Learning.   The teacher asks each research group to compile and define important vocabulary and new vocabulary as they read (**vocabulary self-selection strategy**). She discusses that the whole class needs to learn specific definitions for some words, such as *child*, while other words, like *laceration* or *noncompliance,* may apply to only one research group. Each research group selects its most important words to contribute to a class vocabulary list.

The teacher monitors the class list and each research group's list, checking that the meaning of the words fits the topic of child labor. In addition, she monitors certain students who might have difficulty defining words and those who tend to use "big" words without understanding their meanings.

Refining Phase: Organizing Initial Understandings

At this point, the teacher plans to have the students organize and summarize what they have learned from library sources. They will apply that knowledge in the second part of their investigation when they collect their own data.

Teaching/Assessing Tools for Organizing and Summarizing Library Information. Since not every person in a research group has read every source, the group members need to pool their information. To help her students review their subtopic questions and compare their notes, the teacher suggests that each group address the following **questions as a guide** for their **summary**:

- Where do you have similar information that you could condense and summarize?

- Where might you find unique information worth adding?

- What information have you gathered that would be useful when the class surveys businesses, agencies, and other people knowledgeable about child labor?

- What new questions does your group have?

Because this summary is an interim stop in the research project, the teacher doesn't require a written report of the findings. Instead, each research group summarizes its information on a **graphic organizer** and then orally reports or explains the graphic organizer to the class.

Having enhanced their background knowledge through their library research, the class is now ready to investigate the issue and gather their own data from which to formulate their own positions. Thus, the students will recycle through the three phases (see Figure 7.7).

Recycling to Generating Phase Strategies

To gather their own data, the teacher and students **brainstorm** local businesses, governmental agencies, and other community sources, such as the local legal services office and the local hospital emergency room, where they can interview people about child labor. Using the Yellow Pages for additional sources, the class creates a table identifying sources for additional information or data (see Table 7.2).

Next the teacher proposes reorganizing the class in jigsaw fashion (Chapter 3) into three new data groups: a business group, an agencies group, and an other community sources group. She discusses with the class how the new data groups can benefit from the knowledge gained from the previous library research groups on regulations, working teens, minors overseas, and history. The students choose which type of source they want to contact for additional information: businesses, agencies, other community sources.

Figure 7.7   Recycling Through the Three Phases

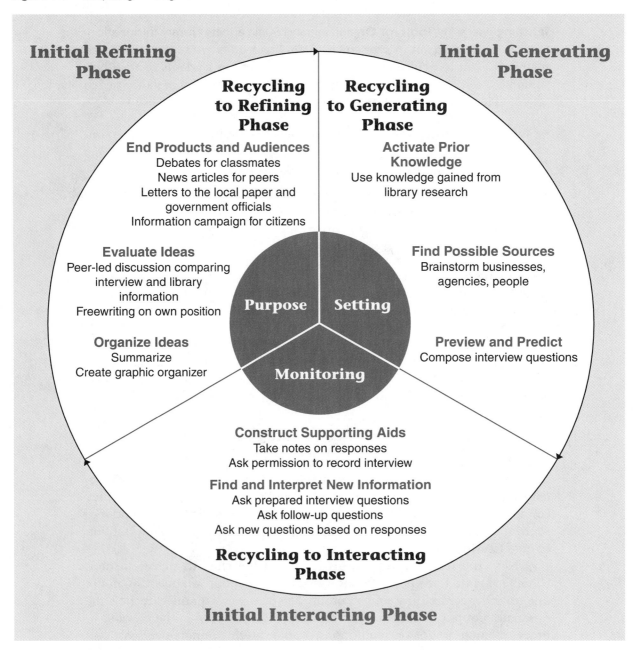

Table 7.2   Sources for Additional Information or Data

Businesses	Agencies	Other Community Sources
Local fast food restaurants	State attorney general: Fair Labor and Business Practices Office	Labor lawyer
Local grocery stores		Local bar association
Local car washes	State Office for Children	Union official
Local clothing stores	U.S. Labor Department Regional office: Child Labor section	Legal services office
Reebok		Local hospital emergency room or physician
Nike	Occupational Safety and Health Administration regional office	Local newspaper
Patagonia		Teens who work
Gap	National Institute of Occupational Safety and Health	High school principal
Liz Claiborne		Teachers
Pizza Hut		
Domino's		

However, the teacher places one condition: at least one student from each library research group must be present in the new data groups.

In their three new data groups, the students formulate **new questions** to ask specific people. For example, the students in the new data group for businesses list some questions appropriate for several businesses, such as:

- Do you employ teenagers? How many? What ages?
- What hours and days do they work?
- Do you make any distinction between your teenage workers and your workers over eighteen years old?
- What training do you provide, especially for teenage workers?
- What is your overtime policy?

In addition, they ask questions that apply only to specific businesses, like fast food restaurants:

- What hazardous machines are used in your business?
- How do you ensure the safety of your workers?
- What are the procedures when an injury does occur?
- How do you ensure that teenagers do not operate some machines, like slicing or mixing machines?
- What are the qualifications to be a driver who delivers to customers? How do you advertise for drivers?

The teacher reminds the students that their interview questions should be framed in a positive manner because they are inquiring to form a position, not to enforce a regulation. She instructs the students that they can ask agencies and officials questions about businesses' compliance with regulations.

Recycling to Interacting Phase Strategies

The teacher reviews the purpose of the interviews: to **find and interpret new information** about the conditions of child labor from the point of view of business owners, governmental agencies, and other interested people like working teenagers, high school teachers, and doctors. Although they will concentrate on local sources, they will also try to gain information from national and multinational businesses.

For a practice session before the actual interviews, the teacher invites several parents and senior citizens to class to be interviewed about their work experiences as a teenager and as an adult. After reminders about courtesy, the students ask questions and listen carefully in order to ask follow-up questions or new questions based on the responses of the interviewee. In some cases, the students ask the interviewee for further information and for evidence to support an opinion. At the conclusion of the practice session, the students ask the interviewee if they could contact him or her again later if they need clarification. The class discusses what they learned about interviewing people.

During the next class period, each group decides specifically the different people to interview and which student will conduct each interview. The students make their own appointments, decide whether to interview in person or on the telephone, and take notes or tape-record, if permission is granted. Throughout the week, the students conduct their interviews and share the new information with their new data group.

Recycling to Refining Phase Strategies

First, the students **organize and summarize** each interview they conducted so that they can identify the main points and the supporting details. Next, each data group—the businesses group, the agencies group, and the other community sources group—**evaluates** the information the whole group has gathered. Since they have interviewed different people, each group compares the information they have gathered from different sources. For example, the students in the business group determine the following information:

- What information gathered from local businesses is similar?
- Is the information from different types of local businesses similar or different?
- Is the local business information different from the national business information?

To present their composite picture to the class, each new data group creates a **graphic organizer**.

After each data group presents its composite picture, the class compares the interview information to the information they gathered from library sources. To guide their comparison, the teacher posts the following questions:

- How does their new information fit with historical information?
- How are businesses and consumers reacting to child labor overseas?
- What are the positions of teenagers, teachers, and business owners in regard to child labor regulations in the United States?
- Do child labor regulations and safety regulations actually protect children?

At the conclusion of the class discussion, the teacher restates the major issue of the investigation: "Should businesses employ minors or child labor in the United States and abroad?" She asks the students to write a personal response or position statement on child labor and include information that supports their positions. In formulating their individual positions, she suggests that the students might consider what conditions are fair in specific situations:

- What is detrimental to the health and welfare of children?
- Are state and federal regulations protecting children's health and welfare, or are they inhibiting teens from earning money?
- When the child's income helps support the family, are different conditions allowable?
- Would the American consumer pay more for items made overseas if companies improved their working conditions?

By assigning the students to write either a personal response or a position statement, the teacher intends that the students will reflect on the information they gathered during the entire unit.

Communicating Learning: End Products for the Project

As students volunteer to share their personal responses and position statements, the students realize the class has a variety of positions on the issue. To culminate the unit, the class decides how to **express** their positions on the question, "Should businesses employ minors or child labor in the United States and abroad?" and to whom they want to communicate their positions.

First, they decide to hold a series of debates among themselves, each centering on a specific proposition—for example:

- Our state regulations are too restrictive.
- Businesses need child labor to maintain competitive prices.
- Children benefit from work experiences.
- The United States should not apply its child labor regulations to foreign countries.

Second, to inform other students through their school newspaper, some students decide to write news articles about the information they have researched. Also, they will write editorials expressing their positions and encouraging other students to take appropriate actions as consumers of products.

And finally, to inform their local community, some students decide that local agencies need more support to check on businesses' policies and safety. They decide to communicate their concerns in a letter to the editor of the local newspaper and in a letter to their governmental representatives who fund the agencies. Other students decide that local consumers would benefit from an informational campaign about manufacturers or businesses supporting fair labor practices. Using their information about unfair child labor practices, these students also organize a petition to change a specific company's policy.

To assess their different end products, the class decides on three criteria: a clear position, supporting evidence, and appropriate for intended audience.

Summary of the Chapter

As a result of reading this chapter, you have a new understanding about the following issues:

- The generating, interacting, and refining phases are interlocking and not separate.
- Sometimes a strategic learner may recycle through the phases.
- Strategic learners choose the strategies that will serve them best.

You also recognize that teachers choose the type of research project that students will pursue:

- Assembling known facts and interpretations
- Investigating a problem or issue to find new data

Teachers choose research projects based on their curriculum goals, the available resources and time, and their students' learning needs. However, we think every student needs the opportunity to experience both types of research projects.

You also know that teachers choose which strategies to teach to their students. They will assess what their students can accomplish independently and select a few strategies to teach now. If the students need more strategy instruction, the teacher will schedule another research project later in the year to teach more strategies.

Finally, we would like you to think about the different end products that your students could complete. We think students benefit from:

- Expressing their learnings to a variety of different audiences in and out of school
- Expressing themselves in oral, written, and artistic presentations

Inquiry Activities About Your Learning

1. Think about a hobby you pursue, an interest in your content area that you have, or a current issue that concerns you. Perhaps you want to research a new hobby, such as rock climbing. You might want to research the new information on volcanoes for your earth science class. Or you might research the issue of high school dropouts. Choose a topic new to you—one for which you have little prior knowledge.

Gather information in three very different ways: read a book or article, interview a person, make an observation, or search the Internet. What different information do you learn from each source?

Record in a journal how you investigated your new topic. During the generating, interacting, and refining phases, what strategies did you use to research? How would you describe your process to your students?

2. Investigate topics you might teach in your content area. Survey the topics in a textbook or a curriculum guide (see also Part Three). Look for topics that you could extend into research projects. Skim professional journals in your content area and think about what questions are being asked that you could convert into research projects for your students. Skim newspapers and magazines for current issues in your field that your students could investigate.

Compile a list of curriculum topics and possible research projects that you and your students might pursue in the future.

Inquiry Activities About Your Students' Learning

1. Interview a struggling student and a thriving student. What types of research projects do they complete in school? What types of end products do they complete? How much choice do they have in the topics they research? Do they receive guidance or instruction? Do they do most of the work at home or in school? What suggestions do they have for teachers who assign research projects?

2. Investigate a topic in your content area with a student. Record the strategies the student uses independently. What strategies would help the student? Choose one or two strategies to teach the student.

Information and Resources

Professional Books

Atwell, N. (1998). *In the middle: New understandings about writing, reading, and learning* (2nd Ed.). Portsmouth, NH: Boynton/Cook.

Describes how Atwell teaches and explores literacy with adolescents.

Dillon, J. T. (1994). *Using discussion in classrooms.* Philadelphia: Open University Press.

Defines discussion and outlines how to conduct discussions.

Fulwiler, T. (1987). *The journal book.* Portsmouth, NH: Boynton/Cook.

Defines the benefits of journals and discusses journals in different content areas.

Langer, J. A. (1995). *Envisioning literature: Literary understanding and literature instruction.* New York: Teachers College.

> Presents a rationale and describes teaching and exploring literature based on collaborative research with secondary teachers.

Professional Journals

Bulgren, J., & Scanlon, D. (1998). Instructional routines and learning strategies that promote understanding of content area concepts. *Journal of Adolescent and Adult Literacy, 41*(4), 292–302.

> Describes how graphic organizers can support students' learning of strategies in social studies.

Burns, B. (1998). Changing the classroom climate with literature circles. *Journal of Adolescent and Adult Literacy, 42*(2), 124–129.

> Describes how a sixth-grade teacher began literature circles and includes the sixth graders' positive reactions.

Childress, J., & Hall, J. (1998, October). Oil spill ecology: Students help scientist assess the damage in Prince William Sound. *Science Teacher,* 32–35.

> Describes the Youth Area Watch, students' research projects, and the communication of results to different audiences.

Crocco, M. S. (1998). Putting the actors back on stage: Oral history in the secondary school classroom. *Social Studies, 89*(1), 19–24.

> Discusses the rationale for oral history projects, describes a high school project, and gives checklists for interviewing and for assessing students' progress and their final reports.

Ford, B. (1998). Critically evaluating scientific claims in the popular press. *American Biology Teacher, 60*(3), 174–180.

> Explains the strategies and presents a chart (study guide) for evaluating science reports in newspapers and magazines.

Harmelink, K. (1998, January). Learning the write way. *Science Teacher,* 36–38.

> A high school chemistry teacher's description of how she uses student journals.

Holt, P. W. (1998). The Oregon Trail: Wyoming students construct a CD-ROM. *Social Education, 62*(1), 41–45.

> Explains how high school students research, evaluate, and select primary source documents to make a CD-ROM for fourth graders.

Mathews, R., & Chandler, R. (1998). Using reader response to teach *Beloved* in a high school American studies classroom. *English Journal, 88*(2), 85–92.

> Presents a rationale for reader response and outlines how the authors prepared, supported, and challenged their students to respond to the difficult text.

Morrison, T. G., & Chilcoat, G. (1998). The "Living Newspaper Theatre" in the language arts classroom. *Journal of Adolescent and Adult Literacy, 42*(2),104–115.

Explains how to dramatize a "Living Newspaper Theatre" (popular in the 1930s) in secondary history/English classrooms and presents a model script on the issue of child labor.

Ricker-Wilson, C. (1998). When the mockingbird becomes an albatross: Reading and resistance in the language arts classroom. *English Journal, 87(*3), 67–72.

Describes the problems one teacher encountered when diverse students read *To Kill a Mockingbird* and her solution the second year she taught it.

Ridgeway, V. G., & Padilla, M. J. (1998, November). Guided thinking: Using three-level thinking guides to promote inquiry in the classroom. *Science Teacher,* 18–21.

Explains the three-level comprehension guide and gives an example from a kinetic molecular theory lab.

Tanner, M. L., & Casados, L. (1998). Promoting and studying discussions in math classes. *Journal of Adolescent and Adult Literacy, 41*(5), 342–350.

Explains how Casados's students learn how to discuss their math textbook using a fishbowl technique, debriefings, and videotapes and find they learn better as a result.

Taylor, K. L., & Sobota, S. J. (1998). Writing in biology: An integration of disciplines. *American Biology Teacher, 60*(6), 350–353.

Describes using clustering (brainstorming a graphic organizer), active reading (questions about strategies), and peer editing in biology classes.

Weir, C. (1998). Using embedded questions to jump-start metacognition in middle school remedial readers. *Journal of Adolescent and Adult Literacy, 41*(6), 458–467.

Explains guidelines for writing questions to support students' literacy strategies as they read and gives examples from students.

Internet

http://www.whyfiles.news.wisc.edu (The Why Files).

Publishes monthly articles explaining the science behind the news and keeps archives of past articles geared to secondary teachers and students.

http://www.scout.cs.wisc.edu/scout/KIDS/index.html. (KIDS, Kids Identifying & Discovering Sites).

Web sites for K–12 students that are evaluated by intermediate, middle school, and high school students according to their published criteria.

http://www.graphic.org/links/html (The Graphic Organizer).

A source for graphic organizers submitted by content-area teachers.

http://www.gsh.org (The Global Schoolhouse).

Internet learning projects linking students and teachers across the world. Teachers can register their project ideas to find teachers from other schools to participate. Free membership for teachers required.

Multimedia

Cultural debates. CD-ROM. Watertown, MA: Tom Synder Productions, **www.teachtsp.com**.

Video on aspects of an Indonesian culture (education, medicine, ecotourism) and related issues presented for debate.

Decisions, decisions. CD-ROM. Watertown, MA: Tom Synder Productions. **http://www.teachtsp.com.**

Series of fourteen kits, such as Cold War and Violence in Media, in which students analyze the situation, consider options, make decisions, and examine the consequences.

Inspiration. **www.inspiration.com.**

K–12 and Professional software that has graphic organizer templates and 500 symbols to make your own. Has the capacity to convert the graphic organizer to an outline.

	Single Subject/ Departmentalized	Coordinated/ Parallel Disciplines	Integrated
Disciplines	Separate disciplines; units have discipline-based objectives	Teachers in two or more complimentary disciplines confer	Teams of teachers from different disciplines work together; disciplines serve the problem, issue, theme
Planning	Independent planning and teaching	Together teachers plan to link objectives and activities in their own discipline to occur at similar times with that of other disciplines	Teams of teachers collaborate to plan and implement one curriculum
Time/ Schedule	Activities planned for regular class periods	Units taught at the same time of year; little or no change in class time/regular class schedule for each discipline	May remain in usual class periods or combined in blocks for students and teachers; may be scheduled for different lengths of time (week, semester, year)
Connections	Often no deliberate attempt to show relationships among disciplines or to connect with other teachers	Two units or topics have complementary content that connects them; teachers identify related content in their disciplines, however, the connection is not always made explicit for students	Focus on problems or issues; disciplines used to solve, to investigate, to provide information

In Part Three, *Enhancing Learning Through the Disciplines*, we focus on the importance of curriculum design that emphasizes major understandings and the use of literacy and learning as underpinnings in every discipline. Chapter 8, *Designing Curriculum for Learning: Teaching for Major Understandings*, discusses the recent standards movement and how to develop a unit. Chapter 9, *Single Discipline-Based Learning and Literacy*, describes single subject teaching and the connection of literacy learning (outlined in column 2 of the graphic). Chapter 10, *Coordinated Curriculum: Enhancing Learning Among Disciplines*, emphasizes two discipline-based teachers working together (column 3). Chapter 11, *Integrated Curriculum*, focuses on teams of teachers creating curriculum (column 4).

We close this part with Chapter 12, *Continuing to Grow as a Reflective Professional*, which emphasizes the role of the teacher as reflective practitioner and inquiring learner, a theme that runs throughout the book and impacts a teacher's career no matter what the discipline or the level taught.

Enhancing Learning Through the Disciplines

Chapter 8:

Designing Curriculum for Learning: Teaching for Major Understandings

Chapter 9:

Single Discipline-Based Learning and Literacy

Chapter 10:

Coordinated Curriculum: Enhancing Learning Among Disciplines

Chapter 11:

Integrated Curriculum

Chapter 12:

Continuing to Grow as a Reflective Professional

Information and Resources

8

Designing Curriculum for Learning: Teaching for Major Understandings

When you hear the term *curriculum* in conversation or when you read about curriculum in journals or newspaper articles, what do you think of? What personal associations do you have with curriculum? Have you heard of curriculum referred to outside of a school, college or university setting? Is this term always used in conjunction with courses and programs of some sort? Perhaps when you did a field placement as part of your teacher education program, you were asked to implement either a middle school or high school curriculum in the content area you are specializing in. Perhaps you have been asked to survey a curriculum guide that goes along with the mathematics or biology textbook the students and the teacher were using as their major resource in a particular course.

Most experienced educators, no matter what their level or their setting, are likely to be able to share with you firsthand experiences they have had as both an implementer and a developer of curriculum in their discipline or area of expertise. As a beginning teacher, you will most likely study and implement curriculum that educators more experienced than you have developed. As you will learn in this chapter, some important factors currently are shaping curriculum in every discipline across the country, among them the national curriculum standards. You will also learn about some models for delivering curriculum as well as of developing curriculum that help teachers across disciplines and levels plan and carry out instruction with their own students.

We hope you will approach curriculum development and adaptation as both an opportunity for you to continue to keep your own content knowledge current and as a necessity in order to create meaningful learning opportunities for your students now and in the future.

As you read this chapter, we suggest you ask yourself some questions related to curriculum that we believe you will continue to come back to no matter what your particular discipline, the grade level you teach, or your particular student population:

Purpose-Setting Questions

1. How do I identify the major understandings in my discipline to which I want to expose my students?

2. What are the pervasive factors or new knowledge and content I should consider in shaping curriculum in my field?

3. Are there models that will help me design or modify curriculum in my discipline?

4. Is there a way to design or modify curriculum so that the emphasis includes the theory advocated in Part Two where literacy and learning act as underpinnings in every discipline?

Defining Curriculum

We define *curriculum* in the broadest sense as a school's entire program of studies, comprising discrete disciplines and the individual courses that are available to students in those disciplines. The major discipline areas most prevalent in schools today are mathematics, science, social studies, English/language arts, foreign or world languages, health, physical education, and the arts. The curriculum and course offerings in the major disciplines determined by local school districts and guided by individual state mandates are fairly similar in middle schools and high schools across the United States.

Teacher as Inquiring Learner Activity

Think about your own definition of and experiences with curriculum.

• In high school and college, did the year-to-year progression of the science (general science to biology) or the social studies (world history to American history) program make sense to you? Were there connections made and opportunities to link your learning from one year to the next? Were the courses you took treated as discrete elements of your academic experience? How frequently did you have a course that made explicit links to another course of study?

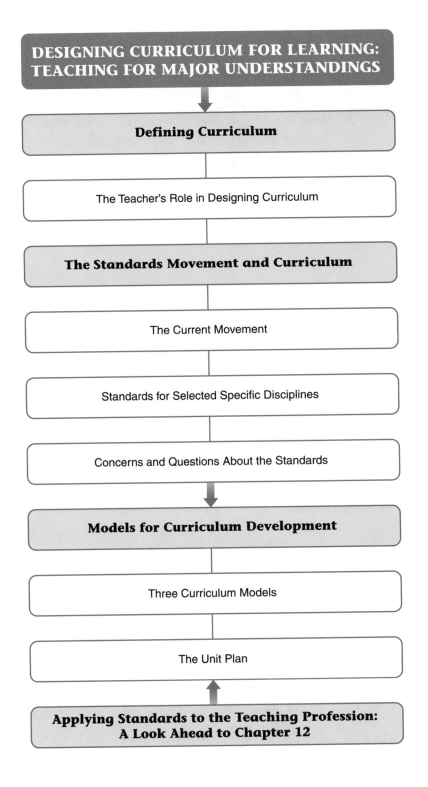

DESIGNING CURRICULUM FOR LEARNING:
TEACHING FOR MAJOR UNDERSTANDINGS

Defining Curriculum

The Teacher's Role in Designing Curriculum

The Standards Movement and Curriculum

The Current Movement

Standards for Selected Specific Disciplines

Concerns and Questions About the Standards

Models for Curriculum Development

Three Curriculum Models

The Unit Plan

Applying Standards to the Teaching Profession:
A Look Ahead to Chapter 12

Think about how these ideas about curriculum have been transmitted in the discipline in which you are now majoring as an educator.

Within each discipline, districts often devise district-level plans for curriculum across the grades. These plans are commonly organized into documents known as *curriculum guides*. Curriculum guides are usually written documents that focus on the major goals or understandings and the experiences that students are expected to have within a given discipline as a whole or in the particular courses comprising that discipline. For example, a science curriculum guide may be an outline of major goals that all students K–12 will be expected to achieve. Students will realize these goals through participation in general science lessons and courses at the elementary and middle school levels and in their discipline-specific courses such as biology, chemistry, or physics at the high school level. Finally, curriculum guides may contain the major goals in a discipline for a single grade level or for all grades, K–12.

In designing curriculum guides for a local school district, teachers and curriculum specialists seek to coordinate and sequence major understandings, concepts, strategies, and skills in their field across the grades. Unfortunately, many curriculum guides have become end products in and of themselves, understood and supported only by the committee that created them. In addition these guides often lead to rigidity in terms of outcomes, activities, and the use of materials within given courses. When this has occurred, curriculum guides that were meant to act as a framework for coherence within a discipline have become barriers to the development of individualized and integrative lessons that would be responsive to particular classroom settings and to the learners in these classrooms. And finally, too often teachers file curriculum guides away in cabinets or bottom drawers because of their misperceptions about the purpose for the guides and their lack of involvement in their development.

We view curriculum guides as a means for establishing major understandings and goals for a discipline at a single grade level or across grade levels. They can be useful in providing continuity from grade to grade or from course to course in a discipline. Such guides should be flexible enough so that teachers can revise them based on student needs, as well as changes in the field and in the outside world. We believe the most important contribution that curriculum guides can make is to stimulate teachers to design creative teaching/learning opportunities for their own learners.

Another predominant source that teachers use to shape curriculum are the major content-area textbooks available in every field and at every level.

The publishers know, as we do, that in designing curriculum guides, teachers and curriculum specialists review textbooks and related materials. District-level committees then choose materials to support the curriculum guides, and teachers design their curriculum based on the materials readily available for the discipline and the grade level in which they are teaching.

Knowing the wide appeal and use of content-area textbooks and anthologies, publishing companies move quickly to incorporate new trends in discipline-based content, as well as strategies or processes that appear in the professional literature and at conferences. Publishing companies often create particular texts and sets of materials that support these new concepts or strategies. They hope their materials designed for the school market will be used to implement the curriculum in schools across the country. For example, social studies educators recently placed an emphasis on economic education and global perspectives. Publishers of social studies materials responded by creating numerous texts and related resources on these topics. Another recent example is the focus on diversity that has affected every discipline. We see multicultural literature in the anthologies and collections of trade books that many companies are publishing to support the English/language arts curriculum as well as the other disciplines. In addition, there are numerous other multicultural resources available in the form of videos, software, and a variety of specialized publications.

Teacher as Inquiring Learner Activity

You may have found a middle school social studies guide in the classroom where you did a field placement recently. Examine a guide and ask yourself some questions.

- Who created this guide? Is the classroom teacher using the guide, or did he or she file it away in a drawer or on a shelf? Was it created by a committee of teachers in the school or by a districtwide committee? Or is the curriculum guide being used one that was developed by the publisher to go along with their materials?

    Next, think about what you see teachers using to guide their teaching in the middle schools and high schools where you are working.

- Are the instructional focus and the lessons that make up the everyday life of the classroom drawn primarily from a content-area textbook in the subject area where you are working? Is the focus of the curriculum on major understandings, subject-based knowledge, and principles in a particular field of study? Are broad topics or themes—such as the effects of pollution and what we can do about it, or what is meant by a balance in nature and how the building of new highways and bridges near waterways can destroy or alter that balance—used as the organizing focus of the curriculum in the school where you are teaching? Finally, do you see any attempts to link the learners' academic competencies in the classroom to the real world?

▶ ▶ ▶ ▶ ## The Teacher's Role in Designing Curriculum

We realize that if subject matter or grade-level goals are new for a teacher, she or he rely more heavily on a curriculum guide and companion textbook the first year of teaching this material. However, we hope that after that initial year, the teacher will use both the guide and the text as flexible resources. A classroom teacher's most prevalent role is still that of curriculum adapter. Given the particular district or text-based curriculum they encounter, teachers make many decisions related to actual instruction and the implementation of curriculum in their classrooms. Currently most teachers' major role in the curriculum process is focused on modifying the strategies used to meet the learning needs of their own students and to employing different groupings and a variety of resources to support instruction and the learning opportunities for their students.

Another persistent reason teachers note for making change and choices with the curriculum is based on their own attitudes and personal preferences for themes, content, and instructional strategies (Ben-Peretz, 1990). For example, a teacher or group of teachers in different disciplines may focus the curriculum on local history or a local issue in order to give the students real-life experiences with the central concepts in a discipline. Furthermore, a teacher may design a component of the curriculum based on his or her own interests and something that may expose students to a new area, as did the teacher we described in Chapter 7 who created a series of lessons focused on women photographers and the arts. There is currently heightened interest and increasing support for teachers to meet and work with colleagues who are teaching within the same discipline or teaching the same students. Both of these trends stem from an impetus of the educational reform movement focused on the need for more teacher/professional development opportunities and collaboration focused on improved educational opportunities for students that will be reflected in the curriculum offered. We hope you will have opportunities as an individual and in collaboration with other teachers to design curriculum for your own students as you pursue your career as an educator and become more knowledgeable about your discipline and your learners.

In Chapters 9, 10, and 11, we emphasize the role that teachers play as curriculum designers. We will consider the factors that lead to a teacher's or a team's desire to design curriculum. Often in education, an external force such as the national standards movement, state curriculum frameworks, and professional trends such as thematic instruction and global awareness act as stimuli for curriculum revision or change. As you begin your role as a teacher with your own classroom, you will most likely be implementing curriculum. However, we hope you will always be supported in adapting and shaping curriculum based on the needs of your learners, as well as on your own expertise and preferences. Finally, whether you design or adapt curriculum, we hope that you will continue to see yourself as a learner about your students, your content and resources, and your pedagogy throughout your career.

The Standards Movement and Curriculum

You have heard throughout this text that there are many factors that impact a teacher's curriculum design and instructional planning. In this chapter, we will address the impact that the national standards movement is having on every discipline. You will learn about particular trends or issues faced by the individual disciplines. Finally, you will learn about some pervasive concerns and questions that have emerged as a result of the standards movement that, we believe, affect every discipline.

▶ ▶ ▶ ▶ The Current Movement

Educators in many schools across the country are revising their curriculum guides because of the standards movement. Concerns raised in the 1983 report by the National Commission on Excellence in Education, *A Nation at Risk: The Imperative for Educational Reform,* put the nation's educators on notice. In 1989 President Bush and the fifty state governors met, unified by their concern for the quality of American education. The major outcome of this meeting was the creation of six national goals that the president and the governors believed would serve as a framework for excellence in education in the United States. These goals were meant to set a tone for high expectations and equity in educational opportunities for all students in America's schools. Six broad national goals emerged as the substance of the Goals 2000: The Educate America Act (PL 103-227), enacted in 1994:

- All children in America will start school ready to learn.

- The high school graduation rate will increase to at least 90 percent.

- American students will leave grades 4, 8, and 12 having demonstrated competency in challenging subject matter, including English, mathematics, science, history and geography.

- American students will be the first in the world in science and mathematics achievement.

- Every adult American will be literate and will possess the knowledge and skill necessary to compete in a global economy and exercise the rights and responsibilities of citizenship.

- Every school in America will be free of drugs and violence and will offer a disciplined environment conducive to learning.

The federal government realized that these goals were merely a first step to both recognizing and addressing the need for improved education in the United States. Subsequently, the U.S. Office of Education encouraged nongovernmental organizations in subject areas to create discipline-based standards documents that would focus these broad goals specifically on the individual disciplines. Although the various standards documents that have evolved with the standards movement differ greatly in approach and in format, each addresses what students need to succeed in their careers. The national goals and the development of discipline-based standards were meant to ensure that all schools, states, and districts work toward the same ends, although that does *not* mean a national curriculum.

The standards documents are designed to highlight the most important understandings in a discipline and to provide exemplars that identify worthy tasks for students to engage in. Of course, no matter how clear and reasonable they are, the standards cannot alter the quality of education in a state, a district, a school, or an individual classroom. In order to be successful, teams of teachers and administrators within individual districts and individual schools must have time for discussion, planning, and implementation of specific curriculum in the form of units and lessons for their students. The standards can provide coherence to a district's or a school's program. However, the changes indicated in the standards documents can come about only through improved instruction, classroom materials, teacher education, and assessments (Ravitch, 1995). The development of criteria that could be used to judge students' output and the quality of their performance relative to the standards was also considered an important component of the standards documents. Therefore, it is the responsibility of local curriculum development bodies and teachers within each discipline to use the standards and the specific objectives and criteria

As part of the educational reform movement, teachers at every grade level and in every discipline must understand and use the national standards and state curriculum frameworks to design their curriculum and instruction.

© Michael Zide

expressed in the standards documents and to turn these into meaningful curriculum, lessons, and tasks.

A major difference with these standards from earlier curricular reform is the premise that basic skills *are not sufficient for any students at any grade*. Each of these recent standards documents recommends an emphasis on active participation and varied outcomes by students as opposed to the rigid discipline-specific knowledge and memorization of facts that was often the measure of learning in the past.

From across the nation, school-based and university-based educators in various fields have come together motivated by concern for our schools and the students in them. They intend the standards documents to be guides, not prescriptions, for improved curriculum and instruction across the disciplines and across the grades. The individuals who created the standards expect teachers to provide input, and to review and revise the standards as they implement them. The developers of the standards did not intend them to be final or static end points for the students or the schools that serve them. The standards are primarily statements of educational goals. These goals can be realized only if teachers choose to realign their curriculum and instruction, examine the textbooks and other resources that support instruction, and employ multidimensional, authentic assessment of their students' outcomes. Each group responsible for developing the standards hopes that they will foster high expectations for all students, as well as promote equitable educational opportunities for all students (Porter, 1994).

The standards documents were designed to help local educators identify collectively what their students should learn (in the form of central purposes and learning outcomes in each discipline) and how the learning will be assessed (what assessment standards, strategies, and recording systems teachers will use). This use of the standards ties the educational goals and expectations for excellence together across a district, while still recognizing that the actual learning experiences and opportunities for students are in the hands of the classroom teacher who designs and implements the curriculum in an active way every day (Monson & Monson, 1993).

In addition to these national standards, teachers in many schools are being expected to implement state-level curriculum frameworks as well as district-level curriculum goals. For example, middle school math teachers in the Boston Public Schools are expected to be familiar with and to use the standards proposed by the National Council of Teachers of Mathematics (NCTM) to design curriculum and shape units and lessons. Second, they are expected to implement the Massachusetts State Curriculum Frameworks and to prepare their students for state-level assessment on measures directly related to these frameworks. And they are responsible for implementing goals within the discipline that have been presented in a citywide standards document, *Citywide Learning Standards and Curriculum Frameworks* (1996), that emphasizes literacy and communications skills across the disciplines. Most teachers today, and you will be among them, are expected to use this three-tiered set of expectations—national standards, state-level curriculum frameworks, and district-level plans—to design curriculum for all their students across grade levels, disciplines, and courses of study. Think about this recent occurrence. Is it feasible or appropriate for teachers to try to balance three sets of expectations in their discipline? What should be done so that these various documents support or complement one another and the role they will play in enhancing the teaching and learning?

Teacher as Inquiring Learner Activity

Search the Internet for the state-level curriculum frameworks for your discipline, for either the state where you are doing your teacher training or where you think you might teach after you finish your degree. A state's core curriculum standards are often on a web page created by the State Department of Education; therefore, you might enter the following statement: "*State* [the one you are interested in at this time] Department of Education Core Curriculum Standards."

Survey your state web site that has the curriculum frameworks.

- How many different disciplines are covered by separate state documents?
- Which document would be used by teachers in your discipline?
- How is that document organized—how many levels are there within the document, how many standards or strands are there of the particular discipline, are there actual activities to help the teacher plan for instruction, and are there assessment suggestions to go along with the standards?
- Finally, can you determine how students will be assessed on their competencies with these standards?
- How will teachers be held accountable for their implementation and the outcomes in terms of student learning? If this latter information is not available at the state department of education web site, what are some other ways you could pursue to discover how the outcomes and benefits of the curriculum frameworks in your state will be evaluated?

▶ ▶ ▶ ▶ Standards for Selected Specific Disciplines

The many educational commissions and professional organizations that have convened groups to develop discipline-based standards have produced a plethora of reports to guide the development of curriculum and the subsequent instruction in our schools. Kendall and Marzano (1996) have compiled a compendium of forty sets of standards representing recent work on standards across the disciplines. Given that there are so many sources of the standards reports, we have chosen to focus on the standards put forth by either national teacher organizations or major commissions in six major disciplines. The standards we look at were developed by the National Council of Teachers of Mathematics, the National Council of Teachers of English and the International Reading Association, the National Council for the Social Studies, the National Committee on Science Education Standards and

Assessment, the American Council on the Teaching of Foreign Languages, and the Joint Committee on National Health Education Standards (see Table 8.1).

We recognize the striking differences in both the depth and breadth of the understandings included within these six documents. We note as well the great differences among the documents in the specificity of the information they provide and the activities they detail to support teachers' development of lessons and their actual instruction. In examining these standards documents, we also found marked differences in the specificity about student assessment provided. These differences may stem chiefly from differing beliefs by the standards' developers themselves about how the standards will and should be used.

Yet, regardless of the differences, the common goals and overall impetus for the various standards documents are that educators across the disciplines want to see curricula designed and learning opportunities created that will enable all students, elementary through high school, to do the following:

- Solve problems.
- Reason and think critically.
- Apply their knowledge and their strategies in a variety of settings.
- Communicate effectively with others in a variety of forms, both spoken and written.

There are many similarities in these documents as well. Each discipline-based document is designed to highlight the standards of the discipline stated in the form of goals statements or understandings. For example, in foreign language, there are five major areas for understanding that shape the standards. Two of the areas covered by the standards in foreign language are *communication* in languages other than English and *community participation*, focusing on multilingual communities at home and around the world. In science, there are eighteen discipline-based standards delineated into four strands—physical science, life sciences, science and technology, earth and space—that cover all of the separate courses or fields that might be included in elementary or secondary school science curriculum. In addition, each of the science standards is supported by performance criteria for students in the form of objectives for students. These objectives are delineated by levels of difficulty—primary, intermediate, junior high/middle school, and high school—that correspond to the grade levels found in most school districts. The standards and the performance criteria are meant to serve as guidelines for individual teachers, teams of teachers, or departments to help them design courses, units, and lessons.

As you begin your role as a teacher and as a curriculum adapter and developer, think about how you will use the standards within your own courses, units, and lessons. We especially would like you to think about how you will use

Table 8.1 The National Standards Documents: A Summary

Disciplines/ Organization(s)	Levels	Number of Standards/Strands	Information Within Standards	Special Features
Mathematics/ National Council of Teachers of Mathematics	K–4 5–8 9–12	13 standards 13 standards 14 standards	Objectives stated, focus and discussion section with sample teaching/learning activities for each standard at the 3 levels	Separate evaluation standards: General assessment, student assessment, and program evaluation
Social studies/ National Council for the Social Studies	Early grades Middle grades High school	10 standards for each level	Performance expectations stated for each standard	At the early, middle, and high school levels there are 2 to 3 class-room examples for each standard
Science/National Committee on Science Education Standards and Assessment	K–2 3–5 6–8 9–12	18 standards for each of the 4 levels	Objectives provided for each standard at each of the 4 levels	4 major areas of science are used as the macro-organizers: physical science, life sciences, science and technology, and earth and space
English/language arts/National Council of Teachers of English and International Reading Association	Elementary Middle High school	12 standards	Rationale statement and narrative discussion provided for each standard	5–7 vignettes provided for each standard covering situations at the elementary, middle, and high school levels
Foreign languages/ American Council on the Teaching of Foreign Languages	K–4 5–8 9–12	5 standards for each of the 3 levels	Sample performance indicators for each standard at each of the 3 levels	34 learning scenarios that emphasize the use of foreign language in areas as diverse as the newspaper, geography, and fairy tales

Table 8.1   (continued)

Disciplines/ Organization(s)	Levels	Number of Standards/Strands	Information Within Standards	Special Features
Health/Joint Committee on National Health Education Standards	K–4 5–8 9–12	7 standards for each of the 3 levels	Performance indicators focused on concepts and skills students should know by the end of each of the 3 levels	Rationale statement for each standard; opportunity-to-learn standards focused on local, state, and national organizations, higher education, and community roles in order to ensure the standards are met

the literacy strategies we described in Part Two to teach your students and to assess their grasp of the major understandings in your discipline, highlighted in the particular standards document or documents associated with your content area.

Teacher as Inquiring Learner Activity

We think you should be familiar with the standards in your discipline. As a pre-service teacher, you should use the standards to examine the knowledge, strategies, and attitudes you have developed in your own discipline. Find some opportunities to discuss these standards with your peers. Talk about how you could use the standards to design curriculum and day-to-day lessons. Discuss the standards and their implementation with your professors or with the teachers and department chairs in a school where you are working.

- How can you teach or hold your students responsible for understandings and processes with which you are not personally familiar? Why is it important for you to implement the standards of your district as well as of your state as they relate to your content?

You will now have an opportunity to learn about some of the predominant features of the six standards documents listed in Table 8.1. We hope that you will be curious about your own discipline and that you will also read about other disciplines to learn what your colleagues are being asked to emphasize in their respective fields. You may also begin to see some similarities in the focus of the standards documents, which you will be able to use when working with teachers in other disciplines to create curriculum.

Mathematics.   The National Council of Teachers of Mathematics (NCTM) was the first national discipline-based organization to address the need for a new approach to teaching and a new view of the goals of learning for the K–12 population. Once many classroom practitioners and teacher educators recognized the need for an overhaul of the existing math curriculum, they launched a grass-roots effort to shape a set of standards that convey understandings that are necessary for a math-literate population. They developed the following broad goals for all students, from the primary through the secondary years:

- Value math and its many uses.
- Be confident in their own ability to use math operations and computations.
- Become mathematical problem solvers.
- Learn to communicate mathematically using the language of math to clarify or refine a situation or problem.
- Learn to reason mathematically and to gather evidence or to build an argument using mathematical principles, processes and structures. (NCTM, 1989)

Mathematics educators advocating for these standards are convinced that such standards are necessary if students are to improve their academic performance. These advocates also believe that the standards highlight the mathematics understandings and practices necessary if students are to be prepared for a range of employment opportunities. Finally, these educators believe that in order for the average citizen to deal with the everyday demands of the information age and to participate as an informed member of society, they must understand the role that mathematics plays in areas such as defense spending, taxation, and health care.

The standards document comprises thirteen standards each for levels K–4 and 5–8 and fourteen standards for grades 9–12. Each of the three levels has separate standards and objectives. Each individual standard comprises a number of major understandings as well as specific objectives. A discussion section following each standard acquaints teachers with the understandings and principles emphasized at earlier levels. This section also provides suggestions for helping students apply the standards to other disciplines and to the real world. Finally, detailed student activities for levels K–4, 5–8, and 9–12 conclude each of the standards statements. These suggestions are provided to help teachers plan and facilitate learning opportunities for their own students.

In this document, a separate section discusses three distinct areas of assessment:

- Generalizable assessment strategies that cut across grade levels and areas of mathematics
- Criteria of student progress aligned with the standards at each level
- Program evaluation standards with an emphasis on the effectiveness of instruction and the overall quality of the program

Finally, the appendixes provide many rich examples of mathematical connections designed to give students across the grades experience with real-world applications of math. Students who have solved problems in their math classes learn how they can apply mathematical models to another discipline. For example, in social studies, students could use the models they learned in mathematics to quantify economic trends and to show their relationship to an upcoming political race. They can learn to apply problem solving and the use of models in science. For example, students could use mathematical models to display changes in weather patterns. In a lab simulation, students could record data using mathematical models and then see how such data are used in actual weather forecasting. Students should have many opportunities to apply the standards goals in the curriculum you design and in the individual lessons.

Social Studies.   The standards document for the social studies, *Expectations of Excellence: Curriculum Standards for Social Studies* (National Council for the Social Studies, 1994), was designed to help curriculum specialists and teachers address four key questions in the field of social studies:

- Why should social studies be taught?
- What should be included in the curriculum?
- How will we teach what we decide is of value for all students?
- How will we assess whether students can apply what they have learned? (National Council for the Social Studies, 1994)

The developers of these standards believe that students will not benefit from curriculum that emphasizes only discipline-specific knowledge. Rather, the curriculum and the lessons should focus on helping students become adept with strategies and skills that will enable them to acquire information on their own by reading, studying, or searching for information. Like their math colleagues, these educators advocate for teaching and learning events in social studies that will help students learn how to deal with issues and resolve differences in the real world. Furthermore, they believe students need literacy strategies and communication skills infused into the social studies so that they will be able to demonstrate their personal understandings, as well as applications of various social studies principles. For example, after studying the First Amendment in a government or civics course, students might discuss current issues related to censorship on the Internet and decide whether their own rights or those of others in their community have been infringed on.

This standards document is organized into ten thematic *strands,* or areas of major understanding, to give a broad vision of social studies and to highlight areas of emphasis. These strands range from a historical focus on power, authority, and governance to an economic focus on production, distribution, and consumption, to a focus on global connections. For each of the ten strands, a set of separate but closely aligned guiding principles for the early, middle, and high school years is provided. For example, accompanying the first strand, Culture, a number of age- and grade-appropriate experiences are recommended to enable students at each of these levels to learn about various cultures around the world and the cultural diversity represented in their own country.

Performance expectations for students analogous to objectives in the math standards are the second component of the social studies standards. These expectations have been provided to assist teachers and curriculum specialists in designing activities for students that will lead to opportunities for students to demonstrate what they have learned. Using another example from Standard 1, Culture, students at the high school level might be asked to study a variety of resources and to compare the ways in which groups, societies, and cultures have addressed human needs and concerns in the past and today.

Each standard has specific activities for the three levels. These sample activities can be used to shape learning experiences within the different courses of study that make up a typical social studies department. For example, at the high school level, the following classroom-based problem provided as a sample vignette related to Culture might be used:

> "I don't see why we can't have prayer in the school," says 17-year-old Marcus to his teacher, Bill Tate, and the rest of the U.S. government class. "After all," continues Marcus, "every important document of this country makes reference to God. When a president or judge is sworn in, they place their hands on the Bible. You place your hand on the Bible before you testify in court. What is the big deal?"
>
> "What is the big deal?" Tate asks the class. "Marcus makes an interesting point."
>
> "Well for me the big deal is that I'm Buddhist," says Amy Wantanabe. "My concept of God and religion is probably different from what Marcus is talking about."

[Additional student comments are included.]

Tate records the students' comments on the board in columns that represent positions that are either for or against religion in the schools. As he writes, more students chime in their opinions. . . . As the period draws to an end, Tate presents the students with a case study about a city's decision to have a nativity scene on public property. For homework the students are to state which side of the argument they agree with and list all of the reasons with which they can support their opinions. In addition, they are to research analogous historical or contemporary situations.

In the next class session, students present their homework in small groups. Each group is given a recording chart to list the points students make to support their opinions. The results are presented to the class and compared. Tate evaluates the individual assignments and group charts on the basis of the clarity of presentation and reasoning and the demonstrated understanding of the historical or contemporary comparisons used to support the argument. (National Council for the Social Studies, 1994, pp. 111–112)

The issue focused on and the questions asked concerning Culture found in this vignette could be applied to a history, a civics, or a government class within the social studies departments of most high schools.

We believe the social studies standards provide a framework for rich curriculum development beyond a single discipline or course. The standards can be enacted in a single discipline or course, they can be used in different courses within the same discipline, and they can act as a stimulus for coordinating disciplines.

Science. In science there has been an evolution of reports and standard-setting attempts in the past decade. The seminal work aimed at improving science education was *Science for All Americans: A Project 2061 Report on Goals in Science, Mathematics and Technology,* written in 1990. *The National Committee on Science Education Standards and Assessment* (1994) builds on *Project 2061's* emphasis on scientific inquiry, scientific knowledge, and the importance of scientific processes. The National Committee on Science Education Standards and Assessment document that we look at here organizes the study of science into four major areas: earth and space, life sciences, physical science, and science and technology. Eighteen standards related to major understandings and processes in science are subsumed under these four major areas. For example, in the area of life science, a specific standard is that students will know "about the diversity and unity that characterizes life" (Kendall & Marzano, 1996, pp. 82–83).

Specific objectives of differing levels of sophistication are provided for each of these eighteen standards for grade levels K–4, 5–8, and 9–12. Teachers can use these grade-level objectives when planning for their own students. The developers of this document also believe strongly that the objectives and related learning activities at one level should be used to prepare students for more complex understandings at successive levels. For example, in the life science area, students in grades K–2 are taught "that plants and animals have features that help them thrive in different environments." Later, at the high school level, the more sophisticated expectation in the life sciences is that students will "know that organisms are classified into a hierarchy of groups and subgroups based on their similarities and reflecting their evolutionary relationships; and that the similarity of organisms inferred from similarity in their molecular structure closely matches the classification based on anatomical similarities." Clearly a high school student studying biology, botany, or zoology would have difficulty grappling with the knowledge expressed in the objectives for grades 9–12 without having prior experiences and knowledge related to the differentiation of plant and animal species focused on for grades K–2.

English/Language Arts.   The English/language arts standards, the most recent of the standards documents to be completed under the auspices of a professional teaching organization, were created jointly by the National Council of Teachers of English and the International Reading Association, two national organizations focused on literacy education from early childhood through the college levels. The educators who wrote this document developed twelve broad standards as a framework for literacy education.

Unlike the mathematics and science standards documents, which include specific objectives for each standard or strand, each of the twelve English/language arts standards statements is followed by a narrative explanation applicable across grade levels. A separate section of the document contains sample vignettes that highlight actual classroom practice in varied elementary, middle, and high school settings. Following each vignette are questions appropriate for consideration by in-service as well as preservice teachers. In order to use the English/language arts standards to shape curriculum, teachers might begin by examining the genres and themes they are currently focusing on in their courses. They could then use the standards to make some changes or revisions in the existing curriculum rather than starting from scratch. For example, Standard 9 is focused on students' "developing an understanding of and respect for diversity in language use, patterns and dialects across cultures, ethnic groups, geographic regions and social roles" (p. 41). Teachers in a middle school using a folk tale unit might consider what changes they would make in their own classrooms to enable students with limited English proficiency to affirm their own primary language and culture while at the same time being encouraged to work toward proficiency in English while learning about folk tales from their own and from different cultures.

Foreign Languages. *Standards for Foreign Language Learning: Preparing for the 21st Century* (1995) was developed as a collaborative effort of the American Council on Teaching of Foreign Languages and the three language-specific organizations for teachers: the Associations of Teachers of French, Teachers of German, and Teachers of Spanish and Portuguese. The educators who contributed to the national standards document created five broad standards designed to act as major goals for all students engaged in foreign language learning for the elementary (K–4), middle school (5–8), and high school levels (9–12).

Among the goals that the *Standards for Foreign Language Learning* emphasize are those that focus on the active role and everyday applications of a second language:

- Use the target language to engage in conversation expressing their personal feelings and thoughts.

- Comprehend and use written and spoken language on a variety of topics and from a variety of sources, individuals as well as media.

- Have knowledge and understanding relative to the target culture of the language being studied (its institutions, traditions, literary, and artistic expressions).

Each of the five standards cites specific yet broad performance objectives for students, which are included to assist teachers in the design of curriculum for their individual language-specific courses.

This document contains a strong recommendation that students have opportunities to reinforce their knowledge of foreign language in other disciplines, as well as opportunities to acquire information from authentic documents such as foreign language newspapers, which can be used in studying other school subjects. Since most secondary schools are organized into separate departments, it may be difficult for a teacher of a foreign language to assess whether students have appropriate opportunities to integrate foreign language materials and understandings into other disciplines. We believe that it would be equally difficult for the teachers of the non–foreign language courses to determine when to encourage students to include understandings from materials available in a foreign language into their particular courses.

Although it may not be simple to implement or to assess these real-world applications of a foreign or second language, this seems to be an important educational goal, which could be enhanced by coordinated or integrated curriculum described in Chapters 10 and 11 of this book. The *Massachusetts World*

Language Curriculum Framework (1996) states, "In our society knowing another language is an essential part of every student's education, not just for the many benefits it brings the individual, but for the important lessons it provides in local and global cross-cultural understanding" (p. 5).

A current point of debate among the community of educators directly responsible for the development and implementation of national standards and state-level frameworks related to foreign language is the question pertaining to the purpose and value of studying and speaking a second language. Educators and politicians in states with significant numbers of speakers of languages other than English have committed themselves in their latest state frameworks to all students' being able to read, write, and converse in at least one language other than English. In fact, the introduction to the recent *Massachusetts World Language Curriculum Framework* (1996) states, "Multilingualism expands our sense of community. By crossing cultural and linguistic boundaries to talk to one another we gain respect for others and learn about the similarities we share" (p. 7). This entire frameworks document is built on the premise that knowing another language helps individuals understand their own responsibilities and opportunities as citizens of the world and helps them analyze and understand world events more effectively as a result of their exposure to the language and culture of other people.

Health.   The final set of national standards we include is the *National Health Education Standards: Achieving Health Literacy* (1995), which a committee of educators and health professionals developed. The seven standards in health education that students across the grades are expected to have are these:

- Comprehend concepts related to health promotion and disease prevention
- Demonstrate the ability to access valid health information and health-promotion products and services
- Demonstrate the ability to practice health-enhancing behavior and reduce health risks
- Analyze the influence of culture, media, technology, and other factors on health
- Demonstrate the ability to use interpersonal communication skills to enhance health
- Demonstrate the ability to use goal-setting and decision-making skills to enhance health
- Demonstrate the ability to advocate for personal, family, and community health (p. 8)

There are many overlaps between health education and the disciplines of science and physical education. In fact, documents such as the *National Science Education Standards* (1994) and *Project 2061*, the work of the American Association for the Advancement of Science (1993), were used to design the health standards. Concern for the interaction between the environment and human beings is linked to the disciplines of health and science as well. Similarly, health education is connected to physical education, especially concerning the belief today that each individual, no matter what his or her age, should maintain a level of physical fitness.

Each of the standards in the national health education document is supported by knowledge and skills statements written as objectives that are appropriate for students at each of three levels: K–4, 5–8, and 9–12. In addition, what a student learns at the elementary level about health should serve as background knowledge for more sophisticated understandings emphasized at the secondary level. For example, at the elementary level, students learn about a variety of causes of pollution (e.g., air, ground, noise, water, and food) in their own communities. At the high school level, students learn how environmental and other external factors affect individual and community health. The emphasis for the older students will be on seeing how, as informed citizens, they can use public health policies and government regulations to safeguard and improve their own lives and that of others in their community.

Teacher as Inquiring Learner Activity

Look at the standards and the objectives listed for the high school level in your discipline.

- Do you think your classroom experiences and the learning outcomes you were responsible for in high school were shaped by these standards? What understandings, content, and issues did your teachers emphasize in the courses you took? Are there any areas that you feel particularly weak in?

  If you are in the arts or physical education, you will find that there are standards documents for you to survey also. Check with individuals in your discipline for the documents they are using, or consult Kendall and Marzano's recent *Content Knowledge: A Compendium of Standards and Benchmarks for K–12 Educators* (1996), available in text format and on the Internet, to find the standards for your discipline.

Finally, discuss with other students in your discipline and with preservice teachers in other disciplines what the implications of these standards are for your preparation as a teacher.

▶ ▶ ▶ ▶ Concerns and Questions About the Standards

These standards and the standards movement itself are not without critics. As some educators and politicians push for a national curriculum, others contend that no national force exists that can make these standards a reality in all schools. We live and teach in a country with an enormous and complex educational system and a student population that is extremely diverse. These factors alone make any attempt to set national standards difficult and challenging.

Another group of critics looks at the range of formats and the number of discrete disciplines developed in standards movement. These critics are concerned with the sheer number of the standards documents and the implications for what teachers will teach and what students will learn. Indeed, the expectations for teachers and students to cover these newly created standards do seem staggering.

Finally, educators who have begun to work toward more integration within the curriculum fear that these standards will lead to increased fragmentation in schools. They believe that teachers held accountable within their own discipline for the standards for their field will not have the time to work with their colleagues in other disciplines on integrated curriculum. They believe the time and energy necessary to examine and to validate or change one's own curriculum area using the standards will counter the integrated work with colleagues that has begun to infuse our schools in positive ways.

The national standards are meant to act as goals for their respective disciplines. The standards are *indicators* of what should be emphasized through the curriculum; they are *not* the curriculum. In most instances, these documents do not designate specific content or subject matter. The content, pedagogy, and resource decisions are left up to individual teachers, departments, and curriculum committees. Using the standards as a framework of expectations for discipline-specific knowledge and strategies, teachers or teams of teachers will still need to develop their own curriculum. They will also have to carry out their own planning in order to create curriculum that will accommodate their student population and the setting in which they teach. Content-area teachers engaged in curriculum planning in which they are attempting to embed the national and perhaps state frameworks have many decisions to make about content, the manner in which they will organize and carry out teaching/learning experiences, and the approaches they will use to assess their students' learning.

Models for Curriculum Development

The national standards have had a profound effect on curriculum development in states, school districts, and publishing companies across the country. In each of the disciplines, classroom teachers and other educators are struggling with which priorities or expectations to focus on, how best to design and implement curriculum that will reflect the standards, and how to assess the outcomes.

In each discipline, individual teachers as well as teams of teachers and curriculum committees are working to interpret the national standards in their discipline in order to turn these standards into viable curriculum that will guide their teaching and their students' learning. Additionally, as a result of the Education Reform Act of 1994, states are developing and disseminating curriculum frameworks for each discipline. Teachers today find themselves needing to demonstrate how the curriculum they develop, and the lessons they carry out, are responsive to the national standards and the state-level curriculum frameworks in their discipline, as well as to district-level guidelines and schoolwide expectations shaped by the demographics and the learning needs of their particular student population. Finally, teachers have to consider the texts and other resources available in their schools to complement the content and the understandings they will emphasize in the curriculum they are adapting or designing for their own students. (See Figure 8.1)

To demonstrate more clearly how to use the national standards and curriculum frameworks to shape curriculum, we will examine three curriculum models currently used in every discipline and at every level: single discipline, coordinated, and integrated. We briefly describe them in this chapter and then look at them in depth in the following three chapters. And finally in this chapter we will discuss the unit plan and its components, which we also look at in depth in the following chapters.

▶ ▶ ▶ ▶ Three Curriculum Models

Curriculum at the elementary and secondary levels is designed and carried out in one of three models: a single discipline model, a coordinated model where parallel work is done in a pair of disciplines, or an integrated model where two or more disciplines are closely interrelated.

Figure 8.1

Shaping and Designing
Curriculum

National Standards for a particular
discipline and the accompanying objectives
and performance indicators related to the standards

State Curriculum Frameworks for each discipline

Districtwide Guidelines and Schoolwide Expectations

Textbook and Other Published Programs/Materials

examined by

**Individual Teachers, Departments, Teams,
Curriculum Committees**

for priorities and emphasis of content

distilled by

Individual Teachers or Teams of Teachers

in terms of their own content, pedagogy, and
materials, as well as their expertise and interest
and
their particular students' strengths and needs

to adapt or design

units with lesson plans

Source: From *Expectations of Excellence: Standards for the Social Studies*, 1994, pp. 111–112. Used by
permission of the National Council for the Social Studies.

Single Discipline Model. The most prevalent model in the middle school and the high school is the *single discipline model*, where teachers teach their subject matter as a separate entity. The advantage is that teachers and students can "cover" a discipline's major topics and study specific topics in the field in depth. The disadvantage is that often students in such classrooms see the content, the processes, and the strategies that they are learning in one discipline as separate from everything else they are doing in school. In addition, students may see their courses as separate from anything they are doing outside school.

Even within this model, however, segregation of curricula from school and the rest of life does not have to be the case. Many single-subject teachers do connect their subject matter to other areas of the curriculum on a regular basis, as well as to applications in everyday life. For example, a middle school teacher of geometry linked what the students were learning about mathematics principles to the arts and social studies. Students examined the prevalence of geometric forms in the architecture of the Greek and Roman civilizations and geometric forms found in the beautiful quilts crafted by the Mennonites and the blankets and pottery of the Navajos. Such an emphasis in content-area classrooms can demonstrate the link between the arts and the world of mathematics in a natural way within the single discipline curriculum model.

Coordinated Curriculum. In *coordinated curriculum*, teachers in one discipline plan their lessons to coincide with lessons in another discipline in order to reinforce and expand student understandings of related topics or issues found in both disciplines. For example, at the same time as an eighth-grade class was studying the American Revolution in social studies, their English teacher chose a book of historical fiction, *My Brother Sam Is Dead* by James and Robert Collier, set in the same time period. Through such a coordinated experience, students used their recently acquired background knowledge from history to evaluate the authors' authenticity in representing a fictional family's experiences during the Revolutionary period. This type of coordinated planning is one of the simplest ways to connect different disciplines and frequently is seen in the middle school setting. For coordinated curriculum to work, teachers across disciplines must communicate with one another about the topics and themes they are covering in their courses.

Coordinated curriculum is not limited to efforts that two different teachers make in different disciplines. An individual teacher can design a lesson or a unit in his or her own area and connect it to related material from another discipline. For example, a science teacher who has created a unit that focuses on weather from a scientific standpoint can extend students' understandings by having students focus on how the weather affects human beings. This extension that focuses on a social studies perspective related to weather could be carried out by having students read informational texts or primary sources about individual explorers who spent time in remote areas with extreme weather conditions, such as the Arctic or the rain forests of Brazil. Students could use their scientific knowledge about weather to understand more fully both the physical and the emotional effects that extreme weather conditions have on human beings who live in or explore such regions of the world.

As another example of coordinated curriculum, mathematics and social studies classes could study the history of and use of the census in the United States. The mathematics teacher teaches students about the variety of mathematical procedures that professionals use in obtaining and analyzing census data. For example, census takers use statistical methods to track population shifts. By applying means and averages they learned in mathematics, students could see how various categorization systems classify population groups within the United States. The social studies teacher could build on the understanding of graphs that students have gained in their mathematics class to help students see how data are analyzed and arranged to make determinations about immigration quotas and how funds for a variety of school programs and community services are determined by census data. Many more examples of coordinated curricula are the focus of Chapter 10.

Integrated Curriculum.   The primary emphasis of *integrated curriculum* is on the value of interrelatedness and the importance of finding natural connections among disciplines. The overarching goal of integrated curriculum is to deepen students' understandings of themselves, their communities, and the world rather than to focus on specific discipline-based content or processes.

Let's take an example of coordinated curriculum related to the census and transpose it to an integrated curriculum situation where the content related to the social sciences and the tools of mathematics were combined in a coordinated curriculum model to help students understand the purpose and use of the census in the United States. If this were an integrated curriculum setting instead, the focus might be on looking at issues related to immigration laws and patterns in the United States. Students could apply their mathematical understandings to examine trends in the census rather than simply trying to understand the collection and use of census data. Students could study recent immigration trends, look at laws about quotas, and learn how actual people have experienced the immigration quotas and laws. The students could read informational books for young adult readers, such as *Illegal: Seeking the American Dream* (P. Anastos & C. French, 1991), *Dan Thuy's New Life in America* (K. O'Connor, 1992), and *Still a Nation of Immigrants* (B. K. Ashabranner & J. Ashabranner, 1993), to learn about the issues immigrants face, especially immigrants in their same age group. Through these nonfiction accounts of young people, students could begin to gain a better understanding of how numbers and statistics are used to make decisions that affect real people. The social studies, mathematics, and English/language arts teachers working within this integrated curriculum model could help students form their own opinions about immigration laws and the use of the census in the United States today. Teachers could encourage students to find avenues to communicate their knowledge and opinions. They might write a letter to the editor of a local newspaper or communicate over the Internet with other individuals who have similar concerns or issues. Through integrated experiences such as these, students would begin to see how the interrelatedness of the disciplines sheds light on real and important questions about their world.

▶ ▶ ▶ ▶ **The Unit Plan**

Curriculum revisions, changes, and additions are an ongoing concern of teachers. Numerous sources might provide an impetus for teachers to engage in planning a new unit or new curricula: courses they take, staff development sessions, changing areas of focus in a discipline, documents like the national standards or state-level curriculum framework, and even textbook changes. Before putting significant time into exploring or developing a new unit or changing curriculum, teachers should ask themselves some important questions about their existing curriculum or course of study:

- Is there an existing curriculum guide? If so, how widely and effectively is it used?

- Is there a required textbook or any other associated material such as lab manuals or software in place?

- What are the strengths of the unit, and are there any problem areas especially with regard to how particular content or concepts are handled?

- How well are students performing within the existing curriculum? (What content, processes/strategies, and skills are they learning? Are students able to apply these to real-life situations and to connect them to other areas or disciplines?) (Tchudi, 1991)

Whether your curriculum work is single discipline, coordinated, or integrated, the *unit plan* is a widely used organizational framework for the design of curriculum and the delivery of instruction. Figure 8.2 sets out the typical components of a unit plan, which you may create yourself or which you may find in published material. Earlier in this chapter, you saw in Figure 8.1 that

Figure 8.2

Developing a Unit Plan

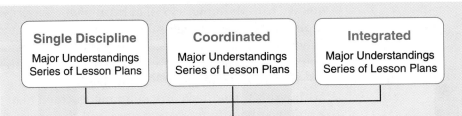

Single Discipline	Coordinated	Integrated
Major Understandings Series of Lesson Plans	Major Understandings Series of Lesson Plans	Major Understandings Series of Lesson Plans

Planning and Setting Up a Unit

Unit title and focus—rationale, philosophy, values related to
content and concepts
Time allotments—semester, weeks, days
Major understandings and goals—written in the form of generalizations
Specific content, strategies that will shape the lessons in the unit
Text, other resources—instructional materials and media for
teachers and students

Teaching the Unit: Series of Lessons

Focused on the content, concepts, facts, theories, and ideas related to the
major understandings and goals of the unit

(Varying numbers of lessons may be developed for each phase; phases are
determined by the discipline content and needs of the learners)

Generating Lessons
Content objectives
Strategy objectives

Interacting Lessons
Content objectives
Strategy objectives

Refining Lessons
Content objectives
Strategy objectives

Evaluate the Unit

Evaluation of students—assessment of student learning in terms of major
understandings and objectives
Evaluating the design and implementation of the unit—materials,
time allotments, lessons

Source: Adapted from M.A. Laughlin and H.M. Hartoonian. *Challenges of Social Studies Instruction in Middle and High Schools* (Orlando, Fla.: Harcourt, Brace, 1995); A.A. Glatthorn, "Alternative Processes in Curriculum Development" (paper presented at the Annual Meeting of the American Educational Research Association, San Francisco, 1986).

there is an overall relationship between the factors that influence curriculum development, such as the national standards, state curriculum frameworks, and teacher interest and expertise, and the unit plans and lessons that comprise the unit being designed and enacted in classrooms or courses every day.

In Chapter 3 you learned that individual lessons are built on specific content and strategy objectives that guide student learning outcomes. You saw how the lesson plan format we proposed supported the design of instruction in a science lesson focused on nutrition and the importance of interpreting graphs. The content-area lesson example in Chapter 3 was a single component of a larger organizational structure used to design instruction: the unit. The modeling and explaining scripts for mini-lessons on particular strategies found throughout Part Two are another component of content-area unit plans.

Planning and Setting Up a Unit.   Once you decide to spend time planning a new unit or course of study in your own discipline or in a coordinated or integrated effort with other teachers, consider these questions:

- How will the new course or unit relate to existing courses in the school's program of study? Is it part of a proposed sequence of courses? Is it intended to relate closely to the content of other courses?

- What are the general course or unit outcomes? What general concepts and skills do we hope to develop?

- For which group of students is the course or unit primarily intended? (Glatthorn, 1986, p. 10)

You should continue to refer to Figures 8.1 and 8.2 as you read the next sections. The figures will guide you through the components of a unit and help you see how units are related to the larger picture of curriculum design and instruction.

You begin planning a unit by establishing major goals or understandings that are inherent in the topic to be studied. For example, in a unit titled, "Why Study Economics?" intended as an introductory area of study for juniors and seniors in high school, the focus may be on helping students understand the basic premises of economics. The principle that choices in our society are driven by the need to meet unlimited wants with limited resources and that both personal and national economic policies have implications for individuals and for society as a whole is an example of such recurring generalizations in economics (Laughlin & Hartoonian, 1995).

As you plan a unit, you should ask yourself what strategies and skills students will need in order to comprehend the content's major understandings as well as how you will expect students to demonstrate these understandings. In the planning stage of the unit, you should decide on specific concepts, strategies, and skills directly related to the content and goals of the unit. You should emphasize them as well in the lessons through the teaching/learning experiences that occur throughout the unit. For example, in the "Why Study Economics?" introductory unit, the goal should be to help students acquire an understanding of key economic concepts, such as needs and wants and producers and consumers. They might also learn about different economic systems such as capitalism and socialism. If students have had no prior experience with economic material, they will need specific literacy strategy instruction and practice such as finding and interpreting information on economic charts, tables, and graphs in order to read and interpret various sources and to be able to apply their understandings to current economic issues. Students may require assistance in analyzing data from a number of sources and in using data to make predictions about the issue at hand.

Another important decision in the early planning of a unit concerns determining what materials and resources will complement the area of study. You must take into account the focus of the unit, the disciplines you will incorporate, the needs of the learners, and the availability of resources. When you study the generic unit plan format in Figure 8.2 with the economics unit for juniors and seniors in high school in mind, you will probably decide to incorporate some or all of the following types of materials to support instruction:

- A chapter or chapters from a secondary economics textbook such as *Economics* (J. B. Taylor, 1998)
- A handout entitled "Economic Headlines"
- Editions of local and regional newspapers
- The film *Very Basic Economics* or the computer program Economics: What, How and for Whom? by Focus Media for demonstration purposes (Laughlin and Hartoonian, 1995, p. 226)

You might want to check back to Chapter 3 for a detailed discussion about choosing materials.

Teaching the Unit: A Series of Lessons.   The day-to-day or class-to-class enactment of a unit is made up of a series of lessons using the format we developed in Chapter 3. The lessons themselves are shaped by both the content in a particular discipline or disciplines and the literacy strategies needed to understand and use that content. One or more lessons in a unit may be focused on generating ideas, interacting with ideas, and refining and reconstructing ideas, determined by the major understandings being pursued, the particular content, and the resources that support the unit as well as by the learning needs of the students.

Generating Ideas.   An *initiating activity* or *introductory lesson* usually begins a unit. The focus in this lesson is on students' generating ideas about the text being used and the topic being studied. The emphasis in the initiating lessons of the unit should be on helping students set purposes for studying the topic using strategies such as making predictions and activating prior knowledge found in Chapter 4. In the initiating lessons, students engage in using tools such as brainstorming, freewriting, and anticipation guides to activate their prior knowledge and generate ideas related to the topic being studied. You should decide on key vocabulary related to the content to explore as part of the generating process.

Interacting with Ideas.   The core of the unit is made up of lessons that emphasize students' interacting with ideas. Students are actively engaged with texts and other resources, and many of the strategies we described in Chapter 5 come into play at this stage in a unit. Therefore, the emphasis in these lessons, which make up the core of the unit, is on students' finding and interpreting important information within the materials they are using. The emphasis should be on students' increasing their understandings of a topic or theme. The reading in various texts and the activities the students are participating in should be focused on students' deepening their understandings. Students can communicate their increasing understandings in spoken and written form throughout the unit. Lessons that incorporate teaching tools such as pattern guides and the DRTA or ones that emphasize the use of study guides and the value of discussion groups as well as the tools necessary for the interpretation of different types of graphic aids are essential to the development of these central lessons in a unit. In these lessons, you should model for students how to use supporting strategies, such as note taking, graphic organizers, and story maps and frames, so that they will better understand the content and concepts they are studying.

Refining.   To bring a unit to culmination, you should ensure that the lessons focus on students' ability to refine or reconstruct their understandings, to organize and revise their ideas, and to connect ideas and information from different sources and other disciplines. At this stage, students can reflect on and find personal meanings in the material they have studied. You can instruct students on the tools they need in order to share their knowledge with others. Students can learn how to write summaries or reviews, give book talks, or design projects that will demonstrate their understandings and their personal interpretations of the content or issues they have studied.

Students often share their culminating experiences or final lessons in a unit with the entire class. During such concluding lessons, students should have opportunities to explain their personal interpretations as well as to compare their individual or small group learning experiences with one another. At this stage in the unit, the emphasis should be on students' collectively having opportunities to revisit, discuss, and even debate the unit's major understandings.

Students should have many opportunities to use their knowledge and to demonstrate their new understandings related to the topic they are studying. For example, students could read their textbooks and survey current newspapers or periodicals such as *Zillions* or *Consumer Reports* for articles related to economics. They could participate in class simulations and discussions about economic issues that are important to them and to their own communities. Students engaged in an economics unit focused on everyday applications of economics could then be expected to explain why the study of economics is important in their lives as teenagers and as citizens of the United States.

Students might be expected to participate in a discussion about the types of important economic choices that leaders in countries around the world must make today. They could focus on recent decisions made in the United States, such as a change in the consumer price index or the rising cost of child care or medical care, that will affect their own lives or those of their family and their community. Students could also discuss such topics as what a change in the availability of natural resources such as lumber or natural gas, widely used in their region of the country, would mean for them personally or for other individuals or companies in their own community.

Evaluating the Unit.   Every unit incorporates two types of evaluation: one that is ongoing (formative) and one that is final (summative). Both types should inform teachers about their instruction and students about their learning. *Formative evaluation* takes place when the teacher uses teaching tools and observes student responses during a lesson. Throughout the lessons that make up the unit, teachers can evaluate student learning as students participate in discussions and create various written products. Teachers can assess and give feedback to students as they examine work in progress, such as field notebooks, note cards, or retellings. They can do this while conferencing with an individual student or a group of students engaged in ongoing study or product development related to the topic being studied. Based on students' and teachers' ongoing, formative evaluation of the students' learning, teachers should revise planned series of lessons so that instruction better matches the students' strengths, needs, and interests that emerge during classroom interactions between student and student and between student and teacher.

Concluding lessons and activities in a unit include within them natural opportunities for evaluation of student learning. In the final evaluation, known as *summative evaluation*, teachers can look at the outcomes or student products in order to assess their instruction as well the students' learning. The focus on evaluation at this stage is often on students' application of their understandings from the course of study or the unit to solving everyday problems or concerns. In a unit like the one on basic economic principles, students could discuss why the states of the former Soviet Union are having such massive economic difficulties since the collapse of communism and the ending of the cold war. Students might consider how this dramatic economic change is affecting the Russian government as well as the day-to-day lives of individual citizens, and they might propose some economic solutions for the future.

A concluding assignment that would be evaluative in nature and would necessitate that the students apply what they have learned about economics to their own lives might be to ask them to bring a current newspaper or magazine article related to economics the following day to share with the class or watch one of the network news programs and report on economic news contained in the newscast. Then the focus of the discussion the next day and the enabling activity would be for the students to think about how economic events influence our (their) daily lives and what some likely consequences are of the events they have heard or read about.

Applying Standards to the Teaching Profession: A Look Ahead to Chapter 12

I n the next three chapters you will have the opportunity to see how middle school and high school teachers in different disciplines have tackled the task of extending their existing curriculum as well as the development of new curriculum using single discipline, coordinated, and integrated curriculum models. Through the sample units in these chapters, you will see how these teachers continue to ask themselves questions about their discipline, their students, and their settings in order to inform their practice on an ongoing basis.

Although we know you will take on a variety of roles in your career as a teacher—content-area specialist, evaluator and diagnostician, curriculum developer and adapter, and instructor—-we know it is in the last role where you will focus your time and your energy. From our own work in the classroom and our work with both preservice and in-service teachers, we believe this will be the case whether you teach in a middle school, a junior high school, or a high school; whether you teach as part of a team, a department, or a cluster; and, finally, whether you teach from a single discipline, a coordinated, or an integrated model of curriculum.

You recall that we began this chapter on curriculum development by discussing the standards movement. The standards movement is affecting curriculum development and instruction for students, and also the credentialing or professional standards being established for teachers. Thus, in Chapter 12, when we conclude Part Three of this text, we will return to the standards movement and your own continuing professional development. You will see why we are advocating that you continue to grow personally, contribute to your field and to your school, and, above all, improve instruction for your learners as you engage in reflective practice focused on your multifaceted role as an educator.

Summary of the Chapter

We began the chapter and concluded it by focusing on teachers like you. We discussed two important topics:

- The teacher's role as an adapter and as a designer of curriculum
- The relationship of a teacher's role in curriculum development to his or her own ongoing professional development

Second, we discussed the major force that is affecting the development of curriculum across the disciplines today, the national standards movement, and emphasized the following:

- Important features of the standards in six major disciplines
- Concerns and questions about the standards movement as a whole and the use of the standards documents
- The relationship of the national standards to state curriculum frameworks, districtwide guidelines, schoolwide expectations, and individual teacher expertise and preference

We briefly discussed three models for curriculum development: single discipline, coordinated, and integrated.

Finally, we presented a unit plan structure for teachers to use, both to adapt and to design curriculum for their own courses and learners. We have focused on the components of the unit plan as well as the relationship of the individual lessons you learned about in Part Two to the development of an entire unit. As you begin the following chapters focused on single discipline, coordinated, and integrated curriculum, think about how you will combine the literacy strategies you learned in Part Two of this book and the major understandings of your own content area to create meaningful learning opportunities in the form of units and lessons for your own students.

Inquiry Activities About Your Learning

1. Talk with your cooperating practitioner, supervisor, or instructor to see whether he or she has been involved in some recent curriculum development work. Ask what the impetus was for the work: new standards in the field, reorganization of a department, issues in the community, or something else. Find out if the teacher worked alone, in a team, or as part of a committee and what role he or she played in the project. Ask how he or she would characterize the experience as a professional and whether he or she implemented this curriculum. If the person has implemented the new curriculum, find out what the outcomes were for the students.

2. Examine the national standards or the state curriculum frameworks in your discipline, particularly at the objectives for the high school level, to note whether there are any explicit applications of literacy within your discipline. Since the focus of this textbook and the course you are now taking is on literacy and learning in your content area, we'd like you to notice how literacy and communication are interwoven in the discipline. Can you find some concrete examples of students' being required to use their reading, writing, listening, and speaking skills and strategies in either the classroom or in real-world applications related to your discipline? How effectively have the developers of these standards helped content-area teachers like you design curriculum for your own students that will enhance both their literacy and communication skills and their content-area knowledge?

Inquiry Activities About Your Students' Learning

1. In this chapter we have discussed three curriculum models that teachers use in schools today. Interview a student at the middle school level and one at the high school level, and ask them to tell you what they are studying in each of their major subjects. Next, ask each of the students whether currently or in the past they have studied a topic from the perspective of two of their content areas (coordinated curriculum). Finally, ask each of the students if they have studied any topic or issue using information and understandings from multiple content areas. If they have participated in coordinated or integrated curriculum, what can they tell you about the advantages or disadvantages they experienced when one teacher or several teachers focused on connections among the content areas in their program of studies? What do the experiences of these students tell you, and how will you use their experiences to inform your future curriculum work when you student-teach or when you have your own classroom?

2. In this chapter we have emphasized how important it is for all content-area teachers to focus on major understandings as well as critical thinking and communication skills within their discipline. We have also stressed the importance of students being able to apply content-area knowledge to their everyday lives.

Interview either a high school or a middle school aged student and ask them to tell you in their own words what major understandings or topics are being emphasized in the course/discipline you are planning to teach. Ask this student what types of assignments they have had in their course. Try to determine whether the student has had an opportunity to apply his or her knowledge concretely. Finally, ask the student if he or she has discovered on their own or if any specific connections have been made between what they are studying in school and what is happening in their everyday world.

Reflect on what you have learned from this student and think about how in the future you would want your own students to respond to these questions.

9

Single Discipline-Based Learning and Literacy

Historically most curriculum, middle school through college, has been focused on discrete disciplines. Single discipline–based learning is a particularly important topic because recent data indicate that most middle schools and secondary schools are still organized around separate disciplines. Although this often means that there is an accompanying emphasis on isolated, subject-specific content rather than on thinking, problem solving, and application of knowledge, it does not have to have this meaning at all. The best of separate subject/single discipline teaching demonstrates a teacher's depth of knowledge and thoroughness of instruction, which in turn leads to students becoming knowledgeable about important concepts and generalizations associated with a given discipline (Ediger, 1998). Most individuals who become middle school or high school content-area specialists do so because they have a strong personal interest in the subject matter associated with a particular domain of a discipline such as biology or chemistry in science or American history or economics in the social sciences. These individuals, who are probably very much like you, decided to share their interest as well as their knowledge with young people and to become a teacher.

Exemplary teachers of every discipline have some shared characteristics. They probably demonstrate in-depth content knowledge as well as firsthand experience with the materials and tools of their discipline. These teachers are also well versed in the craft of teaching, which includes many of the strategies and techniques that have been emphasized in your own teacher preparation program as well as the literacy strategies we emphasized in Part Two in this text.

These teachers probably have all or many of the characteristics associated with good subject matter teaching:

- The ability to choose materials that foster a balance of breadth and depth related to a subject or topic and that match the needs of one's students
- The ability to present information or do demonstrations; to model for and to respond to one's students in order to assist students in constructing meaning of their own about the content being studied
- The ability to shape learning experiences that will help students acquire problem-solving and critical thinking skills useful in the discipline and applied to actual contexts
- The ability to create a learning community built on dialogue between teacher and students, between individual students, and among groups of students

These competencies can serve as goals for your own teaching in your discipline.

No matter what the discipline, the priority in a classroom should not be to teach subject matter alone, but to teach students in a manner that challenges their misperceptions and emphasizes their linking prior knowledge to new experiences and new knowledge. The classroom in which such teaching is enacted is characterized by question asking by students as well as by the teacher, dialogue between students and between students and teacher, as well as many opportunities for elaboration and explanation related to the topic under study. Finally, students in these classrooms have numerous opportunities to synthesize and to evaluate their own learning.

Remember, too, as we pointed out in Chapter 8, that thoughtful single-subject teachers make connections all the time—to other subject areas and to real life experiences—directly within the individual content-area classrooms. Isolation and rigidity of content do not have to characterize single-subject teaching.

In this chapter we first explore the concerns common to all content-area teachers, particularly those teaching at the middle and high school levels, because there are certain key issues that cross subject boundaries. We next look at some of the specific challenges that particular disciplines pose and how students can use literacy strategies to meet discipline-specific challenges. And finally we demonstrate in two different sample units how teachers can teach effectively and well their own discipline and important learning and literacy strategies well within a single discipline–curriculum approach.

Purpose-Setting Questions

1. What are the common concerns that content-area teachers today face at the middle and high school levels? What issues cross subject boundaries?

2. What specific challenges face each of the disciplines today?

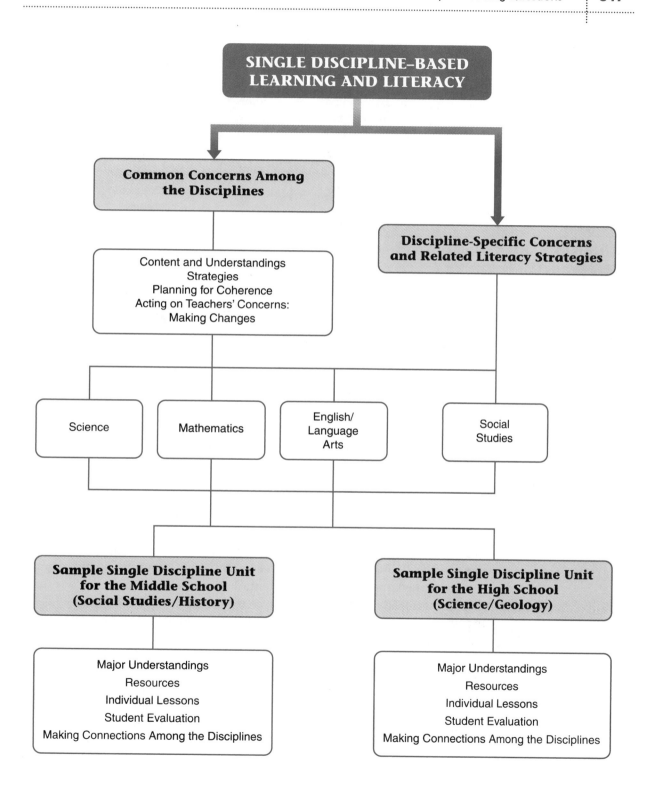

SINGLE DISCIPLINE–BASED
LEARNING AND LITERACY

Common Concerns Among
the Disciplines

Discipline-Specific Concerns
and Related Literacy Strategies

Content and Understandings
Strategies
Planning for Coherence
Acting on Teachers' Concerns:
Making Changes

Science

Mathematics

English/
Language
Arts

Social
Studies

Sample Single Discipline Unit
for the Middle School
(Social Studies/History)

Sample Single Discipline Unit
for the High School
(Science/Geology)

Major Understandings
Resources
Individual Lessons
Student Evaluation
Making Connections Among the Disciplines

Major Understandings
Resources
Individual Lessons
Student Evaluation
Making Connections Among the Disciplines

3. What particular literacy tools will help students handle challenges inherent in each discipline?

4. Given two sample units that demonstrate a single discipline–curriculum approach, one at the middle school level and one at the high school level, what are the literacy and learning strategies emphasized in each, and what do you find in these samples that is applicable to your own content area and to your practice as a teacher?

Common Concerns Among the Disciplines

There is not a text written today focusing on educational pedagogy, policy, or curriculum that does not highlight the need for innovation and educational reform. All educators and many policymakers and parents are asking whether the current view of educational reform evidenced in documents such as the national discipline-based standards, curriculum frameworks, and professional teaching standards will lead to visible, long-lasting changes in our schools and classrooms, as well as tangible benefits for students. Everyone you talk with in education today seems to be either implementing or assessing the impact of the various standards and frameworks and the school restructuring efforts that often accompany them.

This current call for reform emphasizes the need for students to meet higher expectations in problem solving, communication skills, and application of knowledge across the disciplines and the domains of everyday life. Furthermore, recent concerns that teachers, curriculum developers, and subject matter experts have expressed are similar across the disciplines. We do recognize, however, that there are long-standing disagreements regarding the term *discipline* itself and that scholars and educators within every field are engaged in debating what constitutes the essential structure or the major understandings in their field. Think about the recent standards movement and the documents we discussed in Chapter 8. The clearest example of such dissension within a discipline is in social studies.

The standards movement and its emphasis on identifying essential understandings seems to have exacerbated the differences among the fields commonly associated with the social sciences: history, geography, civics, and social studies. The unfortunate result is that there are now four different sets of standards for social studies, each claiming to be the most necessary standards for the study of social studies. How will middle school and high school teachers decide which set of standards to use as a framework for their own social studies curriculum? This dilemma and similar ones in other disciplines have left individual teachers, departments, school districts, and even publishers trying to decide what to focus on in courses and curriculum and in the materials that support these various endeavors.

Table 9.1 shows some of the more prevalent domains or areas of focus being touted as appropriate organizers for courses and curriculum today. Think about this chart and what it says about the dilemma facing educators in secondary schools. What courses were available to you in your own secondary program? How is the content in the discipline you are now studying organized into courses at the college level? If you've looked at a local school district's standards of learning or state-mandated curriculum frameworks and accompanying tests, do you think the courses you are taking match with what you need to know in order to teach your future students?

Beyond the issue of what content to focus on and what domains are central to the development of secondary school programs, educators in each content area are trying to answer three overarching questions in an effort to shape a more responsive curriculum:

- What are the essential understandings in the field of knowledge?

- How do we enhance students' ability to problem-solve, to think critcally, and to apply their understandings of content to everyday life using effective strategies, particularly the literacy strategies of an effective reader and writer?

Table 9.1 The Content Domains

Mathematics	Social Studies	Science	Language Arts
Mathematics	U.S. history	General science	American literature
Discrete math	World history	Biology	British literature
Algebra	Geography	Chemistry	World literature
Geometry	Civics	Physics	Spelling
Calculus	Economics	Ecology	Writing/composition
	Anthropology	Life science	Grammar
	Political science	Physical science	
	Sociology	Earth and space science	
		Technological science	

- How do we ensure time to plan and coordinate these understandings and strategies across each discipline and across the curriculum from level to level and grade to grade in some cohesive fashion?

▶ ▶ ▶ ▶ **Content and Understandings**

Each of the standards documents discussed in Chapter 8 emphasizes the importance of big ideas and overarching principles as the cornerstone for the individual discipline. Each of the standards documents is explicitly designed to communicate essential, long-standing, and valuable understandings in their field. Therefore, the discipline-based standards are meant to provide a framework of important understandings from which curriculum can be shaped. The second overarching goal being suggested by each of the standards documents is that all students in our schools receive a quality, equitable education that stresses important understandings in the discipline, thinking and problem solving, and application of content to real-life situations and issues. No matter what courses students take within a discipline, these overarching curriculum goals should be the same.

Teacher as Inquiring Learner Activity

In order to understand the dilemma about what to teach in your discipline, examine several texts at a specific grade level in the subject you hope to teach. For example, if you are an English major, look at three anthologies of literature for the tenth grade, or if you are a science major, look at several texts written for high school earth science courses. Examine these texts and ask yourself the following questions:

- Are any topics mentioned in all of these texts or in two out of the three? What fundamentals or key principles associated with the discipline are explicitly made and covered in depth within each text? What sorts of activities associated with the discipline are emphasized in the activities or the "to-do" sections of the text? What literacy and learning strategies are incorporated into the content area materials? What everyday applications or career-related examples are provided for students in this text?

As a teacher, you may be in a position to choose specific content from your domain to carry out the national, state, or local curriculum standards or goals. The choices you make will determine the learning experiences you provide and the outcomes of learning for your students. Selecting content carefully helps you keep your focus on the major understandings in your field and also helps you maintain a balance between what is surveyed and what is studied in depth in your discipline.

You may feel overwhelmed when you realize how rapidly your discipline is changing and how difficult it can be to sort through the information explosion affecting every area of your life. Nevertheless, several important principles or guidelines can help you select the content and the understandings to focus on, no matter what your discipline or the level you teach. These guidelines are closely linked to the knowledge you have about your students, the knowledge you have pertaining to materials, and the knowledge you have about strategies to promote literacy and learning.

- Choose durable content closely aligned with the main ideas or concepts in a field; avoid minor ideas and trivial details associated with the subject to be studied.

- Think about your particular learners to determine the content and how it is presented with special attention to the life experiences and background knowledge they bring to learning.

- Seek to illuminate and to contextualize the content with data from other fields as well as from students' previous learning (Doll, 1996).

Finally, no matter what your discipline, we think you might find a set of guidelines that the National Science Teachers Association (Texley & Wild, 1996) recently developed to accompany its curriculum frameworks helpful as well. We have turned these guidelines into questions you can ask yourself about your own curriculum and the content you focus on:

- Is the content connected to other areas of learning both within the discipline and beyond?

- Does the curriculum provide the necessary tools of the discipline (e.g., math for science, writing for language arts and social sciences)?

- Is the curriculum supported by time, space, and equipment?

- Is the curriculum designed to give diverse learners equal footing and to provide background knowledge when necessary?

- Is the curriculum supported by the faculty and the school community, and has it been assessed and renewed?

▶ ▶ ▶ ▷ **Strategies**

The second issue that teachers in every discipline wonder is how they will enhance their students' independent thinking and use of strategies. Think about the strategies you use on a regular basis to solve problems or to answer questions in your content area. When you read, write, collect data, or do research to investigate new topics in your field or connect past understandings to new knowledge, what strategies do you use? As you explored the strategies detailed in Part Two, did you add some new strategies to your repertoire? This is a good time to review your own learning patterns and the literacy strategies you use regularly and those you explored as you studied Part Two. You are most likely to be able to model and to explain with credibility to your own students those strategies with which you have had firsthand practice.

As you build expertise in your discipline, we hope you will continue to explore being a strategic reader and writer in order to use increasingly more complex materials and to link new knowledge and understandings to prior knowledge in your own discipline. For example, if you are a life science major, you may have studied biological science in depth. When you take a different type of course in, say, earth science, you would learn more about this new field if you approached it looking for connections to what you already know about science in general. For example, biologists always attempt to identify structures and systems of a particular organism they are studying. Your new exploration of earth science could begin with your looking for structures and systems in the earth.

We also believe the teacher's role, no matter what the content area, is to explain and model strategic applications of the understandings in a field through "think-alouds" and modeling and explaining scripts like those we explained in Part Two. We think teachers can help their students be more strategic by engaging them in new learning experiences in a coaching mode rather than a didactic mode. Teachers should use appropriate teaching and assessing tools to support their students and to enable them to process content, to make knowledge their own, and to apply understandings to authentic problems and real-world contexts that have meaning beyond the classroom walls. The major goal in every subject area is for students to explain principles and concepts in their own words and to be able to apply understandings both in and out of school.

▶ ▶ ▶ ▶ Planning for Coherence

The third issue teachers in every discipline are dealing with is the lack of coherence in the curriculum from grade to grade and from level to level. Think back to Chapter 1 and our recommendation that you reflect on the essence of your content area and how you will convey that to your own students. What cross-grade opportunities have you seen or have you been able to participate in through a field experience at the middle school or the high school level? When you did your student teaching, did you see your cooperating teacher or mentor work with another teacher in the same discipline? Is there any evidence that the faculty at the institution where you are now participate in any

In their study of current events, students locate information from a combination of sources—newspapers, maps, and globes.

© Michael Zide

sort of coordinated work on curriculum? What opportunities do you think you will have as a new teacher to learn from an experienced teacher?

Teachers at every grade level and in every discipline have very little planning time scheduled during the school day. The usual time structures and schedules in both middle schools and high schools, even when the teachers are organized by discipline, do little to foster discussion and planning of content from grade to grade. Even in middle schools where there are interdisciplinary teams, subject matter teachers at different grade levels rarely meet or plan with one another to create coherence within a discipline from year to year and from grade to grade.

One of us recently saw the benefits of cross-grade discipline meetings firsthand. Middle school teachers in a large urban middle school who were part of a grant focused on the English/language arts voluntarily met in discipline-based groups with a university subject matter specialist for one semester. When the participating teachers were asked to evaluate the benefits of the grant, a number of them cited these cross-grade discipline-based sessions as the most useful and invigorating experiences that the school-university partnership provided (Lesley College/Lewenburg Middle School, Balfour Foundation Grant, 1996–1997).

As a beginning or new teacher, we suggest that you seek out colleagues in your discipline, or at least one "buddy," with whom you can discuss the content you are teaching and the teaching and assessing tools you are using in your discipline. We are encouraging our college students to stay in contact with one another using e-mail in order to maintain the support system they developed during their teacher training. You can begin the curriculum development process in small, manageable increments as you get to know your students, the curriculum, and the context in which you are working. If you focus on assessing your students, becoming familiar with the existing curriculum and materials, and getting to know the community in which you are teaching, you will have a great deal of data to inform your own course development and your day-to-day teaching, particularly after the first year in a setting. Keep in mind that as a subject matter specialist and as an individual with unique interests, strengths, and experiences, you have much to contribute to a school and to its curriculum and how it is taught.

▶ ▶ ▶ ▶ ## Acting on Teachers' Concerns: Making Changes

When you, and some of your colleagues in the future, are ready to make changes in the curriculum in a particular discipline, there are some steps you can follow that will help you gain more satisfaction from the effort and lead to greater benefits for your students as well. First, talk with your department chair, assistant principal, or principal about your idea and its rationale. Second, thoughtfully examine the existing curriculum. Next, consider community needs, issues, and interests, and find ways to connect what is covered in the classroom to what is relevant and authentic in the real world outside the classroom. Fourth, assess your particular learners to determine their background knowledge, their strategies, their skills, and their interests. Finally, consider how you might share your ideas and even your strategies with peers, perhaps in a department meeting or a staff development workshop. Table 9.2, a chart for curriculum development, was developed for the language arts, but it can be applied to curriculum development in all disciplines. It can serve as a road map for you and your future colleagues when you are considering curriculum change and development in your own discipline, grade level, department, or school.

Discipline-Specific Concerns and Related Literacy Strategies

This section looks at some discipline-specific concerns and challenges that middle school and high school educators are facing today. We think it is important for you to know about these challenges and to become familiar with content areas other than your own for several reasons. First, we think the knowledge of other disciplines expands your view of

Table 9.2   Curriculum Development Guide

1. *Study Existing Curriculum*

   - Identify basis of existing curriculum—guidebook, adopted text, individual teacher choices.

   - Identify points of excellence and what is working.

   - Identify where there is dissatisfaction.

   - Identify projects or programs that seem most ready and of highest priority for improvement in this setting.

   - Create a list of what in the best of all worlds is desirable for students in this content area.

   - Create a target list for possible changes.

2. *Assess the Community Needs and Interests (Educate While Collecting Data)*

   - Interview parents regarding concerns for their children (be certain to include second language learners and children with special needs).

   - Conduct informal workshops or information sessions on new curriculum directions.

   - Involve parent volunteers in meetings where they can get firsthand understanding of the change or innovation.

   - Interview representatives of the business community to see their perceived needs for the workforce.

   - Carry out a formal needs assessment of the community.

3. *Assess Students*

   - Determine students' background knowledge and language related to the content area or topic being proposed for study.

   - Determine skills and strategies necessary to carry out the area of study. (For example, in a new area of literature, what writing skills, oral language, and reading skills do students need; what strategies would they be expected to use in studying the new topic or genre; and what skills and strategies would be embedded in the study itself?)

   - Seek information from standardized tests or other tests such as state assessment tools being developed to align with the curriculum frameworks that are given on an ongoing basis in the school or district.

   - Determine what information is available from ongoing student documentation in the form of journals and portfolios and what instruments should be employed to gather specific data.

Table 9.2   (continued)

4. Assess Faculty Interests and Imperatives

- Develop a profile of faculty expertise in the discipline. In language arts, teachers may have expertise and interest in drama, in poetry, or in coaching young writers to write for publication. (Do not assume that discipline teachers have a generic background and broad understandings of their field.)

- Use study teams to look at innovations or new directions in the field and to report back to their colleagues. Have language arts or social studies teachers investigate the use of media or technology in their field or look at the implications of second-language learning for their discipline and the topics they are teaching.

- Provide opportunities for teachers to attend institutes or conferences where they can talk with and interact with others in their discipline. Especially encourage them to participate in experiences where they can get firsthand experiences with new techniques, strategies, and materials.

- Identify imperatives in the field such as national standards or state curriculum frameworks that teachers are responsible for. Find ways to address these while at the same time revising the curriculum using the preceding considerations with regard to content, community, and students.

- Identify the school or curricular conditions that would help teachers more effectively reach the desired curriculum (schedules, resources, etc.).

Source: Adapted from S. Tchudi, *Planning and Assessing Curriculum in English/Language Arts* (Alexandria, Va.: Association for Supervision and Curriculum Development, 1991), chap. 5.

education and provides you with some additional background knowledge to link to your own discipline and your knowledge of pedagogy and practice that you are enhancing in your role as a professional educator. Second, we think it is useful as a classroom teacher to know something about what your students are learning in other disciplines so that you can connect the content and the strategies of your discipline to other content areas. Third, we think that opportunities to learn about what challenges other disciplines face as well as about their standards, the focus of Chapter 8, will help you identify opportunities for coordinated and integrated curriculum, the emphasis in Chapters 10 and 11, respectively. Last, because this text and the course you are taking are focused on literacy learning and helping your students as readers and writers in the disciplines, we have concluded each discipline-based section with a focus on particular literacy strategies we introduced in Part Two. These strategies will help your students deal with the challenges presented by the subject matter and the resources being used for study in each discipline.

We focus on the concerns found in the four core disciplines that comprise the required curriculum for all high school and middle school students in schools across the country: mathematics, science, social studies, and English/language arts. In addition, we consider courses in foreign or world language and health (and physical education) detailed in Chapter 8, as well as those in the arts and vocational education, to be very important for students to have a balanced curriculum and to have choices that align with their interests and needs. We have found that many of the concerns as well as the major goals expressed in the health standards are also found in the science standards and existing curriculum. And there are many similarities between foreign or world language goals and those of the English/language arts and even of the social studies. Therefore, we think focusing on the concerns of the four core disciplines gives new teachers like you, no matter what your discipline, valuable and useful insights about your own discipline as well as about the curriculum as a whole for middle school and high school students.

▶ ▶ ▶ ▶ **Science**

For too long science curriculum across the United States has been a disjointed array of topics and concepts. In many classrooms, students spend at least 50 percent of their time using content-area textbooks (Checkley, 1997; Dillon, O'Brien, & Moje, 1994). In an attempt to give a complete and current view of the field, these texts often do no more than mention a great variety of topics. Furthermore, these texts rarely give teachers using them suggestions about how they might connect these myriad of topics to one another or how they might connect this subject matter to their students' everyday life.

In addition, most science curriculum in the past was focused on scientific processes, models, and procedures, with little emphasis on scientific application to everyday life. Until recently, the major uniformity in the delivery of the science curriculum from school to school or from district to district has been the focus on earth science in grades 8 or 9, biology in grade 10, and chemistry and physics at grades 11 and 12. Although these domains are still recognized as major vehicles for delivery of science education, the emphasis has begun to shift from single domains of study to a focus on key understandings in science that pervade and connect the domains (National Committee on Science Education Standards and Assessment, 1996). In order to achieve this emphasis on the important understandings of science as a whole, science educators in every field have begun to advocate that elementary, middle, and high school curriculum be focused on all students' gaining important understandings about the life sciences, physical sciences, earth and space sciences, and technology and their application to everyday life.

Recent studies have shown that the majority of the public in the United States is scientifically illiterate (Kyle, 1995). Too often students have left their required science courses with limited textbook knowledge about what science is and how it pertains to their own lives. Middle school and high school students need relevant opportunities to use their science understandings to act on issues and challenges in their real world. All students need to understand and be able to apply the advances of science that relate to their lives as consumers. Finally, you and your students have a right to expect science and scientific discoveries to improve your world. At the same time, as citizens of this planet, you and your students also need enough scientific knowledge to monitor the use of science in a world that we all inhabit.

If we believe that basic science understandings are essential in today's world, then scientific literacy goes hand in hand with the communications skills and literacy we focus on in this text (Allen, 1989). The use of appropriate literacy strategies can provide students with the tools they need to learn science content and to become independent learners who can read and write about these content-based understandings in their academic life and their everyday life.

Because many students come to science with limited prior knowledge and misperceptions related to facts and principles that explain their universe, teachers may find that modeling and explaining how to preview a chapter (Chapter 4) or how to use a graphic organizer like a concept map (Chapter 5) will help students distinguish between important information and supporting details and unimportant or irrelevant information (Santa & Alvermann, 1991). Since science material is often filled with technical and specific content words, direct instruction on morphemic analysis and common roots in science help students (Chapter 4), as do strategies such as semantic feature charts (Chapter 5) that focus on similarities and differences among concepts or attributes within an area of study in science.

Finally, with the current emphasis on writing to learn as well as reading to learn across the disciplines, you can help your students use learning logs or journals in their science courses in order to record their initial prereading thoughts and questions (Chapter 4), to guide their reading (Chapter 5), and to record what they know and what they are confused about after reading (Chapter 6). Logs and journals are also excellent resources for students to use in order to share in discussions with peers or with teachers as they seek clarity about the understandings they are developing and the connections they are making in a particular area of science.

▶ ▶ ▶ ▶ **Mathematics**

Mathematics suffers from many of the same criticisms and issues as science does. Mathematics is rarely connected to other fields or disciplines within the curriculum, and there is very little emphasis on the applicability of mathematics to real life. Mathematics has been taught as a separate core subject offered once a day (like a good vitamin) from the elementary grades through high school. Schools have failed to emphasize the humanizing quality of mathematics and the incredible phenomenon that all cultures have developed some manner of mathematics in order to conduct their daily lives. Human beings have used mathematics to keep records and to allocate resources, and they have always used mathematics to design and to construct their dwellings.

Eighth-grade students in the United States have failed to show improvement in mathematics when their scores were compared across the country (*Math Report Card for the Nation and the States*, 1996). Furthermore, an international study released in 1997 (*Third International Mathematics and Science Study*) showed that eighth-grade students in the United States ranked twenty-eighth, or just at the midpoint, when compared with students of the same age in other nations. Researchers at the University of California who examined videotapes of classrooms in Japan, Germany, and the United States concluded that students' scores across cultures appear to reflect the implicit value placed on mathematics in the curriculum as well as the level of the content and the manner of pedagogy employed in these classrooms. The scores of students in other cultures are higher in mathematics and appear to be benefiting from more uninterrupted time for mathematics instruction and problem solving than students in the United States. Middle school–aged students in other cultures also appear to have more opportunities to apply their mathematical knowledge to real problems and more opportunities to deal with both algebra and geometry at lower grades than do students in the United States (Lynch, 1997).

Mathematics provides us with language and with procedures that help us quantify, measure, compare, and identify patterns useful in all of the other disciplines. Whether we are using a time line in history or a comparison chart showing characters' positive and negative characteristics in literature, we are using mathematical concepts and understandings applied to other disciplines. For example, recently a middle school unit entitled "Yesterday and Tomorrow" was designed to foster students' ability to observe and to think about things mathematically in the world around them. Students focused on examining and learning about change in their own community. They used the comparative data to reflect on why the population had grown or why the population had declined in their area. By carrying out this type of analysis, the students began to understand how changes in agriculture, industry, and availability of natural resources had affected their community. By studying current population numbers and census figures, the students also began to understand what these numbers meant and what impact they would have on schools, transportation, and even the size and types of businesses that existed in the community at present as well as what may be needed for the future. Through participation in a unit such as this one, the students gained firsthand experience using their mathematics understandings and seeing how relevant these understandings are in their everyday lives (Kleiman, 1991).

Whenever students are applying mathematics in a variety of discipline-based endeavors or in everyday life, they need to perceive symbols, to attach literal meaning to numbers and symbols, to analyze relationships, and to solve word problems (Earle, 1976). Literacy strategies that focus on students' text-based and schema-based connections, the focus of Chapter 5, are particularly useful when doing mathematics. A comprehension study guide that fosters the use of literal and interpretive questions can be used in order to help students read the graphs and statistical tables present in many content-area materials as well as in newspapers and magazines. Second, many students need assistance in mastering specialized, technical mathematics vocabulary, particularly when it is used in word problems in mathematics and in other content areas such as chemistry, economics, or geography. Strategies such as morphemic analysis (Chapter 4), multiple meanings/multiple terms and connotative/denotative meanings (Chapter 5), as well as the use of context clues and glossaries (Chapter 5), help students with the vocabulary demands of mathematics. Finally, auxiliary aids such as text pattern guides and visuals in the form of diagrams or charts (Chapter 5) help students figure out what facts they have and what relationships are present, as well as what processes to use when attempting to solve word problems.

▶ ▶ ▶ ▶ English/Language Arts

In the English/language arts curriculum, the major debate is about how best to provide a coherent set of literature experiences that will be both challenging and supportive of students who vary widely by linguistic and cultural background. The depth of the controversy between the "new" (expanded) and the "traditional" (the canon) literature is highlighted by a recent occurrence in Massachusetts. When the newly created statewide English/Language Arts Curriculum Frameworks were disseminated, participants on the planning and the review teams who represented two very different factions insisted that two appendixes of "acceptable works" accompany the document. One list included many works written from a multicultural perspective; the other list contained the traditional "great works." With the two lists in hand, Massachusetts teachers and administrators will have to decide which of the two lists to select from, as well as what implications their choices will have for them and for their students.

We are concerned about the schism among educators in the language arts concerning appropriate choices of literature. Two recent studies, one of English department chairs and one of secondary school teachers of English, have pointed to a national movement toward a greater variety of authors and topics being included in the curriculum in grades 7–12. Currently about half of the forty-three most commonly used books at the secondary school level are written by American authors. In addition, almost 20 percent of these same forty-three widely used books focus on twentieth-century American life (Stotsky, 1995; O'Neill, 1994).

There is a second set of issues associated with the choice of literary works that teachers make for their students. Advocates of multicultural and contemporary books for middle school and high school students believe that literature exposes students to both tensions among groups and positive interactions between different racial and ethnic groups represented in this country. However, some critics of the newer, more multicultural books built on contemporary themes argue that many of these books place too much emphasis on the negative aspects of race and ethnic relations rather than showing a balance of positive and negative interactions among individuals and groups (Stotsky, 1995).

Another group of critics of current multicultural literature question how accurately and authentically the diversity of the United States is being portrayed in the books most widely chosen by teachers and curriculum developers for middle school and high school audiences. These critics point out that students may in fact be seeing only the groups represented by affirmative action in the literature they are reading. Therefore, these critics caution that students may be getting a narrow view of this country's diversity through the literature they are being exposed to in school (Stotsky, 1995).

Although a significant percentage of the literature being used in the schools should be focused on recency and multiculturalism, there is a concern that traditional readings and authors appear to be slipping out of the curriculum altogether. We believe that the use of some "great works" can challenge students to recognize some of the universals that connect their own personal experiences with those of individuals who lived in other ages and in other cultures. A classical work such as Shakespeare's *Hamlet*, which focuses on a young person's dealing with a personal dilemma, can be compared to contemporary realistic fiction such as *Scorpions* (Walter Dean Myers, 1988) or *Park's Quest* (Katherine Patterson, 1988), which also focus on young people facing dilemmas in situations with which students can identify. Rather than seeing literature like Shakespeare's *Macbeth* or Arthur Miller's *The Crucible* as portrayals of people and situations that are unrelated to their lives, you can lead your students to make connections between the past and the present through literature just as in history they make connections between events happening today and those that took place in the past. Building on the themes of these two works, you can help students identify their own prejudices and see that there are concerns about witchcraft activity today in many areas of the country. In other words, you can help your students see the universality in the human experience and even see how their own lives are connected to those of the characters in the books they read.

The current emphasis in literature is for students of all ages to be exposed to a wider range of literature works, those in "the canon" and those that reflect contemporary relevance and cultural diversity, and to more and varied styles or genres of literature. Students need to be taught how to use story maps as supporting strategies in order to read narrative text and to use text pattern guides to understand the different organizational patterns in the expository or informational texts they will read in all of their content areas (Chapter 5).

Deciding on the particular meanings of words is another challenge for many readers as they meet settings, cultures, and characters very different from themselves in the texts in their literature courses. Students need to learn to be strategic and to learn how to use context clues effectively to deal with new vocabulary and ideas in the books they read for class or on their own as well as when and how they can use the dictionary for determining precise word meanings (Chapter 5). Students also need direct vocabulary instruction and opportunities to apply strategies such as how to discern connotative and denotative meanings in the literature they are reading and how to use vocabulary tools (Chapter 5).

Finally, when students read literature, you can assist them in the creation of a discussion web or journal responses (Chapter 5) to help them prepare for expressing their own ideas as they interact with text. You can show them how they can use these webs or journal entries to refine their ideas as they participate in a variety of small group peer-led discussions such as those described in Chapters 5 and 6.

▶ ▶ ▶ ▶ **Social Studies**

There are also pervasive concerns about the current curriculum, the materials, and the pedagogy in social studies. The *History Report Card: History Assessment at a Glance* (1994) highlighted how narrow and detail oriented most middle school and high school social studies courses and programs were. The social studies knowledge of many middle school and high school students appears to be a collection of unrelated historical facts, dates, and names of famous people. The National Center for History in the Schools is one organization that has developed standards specifically for history education in grades 5–12. Its emphasis has been on helping teachers create learning experiences that will require their students to use their historical understandings to interpret the past, to understand the present, and to project to the future. Social studies educators from the National Center advocate learning experiences that will involve middle school and high school students in using their historical knowledge to think and to problem-solve rather than in memorizing information limited to people, facts, and dates.

Another concern with the social studies curriculum, and particularly with history, the most widely studied of the social studies in our schools, has been its Eurocentrist and almost Anglocentric focus (Cohen, 1995). This tradition has recently been challenged by advocates of a pluralistic, multicultural approach to social studies. In addition to demanding an emphasis on a more inclusive perspective in the social studies taught in middle schools and high schools, social scientists and educators alike are attempting to incorporate more of the domains associated with social studies within the middle school and high school curriculum. There is a movement to expose students to more of the fields of social studies and to bring these fields together in order to help students study real problems and issues related to the social sciences.

The pedagogy and materials used in social studies are changing as well. Even in the early grades, primary sources and oral histories are being used as subject matter, and investigative research is modeled and supported in age-appropriate ways. An emphasis is being placed on students' reading authentic historical materials rather than relying solely on secondary sources. Teachers are modeling for their students concepts such as how to find an author's intent in the materials they use (Chapter 4 and 6). Teachers are also helping their students to interpret history and are encouraging them to look for cycles and trends as social scientists do rather than focusing solely on facts and dates (Chapter 6). Students are also being encouraged to ask questions and to set purposes for their own reading in the social sciences. Strategies such as a KWL chart, a QAR or a DRTA , various note-taking techniques, and the use of graphic organizers that social studies teachers model will help students in the middle and secondary grades gain confidence in their ability to use their social studies understandings in the classroom as well as in the real world. In all social studies courses at every level, teachers should encourage students to participate in discussion groups and to write in order to demonstrate their own learning and understanding.

The major goal of all social studies courses and curriculum should be to empower students to become active participants in their communities. Therefore a priority in the social studies classroom should be students' working to understand why things happened as they did in the past. In each of the social sciences, teachers should encourage students to think about how issues such as human rights, affirmative action, and censorship are dealt with and what impact decisions made today may have on the future (Van Sledright, 1994). Teachers should encourage students to reflect on what they can learn from the past to improve their lives and those of others in their communities. These students will then become active citizens.

Sample Unit Plans

Sample Single Discipline Unit for the Middle School

In Chapters 9, 10, and 11 we have developed sample middle school and high school units to demonstrate the enactment of single discipline, coordinated, and integrated curriculum, respectively. Each of the scenarios, which we developed for this text, represents an amalgam of real classroom events and lessons we have witnessed or heard about and settings and programs that classroom practitioners have described at national and regional conferences that we have attended. These scenarios were also drawn from the goals, performance standards, and vignettes in various national standards documents and curriculum frameworks, as well as teaching/assessing ideas we have drawn from various books, journals, ERIC documents, and sources on the Internet dealing with curriculum development for specific subject areas. As you read these sample units, imagine yourself participating in these scenarios as a middle school or high school teacher working with your own students or as a student teacher working in a classroom doing a field placement.

We designed this middle school single discipline unit focused on the domain of history. It is designed to demonstrate how a single subject teacher at the middle school level can enact the three principles outlined earlier in the chapter: understandings, strategies, and connections. It was developed drawing on a unit described in The Theme Immersion Compendium for Social Studies *(Manning, Manning, & Long, 1997), the goals of the national social studies standards (National Council for the Social Studies, 1994), and the literacy strategies for learning we emphasized in Part Two of this book. This unit was designed as part of an eighth-grade course on twentieth-century U.S. history.*

Major Understandings

In this unit, the students study the major conflicts the United States has engaged in since World War II: the Korean, Vietnam, and Gulf wars. Students are expected to learn why each of these wars was controversial among citizens and politicians in the United States. They also learn that the big questions that the opponents of each of these conflicts asked were whether the United States should be involved in regional conflicts and whether the United States had an obligation to serve as the "world's peacekeeper." We are still asking these difficult questions about our role in such conflicts around the globe today.

The major understandings or goals for this unit were drawn from the recent standards document published by the National Council for the Social Studies discussed in Chapter 8. The important ideas for students to grasp related to this unit focus on the U.S. involvement in the Gulf War, included in Standard VI, Power, Authority and Governance, and Standard IX, Global Connections and Interdependence.

First, in conjunction with Standard VI (Table 9.3), students come away from this unit with a heightened sense of how individuals and groups create and change structures associated with power, authority, and governance in their own society. The students participating in this unit acquire the ability to explain in their own words the conditions, actions, and motivations that contributed in the past and continue to contribute to conflict within and among nations.

Table 9.3   Excerpt from Standards for Social Studies: Thematic Strand VI

Thematic Strand VI.—Power, Authority and Governance

Social studies programs should include experiences that provide for the study of how people create and change structures of power, authority and governance so that the learner can:

Sample Performance Expectations for the Middle Grades

c. Analyze and explain ideas and governmental mechanisms to meet needs and wants of citizens, regulate territory, manage conflict, and establish order and security

f. Explain conditions, actions, and motivations that contribute to conflict and cooperation within and among nations

g. Describe and analyze the role of technology in communications, transportation, information-processing, weapons development, or other areas as it contributes to or helps resolve conflicts

i. Give examples and explain how governments attempt to achieve their stated ideals at home and abroad

Source: From *Standards for Social Studies*, 1994, p. 94. Used by permission of the National Council for the Social Studies.

Second, as a result of the lessons and learning experiences focused on in this unit, middle school students gain an understanding of Standard IX (Table 9.4), focused on Global Connections and Interdependence—that is, to be able to explain in their own words the relationship between the U.S. need for national sovereignty and its global interests. Third, this unit helps students become aware of the issues related to the protection of universal human rights. Finally, students involved in this unit become aware of how easily differences in language, art, music, and other cultural dimensions can cause misunderstandings among peoples or nations and ways in which greater understanding can be facilitated.

Resources

The major resource used at the beginning of the unit was a common text, *War in the Persian Gulf* (Bratman, 1991), chosen because it is appropriate in reading level and a challenge for a heterogeneous class of eighth graders. In addition, the teacher guides the students to select articles from student periodicals in the social sciences such as *Cobblestone* and student weekly newspapers like *Junior Scholastic*. Students carry out research to find articles and political cartoons in newspapers written at the time of the Gulf War in order to learn how different perspectives about the conflict were expressed. The teacher guides the students toward *USA Today* and local newspapers because they are more ap-

Table 9.4   Excerpt from Standards for Social Studies: Thematic Strand IX

Thematic Strand IX.—Global Connections

Social Studies programs should include experiences that provide for the study of global connections and interdependence, so that the learner can:

Sample Performance Expectations for the Middle Grades

b. Analyze examples of conflict, cooperation, and interdependence among groups, societies, and nations

e. Describe and explain the relationships and tensions betwen national sovereignty and global interests in such matters as territory, natural resources, trade, use of technology, and welfare of people

f. Demonstrate understanding of concerns, standards, issues and conflicts related to universal human rights

Source: From *Standards for Social Studies*, 1994, p. 102. Used by permission of the National Council for the Social Studies.

pealing and more readable than major national papers like the *Washington Post* or the *New York Times*. Some students also use the Internet to get newspaper and journal information

Another source that students can access is the Social Studies School Services media collection on wars in U.S. history. Some students might also check the listings of cable TV's History Channel to see if there were upcoming programs or videos in the archives that would help them gather data and understand events at the time of the Gulf War. Using the Internet, the students can find World Wide Web sites focused on wars and battles. By going to these sites, the students are able to study maps, photographs, and even interviews pertaining to most of the major wars that the United States had participated in throughout its history. Finally, the teacher may use a comprehensive Web site such as the History/Social Studies Web Site for K–12 Teachers (**http//www. exe.cpc.com/~dboals/boals.html**) to see whether there were any lessons or units that other teachers had created for their own middle school classes on this topic.

Individual Lessons

The teacher introduces the unit with a generating activity that engages her students in a discussion about factors they thought might lead to conflicts between nations. The students then participate in a series of lessons to extend their prior knowledge as they interact with a range of resources and a variety of information. They conclude the unit with a series of lessons that help them refine their knowledge and also help them gain personal ownership of the content and the major understandings on which the unit was built.

Generating Phase Lessons.   In response to the teacher's initial question, the students create a brainstormed list to record their ideas about factors they think lead to conflicts between nations. The teacher reminds the students to think about conflicts the United States has been involved in that they have learned about in other courses or that they have read about, heard about, or seen portrayed in movies and on television. After the students have time for brainstorming and sharing their ideas as a class, the teacher informs the students that the unit they are going to focus on would help them understand more fully what contributes to conflict between the United States and other nations today. The teacher points out that they were going to start with a war the United States was involved in during their own lifetime: the Gulf War. The students then brainstorm what they heard recalled about the Gulf War of 1991 or what they remembered about the more recent threat of war with Iraq and the destruction of weapons' sites in 1998. The whole class activity motivates the students and builds on their prior knowledge. This activity also helps the teacher assess the background knowledge the students shared as well as misperceptions they have about the topic they were about to study.

The students' general information and their recollections about the Gulf War are tapped in an additional generating activity. Using tools described in Chapter 4, the students organize the data they have into major categories on a web made up of key questions related to this unit's focus on conflict. Groups of four to five students synthesize what they know about (1) the causes of the Gulf War, (2) why the United States was involved in the conflict, (3) how the conflict ended, and (4) what happened as a result of the conflict. Each group placed its information on its own web, and then the small groups compared their webs.

Finally, the teacher models how the students could take information that represented their prior knowledge from their small group webs to create a KWL chart. The chart is used to record **what they already knew about the war**. It also helps them decide and then to articulate **what they now wanted to know about the war**. And at the conclusion of the unit, after the students have read and discussed their common text and carried out some research on their own, they could come back to the KWL chart and record **what they had learned about the Gulf War**.

Interacting Phase Lessons.   In the next group of lessons, students interact with text in a variety of ways. They find and interpret information related to **what they now wanted to know about the war** using the common text, *War in the Persian Gulf*. The teacher creates a comprehension study guide as a teaching tool to help the students with their reading of the text and to guide the students' individual, small group, and whole class research about the Gulf War. The comprehension study guide helps the students as they attempt to prove, to disprove, and to add to what they already know or believe about the topic being studied. Using their study guide, the students are directed to find (1) data related to causes of the war; (2) data that showed the involvement of the United States, other countries, and the United Nations in the war; (3) the cost of the war in terms of civilian and military lives; (4) the resolution of the conflict; and (5) the outcomes of the conflict for each of the countries involved.

Students who had previously learned how to construct supporting aids such as notes kept in a journal or two-column notes are reminded to use these tools for this activity. In addition, the teacher models and explains using notes to record the data they were finding and to answer the questions on the study guide. The teacher also uses this time to observe the students informally as they work independently and in small groups.

After the students conclude their reading of the common text, they come together for a discussion to clarify their understandings about the information in the book. Some students mentioned during the brainstorming activity in the generating phase lessons that they had heard that there was a great deal of opposition to the Gulf War. Now that they have read the text and gained some more accurate knowledge about the war, the teacher asks the students to do freewriting to explain why they think there was opposition to the war and the role the United States played in this conflict in the Middle East.

An additional activity that helps the students answer the questions the teacher posed in the comprehension study guide was to work in pairs to explore how the media presented information during the war and what opposing viewpoints about the U.S. involvement in the Gulf War were expressed. Each pair of students is assigned to find one news article and one political cartoon written during the war. The students carry out discussions among themselves and list on a discussion web what they think are the facts about the war and what they think were the reporters' and the cartoonists' opinions about the conflict. The pairs then meet in groups of four to discuss what they agree to as a group and what they disagree about. The teacher encourages the students to create a graphic organizer to help them clarify their ideas as well as to be prepared for a future whole class discussion on the Gulf War. If they cannot agree on what were the facts and what were the opinions, the teacher suggests they create a minority report that could also be shared to inform the whole class discussion.

Refining Phase Lessons. Once students in the class have completed the interacting activities, they move to the final phase of the unit and some lessons focused on refining their ideas and clarifying their knowledge. First, the students revisit the class KWL chart and fill in the column that records **what they know now**.

In order to extend the students' understanding of the Gulf War, the teacher guides the students to consider the U.S. involvement in the war and the persistent debate about whether the United States should continue to be involved in conflicts and wars around the globe. The students make a list of the people or groups they could interview who would be knowledgeable about the Gulf War or about other conflicts in which the United States has been involved. Their list includes male and female veterans of the war, current members of the military, local war historians, history teachers from local colleges and secondary schools, and representatives from groups like ESR (Educators for Social Responsibility) that opposed the war. The teacher also suggests they contact the U.S. senator's office from their state to see what the senator's position is on the war and why.

For students who had not already been taught to interview, this was a perfect opportunity for the teacher to teach them the skills they need and the tools to use in conducting a good interview. The teacher may decide to prepare the students for carrying out their interviews by having an individual come to the class for a practice session before the students go out to interview their own resource people. Each student's participation during the in-class activity, as well as his or her preparation of interview questions modeled on what was done in class, provided the teacher with a rich opportunity to collect informal assessment data about the students during the ongoing teaching/learning part of the unit.

Student Evaluation

This teacher has numerous opportunities to assess students' learning and understanding of the topic they are studying during the ongoing lessons comprising this unit. The teacher is able to work with students individually and in small groups to modify assignments and to introduce new strategies as the students needed them throughout the unit.

The students use a variety of teaching tools that lend themselves to their teacher's ongoing evaluation. Student participation in the brainstorming activity at the beginning of the unit, their participation in the periodic discussions positioned throughout the unit, and their contributions to and use of the class KWL chart informed their teacher about the understandings and knowledge individual students are acquiring as well as which understandings, strategies, or materials were giving particular students difficulty. Each student's individual use of the comprehension study guide and ability to take notes after the teacher models this strategy provides the teacher with an additional indicator of how well each student is understanding the concepts and using the materials in the unit and whether individual or entire class modifications are necessary.

Since previous social studies lessons have focused on group participation and the use of expressive language in spoken as well as written work, students are expected to monitor their own performance during the discussions in this unit. Each student fills in the form entitled "Student Self-Evaluation in Discussion Groups" (see Figure 9.1) to monitor his or her own participation and contributions to both the small group and whole class discussions.

The teacher's overall evaluation of each student's learning and growth focused on the products each created individually as well as on what students contributed to in group activities. At the end of the unit, each student writes a composition to express his or her own personal understanding or point of view about the major understandings on which the unit was built. The stu-

Figure 9.1

Excerpt from the Form
for Student Self-
Evaluation in
Discussion Groups

	Yes	No	Sometimes
2. Do you state clearly your views about a problem or issue?	X	—	—
3. Do you know how to find the facts?	X	—	—
8. Do you respect the opinions of others?	—	—	X
9. Do you monopolize the discussion or take your turn?	—	—	—
14. Do you change your mind if you find your position is weak or wrong?	—	—	—
15. Are you willing to become informed about alternative positions?	—	—	—

Source: Reprinted by permission of Maryann Manning, George Manning, and Roberta Long: *The Theme Immersion Compendium for Social Studies Teaching*. (Heinemann, A Division of Reed Elsevier, Inc., Portsmouth, NH, 1997).

dents then place this end-of-unit product in their portfolios as evidence of their "best social studies work" for the year, for the semester, or for the grading period.

Earlier in this unit during the interacting phase lessons, the students had done freewriting about why they thought so many individuals, private citizens and politicians alike, were opposed to the U.S. involvement in the Gulf War. At the conclusion of the unit, the teacher wants them to reflect back on what they had written before they had become informed about the conflict through their reading, researching, and discussions. The teacher asks the students to look at their freewriting and to write a revised piece that reflects their own current thinking about the role the United States played in the Gulf War, as well as their opinion about the ongoing debate in our country focused on, **"What is our role as a nation to be the peacekeeper of the world?"**

The students fill in a "Unit of Study Checklist" (see Figure 9.2), which they and their teacher had created collaboratively at the beginning of the unit. The students use this form to assess their own growth and to help them decide which items they might want to place in their portfolios. Figure 9.2 shows a portion of the checklist these eighth-grade students and their teacher use at the culmination of the unit.

Making Connections Among the Disciplines

We think that students benefit from curriculum that is connected to other disciplines. All students need many opportunities to see the interconnections among

Figure 9.2

Sample Unit of Study
Checklist

	Excellent	Proficient	Needs Improvement
1. Works cooperatively with other group members.	—	—	—
2. Uses a variety of resources in addition to the required text.	—	—	—
3. Records notes when reading and organizes notes before writing or speaking.	—	—	—
4. Participates actively in group discussion.	—	—	—
5. Uses available technology to access information and to solve problems.	—	—	—
6. Written final product shows revision of content and mechanics.	—	—	—

Source: Reprinted by permission of Maryann Manning, George Manning, and Roberta Long: *The Theme Immersion Compendium for Social Studies Teaching.* (Heinemann, A Division of Reed Elsevier, Inc., Portsmouth, NH, 1997).

disciplines and to see how these interconnections inform them about the topic they are studying. The middle school teacher who carried out this unit saw several logical connections to other areas of the curriculum for her middle school students. One was to extend the students' understandings of the Gulf War by focusing on its effect on individuals their own age by using literature about the war and about the Middle East. Students could read fictionalized stories about young people in the Middle East such as Elizabeth Laird's Kiss the Dust *(1992) or Barbara Cohen's* Seven Daughters and Seven Sons *(1990). In addition, they could read biographies and autobiographies about real individuals who played significant roles in Desert Storm, such as General Colin Powell* (Colin Powell: A Man of War and Peace, *1992) or General Norman Schwarzkopf* (Schwarzkopf: Hero with a Heart, *1992). Students may want to read too about former President Bush's role and viewpoint related to this conflict.*

Given the focus of this unit, the teacher and students could explore many connections among the social studies domains to create the desirable coherence within a single discipline. When the United States became engaged in a conflict in the Middle East, the teacher who created this unit, like many other adults in this country, realized how little she knew about the many countries and customs in the Middle East. For this reason, the teacher thinks that a second extension would be to have the students study the cultures of the Middle East. Given the intense focus on multiculturalism and cultural plurality in the United States today, as well as the emphasis on a global society, students would benefit from learning about people in the Middle East by studying their customs, their religions, the geography, and the social and political structures prevalent in this part of the world. Students could learn more about the cultures in the region using a cultural anthropology magazine like *Faces,* written especially for young people, or by finding information from the Internet such as a source for students and teachers called the "Multicultural Pavilion" (**http//curry:edschool.Virginia.EDU/go/multicultural**).

The third possible extension for this unit that would connect the topic to two additional social science domains would be to have students study the geography and the ecology of the desert, which makes up so much of the Middle East. Students could learn about the special medical precautions and special training that the American soldiers took who went to the gulf because of its terrain and the climate. In this way, the middle school teacher could connect her history unit on the Gulf War directly to another of the social studies documents, *Geography for Life*: *National Geography Education Standards Project* (1994).

A fourth interesting extension of this unit would be to have students explore some specialized career options that are related to studying the Middle East. For example, because the Middle East is the site of many ancient civilizations and the birthplace of the world's major religions, it would be interesting in conjunction with this unit to look at the work that archaeologists or cultural anthropologists do. Students could learn about individuals in these fields, what their work is like, and how they each help us understand the past.

Finally, a history unit such as this one could be connected to individual student interests or hobbies. For example, if some of the students collect coins or stamps or have a passion for art, this would be a perfect time to help them make personal connections to this part of the world by studying the coins, the stamps, or the artwork found in the region today and in the past.

Sample Single Discipline Unit for the High School

The high school single discipline unit created for this chapter focuses on science, specifically the domain of geology. The national standards dealing with earth and space science for grades 9–12 emphasize a focus on earth science that will help all secondary students understand local, national, and global challenges to the earth, as well as natural hazards like tornadoes, volcanoes, and floods and the challenges that humans create. We built this sample unit based on the national science standards for the high school level (see both Chapter 8 and Table 9.5), a ninth-grade

Table 9.5   Excerpt from Standards for Science

I. Earth and Space

   #1. Understands the basic features of the Earth

   #2. Understands basic Earth processes

   #3. Understands essential ideas about the composition and structure of the universe and the Earth's place in it.

   Sample performance expectations for Level III (Grades 9–12)

   • Knows that the "rock cycle" consists of the formation, weathering, sedimentation, and reformation of rock; in this cycle, the total amount of material stays the same as its form changes.

   • Knows that geologic time can be estimated by observing rock sequences and using fossils to correlate the sequences at various locations; recent methods use the predictability of decay rates of radioactive isotopes in rock formation to determine geologic time.

   • Knows that evidence for simple, one-celled forms of life such as bacteria and algae extends back more than 3.5 billion years; the evolution of life resulted in dramatic changes in the composition of the Earth's atmosphere, which did not originally contain oxygen.

II. Life Sciences

   (Standards #4–#9)

III. Physical Sciences

   (Standards #10–#13)

IV. Science and Technology

   (Standards #14–#18)

Source: National Committee of Science Education Standards and Assessment, J. S. Kendall and R. J. Marzano, *Content Knowledge* (Aurora, Ohio: Mid-continent Regional Educational Laboratory, 1996).

classroom vignette included in Pathways to Science *(Texley & Wild, 1996), and the literacy and learning strategies we addressed in Part Two.*

An experienced general science teacher wanted to find an interesting way for her students to meet the standards focused on understandings about geology and the origin and the evolution of the earth system. She wanted to enhance the students' awareness about local geology and what the study of earth science means in their own community. In addition, she designed this unit in order to clear up misunderstandings that her students had about the great age of the earth and about the geologic record because she realized that many of her students' only knowledge about the earth came from what they had seen in the science-fiction media that rely largely on a supernatural or magical approach to how the earth and its layers evolved.

The teacher in this sample used a plan book to write up her ideas for content understandings and strategies to be taught, activities for the students and the teacher to carry out, and resources the students would use. (In this chapter and again in Chapter 10, which focuses on coordinated curriculum, you will find one sample unit in narrative form and the other in a plan book format.) During the planning stage, the teacher reflected on what she had done in the past with this topic, what resources were available to her and the class, and how she could incorporate the new standards into her curriculum.

The outline format we use here for this ninth-grade geology unit is similar to what many teachers use in their own plan books. Each of the components necessary for the development of a unit—the resources, the understandings and strategies, the connections to other disciplines, and the student evaluation—is included in this format. This outline developed during the planning stage of the unit would guide the teacher's development of specific lesson plans. Of course, the specific lessons would be determined by particular content as well as by the students' needs and levels of understanding as the unit progresses.

Major Understandings

Students engaged in this unit will develop understandings about the origin and the evolution of the earth system and its changes in order to understand better issues and challenges and how they as well as other inhabitants of earth can evaluate the earth and its changes. The students will be engaged in firsthand opportunities to apply and to observe processes that geologists use to study such things as constancy and change and evolution and equilibrium in relation to current status and the development of the earth's crust. Students will see how these understandings have meaning not only in the science classroom, but also how they help them understand the particular environment where they now live.

Resources

Reference Tools

- *Fossils: A Guide to Prehistoric Life*, a nature guide by Golden Books, for all students to use and share in small working groups

- Geology resources to accommodate a range of reading levels, such as *First Look at Rocks* (Millicent E. Selsam, 1984), *Rocks and Minerals* (Tracy Staedter,

1999), and *Rocks and Minerals* (Chris Pelilant, 1992), to provide all students with informational material they can read on their own

- Other reference tools on paleontology and historical geology from the library
- Information on geology from the Internet
- A large geologic map

Artifacts

- Class collection of specimens of fossils* from the local area that students sort and label as they are brought into the classroom over a two-week period before the unit was begun.

*These were built on a collection of geologic specimens the teacher had collected over the years.

Science Tools

- Hand lenses, stereo microscopes, old dental tools, toothbrushes and wire brushes to clean and expose the fossils, and glue to fix broken specimens.

Individual Lessons

Generating Phase

- As an introduction and motivating activity to the unit, the students collect specimens from the local area over a two-week period.
- Students use their collected specimens and ones that the teacher has and **ask questions that can frame the guided reading and research** the students will do using various natural history guides. Some questions might be:

  What is it [the fossil]?

  What present-day form is it related to?

- Teacher models and explains **how to read diagrams, illustrations, and captions in the guides*** and how to connect to the text.

*Many of the guides tend to be dense in their use of pictorials and graphic aids as well as their use of keys. Therefore, students will need specific modeling and strategy instruction in order to interpret as well as to connect these aids to the brief, highly detailed descriptive text found in most natural history guides.

- Students **preview** the format of the guide they are using so they will be able to match their fossil specimens to the appropriate pictorial aid and to gather information from the descriptions in the text.
- Students **recall and review some Latin and Greek root words** they have studied associated with science that will help them understand the

vocabulary used in geology; affixes such as *pre-* and *meta-* associated with time and size are examples.

Interacting Phase

- Students **connect graphic information**, such as illustrations and diagrams to text, in the guides they are using.

- Students **connect fossils with graphic aids and text** to begin the identification process and to answer the questions posed during the collection stage.

- Students individually **find other sources** to clarify and support their identification (the teacher may recommend sources to particular students based on her informal assessment of their needs).

- Students **construct supporting aids** such as diagrams, sketches, and notes to organize their findings and to keep track of how certain types of fossils were related to one another (for example, students note which types of fossils are found in certain types of rock).

- Students use their information from these aids to **participate in discussions** related to the three questions posed in the generating phase stage; students' responses serve as a source of informal assessment.

- Teacher **models the use of a local geologic map, a special type of graphic organizer**, so that students can plot findings about their own specimens and determine in what age and in what environments their fossils were found.

Real-life example of a similar unit: Students in a ninth-grade class in New York State recently carried out a similar unit and plotted their findings on a geologic map. Among their fossils there were many types of coral, as well as cynobacteria, trilobites, and a starfish, which they then associated with a number of geologic periods ranging from the earliest Precambrian to the Pleistocene eras. The students with the help of their teacher also found that their fossils came from many different environments, and they had a first-hand experience seeing the role that glaciers played in altering and shaping the earth's crust (Texley & Wild, 1996).

Refining Phase

- Students **prepare a brief written summary** about one type of fossil found in their area to include in a sharing session that will bring all of the students together; students use their own diagrams and drawings as well as those created by other students in their small study groups

- Whole class discussion focused on the variety of sources and eras of geology represented in their own immediate environment.

- Teacher informally assesses each student's understandings based on the depth and clarity of their individual presentations as well as on their **use of new scientific vocabulary in both their spoken and their written work**.

- Students will **look back and reread what they have written and drawn** to refine their understandings about this topic. At this stage students in small groups decide whether they want to **do further reading or investigations** before creating a final written report supported by drawings and other graphic aids; students will check their report(s) against the **rubric** for creating science reports that they developed in class earlier in the year; a copy of their group's report could be placed into their individual science folders or into their cross-discipline "best works" portfolio.

- In addition to discussing and writing about the fossils they have collected, students may take **a more extensive geologic field trip** in their community in order to gather more samples as well as to extend their data pool for drawing conclusions and understanding the geologic history of their environment.

- Students **refine** their ideas about this important topic by thinking about how the geologic environment in their area shaped the lives of the local inhabitants. Students **discuss** what building materials are commonly used in the area, such as fieldstone in Pennsylvania or granite in Vermont. They **discuss** constraints that land and rock formations create for the buildings or highways in their area. Students **investigate** the effect that rocks and land formations have had on people's lives or work as well as on the economy where they live.

Student Evaluation

During the Lessons

- Students read and understand text and graphic aids demonstrated by their note taking, drawings, and participation in small group activities and their whole class activities.

- Students match fossils with certain types of rock based on information found in various reference tools and the ability to place the information on a geologic map (a particular graphic organizer used in this unit in the interacting stage).

- Teacher assesses students' appropriate use of new vocabulary words related to the study of geology.

- Students' self-evaluation of their own participation in discussion in both small groups and whole class activities.

After the Lessons

- Students place small group written and illustrated reports into their own science folders or into their cross-discipline portfolio.
- Students evaluate their individual and their small group written reports using the rubric for evaluating science reports that the class developed earlier in the year.
- Each student fills in a portfolio assessment sheet that explains why he or she chose the piece for his or her portfolio; the teacher may also complete a response form.

Making Connections Among the Disciplines

Other Possible Areas of Science

- Study of glaciers and their movement as these relate to geological findings
- Study of volcanoes and the geologic findings in areas where there are ancient volcanoes and where there is more recent volcanic activity (e.g., Mt. Saint Helens in Washington State)
- Study of major natural hazards such as earthquakes and floods and the interrelationships with the geology of an area (e.g., recent floods in the midwestern part of the United States, earthquakes in California)
- Study of the relationship of weather and geology (e.g., global warming and the coming of another ice age)
- Links to astronomy and space exploration and the evolving study of Mars and its geology
- Links to paleontology and the study of dinosaurs (especially with the heightened interest promoted by blockbuster movies like *Jurassic Park*)
- Use of resources found on the Internet that would support these explorations such as the specialized web site where students as well as teachers can ask questions about rocks and earth forms, called "Ask a Geologist," (**http://walrus.wr.usgs.gov/docs/ask-a-ge.html**) and the *USA Today* weather site (**http://www.usatoday.com/weather/wreach.htm**)

Literature

- Study the mythology of various cultures to see how the formation of the earth and various land formations are explained (e.g., Native American, Greek and Roman, Norse)

- Study folktales and tall tales from various cultures to see how they explain the formation of the earth and various land formations (e.g., Paul Bunyan in the U.S. Midwest; study of the creation myths using sources such as Virginia Hamilton's *In the Beginning*)

Mathematics

- Connect the use of statistics and various types of charts and graphs needed to record geological change.
- Learn about scientific notation and the chemical makeup of various rocks they are studying.

Summary of the Chapter

In this chapter focused on individual disciplines, we have shown how the theory and practice related to understanding your content, knowing your learners, and being knowledgeable about literacy strategies can come together in coherent discipline-based units at the middle school and high school levels. We have emphasized the common concerns among the disciplines centered on how teachers, regardless of their subject matter, help their students:

- Realize major content understandings.
- Become strategic learners.
- Experience coherence within the discipline.
- Recognize connections between what they are learning in one discipline to other disciplines and to the real world.

In addition to looking at common concerns, we have explored some of the individual concerns and areas of debate within each of the core disciplines—science, mathematics, English/language arts, and social studies—that prevail at both the middle and the high school levels. Finally, we have emphasized particular generating, interacting, and refining phase strategies we described in Part Two that are useful for students to deal with the literacy challenges found in each discipline.

In order to assist you in thinking about how to develop curriculum in your own discipline that emphasizes major understandings in the field and lessons that focus on helping students become strategic learners, we have provided both a middle school (social studies/history) and a high school (physical science/geology) single discipline unit. These two detailed units provide you with a five-step model to use when you do your own curriculum development or when you modify existing curriculum to meet the needs of your learners. In this chapter as well as in previous chapters, we emphasize your making thoughtful decisions about:

- Major understandings (see Chapter 8)
- Resources (see Chapter 3)
- Lessons that use generating, interacting, and refining phase strategies (see Chapters 4, 5, and 6)
- Student evaluation (see Chapters 2 and 3)
- Connections within your own discipline to other disciplines and to the real world (see Chapters 8 and 9)

You should thoroughly think about and plan for these five steps before you engage your students in a specific unit and the lessons that comprise it. Finally, as you probably already have learned, the best written plan is simply a road map for action. It is the actual doing of a lesson or a unit that informs you as the teacher working with real students how to shape what is on paper to addressing the needs of your own students. The true challenge of teaching in every discipline is to ask, "How will I bring worthwhile content and major understandings to all of my students, and how will I help them connect those understandings to the real world?"

Inquiry Activities About Your Learning

1. Think about a topic you have studied in your own discipline or one that was a focus in the middle school or the high school where you have done a practicum or an observation for a field-based assignment. Revisit that topic now that you have learned about the importance of designing units that promote in-depth understandings of a topic, as well as use of literacy strategies as tools for understanding to help students be effective readers and writers within a discipline.

How would you change and enrich the unit you participated in or witnessed in the middle school or high school classroom where you worked or visited? Jot down some notes, and perhaps investigate a few new sources on the topic. How would you carry out your own research and extend your understandings using these steps and procedures so that you connected your discipline to other disciplines and to the real world? Who might be able to help you plan this unit?

2. Refer back to Chapters 4, 5, and 6. Review your own understandings of the literacy strategies we focused on in Part Two of this text. Look specifically at the graphic organizers at the beginning of each chapter to assist you in your review. Jot down strategies that you use regularly in your discipline. In addition, jot down particular generating, interacting, or refining phase strategies that you have not tried yet but think might be helpful to you in the future. Think about which strategies you will need to master so that you can model and explain them to your own students when they are engaged in a topic and need to use a variety of resources to study it.

Inquiry Activities About Your Students' Learning

1. Have the students in your class do an interest survey and a reading survey. You might discuss with the students whether there have been any connections made between their own interests or their leisure reading (newspapers, sports magazines, trade books) and their work in any of their subject matter. Share with the students how some of your own interests connect to what and how you teach and how you make choices about possible topics and materials. See if the students can think of some ways in which they could connect their interests and their reading as well as their media habits to content they are studying. Have students with related interests brainstorm a list of possible connections.

2. Think of a topic or theme that your students have recently been engaged in within your discipline that has many real-world connections (e.g., the current and projected long-term effects of pollution or of global warming). See if the students can generate some connections or applications of the discipline on their own. Then have your students go into their communities to look for more real-world applications of these topics and understandings. Students could gather data from observations of events in their community and through interviews of people in various roles and professions. They could read their local newspaper or listen to the news on television. Finally, you could have your students survey a variety of settings represented in their communities such as libraries and other cultural institutions, businesses, and government and service agencies to find possible connections and applications of the science, mathematics, social studies, and English/language arts they are learning in school.

10

Coordinated Curriculum: Enhancing Learning Among Disciplines

Students at every stage of development and at every grade level gain depth of understanding about a topic when the disciplines or courses they are studying are brought together in meaningful ways. The second model of curriculum that we examine in this text is coordinated curriculum, an approach that focuses on teaching complementary topics concurrently in two different disciplines to the same group of students. When the activities planned, the methods used, and the materials chosen are focused on a common topic and objectives in more than one discipline, students appear to learn more and to take more ownership of their own learning than they do with the usual discrete, single discipline approach.

Imagine how much more knowledgeable students would be whose high school curriculum included a coordinated unit where mathematics, biology, and art all looked at symmetry at the same time. In such a situation, complementary views from the different disciplines would enhance the students' understanding of this important concept. Students could learn to use the principles of symmetry in plane and solid geometry as well as see its many everyday applications in the structures around them. They could also learn how useful symmetry is in biology when applied to studying different forms of life, from the smallest protozoa to the largest mammals. Furthermore, students' ability to create and appreciate art works is enhanced with an understanding of symmetry.

In this chapter on coordinated curriculum, we stress the importance of connecting subject matter, using literacy strategies for learning, and providing students with opportunities to apply their knowledge. In particular we look at the benefits of a coordinated curriculum for both students and teachers, and we address how teachers can accommodate coordinated curriculum given the usual middle school and high school schedules. In order to help you envision designing such curriculum in your own classroom in the future, we provide two sample coordinated units—one at the middle school level and one at the high school level.

As you read this chapter, keep the following questions in mind. Ask yourself what will be the same and what will be different for you and for your future students if coordinated curriculum is the approach to curriculum you use as compared to the usual single discipline model that still pervades most middle schools and high schools.

Purpose-Setting Questions

1. Given what I have studied in my courses and what I have seen focused on in the middle schools or high schools with which I have had contact, are there advantages for my students or for me to seek opportunities to coordinate with teachers in other disciplines? Are there particular disciplines or domains within the disciplines (biology or chemistry in science, for example) that have strong connections with my own discipline?

2. During my field experiences, have I seen any alternatives in scheduling to the usual six or seven separate periods a day? Did I notice any benefits for either the students or the teachers involved in these alternatives?

3. What sort of planning do teachers need to do in order to design and to implement the type of coordinated curriculum efforts described in this chapter?

4. In the real world, many problem situations are tackled by people from different disciplines working together on teams. What are some of the real-world connections for your discipline, and how could these be enhanced through connection with another discipline?

5. Given the two sample units that demonstrate a coordinated curriculum approach, one at the high school level and one at the middle school level, what are the literacy and learning strategies each emphasizes, and what do you see in these sample units that is applicable to your own content area and to your practice as a teacher?

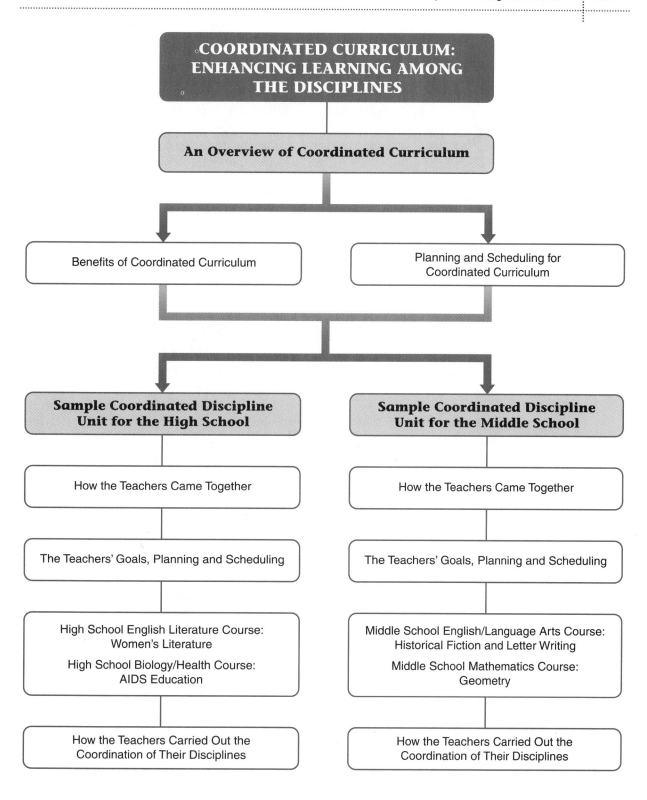

COORDINATED CURRICULUM: ENHANCING LEARNING AMONG THE DISCIPLINES

An Overview of Coordinated Curriculum

Benefits of Coordinated Curriculum

Planning and Scheduling for Coordinated Curriculum

Sample Coordinated Discipline Unit for the High School

How the Teachers Came Together

The Teachers' Goals, Planning and Scheduling

High School English Literature Course: Women's Literature

High School Biology/Health Course: AIDS Education

How the Teachers Carried Out the Coordination of Their Disciplines

Sample Coordinated Discipline Unit for the Middle School

How the Teachers Came Together

The Teachers' Goals, Planning and Scheduling

Middle School English/Language Arts Course: Historical Fiction and Letter Writing

Middle School Mathematics Course: Geometry

How the Teachers Carried Out the Coordination of Their Disciplines

An Overview of Coordinated Curriculum

*C*oordinated curriculum is not the only term used to apply to the concept we are discussing here. For the purposes of this chapter, we define *coordinated curriculum* as those curriculum endeavors in which two or more discrete disciplines are linked to help students understand a topic more fully. The coordination among disciplines that we will look at occurs when a pair or small group of teachers decide to focus on a shared "big idea" or topic while still teaching in the traditional separate subject configuration. Coordinated curriculum is shaped by the same three guidelines that shaped the single discipline units we explored in Chapter 9. Therefore, these coordinations among the disciplines should emphasize major understandings and big issues in the disciplines, the use of strategies for literacy and learning that we proposed in Part Two, and interconnection among the disciplines as well as connections from the disciplines to the real world.

In most efforts toward coordinated curriculum, two teachers in different disciplines seek to help their students gain depth of understanding of a topic in one discipline through the connection, reinforcement, and extension of a second discipline dealing with the same or complementary subject matter. For example, the teacher in a high school general science class on nutrition examining the various nutrients the body needs and how the body uses food throughout the life cycle coordinated with the mathematics curriculum and a focus on the chemical and nutrient balance the body needs. Students practiced reading labels on various foods and applying the use of measurement terms they had learned in mathematics to interpret weight and height tables as well as on calorie charts (Illinois State Board of Education, 1998). Coordinated teaching and learning experiences such as this appear to help diverse learners see how subject matter is related and, more important, to see how knowledge in different disciplines is related and can be used to solve problems in the real world. In addition, more in-depth exposure to important ideas and the repeated application of understandings in different domains appear to increase students' retention of subject matter, as well as to increase the likelihood that they will make this knowledge their own and use it in the real world (Ediger, 1990).

There are examples in everyday life of how coordination among professionals in different fields has helped solve problems and challenges. For example, nutritionists are working with neurologists and special educators to determine if a chemical imbalance or if allergies might be the cause of or at least be related to a number of learning disabilities. Because such coordination among disciplines occurs in everyday life and in the work world, it is important to look for these opportunities and model coordination in our classrooms.

▶ ▶ ▶ ▷ **Benefits of Coordinated Curriculum**

Both students and their teachers can benefit from coordinated curriculum experiences. Students benefit from coordinated curriculum because the teaching and learning activities they meet in one subject and those they meet in another complement one another. The experiences students have when different disciplines are connected around an important idea or understanding create a more holistic learning experience than in the usual single discipline delivery model of curriculum. In classrooms where coordination is implemented, what students learn in one discipline becomes background knowledge for the other discipline. Such experiences enhance the likelihood that students will acquire real rather than superficial understandings of important topics and ideas that cross disciplines.

For example, some tenth-grade students in an American history course were studying the Industrial Revolution in the United States. They explored what led up to this era and what it meant for the people who worked in the factories and mills that sprang up across the East and the Midwest. Think about how a coordinated literature unit using historical fiction set in this same time period using such books as *Lyddie* (1991) by Katherine Patterson or *The Bobbin Girl* (1996) by Emily Arnold McCully would be enhanced by the factual knowledge the students would be aware of if they were studying the same time period in their history class. Think also about how historical fiction that focuses on portrayals of individuals living and working during the Industrial Revolution in America might prompt students to raise questions about the period that perhaps their history text did not deal with. The English teacher could use these fictional works to delve into how an author constructs an accurate historical novel and how authors weave fact and fiction into a story to make it compelling. Students could use their own understandings of this period that they acquired from their history course to judge each author's authenticity as well (Norton, 1995).

Such coordination between history and literature could also be an impetus for students to revisit historical sources for verification of the historical information used in the works of fiction. Once students have read a poignant story about a young person like Patterson's *Lyddie*, they might be curious about the impact the Industrial Revolution had on real individuals and on their families. Coordinated curriculum work drawing on the social sciences might help the students understand why various laws were enacted during this period that are still in place specifically to protect children and women workers.

Teachers we know always point to the benefits they gain from opportunities to get information, advice, and support from colleagues who are teaching at the same grade level or in the same discipline as they are. As two tenth-grade high school teachers from Brattleboro, Vermont, who were presenting at a national conference of English teachers pointed out, the administration can mandate cooperation among curriculum areas and can give teachers the same schedule; however, they cannot mandate real collaboration (Appel & Andreoli, 1996). This particular pair of history and English teachers, who were collaboratively teaching an American studies curriculum for the third year to high school students, identified a number of factors that they believe helped their collaboration and the development of their coordinated curriculum. As you might expect, many of the points they made were directly related to a teacher's approach to teaching and to the subject matter. However, the last point made is related to the role the administration plays when teachers are attempting to coordinate curriculum as well as personal collaboration. These two teachers emphasized that teachers attempting to coordinate curriculum need to:

- Have a shared curriculum and goals
- Have shared performance standards for students
- Have a willingness to explore a topic and some different pedagogy
- Function in a collegial manner
- Approach curriculum, one's discipline, and teaching flexibly
- Demonstrate willingness to work out of one's own discipline
- Obtain support from the department and building-level leadership

Teacher as Inquiring Learner Activity

Think about your own discipline and the many topics you have studied since you have chosen your subject matter specialization.

- Was each course you took taught as a discrete set of information and understandings to be covered? Were you encouraged to think about the connections of what you were studying to other areas within the discipline, such as the connections between botany and zoology? Were you ever asked to link what you were learning in your discipline to some understanding or some issue in another discipline? Did you have any courses from different disciplines that were taught concurrently or that were linked to one another by the professors teaching them?

If you have personally experienced coordinated curriculum in college or have had the opportunity to observe it in operation in a middle school or a high school where you have done a field experience, you have a model to use when you have your own classroom. If you have not had such an experience, think about a major understanding or an issue in your discipline that could be enhanced by the knowledge and the perspective of a person from another field. Think about how you asked peers for their opinions on an issue in Chapter 8. If you are a history major, ask an English major if he or she knows of a story set in a particular period that you have an interest in, and compare the impressions of the period your classmate has from literary works with your knowledge of history. If you are a biology major, talk with a health or physical education major, and see what you each know about the human skeletal system and what you each think are the issues for athletes in different sports.

▶ ▶ ▶ ▶ Planning and Scheduling for Coordinated Curriculum

Coordinated curriculum efforts at the middle school and at the high school levels fall along a continuum determined largely by the planning time available to the teachers before and during the unit. In every instance, the amount of actual time available for teacher-to-teacher and teacher-to-student collaboration has much to do with what is feasible given the broader school schedule and organization.

A necessary factor in any of these joint ventures is for the teachers to have planning time together. The planning to develop and to carry out coordinated curriculum helps teachers think about and identify the priorities or big ideas that they hope to convey to their students. When teachers plan for and implement coordinated curriculum, they often are able to solve some of the prevailing issues that stem from an overcrowded curriculum. Such efforts among teachers often lead to more creative use of the physical space and resources in their setting, as well as to a greater variety of ways to meet the learning needs of their students.

There is no one absolute or correct way to set up planning that will work within every context. It is very difficult to do justice to the understandings, strategies, and applications that are the benefits of coordinated curriculum efforts within the typical single forty-five-minute class period and situations where students are dealing with seven different subjects and changes each day. Nevertheless, currently most attempts at coordinated curriculum are carried out by teachers who are following the usual six- or seven-period class schedules and are teaching a required curriculum, while at the same time they are finding an opportunity to work with other teachers and to connect their disciplines in new ways.

As we will discuss in more detail in Chapter 11, teachers at both middle school and high schools levels must work with their colleagues in different disciplines and with the administration to create schedules that are more flexible and begin to be perceived as a resource to support strong, innovative curriculum rather than as a barrier to teachers and students working together. In this chapter, we will examine some planning and scheduling ideas that we think can help to encourage teachers in a variety of settings to try coordinated curriculum that will enhance the content-area learning and the literacy learning of middle school and high school students. We deal with this concern with planning and scheduling as well as the particular issue of time needed to carry out curriculum innovations in further detail in the next chapter, which examines integrated curriculum.

Numerous variables determine the exact scope and focus of a given effort by teachers of different disciplines to create coordinated curriculum. At the simplest level, two teachers identify complementary strands or content and shared understandings in their individual courses, and they teach these to a given group or groups of students during a semester or marking period. For example, two teachers could arrange the study in geography of the Midwest plains states to occur at the same time that students are reading fictional works such as Patricia MacLachan's *Sarah, Plain and Tall* (1985) or Willa Cather's *My Antonia* (1918/1999) or nonfiction works such as Russell Freedman's *Children of the Wild West* (1983). The teachers may make varying attempts at explicit connections between their two subjects and the content and understandings at hand depending on the physical structure of their school and classrooms, the length of class periods, the teachers' own planning time, and the overall degree of flexibility they have given the other courses in the curriculum and the broader school schedule.

Teachers who choose to do coordinated curriculum need planning time together before the unit begins and, at the very least, some time to check in with one another during the implementation of the coordinated unit. Given the realities of many high schools and even middle schools organized in a team structure comprising discipline-based teachers for each core subject, the only times teachers are assured they can meet and plan are during shared lunch periods or before and after school on their own time. Occasionally two teachers find they have a shared preparation period (often the very time in which their ideas for coordination were sown during informal conversation, as is the case in the sample units you will read about later in this chapter).

With the increasing number of schools at the middle school level that use teams, more teachers may have a scheduled planning period with teachers from the other disciplines on their team, and therefore the time to do coordinated curriculum planning. With the recent emphasis on professional development for teachers throughout their teaching careers, there may be more opportunities and more incentives for you and your future colleagues to work with one another on curriculum development as a form of staff development. Finally, teachers such as the biology and literature teachers described in the sample high school unit later in this chapter, can seek support for summer work through grants from their own district or from state education departments, as well as from an increasing number of professional organizations that are fostering teacher scholarship and research.

Another variable that seems to determine the overall quality and the depth of a coordinated unit is the scheduling of the students and their teachers and the possibilities during the school day for the teachers and students involved in a unit to work together. In the sample middle school unit detailed later in this chapter, the two middle school content-area teachers were part of a team serving the same groups of students throughout the year. Therefore, the teachers were able to implement both their single discipline curriculum and the newly designed coordinated unit using their class periods that were scheduled back to back each day of the week. Furthermore, these teachers occasionally were able to create a double period to enhance the connectedness of their disciplines as well as the opportunities for the students to apply their knowledge at key times throughout the unit without disturbing either the curriculum or the schedules of the other members of their team.

At the high school level, which is still largely organized and scheduled with a priority given to academic departments and the domains within those departments (see Table 9.1), it is most likely that teachers of different disciplines will design their coordinated curriculum for the particular students they have within a period or within a common block of time that occurs in a daily or weekly schedule. Such arrangements deal with the reality of the high school schedule and enable the teachers and the students to come together at few key points during the coordinated unit, even if it is only for a culminating activity such as the discussion and debate that concludes the sample high school unit that brings together biology and twentieth-century American literature described later in this chapter.

Teacher as Inquiring Learner Activity

We hope you have begun to think about the benefits of coordinated curriculum for yourself as a content-area teacher and for your future students.

- If you believe that your students' learning will be enhanced if you are able to coordinate with teachers at the same grade level or in other disciplines, how will you as a new teacher attempt to deal with the usual scheduling and planning dilemmas?

Talk with your classmates and see if you can come up with a list of possible ideas. This is also a good time to engage in discussion with the professor teaching the course you are now taking to see what ideas or suggestions she or he has about coordinating with individuals in other disciplines. You might also want to interview a teacher at the middle or high school level who has had some experience personally coordinating with colleagues in other disciplines. As you read the rest of this chapter and the sample coordinated units, see if you can add some topics you might consider coordinating with various content in your own discipline.

Sample Unit Plans

Sample Coordinated Discipline Unit for the High School

This first unit that we have designed for this chapter brings together the teachers and students in a junior-level course in biology with a focus on disease and health and an English/language arts course with a focus on twentieth-century women writers. We developed the science component by drawing on a recent science resource for teachers looking at the role of women in the physiological sciences, Women in the Life Sciences: Past, Present and Future *(Matyas & Haley-Oliphant, 1997) and the goals of the national science standards at the high school level, particularly the strand emphasizing the life sciences (refer to Table 8.3). We based the English/language arts component primarily on an actual unit of study entitled "Engaging Students in Women's Literature" developed and implemented by two classroom teachers and shared at a recent state-level language arts conference. In addition, we used specific standards from the English/language arts standards document created jointly by NCTE and the IRA (see Table 10.1), several ERIC sources (Sandel, 1989;*

Table 10.1   Four Standards for the English/Language Arts Emphasized in the Sample Coordinated Unit for the High School

2. Students read a wide range of literature from many periods in many genres to build an understanding of the many dimensions (e.g., philosophical, ethical, aesthetic) of the human experience.

5. Students employ a wide range of strategies as they write and use different writing process elements appropriately to communicate with different audiences for a variety of purposes.

7. Students conduct research on issues and interests by generating ideas and questions and by posing problems. They gather, evaluate, and synthesize data from a variety of sources (e.g., print and non-print texts, artifacts, people) to communicate their discoveries in ways that suit their purpose and audience.

11. Students participate as knowledgeable, reflective, creative, and critical members of a variety of literacy communities.

Source: *Standards for the English Language Arts*, by the International Reading Association and the National Council of Teachers of English. Copyright © 1996 by the International Reading Association and the National Council of Teachers of English. Reprinted with permission.

Terner et al., 1988) focused on the importance of biography in the content areas and the recent AAUW report, How Schools Shortchange Girls *(referred to in Chapter 2) to shape this coordinated unit. Finally, the literacy strategies for learning that we focused on in Part Two served as a framework for the students to grapple with the resources chosen and the understandings emphasized in this unit.*

How the Teachers Came Together

The high school biology teacher was in the midst of a unit designed to link biology and health together in order to focus students' attention on the application of biology to their own lives and on current infectious diseases—AIDS, in particular. Students in a literature class had been examining the changing experience of women in this country as shown in the works of twentieth-century women writers from different parts of the country: works such as Annie Dillard's *An American Childhood* (1988) and Eudora Welty's *One Writer's Beginnings* (1984), as well as works from different racial and ethnic groups such as Jamaica Kincaid's *Annie John* (1983) and Judie Snow Wong's *The Fifth Chinese Daughter* (1945). These two teachers had independently read the AAUW report, *How Schools Shortchange Girls: A Study of Major Findings on Girls and*

Education (1995), and the flurry of related newspaper and professional journal articles that followed. As they chatted one day in the teachers' lounge, they realized that they and their tenth-grade students, both the boys and the girls, might benefit from the findings of this report and its implications for their own classrooms and curriculum. The two teachers began to wonder if there were some interesting way for them to connect their disciplines.

The biology teacher pointed out that the person who had discovered the AIDS virus, which the students would learn about in this unit in the biology course, was a young female scientist named Linda Laubenstein. She sighed that she rarely had time to go into the lives of the scientists who were responsible for the principles in biology that her students were studying. As the two teachers continued to talk, the biology teacher mentioned to her colleague that she had also been trying to figure out how to use the biographical sketches and annotated bibliographies about living female scientists that were included in a new resource she was using, *Women in the Life Sciences: Past, Present and Future* (Matyas & Haley-Oliphant, 1997).

The English teacher acknowledged that the required readings in her women's literature course included few autobiographies and no biographies at all. She said that she felt her students would benefit from the study of these two genres within the course, but she had not had time to revise her course and research some of the readings she might use. She commented that the readings and the written assignments throughout her course emphasized the universality expressed by women authors who used their writing to find themselves and to understand their world. She wondered if her students would gain more personally from the emphasis on contemporary women and their world if they could read about women other than authors.

The Teachers' Goals, Planning, and Scheduling

What if these two high school teachers could each use biography or autobiographies in their respective courses to focus their students' learning on women who had succeeded in a variety of fields? Could the use of autobiographies and biographies extend their individual course content and understandings while at the same time providing their students with powerful role models across disciplines and fields? As a result of these informal conversations, the two teachers were inspired to apply for a planning grant that was available in their school system for summer curriculum development work. They felt that their ideas could be shaped into a worthwhile coordinated learning experience for the students in both the biology and the literature courses. The two discipline-based teachers also believed that the coordinated focus on women in nontraditional roles through the genres of biography and autobiography would be beneficial whether individual students were taking one of their courses or both of them during the same semester. These teachers also believed that their idea was a realistic way to attempt some curriculum coordination within their curriculum and high school structure.

Coordination had become the buzzword in their school system as well as in their respective professional organizations. With what they thought was a good idea, they were now eager to try some coordinated curriculum development on their own. The teachers realized that they would have to think carefully about both scheduling and planning hurdles that they would face if they were to implement such a coordinated unit. They knew that they would have to work with their respective department chairs and their principal in order to implement their idea, especially if it were to include some joint meetings of their students. Nevertheless, these teachers were enthusiastic about working together and believed that once they had developed a working plan, they could come up with a reasonable way to carry out the unit and get the administrative support they needed. They also saw this opportunity to explore coordinated curriculum as a way to enhance their own professional development.

Additionally, the two teachers knew from their professional literature that the examination of the lives of real individuals through biography and autobiography has become an increasingly powerful form of literature across the disciplines (Sandel, 1989). Each had heard about how students at all ages seem to benefit greatly from entering subject matter through the eyes and the experiences of someone who has actually lived the event or the period under study. Therefore, these teachers were eager to attempt this coordinated unit for many professional and personal reasons.

Before you look at the coordinated unit that was the outcome of the teachers' summer planning, we think you should see what the English/language arts and the biology teachers did independently with their students before they engaged in the coordinated component of this unit. The work done in each of the separate disciplines was built on the existing curriculum with which these two teachers were already experienced. Their summer work led them to more thoughtful planning of activities within their respective courses, as well as to the use of a greater variety of resources and an emphasis on literacy and learning strategies.

High School English Literature Course: Women's Literature

Major Understandings.   Students see how women writers have found themselves through their writings, built on a quotation from the book by Kate Chopin, *A Pair of Silk Stockings and Other Stories* (1996) and the suffragette movement: "Her development, her freedom, her independence must come from and through herself." Students come to value themselves as individuals and to find themselves by reading about a person who shares an interest of theirs.

Resources.   Five core readings by American women writers served as the primary resources: a poem ("Caged Bird" from *Shaker Why Don't You Sing,* 1983, Maya Angelou), an essay ("My Name" by Sandra Cisneros from *The House on Mango Street),* 1991, a short story, which had also been a made-for-TV drama ("The Yellow Wallpaper" by Charlotte Perkins Gilman, 1892), and two novels (*The Awakening* by Kate Chopin, 1899) and *Their Eyes Were Watching God* by Zora Neale Hurston, 1937).

Individual Lessons

Generating Phase Lessons

- Students do **freewriting** based on the quotation from *Silk Stockings.*
- Students participate in small group **brainstorming** and then creating a "Then and Now Chart" that helps them think about the issues related to gender that they know about—ones they have heard about or learned about in the past through other courses (such as history) and ones that they know about today in their own lives or those of women they know. They **discuss** whether there are particular issues, concerns, and questions that face women because of race, religion, or ethnicity.

Interacting Phase Lessons

- The whole class **discusses** the poem and the essay in the core readings and then reflects on the message these two authors convey related to the major understanding.
- Students use selected paragraphs from "The Yellow Wallpaper" to focus on vocabulary analysis with an emphasis on **connotative** meanings of words and phrases.
- Students write **personal responses** in a journal and then participate in a **jigsaw activity** to share their responses with other students.
- Students use a **character web** to take notes focused on understanding the protagonist in the two novels—looking for events and interactions with other people that shaped the experiences and helped the particular protagonist find herself.

Refining Phase Lessons

- Students demonstrate their understanding of the main character through **creative writing assignments** in which they place one or more of the characters from the stories they have read in a hypothetical situation; students also **role-play** the main character's thoughts and actions and share these with their peers.

Evaluation of Students

- Students' **freewriting** and the **brainstorming activity** demonstrate prior knowledge.

- Students' vocabulary **journals** and **character webs** demonstrate understanding of the five core reading selections.

- Students' small group **written responses** and whole class **discussions** demonstrate comprehension of the readings and of the topic as a whole.

- Students place their vocabulary logs, character webs, and creative writing samples into their individual English/language arts folders or into their cross-discipline working portfolios.

- Students assess their products and place one or more in their showcase portfolio, accompanied by a checklist and an explanation (see Figure 10.1) for their choice(s).

Figure 10.1

Student Self-Evaluation for a Showcase Portfolio

In order to choose items for your showcase portfolio, ask yourself the following questions and share the answers with the audience who might view this portfolio:

1. What did I learn from writing (or creating) this piece?
2. What would I have done differently if I had more time?
3. What are the greatest strengths and the greatest weaknesses of this sample?
4. What problems or obstacles did I experience when doing this? How will I overcome these obstacles or problems next time?
5. Is this my best work? Why or why not?
6. What will I do for my next work?

Source: J. M. McMillan, *Classroom Assessment: Principles and Practices for Effective Instruction* (Needham Heights, Mass.: Allyn & Bacon, 1997).

Making Additional Connections Within and Among the Disciplines

English/Language Arts

- Students read autobiographical works by other women writers such as Margaret Mead's *Blackberry Winter* (1972).

- Students read literary works that have portrayed women finding themselves made into movies, such as Alice Walker's *The Color Purple* (1982) or Karen Blixen's *Out of Africa* (1938/1987).

Social Studies

- Students read women writers whose works help readers today understand different times and events in American history, such as Harriet Beecher Stowe's *Uncle Tom's Cabin* (the Civil War) or Willa Cather's *My Antonia* (life in the West in the nineteenth century).

Mathematics

- Students carry out a survey to identify the range of fields women are in today and where they predominate.

- Students look at some of the current periodicals devoted to women in the workplace, such as *Working Woman* for statistics or articles focused on women in the workforce and the issues they are facing.

High School Biology/Health Course: AIDS Education

Major Understandings.   Students learn why it is important to be informed about a disease that affects people today. Students understand how a disease can be spread, and they understand how this knowledge can help them as individuals now and how it will help them as they participate in their communities in the future.

Resources.   The lab is set up for a simulation of how disease is spread. There are enough eyedroppers, test tubes, solution of normal sodium hydroxide, and water. Step-by-step lab procedures are supplied for carrying out a disease-transmission simulation such as "AIDS, Who Me? A Disease Transmission Simulation" (Matyas & Haley-Oliphant, 1997). Finally, all students have a lab notebook to record the results of simulation and to analyze the data.

Individual Lessons

Generating Phase Lessons

- Students **create individual lists** of what they know about AIDS; they share their lists and create a **cumulative class list**. Then the teacher asks students to think about which concepts or ideas are scientifically or biologically related and which are socially related. The teacher creates a **comparison chart** on the overhead to display these ideas.

- In order to **establish a purpose** for the series of lessons that will follow, the teacher poses a question, "Should teachers and students have the right to be aware of the health problems others in the same room have? Would you be willing to work with a partner carrying a contagious disease, or is the individual's right to privacy the overriding concern?" (Matyas & Haley-Oliphant, 1997, p. 112).

- Following the discussion, the students read the directions and carry out a **simulation** (see Figure 10.2) of disease transmission; they gather and analyze the data and then return to the question the teacher asked earlier for **discussion**.

Interacting Phase Lessons

- Students first **interpret information on charts** with AIDS statistics to see how many people have been infected and who they are by age, race, and gender; to see what the statistics show about life expectancy and to see the prevalent ways in which people become infected with HIV.

- The teacher **creates a study guide** to help students read articles from the popular press and from scientific magazines to find information and statistics related to the spread of AIDS since the early 1980s, when it was discovered, and to focus on identifying changes since its onset and the progression of the disease to date.

Refining Phase Lessons

- Students as a class revisit the scientific and social aspects of the disease that they listed at the beginning of the unit and **add new information** that they have from their simulation and from the research they have done.

- Students look at cases like the ones on p. 117 in *Women Life Scientists* (Matyas & Haley-Oliphant, 1997) that highlight opposing points of view regarding AIDS issues. They **role-play/debate** how they would handle the situations that are described in the cases found in the text (see Figure 10.3), focusing on the fact that there are no "right" answers.

Figure 10.2   Science Simulation Activity

Activity #1: AIDS? Who, Me? — A Disease Transmission Simulation

PURPOSE

In this activity, you will find that a single carrier of a disease can infect large numbers of individuals when the spread of the disease is exponential rather than geometric. Also, you will learn how epidemiologists can trace the original source of an infectious disease organism. You will also sharpen your data collection and analysis skills.

MATERIALS

- 1 test tube or cup of prepared fluid
- 1 eyedropper

PROCEDURE

- Each student will receive a test tube or cup of liquid that represents a sample of "blood." All but one of the samples is untainted, or disease free. One of the samples (which looks just like all the others) contains an additional chemical representing a certain strain of disease. Only your instructor knows the identity of the one "infected" individual.

- At your teacher's signal, exchange "blood" with another student in the following way:

  1. Pull about half of the liquid in your tube or cup into the eyedropper; your partner should do the same.
  2. Put the liquid in your eyedropper into your partner's tube; he/she should put the liquid in his/her eyedropper into your tube.
  3. Swirl the liquid in your tube to mix it (or use your eyedropper to mix it with an up and down motion).
  4. Record the name of the person with whom you exchanged "blood" on your "Data Table." It is important that you record your exchanges in the order in which they occurred!

- Next, find a new partner (someone you have NOT exchanged "blood" with before) and wait for your instructor's signal, then repeat *steps 1–4* above.

- When you have made all the exchanges (ask your teacher how many), bring your tube to your teacher to test for "infection." A dark orange color in the tube means that you are infected with the disease. Record whether you are "infected" or "disease free" on your "Data Table."

- By careful sharing, organization, and interpretation of the data, determine who among your classmates had the original "disease carrier" tube or cup. Good luck and start thinking!

DATA TABLE

Exchange number	Exchange person
1	_____
2	_____
3	_____
4	_____
5	_____

After five exchanges, add the indicator to determine whether your "blood" sample is infected with the disease.

Is your sample **"disease free" (yellow)**, or **"infected" (dark orange)?** _____

Who had the original tube/cup that carried the disease? _____

QUESTIONS

1. What methods of sharing and organizing data proved most successful in your analysis? What did you do that did not assist in your interpretation of the observations?

2. Is it possible for two people to exchange fluids and, at the conclusion of the exercise, one person be "infected" while the other remains "disease free"? Is this true for a disease such as AIDS?

3. Who was the original "disease carrier" in your class? How did you come to that conclusion?

4. What other technological or societal issues of our day require extensive exchange and analysis of data in working toward a common goal?

The science teacher guides the students as they read the directions, conduct the experiment, and record their observations.

© Michael Zide

- Students decide where else and from whom in their community (social workers, public health official, nurses, or doctors, for example) they could get more information about this disease. Students **prepare questions** that are related to areas of confusion or disagreement that they have found; individuals come to speak on a panel or to be interviewed by the members of the class.

- Students **create a poster or other informational piece** to share their knowledge about AIDS and to inform others in their school community.

- Students **read a biographical sketch** about the woman who discovered the AIDS virus (included in the teacher resource, *Women Life Scientists: Past, Present and Future* [Matyas & Haley-Oliphant, 1997]), and discuss additional information they learn about AIDS as well as what they learn about this woman as a scientist and as an individual.

Evaluation of Students

- Students develop **comparison charts** showing the biologically and scientifically related ideas associated with AIDS and the socially related ideas and issue.

- Students **make notes** on the study guide as they read and react to the material.

Figure 10.3

Sample Case for
Discussion

Perez .... Allen

Perez believes that names of persons who have a positive result of the AIDS antibody should be kept private. That is, only persons chosen by the individual tested and those involved in the health care of the person should know. Allen believes that positive test results should be available to persons wanting them. Employers, school officials, and landlords, for example, have the right to know who has the AIDS virus.

What is your opinion? _____

_____

_____

_____

_____

Source: M. L. Matyas and A. E. Haley-Oliphant, *Women in the Life Sciences: Past, Present and Future* (Bethesda, Md.: American Physiological Society, 1997), pp. 119.

- Students **prepare questions** for the panel.
- Students **create posters** for a community awareness campaign.
- Students do lab work and **write responses** with a partner during the simulation activity.

Making Additional Connections Within and Among the Disciplines

English/Language Arts

- Students read an article, such as "Shortchanging Boys and Girls" (*Educational Leadership,* May 1996) based on the AAUW report, *How Schools Shortchange Girls,* and discuss the relationship of the report's findings and the fact that fewer women than men are found in science.

Mathematics

- Students examine statistics and graphs that show information about other infectious diseases and analyze the findings and the implications like they did with the AIDS data used earlier in the unit. Popular press resources like *USA Today* and the Internet are particularly useful and accessible to students.

Social Studies/History

- Students study instances in the history of the United States and of other countries and cultures when the spread of disease has changed or altered society (e.g., the spread of and the devastation caused by measles, a European disease brought to the Americas, to the Native American population of the United States during the colonial period or the spread of the bubonic plague, or the Black Death, throughout Europe during the late 1340s).

How the Teachers Carried Out the Coordination of Their Disciplines

Both teachers individually carried out their single discipline courses emphasizing the major understandings of the unit they were engaged in, as well as the various discipline-specific processes and the literacy strategies that their students needed. To begin the coordinated component of the unit, each teacher independently introduced her students to the use of and the value of autobiographies and biographies as they pertained to her own discipline. The series of lessons that made up the single discipline work and the movement into the new connected material were planned to run concurrently in the two disciplines.

In the biology course, the students shared the biographical sketch taken from *Women in the Life Sciences* (1997) written about Linda Laubenstein who discovered the AIDS virus. This brief biographical sketch served as a jumping-off point for the students to understand the role that biographies can play in helping them gain insight into the real world of science through the eyes and the experiences of individuals who are "doing" science. The teacher encouraged the students to identify an area of science that interested them, such as astronomy or marine biology, and to find an individual who excelled in that field. The teacher also encouraged the students to focus on women living and working in the twentieth century. Among the women in science the students chose to read about were Diane Fossey, the animal biologist, and Sally Ride, the astronaut, whom they had heard about in the news and in the movies, as well as women from minority groups in the sciences (including mathematics and engineering). Resources such as *Facts on File*, the collective biography *Women Scientists in the Twentieth Century* (1997), and books for young people like *Twentieth Century American Women Scientists* (Yount, 1996) and *Extraordinary Women Scientists* (Stille, 1995), all written relatively recently, were introduced to the students to get them started on their individual research and to ensure that there was reading material that would appeal to students at a variety of levels.

Meanwhile, students in the literature course had been reading the works of women writers in the twentieth century who had found themselves through the stories they told about others and about themselves. They had read and analyzed poetry, essays, short stories, and novels written by an array of twentieth-century female authors. For this coordinated component of the unit, the students read a common source, "The Book as Revelation," a chapter from Milton Meltzer's *Non-Fiction in the Classroom* (1994). The students and the teacher discussed how biography is different from the genres they had already read in their literature course. The students and the teacher discussed how writers often use biography to focus on a real individual, living or dead, whom they admire or are intrigued by.

At this time in the coordinated unit, the students in both classes were engaged in reading a biography or autobiography about the person they had chosen to study. The students then created a character map that displayed such things as their chosen individual's personality characteristics, people who had influenced this person, and issues or difficulties their subject had faced in her life or her work. For the students who had not had the experience of creating a character map before, the teachers modeled the procedure using the biographical sketch that the biology students had shared as a group earlier in the unit.

While the students were researching and reading about their own subject, both teachers conducted informal discussions about why the students in both classes were reading biographies at the same time. When the planned time for the two classes to come together arrived, the students in both classes had already engaged in conversations and had thought about why they were using the genre of biography in two very different disciplines. When the two groups of students and their teachers convened for a joint class planned for and scheduled during the teachers' collaborative summer planning, this topic about the same work in two separate disciplines became the basis for the group's discussion and debate. In addition, the high school students found themselves focusing on concerns related to gender equity in a number of different fields they had read about, as well as whether there were any common characteristics held by individuals, men or women, who have become recognized as innovators and leaders in their respective fields.

Sample Coordinated Discipline Unit for the Middle School

We designed this unit to focus on coordination between two members of a typical middle school team: the mathematics and the English/language arts teachers. The mathematics component was inspired by an actual classroom project that one of us had the opportunity to learn about while participating in a university-school partnership grant in a large urban middle school. In addition, the National Council of Teachers of Mathematics Standards (1989) (see Table 10.2), a number of state curriculum frameworks (Illinois Learning Standards, Florida Sunshine State Standards, and New Jersey Core Content Standards), and the findings from the Third International Mathematics and Science Survey Report (1997) focus on geometry and its applications at the middle school level.

The English/language arts component was based on a chapter in Doing History: Investigating with Children in Elementary and Middle Schools *(Levstik & Barton, 1997) that emphasizes the use of historical fiction to examine the connection between history and literature, in particular, the study of the pioneers and the westward movement is often covered in eighth-grade American history courses. This emphasis was also detailed in a unit called "Hats Off and Hats On: A Trip Westward," which was presented by two middle school teachers at an annual National Council of Teachers of English Conference. Finally, a teacher's personal interest in quilts, in this case one of the author's, served as an inspiration for this coordinated unit that connected geometry and the English/language arts within a particular period of history.*

Table 10.2 Excerpt from Curriculum and Evaluation Standards for School Mathematics, Grade 5–8

Standard 12: Geometry

In grades 5–8, the mathematics curriculum should include the study of the geometry of one, two, and three dimensions in a variety of situations so that sutdents can—

- Identify, describe, compare, and classify geometric figures

- Visualize and represent geometric figures with special attention to developing spatial sense

- Explore transformations of geometric figures

- Represent and solve problems using geometric models

- Understand and apply geometric properties and relationships

- Develop an appreciation of geometry as a means of describing the physical world

How the Teachers Came Together

Two teachers on an eighth-grade team in a large middle school found them-selves reflecting on the efforts to create thematic units and to coordinate cur-riculum in their school. These teachers discussed the benefits of the recent ef-forts at coordination for their particular team—for both the teachers and the students.

One of the teachers, who taught mathematics, realized that although she was aware of some of the topics and themes that other members of her team had been working on, she herself had been only peripherally involved. She had worked with the science teacher on the team in order to coordinate some of the mathematics processes she was teaching with the skills and processes the students needed in order to carry out various science experi-ments and projects. However, this mathematics teacher and her colleague, the English/language arts teacher, realized that they had never explicitly con-nected their two disciplines. The teachers wondered if there was some way for them to find a connection between their disciplines that would enhance their students' learning and extend some topic they were already studying in their curriculum. Each agreed to think about their own curriculum and the topics and major understandings that they covered. Then they agreed to meet again in two weeks to see whether they could find a way in which they could coordi-nate mathematics and English/language arts.

The Teachers' Goals, Planning, and Scheduling

When the two teachers met a few weeks later, the English teacher shared with the mathematics teacher an idea that she had always hoped to carry out with her students when her class did a unit on historical fiction and letter writing that complemented the study of westward movement in their social studies course. She thought that the students would gain a great appreciation of the period if they created a group quilt. The English teacher explained how impor-tant quilts were in many stories, both fictional and real, about families mov-ing West. She told the math teacher about *The Quilt Block History of Pioneer Days* (M. Cobb, 1995), a book that explains various American quilting pat-terns and how they were created and named for the events of the trip West and for the daily activities of frontier life. The English teacher also thought such a project would give some of her students who were artistically talented a chance to shine in a group venture.

The mathematics teacher said that she had not thought about a topic or project as concrete as the one the English teacher mentioned, but that she had done a great deal of thinking about an area in the current mathematics pro-gram that needed more emphasis. She pointed out to her colleague that stu-dents were not getting enough opportunities to apply the mathematics they were learning to real-life situations. She stated that this was clearly shown in some of the findings of recent studies that compared eighth graders in the United States with their grade-level peers in other countries (TIMSS Report, 1997). These studies demonstrated that eighth graders in the United States are not as competent in mathematics, and particularly in geometry, as their same-age peers in other countries. The findings concerned her. She stated that she was also trying to find more ways of having her students apply math beyond the classroom in order to comply with the *Curriculum and Evaluation Standards for School Mathematics* (NCTM, 1989). As she listened to the English/language arts teacher talk about the idea for a quilt, she began to envision the possibility of connecting the geometry she taught with the literature unit focused on historical fiction portraying the western movement.

The two teachers thought that they were on to an exciting idea that had significant possibilities for coordination of their two disciplines. They decided to spend some additional time planning this coordinated venture, which they thought would complement the topics they would already be studying in the spring: in the English classes, historical fiction with an emphasis on stories set in the westward expansion period, and in the eighth-grade mathematics classes, geometry. The two teachers believed that their coordination on a quilt project should come as a culminating project for the respective units they would carry out with their own classes.

The teachers realized that the next step was for them to figure out how they would orchestrate the creation of the quilt and ensure that they had the resources they and their students needed. They also wanted to be sure that this project would be more than an art project that was tacked on "for fun." In order to coordinate the quilt project successfully, each teacher decided to review the understandings, the materials, the lessons, and the student evaluation that made up their respective units in mathematics and the English/language arts.

In the next part of this chapter you will see the outline of the literature and the geometry units that the students participated in before two teachers introduced and implemented the coordinated component. Keep in mind that the goal of the quilt project was for the students to refine and extend their understandings and the experiences they had in the individual discipline-based units.

Middle School English/Language Arts Course: Historical Fiction and Letter Writing

Major Understandings.   Students understand other people's perspectives through historical fiction focused on the 1880s in America; students learn how experiences shaped people's or characters' lives, and they learn to tell about themselves or a character and to describe unfamiliar settings and situations to a known audience using letters.

Resources

Fiction The teacher used a collection of tall tales and selections from anthologies to meet the needs of students at various levels, plus four works of historical fiction appropriate for young adolescents (two with female protagonists and two with male protagonists): *My Daniel,* by Pam Conrad (1989); *Brothers of the Heart,* by Joan Blos (1985); *Sarah, Plain and Tall,* by Patricia MacLachlan (1985); and *A Stitch in Time,* by Ann Rinaldi (1994).

Books that were on tape were important to the selection process so that the struggling readers in the class could share the content of books appropriate for their age and grade level along with their peers.

Nonfiction The teacher read aloud to the students "Going West" and "Settling Down" in *The Long Road West* (R. Freedman, 1983), to ensure that they all shared background knowledge on the period. Then the students read books about quilts and on making quilts written for adolescents and young adults such as Raymond Bial's *With Needle and Thread: A Book About Quilts* (1996), Kime's *Quilts for Red Letter Days* (1996), and Ellen Howard's *The Log Cabin Quilt* (1996).

Individual Lessons

Generating Phase Lessons (Chapter 4)

- Students read tall tales that take place in the West to stimulate discussion and to tap their **prior knowledge** and impressions of the West.

- Students create a group **KWL chart** to show what they know and what they want to know about the early West and the westward movement, with a particular focus on the experiences that young people like themselves had.

- The teacher reads to the students and engages them in a **DL-TA** using R. Freedman's *The Long Road West* to focus on problems young people faced traveling west and the comparisons of their lives as young people in the United States today. The teacher also acknowledges the experiences of emigrating today, which some of the students or their parents or relatives have recently experienced.

- The teacher does a **book overview** for each of the four trade books to help students make their selection of the book they want to read. The overview contains a discussion of the book cover, any illustrations in the book, and an excerpt chosen about each book to share with the group as a whole. The teacher allows students time to skim the books to make sure their choice is appropriate.

- The teacher creates an **anticipation guide** for each book to help the students set a purpose and begin reading the book of their choice.

Interacting Phase Lessons

- Students participate in **peer-led discussion groups**, making predictions and checking their inferences with a focus on using the anticipation guide that the teacher has created. The students add information to the KWL chart as they find answers to their questions and gain new information about the westward movement.

- Students create individual **character webs** to keep track of the protagonist's feelings, interactions with other characters, and experiences as the story unfolds. They share the information with other students in peer-led discussion groups.

- Students create **graphic organizers** (time lines, route maps, etc.) in order to keep track of details about the place or places where their characters go as they travel west; they share this information in peer-led discussion groups.

- Students keep a **vocabulary journal** of new words or words used in special ways pertaining to the West (e.g., *greenhorns, dugout, prairie schooner, mementos, sentries*).

- Students keep a list of types or forms of writing that the protagonist or other characters in the book use to communicate with others and themselves—for example, journals, diaries, letters, and newspapers.

Refining Phase Lessons

- Students as a class **revisit the KWL chart** they created on the western movement and see what new information they want to add, what they want to change, and what new questions they have.

- Students **compare** the experiences of young people going west across the texts they have read.

- Each student writes a **fictional letter** from the perspective of an individual in the book to someone at home that includes facts and understandings from the history of the period woven into the information from the book they read and about its setting.

- Students have a **conference** about their letter with a partner using a checklist the teacher developed to guide their revisions in this assignment.

- Each student chooses an event, an episode, or a chapter in the book he or she is reading to do an **oral retelling** to the teacher.

Evaluation of Students

- Students participate in **peer-led discussion groups**.

- Students carry out **peer evaluation** of one another's letters from the character's viewpoint using a written checklist with questions, **praise**, problems, and proposals for the author.

- Students develop and use individual **vocabulary journals**.

- Students create and use graphic organizers such as a semantic map or the character web to check their comprehension and to prepare for writing a fictionalized letter.

- Students **create a letter** written by a character in the book describing a new or unfamiliar setting to a known audience (someone back home).

- Students prepare for and do a **retelling** of a favorite event, episode, or chapter in the book they read that the teacher listens to.

Making Additional Connections Within and Among the Disciplines

English/Language Arts

- Students create a month-long journal written by a young person during a trip west in the 1800s basing it on a book they have read in literature and the information they have about what happened from social studies.

- Students create the front page of a newspaper printed during the 1840s or 1850s, including weather, ads, a main story using the events that occurred in the book they read, and even an advice column for people in the East who are considering the trip west.

Social Studies

- Students use the computer simulation "Oregon Trail" to problem-solve and to learn more about this time in history.

- Students view and discuss such videos as The Donner Party, one of the specials in the WGBH American Experience Series (Burns, 1997).

- Students learn more about the Native Americans in this part of the country and the experiences they had as the settlers moved West, with a focus on nations, customs, famous leaders, and a better understanding of the Indian experience from the Native American perspective.

- Students learn more about the history and the geography of the fifteen states that were settled during this period.

- Students learn about the various ethnic, racial, and religious groups who settled this region. They learn where they came from and why they left their homes.

Mathematics

- Students apply principles of measurement and cost in a simulation of a visit to the general store on the frontier or in the preparation of the wagon and supplies for the trip west.

Science/Geography

- Students learn about weather occurrences that are more prevalent in the West, such as droughts, dust storms, and tornadoes.

- Students learn about the deserts of the United States (Death Valley) that many of the settlers faced for the first time and compare these deserts to deserts in other regions of the world.

Middle School Mathematics Course: Geometry

Major Understandings.   Students demonstrate that they can reason and problem-solve using various strategies and selecting appropriate computational techniques (e.g., graph paper, dot paper, computers), and students demonstrate that they can communicate their math understandings in written and oral forms.

Students also understand and apply basic and advanced properties of the concepts of geometry with an emphasis on their combining, subdividing, and changing basic shapes; visualizing geometric shapes in various rotations; and solving real-world problems involving the area of geometric figures.

Resources

Teacher Sources   The major teacher resources are the Standards Document of the National Council of Teachers of Mathematics (1989) and the teachers' individual state standards and curriculum documents.

Teacher and Student Sources   *Passports to Mathematics, Book 2* (R. E. Larson, L. Boswell, & L. Stiff, 1997), a text designed for middle school students that emphasizes the review and extension of mathematics learned in the elementary grades and new understandings and applications in geometry and algebra.

Individual Lessons

Generating Phase Lessons

- Students review the names and properties of geometric shapes and participate in a **freewriting** activity in which they respond to this question: "What shape do you think is used the most often in society, and why?"

- Students **review the meaning** and use of mathematical concepts and terms: parallelism, perpendicularity, congruence, and similarity. They do some sample applications with various geometric figures and respond to and explain their answers to a set of true-or-false statements, for example, "A square is the only quadrilateral with four congruent sides."

Interacting Phase Lessons

- Students **investigate** the idea of area using tangrams of seven common geometric figures (e.g., square, rectangle, parallelogram) and manipulate these figures to understand how these shapes compare to and fit with one another. Students also learn how to compute the area of a parallelogram.

- Students **explore** the idea of similarity and congruence using squares, rectangles, triangles, and parallelograms. They look for real-world examples of similarity and congruence between such things as baseballs and softballs, a photo and its enlargement.

Refining Phase Lessons

- Students apply their mathematical understandings and organize their ideas to **compare** the area of a single shape and how different shapes fit into a larger surface (e.g., to see how the area of two triangles and a rectangle within a parallelogram compares to the area of the parallelogram).

- In order to apply their knowledge to new situations, students **create** an object for which they have to do calculations and measure fabric or paper in certain shapes (e.g., a kite made up of triangles or a quilt made up of squares).

- Students use their understanding of the principles of geometry and the language of mathematics to **interpret** directions and to carry out word problems.

Evaluation of Students

- Students demonstrate their knowledge of mathematical terms and concepts in a **prewriting** activity.

- Students demonstrate their knowledge of technical vocabulary used in geometry in **discussions** and when they **explain procedures** during the application activities.

- Students demonstrate their knowledge and understanding in application activities, such as comparing areas and shapes or creating a kite, a quilt, or other product.

Making Additional Connections Within and Among the Disciplines

Social Studies/Geography

- Students look at the states that were in the original thirteen colonies, and determine their area individually and collectively compared to the United States today.

- Students look at the states that were settled during the westward movement, such as Oregon, Nevada, and Montana, and see how many are in the shapes of parallelograms.

- Students determine the area of these states and draw some conclusions about why, when these territories went for statehood, they had particular boundaries and shapes.

- Students look at a map of their own state and see if they can determine its area as well as that of the county they live in.

Fine Arts

- Students look for and use various geometric shapes within any visuals they create, such as drawings, paintings, sculpture, or models they create at home related to a hobby or a project in school.

- Students create models of real-world objects linked to their studies in science, social studies, and literature.

- Students look at the use of geometric shapes in the architecture found in their community and in fabrics used in clothing.

How the Teachers Carried Out the Coordination of Their Disciplines

Because the two teachers who carried out this unit were part of the team that taught these same students, planning time for the teachers and scheduling of students were already built into the existing structure. These factors made the coordination more manageable than it had been for the two high school teachers who collaborated to create the biology/health and English/language arts sample unit described earlier in the chapter. The two middle school teachers were able to use their alternate-week open planning time to work together on this unit. In addition, the schedule these teachers and their students had for the spring placed math and English/language arts back to back twice a week. This scheduling arrangement enabled the teachers to allocate some double periods to the quilt project. These longer blocks of time made the project seem more manageable since each student would be designing and then constructing a block for the quilt as well as looking at resources on quilting and conferring with other students and with the teachers. An additional advantage of such a coordinated unit is that students had two teachers to answer their questions and to help them design and make their own blocks for the quilt. Because of other units and themes planned for the latter part of the semester, these teachers had only three weeks in which to carry out this coordinated component of their unit.

The teachers began the coordinated component of the unit by reading a selection from M. Cobb's *The Quilt Block History of Pioneer Days* (1995) to all of their students. Because of the diversity of the students, especially those with learning disabilities within their classes, the teachers guided their students' listening with a DL-TA. The selection focuses on friendship quilts, which were very popular during the mid-nineteenth century. These quilts were made up of individual blocks stitched and autographed by each family member or friend who worked on the project. Students learned about how friendship quilts were traditionally given to a family at a going-away party in their honor before they left for the West. After the teacher read the selection, the entire class looked at some photographs and samples of quilts. The two teachers found a number of resources on quilting because of the revival of quilting in the United States today. They found books to inform them as adults about this topic, as well as a number of books of fiction (*A Stitch in Time*, by A. Rinaldi, 1994, and *Sweet Clara and the Freedom Quilt*, by D. Hopkinson, 1993) and nonfiction (*With Needle and Thread: A Book About Quilts*, by R. Bial, 1996, and *Quilts for Red Letter Days*, by J. Kime, 1996) about quilts written with a middle school audience in mind.

After the introductory read-aloud activity, each teacher asked the students to make some predictions about why they were learning about quilts at this point in the curriculum. The teacher asked the students to think about whether they saw any connections between quilts and their recent study of quadrilaterals in their mathematics course. Students were also asked this question to see if they could identify any connections between quilts and their study of the western movement through literature. Many of the students made the connection between geometric shapes and quilts once they saw some of the photographs and samples that their teachers had assembled. Some students in the class who had seen a quilt at home or in a museum were able to make a connection between quilts and geometry from their own firsthand experiences. Students who had read books in The Little House series or *A Stitch in Time* were able to make some connections between quilts and the westward movement in the United States during the mid-nineteenth century.

The teacher then told the students that they would all participate in making a class quilt to connect their understandings about the westward movement from social studies and literature and their knowledge of geometry. In order to apply their mathematical knowledge about squares and measurement, the students had to figure out how large a block each of them would have to make in order to create a quilt that could serve as a wall hanging for display in the school foyer. Students started by measuring the wall in the school where the quilt would be hung. Then they figured out mathematically, given the number of students in the class, how many blocks of what size they needed to fill the space. They determined that each student could create an eight-inch square for the project.

In order to work on their quilt blocks, the students had to use their literacy skills and strategies throughout the coordinated unit. They had to read and interpret the directions that their teacher provided them about how to design and put together their quilt block. The teachers gave the students a number of choices related to the design of their block and to its construction. Each student was then required to come up with a design for the block that would clearly show something he or she found to be particularly interesting about the westward movement. The teachers suggested that each student design a block that showed a map and the trail that a particular group followed, some memorable scene in the nonfiction or fiction sources they had read, or an adaptation of a quilt pattern like the "broken plate," which told a story about frontier life. Before settling on their final design, the students engaged in using the various resources the teachers had collected, as well as studying some slides provided by the National Quilt Museum and information they found on the Internet about quilts (**http://www.antiquequilts.com**) and an educational site (**webmaster@forum.swarthmore.edu**) that brings together projects that connect geometry to a variety of real-world situations. Students took on other math challenges as well in creating their block. Some students created a block using one of the quilt patterns that pioneers widely used during the 1800s. Many of these patterns the students chose were made up of quadrilaterals they had recently studied in geometry. Patterns like the multiple rectangles in the log cabin pattern and in the rail fence pattern were just two examples of what the students chose to create. Once the students designed their own block for the quilt, they had to figure out the size and shapes of the pieces they needed to fit their design into their own eight-inch block.

Finally, the students were given the option of sewing, gluing, or using a new iron-on material, known as Wonder Under, to put the pieces together on their individual block, and they had to follow directions for the method they chose.

Students had many opportunities to practice their literacy competencies as writers and as speakers in additional activities throughout this coordinated project. All students prepared a brief oral presentation to explain to classmates why they had created their block as they did. In order to explain the block as a personal statement, all students had to reflect back to what they had learned about the westward movement and what classmates knew and, in particular, what new information they had learned from the sources the teachers read and the chapter books they had read in small groups. This activity also enhanced the students' ability to express their own opinions and perspectives about a topic. The teachers linked their individual creation of a personally meaningful block for the quilt to the same kind of perspective taking the students had done in the letter writing activity based on works of historical fiction that was part of the eighth-grade English/language arts curriculum.

During work time, the teacher encouraged the students to share their rationale for their design and to compare ideas. The students had discussions about how they would arrange their individual blocks to compose the class quilt. As the students shared their ideas, they realized that many of them had been influenced by the hardships that the pioneers experienced and how these experiences contrasted to their own lives in the twentieth century. They were struck by the great distances that the pioneers traveled in crude wagons and rafts, as well as by foot, and the number of cities today that began as small settlements between the 1840s and the 1860s. Finally, in addition to the language arts—related skills and strategies that were enhanced by this project, the students' ability to carry on discussions using the language of mathematics was also enhanced as they talked about the design, size, and color choices they made for their blocks.

Once the group put the quilt together, they came back together once more for a discussion centered on the experience they had as a community in creating something tangible for their school. The teachers focused the discussion on the sense of community that grew as the students worked together. They asked the students if they had any new ideas about the role that quilts played in pioneer life. The teachers also introduced the students to some of the other types of quilts that were important in the history of the United States, such as the brightly colored quilts of the Amish and the story quilts of African Americans. The discussion concluded with the teachers asking the students if they knew of any current projects where people have contributed to a quilt to form a special kind of community. Some students had heard about the AIDS Quilt, which has traveled around the country and has been displayed on the Washington, D.C., Mall. Some of the students in this class, which was in the Midwest, knew about the Scrap of Pride Quilt that citizens in northeastern Ohio crafted to commemorate Cleveland's bicentennial and to demonstrate the diversity of their region's population. Finally, the teachers pointed out that with the enormous current interest in family histories, quilts are considered important artifacts and heirlooms. Some students volunteered that they had quilts from their own family that linked generations past with those in the present and would link their own present with the future.

Summary of the Chapter

In this chapter, we have given you some guidelines on coordinated curriculum experiences:

- How and when coordinated curriculum experiences will enhance the teaching and learning in your classroom and will benefit both you and your students

- The benefits of coordinated curriculum for both teachers and their students at the middle school and high school levels

- The importance of careful planning and scheduling

Finally, we have provided a few specific guidelines for you to consider as well as several suggestions that are useful in supporting and enhancing the possibility for successful connections within and among the disciplines.

We believe that the sample units in this chapter should help you design coordinated units and meaningful learning opportunities for your own students. As the teachers in the sample units demonstrated, you and your colleagues should begin all curriculum development work with a particular set of learning experiences and content in mind. You should also give careful thought to the particular grade or grades and the particular group of students who will participate in the unit. Finally, we believe that you should always ask yourself the following questions:

- Have I built this unit on essential content in my discipline? Will it help students focus on major understandings, themes, or issues in the field?

- Do I have a range of appropriate resources that both complement the content and meet the various needs and strengths of the students who will participate in this unit?

- Did I choose teaching and learning strategies to shape the lessons within the unit? Do these strategies complement the learning strategies in the content area I am teaching? Will students have opportunities to apply the strategies on their own in order to become more independent as learners?

- Have I included a variety of formats and opportunities for student evaluation that will inform me about my students' learning and literacy and help the students be more aware of their own learning?

- What possible connections are there between my content-area focus and other subjects in the curriculum? What connections are there between the focus of this unit and the real world?

As a new teacher, or even as an experienced teacher, you may be required to use curriculum that other members of your team or other teachers in your department developed. You may also be required to use curriculum that was developed by a districtwide committee or, in some cases, you may even be required to implement curriculum that has been developed by the state in which you work. Perhaps you will have an opportunity to implement a unit you designed during your teacher preparation program because it is a good match with your learners' needs as well as with the school or the district's curriculum. We hope that you will look for opportunities to coordinate your content area with others in the school. We hope that you will make connections between your own discipline and other disciplines in order to enhance your students' learning, as well as to benefit you as a teacher and as an individual who is always learning from your own teaching.

Inquiry Activities About Your Learning

1. Look back through Chapter 9 and this chapter at the sample units. Did you read about any topic, issue, or theme that you could connect to content you are familiar with in your own discipline? List the ways in which two disciplines can be connected. See if you can create a statement of a major understanding or of a goal that these two areas could enhance. What are some resources you would use as a teacher in order to help you design a coordinated unit? Can you also find at least three different resources on the topic that would be appropriate for the variety of students found in a middle school or high school where you have observed or done your student teaching?

2. In Part One of this text and again in Chapter 9 and this chapter, we explain that good teaching and learning experiences are created when the needs of the learner, the instructional goals, and the context mesh. Teachers are not unlike their students in that they teach well what they are interested in and confident about. Think about your own discipline and something you would enjoy learning more about. For example, when the middle school English/language arts and mathematics teachers decided to do the quilt project, the literature teacher used this opportunity to build on her own long-term fascination with quilts and to investigate her interest.

Reflecting on one of your own interests, think about a way in which it could complement or connect with a topic in your discipline. Once you have decided on a topic, find at least three print resources (fiction and nonfiction) that would be appropriate for your students. See if you can identify some artifacts or simulations that would give your students a hands-on experience that would complement the topic. Finally, identify an Internet source where you can exchange ideas with other teachers interested in the same topic or find an Internet source that would be appropriate for your students to use.

Inquiry Activities About Your Students' Learning

1. Interview a student who does well in your content area and a student who does not do well. Ask each student a series of questions about his or her experiences as a learner in the discipline. These questions to the two students and the analysis of their answers should help you gain some insights about the things you might consider when you are a teacher and planning curriculum for a variety of learners.

You might ask the students what they find difficult and what they find easy in the discipline; you might also ask them to think of what they have found interesting about the content and what was confusing. Ask the students about the sorts of resources they have used; find out which were required in the course and whether there were any resources that they used on their own. Ask them about the kinds of written assignments they have had in their course, and whether they have had to prepare anything for speaking or discussion. You might also want to know about the grouping arrangements they have participated in—cooperative groups, partner work, whole class—and which ones they found most beneficial. Finally, you should ask the students what strategies they use and what sources they find most useful as a learner—books and other print material, audiovisuals, or manipulatives.

This type of information is necessary to collect if you are to know your students better so that you can make conscious choices about the teaching and learning activities that will predominate in your own classroom. This information will also help you design curriculum, whether it be single discipline, coordinated, or integrated, the topic of Chapter 11.

2. Think about a coordinated unit you have carried out or one that you are familiar with in your discipline. Reexamine a single discipline unit you have already carried out. How could you make that unit into one that coordinated with another discipline? What important understandings would be enhanced through the connection of the two disciplines around a common topic? What literacy strategies and tools would you include in this new unit? How would you assess your students if they were to engage in the unit you are thinking about? How would you assess whether your students have adequate background knowledge and the necessary strategies to carry out the unit? In other words, what are the prerequisites students would need in terms of content knowledge, skills, and strategies? Second, what strategies would students use when they participate in the variety of activities and use the resources required in your unit? Finally, what are the particular literacy strategies and tools that you could teach and then assess as the unit proceeds?

11

Integrated Curriculum

In this chapter, we shift our emphasis from studying discrete discipline-based content and process to the interrelatedness of the subject areas and a more holistic approach to curriculum design and planning. We look at the issue-based or problem-solving process and content that ignores rigid discipline boundaries.

In many middle schools and high schools, the usual procedures teachers use for curriculum development and the usual class scheduling patterns appear to have placed artificial barriers between disciplines. Barriers even exist between subject matter in related disciplines, such as history and civics or biology and botany. Yet in the real world, experts don't work on issues alone and in discrete forty-five-minute segments. For example, chemists, physicians, social workers, and political activists work together, each lending expertise, to find answers and solutions to the spread and the treatment of AIDS.

In the classroom, teachers' and students' lives are increasingly fragmented and overcrowded because the knowledge explosion and the expanded impact of technology have collided with the prevalence of numerous stand-alone courses and separate discipline study. In addition to too much content in each of the disciplines for teachers and their students to cover adequately, large-scale national assessments like the National Assessment of Educational Progress (1994) show that few middle and secondary school students demonstrate creative or critical thinking skills. Furthermore, there are indications that most students tested cannot apply the knowledge they have gained in school to problems and issues they encounter in the real world.

In an integrated curriculum approach, the focus is on enhancing connections between disciplines and topics and on students' active learning. Through investigating issues in an integrated curriculum, your students will have opportunities to use critical thinking and problem solving. We think that integrated curriculum can encourage teachers to collaborate with other teachers and challenge students to think and problem-solve in an active manner. We also believe that collaboration and shared experiences among teachers and their students can extend and enrich all content-area study.

This chapter will help you learn to foster major understandings as well as content-specific skills and strategies and literacy learning in your discipline. As you read the chapter and apply it to your own discipline, ask yourself these questions:

Purpose-Setting Questions

1. Can I create a working definition and rationale for integrated curriculum that works for me now and that I will be able to use in my career as a classroom teacher?

2. Do I understand what is meant by a thematic approach as it is used in this chapter, and can I find some current themes linked to my discipline using the sources suggested as well as current professional literature in my field and discussions with peers, classroom teachers, and my professors?

3. Do I understand the special importance of preplanning when designing integrated curriculum? How does the model of curriculum development suggested in this chapter compare with the curriculum models introduced in Chapters 9 and 10?

4. Do I understand how the types of authentic assessment introduced in Chapter 3 and interwoven throughout Part Three benefit both teachers and students as well as how I might implement some of these in my own discipline?

What Do We Mean by Integrated Curriculum?

In this section we clarify what we mean by integrated curriculum and explain how it is different from single discipline and coordinated curriculum. (Table 11.1 outlines this information.) In addition, we clarify what we mean by the terms *interdisciplinary, integrated,* and *thematic,* which are often confused with one another. We also discuss our rationale for including integrated curriculum as an approach in this part of the text focused on curriculum development and the use of literacy strategies across the disciplines.

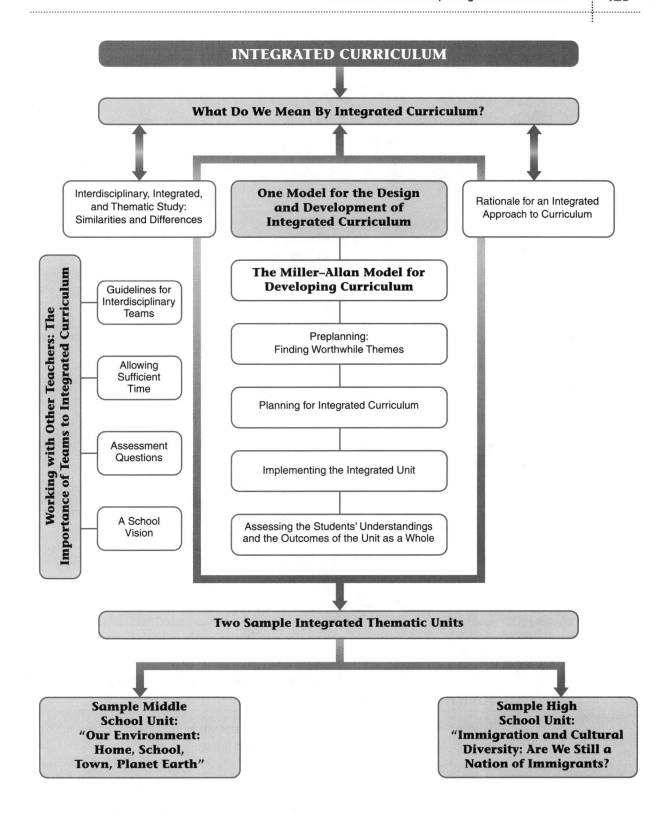

INTEGRATED CURRICULUM

What Do We Mean By Integrated Curriculum?

Interdisciplinary, Integrated, and Thematic Study: Similarities and Differences

One Model for the Design and Development of Integrated Curriculum

Rationale for an Integrated Approach to Curriculum

Working with Other Teachers: The Importance of Teams to Integrated Curriculum

Guidelines for Interdisciplinary Teams

Allowing Sufficient Time

Assessment Questions

A School Vision

The Miller–Allan Model for Developing Curriculum

Preplanning: Finding Worthwhile Themes

Planning for Integrated Curriculum

Implementing the Integrated Unit

Assessing the Students' Understandings and the Outcomes of the Unit as a Whole

Two Sample Integrated Thematic Units

Sample Middle School Unit: "Our Environment: Home, School, Town, Planet Earth"

Sample High School Unit: "Immigration and Cultural Diversity: Are We Still a Nation of Immigrants?"

Table 11.1   Three Curriculum Design Options

	Single Subject Departmentalized	Coordinated/Parallel Disciplines	Integrated
Disciplines	Separate disciplines Units have discipline-based objectives	Teachers in two or more complementary disciplines confer	Teams of teachers from different disciplines work together Disciplines serve the problem, issue, theme
Planning	Independent planning and teaching	Together teachers plan to link objectives and activities in own discipline to occur at similar times with that of other disciplines	Teams of teachers collaborate to plan and implement one curriculum
Time schedule	Activities planned for regular class periods	Units taught at the same time of year Little or no change in class time; regular class schedule for each discipline	May remain in usual class periods or combined in blocks for students and teachers May be scheduled for different lengths of time (week, semester, year)
Connections	Often no deliberate attempt to show relationships among disciplines or to connect with other teachers	Two units or topics have complementary content that connects them Teachers identify related content in their disciplines; however, the connection not always made explicit for students	Focus on problems and issues Disciplines used to solve, to investigate, to provide information

Source: P. S. George, and W. M. Alexander *The Exemplary Middle School* (2nd ed.) (Fort Worth, TX: Harcourt Brace, 1993), and H. H. Jacobs (ed.) (1989). *Interdisciplinary curriculum: Design and implementation.* (Alexandria, VA.: Association for Supervision and Curriculum Development.)

▶ ▶ ▶ ▷ ## Interdisciplinary, Integrated, and Thematic Study: Similarities and Differences

As you begin to refine your study about curriculum development in your discipline, you may be confused about the differences among the terms *interdisciplinary, integrated,* and *thematic study*. These terms are often used interchangeably because all three refer to cross-discipline study. Acknowledging that no single definition or model for integrated curriculum exists, we will explain working definitions for each of these three important terms that we use throughout this chapter.

Interdisciplinary Perspective.   Let us begin with the broadest term, *interdisciplinary perspective* (also referred to as *multidisciplinary* and *transdisciplinary*). Teachers using such a perspective make deliberate attempts to identify the relationship between disciplines and to demonstrate how perspectives from different disciplines contribute to the understanding of a particular topic or issue. When you use an interdisciplinary perspective to shape your curriculum, your students will see how disciplines can work in concert with one another. When we talk about designing curriculum from an interdisciplinary perspective, we identify it as *integrated curriculum*. Integrated curriculum is the heart of this chapter. You will read about integrated curriculum in detail in the next section and will see how to use an interdisciplinary perspective to shape units that are built on key content understandings and incorporate appropriate literacy strategies. Before we explain how integrated curriculum is a manifestation of an interdisciplinary perspective, we want to point out that an interdisciplinary perspective can be accomplished within the single subject or coordinated curriculum.

You could accomplish this interdisciplinary perspective in a modified manner as a single subject teacher by bringing in examples from different disciplines or by having your students extend their understandings of a topic they are studying in your discipline by looking at how other disciplines or sources deal with the same topic (our single discipline model in Chapter 9). Furthermore, if you are coordinating the work in your discipline with that of another subject-area teacher (the subject of Chapter 10), each of you could look at the topic or theme from your own discipline's vantage point and then you could have students see how the information in the two disciplines complements one another. Students could compare and contrast what they learn about the topic from each discipline.

For example, if you were a biology teacher whose class was studying the respiratory system, you might link this topic to a real-world concern, such as the effects of smoking or second-hand smoke on the respiratory system. You might also have your students explore what is being said and written about the benefits of a smoke-free environment. This area of study in science could be coordinated with the social studies teacher's current emphasis on government and the role that lobbyists play in their interactions with legislators. In this manner, students could study recent efforts related to smoking and efforts for and against a smoke-free environment from the vantage point of two separate yet coordinated disciplines.

Before you and the other teachers you are working with engage in time-consuming integrated curriculum planning, you should determine whether exploring interconnections among the particular disciplines will lead to greater insights by your students, and whether knowledge of one content area will actually complement the students' understandings or concepts in another area. All too often curriculum that has been labeled as interdisciplinary has evolved into artificial attempts to connect discipline areas and courses that are present in the existing curriculum. Therefore, when you design your own curriculum, you want to be certain you are emphasizing important understandings and strategies related to the disciplines and that you are not focusing on trivial content or superficially stretched ideas that are not worthy of your own or your students' time and energy.

Integrated Curriculum. We use *integrated curriculum* to designate study that focuses on issues, problems, and themes rather than on specific content within preselected curriculum areas or disciplines. The departmentalized structure predominant in secondary schools today gives students a false notion that information is organized into discrete subject areas with very little, if any, connection. When we design integrated curriculum, the emphasis is on helping our students make sense of their world, not on simply studying science or literature or art. When the focus is on issues, themes, and problems rather than on the traditional disciplines or subject areas found in most middle schools and high schools, the expectation is that students will use the concepts and their understandings from the disciplines as tools to learn about and to understand their world.

Too often integrated curriculum is associated with any curriculum approach that moves beyond strictly separate subjects. But truly integrated curriculum is not about doing the same things somewhat differently, such as rearranging the usual course schedule or modifying subject-based tasks or using different methods of assessment. In its purest form, integrated curriculum is created when the entire schedule evolves around projects rather than subjects and when disciplines come into play as resources to be drawn from in the context of the theme and its related issues and activities (Beane, 1995).

The theme, problem, or issue chosen for study should always be the context and the motivation for using a particular discipline and its content, not merely the fact that it is one of the subjects that has to be covered in the curriculum. For example, we could begin with an issue such as the desirability and possibility of a smoke-free environment by the year 2000.

Building on the interdisciplinary connection between a biology and social studies teacher, we could explore the possibility of using facts, strategies, and understandings from a number of disciplines to study a real-world issue.

In biology, students could examine the effects of smoking and second-hand smoke on the human body, specifically the respiratory system. The mathematics teacher could instruct the students in how to design surveys as well as how to organize and analyze data so that they could survey local restaurants and sports facilities to see what effect current or proposed policies related to smoking have had or will have. The English/language arts teacher could direct students to collect advertisements and editorials pertaining to smoking and bans on smoking. They could study how the media use facts and opinions to create persuasive arguments to persuade people about important issues. And from a social studies perspective, students could contact their congressional representative to learn about bills in the legislature pertaining to smoking. In this manner, the disciplines that make up the curriculum of most middle schools and high schools could be integrated and focused on students' learning for real purposes and to solve a real societal problem—not on learning history, literature, or geometry for school, for a grade, or, worse yet, for a test.

We encourage you to incorporate an integrated curriculum unit into your teaching and to experience the benefits for both you and your students. Well-designed integrated curriculum enables you to do the following:

- Capture student interest through focusing on relevant and real topics.
- Surmount overcrowded curriculum because in a single unit you can merge perspectives and skills from several disciplines.
- Gain a new perspective on basic skills as you work to identify the strategies, skills, and content principles that have widespread applicability in both the classroom and in the real world.
- Collaborate with colleagues and find new ways of working in your school and your classroom (Willis, 1992; Drake, 1993).

Thematic Study.   We see *thematic study* as a particular means to achieve integrated curriculum, not as an end unto itself. The identification of a theme serves as a tool and an important first step toward integrated curriculum. With well-chosen thematic units, teachers and students have an opportunity to participate in holistic learning at its best (Meinbach, Rothlein, & Fredericks, 1995). Well-chosen themes can lead to the exploration of ideas, can help students pull ideas together, and can stimulate students to form their own interpretations and conclusions. In addition, well-chosen themes create natural connections between the disciplines, as well as between students' in-school and out-of-school lives.

In order to create a thematic unit, you should keep in mind that the theme should challenge your learners, should interest you, and should promote powerful linkages among the disciplines. First, you might find interesting themes in existing curriculum or courses that are linked to the usual academics, such as the pioneer experience. With the pioneer experience as your theme, you and your students could focus on a comparison of the pioneer experience in the 1800s and today's pioneering explorations in outer space or in the depths of the ocean. Second, major themes, such as the solar system and space or culture and multiculturism, expressed through the strands in state curriculum frameworks and national standards documents are another rich source for themes that are linked to the existing academic requirements in the schools.

Third, we believe the most compelling source for themes remains the immediate community in which students live. Local concerns and issues like pollution and the effect on water quality or the effect of a recent natural disaster like the floods in California or hurricanes and tornadoes in Florida are compelling topics to explore and to use to shape curriculum. Controversial local topics are also good choices because students can investigate using authentic sources they can find in their own communities and that are related to the lives of people they know. Community issues, such as the damage caused by dumping toxic wastes into a previously clean and scenic river can pique your students' interest as well as provide a variety of topics to investigate and study and a natural way to bring the disciplines together in a meaningful way. By interviewing citizens as well as community leaders, your students will see the range of opinions about any controversial issue. An integrated unit shaped by a specific local issue has the advantage of providing immediate relevance and authenticity for both students and their community.

Fourth, in addition to local issues and community-centered issues, students and their teachers might find the themes they wish to explore in more universal problems, such as starvation and other population issues, wildlife protection and extinction issues, and global warming and pollution-related issues. Such issues or problems will have a widespread effect on the students' own lives, and as the adult generation of the next century they should be involved with the solutions for these problems. What better place to start with that problem-solving stance than in the integrated curriculum and authentic experiences with real-life issues in their middle or high school programs?

We also realize that sometimes these local issues touch a nerve. This is especially so when students start asking tough questions of lawmakers and officials in their own communities. We know of a recent example where a team of teachers and their students were trying to understand what was getting in the way of legislation to support the building of a bicycle path in their community. During the process of their investigation into the issue, the students stumbled on some thorny local politics. The issue became so sensitive that the superintendent of schools asked the teachers not to include this topic in their curriculum in the future. Once you have identified an issue, you should probably discuss the topic with other teachers in your school and community as well as with your principal before you engage in planning and implementing an entire unit of study.

Keep in mind that thematic units can be both expansive and time-consuming when designed to include many disciplines, or they can be focused and contained in a relatively short time frame and focused on one or two disciplines. For example, recently in a Virginia high school, the mathematics, earth science, history/geography, art, English, vocational, and business teachers and their students engaged in a nine-week thematic unit, "Cleaning Up the Chesapeake Bay," which focused all of their efforts on an important regional concern (Richardson & Morgan, 1997). By comparison, a three-week-long thematic unit on survival was based on the theme of Jack London's *Call of the Wild*, the novel being studied in a middle school English class (Richardson & Morgan, 1997). In this second example, the students and their teacher explored the particular period and location in which the story took place, as well as the insights about human nature that are central to London's works. To broaden this into a thematic study, the teachers drew on different disciplines to focus on survival and life in the Northwest during the period in which the novel was set as compared to the Northwest today using the interconnections of the terrain and the climate (geography); the interdependence of humans and animals, both those that are domesticated and those that are native to the area (science); and laws that govern the use of natural resources (the social sciences).

In summary, then, the most compelling reasons for engaging in thematic study are that it fosters the following goals (Fredericks, Rothlein, & Meinbach, 1992):

- Establishing a clear purpose for students' learning at the outset

- Emphasizing relationships among areas that contribute to understanding a particular issue or question

- Applying both content and strategies in meaningful contexts

- Developing students' ownership as students answer their own questions and see value in their processes for solving problems

- Enhancing students' learning as they probe, explore, and uncover the aspects of an intriguing issue, problem, or theme

- Building cooperation between teachers and between teachers and students to create a community of learners

▶ ▶ ▶ ▶   **Rationale for an Integrated Approach to Curriculum**

When you are a teacher at the middle school or high school level, you will want to use integrated curriculum selectively. This model of curriculum development is not a new way to string your existing discipline-based lessons or units together or an approach that should replace the study of significant content or concepts that are central to understanding and applying your discipline. However, when you identify issues of significance or themes that have widespread appeal and durability, you can use them as the core experiences or building blocks for designing an integrated curriculum.

Think about how interesting it would be for you to study a topic or an issue closely related to your discipline in a new way. For example, as literacy teachers and writers, we are very interested in why issues about censorship keep emerging. We ask ourselves what new censorship issues will arise in the next century as we become a more technologically sophisticated society with fewer restrictions on modes of communication. We could examine the censorship issue from a single discipline perspective in language arts. However, we realize that information from other disciplines and different perspectives could help us and students understand this important issue. We could collaborate with social studies teachers who have studied civics and law, or look at censorship issues with e-mail and the Internet by talking with technology experts to see what issues they may have encountered. We could learn about personal and professional real-life, day-to-day experiences that individuals in the community have had with censorship by talking with a librarian, a local newspaper editor, and even school administrators.

Finally, no matter what the form of integration you choose and no matter what portion of the total curriculum you devote to integration, you can ask some questions that will help you decide the merit of this experience for your students and for you and for colleagues. Before you engage in the detailed planning and implementation necessary for quality integrated curriculum, consider your responses to these questions (Jacobs, 1989):

1. How valid are the concepts being fostered within each designated discipline? Is the emphasis on concepts that are important and relevant?

2. How valid is this discipline as a means to explore this theme? Is this a legitimate topic through which to encourage students to use multiple lenses?

3. How important is the central idea? Will it promote flexible thinking and help the students accept multiple views or new ways to solve problems?

4. Will pursuit of this theme enable students to practice an approach to problem solving that will have far-reaching applicability?

One Model for the Design and Development of Integrated Curriculum

If you and your colleagues decide to explore curriculum development using an integrated curriculum approach, we hope the impetus will come primarily from the needs and interests of your students and your own need to challenge yourself as an educator. Above all, we hope the interest in some compelling theme, issue, or problem that demands the attention and a team effort by you, your colleagues, and your students is the driving force behind the integrated curriculum you create. In this section we suggest a model for the development of integrated curriculum and some useful ways for you to identify themes that can shape such integrated curriculum.

▶ ▶ ▶ ▶ The Miller-Allan Model for Developing Curriculum

We recognize that integrated curriculum takes a great deal of time. If you and your colleagues attempt to integrate the curriculum, you will have to balance its demands with the many other pulls that are part of your ongoing work as a teacher of a particular subject in a particular setting. However, we believe that well-designed integrated curriculum can help you consolidate some of the components of the already overcrowded curriculum, identify appropriate ways to assess your students, and create clearer links between national, state, and district curriculum frameworks and standards.

Integrated curriculum does not occur automatically; time and teamwork are both necessary. When you decide to explore and then to plan and implement integrated curriculum with other teachers in different disciplines, you and your colleagues may discover that you need training in curriculum design or in team teaching to achieve the goals and benefits you envision for yourselves and your students. Also, you will need support from the administration in order to change the usual scheduling of your teaching and planning time, as well as the instructional time for the students with whom you plan to carry out the unit. You may even decide to plan the unit during one semester and carry it out the following semester or the next year. Teams for designing and implementing integrated curriculum should have the following characteristics as baseline requirements if they are to succeed (Furner, 1995, p. 5):

- Two or more teachers are involved.
- All teachers share common planning time.

- All teachers share the same students.
- All teachers have skill in and are committed to collaboration, consensus building, and curriculum development.

Even when an appropriate theme is identified with clear objectives and purpose, other factors can inhibit the success of an integrated unit. First, if the project is too broad in scope and length or if it necessitates obtaining a large number of new or varied resources, there is a likelihood of failure. Second, if a study involves too many teachers, students, or outside participants, the chances for failure rise. And if administrative and collegial support are not part of the culture of the school, the chances for fully implementing and sustaining integrated curriculum are greatly reduced.

We recognize that there are an increasing number of models designed to help teachers who wish to engage in integrated curriculum planning (Meinbach, et. al., 1995; Cooper, 1993). Our recent work with student teachers as well as with practitioners in the schools has led us to a model (set out in Figure 11.1) and a set of steps for the development of integrated curriculum that we will use as we examine integrated curriculum design in the remainder of this chapter.

▶ ▶ ▶ ▶ **Preplanning: Finding Worthwhile Themes**

Thoughtful preplanning can enable you to identify the right theme for both you and your students to study. Recall the four sources for finding a worthwhile theme or question discussed earlier in this chapter: goals in the existing curriculum, strands from the national standards or state curriculum frameworks, local issues, and universal problems and concerns. Three specific approaches for finding and focusing on significant themes begin this section of the chapter. In addition, keep in mind that generating phase activities can also help you and your students find and refine worthwhile themes and issues for study.

Three Approaches for Turning Goals and Issues into Viable Themes. Martinello and Cook (1994) have identified three approaches that can assist you in finding significant themes and in turning compelling issues or topics into viable themes for integrated curriculum.

The Question-Driven Approach. Using this approach to finding important themes for integrated curriculum, your team would ask, "Given this topic, how would individuals trained in different disciplines go about exploring this topic? What big ideas are suggested?" As an example, let's take a group of sixth graders in a middle school who ask, "Is it possible that a local species

Figure 11.1

Miller-Allan
Model for Developing
Curriculum

1. **Preplanning to Identify Theme/Focus**
   a. Approaches and activities for finding a significant theme and focus of study
   b. Relation to core curriculum standards and local curriculum requirements

2. **Planning**
   a. Identifying what students might learn
      - Emphasis on constructing meaning—concepts and ideas
      - Strategies and skills to be learned, enhanced, and applied
   b. Selecting a wide range of resources
      - Print sources—fiction and nonfiction, magazines, primary sources, on-line sources
      - People sources—experts, community leaders, citizens in various roles and specializations
      - Community sources—museums, agencies, businesses
   c. Organizing for implementation
      - Designing teaching-learning events, activites, or lessons that may be generating, interacting, or refining
      - Outlining a tentative schedule or time line
      - Organizing the setting—arranging the classroom learning space, modifying schedules for teachers and students
      - Seeking support within the school—teachers at other grade levels or in other disciplines; librarians; technology or media specialists; those in the arts; administrators

3. **Implementing the Integrated Unit**
   a. Activities for generating ideas or initiating the unit (whole class or small group)
   b. Activities for interacting ideas or developing the unit (whole class and small groups)
   c. Activities for refining ideas or ending the unit (small groups, pairs and individual learners)
   d. Formative evaluation guidelines

4. **Assessing students' understandings and the outcomes of the unit as a whole**
   a. Self-evaluation by individual learners; small group evaluation
   b. Sharing with peers and appropriate audiences
   c. Evaluating the team effort and collaborations among students and teachers
   d. Summative evaluation guidelines

like the red-tailed hawk will become extinct?" In asking this question, you realize that a focus on this local concern that your students have expressed is related to a more expansive question: "Can animals, including humans, survive their changing environment?" For their study, your students can discover what adaptation has meant in the past, what it means for the present, and what the implications are for the future. By carrying out this study, students will address their own question about the red-tailed hawk as well as the broader question about survival for all species.

The Significance Approach.   You can use this approach to examine a possible theme or generalization and to decide on its long-term merit as the basis for curriculum design and implementation. For example, if you were using this approach for the hawk issue described above, you would focus on a question about how and why a changing habitat threatens species like the hawk. Your examination would undoubtedly result in your concluding that this is a significant concept worthy of extended study. You would then need to assess whether this question legitimately promotes connections among several disciplines in the existing curriculum such as science, mathematics, and literature. Finally, you could test the theme's or question's significance by asking yourself whether this theme would help students expand their understanding of major issues in the real world.

The Literature-as-Source Approach.   Many universal and significant themes are found in good current young adult fiction and nonfiction. You can tease them out from literature sources yourself. You can get ideas for themes from your students' reading and questions, or you can use a number of recent teacher resources such as *Using Literature in the Middle Grades: A Thematic Approach* (Moss, 1994) or *Books and Beyond: Thematic Approaches for Teaching Literature in the High School* (Gregg & Carroll, 1998) to identify appropriate themes supported in good adolescent and young adult literature. For example, individuals often face conflict when they find themselves living between two worlds—between the customs and the expectations of their own native culture and that of a new land they may have immigrated to. A student could read Diana Kidd's *Onion Tears* (1991), a fictional account of a young person's experience, as well as two nonfiction pieces, Linda Crew's *Children of the River* (1991), and Brent K. and Melissa Ashabranner's *Into a Strange Land: Unaccompanied Refugee Youth in America* (1987) to learn more about the Vietnamese experience in America. Another example of a universal theme is the question of how individual human beings have maintained their nobleness and morality in the face of evil and personal peril in times of tremendous political and societal upheaval. For example, a nonfiction book such as Milton Meltzer's *Rescue: The Story of How*

Gentiles Saved the Jews in the Holocaust (1988) or Lois Lowry's 1994 Caldecott winner, *Number the Stars,* lend themselves to this long-standing, universal problem.

Using Generating Strategies to Find a Theme.   You remember we discussed generating strategies and activities for your students in Chapter 4. You can use these same strategies to find a significant theme for your unit. Brainstorming and webbing are two strategies particularly well suited to the initial process of finding a problem or theme for study.

Brainstorming.   This is a highly useful process for beginning to find themes in the preplanning stage of integrated curriculum development. You and your colleagues can brainstorm many topics or issues arising from multiple sources. You will realize that some of the ideas that surface during your brainstorming will not lead to viable topics or issues for study, while others will appear to be quite viable and worthy of pursuit. The brainstorming process will give you some ideas, as well as questions and resources from which to begin the sorting and prioritizing necessary to shape a thematic study and integrated curriculum.

Webbing.   A process like webbing is also useful in identifying a major topic and related topics and in determining a viable theme or key question to focus on. Once you have brainstormed interesting and relevant topics, you can select one or two of the most significant ones and categorize ideas, concepts and related topics on a web, the graphic organizer we presented in Chapter 4.

For example, a group of middle school teachers decided on the significance of an issue during the preplanning phase of a unit. They knew their students were concerned about how carefully recycling was being carried out in their area and what this meant for safeguarding their environment now and for the future. The teachers brainstormed how their students could pursue this question. Most important, these teachers realized that by having their students participate in a variety of activities in each of their disciplines, they would experience the interconnectedness of the disciplines for studying significant real world issues firsthand.

Teacher as Inquiring Learner Activity

Think about a recent issue or question that has arisen related to your discipline. In pairs or groups of four, talk with some of the other students in this course who are in the same field or discipline to see if they have a similar concern. Next, meet in small groups of three (with students from different disciplines), and talk about the issue or question that you all share. Focus particularly on how different perspectives or different lenses can be used to study an issue or problem. Record these possibilities along with key questions related to the issue that need to be answered. Be certain to discuss how each discipline could help with an exploration of this common issue or question.

▶ ▶ ▶ ▶ **Planning for Integrated Curriculum**

In an integrated curriculum model, students can come to a better understanding of their environment, make decisions, test out assumptions, and develop ownership for the knowledge they are acquiring. Many students, particularly those beyond grade 8, are weak in critical thinking and problem-solving abilities (NAEP, 1994). You can encourage students to become active learners and problem solvers as well as critical thinkers by identifying specific concepts and ideas as well as strategies and skills, by selecting a wide range of resources, and by planning and organizing the schedule and design of lessons and activities that comprise the day-to-day enactment of that curriculum in your own classroom.

Identifying What Students Might Learn: Content Understandings and Strategies.   You should provide experiences for your students that help them acquire the strategies they need to deal with current curricula as well as with future academic and real-world problems. For example, students can apply strategies used to solve problems involving size, quantity, or distance in mathematics to a variety of independent problems and projects beyond the mathematics class. And students who have learned to support an argument using either a letter to the editor or a letter of complaint to a town official as a focus of writing in the language arts will know how to use these strategies in the future when they are disturbed by political or environmental issues in their own community.

Many of the strategies we detailed in Part Two foster students' constructing knowledge as well as ownership and independence in their own learning. These strategies not only help your students be more aware of what they already know, but they also help the students confirm, extend, or refute ideas, concepts, and knowledge they have about the issue or theme under study. Generating strategies such as freewriting, brainstorming, and anticipation guides (described in Chapter 4) help students tap into their background knowledge and the experiences they bring to the unit. At the generating stage, you can model strategies to help your students identify a range of resources, including artifacts and people, that might help them study their issue and find answers to their questions. You can select interacting strategies such as the DR-TA or text pattern guides found in Chapter 5 to support students in finding and interpreting important information in texts as well as in various media and technological sources. To assist students in refining or reconstructing their knowledge, the focus of Chapter 6, you may choose to include summarizing or semantic feature analysis charts, for example. Or you may decide to use the KWL variations described in Chapter 4 and extended in Chapter 7.

Selecting Resources and Gathering Materials to Implement the Study. Since your role as teacher is to act as a guide and facilitator in the initial stages of interdisciplinary theme studies, you may select resources that will assist the students with their study, such as an overview of the topic or ones that will highlight different positions or questions related to their issue or theme. You will need to choose enough sources to make the study feasible for the students at the beginning stages as well as to ensure that there are varied sources, especially related to the students' reading levels, available to them for their own investigations. A variety of objects and artifacts, audiovisuals, and print resources as well as technological support, particularly through the Internet, should be available to involve all of the students engaged in the study in meaningful interaction and investigations. Keep in mind that the resources you find can influence or change the direction of the students' study as well as the direction of your entire unit.

Searching for resources takes a significant amount of time. Therefore, be certain to build this time into your planning, and enlist the help of the librarian or media specialist, technology expert, and other teachers on your team. Divide up tasks, such as finding resources, by topic or type of material. Reach out into the community to identify a variety of sources—texts, people, and community sources that are available and have relevance for the study. The planning stage is an important time to inform others in the school and the local community at large about the theme or issue that is under consideration.

In this role as facilitator or guide for your students' inquiry, there are some useful questions to consider regarding the resources needed to support the issue or theme (Martinello & Cook, 1994, p. 147):

• Where can I find the most appropriate resources for theme study?

• How do I prepare my students to understand the connection between the questions asked and the type of resources to be used?

Teachers and students consider a variety of informational sources in order to answer their resource questions.

CREDIT: © Susie Fitzhugh

- How can I involve my students with the resources so that they can select meaningful data from them?
- How will the students analyze the data they collect by examining these resources? What methods of recording data will they use? What new questions will emerge from the use of these data?

We would add one more question:

- How do I know whether my students have the generating, interacting, and refining strategies or the discipline-based skills to use these resources on their own?

Teacher as Inquiring Learner Activity

In pairs or groups of three or four individuals, discuss the resources that are widely used in your field that you think middle school or high school students should be exposed to and be encouraged to use in classroom and independent investigations—for example, computer simulations, sites on the Internet, references such as atlases or almanacs, or certain science instruments such as microscopes and barometers.

Make a list of some of the resources you use when pursuing work in your discipline or ones that are used in real-world applications of your discipline. Then think about which of these would be especially useful to your own future students. For example, when working with students while pursuing a topic like "Pollution Prevention," your list could include the science text the class is using, which has a chapter on environmental concerns, informational books from the library such as Earth Works Group, *50 Things You Can Do to Save the Earth* (1989), recent newspaper articles, and pamphlets and other documents obtained from the regional EPA center or the Department of the Interior.

Organizing for Implementation. We recognize that to a large degree in elementary schools, teachers have a great deal of autonomy and make decisions about how to shape the day and to weave in disciplines, content, and strategies. At the other extreme, in most high schools, teachers have little to say about their own schedule or those of their students. Most often in the high school, the arrangement to accommodate the different disciplines and the numbers of students is a departmentalized structure, with teachers grouped together who teach in the same discipline area. The usual department structure tends to lead to rigidity and lack of integration among subject areas, as well as to barriers between teachers' and students' working together. The department structure also reinforces the notion that knowledge is compartmentalized by the separate disciplines. The goal to create integrated curriculum fosters cross-discipline mini-departments between and among teachers of different disciplines.

At the middle school level, however, we are finding increasing numbers of teams of teachers working together to create and implement comprehensive academic programs for specific groups of students at a single grade level. In fact, 86 percent of the so-called "schools for excellence" designated by the U.S. Department of Education were made up of small teams of four to five different subject-area teachers working with the same students in the same building area and planning together what their students would study across disciplines.

No matter what the organization or scheduling decisions are in your school, they should be aligned with the curriculum priorities and the themes and topics being studied—those that are mandated and those that a particular group of teachers creates to serve the academic and future needs of a particular population of middle school or high school students. Scheduling arrangements should accommodate interconnections of the disciplines as well as coordination among teachers and their students. Any group of teachers attempting to integrate their disciplines would find the following principles pertaining to planning and flexible scheduling very helpful (George & Alexander, 1993):

- Prioritizing—focusing on what is most important
- Keeping instructional responsiveness to students at the forefront of all planning
- Viewing scheduling as a collaborative effort to facilitate work with other teachers as well as a way to meet students' needs
- Viewing teaching and learning as the goals that the schedule allows you to reach
- Seeing scheduling as a never-ending process indicative of change that is necessary as mandates in the discipline or the district change and as students change

The *block schedule,* an increasingly popular scheduling approach, fosters teachers of different disciplines working together with a common group or groups of students. The two most common arrangements of the block schedule are the equivalent of two class periods being used for a single course or unit or the split between courses with two teachers working together and sharing the planning and implementing of two consecutive periods. In either case, the teachers need time in their own schedules beyond the periods in which they are working with students to develop shared curriculum goals and to have sufficient discussion and planning time before implementing any new courses or units. When the schedule in a middle school or a high school is altered to accommodate new courses or units of study, everything in the school day will be affected: staffing patterns, course offerings, meeting students' individual needs, and even the allocation of resources (labs, technology, libraries) shared throughout the school. Therefore, the teachers who engage in such an effort should be mindful of the impact of the curriculum innovation they are involved with in order to maximize their own chance for success and to lessen any disruption to other teachers and students' ongoing course work and curriculum needs.

A block schedule such as the one in Table 11.2 is generally characterized as a plan that permits teachers of different disciplines interested in implementing integrated or thematic curriculum to have longer periods in which to work with a given group of students as well as with one another. You can see

Table 11.2   Sample Block Schedule for a Sixth-Grade Middle School Team

Student Group A

Time blocks (in minutes)	75	75	Lunch	50	50	50
Courses	Language arts Reading	Science Social studies		Math	Physical education	Exploratory (arts, vocational)

Student Group B

Time blocks (in minutes)	50	50	50	Lunch	75	75
Courses	Math	Physical education	Exploratory (arts, vocational)		Language arts Reading	Science Social studies

Note: At mid-year the students would switch their schedules, allowing for each group to have the longer blocks (75 minutes) with the major disciplines in the morning.

Source: P. S. George and W. M. Alexander, *The Exemplary Middle School* (2nd ed.) (Fort Worth, TX: Harcourt Brace, 1993).

in the table that language arts, reading, social studies, and science are offered in 75-minute blocks back to back every day of the week. This arrangement would enable a sixth-grade middle school team a great deal of flexibility throughout the year. The team could focus on single or coordinated discipline work within the 75-minute time blocks, and they could have as much as 150 minutes with an entire group of students for work on an integrated unit.

Students and their teachers benefit from flexibility in the schedule because differences in learning needs can be met more effectively and different types of content and resources can be used. When there is the possibility of longer time periods than the usual 45 minutes per subject, accommodations can be made for large group instruction, lab experiments and computer simulations, small group work, and individualized or independent study opportunities for students. When the administration supports teachers' scheduling days, weeks and even semesters creatively and flexibly to meet the needs of their students and to complement the subject matter, often the best teaching and learning ensues.

Teacher as Inquiring Learner Activity

Think about the schedule you followed when you were a middle school (or junior high school) and high school student.

• Did the schedule make sense to you? Did you feel your schedule added continuity to your academic experience, or did it tend to reinforce the separation of the disciplines from one another and from your everyday life? Did you ever get confused by the schedule or have trouble fitting in both your requirements and choices you wanted, such as art or orchestra? Did you ever have a period longer than forty-five or fifty minutes for a given course? Did you ever participate in a class or a course that two teachers from different disciplines taught?

Now that you have reflected on your own experiences, think about what you have observed recently as a student teacher at the middle school or the high school level.

• Did you have any difficulty getting accustomed to the schedule of the classes you taught or to getting to know who your students were, much less their abilities and their needs?

Talk with classmates in your same discipline and with classmates in other disciplines who are interested in teaching at the same grade level as you are to see what their experiences have been related to the scheduling of classes.

▶ ▶ ▶ ▶ **Implementing the Integrated Unit**

Teachers need to model and to provide many opportunities for students to engage in their own learning (*Breaking Ranks,* 1996). The activities you develop and the learning environments that you create for your students should give them opportunities to think critically when they are presented with an issue or problem that they have to clarify or sort out. Your students should have a number of opportunities to compare and contrast information from different sources, as well as to find patterns and relationships. They should be helped to synthesize information when they try to brainstorm solutions to problems, when they make predictions and attempt to confirm these predictions, and when they create a model, a diagram, or a plan to explain something they have discovered or developed to others.

Throughout the implementation stage of a unit, you can provide choices for your students to help them gain confidence in their own decision-making ability and to experience alternate routes to solving problems. First, you should continuously model and support the strategies you want students to use. Second, if you want your students to develop problem-solving abilities and be able to apply both strategies and skills, you should provide opportunities for them to gather and analyze data on their own. And finally, you should foster opportunities for your students to share their findings with the community in the form of information and service. Encourage the community to regard the school as a place where problems and issues that affect everyone are being investigated and as a place where they can raise questions and issues to inform the curriculum.

Many of the strategies we explained in Part Two are useful in helping students deepen and extend their ownership of content and the concepts and ideas from different disciplines related to an issue being studied. These strategies also foster connections between students' current understandings of data and their implications for future situations in the real world.

Activities for Generating Ideas or Initiating the Unit. In any content area when your students' background knowledge is activated, their learning is enhanced. As we demonstrated in Chapter 4 on generating ideas, prior knowledge includes not only content-specific knowledge and past experiences but also information about effective strategies for learning. The concepts, feelings, and experiences students access are part of their schemata to use to understand new content, materials, and situations. The initial lessons of an integrated unit may focus on having a number of shared experiences for the entire class using the same materials such as viewing a video or working with a computer simulation. At this initiating stage, the goal is for your students to begin investigating the topic or theme by building on their prior knowledge in a meaningful way related to this issue or topic.

When planning your daily lessons in your integrated unit, you'll want to use generating activities such as brainstorming and webbing to introduce your unit and to create a common initiating activity for all students. Webs and other graphic organizers are also particularly useful in integrated curriculum because they enable teachers and students to examine how different disciplines explore an issue or question. When individual students or small groups share their graphic organizers, differences of opinion and additional questions about a topic often surface. Such differences or contradictions related to a topic frequently come to be the basis for the investigations that students pursue during the interacting phase of the unit.

During the initiating phase of a unit, students should begin to use the resources you have collected during the preplanning stage. You may choose to adapt the tasks and materials to meet the individual needs of different learners in your class. You may decide to use tools such as the anticipation guides described in Chapter 4 to help your students use new texts or resources.

At this stage, you can also model previewing and predicting as strategies for your students to use with their texts. If you have introduced these strategies to your students earlier and your informal assessment during this phase shows that the students are not using them effectively, you should remind the students or review the procedures with the content at hand. You may also need to enlist the aid of resource staff members such as the reading specialist, a resource teacher for learning disabled students, or the English as a Second Language teacher to help the students complete activities and to use resources supporting the integrated curriculum unit.

Activities for Interacting with Ideas or Developing the Unit.   While your students are grappling with new information they have found in the resources you provided, comparing this information to prior knowledge, and integrating new information with prior information, they are transforming their thinking on a subject and interacting with ideas. Overall the emphasis at this stage is on helping students find what is important related to the topic, issue, or theme they are studying, as well as how ideas and concepts connect.

Each student should be guided to look for the important big ideas in text they are reading, videos they are viewing, and technology they are interacting with. You should also encourage your students to find supporting details related to the major ideas from a number of sources at this stage. Do not overlook the value of a core text or set of readings for the entire class to use. DRAs, comprehension guides, and text pattern guides are particularly useful tools to assist students at this stage in their work.

As students find important information that is directly related to the questions, they might need the supporting strategies of constructing auxiliary aids, such as the note-taking graphics we introduced in Chapter 5. They may need to learn how to record data and how to organize various pieces of data from their own search. By introducing your students to different formats such as note taking, math notations, oral recordings, and graphic organizers, as well as schematic representations, you can continue to give them tools useful for demonstrating their thinking in classrooms as well as in the real world.

You will notice that there is much fluidity at this stage in the unit. Students are working with and interacting with various peer groups and alone. Strategic learners will continue the task with little or no guidance. You can support the nonstrategic learners with teaching tools that will introduce them to appropriate strategies. You and your colleagues who are working on an integrated unit will also find yourselves in a variety of roles as you model particular strategies for the entire class or a small group, confer with small groups who are engaged in discussions or working with certain resources, and helping individual students interact with the text and the content they are attempting to understand and to use on their own.

Activities for Refining Ideas or Ending the Unit.   At this third stage, the refining stage, which is the focus of Chapter 6, you should ask strategic learners to view the theme or topic as a whole. For this reason, much of the work at this stage centers on opportunities to bring the entire group or class together. Students may review the thinking they did at the prereading stage of the unit. They can identify what similarities or contrasts among data have been uncovered by their classmates and what new information has been found. The most useful strategies at this stage are categorizing ideas and summarizing, which were described in detail in Chapter 6. Encourage students to reflect on the different ideas and views they have been exposed to in order to draw conclusions about the topic or issue. At this stage, you can instruct and help students add to the notes or outlines they have created in the interacting stage of the unit. Because the emphasis is on taking time to review, reflect on, and revisit information, you should plan for sufficient time for individuals, pairs, and small groups to refine and reconstruct the ideas they have developed during the generating and interacting phases.

By writing drafts, summaries, and graphic organizers, students at this stage often refine their purpose or revise their thinking about a topic. As students summarize their findings in these ways, you will notice where there are missing pieces of information and where there are conflicting views or opinions. You should encourage your students to revisit text that they have previously studied and to seek additional sources that might answer their new questions or solve a dilemma that has arisen. When new questions also emerge at this stage, you should encourage your students to research those and to follow the various paths of inquiry that they dictate. At this stage, students might do surveys or carry out experiments, and they will need the strategies and tools we discussed in Chapter 7.

If the problem your students pursue is to have authentic implications, they must have opportunities to communicate their findings to others whom it affects. Therefore, you should encourage students to share the results of their investigations with others in their immediate setting, like the students at their own grade level or their entire high school population, others in the field or profession that deals with the issue or topic studied, or others in the broader community in which they live. They can do this in the form of pamphlets, how-tos, speeches, or panel presentations as well as letters to the editor of a local newspaper or articles for a school newspaper. Each of these communications provides a powerful culminating activity for your students, as well as a means for them to influence appropriate audiences, in school and in the larger community, in a real way.

▶ ▶ ▶ ▷   ## Assessing Students' Understandings and the Outcomes of the Unit as a Whole

Students who are working with integrated curriculum units should have many opportunities to engage in interactive and meaningful assessment authentically related to the issue they are studying. They should state and support their conclusions or opinions; critique something they have read, seen, or heard; or establish criteria for a situation or an event based on their firsthand experience.

During the planning stage of the unit, you and the other teachers you are working with can identify assessment tools and criteria for performance that correspond to the objectives of the unit. As you recognize the students' different learning needs and their use of different strategies, you should encourage the students to demonstrate their understandings through a variety of modalities—for example, interviews, observations, and a wide variety of written forms like journals, logs, outlines, and drafts. Students will also demonstrate their understandings of the theme, issue, or problem when using various project-related assessment tools like checklists and inventories, as well as through their creation of videotapes and audiotapes and their participation in the visual and performing arts.

Multifaceted Assessment and Integrated Curriculum.   A multifaceted approach to assessment will enable each student to demonstrate understanding in appropriate and meaningful ways. You and the other teachers in the team can use the various formats your students develop during the refining stage of a unit, such as pamphlets and how-tos, letters to the editor and to town officials, and displays and models, to evaluate your students' individual and collective understandings of the theme or issue focused on in the integrated unit. For example, students who studied the impact of pollution on their own lives might engage in a schoolwide pollution prevention campaign, which could include a focus on their own school and the role of their peers in an effort to reduce waste in the school lunchroom. In addition, based on the knowledge they have gained during their research on the problem, students might write letters to the city council, the mayor, or the planning board to try to initiate changes in the local laws that would make people and industries in their area more environmentally responsible. Through such authentic school- and community-based activities, students would be able to see the impact their investigations might have on their own lives and others they know. In addition to teacher evaluation and feedback, students need opportunities to engage in self-evaluation of their learning using the criteria or rubrics developed to go along with their projects.

Looking at students' work in progress (as seen in the teaching/assessing tools covered in Chapters 4, 5, and 6), teachers and the students get a more complete picture of how effectively students are gaining new understandings and using their skills and competencies. In particular, students' work done individually or that done with a partner or small group during the interacting and refining phases of study provides many rich opportunities for both teachers and learners to assess understandings and progress. Students' individual work in progress such as math calculations to solve a word problem, drafts of lab reports in science, story maps or learning logs to record impressions and understandings of a chapter book in literature reflect work in progress during the interacting phase. Likewise, a student's participation in a group discussion, a lab experiment with a partner, or feedback during peer writing conferences provides valuable data to both the student and teacher.

Teachers can use data from ongoing assessment of their students to add to and to modify groupings they planned at the beginning of a unit. Teachers view individual students' work in progress and the day-to-day work of the class as the data for evaluating their students' learning as well as material for shaping and revising their own ongoing modeling and explaining and direct instruction. Anecdotal records and observations are very important tools for the teacher at this stage. For example, a teacher's collective observations of several pairs of students struggling as peer editors with an effective paragraph structure may lead the teacher to develop a mini-lesson focusing on the structure and purpose of introductory and concluding paragraphs in expository writing.

Another benefit of the assessment associated with integrated curriculum that benefits teachers and ultimately the students is the information that teachers share about how well the students as a group and individual students are grappling with the major concepts and content of the unit. In other words, teachers in one discipline may learn about a student's strategies (or lack of strategies) from their observations, interviews, and conferences with students in their discipline that will be useful to other teachers on the team as they organize groups or carry out instruction for the class as a whole or attempt to meet an individual student's needs. Often specialists such as the reading specialist, the English as a Second Language teacher, or the special needs teacher can offer insights and suggestions from their ongoing assessment of the students they work with to support learning by all students involved in the integrated unit. Because teachers are experts in different disciplines with different learning demands, they may get different impressions of what students know and can do. Using cross-disciplinary assessment data to plan and to modify the teaching and learning activities of the integrated unit is another positive outcome of a team effort that benefits both the teachers and their students.

Teachers involved in collaborative planning and implementation often create criteria that work across the disciplines and therefore align their assessment procedures and their evaluation of students. The development of criteria across disciplines helps teachers strengthen and clarify the overarching goals of the curriculum, the purpose of their teaching, and the measures of accountability for their students. For example, a team of high school teachers adopted a generic rubric for writing research papers across disciplines to be used in an integrated unit connecting English/language arts, history, and the arts. The teachers discussed what was necessary at the high school level to qualify as a quality research paper and provided the students with a generic rubric (shown in Table 11.3), which the students could continue to use and to refine throughout their high school experience.

The Role of Portfolios in Integrated Curriculum.   The role that portfolios play in integrated curriculum highlights the relationship between authentic assessment and instruction and the emphasis on process learning within a realistic framework. Collectively, portfolios are a powerful source of data from which a teacher or team can assess the outcomes of their instruction and the activities in their content-area classrooms, as well as the development and implementation of the unit as a whole. No matter what the precise format or purpose, portfolios that accompany integrated curriculum as well as the single or coordinated discipline work, which make up any given student's school experience should meet these guidelines (Mcmillan, 1997, p. 232):

- Based on specific learning targets
- Systematic, well organized
- Built on preestablished guidelines for selecting content and for the evaluation of work samples
- Demonstrative of student engagement in selection of products as well as reflection on their work
- Inclusive of student-teacher conferences to review progress, identify areas for improvement, facilitate student reflection

Portfolios may differ in purpose, in format, and in use. They may be as individual as the students who create them. Regardless of whether the portfolio is the *collection type*, with many works in progress as well as finished projects, or a *showcase portfolio*, with carefully selected works meant to represent the student's best work for a unit, a semester, or an entire academic year, it may be constructed for a single discipline or across disciplines.

In addition to their own work, you should encourage students to include in their portfolios assessment data that other teachers have contributed, such as conference notes, entries in a dialogue journal, or a discussion checklist.

Table 11.3   Rubric for a High School Research Paper

	Criteria for Writing Component		
	Distinguished	**Proficient**	**Not Proficient**
Thesis	Clearly defined and sustained throughout Topic effectively limited	Stated Attempt to limit topic	Unclear or unidentifiable No attempt to limit topic
Development	Topic thoroughly developed throughout with specific examples to support thesis	Topic developed General supporting evidence	Topic not developed clearly Unnecessary information
Organization	Highly organized plan with effective transitions Superior introduction and conclusion clearly relate to whole	Logical organization, but with inconsistent transitions Introduction and conclusion relate to whole	No organizational plan No attempt to create unity No transitions
Research	Four or more qualified sources cited appropriately Bibliography includes three or more types of sources (books and interviews, for example)	Three qualified sources cited Bibliography includes two types of sources (books and interviews, for example)	Fewer than three qualified sources cited Bibliography includes only one type of source
Mechanics	Superior editing (fewer than four total errors in paper) in the following areas: • punctuation • capitalization • spelling	Careful editing (no more than one error per page) in the following areas: • sentence structure • run on/fragment • verb usage	Careless editing (more than one error per page) in the following areas: • subject/verb agree • pronoun usage • point of view • manuscript form

Source: Sills-Briegel, T., Fisk, C. & Dunlop, V. (1996/1997), "Grading by Exhibition" *Educational Leadership*, 54, (4), p. 68. Used by permission of the Association for Supervision & Curriculum Development. Copyright © 1985 by ACSD. All rights reserved.

They should also include evaluations that peers have contributed to, such as evaluations of their oral or written retellings, peer editing comments on a story or expository piece, or written feedback on a culminating project.

The greatest benefit that portfolios provide to students is the student's own metacognitive reflection on the knowledge gained, the strategies that worked, and the pride and motivation he or she experienced while carrying out the varied tasks and creating the different products in the unit. By participating in the setting of criteria for judging the merit of their work, selecting which items will be representative of them as a student, and carrying out self-evaluation and reflection on the items themselves and on their process as a learner, students participating in portfolio assessment gain a new depth of understanding and a new sense of ownership that extends beyond any single assignment and beyond the particular unit or content. Therefore, although portfolios may be included in both single discipline or coordinated discipline settings, we include them with integrated as well because reflection on process and product, which is an important aspect of the portfolio approach, aligns closely with integrated curriculum's emphasis on students' achieving ownership of their learning as well as competency as problem solvers and critical thinkers.

Teacher as Inquiring Learner Activity

Review the different types of data collecting (assessment) sources we set out in this chapter as well as the teaching/assessing tools we examined in Chapters 4, 5, and 6.

- How many of the sources we have discussed and explained have you had firsthand experience with either as a student or as a teacher?

List the types of data collecting you are familiar with and the examples you remember producing yourself or seeing students produce in the classes where you have observed or have student taught. Compare your list with someone who is in the same discipline, and see if you have any assessment tools in common. Decide whether these assessment tools have particular relevance to your field and the sorts of activities an individual who is a scientist, a historian, or an economist uses daily at work. Now compare your list with that of someone in another discipline and see which tools are the same and which are different. Choose one assessment tool to focus on.

- What can you learn about students from this assessment tool? How do you think a good student's performance would differ from a poor student's? What criteria would you use to judge students using this tool?

Working with Other Teachers: The Importance of Teams to Integrated Curriculum

We have indicated throughout this text that no one model of curriculum design or instruction is consistently appropriate for a single teacher or a group of teachers. Nevertheless, we do believe that the team approach is absolutely necessary in order for the interdisciplinary connections of an integrated curriculum to work. Quite simply, cooperation among teachers of different disciplines is essential.

Teachers who have participated on effective teams often mention significant changes for themselves as professionals in terms of their own heightened sense of competence in decision making. Many teachers say that the support of the team enabled them collectively or individually to work more effectively with the administrators, parents, and counselors who are also involved with their students. Among the benefits teachers mention are these:

- More approaches to deal with an overcrowded curriculum

- More opportunities for student individualization and less isolation for students

- More support to deal with external demands such as standards for their students and professional expectations for themselves

- More resources (human) to deal with the increasing diversity and heterogeneity in the student populations found in their schools and classrooms

- More opportunities collectively and individually to work effectively with other constituencies: administrators, parents, and counselors

- More opportunities as a group to do in-depth planning and creative problem solving beyond what any one individual could have achieved alone

Teacher as Inquiring Learner Activity

Determine whether there are any teams of teachers working on curriculum in the middle school or high school where you are doing your field-based experience. Also consider whether your own college or department offers any integrated courses or programs. Many undergraduate colleges now offer programs focused on community service-learning, which is often interdisciplinary in nature. For example, in our college, a team of social studies, science, and technology faculty are working on a new course, entitled Interdisciplinary Curriculum for the Middle School, which will emphasize many ways in which the disciplines can be interconnected as well as how technology is integrated across the curriculum.

Interview a teacher who is a member of a team. Find out what the stimulus was for the team to be created and what its major purpose is. Ask the individual to describe what the advantages are for him or her personally as an educator and what the advantages are for the students. Be sure to ask if there are any disadvantages or weaknesses in the model for him or her personally or for the students. Record your findings, and then share them with other students in your class who have talked with individuals in other disciplines and in different settings.

- Have your classmates found some of the same advantages and some of the same frustrations with team teaching that you have found?

▶ ▶ ▶ ▶ Guidelines for Interdisciplinary Teams

In order to design and develop the kind of integrated curriculum that we have described at the beginning of the chapter, we believe a team approach is the most useful structure. Just like any other team situation, there are rules or norms that maximize the possibility that a curriculum team can succeed as an entity and that a successful integrated unit will be the result of their work together. Certain guidelines for team building seem to help maximize the potential for success at the beginning of the team unit building process. Too often when teachers who are each experts in their own domains come together, they do not attend to the early stages of team building that are highlighted in these guidelines, and their efforts are minimized or even doomed from the beginning. You might even use these same guidelines when you and a group of your classmates set out to do a collaborative class assignment in the future (Maurer, 1994).

Guidelines for Collaborative Curriculum Building

1. Start with an aim to clarify your purpose and arrive at a unified sense of the reason for doing this project together.

2. Make decisions by consensus, not by majority, and be able to admit that conflict may exist.

3. Work toward and value active listening that will lead to understanding differences.

4. Gain administrative support for the team and its work.

5. Pilot a few lessons as a first step, and examine the results.

6. Solicit, examine, and value feedback from parents, administrators, and students both during and at the culmination of the project.

7. Place the goals and purpose of the team as the focus of each individual's participation, while honoring the other memberships and responsibilities a member may have.

▶ ▶ ▶ ▷ ## Allowing Sufficient Time

Once you and a group of colleagues decide to pursue integrated curriculum and to use the team model, the single most important factor that appears to determine whether a team will succeed is their awareness of and their acceptance of the amount of time collaboration takes (see Figure 11.2). Teaming to achieve integrated curriculum appears to be an evolutionary process. Before any real curriculum development work can be done, the team members need time to organize the working structure of the team and to decide on the various roles for the participants. In essence, just like with a sports team you have participated on, in order to function as a unit, teachers need time to get to know one another and to build community among themselves. They need time to get to know one another's strengths and interests that can be brought to bear on the project at hand.

In the early stages of integrated curriculum, it is important for the team to take the time to disseminate information about the project on an ongoing basis in order to gain the support for and the understanding of the goals and the outcomes within the school, the district, and the community. Once the interdisciplinary thematic study is launched, the plan is in place, and the implementation of instruction has begun, team members need time to meet in order to assess and revise their instruction. Team members also need time throughout the implementation to meet with other constituencies such as administrators, parents, and community representatives as well as to contact and work with people and agencies outside the school to further the particular theme or topic.

Finally, team members and students participating in the study need time to assess the outcomes in terms of student performance and learning and to use that information to refine and to build curriculum. Throughout the team process, participants should assess the effectiveness of the unit to see how effectively it is meeting the designated goals and outcomes related to the issue or theme under study. The effect of the team effort on the participants, both the teachers and their students, should also be continuously evaluated.

Figure 11.2

Time Allocation and
Integrated Curriculum

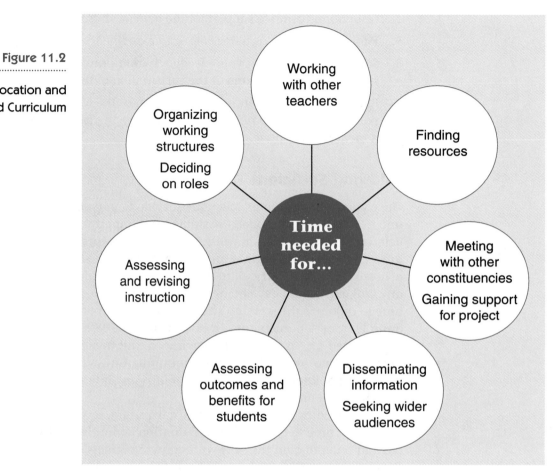

In addition to the importance of time and all of its implications, if teachers are going to attempt to do things differently instructionally and organizationally, they need incentives that will explicitly confirm the commitment of the administration while at the same time support the changes they are attempting. Such things as relief from some usual building assignments, block or cohort programming with other team members, and classroom coverage for interventions and training opportunities seem to make the most significant difference to the teachers who are engaged with their colleagues in designing and implementing integrated curriculum (Beane, 1995). Finally, teachers need to have the support of and understanding by the administration and their colleagues that the first attempts with integrated curriculum are pilots from which everyone—the administration, the teachers, and the students—can benefit and learn. These teachers need to be able to show other teachers in their school, especially those in their departments, that their success can be reasonably replicated in other classrooms.

▶ ▶ ▶ ▶ Assessment Questions

Before a new unit becomes a permanent part of the curriculum and before other teachers are asked to replicate what one team has done, the teaming effort and its effectiveness in meeting its goals related to creating integrated curriculum that benefits both students and teachers should be assessed, and each team participant should be expected to respond. An assessment instrument might be developed to include questions designed for the three important constituent groups affected by the teaming effort and the integrated curriculum: the students, the participating teachers, and the parents. In order to refine or improve the integrated curriculum they have designed and implemented, teachers should evaluate the effectiveness of their team and the outcomes of its planning and collaboration through such questions as these (Rehbeck in Lounsbury, 1992):

1. Were the activities for students planned to involve all students without competition?
2. Were different activities planned that encouraged students with diverse needs and interests to interact with their peers?
3. Were parents invited to join school activities, and were they informed of student academic achievement and behavior?
4. Were team members cooperative, and did they support one another?
5. Were responsibilities for collecting resources and designing activities as well as decision making shared by the team members?
6. Did curriculum planning occur as a team?
7. Were students involved in the planning and in the decision making?
8. Did the team members acknowledge both the accomplishments and the shortcomings of the team effort as it affected both them and their students?

▶ ▶ ▶ ▶ A School Vision

All of the benefits of teaming and the development of integrated curriculum in middle schools and high schools will be fruitless unless they are part of systemic planning and commitment by a number of constituencies: the teachers in the team and their other grade-level or discipline-based colleagues, the building-level administration, and even the central administration. In order to support integrated curriculum, a school community needs to develop a school vision or goal that places value on integration and connectedness across the disciplines, teacher involvement in and commitment to the vision, administrative support for teaming, and planning time and in-service for the teachers who will design and implement the integrated curriculum. If the schools in which you work are going to be transformed by integrated curriculum, there must be commitment to the development and maintenance of a variety of internal structures like the scheduling of students and courses, planning time for teachers, and the reallocation and the addition of resources to foster this approach. No matter how appropriate the theme you have chosen and how carefully you and your colleagues have pursued the preplanning and planning steps of designing integrated curriculum, if the structures are not in place to support your teaming with other teachers and alternative scheduling for your students, you and your colleagues will not be able to change our schools and the learning opportunities for your students with integrated curriculum. Integrated, interdisciplinary curriculum and the challenges and promises it offers to middle school and high school teachers and their students is at its very core school reform. "Though far from a panacea . . . the interdisciplinary [integrated] model is still the most powerful and appropriate way to reconstruct our classrooms [today and for the future]" (Panaritis, 1995, p. 628).

Two Sample Integrated Thematic Units

You will now have the opportunity to see how two different teams of teachers, one at the middle school level and one at the high school level, planned, implemented, and assessed an issues-based integrated curriculum unit. You will learn what the impetus was for the topic focused on, and you will see how two teams of teachers used the Miller-Allan Model for Developing Curriculum (refer back to Figure 11.1). You will also get a clear sense of how teachers in different disciplines work together to support one another, their students, and the unit as a whole. A planning web accompanies each thematic unit. Each web shows the activities explicitly described in the text as well as some additional connections that could be made to other disciplines. These additional suggestions would allow teachers to tailor the unit to meet specific learning needs and interests of their own students more effectively, as well as to meet the particular curriculum frameworks in their state or guidelines in their districts.

Sample Unit Plans

Sample Middle School Unit: "Our Environment: Home, School, Town, Planet Earth"

This unit, described in an article in the Journal of Adolescent and Adult Literacy *(Heller, 1997), uses a big issue—the state of the environment as we envision the future and the year 2000—to look across the curriculum and see how integrated curriculum might be implemented. Applying the Miller-Allan model for the development of a thematic, integrated unit, you can see where questions were explored and where various strategies and skills were used by the sixth-grade middle schoolers who were engaged in this collaboratively constructed two-week thematic unit. (See Figure 11.3 for a graphic overview of the unit and the disciplines covered.)*

Preplanning

The thematic unit was a collaborative effort between a university researcher/teacher educator and a sixth-grade middle school teacher interested in exploring the use of student-centered thematic study to help the students find relevance in the content and to become more actively engaged in learning. The focus of the thematic unit was on the sixth-grade students' studying the concepts of conservation, preservation, and estimation in the context of their reading/language arts, social studies, science, and mathematics curricula in order to envision the state of the environment in the future and what role they as citizens could play in determining that future.

Planning

The teachers identified what students might learn in the form of specific objectives and learner outcomes:

- An awareness and understanding of the concepts of conservation, preservation, and estimation in the context of environmental issues

- Enhanced critical thinking through conversation and discussion about environmental issues and their immediacy for the students and their world

- Development of critical and creative writing inspired by study of the environment in children's literature, print and nonprint media, and discipline-based readings and activities

Figure 11.3 How the Disciplines Work Together in a Middle School Thematic Unit

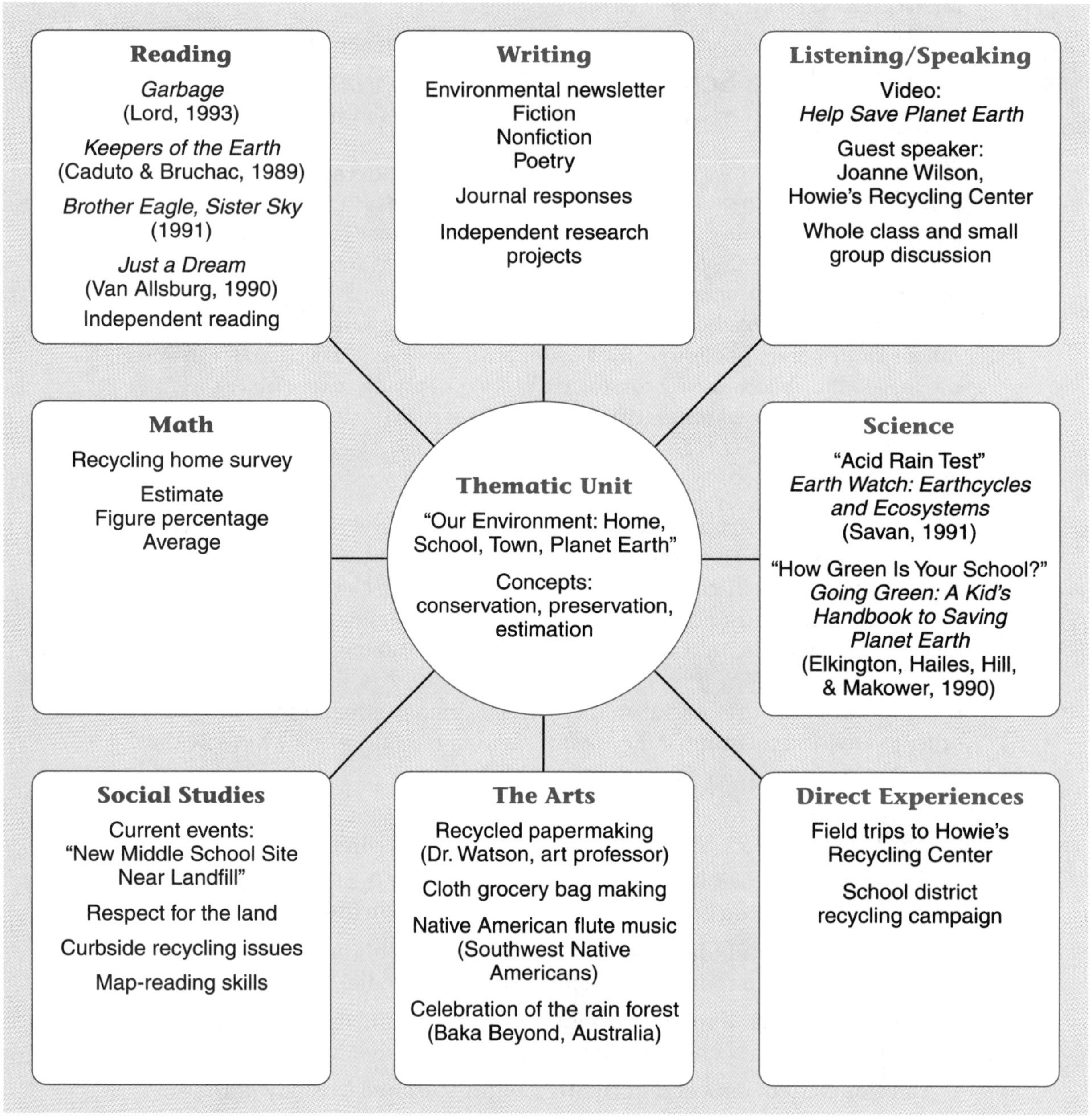

Reading

Garbage
(Lord, 1993)

Keepers of the Earth
(Caduto & Bruchac, 1989)

Brother Eagle, Sister Sky
(1991)

Just a Dream
(Van Allsburg, 1990)

Independent reading

Writing

Environmental newsletter
Fiction
Nonfiction
Poetry

Journal responses

Independent research
projects

Listening/Speaking

Video:
Help Save Planet Earth

Guest speaker:
Joanne Wilson,
Howie's Recycling Center

Whole class and small
group discussion

Math

Recycling home survey

Estimate
Figure percentage
Average

Thematic Unit

"Our Environment: Home,
School, Town, Planet Earth"

Concepts:
conservation, preservation,
estimation

Science

"Acid Rain Test"
*Earth Watch: Earthcycles
and Ecosystems*
(Savan, 1991)

"How Green Is Your School?"
*Going Green: A Kid's
Handbook to Saving
Planet Earth*
(Elkington, Hailes, Hill,
& Makower, 1990)

Social Studies

Current events:
"New Middle School Site
Near Landfill"

Respect for the land

Curbside recycling issues

Map-reading skills

The Arts

Recycled papermaking
(Dr. Watson, art professor)

Cloth grocery bag making

Native American flute music
(Southwest Native
Americans)

Celebration of the rain forest
(Baka Beyond, Australia)

Direct Experiences

Field trips to Howie's
Recycling Center

School district
recycling campaign

Source: Figure from Heller, Mary F. (1997, February). "Reading and Writing About the Environment: Visions of the Year 2000" from *Journal of Adolescent and Adult Literacy 40*, (5), 332–341. Reprinted by permission.

Figure 11.4

Sample Items from the
Self-Assessment
Checklist

____ I made a recyclable materials cover for my Environmental
Awareness portfolio.

____ I completed the survey of environmentally safe and recyclable
products found in my home.

____ I made suggestions for our list of enviromental research questions
and tried to find the answer to one or more of the questions from
current news articles or other media sources.

____ I read at least one book about environmental issues and
responded in my journal.

Source: M. F. Heller (1997). Reading and Writing About the Environment: Visions for the Year 2000. *Journal of
Adolescent and Adult Literacy*, 40(5): 335.

The teachers developed an overview of the entire unit. Then they turned the
overview and major goals into a self-assessment checklist, "Our Environment—Home, School, Town, Planet Earth," for each of the students to use as a
guide in their whole class, small group, and individual study for the two-week
period of the unit. (See Figure 11.4.)

Implementing

Activity for Generating Ideas or Initiating the Unit.   The teachers began
the unit by posing the following question to the students in a whole class setting: *"What concerns you most about our environment as we approach the year
2000?"* This question provided the middle school students with a framework
for discussion. It also gave the teachers and the students a chance to see what
background knowledge the students had about the environment. The discussion made apparent what questions the students had and what might be interesting topics about which they could do further writing, reading, and research related to the environment. The environmental issues that the
students believed most touched their lives were air, water, and land pollution;
the need to recycle; and the concern for endangered plant and animal life,
particularly on the prairie of the United States, where they lived.

Activities for Interacting with Ideas or Developing the Unit.   Next, the
teachers distributed a one-page home survey of questions in order to
heighten the students' awareness of the day-to-day impact of these environmental issues and to connect the study to the real life of the community (see

Figure 11.5

Some Sample
Questions
on the Survey

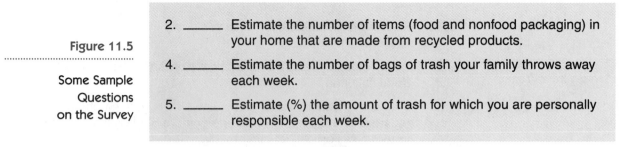

2. _____ Estimate the number of items (food and nonfood packaging) in your home that are made from recycled products.

4. _____ Estimate the number of bags of trash your family throws away each week.

5. _____ Estimate (%) the amount of trash for which you are personally responsible each week.

Source: M. F. Heller (1997). Reading and Writing About the Environment: Visions for the Year 2000. *Journal of Adolescent and Adult Literacy*, 40(5): 336.

Figure 11.5). This survey also functioned as a vehicle to involve the parents in the study.

The survey inspired much class discussion as the students began sharing their results with peers, teachers, and parents. The survey results prompted an interest in further research in the form of some scientific experiments that the students could carry out in the classroom. This survey offered numerous opportunities for the students to apply understandings and strategies they had learned in mathematics in meaningful ways. They charted the data and figured the percentage of surveys returned each day. In addition, students had opportunities to practice their skills in estimating, averaging, and figuring percentages using the data that they were compiling from the surveys.

The class as a whole viewed a public service video, *Help Save Planet Earth,* to help them identify significant environmental issues around the world. The teachers encouraged the students to discuss and to write their personal responses to this video as a way of interacting with media and helping them focus their investigations about the environment on issues and ideas that were beyond what they already knew or believed about the topic. The teachers read aloud from fiction, such as recent picture books (Lynne Cherry's *The Great Kapok Tree* [1993] and Susan Jeffers' *Brother Eagle and Sister Sky: A Message From Chief Seattle* [1993]), from nonfiction sources (such as Paul Shower's, *Where Does the Garbage Go?*, 1974), and from environmental poetry (such as Shel Silverstein's "Sarah Cynthia Sylvia Stout" in *Where the Sidewalk Ends* [1974]). The teachers read to the students daily to extend the students' knowledge of the topic, to raise additional questions for the group to consider, and to provide models for students' own written responses. After the read-alouds, the teachers asked the students open-ended questions to stimulate critical and creative thinking about the environmental issues they were studying.

In addition, every student read and responded to a self-selected book dealing with an environmental issue. The students researched an environmental issue by reading a variety of texts and specialized periodicals such as *Audubon* and *Sierra* focused on a wide array of environmental issues.

Throughout the two-week unit, each student kept a collection portfolio with drafts of their writing and other supporting materials that they felt displayed their personal thinking and learning about these environmental issues. One of the major sources for these collection portfolios were the students' individual response journals, which contained their written responses to what they were exposed to in their own reading and in their listening to the read-alouds as a group, to the ideas they learned in their independent study, and to the ideas they encountered in the world outside the classroom. The teachers encouraged the students to think critically and to become reflective about what they and others should do to preserve their world. These journals and the collection portfolios provided the teachers with ongoing, informal data that they needed in order to inform their instruction and to individualize the learning experiences for their sixth-grade students.

Activities for Refining Ideas or Ending the Unit.   Due to the fact that this entire unit was done in a fairly concentrated time period and the fact that the various disciplines were brought together by the teachers who planned it, the revising of understandings that we described in Chapter 6 happened alongside the interacting with text and other sources. Students were constantly revising their views about the environment and the pressing issues based on class discussions, their own reading, and the teachers' read-alouds, data they were collecting and analyzing from the home environmental survey, and their personal reflections in their journals.

The final written product for this unit was a class newsletter that the students published and distributed on the annual celebration of Earth Day. The *Recycler's Digest,* as they named it, demonstrated the range of student interests and writing styles. The newsletter contained informational pieces with recipes for natural cleaning products, an interview with an industrial hygienist, and fictional pieces such as "The Life of an Aluminum Can" and "The Vanity of Asphalt." By using this real-life communication product and choosing this particular date, the teachers were helping the students see how their knowledge could inform a wider audience about a topic that affects everyone's life.

Assessing Student Understanding and Outcomes of the Unit as a Whole

The newsletter also served as an assessment tool for the teachers. They were able to evaluate the quality of the students' work as well as the outcomes of their planning and their teaching. In addition to the newsletter, which gave the students a chance to share their new knowledge and to inform the wider community, the teachers learned that some of the students had become "environmental junkies" at home and showed evidence of having come away from this unit as more conscious and committed guardians of our environment. What better way for the value of integrated, thematic study to be evaluated and validated than to see it have a lasting impact on these middle schoolers who when they are adults will be making decisions about our environment.

Sample High School Unit: "Immigration and Cultural Diversity: Are We Still a Nation of Immigrants?"

Immigration and cultural diversity is a timely and significant theme for the development of integrated curriculum at the high school level. It is important that young people realize that questions about immigration, assimilation, and cultural pluralism are not unique to those of us living now but are in fact long-standing questions embedded in our history as a nation founded by immigrants. An additional impetus for focusing on this theme in an interdisciplinary, integrated manner in the curriculum is the fact that these issues are emphasized in national standards documents like Expectations for Excellence: Curriculum Standards for the Social Studies *(National Council for Social Studies, 1994) and in many of the recent state curriculum frameworks, especially those focused on history and the social sciences and on foreign or world languages (Massachusetts Curriculum Frameworks, 1998).*

Applying the Miller-Allan model (refer back to Figure 11.1) for the development of an integrated issues-based unit, a group of ninth-grade teachers created a four-week unit entitled, "Immigration and Cultural Diversity: Are We Still a Nation of Immigrants?" These teachers were particularly interested in this issue because they and their students, as well as the rest of their community, faced these concerns on an ongoing basis; this was an authentic issue that was literally in their backyard. The ninth graders had come from two different middle schools in their district. Therefore, the teachers believed that an integrated unit at the beginning of the school year could do as much to foster understanding of one another and to create a more cohesive academic setting for the students as it would give them a chance to deal firsthand with a significant historical and social issue affecting their own lives at the present.

Preplanning

The collaboration in this unit was prompted by a ninth-grade history teacher's desire to find a compelling way to introduce his students to a newly required two-year sequence of American history courses (colonialism to 1865 and 1865 to the present). The issues immigrants face and questions those already living in a community ask were interesting and real for this teacher because his own community was facing an influx of new immigrants. In addition, this teacher had recently attended a session at a social studies conference that focused on the importance of using relevant subject matter and attention to social issues that students in high schools today would be expected to deal with as adults.

This teacher wondered if he and his colleagues could create an integrated unit in which the students examined the status and implications of immigration today in the United States. To explore the feasibility of connecting a number of disciplines around this issue, the social studies teacher asked a group of his ninth-grade teaching colleagues in different content areas (English/language arts, mathematics, science, and foreign language) to meet for a brainstorming session. The teachers came away from this meeting with an interest in the proposed theme, a commitment to reflect on the role their own discipline could play in its study, and a decision to meet again to develop a planning map similar to the one developed for the middle school unit described earlier in the chapter. The outcome of their second meeting can be seen in the thematic map in Figure 11.6.

Planning

The discussions led the teachers to realize that exploring this issue would enable them to pursue some curriculum goals they held in common for their students. The teachers next developed four overarching objectives and learner outcomes to guide their own work and that of their students who would be engaged in the integrated unit:

- An awareness of patterns of emigration to the United States from other lands, with particular focus on the countries and reasons that people are coming here today (drawing on history, geography, and economics)

- An understanding of the topics that are most often debated in relation to immigration: costs for schooling, health care, and welfare needs; implications of the variety of languages and cultures present in the United States today; and economic implications, especially with regard to competition for jobs between immigrants and citizens

- An understanding of the principles and laws pertaining to citizenship rights in the United States and the rights and benefits of legal immigrant residents

- Refinement and extension of the students' research skills and their use of technology for research as well as their critical writing and speaking skills and a focus on evaluating a variety of sources on one topic with differing viewpoints expressed

Figure 11.6   How the Disciplines Work Together in a High School Integrated Unit

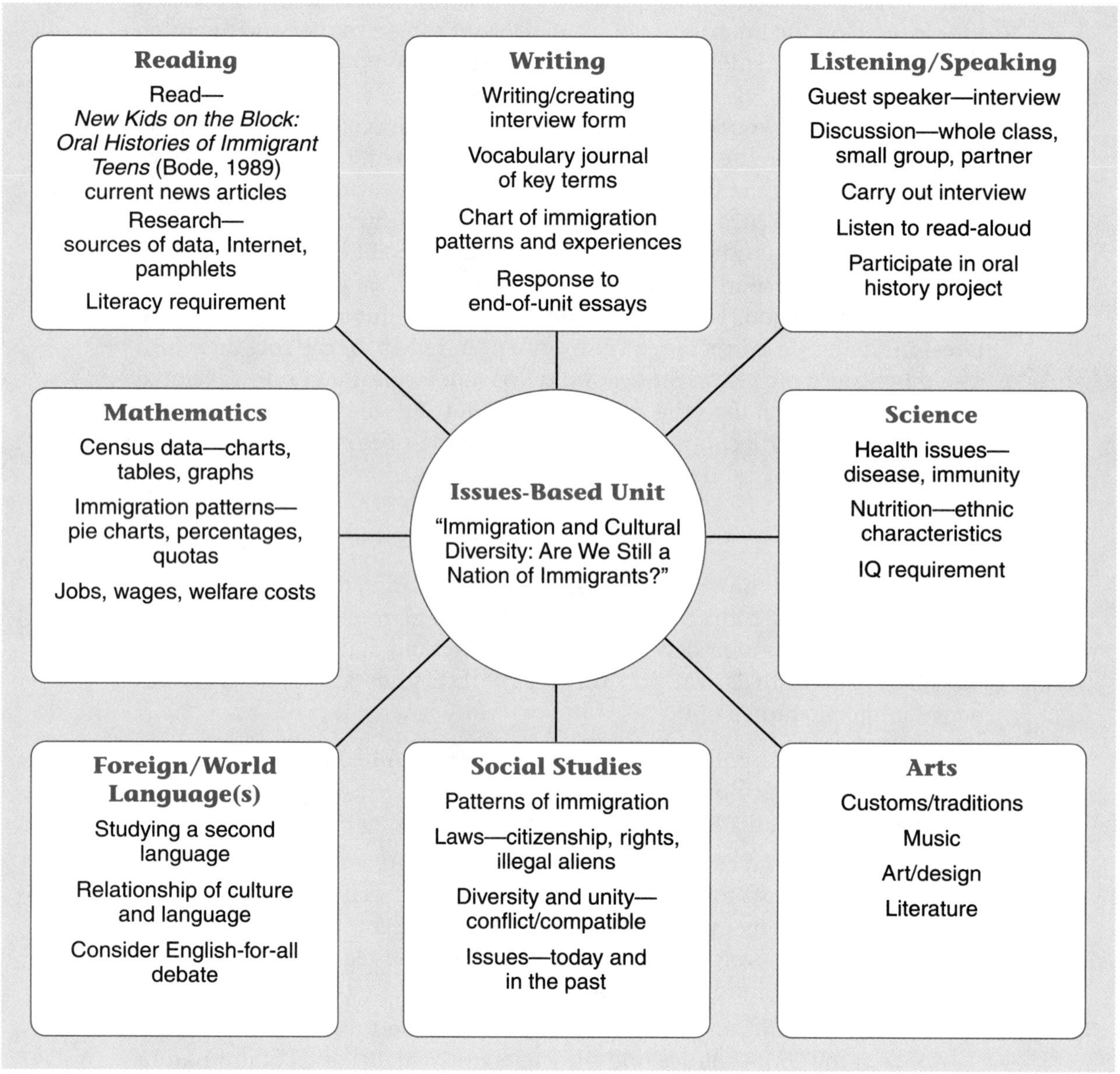

Reading

Read—
New Kids on the Block: Oral Histories of Immigrant Teens (Bode, 1989)
current news articles

Research—
sources of data, Internet, pamphlets

Literacy requirement

Writing

Writing/creating interview form

Vocabulary journal of key terms

Chart of immigration patterns and experiences

Response to end-of-unit essays

Listening/Speaking

Guest speaker—interview

Discussion—whole class, small group, partner

Carry out interview

Listen to read-aloud

Participate in oral history project

Mathematics

Census data—charts, tables, graphs

Immigration patterns—pie charts, percentages, quotas

Jobs, wages, welfare costs

Issues-Based Unit

"Immigration and Cultural Diversity: Are We Still a Nation of Immigrants?"

Science

Health issues—disease, immunity

Nutrition—ethnic characteristics

IQ requirement

Foreign/World Language(s)

Studying a second language

Relationship of culture and language

Consider English-for-all debate

Social Studies

Patterns of immigration

Laws—citizenship, rights, illegal aliens

Diversity and unity—conflict/compatible

Issues—today and in the past

Arts

Customs/traditions

Music

Art/design

Literature

At the preplanning stage, the teachers also spent time selecting a range of resources to meet the learning needs and levels represented by the students in their ninth-grade class. They also selected a range of sources appropriate for research on the theme they chose for their unit. The English teacher identified fiction works such as Sandra Cisneros' *The House on Mango Street* (1991), Fran Leeper Buss' *The Journey of the Sparrows (1993),* and Maureen Crane Wartski's *A Long Way from Home* (1982) and nonfiction works such as Janet Bode's *New Kids on the Block: Oral Histories of Immigrant Teens (1989).* The social studies teacher contributed such resources as a public issues series developed by the Social Science Education Consortium and the Lucent Overview series focusing on social, political, and environmental issues and written for middle and high school audiences. The teachers located specialized research tools such as almanacs and yearbooks and sources on the Internet to support the development of this unit. In addition, they selected media sources such as recent feature stories and editorials in the local newspaper, as well as films, videos, and television documentaries. Finally, the teachers did some research on their own community to find out about its ethnic makeup represented by its clubs and churches, specialized stores, or restaurants as well as census information related to its ethnic and cultural background. They contacted local government officials as well as the school administration to find out about current issues related to immigration that they were knowledgeable about.

Implementing

Activities for Generating Ideas or Initiating the Unit.

The history teacher began the unit with a role play in which he played his grandfather from Latvia who came to the United States in 1910 at the age of ten. During the role play, the students learned why his grandfather came to the United States, what his native country was like then, how he traveled and who he traveled with, and what his initial experiences were like. The other content-area teachers who were participating in the unit and the students were asked on a volunteer basis to share where their families came from and why they had come to the United States. The students began a chart to show the countries represented in their community and the reasons they or their ancestors came to the United States. Many similar reasons for emigrating emerged. This whole class activity identified similarities between the students who were born in the United States and their classmates who were the newer immigrants.

Following this discussion, the teacher showed a cartoon on the overhead and asked the students to define the words *immigrant* and *emigrate,* highlighted in the cartoon (see Figure 11.7). They listed several other words and phrases: *assimilation, pluralism, diversity, equality, the American way,* and *melting pot* and

Figure 11.7

Cartoon Used to
Enhance Vocabulary
Instruction Within
a Unit

Source: Cobblestone (1982). Peterborough, N.H.: Cobblestone Publishing Company. Reprinted with permission of the artist.

salad bowl. Using a vocabulary chart such as the one introduced in Chapter 4 (see Figure 4.5), the teacher asked the students to write their own definitions of the words or phrases that they thought they knew. The students got together in small groups of three to four to share what they knew and thought about these words and phrases. Finally, the teacher asked the students to consider how these words and concepts applied to them personally and to their community. These two activities set the stage for the teachers to pose the key questions for the unit: "Are we still a nation of immigrants?" and "As we enter a new century, what is the immigrant experience today, and what should it be for the future?"

The generating activities laid the foundation for the students to decide on questions they would ask someone in their own family or someone in their community who had emigrated recently. With the teacher's support, the students created an interview form that contained what they considered to be the most important questions (see Figure 11.8).

Activities for Interacting with Ideas or Developing the Unit.   Using the interview questions that the class generated, the teachers decided to arrange a group interview to sharpen the students' questioning abilities and to give them an opportunity to practice their listening and their note-taking skills before they interviewed an individual on their own. One of the teachers asked a Cambodian couple who had recently immigrated to their community to come to the class in order to share their experiences and to be interviewed.

While the students were preparing for their interviews, and realizing that there were various ability levels and language levels among the students in the class, the English teacher decided to do a read-aloud of *The House on Mango Street,* a young adult novel about the immigrant experience. She chose this story for its overall literary value as well as the fact that it shows a young person's perspective on how the immigrant experience can be both positive and negative. After some discussion of the story, the teacher suggested that the students create a list of positive and negative immigrant experiences in the book to which they could add the firsthand experiences being shared by the people they were individually going to interview.

Each student was independently reading the nonfiction accounts of young people like themselves coming to the United States found in *New Kids on the Block: Oral Histories of Immigrant Teens* (Bode, 1989). The book focuses on

Figure 11.8

Immigrant Interview Questions

1. What country did you come from?
2. Why did you immigrate?
3. What difficulties did you have when you first arrived?
4. Was the United States what you expected?
5. How much did it cost you to come here?
6. Who was your sponsor? *or* Who did you know here?

Source: Adapted from L. S. Levstik and K. C. Barton, *Doing History* (Hillside, N.J.: Erlbaum, 1997).

why each of these young persons came to the United States, whom they came with, and what experiences they are having as recent immigrants. The students in the class were encouraged to share their thoughts and impressions with a partner and to record these discussions on a discussion web, such as the one presented in Chapter 5. The students added the positive and negative aspects of the immigrant experience they found in these personal accounts to the class chart they had begun earlier in the unit.

Throughout this phase of the unit, students refined their knowledge of the vocabulary and the key concepts identified during the generating phase of the unit. All students kept a vocabulary journal in which they recorded clarifications and ideas related to the terms *immigration, diversity, assimilation,* and *pluralism.*

As the students read with their partners and discussed current news articles in their local newspaper, they became increasingly curious about U.S. citizenship laws and how census data were collected and used in the United States. The mathematics, science, and social studies teachers helped the students research these areas of interest. This research component of the unit, triggered by real questions and concerns, enabled the students to use a variety of community-based sources other than texts: newspapers, Internet sources focused specifically on immigration issues on the Immigration Home Page(**http:www:bergen.org/AAST/Projects/quickview-3.html**) and on a web site focused on immigration issues at the University of California at Davis (**http://heather.cs.ucdavis.edu/pub/Immigration//Portes.html**), as well as informational pamphlets and brochures such as the Department of the Interior's *Guide to Citizenship.* The social studies teacher created study guides for the students to use to find answers to their questions using some of the specialized resources they identified during the preplanning stage. The mathematics teacher helped the students contact local government representatives to gain current information about how the census data were being used in their community. This teacher helped the students use graphs and charts to interpret the census data. The students also learned how the census data were used to allocate funds for services to community agencies such as schools for programs like Chapter I and free lunch or breakfast programs for children of school age. Another group of the students, prompted by a recent newspaper article, "Immigration Curbs Urged to Protect Wages" (*Boston Globe,* January 23, 1998), explored a prevalent economic concern in communities such as theirs with large influxes of new immigrants. The students wanted to find out what the real impact was on the availability of jobs in their own community.

Throughout the month, all students kept a collection portfolio that contained their written reflections related to the key questions, their personal vocabulary journals, and other supporting materials that demonstrated their meeting the learning goals of the unit. Furthermore, the data in these portfolios (as well as what was not there) helped the teachers identify individuals or groups that needed coaching, conferencing, or direct instruction. The portfolios were the most helpful sources for teachers to use in order to individualize the learning experiences for the variety of ninth-grade students in their classes. They provided the teachers with a source of data useful in selecting resources, strategies, and grouping patterns to help each student gain the most from this integrated unit.

Activities for Refining Ideas or Ending the Unit. As they moved into the final phase of this unit, the teachers wanted to ensure that each student had individually grappled with the issues and questions posed at the beginning of the unit. Second, they wanted the students to see that the immigrant issue has persisted since our earliest settlements. The teachers wanted the students to use these questions—"*Are we still a nation of immigrants?*" and "*What is the current immigrant experience?*"— and their new understandings about immigration as a framework for the upcoming study of American history from the colonial days to the present, which was the statewide social studies requirement for the ninth and tenth grades.

The teachers designed two culminating activities for this unit: an individual activity and a group project that extended the unit into the real life of their community. First, each student was to write an individual opinion piece based on research throughout the unit, discussions of readings with partners, and the information he or she learned in small research groups and from whole class discussions (see Figure 11.9). The students chose one of the two essay questions designed by the team of content-area teachers involved with the unit.

Because the integrated unit on immigration coincided with the students' town's year-long centennial celebration, the students and their teachers decided to pull the information they had learned about their community and its immigrant groups together into an oral history project. Finally, the students used their newly acquired knowledge about their community and its ethnic heritage to help the town's board of selectmen and the town's historical society plan and implement a Heritage Pride Day for their town's special celebration.

Assessing Students' Understandings and the Outcomes of the Unit as a Whole. Each of the essays was written for a certain purpose. The essays were a response to one of the questions designed to demonstrate students' critical-writing ability, their knowledge of the vocabulary and concepts dealt with in the unit, their ability to express their personal opinion, and their ability to assimilate and use data from a variety of sources.

Figure 11.9

Final Individual Response Questions for the Immigration Unit

Question #1: Place yourself on these two continua.

Views of the United States

Refuge for the Oppressed .... *America for "Americans"*

Views of National Character

Strength through Diversity .... *Strength through Unity, Assimilation*

Consider what has most influenced your placement on the two continua. Has your own view changed since we began the unit, and if so, how? Finally, do you think Americans will ever reach agreement on these issues? Why do you think it is so difficult to reach agreement on these issues?

Question #2: Reflect on both the positive and the negative experiences immigrants face or have faced in the American culture. Think about a person proud of their ethnic/cultural heritage or a person who wants to hide their foreign background. How would that person react to specific immigrant experiences? Would the individual you are thinking about have a different viewpoint if he or she had settled in another part of the country? If they settled in our community how would they react? If they came here as a child or teenager, would they react differently?

Source: Adapted from Social Science Education Consortium (1988). *Immigration: Pluralism and National Identity*. (Boulder, CO: Social Science Education Consortium.)

The second culminating project, the group oral history, allowed the students to focus on the ethnic makeup of their community, which they had learned about through their investigations using the census data as well as through their personal interviews with a variety of individuals living and working in the community.

Summary of the Chapter

This chapter concludes the part of the text devoted to the development of curriculum and the enhancement of literacy learning across the disciplines. In this chapter, we have emphasized:

- The role of integrated curriculum
- The interrelationships among disciplines to solve problems and issues and to explore significant themes

We began the chapter by explaining our definition for integrated curriculum and pointed out where there is confusion in the terminology. Then we provided a rationale for pursuing this form of curriculum development and collaboration with colleagues in different disciplines.

We presented a refinement of the unit plan model we introduced in Chapter 8 and implemented in Chapters 9 and 10, designated the Miller-Allan Model for Developing Curriculum. This plan has four components:

- Preplanning and finding significant themes
- Planning the unit, with emphasis on working with colleagues, scheduling, and finding resources
- Implementing the unit with emphasis on the content understandings and literacy learning using teaching/assessing tools
- Assessing the unit with an emphasis on the role of portfolios in evaluation and the benefits for both teachers and students

Since integrated curriculum involves working collaboratively with other content-area teachers over time, we include some guidelines for teachers working in interdisciplinary teams. We also provide some recommendations for teams of teachers to consider in order to ensure that their setting will support and accommodate the curriculum they have designed.

Finally, we concluded this chapter with two sample integrated units, one at the middle school level and one at the high school level. Both show in detail how the content-area teachers and their students used the Miller-Allan Model for Developing Curriculum in order to study a significant real-world issue.

Inquiry Activities About Your Learning

1. Think about the themes of the sample middle school and high school units in this chapter. Now consider your own discipline, courses you have taken, and real-world occurrences with which you are familiar. Look at the planning webs on the environment and on immigration and decide what you could add from your academic or personal experiences to extend each of these integrated learning maps.

2. Look at the national standards or curriculum frameworks in your discipline. Identify one or two topics or understandings in your field that you think you could link to one or more other disciplines. Discuss the possibilities with peers who are subject matter specialists in other areas to get their ideas and reactions.

Inquiry Activities About Your Students' Learning

1. The issues or problems that face the students' own communities are a rich source of integrated curriculum themes. Have your students survey their community for issues by reading the newspaper, listening to the local news station, and talking with friends and neighbors as well as officials in law enforcement, education, or community service positions. Help the students identify areas of concern like recreation, the environment, civil and political rights, health, education, and job- and employment-related issues. Once the students have had a chance to survey their community, see whether the students have come up with similar or related concerns. If so, discuss with the students how they could explore these issues in any one of or in a combination of the disciplines that make up their school's existing curriculum.

12

Continuing to Grow as a Reflective Professional

As you approach student teaching, you are about to embark on a career that will sustain and fulfill you for more than thirty years. You will certainly experience tired feet, mounds of student papers and lab reports to correct, satisfaction when a struggling student "gets it," and exciting work opportunities with colleagues as well as challenges from new mandates, new curriculum, and new students. What will sustain you is being a lifelong learner. This will happen if you keep exploring and building on the *act* of teaching and the *art* of teaching.

Throughout this text, we have emphasized the reciprocal nature of teaching and learning. We have also emphasized that to be an effective teacher, you must remain an active, ongoing learner throughout your career. We believe that as a preservice teacher, you have had many opportunities to become informed about the *act* of teaching, which includes knowledge of your content area (discipline), your learners, and your growing repertoire of content pedagogy and knowledge of curriculum materials and resources. Now you must continue that learning on your own. We also believe that you have begun your personal journey toward acquiring the *art* of teaching: your reflection in action and your ability to call on the repertoire of tools you have and your reservoir of knowledge as well as your ability to match these to the diverse students in the settings in which you find yourself. We think you have begun this journey as you have tried various activities suggested in this text and in your other courses, which have given you the opportunity to apply and to reflect on what you are learning about content, students, pedagogy, and resources.

Furthermore, we have suggested that you share your experiences as a learner as well as a teacher with peers (colleagues) in the same discipline, with peers interested in students at the same level (middle school or high school), and even across disciplines. We began this focus on connections with others in your profession in Chapter 1 to encourage you to see yourself as part of a community of educators. We did this to foster models of collaboration in your preservice experience that we hope you will take with you into your own schools and classrooms in the future.

We believe that by engaging in the activities and using the strategies we suggest in this text, in combination with your other course work and your ongoing field-based experiences, you are becoming the professional educator, the "good teacher," that so many recent reports, such as *Turning Points: Preparing American Youth for the 21st Century* (1990) and *Breaking Ranks: Changing an American Institution* (1996), as well as the standards documents and new credentialing initiatives, are focused on to provide the leadership in our schools for the next century. The essential attributes of a "good teacher" are well stated in the summary report of the National Commission on Teaching and America's Future, "What Matters Most: Teaching for America's Future" (*Report of the National Commission on Teaching and America's Future,* 1996). The teachers they envision—and we believe you can be among them—have the following attributes:

- Subject matter expertise (content knowledge) and understanding of how children learn and develop (knowledge of learners)

- Skill in a range of teaching strategies and technologies (content pedagogy)

- Effectiveness in working with students from diverse backgrounds (knowledge of learners)

- Ability to work well with parents and colleagues

- Assessment expertise and know-how to use results to affect instruction for students (content pedagogy)

In this text we suggest many in-class inquiry activities and simulations to help you focus on the activities, the questioning, and the problem solving required of an educator who will teach tomorrow. We hope these opportunities have helped you try on your role as a teacher and have given you many tools for your future in the classroom.

We have focused on your learners and your role as an effective teacher of literacy and learning in your particular discipline. As you read this concluding chapter, you may want to ask yourself some questions focused on yourself as both a learner and a teacher.

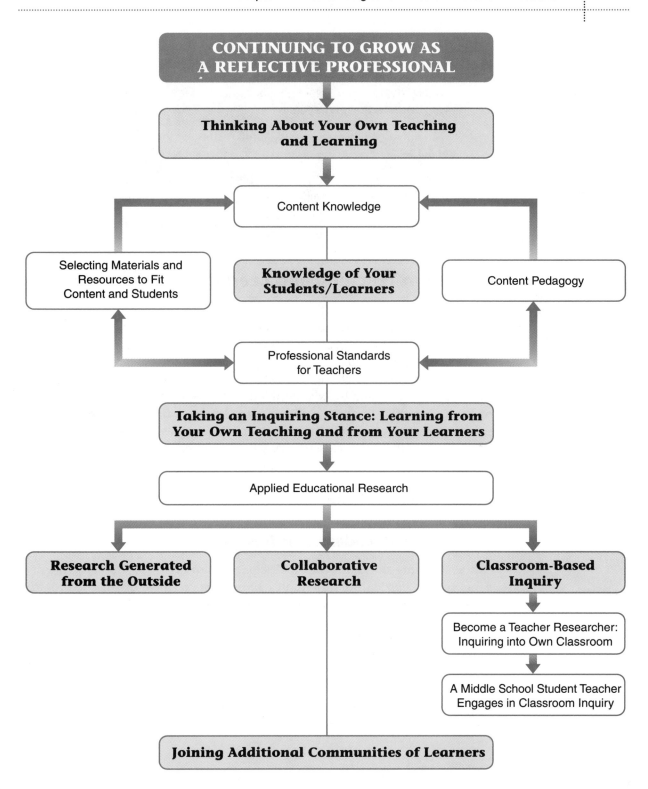

Purpose-Setting Questions

1. What is meant by professional teaching standards, and how do they apply to you now and in the future?

2. What do you know about educational research? Who does it, and what impact will it have on the classroom where you teach?

3. Have you ever heard about classroom inquiry? What do you think we mean when we say another role we'd like to add to your repertoire of choices is that of a teacher researcher?

Thinking About Your Own Teaching and Learning

In order to be the continuous learner we discussed in Chapter 1 and to meet the standards of the profession throughout a career of teaching, teachers need time devoted to learning about new initiatives like the national discipline-based standards, changes in subject matter relevant to their discipline, and teaching/assessing tools designed to enhance student learning. Teachers at every level and in every discipline need time to find and to develop resources to support the teaching and learning activities that will make up the daily fabric of their own classrooms. You too will have these needs as you attempt to meet the myriad of expectations placed on you as a teacher and curriculum developer trying to create relevant and long-lasting learning experiences for your own students.

▶ ▶ ▶ ▶ Professional Standards for Teachers

Just as there are standards for the disciplines that are meant to guide the development of curriculum and quality of instruction, there are also standards being developed for teachers who are the primary agents for school reform and the major developers of curriculum in schools today. Three areas are being focused on to establish quality within the teaching profession. First, standards are being proposed for institutional or program accreditation, whereby an institution's program or program for the preparation and entry of individuals into the field of education is approved or accredited by a state, regional, or national agency responsible for teacher education. If you have not already done so, you might want to look at your institution's course catalog or program booklet provided. Can you determine by which agency or agencies your teacher education program is accredited?

Second, once you have successfully completed your program of study and one or more field-based experiences such as student teaching or an internship, you will receive your first credential or certificate to teach. This certificate is granted most often by the department of education in the state in which your college or university is located. Currently, forty states require a passing score on a teacher test, which usually focuses on communication skills and subject matter knowledge, in addition to the successful completion of an accredited program at a college or university before one can become credentialed as a teacher.

Finally, as a result of recent concerns about the quality of teaching in our schools and equitable opportunities for all students, states have individually designed rigorous recertification programs for in-service teachers in all fields. A number of states and professional organizations have also joined together to establish national performance standards and tests of competence for beginning and experienced teachers. The developers of these standards believe that the standards and accompanying tests will weed out poorly prepared and ineffective teachers and that they will serve as a means for comparability of teacher education programs from state to state. In addition, the developers of these standards hope that such unified professional standards will create a teaching force that is capable of producing comparable, quality instruction for all students across the country.

Recommendations related to the preparation of teachers, qualifications for entry into the teaching profession, and guidelines for continuation in the field of education have many similarities. Regardless of whether you are a beginning or an experienced teacher, it is expected that teachers can demonstrate competencies as educators in a variety of ways appropriate to their particular grade level and discipline. Knowledge of your content, your students, and your pedagogy, which we have emphasized throughout this text, is at the heart of the many standards documents and the teacher assessment instruments being developed for both new and experienced teachers.

▶ ▶ ▶ ▶ Content Knowledge

From the beginning of this book, we have urged you to continue to build your knowledge and expertise in your discipline. Think back to the activity in Chapter 1 where we asked you, first with your peers and then with experienced professionals, to see if you could come up with a shared list of important understandings in your field. The recent discipline-based standards documents that we examined in Chapter 8 are another source to use as you try to create such a list to guide your teaching. The practitioners and scholars who have contributed to these documents have sought to identify key understandings in their respective disciplines. These educators have sought to identify the essentials in each discipline in an attempt to put some cohesiveness and coherence into the curriculum across the country. In many of these standards documents, you will notice that students across grades and levels are exposed to similar key ideas and understandings. This is not coincidence. The educators who designed these standards know that we all learn best when we have a chance to revisit and gain depth about a topic and have opportunities to apply knowledge on our own and to connect it to prior knowledge.

The topics we have chosen for the sample middle school and high school units in Part Three exemplify the current focus on both relevancy and major understandings across the disciplines. A recent conversation between two middle school educators demonstrates the difference between a focus on a particular topic and the focus on big ideas and understandings related to a topic. The two educators were debating how teachers in the social studies determine what should be taught and whether there is a core of knowledge in their discipline. The conversation went like this:

Educator A: It is clear that all eighth graders should know the Bill of Rights.

Educator B: What is the Seventh Amendment?

Educator A: Well . . .

Educator B: I think this shows the essence of the current argument in social studies.

We want students to have an understanding of what these rights mean for them as citizens of the United States. And we want them to see how often in their day-to-day lives, these laws are called into action to settle disputes and to protect individual rights.

▷ ▷ ▷ ▷ **Knowledge of Your Students/Learners**

The second area we have emphasized is knowing who your students/learners are. We have pointed out that you must always remind yourself that you are teaching students, not content. The race, class, ethnic background, gender, and learning differences of your students must dictate which tools and resources you use to facilitate your students' learning. The standards and goals manifested in the curriculum you design should be equitable for all students, and the understandings and content you choose should have relevance and long-term importance related to students' becoming citizens and consumers in the real world beyond the classroom today and for their future.

Once you have made careful and thoughtful decisions about the content and the understandings that your curriculum will emphasize, your major responsibility is to meet the diverse needs of your students so that each can participate and successfully learn in your classroom. We believe that you can best do this by implementing a range of literacy strategies and teaching tools for your students to use, as well as to provide a variety of resources related to the topic and content being studied. In addition, we have stressed how important it is that you become familiar with a variety of different assessment tools that will inform both your instruction and evaluation of your students' learning and will also inform students about their own learning.

▶ ▶ ▶ ▶ **Content Pedagogy**

In both Parts Two and Three of this text, you have had many opportunities to see given strategies, such as KWL charts, concept maps, journals, or learning logs, recommended to learners trying to understand and to make use of an array of different content (biology, geology, law, history) from an array of different resources (textbooks, newspapers, magazines, trade books). This text has been designed to help you extend your own use of literacy strategies and teaching tools. You have had the opportunity to apply these strategies in your own discipline with your own resources. We hope you have discussed with peers how these strategies work in their disciplines. And, most important, we hope you have some opportunities to model and explain these strategies with students of your own. Finally, if you use the teaching tools we have suggested in this text not only as teaching tools, but also as learning and assessment tools with your own students, we believe you will be able to create a community of learners in your classroom where you share with your students the ownership of knowledge and understanding.

Whether your students are engaged in work with partners, cooperative learning groups, or discussion groups of various sizes, you will want to interact with all of your students and assess their participation and learning. This information you have gained from careful observation of authentic classroom activities will help you make decisions related to what teaching tools to use, what additional resources are needed, and what changes in grouping or organization you need in your own classroom. All of these decisions will be intimately tied to the manner in which you decide you can best connect the content you are teaching and the understandings you are emphasizing with your particular students and their world. This is the challenge of teaching: the constant need to assess your learners and to make decisions about the content and your pedagogy that are specific to your learners and your classroom setting.

▶ ▶ ▶ ▷ ## Selecting Materials and Resources to Fit Content and Learners

If you know the understandings you wish to focus on, some resources that support the content, and, most important, your students, you have the essentials to make well-informed decisions matching students and materials. In Chapter 3 we introduced you to some components of text that can assist you in making an assessment of the materials available as well as an appropriate match of materials and your learners. We pointed out how you can use readability formulas, leveling of books, and text approachability or friendliness to examine the materials you will use with your own students. Over and over again as an educator, you will need to apply these criteria to the resources that support your curriculum if you are going to meet the learning needs of your students, who will change from year to year and from class to class.

We have emphasized how important it is once you have determined the text you will use that you determine the literacy and learning strategies that will give students access to both the material and the ideas and concepts contained within. When you encourage your students to use a variety of materials, they are more likely to gain personal understanding and to have ownership of the content and their knowledge. For example, you might want to determine whether your students use any generating strategies on their own before they begin reading a new text. If your students don't use these literacy and learning strategies on their own, you may decide to teach them how to use prediction strategies and how to preview a text before they begin reading. Similarly, if you know the needs of your students and the demands of the text, you may decide to introduce a text study guide to help them focus on the important information in the text. Such decisions, which we emphasized in Part Two of this book, are necessary to meet the diversity needs of your learners so that they can effectively learn the content and the concepts your curriculum is focusing on.

Taking an Inquiring Stance: Learning from Your Own Teaching and from Your Learners

As you prepare to be a teacher, your ideas about teaching and learning have probably been shaped by your own experiences as a student as well as by the courses you have taken and your field experiences in a middle school or a high school. As you have thought about the pedagogy, strategies for learning literacy, and content and assessment tools you have learned about recently, have you ever wondered where these ideas came from? Even if you have not explicitly been told, no doubt you have already been influenced by an array of educational research, and you will continue to be affected by research throughout your career as an educator. The array of research likely will affect what you think and do as a teacher:

- *Large-scale studies* with an emphasis on the collection of and analysis of comparative data focused on broad educational issues such as achievement in mathematics of students in the United States as compared to other countries (the TIMMS Report) or the literacy, mathematics, science, and social studies competency of fourth, eighth, and twelfth graders compared by region of the country as well as demographics in the National Assessments of Educational Progress Reports (1992, 1994, 1996).

- *Basic* or *laboratory research* carried out by a single researcher or a group of researchers primarily interested in testing a theory related to a particular strategy (e.g., schema theory), grouping procedure (e.g., cooperative learning), or assessment method (e.g., the use of retellings).

- *Applied educational research* focused on classrooms and teaching practice. This research can take a number of forms, ranging from research initiated by a university researcher interested primarily in proving a theory to collaborations between researchers and classroom practitioners interested in finding outcomes that can be generalized from one classroom to many classrooms and, finally, to practice-driven research initiated by teachers in their own classroom settings. In the last, often referred to as *classroom inquiry,* teachers are most interested in solving problems or answering the questions that arise naturally in the day-to-day workings of their own classrooms and settings.

▷ ▷ ▷ ▷ **Applied Educational Research**

Applied educational research is the broad term used to describe research carried out in real classrooms focused on students and teachers actively engaged in teaching and learning. What differs most in the different forms of applied educational research is whether the question or problem is generated from outside the classroom by a researcher, university faculty member, or staff developer and is then studied within a classroom or whether the question is generated from within the classroom by the teacher/practitioner. Two other factors that determine the form that the applied educational research takes are the role the teacher plays in designing and implementing the research and in what manner and by whom the results of a study are used (Oja & Smulyan, 1989).

Research Generated from the Outside and Applied to the Classroom. Researchers and experts outside the classroom have conducted a great deal of educational research. Often these researchers seek to develop theories and teaching practices to guide behaviors of both teachers and their students in elementary, middle school, and high school classrooms that can be generalized to schools and classrooms across the country. In these situations, the classroom teacher's role is usually designated to disseminating or carrying out what the researcher has "discovered." Usually the teacher's role is to carry out a prescribed task with students. The researcher then collects and analyzes the data and interprets the results and conclusions. Researchers see a given classroom of students and teachers as representative of an age or grade-level population they are interested in studying rather than as individuals they will teach, and the results of their research are used to inform a wide audience. This form of applied educational research, often described in professional teacher education journals and in texts used in education courses like the ones you are taking, is meant to inform classroom practice and improve instruction for a wide range of teachers and their students.

Collaborative Research: Researchers and Teachers Working Together. A second form of applied educational research invites researchers and teachers to be *collaborative participants* (such as Raphael's work with teachers in book clubs or peer-led discussion that we examined in Chapter 5). This research model, first conceptualized in the 1930s, is more focused on the day-to-day problems that teachers encounter in their own classrooms. However, even in these instances, the questions and the theories being tested are generated by researchers outside the classroom—-an agency, a university professor or team, a curriculum coordinator. In this form of applied educational research, teachers may help with the planning of the study and with the data collection as it pertains to their own classrooms and students; however, they are still testing someone else's theory or hypothesis about their students and their students' learning. Teachers bring their practicality about real classroom life and the knowledge of their students to this shared endeavor, and often they can influence the progress of the research as well as how the study is implemented. Together the teacher and the researcher analyze and interpret the data; there is also more of an opportunity for the teachers to influence how the outcomes of the research are used.

In such collaborative educational research between classroom practitioners and outside researchers, each constituency is contributing an important role in the research endeavor. The outcomes of this research have the potential to influence a wide audience of teachers who teach in the same discipline or have a similar student population to the teachers involved in the study and who will therefore find the outcomes and the implications credible and usable for their own classrooms. Perhaps when you have your own classroom, you will have an opportunity to collaborate with someone at your college or university on such applied educational research and contribute to the research about teaching and learning in your own field.

Classroom-Based Inquiry: Teacher Initiated.   A third form of applied educational research that has gained momentum is *teacher research*. In this form of research, teachers identify the issues and concerns they have about their own practices, their own students, and their own settings that they feel need to be examined. Teachers often realize that they have data from their ongoing practice that will yield valuable information if they can study and analyze the data with a particular question in mind. In addition, teachers select research tools that will give them needed information about their students and their students' learning. These may be the teaching/assessing tools we looked at in Part Two. The individual teacher collects, organizes, analyzes, and interprets these data. Finally, the teacher uses his or her own interpretation of the findings to inform and perhaps to alter or change classroom practice. The teacher research or classroom inquiry is done primarily for the teacher's own continuous learning (discussed at the beginning of this text in Chapter 1) and to enhance the learning of the students.

At the core of classroom inquiry or teacher research is a teacher's desire to understand his or her own teaching practice rather than to prove a specific teaching practice works. Effective teachers have always sought to learn from their students, as well as to use new teaching tools to improve their students' learning and understanding. However, what is different about being a teacher researcher is that these teachers collect and analyze their data in an organized, systematic manner in order to answer specific questions about their classrooms and their classroom practice. Rather than relying on hunches and impressions about the effect of their classroom practices, teacher researchers follow focused plans to produce findings and to draw conclusions about classroom practices. Their findings inform their future practices and can be shared with others—-colleagues, supervisors, parents, and the students themselves. In this manner an individual teacher researcher assumes the responsibility for change within his or her own classroom based on the results of research and findings.

Throughout this text, and especially in Part Two where we examined the literacy strategies and teaching tools, we have encouraged you to approach your teaching with an inquiring stance. We have advocated that you try out many of the teaching/assessing tools we have discussed with a small group of learners at a grade level or within a discipline in which you hope to teach. In doing this, we suggest you continue to ask yourself about your practice as a teacher as well as about your students' learning. For example, after we introduced you to a pattern guide to be used with a new resource in your discipline in Chapter 5 or a categorization chart to organize information from sources in Chapter 6, we suggested you try these strategies yourself as a learner and then with your own students.

In addition we have suggested in the Teaching as Inquiring Learner Activities embedded in the chapters and the Inquiry Activities About Your Learning and the Inquiry Activities About Your Students' Learning at the conclusion of each chapter that you continue to think about and learn more about your discipline, your teaching methodology (especially your use of teaching tools), a variety of curriculum materials and resources, and, most important, your learners. We have done this by:

- Asking you throughout the chapters to question, analyze, and reflect on the understandings and the philosophy you have pertaining to your field or discipline

- Encouraging you to think about how you use literacy strategies to learn from different resources

- Asking you to assess your own background knowledge, your perceptions and beliefs, and your values in order to understand yourself as both teacher and learner

- Suggesting that you think about how different students respond to a topic being studied such as girls versus boys, the strongest students in the content area versus the weaker ones, the students who have some background knowledge and the ones who have little or none

While taking this questioning stance integral to the multifaceted role of a teacher, you have been engaged in reflecting on your own actions in the classroom. (Schön, 1983). Without knowing it, you have been doing what is currently being referred to as "classroom inquiry" and have begun to take on the characteristics of a teacher researcher.

Teacher as Inquiring Learner Activity

Perhaps you kept a field notebook or a journal like the one we recommended in Chapter 1 in conjunction with your courses or when you did a prepracticum or engaged in other field-based experiences as part of your teacher education program. Perhaps when you student teach or when you do a field placement, you will be advised to keep a journal or a log to record the most significant events of your day or your week. You may share these with your cooperating teacher, with your supervisor, or with other students in your seminar in an attempt to understand your perceptions and your concerns as a teacher in training.

We believe a teaching log or journal is one of the best tools for any teacher, whether new or experienced, to think about classrooms and to find questions that can shape future classroom inquiry as well as to inform future teaching practice. Look back at your own log to see how many of your observations were related to your discipline, your own teaching, the materials you were using or were trying to use, and your students and their differences and needs. As you look at your journal over a semester or even over a few weeks, perhaps what at first appeared to be random thoughts may begin to take on a pattern, and you will realize that there are some recurring questions related to your students or your role as a teacher.

For example, perhaps you find that you often mention your concern with a specific student's lack of attention or failure to participate in group discussions, or perhaps you are concerned about a bilingual student's inability to read and comprehend a required social studies textbook. Perhaps you have ended your entry with questions such as, "How could I help this student? or "Are there materials available on tape for the two students who are struggling with the reading level of the major resource?"

Finally, discuss your findings with another student in your discipline or at your level, middle or junior high school or high school, and see whether she or he has similar questions about pedagogy, students, or even the content area.

▶ ▶ ▶ ▶ Becoming a Teacher Researcher: Inquiring into Your Own Classroom

In order to be a teacher researcher, the most important ingredient is finding a question, a puzzle, or a dilemma you want to answer or solve that is evident from your ongoing practice. To date we have suggested literacy strategies and teaching/assessing tools for you to learn about and for you to try yourself and with your own students. We have guided your question asking and inquiry and your reflection on your practice.

We believe that good teachers are those who keep asking questions about their students, their own teaching/assessing practices, the resources they are using, and the strategies, skills, and content they are presenting to their students. When you are doing inquiry in your own classroom, we hope you realize that interesting questions won't appear in some perfectly obvious and neat form, nor will they come from some outside sources. Questions come from the surprises, the puzzles, and the concerns you experience in your own classroom.

We have worked with our own student teachers and with experienced teachers in order to support their classroom inquiry and to help them become teacher researchers. Both student teachers and experienced teachers we have worked with have followed a three-step model of classroom inquiry:

1. Finding or framing a question

2. Deciding what data or information they already have and what additional data they need to collect to answer their question

3. Knowing when the analysis or study of data has provided them with answers to their questions that will help them understand their teaching and the students in their classrooms

Finding and Framing a Question.   We ask our student teachers to look at the journals they have been required to keep during the first several weeks of their student teaching. We ask experienced teachers to look over journals, conference notes, or anecdotal records they have kept as part of their ongoing classroom record keeping. The teachers in each of these groups are likely to find within their reflections some wondering or question about a particular student, a group, or a teaching practice that keeps worrying or annoying them. Looking at these raw notes often leads them to find that some patterns emerge or that certain puzzles or surprises stand out from the rest of their notes. We suggest at this stage that they create a tentative question related to the topic, the issue, or the student or students that intrigues them. Question stems (see Figure 12.1) like the ones we offer the teachers we work with carrying out an inquiry project might also help you if you carry out classroom inquiry. We also suggest to our students at this stage, whether they are experienced teachers or student teachers, that they share their question with a partner and take

Figure 12.1

Sample Question Stems for Classroom Inquiry

What is the role of . . . . . ?
How do . . . . . ?
What procedures . . . . . ?
What happens when . . . . . ?
Do (does) **X** change **during/over time/after** . . . . . ?

Figure 12.2

Working Plan for Classroom Inquiry

- What is your question?
- Who is involved?
- When will the activity occur?
- What is to happen?
- Would it be helpful to know what the students already know, think, or feel? If so, how will you find that out?
- How will you know you've answered your question? *or* What data will you collect to answer your question?

some time to talk about their questions in an effort to clarify what they are really interested in.

We give our students, experienced teachers and student teachers alike, the plan shown in Figure 12.2, which is designed to help teacher researchers keep focused on their question and to make the inquiry process reasonable and doable within the normal flow of classroom life. Once you decide on a question, we recommend that you use a working plan to guide your data collection and analysis and your question answering.

Although you may be tempted to use classroom inquiry to help all of your students, we recommend to the teachers we work with that they limit their sample or select only a few students to study. We recommend that they select a single student, perhaps the most puzzling one for them, or that they select a high, an average, and a weaker student to compare in the use of a new strategy or content-area material. They may also choose a few contrasting students who differ by gender, regular education or special education placement, or ones who are more verbal and ones who are less verbal to observe carefully as they are engaged in ongoing classroom practice.

Deciding on Data Collection. Rather than trying to use new data collecting tools, we recommend you take classroom inquiry as an opportunity to look more systematically at what you are already doing and what data are readily available in your classroom. You should look for available data in the field notebook you have begun when you were finding your question, your notes as you used various teaching/assessing tools with your students, and the evidence of your students' learning found in their ongoing work and in their culminating projects and products.

First, we recommend that in addition to relying on student work, teacher researchers sharpen their own observational and listening skills in order to collect data from ongoing classroom interactions more effectively. Many teacher researchers keep a field notebook in which they jot down observations, comments, and questions they have during the day that are related to the question they are probing, the students they are focused on, or the strategy they are studying. They may write notes to themselves and keep these in a notebook. Daily or weekly the teacher researcher can look over these notes and write reflections or interpretations about what is occurring in the class in what is often referred to as a *double-entry notebook* (Figure 12.3). Although such double-entry notebooks are not the only means for collecting and analyzing rich, ongoing classroom data, we feel they are one of the most effective tools a teacher researcher, no matter what the discipline or the level he or she is teaching, can use. In addition, you may have anecdotal notes that you kept as you observed individual students or groups in process within your classroom; conference notes you keep during writing or reading conferences and workshops or during group discussions or cooperative group work are other sources of ongoing classroom procedures that are also rich sources of data readily available in your classroom.

For example, a teacher whose question was, "What is the best method for grouping ninth-grade students for cooperative science activities: assigning groups for the students or allowing them to choose their own groups?" recorded observations over several days to note which students were participating consistently in the recently formed cooperative learning groups. When the teacher carefully looked at her field notes at the end of the week, she realized that the two students with learning disabilities with whom she was most concerned had each volunteered an answer twice during the small group sessions, whereas neither had ever voluntarily responded during previous whole class discussions.

Figure 12.3

Double-Entry Field Notebook for Classroom Inquiry

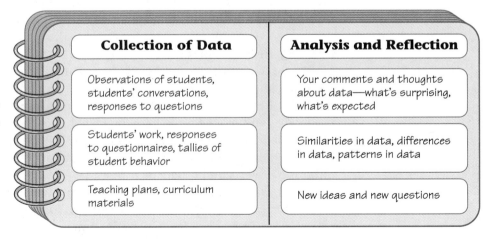

Collection of Data	**Analysis and Reflection**
Observations of students, students' conversations, responses to questions	Your comments and thoughts about data—what's surprising, what's expected
Students' work, responses to questionnaires, tallies of student behavior	Similarities in data, differences in data, patterns in data
Teaching plans, curriculum materials	New ideas and new questions

Second, you have used various teaching/assessing tools like those described in Part Two to meet the learning needs of your students. Teacher researchers undoubtedly use these tools to inform their own practice as a teacher as well as to help their own students judge themselves as learners. Now these teacher researchers can look at these sources of data more closely and more systematically than they have before. They can organize and analyze the data in new ways to answer a specific question they have framed about their own ongoing practice and can use their analysis and its implications to inform future practice.

Finally, we advise experienced teachers and the student teachers with whom we work to look at what student work (writing samples, projects, reading lists, lab reports, and field notebooks) and what assessment data (test results, rubrics, checklists, and portfolios) are available as part of their and their students' regular classroom routine. These products will show what literacy strategies students are using effectively as readers and writers and what content understandings they have acquired, as well as where there is need for additional or new teaching and learning.

Teacher as Inquiring Learner Activity

Although we recommend that you as a beginning teacher researcher and as a new teacher put your energy and your time into using the teaching/assessing tools in your classroom for the data when you do your inquiry, at some point you may want to try some other tools teacher researchers widely use. Several of the most widely used and accessible tools for collecting data in one's own setting are interviews, surveys, sociograms, and videotapes and audiotapes (Hubbard & Power, 1993; Anderson, Herr, & Nihlen, 1994).

- Have you ever been a respondent to any of these forms of data collecting tools as a student in middle school, high school, or college? Have you seen your cooperating teacher or supervisor or a college instructor use any of these tools to collect data about students and about students' learning? Do you think the information from these tools helped the particular teacher work more effectively with his or her students?

Analyzing and Interpreting Data.   So much of what an experienced teacher does is on-the-spot decision making about individual students, groups, pedagogy, and even resources based on their reflection in action. Teachers revise a lesson on the spot based on the cues they are receiving from their learners. We know that this is something in which you will gradually build confidence; at first you will feel wedded to that lesson plan that you have spent so much time writing and planning. An important goal for our student teachers or beginning teachers is to learn to switch their focus from what they are doing during a lesson to what evidence their students show of thinking and learning. After a lesson you may reflect on action alone or with your cooperating teacher or with your college supervisor.

Periodically as you collect data that you have decided will inform your classroom inquiry question, you should look over your field notes and some of your data samples and take the time to do freewriting. Ask yourself, "What is emerging?" "What could this mean?" Teacher researchers do this careful reflection on action on a regular basis aided by the data they have collected during the second phase of their classroom inquiry. This process of looking with a critical eye at the notes you have taken and the observations you have recorded is referred to as *cooking the data* (Hubbard & Power, 1993). At this

The student teacher, cooperating practitioner, and college supervisor discuss and reflect on what the sixth graders learned during the student teacher's lesson.

CREDIT: © Frank Siteman/ PHOTO EDIT

stage the teacher researcher is engaged in a discovery process trying to understand what their data means and whether they have answered their own question. Look back to Figure 12.3 to see the double-entry notebook that many teacher researchers find very useful and manageable for collecting and sorting data and impressions associated with their ongoing classroom work and their particular inquiry question.

We remind the experienced teachers and the student teachers we work with to look for patterns or characteristics that are naturally occurring in their classroom settings. For example, we suggest that these teachers look for patterns of behavior of students who are speaking most frequently during literature circles in the English/language arts courses or those participating most appropriately during discussions and debates in social studies courses. We also suggest they look for evidence that students are using various graphic organizers (webs or semantic feature charts) or other study aids on their own with content-area materials.

In addition, as the teachers look over their own field notes or their students' ongoing work samples, we remind them to look for surprises and puzzles in the data. For example, a teacher may ask why a usually quiet student chose to participate more on a given day than he or she had in the past. Asking oneself, "Does the student have more background knowledge on this topic or is the composition of the group more conducive to the student's willingness to participate?" might yield some useful information for the future. Finally, we encourage teachers to reflect constantly on their teaching plans (both lessons and units) as well as on their curriculum materials in order to generate new ideas and new questions to inform their classroom practice.

▶ ▶ ▶ ▶ A Middle School Student Teacher Engages in Classroom Inquiry

Recently a student in our middle school program wrote a summary of the classroom inquiry she carried out in the eighth-grade classroom where she did her student teaching. This example, set out in Figure 12.4, shows the evolution of an inquiry question and demonstrates the dynamic nature of the inquiry process. It also clearly demonstrates how carrying out classroom inquiry can help teacher researchers understand their classroom as well as to inform them for the future in a way that can help them and their students. In this example, you can see the question that the student teacher framed, the tools she used to gather her data, how she analyzed her data, and what outcomes and inferences she drew from this inquiry. Finally, you can see how naturally this inquiry fits with her ongoing teaching practice with this particular class, and

Figure 12.4   Summary of Classroom Inquiry

Classroom Inquiry Question

What techniques can I use to interest females in science and eliminate gender differences in participation and interest?

Plan to Answer Question

Who: One class consisting of seventeen eighth graders—twelve boys and five girls

Focusing on different methods of assessing class participation and looking for changes in the amount that each student participates. My goal is to empower the girls to participate more often and to encourage the boys to participate more selectively.

Documenting the inquiry goal by taking notes and making observations myself, and by designating certain students to keep a daily tally sheet (students will be given a sheet that asks them to record *positive participation* (relevant questions or comments), *negative participation* (irrelevant answers or comments), and *beyond negative participation* (put-downs or rudeness of other types) of the members of the group by gender.

Changes Made to Question and/or Plan Along the Way

Deciding to make this goal more of a class effort rather than a teacher-led project. The method of assessment I used was completely student generated. I realized that my original plan to use multiple methods of assessment was too far reaching, so I decided to focus on and analyze only one method. Students were responsible not only for devising a system of assessment, but also for keeping that system in check on a daily basis.

At the end of each class, I delegated a student to go around the room with a class list, asking each person what he or she thought his or her score for the day should be on a system decided by students: *check +* if they participated twice with a thoughtful, relevant comment; *check* if they participated once in an appropriate manner, and *check −* if they didn't participate at all or participated inappropriately.

What Did You Find Out? What Did You Learn?

First, I learned that students at this level become more involved and invested in a project like this when they themselves are responsible for making and following through with the basic ground rules. Second, eighth graders are also more likely to cooperate when they know they are being assessed, or graded.

I also gained some insight into adolescent psychology, in particular when I introduced the project and had the girls and boys each fill out a large Idea Sheet. (This sheet asked each gender group separately why they did or did not participate to date, what could be done, and what they thought the student teacher could do to change what currently existed.) Two things struck me from the sheets: the girls did not feel intimidated by the boys, and the boys perceived themselves as more secure than the girls. I didn't feel that either was true, but it was interesting to consider how the students wanted to be perceived.

What Is a New Question You've Discovered?

Will such a method of student-generated assessment work as well in a class with students of more diverse abilities?

Would introducing this idea at the beginning of the school year create students more willing to participate on their own, without assessment, by the middle or end of the year?

What Would You Do Next Time?

Next time, depending on the makeup of the class, I might choose to discriminate between participators and nonparticipators, rather than specifically between boys and girls. I might also attempt to videotape certain classes in order to determine how often I call on certain students and what effect that has on participation.

Developed by J. P. Walker, May, 1997

Source: Julie P. Walker, Lesley College Clinical Intern, Middle School Master's Program, May 1997.

why she thinks the results will serve to inform her practice as a middle school teacher in the future.

Joining Additional Communities of Learners

In addition to the community of learners you create in your own classroom, we hope that throughout your career you will participate in two other communities of learners:

- The other teachers in your discipline, your grade level, or your team who are your most immediate colleagues
- The larger professional community in which you have entered as a content-area specialist

Each of these communities offers you a wider community of learners to interact with in order to create a collective knowledge base about teaching practice, content, and students. In order to break the isolation of working alone and focusing only on your own classroom and students, collaboration and conversation with other teachers, especially those who know the same student population and the same school setting, are essential. What can be more credible than hearing about the effectiveness of a teaching/assessing tool or a grouping procedure from a colleague who teaches down the hall or who works in the same discipline in another district? We hope that as you go from your role as student teacher to being a professional in the field, you continue to question and to learn from your teaching and you share your triumphs as well as your puzzles with other professionals throughout your teaching career.

We have encouraged you to seek out peers and colleagues as you have considered the literacy and learning strategies we emphasized in Part Two and the application of these strategies within a range of disciplines we explored in both Part Two and Part Three. We hope you have begun to see yourself as a member of a community of learners and that you will continue to seek out colleagues when you become an in-service teacher with your own students and your own classroom. If a new text or a new set of frameworks is introduced for your content area, we hope you will approach their implementation with a questioning stance. In other words, we hope that you will always attempt to identify how well these changes match with your students' needs as well as what literacy strategies and teaching tools you will need to introduce students to in order to complement the demands of new material or new understandings.

If you and a colleague or a group of teachers in the same content area are being asked to pilot a program by your school, your district, or your state, why not consider some peer coaching and support rather than trying to implement the change on your own? Perhaps you and a colleague can observe one another or one another's classrooms in action, or you both can collect the same data from your two classes and compare your observations and perceptions. Such an approach demonstrates that you are taking an inquiring stance to be certain that there is always an appropriate match between your students and the content they are studying and the materials they are using in your classroom.

In order to increase the likelihood that there will be a community of learners among the teachers in a school and that each teacher will continue to grow and to learn in their professional role, Deborah Meier (1996), a researcher and school-based practitioner, advocates that all teachers have:

- Frequent conversations with one another about work

- Access to one another's classrooms

- Time to develop common standards of student performance

- Opportunities to speak and to write about work, attend conferences, and read journals—in other words, to go beyond the own day-to-day concerns about a student or students

Meier's final point highlights the second community of learners we hope you will become part of: the broader professional community associated with either your discipline, such as the National Council of Teachers of Mathematics, or with your level, such as the National Middle School Association. As a beginning teacher, it is easiest to become connected to this type of professional organization by maintaining a membership and a subscription to a journal in your field. Many national and state-level professional organizations also have web sites so that you can constantly be connected to a broader professional community of educators and learners than the one in your school or your district. These resources will help you continue to think and to learn from teachers in your field who may have similar students, similar content, and similar settings.

We also recommend that you seek out a local or regional organization for teachers in your discipline, such as the New England Association of Teachers of English or the Bay Area Association of Teachers of Mathematics. We believe that membership and participation in such professional organizations will give you many opportunities to learn about new teaching techniques and resources, to keep up with standards and frameworks for your students and credentialing and licensing issues that may affect you, and to share ideas and concerns with colleagues across a broader professional base than you can identify with in your own school or district.

Conclusion to This Book

We have built this book on some very specific premises related to being an effective teacher, and we believe that in doing so we have given you a tall order to fill as you become a teacher. In essence we have said you need to be:

- A teacher and a learner
- A collaborator and an evaluator
- A participant and an observer
- A facilitator and a coach
- A developer of curriculum and a critic of content/materials

Throughout this text we have prompted you to try out literacy strategies for yourself as a learner in your own discipline, and to try these strategies and teaching/assessing tools with your own students. We have asked you to reflect on the effectiveness of these strategies and tools with different students and with different resources. Furthermore, we have often recommended you share and compare the outcomes of your learning and your teaching with peers, other preservice teachers, and experienced teachers in the schools where you are doing your field placement. We have challenged you to reflect on your own actions and experiences as a teacher in order to see what works for you and your particular students in your discipline and in the context in which you find yourself, and not merely to believe us as the authors of this text.

We hope you will continue to question and reflect on what you are doing as a middle school or high school content-area teacher. We also hope you will continue to ask yourself questions about your learners, your content, and your pedagogy. We believe your own ongoing learning in the profession is dependent on thoughtful reflections and your willingness to revise and to revamp your practices. As Linda Darling-Hammond (1994) said at an annual conference of the American Association of Teacher Educators, "We are at a moment in education when we are re-evaluating the entire educational system, teachers and students within it and developing a paradigm in support of more professional learner-centered teaching." We concur with Darling-Hammond and believe that a teacher, by the nature of the profession, no matter what the discipline or level, *must be engaged in continuous learning.*

Throughout the text, we have also reminded you about the many choices you will have as an teacher, for both yourself and your students. We have not offered you these choices to confuse or to confound you; rather we have done this to challenge you to review your current situation regularly and to consider everything you have learned as a teacher, as well as all that is in your repertoire, before making educational decisions. If you do this, you will be able to revise and to reshape your role as teacher, your classroom organization, the teaching/assessing tools you use, and the resources you choose based on the learners who are before you at any given moment, *not* on some tenth graders who happen to be taking general science this semester in this school.

We agree with Deborah Meier (1996) when she says, "Teaching is too complex to offer prescriptions for action. . . . There is neither prescription for action nor checklists for observation to assure intelligent and responsive teaching. All that can be offered are guiding theory and abundant examples." We have filled this text with examples of strategies, teaching/assessing tools, and sample content-area lessons and units. We have invited you to add your own examples from your discipline and from your grade levels along the way. Now we believe that you will be able to take the understandings of your discipline, the understandings of your students, and your newly enhanced pedagogy, particularly your knowledge of literacy and learning strategies, in order to use them effectively and reflectively as a capable, professional middle school or high school teacher who will guide the students and shape the schools of the twenty-first century.

Information and Resources

Professional Books

Canady, R. L., & Rettig, M. D. (1996). *Teaching in the block: Strategies for engaging active learners.* Larchmont, NY: Eye on Education.

Provides the rationale and models for block scheduling with an emphasis on classroom structures, such as learning centers and Socratic seminars, and the use of a range of instructional strategies, such as simulations and direct instruction to foster student understanding.

Dickinson, T. S., & Erb, T. O. (1997). *We gain more than we give: Teaming in middle schools.* Columbus, OH: National Middle School Association.

Provides useful historical background for the team teaching concept, case studies that describe different models for teaming, and, most important, guidelines for the design, implementation, and evaluation of effective teams at the middle school level.

George, P. S., & Alexander, W. M. (1993). *The exemplary middle school* (2nd ed.). Fort Worth, TX: Harcourt Brace.

Focuses on the nature of the middle school–aged student, the role of the middle school teacher as adviser, teacher, and team member, and the curricular and organizational parameters necessary for effective middle school education.

Hubbard, R. S., & Power, B. M. (1993). *The art of classroom inquiry: A handbook for teacher-researchers.* Portsmouth, NH: Heinemann.

Describes a clear set of steps for teacher researchers to follow in order to carry out classroom inquiry, from finding and framing a question to analyzing and using data to inform one's own practice.

Levstik, L. S., & Barton, K. C. (1997). *Doing history: Investigating with children in elementary and middle schools.* Hillside, NJ.: Erlbaum.

Designed to help teachers view the study of history from a sociocultural and multicultural context and to build curriculum that fosters in-depth historical thinking using family and personal histories, literature (fiction and nonfiction), and history museums and artifacts in addition to textbooks.

McDonald, J. P. (1992). *Teaching: Making sense of an uncertain craft.* New York: Teachers College Press.

Describes the author's first years of teaching recorded in his journal, his work with a group of teachers reforming their own school, and exemplary teachers, like Eliot Wigginton, the high school English teacher whose students write *Foxfire.*

Tchudi, S. (1993). *The astonishing curriculum: Integrating science and the humanities through language.* Urbana, IL: National Council of Teachers of English.

A collection of essays focused on the role that language plays in connecting science and the humanities in the real world and the classroom. These essays highlight K–12 courses and projects that have fostered learning of language, science, and technology.

Texley, J., & Wild, A. (1996*). National Science Teachers Association: Pathways to science.* Arlington, VA: National Science Teachers Association.

Focuses on middle school and high school science standards, with suggestions for implementation and assessment across the four science strands and useful classroom vignettes.

Professional Journals

Davis, S., & Thompson, D.R. (1998). To encourage "Algebra for All," start an algebra network. *Mathematics Teacher, 91*(4), 282–286.

Describes a professional development project a school district set up so that K–12 teachers could dialogue about weaving algebra principles into the curriculum at all levels.

Schug, M.C., & Cross, B. (1998, March–April). The dark side of curriculum integration in social studies. *Social Studies*, pp. 54–57.

Focuses on myths associated with the benefits of curriculum integration at the secondary level and offers useful cautions for teachers who are thinking about integration, as well as a chart for planning curriculum integration.

Science Teacher (1998, September).

Entire issue devoted to how the implementation and outcomes of the science standards can be assessed as well as to how these are best linked to mathematics and technology and to the teacher's own professional development.

Traill, D. (with the assistance of Harvey, D.). (1998). Team-teaching AP history and English. *Social Education, 62* (2), 77–79.

Discusses planning for instruction and gives the coordinated schedule of history themes and English readings.

Wolf, K., & Sui-Runyon, Y. (1996). Portfolio purposes and possibilities. *Journal of Adolescent and Adult Literacy, 40*(1), 30–37.

Emphasizes that the purpose of a portfolio should determine its form and describes three models, each with a different purpose, and their strengths and limitations.

Internet

http://www.enc.org (Eisenhower Clearinghouse).

Comprehensive web site focused on math and science. Includes a detailed resource finder that can be accessed by grade level and topic, a monthly update of the thirteen most outstanding sites and projects, plus current information on the standards, the curriculum frameworks, and recent national and international studies and reports.

http://www.ipl/teen/ (Internet Public Library).

Compiles information on a range of concerns of and issues for teenagers. Strong in language arts, providing age-appropriate booklists and genre studies, links to authors including their home pages, and an on-line research and writing guide.

http://www.middleweb.com (Middle Web)

Focuses on middle school issues and information designed to be useful to teachers, administrators, and their students. Includes extensive links on assessment and evaluation, curriculum development and instruction, standards-based reform, and professional development opportunities for both principals and teachers at the middle school level.

http://www.ole.net:8081/educator/LINKARCHIVE/index.hbs (On-line Educator)

Designed to link students and teachers to specialized sites from varied discipline areas including physical education and health, many of which encourage interaction and application of content-area knowledge as well as communication skills by students.

References

Alexander, P. A., Jetton, T. L., Kulikowich, J. M., & Woehler, C. A. (1994). Contrasting instructional and structural importance: The seductive effect of teacher questions. *Journal of Reading Behavior, 26*(1), 19–45.

Alexander, P. A., & Judy, J. E. (1988). The interaction of domain-specific and strategic knowledge in academic performance. *Review of Educational Research, 58*(4), 375–404.

Alexander, P. A. & Kulikowich, J. M. (1994). Learning from physics textbooks: A synthesis of recent research. *Journal of Research in Science Teaching, 31*(9), 895–911.

Alexander, W. M., & George, P. S. (1993). *The exemplary middle school.* Fort Worth, TX: Harcourt Brace.

Allan, K. K., & Miller, M. S. (1995). *Purposeful reading and writing: Strategies in context.* Fort Worth, TX: Harcourt Brace.

Allen, S. (1989). *Writing to learn in science* (ERIC Documentation Reproduction Service No. ED 362 883).

Almasi, J. F. (1995). The nature of fourth graders' sociocognitive conflicts in peer-led and teacher-led discussions of literature. *Reading Research Quarterly, 30*(3), 314–351.

Alvermann, D. E. (1991). The discussion web: A graphic aid for learning across the curriculum. *Reading Teacher, 45*(2), 92–99.

Alvermann, D. (1994). Trade books and textbooks: Making connections across content areas. In L. M. Morrow, J. K. Smith, & L. C. Wilkinson (Eds.), *Integrating language arts: Controversy to consensus* (pp. 51–69). Needham Heights, MA: Allyn & Bacon.

Alvermann, D. E., O'Brien, D. G., & Dillon, D. R. (1990). What teachers do when they say they're having discussions of content area reading assignments: A qualitative analysis. *Reading Research Quarterly, 25*(4), 296–321.

Alvermann, D. E., Smith, L. C., & Readance, J. E. (1985). Prior knowledge activation and the comprehension of compatible and incompatible text. *Reading Research Quarterly, 20,* 420–436.

Alvermann, D. E., Young, J. P., Weaver, D., Hinchman, K. A., Moore, D. W., Phelps, S. F., Thrash, E. C., & Zalewski, P. (1996). Middle and high school students' perceptions of how they experience text-based discussions: A multicase study. *Reading Research Quarterly, 31*(3), 244–267.

American Association of University Women. (1992). *The AAUW report: How schools shortchange girls.* Washington, D.C.: AAUW Educational Foundation.

American Institutes for Research. (1998). *Gender gaps: Where schools still fail our children.* Washington, D.C.: American Association of University Women Educational Foundation.

Ames, R., & Ames, C. (1991). Motivation and effective teaching. In L. Idol & B. F. Jones (Eds.), *Educational values and cognitive instruction: Implications for reform* (pp. 247–271). Hillsdale, NJ: Erlbaum.

Anderson, G. L., Herr, K., & Nihlen, A. S. (1994). *Studying your own school: An educator's guide to qualitative practitioner research.* Thousand Oaks, CA: Corwin Press.

Anderson, R. C. (1994). Role of the reader's schema in comprehension, learning and memory. In R. B. Ruddell, M. R. Ruddell, & H. Singer (Eds.), *Theoretical models and processes of reading* (4th ed.) (pp. 469–482). Newark, DL: International Reading Association.

Anderson, R. C., Reynolds, R. E., Schallert, D. L., & Goetz, E. T. (1977). Frameworks for comprehending discourse. *American Educational Research Journal, 14,* 367–382.

Appel, T. & Andreoli, A. (1996, March). *Collaboratively teaching American studies in a block schedule.* Paper presented at the Spring Conference of the National Council of Teachers of English, Boston, MA.

Armbruster, B. B. (1984). The problem of "inconsiderate text." In G. G. Duffy, L. R. Roehler, & J. Mason (Eds.), *Comprehension instruction: Perspectives and suggestions* (pp. 202–217). New York: Longman.

Armbruster, B. B., Anderson, T. H., & Ostertag, J. (1987). Does text struc-ture/summarization instruction facilitate learning from expository text? *Reading Research Quarterly, 22,* 331–346.

Aronson, E. (1978). *The jigsaw classroom.* Thousand Oaks, CA: Sage.

Atwell, N. (1998*). In the middle: New understandings about writing, reading, and learning* (2nd ed.). Portsmouth, NH: Heinemann.

Atwood, R. K., & Atwood, V. A. (1996). Preservice elementary teachers' conceptions of causes of seasons. *Journal of Research in Science Teaching, 33*(5), 553–563.

Baldwin, R. S., Ford, J. C., & Readence, J. E. (1981). Teaching word connotations: An alternative strategy. *Reading World, 21*(2), 103–108.

Ball, D. L. (1991). Research on teaching mathematics: Making subject-matter knowledge part of the equation. In J. Brophy (Ed.), *Advances in research on teaching* (Vol. 2, pp. 1–48). Greenwich, CT: JAI Press.

Ball, D. L., & Reiman-Nemser, S. (1988). Using textbooks and teacher's guides: A dilemma for beginning teachers and teacher educators. *Curriculum Inquiry, 18*(4), 401–423.

Barnes, D., & Todd, F. (1995). *Communication and learning revisited.* Portsmouth, NH: Boynton/Cook, Heinemann.

Beane, J. A. (1995a). Curriculum integration and the disciplines of knowledge. *Phi Delta Kappan, 76*(8), 616–622.

Beane, J. A. (1995b). Introduction: What is a coherent curriculum? *Yearbook for the Association of Supervision and Curriculum Development.* Alexandria, VA: ASCD.

Beck, I. L., McKeown, M. G., & Gromoll, E. W. (1989). Learning from social studies texts. *Cognition and Instruction, 6*(2), 99–158.

Beck, I. L., McKeown, M. G., Hamilton, R. L., & Kucan, L. (1997). *Questioning the author: An approach for enhancing student engagement with text.* Newark, DL: International Reading Association.

Beck, I. L., McKeown, M. G., McCaslin, E. S., & Burkes, A. M. (1979). *The rationale and design of a program to teach vocabulary to fourth-grade students.* Pittsburgh: University of Pittsburgh, Learning Research and Development Center.

Ben-Peretz, M. (1990). *The teacher-curriculum encounter: Freeing teachers from the tyranny of texts.* Albany: State University of New York Press.

Bloom, A. (1987). *The closing of the American mind.* New York: Simon & Schuster.

Bloom, B. S., Englehart M. C., Furst, E.J., Hill, W. H., & Krathwohl, D. R. (1956). *Taxonomy of educational objectives: The classification of educational goals. Handbook I: Cognitive domain.* New York: McKay.

Bos, C. S., & Anders, P. L. (1990). Interactive teaching and learning: Instructional practices for teaching content and strategic knowledge. In T. E. Scruggs & B. Y. L. Wong (Eds.), *Intervention research in learning disabilities* (pp. 166–185). New York: Springer-Verlag.

Bos, C. S., & Anders, P. L. (1990, Winter). Effects of interactive vocabulary instruction on the vocabulary learning and reading comprehension of junior-high learning disabled students. *Learning Disability Quarterly, 13,* 31–42.

Bos, C. S., Anders, P. L., Filip, D., & Jaffe, L. E. (1989). The effects of an interactive instructional strategy for enhancing reading comprehension and content area learning for students with learning disabilities. *Journal of Learning Disabilities, 22*(6), 384–390.

Boston Public Schools. (1996). *Citywide learning standards and curriculum frameworks.* Boston: Boston Public Schools.

Bransford, J. D. (1994). Schema activation and schema acquisition: Comments on Richard C. Anderson's remarks. In R. B. Ruddell, M. R. Ruddell, & H. Singer (Eds.), *Theoretical models and processes of reading* (4th ed.) (pp. 483–495). Newark, DL: International Reading Association.

Brown, A. L., & Day, J. D. (1983). Macrorules for summarizing texts: The development of expertise. *Journal of Verbal Learning and Verbal Behavior, 22,* 1–14.

Brown, D. E. (1992). Using examples and analogies to remediate misconceptions in physics: Factors influencing conceptual change. *Journal of Research in Science Teaching, 29(1),* 17–34.

Buikema, J. L., & Graves, M. F. (1993). Teaching students to use context cues to infer word meanings. *Journal of Reading, 36*(6), 450–457.

Burmeister, L. E. (1978). *Reading strategies for middle and secondary school teachers* (2nd ed.). Reading, MA: Addison-Wesley.

Carnegie Commission Task Force. (1986). *A nation prepared: Teachers for the 21st century.* Report of the Task Force on Teaching as a Profession. New York: Carnegie Corporation.

Carnegie Council on Adolescent Development. (1990). *Turning points: Preparing American youth for the 21st century.* Report of the Carnegie Council on Adolescent Development's Task Force on Education of Young Adolescents. New York: Carnegie Corporation.

Carr, E., & Ogle, D. (1987). KWL Plus: A strategy for comprehension and summarization. *Journal of Reading, 30,* 626–631.

Chambliss, M. J. (1994). Why do readers fail to change their beliefs after reading persuasive text? In R. Garner & P. A. Alexander (Eds.), *Beliefs about text and instruction with text* (pp. 75–89). Hillsdale, NJ: Erlbaum.

Chase, A. C., & Dufflemeyer, F. A. (1990). VOCAB-LIT: Integrating vocabulary study and literature study. *Journal of Reading, 34*(3), 188–193.

Checkley, K. (1997). International math and science study calls for depth not breadth. *ASCD Education Update, 19*(1) 1, 3.

Cochran, J. F., De Ruiter, J. A., & King, R. A. (1993). Pedagogical content knowing: An integrative model for teacher preparation. *Journal of Teacher Education, 44,* 263–272.

Cohen, P. (1995, Winter). Challenging history: The past remains a battle ground for schools. *ASCD Curriculum Update,* 1–2, 7–8.

Collins, A., Brown, J. S., & Newman, S. E. (1989). Cognitive apprenticeship: Teaching the craft of reading, writing, mathematics. In L. B. Resnick (Ed.), *Knowing, learning, and instruction: Essays in honor of Robert Glaser* (pp. 453–494). Hillsdale, NJ: Erlbaum.

Committee for Economic Development. (1987). *Children in need: Investment strategies for the educationally disadvantaged.* New York: Committee for Economic Development.

Conard, S. (1984). *On readability and readability formula scores*. Ginn Occasional Papers: Writings in Reading and Language Arts, No. 17. New York: Ginn.

Cooper, J. D. (1993). *Literacy: Helping children construct meaning* (2nd ed.). Boston: Houghton Mifflin.

Crawford, L. W. (1993). *Language and literacy learning in multicultural classrooms*. Needham Heights, MA: Allyn & Bacon.

Daniels, H. (1994). *Literature circles: Voice and choice in the student-centered classroom*. York, ME: Stenhouse.

Darling-Hammond, L. (1991). The implications of testing policy for quality and equality. *Phi Delta Kappan, 73,* 220–225.

Darling-Hammond, L. (1994, February 17). *Standards for teachers*. 34th Charles M. Hunt Memorial Lecture, AACTE 46th Annual Meeting, Chicago.

Darling-Hammond, L., Ancess, J., & Falk, B. (1995). *Authentic assessment in action*. New York: Teachers College Press.

Delpit, L. D. (1988). The silenced dialogue: Power and pedagogy in educating other people's children. *Harvard Educational Review, 58,* 280–298.

Dillon, D. R., O'Brien, D. G., & Moje, E. B. (1994). Literacy learning in secondary school classrooms: A cross-case analysis of three qualitative studies. *Journal of Research in Teaching Science, 31*(4), 345–362.

Dillon, J. T. (1994). *Using discussion in classrooms*. Philadelphia: Open University Press.

Dole, J., Duffy, G. G., Roehler, L. R., & Pearson, P. D. (1991). Moving from the old to the new: Research on reading comprehension instruction. *Review of Educational Research, 61*(2), 239–264.

Doll, R. C. (1996). *Curriculum improvement: Decision making and process* (9th ed.). Needham Heights, MA: Allyn & Bacon.

Dornan, R., Rosen, L. M., & Wilson, M. (1997). *Multiple voices, multiple texts: Reading in the secondary content areas*. Portsmouth, NH: Boynton/Cook Publishers.

Drake, S. M. (1993). *Planning integrated curriculum: The call to adventure*. Alexandria, VA: Association for Supervision and Curriculum Development.

Duffelmeyer, F. A. (1994). Effective anticipation guide statement for learning from expository prose. *Journal of Reading, 37*(6), 452–457.

Duffelmeyer, F. A., Baum, D. D., & Merkely, D. J. (1987). Maximizing reader-text confrontation with an extended anticipation guide. *Journal of Reading, 31*(20), 146–150.

Duffy, G. G., & Roehler, L. R. (1989). Why strategy instruction is so difficult and what we need to do about it. In C. B. McCormick, G. Miller, & M. Pressley (Eds.), *Cognitive strategy research: From basic research to educational applications* (pp.133–154). New York: Springer-Verlag.

Duffy, G. G., Roehler, L. R., Sivan, E., Rackliffe, G., Book, C., Meloth, M. S., Vavrus, L. G., Wesselman, R., Putnam, J., & Bassiri, D. (1987). Effects of explaining the reasoning associated with using reading strategies. *Reading Research Quarterly, 22*(3), 347–368.

Earle, R. A. (1976). *Teaching reading and mathematics*. Newark, DL: International Reading Association.

Ediger, M. (1990). Designing the curriculum. (ERIC Documentation Reproduction Services ED 336 198)

Eeds, M., & Wells, D. (1989). Grand conversations: An exploration of meaning construction in literature study groups. *Research in the Teaching of English, 23*(1), 4–29.

Elbow, P. (1973). *Writing without teachers*. New York: Oxford University Press.

Englert, C. S., Raphael, T. E., Anderson, L. M., Anthony, H. M., & Stevens, D. D. (1991). Making strategies and self-talk visible: Writing instruction in regular and special education classrooms. *American Educational Research Journal, 28,* 337–372.

Featherstone, J. (1995). Letter to a young teacher. In W. Ayers (Ed.), *To become a teacher: Making a difference in children's lives* (pp. 11–22). New York: Teachers College.

Figueroa, R. A., & García, E. (1994). Issues in testing students from culturally and linguistically diverse backgrounds. *Multicultural Education, 2*(1), 10–9.

Fine, M. (1991). *Framing dropouts: Notes on the politics of an urban high school.* Albany: State University of New York Press.

Flavell, J. H., Miller, P. H., & Miller, S. A. (1993). *Cognitive development.* Englewood Cliffs, NJ: Prentice Hall.

Frayer, D. A., Frederick, W. C., & Klausmeier, H. H. (1969). *A science for testing the level of concept mastery* (Working Paper No. 16). Madison, WI: University of Wisconsin Research and Development Center for Cognitive Learning.

Fredericks, A. D., Meinbach, A. M., & Rothlein, L. (1992). *Thematic units: An integrated approach to teaching science and social studies.* New York: HarperCollins.

Fry, E. B. (1977). Fry's readability graph: Clarifications, validity, and extension to level 17. *Journal of Reading, 21,* 242–252.

Fulwiler, T. (1987). *Teaching with writing.* Portsmouth, NH: Boynton/Cook, Heinemann.

Furner, J. (1995). *Planning for interdisciplinary instruction: a literature review.* Tuscaloosa, AL: University of Alabama College of Education (ERIC Document Reproduction Service No. ED 385 515).

Gambrell, L. B., & Almasi, J. F. (1994). Fostering comprehension development through discussion. In L. M. Morrow, J. K. Smith, & L. C. Wilkinson, *Integrated language arts: Controversy to consensus* (pp. 71–90). Needham Heights, MA: Allyn & Bacon.

García, E. (1999). *Student cultural diversity: Understanding and meeting the challenge* (2nd ed.). Boston: Houghton Mifflin.

García, G. E. (1991). Factors influencing the English reading test performance of Spanish-speaking Hispanic children. *Reading Research Quarterly, 26*(4), 371–391.

García, G. E., & Nagy, W. E. (1993). Latino students' concept of cognates. In D. J. Leu & C. K. Kinzer (Eds.), *Examining central issues in literacy research, theory, and practice* (pp. 367–373). 42nd Yearbook of the National Reading Conference. Chicago: National Reading Conference.

García, G. E., & Pearson, P. D. (1994). Assessment and diversity. In L. Darling-Hammond (Ed.), *Review of research in education* (Vol. 20, pp. 337–391). Washington, D.C.: American Educational Research Association.

Garner, R. (1987). *Metacognition and reading comprehension.* Norwood, NJ: Ablex.

Garner, R., & Alexander, R. (1989). Metacognition: Answered and unanswered questions. *Educational Psychologist, 24* (2), 143–158.

Garner, R., Gillingham, M. G., & White, C. S. (1989). Effects of "seductive details" on macroprocessing and microprocessing in adults and children. *Cognition and Instruction, 6,* 41–57.

Gaskins, I., & Gaskins, E. T. (1991). *Implementing cognitive strategy teaching across the school: The Benchmark manual for teachers.* Cambridge, MA: Brookline Press.

Geography Education Standards Project. (1994). *Geography for life: National geography standards.* Washington, D.C.: Geography Education Standards Project.

George, P. S., & Alexander, W. M. (1993). *The exemplary middle school* (2nd ed.). Fort Worth, TX: Harcourt Brace.

Glatthorn, A. A. (1986). *Alternative processes in curriculum development.* Paper presented at the Annual Meeting of the American Educational Research Association, San Francisco.

Goatley, V. J., Brock, C. H., & Raphael, T. E. (1995). Diverse learners participating in regular education "Book Clubs." *Reading Research Quarterly, 30*(3), 352–380.

Gollnick, D. M., & Chinn, P. C. (1994). *Multicultural education in a pluralistic society.* New York: Merrill/Macmillan.

Goodlad, J. I. (1984). *A place called school.* New York: McGraw-Hill.

Gordon, C .J., & Macinnis, D. (1993). Using journals as a window on students' thinking in mathematics. *Language Arts, 70,* 37–43.

Graves, M. F. (1987) The role of instruction in vocabulary development. In M. G. McKeown & M. E. Curtis (Eds.), *The nature of vocabulary acquisition* (pp. 165–184). Hillsdale, NJ: Erlbaum.

Graves, M. F., & Slater, W. H. (1996). Vocabulary instruction in the content areas. In D. Lapp, J. Flood, & N. Farnan (Eds.), *Content area reading and learning* (2nd ed.) (pp. 261–275). Boston: Allyn and Bacon.

Gregg, G. P., & Carroll, P. S. (1998). *Books and beyond: Thematic appraoches for teaching literature in high school.* Norwood, MA: Christopher-Gordon Publishers.

Grossman, P. L. (1991). What are we talking about anyway? Subject-matter knowledge of secondary English teachers. In J. Brophy (Ed.), *Advances in research on teaching* (Vol. 2, pp. 245–264). Greenwich, CT: JAI Press.

Guthrie, J. T., & McCann, A. D. (1996). Idea circles: Peer collaborations for conceptual learning. In L. B. Gambrell & J. R. Almasi (Eds.), *Lively discussions!Fostering engaged reading* (pp. 87–105). Newark, DL: International Reading Association.

Guzzetti, B. J., & Williams, W. O. (1996). Gender, text, and discussion: Examining the intellectual safety in the science classroom. *Journal of Research in Science Teaching, 33* (1), 5–20.

Haggard, M. R. (1982). Vocabulary self-collection strategy: An active approach to word learning. *Journal of Reading, 27,* 203–207.

Haggard, M. R. (1986). The vocabulary self-collection strategy: Using student interest and world knowledge to enhance vocabulary growth. *Journal of Reading, 29*(7), 634–642.

Hare, V. C., Rabinowitz, M., & Schieble, K. M. (1989). Text effects on main idea comprehension. *Reading Research Quarterly, 24,* 72–88.

Harris, K., & Pressley, M. (1991). The nature of cognitive strategy instruction: Interactive strategy instruction. *Exceptional Children, 57,* 392–404.

Harste, J., Short, K., with Burke, C. L. (1988). *Creating classrooms for authors: The reading-writing connection.* Portsmouth, N.H.: Heinemann.

Hartman, D. K. (1995). Eight readers reading: The intertextual links of proficient readers reading multiple passages. *Reading Research Quarterly, 30*(3), 520–561.

Heller, M. F. (1997). Reading and writing about the environment: Visions of the year 2000. *Journal of Adolescent and Adult Literacy, 40*(5), 332–341.

Herber, H. L. (1978). *Teaching reading in the content areas* (2nd ed.). New York: Prentice Hall.

Hidi, S., & Anderson, V. (1986). Producing written summaries: Task demands, cognitive operations, and implications for instruction. *Review of Educational Research, 56*(4), 473–493.

Hill, M. (1991). Writing summaries promotes thinking and learning across the curriculum—but why are they so difficult to write? *Journal of Reading, 34*(7), 536–539.

Hirsch, E. D., Jr. (1988). *Cultural literacy: What every American needs to know.* New York: Random House.

Hollon, R. E., Roth, K. J., & Anderson, C. W. (1991). Science teachers' conceptions of teaching and learning. In J. Brophy (Ed.), *Advances in research on teaching* (Vol. 2, pp. 145–185). Greenwich, CT: JAI Press.

Hubbard, R. S., & Power, B. M. (1993). *The art of classroom inquiry: A handbook for teacher researchers.* Portsmouth, NH: Heinemann.

International Reading Association and National Council of Teachers of English, Statement on readability. (1984). Newark, DL: International Reading Association.

Illinois State Board of Education. (1998). *Integrated nutrition education.* Curriculum guide developed for the Illinois State Board of Education. (ERIC Document Reproduction Services No. ED 231 505)

Jacobs, H. H. (Ed.) (1989). *Interdisciplinary curriculum: Design and implemention.* Alexandria, VA: Association for Supervision and Curriculum Development.

Jerald, C. D., Curran, B. K., & Olson, L. (August 13, 1998). State indicators. *Education Week on the web.* Available at: **http://www.edweek.org/sreports/qc98/states/indicators/in–1.htm#sta.**

Jiménez, R. T., García, G. E., & Pearson, P. D. (1996). The reading strategies of bilingual Latina/o students who are successful English readers: Opportunities and obstacles. *Reading Research Quarterly, 31*(1), 90–112.

Johnson, D. D., & Pearson, P. D. (1984). *Teaching vocabulary* (2nd ed.). New York: Holt.

Johnson, D. W., Johnson, R. T., & Holubec, E. J. (1990). *Circles of learning: Cooperation in the classroom* (3rd ed.). Edina, MN: Interaction Book Company.

Joint Committee on National Health Education Standards. (1995). *National health education standards: Achieving health literacy.* Washington, D.C.: American Cancer Society.

Jones, M. G., & Wheatley, J. (1990). Gender differences in teacher-student interactions in science classrooms. *Journal of Research in Science Teaching, 27*(9), 861–874.

Kendall, J. S., & Marzano, R. J. (1996). *Content knowledge: A compendium of standards and benchmarks for K–12 education.* Aurora, Ohio: Mid-continent Regional Educational Laboratory.

Kleiman, G. M. (1991). Mathematics across the curriculum. *Educational Leadership, 49* (2), 48–51.

Knapp, M. S., & Woolverton, S. (1995). Social class and schooling. In J. A. Banks & C. A. M. Banks (Eds.), *Handbook of research on multicultural education* (pp. 548–569). New York: Macmillan.

Kozol, J. (1991). *Savage inequalities: Children in America's schools.* New York: Crown.

Kyle, W. C. (1995). Scientific literacy: Where do we go from here? *Journal of Research in Science Teaching, 32*(10), 1007–1009.

Langer, J. A., Bartolome, L., Vasquez, O., & Lucas, T. (1990). Meaning construction in school literacy tasks: A study of bilingual students. *American Educational Research Journal, 27,* 427–471.

Laughlin, M. A., & Hartoonian, H. M. (1995). *Challenges of social studies instruction in middle and high schools.* Orlando, FL: Harcourt Brace.

Lee, O., & Fradd, S. H. (1998). Science for all, including students from non-English-language backgrounds. *Educational Researcher, 27*(4), 12–20.

Lerner, J. (1993). *Learning disabilities: Theories, diagnosis and teaching strategies* (6th ed.). Boston: Houghton Mifflin.

Levstik, L. S., & Barton, K. C. (1997). *Doing history: Investigating with children in elementary and middle schools.* Hillside, NJ: Erlbaum.

Lounsbury, J. H. (Ed.) (1992). *Connecting the curriculum through interdisciplinary instruction.* Columbus, OH: National Middle School Association.

Lozauskas, D., & Barell, J. (1992). Reflective reading. *Science Teacher, 59*(8), 42–45.

Lynch, E. A. (1997). Why Johnny can't add—and Akira can.*The Compass Feature,* ALMANA COMPASS.

Macrorie, K. (1988*). The I-Search paper.* Portsmouth, NH: Heinemann.

Mandler, J., & Johnson, N. (1977). Remembrance of things parsed: Story structure and recall. *Cognitive Psychology, 9,* 111–151.

Manning, M., Manning, G., & R. Long, R. (1997). *The theme immersion compendium for social studies teaching.* Portsmouth, NH: Heinemann.

Martinello, M. L., & Cook, G. E. (1994). *Interdisciplinary inquiry in teaching and learning.* New York: Macmillan.

Massachusetts Department of Education. (1996). *World languages curriculum frameworks.* Malden, MA: Massachusetts Department of Education.

Matyas, M. L., & Haley-Oliphant, A. E. (1997). *Women life scientists: Past, pres-ent and future.* Bethesda, MD: American Physiological Society.

Maurer, R. E. (1994). *Designing interdisciplinary curriculum in middle, junior high, and high schools.* Needham Heights, MA: Allyn & Bacon.

McDiarmid, G. W. (1991). What teachers need to know about cultural diversity: Restoring subject matter to the picture. In M. M. Kennedy (Ed.), *Teaching academic subjects to diverse learners* (pp. 257–270). New York: Teachers College Press.

McDiarmid, G. W., Ball, D. L., & Anderson, C. W. (1989). Why staying one chapter ahead doesn't really work: Subject-specific pedagogy. In M. C. Reynolds (Ed.), *Knowledge base for the beginning teacher* (pp. 193–205). New York: Pergamon Press.

McDonald, J. P. (1992). *Teaching: Making sense of an uncertain craft.* New York: Teachers College Press.

McMahon, S. I., & Raphael, T. E. (Eds.), with Goatley, V. J., & Pardo, L. S. (1997). *The book club connection: Literacy learning and classroom talk.* Newark, DL: International Reading Association.

McMillan, J. H. (1997). *Classroom assessment: Principles and practices for effective instruction.* Needham Heights, MA: Allyn & Bacon.

McQueen, M. E. (1996). Situational drama: An alternative to worksheets. *Journal of Adolescent and Adult Literacy, 39*(8), 656–657.

Meier, D. (1996*). The power of their ideas: Lessons for America from a small school in Harlem.* Boston: Beacon Press.

Meinbach, A. M., Rothlein, L., & Fredericks, A. D. (1995*). The complete guide to thematic units: Creating integrated curriculum.* Norwood, MA: Christopher-Gordon Publishers.

Meyer, L. (1991). Are science textbooks considerate? In C. M. Santa & D. E. Alvermann (Eds.), *Science learning: Process and applications* (pp. 28–37). Newark, DL: International Reading Association.

Miller, G. A., & Gildea, P. M. (1987). How children learn words. *Scientific American, 257*(3), 94–99.

Minami, M., & Ovando, C. J. (1995). Language issues in multicultural contexts. In J. A. Banks & C. A. M. Banks (Eds.), *Handbook of research on multicultural education* (pp. 427–444). New York: Macmillian.

Mitchell, R. (1992). *Testing for learning: How new approaches to evaluation can improve American schools.* New York: Free Press.

Moffett, J. (1983/1968). *Teaching the universe of discourse.* Boston: Houghton Mifflin.

Moll, L. C. (1992). Bilingual classroom studies and community analysis: Some recent trends. *Educational Researcher, 21*(2), 20–24.

Monson, M. P., & Monson, R. J. (1993). Who creates curriculum? New roles for teachers. *Educational Leadership, 51*(2), 19–21.

Moran, C. E., & Hakuta, K. (1995). Bilingual education: Broadening research perspectives. In J. A. Banks & C. A. M. Banks (Eds.), *Handbook on multicultural education* (pp. 445–462). New York: Macmillan.

Moss, J. F. (1994). *Using literature in the middle grades: A thematic approach.* Norwood, MA: Christopher-Gordon Publishers.

Myer, B. J. F., Brandt, D. M., & Bluth, G. J. (1980). Use of top-level structure in text: Key for reading comprehension of ninth-grade students. *Reading Research Quarterly, 16,* 72–103.

Nagy, W. E., & Herman, P. A. (1987). Breadth and depth of vocabulary knowledge: Implications for acquisition and instruction. In M. G. McKeown & M. E. Curtis (Eds.), *The nature of vocabulary acquisition* (pp. 19–35). Hillsdale, NJ: Erlbaum.

National Association of Secondary School Principals. (1996). *Breaking ranks: Changing an American institution.* Report of the National Association of Secondary School Principals in partnership with the Carnegie Foundation for the Advancement of Teaching on the High School of the 21st Century. Washington, D.C.: National Association of Secondary School Principals.

National Center for Education Statistics. (1994). *History report card: History assessment at a glance.* Washington, D.C.: U.S. Government Printing Office.

National Center for Education Statistics. (1996). *Math report card for the nation and the states.* Washington, D.C.: U.S. Government Printing Office.

National Center for Education Statistics. (1996). *The condition of education.* Washington, D.C.: U.S. Department of Education.

National Commission on Excellence in Education. (1983). *A nation at risk: The imperative for educational reform.* Washington, D.C.: The National Commission of Excellence in Education.

National Commission on Teaching & America's Future. (1996). *What matters most: Teaching for America's future.* Report of the National Commission on Teaching & America's Future. Summary Report. New York: National Commission on Teaching & America's Future.

National Council for the Social Studies. (1994). *Expectations of excellence: Curriculum standards for social studies.* Washington, D.C.: National Council for the Social Studies.

National Council of Teachers of English and International Reading Association. (1996). *Standards for the English Language Arts.* Champaign, IL, and Newark, DE: National Council of Teachers of English and International Reading Association.

National Council of Teachers of Mathematics. (1989). *Curriculum and evaluation standards for school mathematics.* Alexandria, VA: National Council of Teachers of Mathematics.

National Education Association. (1997). *Status of the American public school teacher 1995–1996.* Washington, D.C.: National Education Association.

Nelson-Barber, S., & Estrin, E. T. (1995). Bringing Native American perspectives to mathematics and science teaching. *Theory into Practice, 34*(3),174–185.

Nieto, S. (1996). *Affirming diversity* (2nd ed). White Plains, NY: Longman.

Norton, D. E. (1995). *Through the eyes of a child: An introduction to children's literature* (4th ed.). Englewood Cliffs, N.J.: Merrill.

Oakes, J. (1992). Can tracking research inform practice? Technical, normative, and political considerations. *Educational Researcher, 21*(4), 12–21.

Ogbu, J. U. (1993). Differences in cultural frame of reference. *International Journal of Behavioral Development, 16*(3), 483–506.

Ogle, D. M. (1986). KWL: A teaching model that develops active reading of expository text. *Reading Teacher, 39,* 564–570.

Ogle, D. M. (1996). Study techniques that ensure content area reading success. In D. Lapp, J. Flood, & N. Farnan (Eds.). *Content Area Reading and Learning: Instructional Strategies* (2nd ed.) (pp. 277–290). Boston: Allyn & Bacon.

Oja, S. N., & Smulyan, L. (1989). *Collaborative action research: A developmental approach.* New York: Falmer Press.

Olson, L. (February 11, 1998). The push for accountability gathers steam. *Ed-ucation Week on the Web.* Available from: **http://www.edweek.org/ew/vol–17/22accoun.h17**.

O'Neill, J. (1994, June). Move over Dick and Jane, Silas Marner, you too can take a walk. *ASCD Curriculum Update,* 1–4, 7–8.

Palinscar, A. S., & Brown, A. L. (1984). Reciprocal teaching of comprehension-fostering and comprehension-monitoring activities. *Cognition and Instruction, 2,* 117–175.

Palmatier, R. A. (1973). A notetaking system for learning. *Journal of Reading, 18,* 36–39.

Palmer, R. G., & Stewart, R. A. (1997). Nonfiction tradebooks in content area instruction: Realities and potential. *Journal of Adolescent and Adult Literacy, 40*(8), 630–641.

Panaritis, P. (1995). Beyond brainstorming: Planning a successful interdisciplinary program. *Phi Delta Kappan, 7* (8), 623–628.

Paris, S. G., Lipson, M. Y., & Wixson, K. K. (1983/1994). Becoming a strategic reader. In R. B. Ruddell, M. R. Ruddell, & H. Singer (Eds.), *Theoretical models and processes of reading* (4th ed., pp. 788–810). Newark, DL: International Reading Association.

Pearson, P. D., & Gallagher, M. C. (1983). The instruction of reading comprehension. *Contemporary Educational Psychology, 8*(3), 317–344.

Pearson, P. D., & Johnson, D. D. (1978). *Teaching reading comprehension.* New York: Holt.

Peresich, M. L., Meadows, J. D., & Sinatra, R. (1990). Content area cognitive mapping for reading and writing proficiency. *Journal of Reading, 33*(6), 424–432.

Perkins, D. N., & Salomon, G. (1989). Are cognitive skills context-bound? *Educational Researcher, 16*(1), 16–25.

Peters, C. W. (1996). Reading in the social studies: Using skills and strategies in a thoughtful manner. In D. Lapp, J. Flood, & N. Farnan (Eds.), *Content area reading and learning: Instructional strategies* (2nd ed.) (pp. 181–207). Needham Heights, MA: Allyn & Bacon.

Porter, A. C. (1994). National standards and school improvement in the 1990's: Issues and promise. *American Journal of Education, 102*(4), 421–449.

Pressley, M., Goodchild, R., Fleet, J., Sajchowski, R., & Evans, E. D. (1989). The challenges of classroom strategy instruction. *Elementary School Journal, 89* (3), 301–342.

Pugalee, D. K. (1997). Connecting writing to the mathematics curriculum. *Mathematics Teacher, 90*(6), 308–310.

Raphael, T. E. (1986). Teaching question answer relationships, revisited. *Reading Teacer, 40,* 516–522.

Ravitch, D. (1995). National standards and curriculum reform. In A. C. Ornstein & L. S. Behar (Eds.), *Contemporary issues in curriculum.* Needham Heights, MA: Allyn & Bacon.

Readence, J. E., Bean, T. W., & Baldwin, R. S. (1989). *Content area reading: An integrated approach.* Dubuque, IA: Kendell/Hunt.

Reyes, M. de la Luz (1992). Challenging venerable assumptions: Literacy instruction for linguistically different students. *Harvard Educational Review, 62,* 427–446.

Richardson, J. S., & Morgan, R. F. (1997). *Reading to learn in the content areas.* Belmont, CA: Wadsworth.

Richgels, D. J., McGee, L., Lomax, R. G., & Sheard, C. (1987). Awareness of four text structures: Effects on recall of expository text. *Reading Research Quarterly, 22,* 177–196.

Rief, L. (1992). *Seeking diversity: Language arts with adolescents.* Portsmouth, NH: Heinemann.

Robinson, F. (1961). *Effective study.* New York: Harper & Row.

Romano, T. (1995). *Writing with passion: Life stories, multiple genres.* Portsmouth, NH: Heinemann.

Rosenblatt, L. M. (1994). The transactional theory of reading and writing. In R. B. Ruddell, M. R. Ruddell, & H. Singer, *Theoretical models and processes of reading* (4th ed.) (pp. 1057–1093). Newark, DL: International Reading Association.

Rosenshine, B., & Meister, C. (1994). Reciprocal teaching: A review of the research. *Review of Educational Research, 64,* 479–530.

Rowe, M. B. (1974). Relation of wait-time and rewards to the development of language, logic, and fate control: Part one, Wait-time. *Journal of Research in Science Teaching, 11,* 81–94.

Rutherford, F. J. & Ahlgren, A. (1990). *Science for all Americans: A project 2061 report on goals in science.* New York: Oxford University Press.

Sadker, M., & Sadker, D. (1994). *Failing at fairness: How America's schools cheat girls.* New York: Charles Scribner's.

Sandel, L. (1989). *Teaching with biography.* (ERIC Documentation Services Reproduction No. ED 310 372)

Sanders, N. M. (1966). *Classroom questions: What kinds.* New York: Harper & Row.

Santa, C. M., & Alvermann, D. E. (1991). *Science learning: Processes and applications.* Newark, DE: International Reading Association.

Schmidt, D. (1985).Writing in math class. In A. R. Gere (Ed.), *Roots in sawdust: Writing across the disciplines* (pp. 104–116). Urbana, IL: National Council of Teachers of English.

Schneps, M. H. (Project Director). (1988). *A private universe* [Videotape]. Santa Monica, CA: Pyramid Film and Video.

Schön, D. A. (1983). *The reflective practitioner.* New York: Basic Books.

Schunk, D. H., & Zimmerman, B. J. (1997). Developing self–efficacious readers and writers: The role of social and self-regulatory processes. In J. T. Guthrie & A. Wigfield (Eds.), *Reading engagement: Motivating readers through integrated instruction* (pp. 34–50). Newark, DL: International Reading Association.

Schwartz, R. M. (1988). Learning to learn vocabulary in content area textbooks. *Journal of Reading, 32*(3), 108–118.

Scott, J. A., & Nagy, W. E. (1997). Understanding the definitions of unfamiliar verbs. *Reading Research Quarterly, 32*(2), 184–200.

Short, K. G. (1992). Researching intertextuality within collaborative classroom learning environments. *Linguistics and Education, 4,* 313–333.

Short, K. G., & Pierce, K. M. (1990). *Talking about books.* Portsmouth, NH: Heinemann.

Shulman, L. S. (1986).Those who understand: Knowledge growth in teaching. *Educational Researcher, 15*(2), 4–14

Shulman, L. S. (1987). Knowledge and teaching: Foundations of the new reform. *Harvard Educational Review, 57*(1), 1–22.

Sills-Briefel, T., Fisk, C., & Dunlop. V. (1996/1997). Graduation by exhibition. *Educational Leadership, 54*(4), 66–71.

Simpson, M. L. (1986). PORPE: A writing strategy for studying and learning in the content areas. *Journal of Reading, 29,* 407–414.

Singer, H. (1992). Friendly texts: Description and criteria. In E. K. Dishner, T. W. Bean, J. E. Readence, & D. W. Moore (Eds), *Reading in the content areas: Improving classroom instruction* (3rd ed.) (pp. 155–170). Dubuque, IA: Kendall Hunt.

Singer, H., & Donlan, D. (1992). Learning-from-text guide. In K. D. Wood, D. Lapp, & J. Flood (Eds.), *Guiding readers through text: A review of study guides* (pp. 31–33). Newark, DL: International Reading Association.

Slavin, R. E. (1988). Cooperative learning and student achievement. In R. E. Slavin (Ed.), *School and classroom organization.* Hillsdale, NJ: Erlbaum.

Sleeter, C. E. (1997). Reflections on my use of multicultural and critical pedagogy when students are white. In C. E. Sleeter & P. L. McLaren (Eds.), *Multicultural education, critical pedagogy, and the politics of difference* (pp. 415–438). Albany, NY: State University of New York Press.

Sleeter, C. E., & Grant, C. A. (1991). Race, class, gender, and disability in current textbooks. In M. W. Apple & L. K. Christian-Smith (Eds.), *The politics of the textbook* (pp. 78–110). New York: Routledge.

Social Science Education and Consortium. (1988). *Immigration: pluralism and national identity.* Boulder, CO: Social Science Education Consortium.

Sosenke, F. (1994). Students as textbook authors. *Mathematics Teaching in the Middle School, 1*(2), 108–111.

Speigel, D. L. (1987). Using adolescent literature in social studies and science. *Educational Horizons, 65,* 162–164.

Stahl, N. A., King, J. R., & Henk, W. A. (1991). Enhancing students' notetaking through training and evaluation. *Journal of Reading, 34*(8), 614–622.

Stahl, S. A., & Fairbanks, M. M. (1986). The effects of vocabulary instruction: A model-based meta-analysis. *Review of Educational Research, 56*(1), 72–110.

Stahl, S. A., & Vancil, S. J. (1986). Discussion is what makes semantic maps work in vocabulary discussion. *Reading Teacher, 40*(1), 62–67.

Stauffer, R. G. (1969). *Directing reading maturity as a cognitive process.* New York: Harper.

Steffenson, M. S., Joag-Dev, C., & Anderson, R. C. (1979). A cross-cultural perspective on reading comprehension. *Reading Research Quarterly, 15*, 10–29.

Stein, N. L., & Glenn, C. G. (1979). An analysis of story comprehension in elementary school children. In R. Freedle (Ed.), *New directions in discourse processing* (pp. 53–120). Norwood, NJ: Ablex.

Stoll, D. R. (1997). *Magazines for kids and teens* (rev. ed.). Newark, DE: International Reading Association and Educational Press Association of America.

Stotsky, S (1995, April). Changes in America's secondary schools. *Phi Delta Kappan,* 605–612.

Taylor, B. M. (1980). Children's memory for expository text after reading. *Reading Research Quarterly, 15,* 399–411.

Taylor, B. M., & Beach, R. W. (1984). The effects of text structure instruction on middle-grade students' comprehension and production of expository text. *Reading Research Quarterly, 19,* 134–146.

Tchudi, S. (1991). *Planning and assessing the curriculum in English/language arts.* Alexandria, VA: Association for Supervision and Curriculum Development.

Tchudi, S. (1993*). The astonishing curriculum: Integrating science and the humanities through language.* Urbana, IL: National Council of Teachers of English.

Terner, J. et al. (1988). Biographic sources in the sciences. In *Library of Congress Science Tracer Bulletin.* Washington, D.C.: National Center for Science and Technology (ERIC Document Reproduction Services ED 393 727).

Texley, J., & Wild, A. (1996). *National Science Teachers Association pathways to science.* Arlington, VA: National Science Teachers Association.

Thelen, J. N. (1984). *Improving reading in science* (2nd ed.). Newark, DE: International Reading Association.

Tiedt, I. M. (1970, December). Exploring poetry patterns. *Elementary English,* 1082–1085.

Tinajoro, J. V., & Hurly, S. R. (1997). Literacy instruction for students acquiring English: Moving beyond the immersion debate. *Reading Teacher, 50,* 356–359.

U.S. Department of Education. (1997). *To assure the free appropriate public education of all children with disabilities.* Nineteenth Annual Report to Congress on the Implementation of the Individuals with Disabilities Act. Washington, D.C.: U.S. Government Printing Office.

Vacca, R. T., & Vacca, J. A. L. (1999). *Content area reading* (6th ed.). New York: Longman.

Van Sledright, B.A. (1994). *"I don't remember—the ideas are all jumbled in my head": 8th graders' reconstruction of colonial American history.* Paper presented at the AERA Annual Meeting, New Orleans, LA. (ERIC Document Reproduction Services ED 393 727)

Warren, A. R., & McCloskey, L. A. (1997). Language in social contexts. In J. B. Gleason (Ed.), *The development of language* (pp. 210–258). Needham Heights, MA: Allyn & Bacon.

White, T. G., Sowell, J., & Yangihara, A. (1989). Teaching elementary students to use word-part clues. *Reading Teacher, 42,* 302–308.

Whitin, P. E. (1996). Exploring visual response to literature. *Research in the Teaching of English, 30*(1), 114–140.

Wigfield, A. (1997). Children's motivations for reading and reading engagement. In J. T. Guthrie & A. Wigfield (Eds.), *Reading engagement: Motivating readers through integrated instruction* (pp. 14–33). Newark, DL: International Reading Association.

Will, M. (1986). *Educating students with learning problems—A shared responsibility* (A Report to the Secretary of Education). Washington, D.C.: Office of Special Education and Rehabilitative Services, U.S. Department of Education.

Willis, S. (1992, November). Interdisciplinary learning: Movement to link the disciplines gains momentum. *ASCD Curriculum Update,* 1–8.

Wineburg, S. S. (1991). On the reading of historical texts: Notes on the breach between school and academy. *American Educational Research, 28*(3), 495–519.

Wineburg, S. S., & Wilson, S. M. (1991). Subject-matter knowledge in the teaching of history. In J. Brophy (Ed.), *Advances in research on teaching* (Vol. 2, pp. 305–347). Greenwich, CT: JAI Press.

Winograd, P. N. (1984). Strategic difficulties in summarizing texts. *Reading Research Quarterly, 19,* 404–425.

Wolf, D. P., & Reardon, S. F. (Eds.). Access to excellence through new forms of student assessment. In J. B. Baron & D. P. Wolf (Eds.), *Performance-based student assessment: Challenges and possibilities.* Chicago: National Society for the Study of Education and University of Chicago Press.

Wood, K. D. (1988). Guiding students through informational text. *Reading Teacher, 41*(9), 912–920.

Wood, K. D., Lapp, D., & Flood, J. (1992*). Guiding readers through text: A review of study guides.* Newark, DL: International Reading Association.

Index

The AAUW Report: How Schools Short-change Girls, 35, 36, 393
Abstracts, writing, 238
Achievement tests, 44
Admit and exit slips, 171–173
Alexander, P.A., 14, 64, 157
Alexander, R., 10, 17
Alexander, W.M., 71, 440
Allan, K.K., 206, 254
Allen, S., 358
Almasi, J.F., 169, 182
Alvermann, D.E., 23–24, 40, 55, 152, 169, 182, 183, 358
American Association for the Advancement of Science, 329
American Association of University Women, 35
American Council on the Teaching of Foreign Languages standards, 320, 327–328
American Institutes of Research, 35, 36
Ames, C., 42, 43
Ames, R., 42, 43
Analogies, prior knowledge support with, 105–106
Ancess, J., 45
Anders, P.L., 37, 119, 235
Anderson, C.W., 8
Anderson, L.M., 206
Anderson, R.C., 39, 40
Anderson, T.H., 192

Anderson, V., 228
Annotations, writing, 238
Anthony, H.M., 206
Anticipation guides, 114–115
Applied educational research, 481–485; analyzing/interpreting data in, 489–491; classroom-based, 483–493; collaborative, 482–483; data collection in, 487–489; defined, 481; finding questions for, 486–491; outside-generated, 482
Armbruster, B.B., 62, 192
Aronson, E., 70
Art: communicating learning through, 258; as research end product, 271–272
Assessment. *See also* Teaching/assessing tools; admit and exit slips as, 171–173; communication activities as, 237; in coordinated curriculum, 397, 402–403, 410, 413; essays as, 236–237; for evaluating ideas, 253; formative, 76–77, 340–341; of graphic organizers, 102–103, 198, 231–232; of group cooperation, 72; guidelines for choosing, 75–76; in integrated curriculum, 446–450; of integrated curriculum, 430, 455; integrating with instruction, 24; of journals, 185, 186–187; in lesson plans, 83–

84; monitoring/self-monitoring, 77; of note taking, 196, 197; -only tools, 77; for organizing ideas, 236–237; performance measures in, 76; portfolios as, 77, 79, 237, 448–450; of prior knowledge, 100–105; of research projects, 270–273; retelling and, 171; in single discipline-based curriculum, 370–371, 378–379; stan-dardized tests as, 43–47; summative, 78–79, 341; teacher-made tests as, 78–79; tests as, 236–237; think-aloud tool for, 183–184; tools emphasizing schema-based connections, 183–184; tools emphasizing text-based connections, 170–173; tools for literacy, 75–79; of unit plans, 340–341; vocabulary, 123–125
Attention deficit disorder (ADD), 36
Attention deficit–hyperactivity disorder (ADHD), 36
Attitudes, student, 42–43
Atwell, N., 254
Atwood, R.K., 40
Atwood, V.A., 40
Audiences: communicating learning to, 255–260; for summaries, 229
Auxiliary aids, 141, 146; in research projects, 294; teaching/assessing tools for constructing, 195–198

Background knowledge, experiences to build, 106. *See also* Prior knowledge
Baldwin, R.S., 125, 127, 203
Ball, D.L., 8, 54
Barell, J., 173
Barnes, D., 14
Bartolome, L., 33
Barton, K.C., 406
Bassiri, D., 19
Baum, D.D., 115
Beach, R.W., 192
Bean, T.W., 125, 127
Beane, J.A., 426, 454
Beck, I.L., 64, 123, 165
Beliefs, student, 42–43
Ben-Peretz, M., 313
Best-work portfolios. *See* Portfolios, showcase
Bibliographies, 63; annotating, 238
Bilingual students. *See* ESL (English as a Second Language) students
Biology: sample biology/health and English/language arts coordinated curriculum unit, 392–404
Bio-poems, 258
Black English, 33
Block schedules, 440–441
Bloom, A., 65
Bloom, B.S., 155
Bloom's Taxonomy, 155–156
Bluth, G.J., 188
Book, C., 19
Book clubs. *See* Peer-led discussion groups
Books and Beyond: Thematic Approaches for Teaching Literature in the High School, 434
Bos, C.S., 37, 119, 235
Brainstorming; assessing prior knowledge with, 101, 102; to find integrated curriculum themes, 435; in journals, 108; in research projects, 289
Brandt, D.M., 188
Bransford, J.D., 41
Breaking Ranks: Changing an American Institution, 22, 24, 442, 474
Brown, A.L., 166, 228
Brown, D.E., 105
Brown, J.S., 19
Burke, C.L., 185

Burkes, A.M., 123
Burmeister, L.E., 132–133

Carnegie Commission Task Force, 7
Carnegie Council on Adolescent Development, 22
Carr, E., 104
Carroll, P.S., 434
Categorization charts, 228, 248
Certification, teacher; standardized tests in, 44; standards for, 476–477
Chambliss, M.J., 248
Chase, A.C., 201
Chinn, P.C., 30
Citywide Learning Standards and Curriculum Frameworks, 317
Class size, 22
Coaching, 19–21; for teachers, 494; in teacher-student interchanges, 67–68; in using strategies, 74
Cochran, J.F., 7
Cognates, 130
Cohen, P., 363
Collection portfolios, 77, 448. *See also* Portfolios; as assessment, 77, 237; summaries in, 230
Collins, A., 19
Committee for Economic Development, 34
Communication; activities as assessment, 237; activities in language arts and the arts, 255–260; of learning to various audiences, 255–260; roles in classrooms, 66–68; roles of students and teachers, 11; student-student interchanges, 68; teacher-directed, 66–67; teacher-student interchanges, 67–68
Community participation; in integrated curriculum, 428–429; social studies' role in, 363–364
Comprehension levels, 154–155
Comprehension study guides, 168–169
Conard, S., 60
Concept models. *See* Graphic organizers
Concepts, 118–119. *See also* Knowledge; Vocabulary; concept of definition and, 128–129; determining crucial, 119; reinforcing, 235;

semantic feature charts and, 202–203
Conditional knowledge, 21, 74
Conferences, revising first drafts through, 253–255
Connotation, 200, 203
Considerateness, text, 62–64
Content areas. *See also* Coordinated curriculum; Integrated curriculum; Single discipline-based curriculum; activating prior knowledge in, 97–100; becoming teachers in, 5–11; common concerns among, 348–354; common morphemes across, 132–133; concerns in and literacy strategies for, 354–380; content and understandings in, 350–351; domains of focus in, 349–350; and enhancement of strategy use, 351–352; general *vs.* specific strategies for, 18–19; knowledge in schemata, 39–41; knowledge of other, 354, 356; making connections among, 371–373, 379–380; planning for coherence in, 352–354; role of literacy in learning, 15–16; standards for, 315, 318–330; strategies to support learning in, 16–19; teacher knowledge of, 8–9, 477–478; web site, 496
Content-area teaching, learning and literacy in, 14–21
Content variables, textbook, 63–64
Context, clues for vocabulary learning, 203–205
Cook, G.E., 432, 437
Cooking the data, 490–491
Cooper, J.D., 432
Cooperative learning groups, 70–71
Coordinated curriculum, 333–334, 383–420; benefits of, 386–389; benefits of to teachers, 388; defined, 386; discipline coordination in, 404–405; planning/scheduling for, 389–392, 395-396, 407–408; sample biology/health and English/language arts unit for, 392–405; sample geometry and English/language arts unit, 405–417; teacher coordination of disciplines in, 414–417; teacher guidelines for developing, 388

Crawford, L.W., 33, 38
Cultural diversity, 32. *See also* Diversity; cultural awareness and, 37–38; learning strategy choices and, 41–42; schemata and, 40; schemata reconstruction and, 241; social studies and, 324
Cultural identity, 33. *See also* Diversity
Curran, B.K., 44
Curriculum. *See also* Curriculum development; Materials; coordinated, 333–334, 383–420; defined, 309; discipline-specific standards in, 318–330; evaluating existing, 335; integrated, 334–335, 421–472; mandated, 267, 309; planning for coherence in, 352–354; research projects and mandated, 267; single discipline–based, 333, 345–382; sources for, 311–312; standards, 8, 311; standards as indicators for, 330–331; standards movement and, 313–331; state standards, 317
Curriculum development, 308–344; chart for, 354, 355–356; coordinated curriculum model for, 333–334; integrated curriculum model for, 334–335; models for, 331–341; planning web for, 456, 458, 464; single discipline model for, 333; standardized tests and, 45–46; teachers' role in, 313–314; unit plans in, 335–341
Curriculum guides, 311

Daniel, H., 182
Darling-Hammond, L., 44, 45, 495
Day, J.D., 228
Debates, 257
Declarative knowledge, 21, 74
Definitions, concept of, 128–129
Delpit, L.D., 42
Denotation, 203
Derivational suffixes, 131
De Ruiter, J.A., 7
Dialects, 33–34
Dialogue journals, 185
Diamantes, 258–259
Dictionaries, 119; vocabulary and, 205
Dillon, D.R., 23–24, 152
Dillon, J.T., 180

Directed reading activity (DRA), 75, 164–165
Directed reading (listening) thinking activity (DR-TA/DL-TA), 179–180
Disciplines. *See* Content areas
Discovery drafts, 187
Discussions; debriefing after, 183; group size and, 182–183; guidelines for, 182–183; initiating, 181–182; journal writing as preparation for, 185; peer-led, 70, 180–183; student preparation for, 182; student self-evaluation in, 370, 371; teacher-led *vs.* peer-led, 145
Discussion webs, 169–170
Diversity. *See also* Cultural diversity; among learners, 10; gender, 35–36; grouping and, 72; language, 32–34; learning strategy choices and, 41–42; literature choice and, 360–362; prior knowledge mismatches and, 99–100; questioning and, 155–156; racial/ethnic, 30–32; socioeconomic class, 34–35; of special needs, 36–37; standardized tests and, 43–44, 46–47; teaching considerations for, 37–38; in textbooks, 312; text fairness and, 65; web sites, 86–87, 373
Dole, J., 17, 18
Doll, R.C., 351
Donlan, D., 169
Double-entry journals, 185
Drake, S.M., 427
Drama, communicating learning through, 257
Duffelmeyer, F.A., 114, 115, 201
Duffy, G.G., 17, 18, 19

Earle, R.A., 360
Ebonics, 33
Ediger, M., 386
Education reform. *See also* Standards; concern for in disciplines, 348; curriculum and, 313–331; for twenty-first century, 22–24; school vision, 455–456; standardized tests in, 44–45
Education Reform Act of 1993, 331
Eeds, M., 180
Elbow, P., 70, 116
Englehart, M.C., 155

Englert, C.S., 206
English/language arts; activating prior knowledge in, 98; brainstorming in, 101; concerns in and strategies for, 360–362; literature choice in, 360–361; point-of-view guides in, 251; sample biology/ health and English/language arts coordinated curriculum unit, 392–398; sample geometry and English/language arts coordinated curriculum unit, 405–417; standards, 320, 326–327; vocabulary in, 362; vocab-lit strategy, 201–202; web sites, 86–87, 239–240, 496
ESL (English as a Second Language) students, 32–33; cognates, 130; directed reading activity and, 164–165; group discussions and, 183; inflectional suffixes and, 130–131; morphemic analysis for, 130–133; prior knowledge mismatches and, 100; questioning and, 155–156; refining ideas by, 217; special issues in teaching, 38; wait time for, 157
Essay tests, 78–79, 236–237; studying for with PORPE, 252–253
Estrin, E.T., 41
Evaluating ideas, 243–235; assessment, 253; modeling and explaining script, 241, 243–248; teaching/assessing tools, 248–253; writing and, 253–255
Evaluation. *See* Assessment
Evans, E.D., 17
Exit slips, 171–173
Expectations; student, 42–43; teacher, 37–38
Expectations of Excellence: Curriculum Standards for the Social Studies, 323, 462
Expository text organization, 190, 191; teaching tools for, 192–194

Failing at Fairness: How America's Schools Cheat Girls (Sadker, Sadker), 35, 36
Fairbanks, M.M., 119, 205
Fairness, text, 65
Falk, B., 45

Featherstone, J., 27

Fiction: books as texts, 55; modeling/explaining script, 176–178; queries for, 166; story maps for, 191

Field notebooks, 12–13; data collection in, 487–489; double-entry, 488; sample of, 13; text-based connections with, 173–174

Figueroa, R.A., 46

Filip, D., 235

Finding and interpreting information, 142–151; assessment tools, 170–173, 183–184; auxiliary aids and, 195–198; modeling and explaining script, 146–151, 161,174; strategies and tools emphasizing text-based connections, 159–170; strategies and tools emphasizing schema-based connections, 174–183; text organization and, 188, 190–195; types of questions, 153–159; vocabulary and, 198–206; writing and, 173–174, 184–187, 206–207

Fine, M., 32

First drafts, 187; assessing, 273; revising through conferences, 253–255

Fishbowl technique, 183

Flavell, J.H., 16

Fleet, J., 17

Flood, J., 251

Ford, J.C., 203

Foreign languages. *See also* ESL (English as a Second Language) students; standards for teaching, 320, 327–328; student diversity and, 32–34

Formative assessment, 76–77, 340–341

Format variables, textbook, 62–63

Found poems, 258

Fradd, S.H., 32

Frayer, D.A., 128

Frederick, W.C., 128

Fredericks, A.D., 427, 429, 432

Freewriting; for previewing/predicting, 116–117; in teacher research, 490

Fry Readability Formula, 60, 61

Fulwiler, T., 106

Furner, J., 431

Furst, E.J., 155

Gallagher, M.C., 20, 60

Gambrell, L.B., 169

García, E., 33, 38, 46, 47

García, G.E., 33, 130, 217

Garner, R., 10, 16, 17, 161

Gaskins, E.T., 37, 42

Gaskins, I., 37, 42

Gender: and achievement, 35–36; grouping by, 68

Geography for Life: National Geography Standards Education Project, 373

George, P.S., 71, 440

Gildea, P.M., 205

Gillingham, M.G., 161

Glatthorn, A.A., 337

Glenn, C.G., 188

Glossaries, 63; vocabulary and, 205

Goals: in lesson plans, 80–81; of standards, 319; turn to integrated curriculum themes, 432, 434–435; in unit plans, 337–338

Goals 2000: The Educate America Act, 313–314

Goetz, E.T., 39

Gollnick, D.M., 30

Goodchild, R., 17

Goodlad, J.I., 23–24, 54

Gordon, C.J., 133

Grammar, 38

Grand conversations. *See* Peer-led discussion groups

Grant, C.A., 65

Graphic organizers: assessing prior knowledge with, 101–103; assessment of, 102–103, 198, 231–232; categorization charts, 228, 248; defined, 101; for first drafts, 187; in journals, 108; for notes, 196, 198; for organizing ideas, 227, 231; for previewing/predicting, 116; in text pattern guides, 192; vocabulary assessment with, 124–125; web site, 304; in writing, 206–207

Graves, M.F., 99, 126–127

Gregg, G.P., 434

Gromoll, E.W., 64

Grossman, P.L., 8

Groups; assessment of cooperation in, 72; cooperative learning, 70–71; diversity in, 72; ESL students and discussion, 183; expert, 70–71; gender and, 68; learning

disabilities and, 183; modeling participation in, 72; peer-led discussions, 70, 180–183; reader response, 70; size of discussion, 182–183; student-led small, 69–71; student self-evaluation in discussion, 370, 371; whole class, 68–69; writing response, 70

Guthrie, J.T., 180

Guzzetti, B.J., 68

Haggard, M.R., 201

Hakuta, K., 33

Haley-Oliphant, A.E., 392

Hamilton, R.L., 165

Hare, V.C., 190

Harris, K., 37

Harste, J., 185

Hartman, D.K., 143

Hartoonian, H.M., 337

Health: sample biology/health and English/language arts coordinated curriculum unit, 398–404; standards, 321, 328–329

Heller, M.F., 457

Henk, W.A., 197

Herber, H.L., 114, 120, 154, 168

Herman, P.A., 119, 120

Hidi, S., 228

Hierarchical representations. *See* Graphic organizers

High schools: research project in, 267–300; sample units for, 373–380, 392–405, 462–470; scheduling in, 391; for twenty-first century, 22–23

Hill, M., 228

Hill, W.H., 155

Hinchman, K.A., 182, 183

Hirsh, E.D., Jr., 65

History, sample single discipline-based curriculum unit, 364–373

History Report Card: History Assessment at a Glance, 362

Hollon, R.E., 8

Holubec, E.J., 70

Homework, comprehension study guides and, 167–168

How Schools Shortchange Girls, 35, 36, 393

Hubbard, R.S., 490

Hurly, S.R., 32

Idea circles. *See* Peer-led discussion groups

Illinois State Board of Education, 386

Immigrants, voluntary and involuntary, 31–32. *See also* Diversity

Individuals with Disabilities Education Act (IDEA), 36

Inflectional suffixes, 130–131

Informational books: as texts, 55; considerateness, 64

Instructional tools. *See also* Coaching; Modeling; defined, 18–19; direct, 74; modeling/explaining, 19–20, 73–74; student-centered *vs.* teacher-centered, 23–24; teaching/assessing, 74–75

Integrated curriculum, 334–335, 421–472; administrative support for, 432, 454–455; assessment in, 446–450, 455; assessment of, 430, 455; defined, 426–427; finding themes for, 427–429, 432–436; focus of, 421–422; grouping in, 447; identifying content understandings/strategies for, 436–437; implementing units in, 442–450; importance of teams in, 451–456; interdisciplinary perspective on, 425–426; Miller-Allan model for, 431, 432, 433; organizing for implementation of, 439–441; planning for, 436–442; preplanning for, 432–436; rationale for, 430; sample environment unit for, 457–462; sample immigration unit for, 462–470; scheduling and, 421, 439–441; school vision in, 455–456; selecting materials/resources for, 437–438; team design for, 431–432; team guidelines for, 452–455; thematic study in, 427–429; time required for, 429, 453–454

Interdisciplinary perspective, 425–426. *See also* Integrated curriculum

International Reading Association standards, 62, 320, 326–327, 393

Internet: considerateness of, 64; evaluating site quality, 58–59; on-line sources as texts, 58–59; research on, 269, 290; web sites, 58–59, 86–87, 147, 239, 240, 288, 304–305, 367, 373, 379, 416, 468, 498

Interpreting information. *See* Finding and interpreting information

Interpretive comprehension, 154

Interviews as texts, 59

I-R-E pattern, 152, 157–158

I-search papers, 271

Jacobs, H.H., 430

Jaffe, L.E., 235

Jerald, C.D., 44

Jetton, T.L., 157

Jigsaw approach, 70–71

Jiménez, R,T, 33, 130, 217

Joag-Dev, C., 40

Johnson, D.D., 60, 202

Johnson, D.W., 70

Johnson, N., 188

Johnson, R.T., 70

Joint Committee on National Health Education Standards, 320, 328–329

Jones, M.G., 68

Journals, 106–108; assessing, 185, 186–187; dialogue, 185; double-entry, 185; prompts for, 106; reaction, 185; reinforcing vocabulary with, 235; schema-based connections with, 184–187; sketch-to-stretch technique for, 185; as sources of teacher research questions, 486; for teachers, 485; text-based connections with, 173–174; as texts, 59

Judy, J.E., 14

Kendall, J.S., 318, 325

"Kids: Kids Identifying and Discovering Sites," 58–59

King, J.R., 197

King, R.A., 7

Klausmeier, H.H., 128

Kleiman, G.M., 360

Knapp, M.S., 35

Knowledge. *See also* Prior knowledge; conditional, 21; constructing, 14; construction of *vs.* memorization, 15; declarative, 21; explosion, 421; extending with research projects, 267–268; procedural, 21

Kozol, J., 35

Krathwohl, D.R., 155

Kucan, L., 165

Kulikowich, J.M., 64, 157

KWL (Know—Want to Know—Learned), 103–104; Plus, 104; as research tool, 104

Kyle, W.C., 357

Langer, J.A., 33

Lapp, D., 251

Laughlin, M.A., 337

Learning disabilities; categorization charts and, 228; defined, 36; directed-reading activity and, 164–165; group discussions and, 183; learning strategy choices and, 41–42

Learning-from-text guide, 169, 170

Learning logs. *See* Journals

Learning strategies; choice of, 17; communicating content via, 14–21; compared with skills, 18; consciousness/unconsciousness of, 17; defined, 17; diversity of student, 41–42; for English/language arts, 362; general *vs.* discipline-specific, 18–19; for mathematics, 360; modeling/explaining, 74; for science, 358; for social studies, 363; to support content-area learning, 16–19; teacher knowledge of students', 10; teacher knowledge of their own, 10, 16; text variety and, 54

Lectures, objections to, 66–67

Lee, O., 32

Lerner, J., 36, 37

Lesson plans, 79–80; assessment/evaluation in, 83–84; goals/objectives in, 80–81; materials in, 81; parts of, 80; pedagogy/teaching procedures in, 81–83; sample of generic, 80–84

Levels of comprehension guides, 168–169

Levstik, L.S., 406

Limited English proficiency, 33. *See also* ESL (English as a Second Language) students

Lipson, M.Y., 17, 18, 93

Listening, role of in content learning, 15

Literacy; actions defined, 14; role of in content learning, 15–16

Literacy strategies. *See* Learning strategies

Literature. *See* English/language arts; Fiction

Literature-as-source approach to themes, 434–435

Literature circles. *See* Peer-led discussion groups

Lomax, R.G., 145

Long, R., 364

Lounsbury, J.H., 455

Lozauskas, D., 173

Lucas, T., 33

Lynch, E.A., 359

Macinnis, D., 133

Macrorie, K., 271

Magazines; considerateness of, 64; as texts, 57–58

Magazines for Kids and Teens (Stoll), 58

Mainstreaming, 36–37

Mandler, J., 188

Manning, G., 364

Manning, M., 364

Martinello, M.L., 432, 437

Martinez, Victor, 176–178

Marzano, R.J., 318, 325

Massachusetts; English/Language Arts Curriculum Frameworks, 360; State Curriculum Frameworks, 317, 462

Massachusetts World Language Curriculum Framework, 327–328

Materials; choices/decisions about, 53–79; defined, 53; knowledge of for teachers, 7, 11–12; in lesson plans, 81; rationale for variety of texts, 53–54; selecting appropriate texts, 59–65; selecting for integrated curriculum, 437–438; selecting to fit content and learners, 480; types of texts, 54–59

Mathematics: activating prior knowledge in, 97–98; assessment of, 323; concerns in and strategies for, 358–360; sample geometry and English/language arts coordinated curriculum unit, 405–417; standards, 320, 322–323; web sites, 416, 496; women and, 35; writing in, 173–174

Math Report Card for the Nation and the States, 359

Matyas, M.L., 392

Maurer, R.E., 452

McCann, A.D., 180

McCaslin, E.S., 123

McCloskey, L.A., 33

McDiarmid, G.W., 8, 32

McDonald, J.P., 12

McGee, L., 145

McKeown, M.G., 64, 123, 165

McMahon, S.I., 180

McMillan, J.H., 76, 78, 448

McQueen, M.E., 257

Meadows, J.D., 231–232

Meaning construction; role of questioning in, 152–159; strategies for, 141; supporting strategies for, 145–146; text-based/schema-based connections in, 142–145

Meier, D., 494, 496

Meinbach, A.M., 427, 429, 432

Meister, C., 167

Meloth, M.S., 19

Merkely, D.J., 115

Metacognitive awareness; building student, of strategies, 74; defined, 16–17; monitoring as, 135; portfolios in, 450; student lack of, 41

Middle schools; research projects in, 268–269, 274–286; sample units, 364–373, 405–417, 457–462; scheduling in, 390–391; for twenty-first century, 22–23; team teaching in, 390–391, 451; web site, 496

Miller, G.A., 205

Miller, M.S., 206, 254

Miller, P.H., 16

Miller, S.A., 16

Miller-Allan model, 431, 432, 433

Minami, M., 33

Mini-lessons, 67. *See also* Modeling/explaining scripts

Mitchell, R., 44

Modeling and explaining, 19–21. *See also* Modeling/explaining scripts; context clues for vocabulary, 204; dictionary use, 205; group participation, 72; peer conferences, 254–255; research, 268; research projects, 277–278, 279–282, 283–285; strategies for purpose setting, 134–135; strategies for schema-based connections, 174, 176; strategies for text-based connections, 161–162; as teaching tool, 73–74

Modeling and explaining scripts: defined, 93, 95; for evaluating ideas, 241, 243–248; for finding and in-terpreting information, 146–151; for organizing ideas, 217, 219–227; for previewing and predicting, 109–113; sample on algebra vocabulary, 120–123; sample on ancient civilizations, 110–112; sample on e-car (pollution), 146–151; sample on endangered species, 217, 219–227; sample on fiction, 176–178; sample on firearms, 96–97; sample on Pueblo civilization, 241, 243–248; for schema-based connections, 176–178; for vocabulary, 120–123, 199–200

Models. *See* Graphic organizers

Moffett, J., 14

Moll, L.C., 33

Monitoring, 90–91, 134–135; assessment with, 77; checklist for, 136, 208–209, 260–261; and interacting with ideas, 207–209; in refining ideas phase, 260–261

Monson, M.P., 317

Monson, R.J., 317

Moore, D.W., 182, 183

Moran, C.E., 33

Morgan, R.F., 429

Morpheme, defined, 129–130

Morphemic analysis, 129–133; common morphemes across content areas, 132–133; in vocabulary learning, 205; prefixes, 130; root words, 130; suffixes, 130–131

Moss, J.F., 434

Multicultural considerations. *See* Diversity

Multidisciplinary perspective, 425–426

Multigenre papers, 271

Music: communicating learning through, 258

Myer, B.J.F., 188

Nagy, W.E., 119, 120, 130, 205

Narrative text organization, 188

National Assessment of Educational Progress (NAEP); tests, 44, 421

National Assessments of Educational Progress Reports, 481

National Association of Secondary School Principals, 22

National Center for History in the Schools standards, 362–363

National Commission on Excellence in Education, 313

National Committee on Science Education Standards and Assessment standards, 320, 325–326, 357, 374

National Council for the Social Studies standards, 320, 323–325, 364, 365, 366, 462

National Council of Teachers of English standards, 62, 320, 326–327, 393

National Council of Teachers of Mathematics standards, 320, 322–323, 406–408

National Education Association, 32

National Health Education Standards: Achieving Health Literacy, 328–329

National Science Teachers Association, 351

A Nation at Risk, 313

Nelson-Barber, S., 41

Newman, S.E., 19

Newspapers: considerateness of, 64; as texts, 58

Nieto, S., 32

Nonfiction: expository text organization in, 190, 191; queries for, 166

Nonfiction books, 54, 55. *See also* Informational books; considerateness of, 64

Norm referenced, 44

Norton, D.E., 387

Note taking: assessment of, 196, 197; in meaning construction, 146; System for Learning, 195–196, 197; writing from, 272

Oakes, J., 31

Objectives, in lesson plans, 80–81

O'Brien, D.G., 23–24, 152

Office of Special Education and Rehabilitiative Services, 36

Ogbu, J.U., 31

Ogle, D.M., 103, 104

Oja, S.N., 481

Olson, L., 44

O'Neill, J., 361

On-line texts, 58–59

Organizing ideas: assessment tools, 235–237; modeling and explaining script, 217, 220–227; strategies and tools for, 217–240; teaching/assessing tools, 227–235; writing and, 237–238

Ostertag, J., 192

Outlines, 198

Ovando, C.J., 33

Pairs, 71

Palinscar, A.S., 166

Palmatier, R.A., 195

Palmer, R.G., 54

Panaritis, P., 456

Paris, S.B., 17, 18, 93

Partners, 71

Pearson, P.D., 17, 18, 20, 33, 60, 74, 130, 202, 217

Pedagogy. *See also* Instructional tools; assessment tools and, 75–79; choices/decisions about, 65–79; communication roles in classrooms and, 66–68; grouping, 68–73; knowledge of for teachers, 7, 10–11; in lesson plans, 81–83; lesson plans and, 79–84; selecting, 479; teaching tools, 73–75; tool choice in, 19–20

Peer conferences: revising first drafts in, 253–255; revising research drafts in, 272

Peer-led discussion groups; reader response, 70; for schema-based connections, 180–183; writing response, 70

Peresich, M.L., 231–232

Perkins, D.N., 18

Peters, C.W., 232, 248, 249

Phelps, S.F., 182, 183

Picture books as texts, 56–57

Pierce, K.M., 180

Planning/scheduling; benefits of flexibility in, 441; block schedules, 440–441; for coordinated curriculum, 389–392, 394–395, 407–408; for curriculum coherence, 352–354; for integrated curriculum, 436–442; for interdisciplinary teams, 453–455; for text-based teaching/assessing tools, 163

Poetry; communicating learning through, 258–259; as texts, 56–57

Point-of-view guides, 250, 251

PORPE (predict, organize, rehearse, practice, evaluate), 252–253

Porter, A.C., 317

Portfolios; assessment data in, 448–449; assessment with, 77, 79; collection, 77, 448; collection, as assessment, 77, 237; in integrated curriculum assessment, 448–450; for research projects, 270; showcase, 79, 237, 448

Postreading guides, 232–234; point-of-view, 250, 251

Power, B.M., 490

Prediction. *See* Previewing/predicting

Prefixes, 130

Pressley, M., 17, 37

Preview in context, for vocabulary, 125, 127

Previewing/predicting; defined, 82; freewriting for, 116–117; modeling/explaining script for, 109–113; strategies/tools for, 108–117; teaching/assessing tools for, 113–116; vocabulary, 125

Primary sources; considerateness of, 64; as texts, 59

Prior knowledge; activating in content areas, 97–100; direct teaching tools for, 105–106; enhancing, 214; impact of on text comprehension, 139; mismatches resulting from, 99–100; modeling and explaining script for, 93–97; previewing/predicting and, 117; reconstructing, 214; strategies/tools for activating, 91–108; students with, 99–100; teaching/assessing tools for, 100–105; writing and, 116–117

Procedural knowledge, 21, 74

Professional associations, 494–495

Professional development, teacher, 12–13, 313–314, 473–498; applied eductional research and, 481–485; classroom research and, 485–493; content knowledge and, 477–478; content pedagogy and, 479; continuous learning and, 495; joining communities of learners and, 493–495; knowledge of students and, 478–479; material/resource selection and, 480; professional standards and, 476–477; role of inquiry in, 480–493; standards for, 342

Pugalee, D.K., 173–174

Purpose setting, 90–91, 134–136; and interacting with ideas, 207–208;

modeling/explaining strategies for, 134–135; in refining ideas phase, 260

Putnam, J., 19

Queries, 165–166

Question-answer relationship (QAR) framework, 153–154

Question-driven approach to themes, 432, 434

Questioning the author (QtA), 165–166

Questions, 152–159, 170–171; -answer relationship, 153–154; answer wait time, 38; Bloom's Taxonomy of, 155–156; caution with taxonomies of, 157; and comprehension levels, 154–155; in comprehension study guides, 168–169; in directed-reading activity, 164–165; in discussion webs, 169–170; facilitating student understanding with, 156–159; I-R-E patterns in, 152, 157–158; postreading, 232; queries, 165–166; for research projects, 290; supporting, 163; think/wait time and, 157; in this text, 159; types of, 153–156; using statements instead of, 168–169

Rabinowitz, M., 190

Rackliffe, G., 19

Raphael, T.E., 180, 206

Ravitch, D., 315

Reaction journals, 185

Readability, 60–62; Fry Readability Formula, 60, 61

Readence, J.E., 40, 125, 127, 203

Readers' theater, 257

Reading; role of in content learning, 15; women and, 35–36

Reciprocal teaching, 166–168

Reflection; in professional development, 476–480, 484; for teachers, 12–13, 50–51

Reiman-Nemser, S., 54

Report of the National Commission on Teaching and America's Future, 474

Research. See Applied educational research; Research projects (student)

Research projects (student), 264–305; alternatives to term papers in,

270–272; to assemble known facts, 274–286; assessing, 270, 273; end products, 285–286, 300; extending knowledge with, 267–268; introducing, 275–278, 289–290; to investigate issue or problem, 286–301; learning to conduct research in, 268–269; modeling/explaining, 277–278, 279–282, 283–284; purposes for, 267–269; role of end product in, 270–274; sample on child labor, 286–301; sample on outstanding women, 274–286; teacher planning for, 274–275, 288–290; teaching/assessing tools for, 275–277, 278, 282–283; using for learning, 267–274

Resources. See Materials

Retelling, 171

Reviews, writing, 238–240

Revision of first drafts, 253–255

Rewards; extrinsic, 43; intrinsic, 43

Reyes, M. de la Luz, 27, 42

Reynolds, R.E., 39

Richardson, J.S., 429

Richgels, D.J., 145

Rief, L., 271

Robinson, F., 232

Roehler, L.R., 17, 18, 19

Romano, T., 271, 272

Root words, 130

Rosenblatt, L., 70, 139

Rosenshine, B., 167

Roth, K.J., 8

Rothlein, L., 427, 429, 432

Rowe, M.B., 157

Sadker, D., 35, 36

Sadker, M., 35, 36

Sajchowski, R., 17

Salomon, G., 18

Sandel, L., 392

Sanders, N.M., 155

Santa, C.M., 358

Schallert, D.L., 39

Scheduling: benefits of flexibility in, 441; block schedules, 440–441; flexible, 22; for interdisciplinary teams, 453–455

Schema-based connections; assessment tool, 183–184; modeling/explaining script for, 176–178; strategies/tools emphasizing,

174–187; teaching/assessing tools emphasizing, 179–183; writing and, 184–187

Schemata: connecting to texts, 142–145; content knowledge in, 39–41; cultural, 40; defined, 39; as hooks for new learning, 93; reconstructing, 240–255; vocabulary and, 119–120

Schieble, K.M., 190

Schmidt, D., 172

Schneps, M.H., 40

Schön, D.A., 484

Schunk, D.H., 43

Schwartz, R.M., 128, 129

Science; concerns in and strategies for, 357–358; point-of-view guides in, 251; sample biology/health and English/language arts coordinated curriculum unit, 398–405; sample single discipline-based curriculum unit (geology), 373–380; standards, 320, 325–326; web sites, 147, 304, 379, 496; women and, 35

Science for All Americans: A Project 2061 Report on Goals in Science, Mathematics and Technology, 325

Scientific literacy, 357–358

Scott, J.A., 205

Self-efficacy, 42–43

Self-ratings on vocabulary, 123

Self-selection, vocabulary, 201

Semantic feature charts, 202–203, 235

Semantic maps. See Graphic organizers

Sheard, C., 145

Short, K.G., 180, 183, 185

Shulman, L.S., 7

Signals words, 190, 191

Significance approach to themes, 434

Sinatra, R., 231–232

Singer, H., 64, 169

Single discipline-based curriculum: advantages of, 345; chart for development of, 354, 355–356; common concerns among disciplines and, 348–354; discipline-specific concerns in, 354–380; content and understandings in, 350–351; planning for coherence in, 352–354;

Single discipline-based curriculum *(cont.)*: sample units for, 364–380; strategies for, 351–352

Sivan, E., 19

Sketch-to-stretch technique, 185

Skills: insufficiency of, 316–317; strategies compared to, 18

Slater, W.H., 99, 126–127

Slavin, R.E., 70

Sleeter, C.E., 37, 65

Small group discussion. *See* Peer-led discussion groups

Smith, L.C., 40

Smulyan, L., 481

Social sciences, effects of standards on, 348–349

Social studies; concerns in and strategies for, 362–364; sample single discipline-based curriculum unit, 364–373; standards, 320, 323–325, 362–364, 365, 366, 374; web sites, 86, 288, 305, 367, 373, 468

Socioeconomic status, 30, 34–35; standardized tests and, 45–46

Sosenke, F., 259

Sowell, J., 130

Speaking: communicating learning through, 256–257; role in learning content, 13–14; teacher-dominated, 23–24

Special education programs; collaboration with regular education in, 36–37; socioeconomic status and, 35; web site, 87

Special needs students; diversity of, 36–37; self-concepts of, 37; web site, 87

Spiegel, D.L., 55

SQ3R (survey, question, read, recite, review), 232, 235

Stahl, N.A., 197

Stahl, S.A., 119, 124, 205

Standard American English, 33, 38

Standardized tests. *See also* Assessment; characteristics of, 44–45; defined, 44; fair use of, 43–47; teaching to, 45–46

Standards: concerns/questions about, 330–331; content areas content and understandings in, 350–351; current curriculum, 311, 313–318; discipline-based, 315; discipline-specific, 318–330; effects of on dis-

ciplines, 348–349; and enhancement of strategy use, 351–352; goals of, 319; for teachers, 341–342, 476–477; textbooks and, 54; uses of for teachers, 477–478; using, 317, 319, 321

Stauffer, R.G., 179

Steffenson, M.S., 40

Stein, N.L., 188

Stevens, D.D., 206

Stewart, R.A., 54

Stoll, D.R., 58

Story grammar, 188

Story maps, 191. *See also* Texts, organization

Story structure, 188

Stotsky, S., 361

Strategic learners; defined, 16–17; meaning construction strategies of, 142–145; monitoring by, 134–135, 207–208, 260

Structural analysis. *See* Morphemic analysis

Students. *See also* Strategic learners; attitudes, beliefs, values of, 42–43; awareness of learning strategies of, 17; diversity of, 28–38; learning from students, 67; motivation of and communication, 255–260; offering choice to, 267; teacher knowledge of, 7, 10, 478–479; teachers learning from, 480–493

Student texts as texts, 59

Student-to-student interchanges, 68

Suffixes, 130–131

Summaries: expanding student abilities in, 230; modeling/explaining script on, 224–227; preparation for, 228; in research project, 295; writing, 228–230

Summative assessment, 78–79, 341

Taylor, B.M., 188, 192

Teacher-directed communication, 66–67; mini-lessons, 67

Teacher education, 476–477

Teacher-guided discussion, 75; directed reading activity, 74

Teachers: becoming content-area, 7–11; benefits to of coordinated curriculum, 388; characteristics of exemplary, 345, 347; as coaches, 24, 67–68; concerns/questions

about standards, 330–331; decision-making areas for, 51–52; expectations of, 37–38; as facilitators, 24, 67–68; knowledge of other disciplines for, 354, 356; as participant-observers, 68; planning/scheduling time for coordinated curriculum development, 389–392, 394–395, 407–408; professional development for, 12–13, 313–314, 473–498; reflection by, 10–11, 50–51, 484; as researchers, 482–493; role of in curriculum design, 313–314; scheduling flexibility and, 439–441; standards for, 341–342; steps to acting on concerns of, 354, 355–356

Teachers, beginning: becoming content area, 5–11; colleagues and, 353–354; reflection by, 10–11; reliance of on curriculum guides, 313

Teacher-student interchanges, 67–68

Teaching: content-area and literacy, 11–20; diverse students, 37–38; realistic learning about, 10–11; reciprocal, 166–168; for twenty-first century, 4, 23–24; student responses in, 76–77; team, 390–391, 431–432, 439, 451–456; to the test, 45–46

Teaching/assessing tools, 74–75; anticipation guides, 114–115; in assessment, 76–77; brainstorming, 101, 102; comprehension study guides, 168–169; concept of definition, 128–129; for constructing auxiliary aids, 195–198; directed reading activity, 75, 164–165; directed reading/thinking activity, 179–180; discussion webs, 169–170; emphasizing text-based connections, 162–170; for evaluating ideas, 248–253; graphic organizers, 101–103, 198, 231–232; KWL, 103–104; note taking System for Learning, 195–196, 197; for organizing ideas/enhancing prior knowledge, 227–235; peer-led discussions, 180–183; planning for, 163; PORPE, 252–253; postreading guides, 232–234; preview in context, 125, 127; for previewing/predicting, 113–116; for prior knowledge, 100–105; questioning the author, 165–166; reciprocal teaching, 166–168; for research projects, 275–277, 278, 282–283; for schema-based connections, 179–183; semantic feature charts, 202–203, 235; SQ3R, 232, 235; story maps, 191; for students with little prior knowledge, 159; summaries, 224–227; teacher-guided discussion, 75; for text-based connections, 159–170; for text organization, 190–195; text pattern guides, 192–193; for vocabulary learning, 125–129, 200–203; vocabulary self-selection strategy, 201; vocab-lit strategy, 201–202

Teaching groups, 71

Teaching tools. *See* Instructional tools

Technology. *See also* Internet; impact of, 421; integration of, 21

Term papers; alternatives to, 270–272; assessing, 273; making the most of, 272

Terner, J., 393

Tests: as assessment tools, 236–237; classroom and teacher-made, 78–79; creating, 237; essay, 79; standardized, 43–47; studying for with PORPE, 252–253

Texley, J., 351, 374, 377

Text-based connections: assessment tools for, 170–173; modeling/explaining, 161–162; modeling and explaining script for, 147–151; strategies/tools for, 159–174; teaching/assessing tools for, 162–170; writing and, 173–174

Textbooks, 54–55; evaluating definitions in, 129; mandated, 54; previewing, 108–113; shaping curriculum with, 311–312; survey format in, 54–55

Text pattern. *See* Texts, organization

Text pattern guides, 192–193

Texts; considerateness of, 62–64; content variables of, 63–64; defined, 53; fairness of, 65; fiction books, 55; format variables of, 62–63; informational/nonfiction books, 55; magazines, 57–58; newspapers, 58; on-line, 58–59; organization, mixed patterns in, 191–193; organization of expository, 145–146, 190; organization of narrative, 145–146, 188; poetry and picture books, 56–57; primary sources, 59; rationale for variety in, 53–54; readability of, 60–62; selecting appropriate, 59–65; student, 59; textbooks, 54–55; types of, 54–59

Thematic study, 427–429. *See also* Integrated curriculum

Think, Pair, Share, 169–170

Think-aloud tool, 183–184

Think time, 157

Third International Mathematics and Science Survey Report (TIMSS), 359, 406, 407–408

Thrash, E.C., 182, 183

Tiedt, I.M., 259

TIMSS Report, 408

Tinajoro, J.V., 32

Todd, F., 14

Tracking/grouping, 68–73; cooperative learning small groups, 70–71; and instruction focus, 35; instruction purpose and, 68; pairs/partners, 71; peer-led discussion groups, 70, 180–183; practical considerations in, 71–73; same-sex, 68; student-led small groups, 69–71; teacher-led small groups, 69; whole class, 68–69

Transdisciplinary perspective, 425–426

Transitional bilingual programs, 32–33

Turning Points: Preparing American Youth for the twenty-first Century, 22, 474

Tutorial partners, 71

Unit plans, 335–341; components of, 335–336; evaluating, 340–341; generating ideas in, 339; goals in, 337–338; interacting with ideas in, 339; materials/resources for, 338; planning/setting up, 337–338; refining ideas in, 339–340; sample integrated curriculum, 457–470; sample coordinated curriculum, 392–405, 405–417; sample single discipline, 364–373, 373–380; teaching, 338–339

U.S. Department of Education, 36, 439

Using Literature in the Middle Grades: A Thematic Approach, 434

Vacca, A.L., 204

Vacca, R.T., 204

Values, student, 42–43

Vancil, S.J., 124

Van Sledright, B.A., 364

Vasquez, O., 33

Vavrus, L.G., 19

Vocab-lit strategy, 201–202

Vocabulary: assessment of, 123–125; assessment with graphic organizers, 124–125; cognates, 130; concepts and, 118–119; concept of definition, 128–129; context and, 198, 203–205; denotation/connotation and, 203; dictionaries/glossaries and, 205; independent learning of, 146, 198–206; learning in research projects, 294–295; modeling/explaining learning, 198–199; modeling/explaining script for, 120–123, 200; morphemic analysis and, 129–133, 205; preteaching guidelines for, 119–120; preview in context for, 125, 127; previewing, 125; reinforcing, 233; self-ratings of, 123; self-selection strategy, 201; semantic feature charts and, 202–203; strategies/tools for exploring, 117–133; teaching/assessing tools for, 125–129, 200–205; text variety and, 54; vocab-lit strategy, 201–202; writing and, 133; word map, 128–129

Wait time, 157

Warren, A.R., 33

Weaver, D., 182, 183

Webbing, 362; discussion, 169–170; to find integrated curriculum themes, 435

Wells, D., 180

Wesselman, R., 19

"What Matters Most: Teaching for America's Future," 474

Wheatley, J., 68

White, C.S., 161

White, T.G., 130

Whitin, P.E., 185

Wigfield, A., 42–43
Wild, A., 351, 374, 377
Will, M., 36
Williams, W.O., 68
Willis, S., 427
Wilson, S.M., 8
Wineburg, S.S., 8, 165
Winograd, P.N., 229
Wixson, K.K., 17, 18, 93
Woehler, C.A., 157
Wood, K.D., 251
Woolverton, S., 35
Word continuum, 235

Word maps, 128–129
Working portfolios. *See* Portfolios, collection
World Wide Web. *See* Internet
Writing, 13–14; abstracts, 238; annotations, 238; communicating learning through, 258–260; expository, 259; first drafts, 187, 204, 253–255; freewriting, 116–117, 490; graphic organizers and, 206–207; journals, 106–108, 173–174; narrative, 259; persuasive, 259; revising first drafts, 253–255;

reviews, 238–240; role of in content learning, 15–16; summaries, 228–230; summaries for readers, 237–240; vocabulary and, 133

Yangihara, A., 130
Young, J.P., 182, 183

Zalewski, P., 182, 183
Zimmerman, B.J., 43
'zines, 58

Content-Area Curriculum Units exemplify the three curricula models found in middle schools and high schools. Each model includes a middle school and high school example and provides detail on strategies to meet content-area standards.

their planning and their teaching. In addition to the newsletter, which gave the students a chance to share their new knowledge and to inform the wider community, the teachers learned that some of the students had become "environmental junkies" at home and showed evidence of having come away from this unit as more conscious and committed guardians of our environment. What better way for the value of integrated, thematic study to be evaluated and validated than to see it have a lasting impact on these middle schoolers who when they are adults will be making decisions about our environment.

Sample High School Unit: "Immigration and Cultural Diversity: Are We Still a Nation of Immigrants?"

Immigration and cultural diversity is a timely and significant theme for the development of integrated curriculum at the high school level. It is important that young people realize that questions about immigration, assimilation, and cultural plural- ... *t long-standing questions* ... *ts. An additional impetus* ... *ed manner in the curricu-* ... *nal standards documents* ... *ds for the Social Studies* ... *of the recent state curricu-* ... *the social sciences and on* ... *meworks, 1998).* ... *11.1) for the development* ... *e teachers created a four-* ... *re We Still a Nation of Im-* ... *his issue because they and* ... *d these concerns on an on-* ... *their backyard. The ninth* ... *eir district. Therefore, the* ... *of the school year could do* ... *ate a more cohesive acade-* ... *e to deal firsthand with a* ... *es at the present.*

... a ninth-grade history ... his students to a newly ... ses (colonialism to 1865 ... ce and questions those

The teachers realized that the next step was for them to figure out how they would orchestrate the creation of the quilt and ensure that they had the resources they and their students needed. They also wanted to be sure that this project would be more than an art project that was tacked on "for fun." In order to coordinate the quilt project successfully, each teacher decided to review the understandings, the materials, the lessons, and the student evaluation that made up their respective units in mathematics and the English/language arts.

In the next part of this chapter you will see the outline of the literature and the geometry units that the students participated in before two teachers introduced and implemented the coordinated component. Keep in mind that the goal of the quilt project was for the students to refine and extend their understandings and the experiences they had in the individual discipline-based units.

Middle School English/Language Arts Course: Historical Fiction and Letter Writing

Major Understandings. Students understand other people's perspectives through historical fiction focused on the 1880s in America; students learn how experiences shaped people's or characters' lives, and they learn to tell about ... nd to describe unfamiliar settings and situations ... letters.

... a collection of tall tales and selections from an- ... of students at various levels, plus four works of his- ... for young adolescents (two with female protago- ... rotagonists): *My Daniel,* by Pam Conrad (1989); ... an Blos (1985); *Sarah, Plain and Tall,* by Patricia ... *Stitch in Time,* by Ann Rinaldi (1994). ... pe were important to the selection process so that ... e class could share the content of books appropri- ... level along with their peers.

... d aloud to the students "Going West" and "Settling ... t (R. Freedman, 1983), to ensure that they all shared ... e period. Then the students read books about quilts ... en for adolescents and young adults such as Ray- ... *Thread: A Book About Quilts* (1996), Kime's *Quilts for* ... llen Howard's *The Log Cabin Quilt* (1996).

Sample Single Discipline Unit for the High School

The high school single discipline unit created for this chapter focuses on science, specifically the domain of geology. The national standards dealing with earth and space science for grades 9–12 emphasize a focus on earth science that will help all secondary students understand local, national, and global challenges to the earth, as well as natural hazards like tornadoes, volcanoes, and floods and the challenges that humans create. We built this sample unit based on the national science standards for the high school level (see both Chapter 8 and Table 9.5), a ninth-grade classroom vignette included in Pathways to Science *(Texley & Wild, 1996), and the literacy and learning strategies we addressed in Part Two.*

Table 9.5   Excerpt from Standards for Science

I. Earth and Space

   #1. Understands the basic features of the Earth

   #2. Understands basic Earth processes

   #3. Understands essential ideas about the composition and structure of the universe and the Earth's place in it.

   Sample performance expectations for Level III (Grades 9–12)

   • Knows that the "rock cycle" consists of the formation, weathering, sedimentation, and reformation of rock; in this cycle, the total amount of material stays the same as its form changes.

   • Knows that geologic time can be estimated by observing rock sequences and using fossils to correlate the sequences at various locations; recent methods use the predictability of decay rates of radioactive isotopes in rock formation to determine geologic time.

   • Knows that evidence for simple, one-celled forms of life such as bacteria and algae extends back more than 3.5 billion years; the evolution of life resulted in dramatic changes in the composition of the Earth's atmosphere, which did not originally contain oxygen.

II. Life Sciences

   (Standards #4–#9)

III. Physical Sciences

   (Standards #10–#13)

IV. Science and Technology

   (Standards #14–#18)

Source: National Committee of Science Education Standards and Assessment, J. S. Kendall and R. J. Marzano, *Content Knowledge* (Aurora, Ohio: Mid-continent Regional Educational Laboratory, 1996).